THE SCULPTURE OF ANDREA AND NINO PISANO

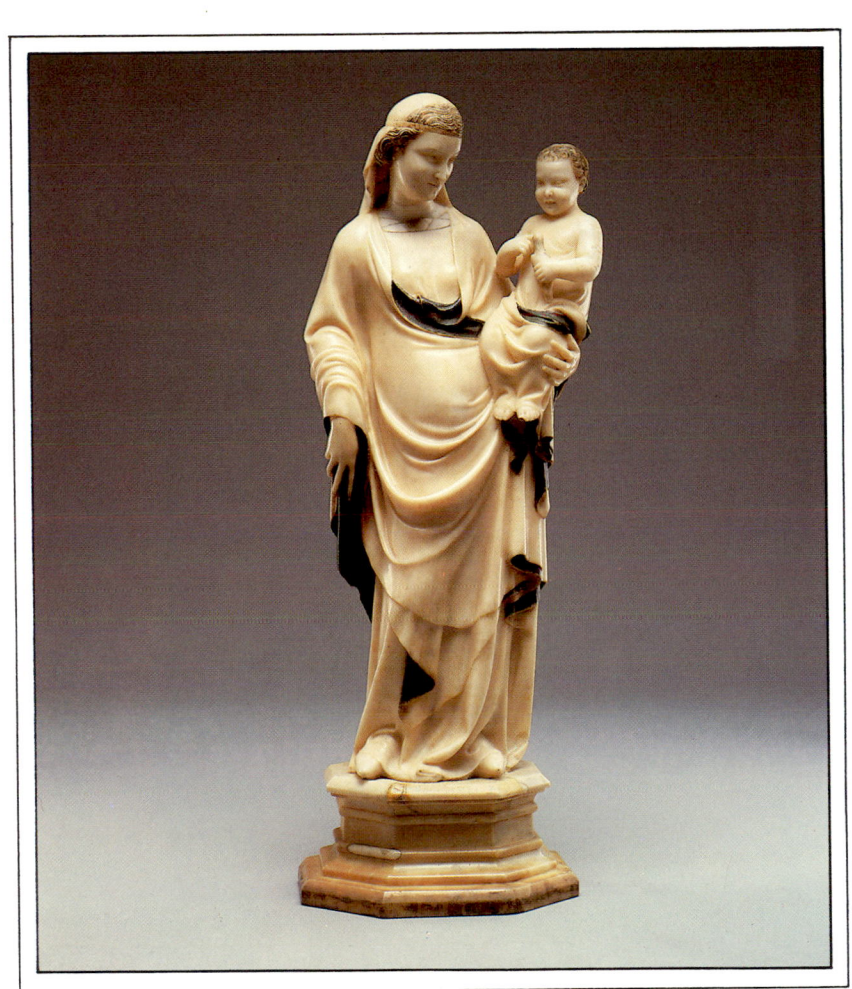

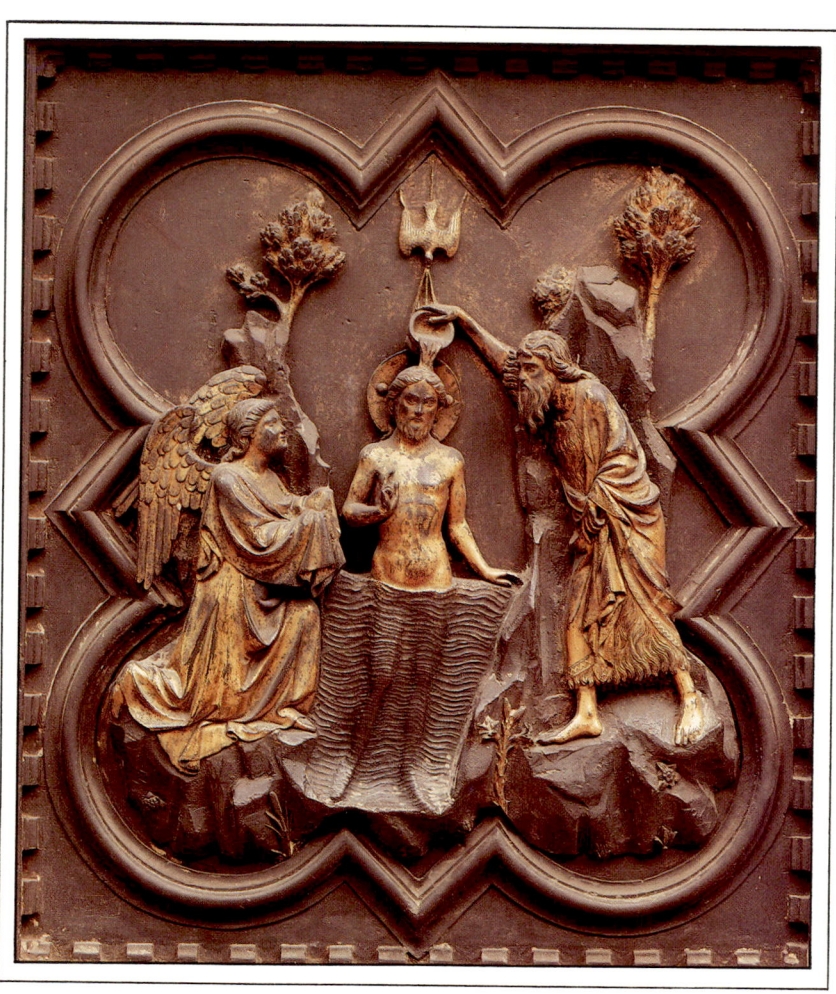

THE SCULPTURE OF ANDREA AND NINO PISANO

Anita Fiderer Moskowitz
Department of Art History
State University of New York
Stony Brook

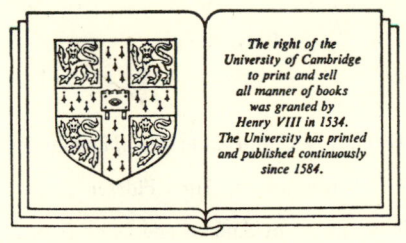

The right of the
University of Cambridge
to print and sell
all manner of books
was granted by
Henry VIII in 1534.
The University has printed
and published continuously
since 1584.

CAMBRIDGE UNIVERSITY PRESS
CAMBRIDGE
LONDON   NEW YORK   NEW ROCHELLE
MELBOURNE   SYDNEY

Published by the Press Syndicate of the University of Cambridge
The Pitt Building, Trumpington Street, Cambridge CB2 1RP
32 East 57th Street, New York, NY 10022, USA
10 Stamford Road, Oakleigh, Melbourne 3166, Australia

First published 1986

Printed in the United States of America

Library of Congress Cataloging in Publication Data
Moskowitz, Anita Fiderer, date
The sculpture of Andrea and Nino Pisano.
Bibliography: p.
1. Pisano, Andrea, 1270–1348? – Criticism and
interpretation. 2. Pisano, Nino, ca. 1315–ca. 1368 –
Criticism and interpretation. 3. Sculpture, Gothic –
Italy. I. Title.
NB623.P39M67 1986 730′.92′2 85–17071

British Library Cataloguing in Publication Data
Moskowitz, Anita Fiderer
The sculpture of Andrea and Nino Pisano.
1. Pisano, Andrea – Criticism and interpretation
2. Pisano, Nino – Criticism and interpretation
I. Title
730′.92′2 NB623.P68/

ISBN 0 521 30754 6

CONTENTS

PREFACE

Andrea Pisano, the creator of the first set of bronze doors on the Baptistry of Florence in 1330–6, is universally acknowledged as the most important Italian sculptor of the fourteenth century, yet he remains a mysterious figure whose origins are obscure and whose artistic range is unclear. A younger contemporary of Giotto, he became the great painter's truest disciple and was the only fourteenth-century master capable of translating the narrative power of Giotto's paintings into the language of sculpture. His receptivity to northern Gothic influence, however, resulted in a more lyrical style than that of Giotto and his strong response to classical sculpture anticipated, in a number of very important ways, the concerns of the Early Renaissance.

Andrea is referred to in the documents as a goldsmith, but he seems also to have worked in wood, was a master of bronze, a supreme carver of marble, and an imaginative and skillful architect. Surprisingly, nothing secure is known of him before his sudden appearance as an accomplished and recognized master in 1330. The question of Andrea's origins has been raised, but not satisfactorily answered, in the two monographs and in several of the articles that have been written about the sculptor. The Baptistry reliefs seem to exist almost outside the context of earlier and contemporary Italian sculpture so that scholars have been hard-put to discern a clear and precise debt to Andrea's great predecessors in the Italian Gothic tradition. Aside from some iconographic similarities, there is little apparent relationship, for example, between the Baptistry doors and the pulpits of Nicola and Giovanni Pisano. Andrea's style is alien to the intense classicism of Arnolfo di Cambio, and its connections to the Sienese traditions of Tino di Camaino and Lorenzo Maitani remain vague. Among the unresolved issues, then, are the origins of Andrea Pisano – in the literal sense of the word, that is, where he came from and what he saw before his appearance in Florence – and the roots of his style.

Andrea's evolution as a sculptor has not been well defined. The Baptistry doors have been discussed, on the whole, as revealing little stylistic variation among the reliefs and therefore involving no growth or evolution on the part of the sculptor. Close examination of the quatrefoils, however, indicates an unexpected degree of experimentation leading to a variety of solutions to specific artistic problems. Andrea's statues, too, have been viewed outside any larger context, as essentially without connection to his relief style, and therefore as exhibiting no internal development. The aim, in part, of the present study is to examine in detail the sculptures that may convincingly be associated with Andrea, to define their salient stylistic characteristics, and to seek out the stylistic variables that reveal, within the scope of a single imagination, changing artistic goals and solutions.

Andrea's sources have received inadequate treatment. Of a perplexing variety, his sources are in fact to be found in the work of Nicola and Giovanni Pisano, French Gothic sculpture and metalwork, Sienese art, Florentine painting, and classical sculpture. This very variety, and the subtlety with which these sources have been integrated, have contributed to the problem of the definition of his style.

These are some of the issues that have continued to evade solutions. Andrea Pisano has remained a "problem," keenly appreciated yet little understood as the complex and eclectic artist that he was.

Andrea's son Nino was a significant and highly appealing sculptor in his own right. To many admirers, the mellifluous rhythms, delicate surfaces, and precious sensibility of the figures that have been associated with his name remain the characteristic expression of the "Gothic" component of Italian Gothic sculpture. His artistic personality, as it has come to be understood, is based, however, almost entirely on uncertain works and later adaptations of his style. The major problem concerning Nino's oeuvre is that his signed or documented sculptures bear little stylistic relationship to the large body of work that has traditionally, from the time of Vasari on, been associated with his name. An uncritical acceptance of Vasari's statements concerning Nino has led, all too often, to forced chronologies that attempt to reconcile the clear stylistic contradictions.

This study offers a reevaluation of the six primary works associated with Nino's name – three that are signed and three ascribed to him by Vasari – followed by a hypothesis concerning their chronology. It also discusses the precise relationship to these six of the numerous later attributions to Nino or his school. A brief discussion of Tommaso Pisano, Andrea's second son, who executed the marble high altar of San Francesco, Pisa, is also included.

Finally, these masters are viewed from several broader perspectives. The relationship of their work to northern Gothic art is explored, as is its place within the evolution of Tuscan sculpture from Gothic to Renaissance. The work of Andrea and Nino Pisano will be seen, on the one hand, to reflect the major interweaving currents in the European arena and, on the other, to herald – and even inspire – some of the artistic achievements of Early Renaissance sculptors in Italy.

ACKNOWLEDGMENTS

✦

This book owes much to friends, mentors, and benefactors. When I took my first graduate seminar at the Institute of Fine Arts of New York University with Professor Marvin Trachtenberg on the sculpture of the Florentine cathedral group, little did I imagine that my report on the Campanile sculptures would lead to a prolonged involvement with the art of Andrea Pisano. That early effort, which led to a doctoral dissertation on the stylistic origins of Andrea, eventually expanded far beyond its original parameters to include a study of trecento sculpture in general and, in particular, Nino Pisano. I shall always be grateful for the encouragement and support that Marvin Trachtenberg gave throughout the evolution of this project. I wish to thank Sir John Pope-Hennessy (whose book on Italian Gothic sculpture remains a source of knowledge and stimulation) for reading an earlier version of my manuscript and for offering a number of valuable suggestions; without his advice and continual support this investigation would have been of more limited scope. Sarah Wilk's reading of the manuscript at an early stage was helpful in many ways, particularly in spurring me on to greater concern with iconographic questions.

Research abroad was made possible by a grant-in-aid from the American Council of Learned Societies during the summer of 1979 and by a fellowship in 1979–80 at the Villa I Tatti (the Harvard University Center for Renaissance Studies in Florence) with support from the Leopold Schepp Foundation. The hospitality and friendly support of Craig Smyth, former director of I Tatti, will always be remembered. The following persons were especially accommodating in permitting the close study and

✦

photographing of museum objects and/or providing me with photographs: Mariagiulia Burresi and Antonino Caleca of the Soprintendenza alle Gallerie in Pisa, Alan Darr of the Detroit Institute of Arts, Patrick de Winter of the Cleveland Museum of Art, Janos Eisler of the Museum of Fine Arts in Budapest, Edith Freund of the Staatliche Museen in East Berlin, Douglas Lewis of the National Gallery in Washington, D.C., and Ursula Schlegel of the Staatliche Museen in Dahlem, West Berlin. Among the many others who offered various kinds of assistance, special thanks are due Father Salvatore Camporeale of Santa Maria Novella and of the Villa I Tatti in Florence, Don Guido Corallini of Santa Caterina in Pisa, and Signor Gianpiero Lucchese of the Primaziale in Pisa. Without the enthusiastic cooperation of Gino Corti, who transcribed unpublished documents or verified the accuracy of previously published ones, the archival material would not have been included. The publication of the color frontispieces was made possible by a generous grant from the State University of New York at Stony Brook.

A warm thank you is due my aunt, Minna Fiderer, who gave generously of her time, assisting with translations and editorial work. My children, Andre and Eva, now grown up, deserve my wonder, respect, and appreciation – not least for their cheerful endurance: The seasons of their childhood years were marked as much by the milestones of their mother's pre- and postdoctoral trials and triumphs as by birthdays and Halloweens. My husband, Martin, with characteristic good humor, not only acted as porter, chauffeur, and housekeeper during the years that this study germinated and developed, but he has also been a sounding board for ideas and literary expressions, and his insights, suggestions, and criticisms have been invaluable. To him I owe my deepest debt of gratitude.

New York, January 1985   Anita Moskowitz

CHAPTER ONE
Andrea and Nino Pisano: Summary Biographies

ndrea's masterpiece, the first of the three sets of bronze doors on the Baptistry of Florence, bears the following inscription on the upper edge of its framework: ANDREAS: UGOLINI: NINI: DI: PISIS: ME: FECIT: A:D: MCCC:XXX (Fig. 1). This monumental door is the creation, then, of a Pisan, not a Florentine artist. According to several documentary references, he was the son of a notary, Ugolino of Pisa, and was born, it would seem, in Pontedera, a small town under the control of Pisa (Doc. 30, 69–71). Nothing remains, however, in the modern village of Pontedera that gives any clue as to the kind of art and architecture Andrea was exposed to during his earliest years. Although his date of birth is not known, it is unlikely that he was much younger than thirty when offered a commission concerning one of the most important and venerated buildings in the city of Florence, a building the Florentine citizens believed had been erected in antiquity.[1] There are no documentary references to Andrea prior to his appearance in Florence but there is considerable evidence that he was trained, probably in Pisa itself, as a goldsmith, for he is referred to several times as *orefice* (Doc. 30, 64, 65, 71). His knowledge of the art and techniques of the goldsmith is apparent in numerous details on the doors including the miniature fragmentary architecture, the tooling on the thrones of the Virtues, and the minute perfection of anatomical and drapery details. A goldsmith's mentality is also evident in certain decorative elements on that part of the Campanile that was designed by him.[2] The attribution of the

[1] Horn (1943), 123ff.   [2] Trachtenberg (1971), 57.

wooden *Annunziata* (Figs. 102–104) and the head of a *Virgin* (Figs. 105, 106) in the Museo di San Matteo places Andrea in Pisa ca. 1320.[3] He also may have been responsible at this time for parts of Santa Maria della Spina during a rebuilding campaign of 1323–25.[4] Finally, numerous elements in his style can be related, as we shall see, to major Pisan monuments of the period.

The city of Pisa, however, seems to have been on the decline artistically, for during the second and third decades of the fourteenth century there was a paucity of commissions and no major project in the works. If he was indeed trained at Pisa, Andrea must have found his opportunities extremely limited. It is therefore likely that he turned to Siena, which was still at the height of its own artistic development and which offered prolific employment opportunities that would have attracted a promising young sculptor.

The situation in Siena differed radically, in several respects, from that in Pisa. During the first three decades of the fourteenth century, a number of major monuments were in progress: The upper part of the Duomo was receiving sculptural decoration, and a Sienese workshop was active in Orvieto producing the most extensive, the most radical, and certainly the most completely realized architectural sculpture of the trecento. Sienese artists were creating monuments for every major and several minor Tuscan cities and beyond these for the towns of Umbria. They even penetrated as far south as Naples, and Messina in Sicily. Furthermore, in contrast to Pisa, where few sculptors deviated from the norm imposed by the power of Giovanni Pisano's artistic personality, Siena experienced a rich sculptural development in which several distinct currents can be isolated. Affinities between Andrea's relief style on the doors and Sienese art have been noted by several observers.[5] We shall find that the most significant characteristics of Andrea's style on both the doors and the Campanile reveal a profound debt to various currents in Sienese sculpture. The evidence, moreover, speaks strongly for a relationship that goes beyond mere influence, a relationship involving a deeply absorbed attitude that would have been inherited during a decisive period of development, if not in Siena itself, then in one of its artistic dependencies. The impact of Orvieto is especially evident in Andrea's Florentine reliefs. It may be significant that the tradition of bronze sculpture flourished in Orvieto: The lunette over the central doorway of the Duomo of Orvieto contains six bronze angels holding a curtain that reveals a marble *Madonna and Child.* On the same level flanking the outer portals are four bronze symbols of the Evangelists.[6] In addition, there is a bronze

[3] See pp. 51–3ff.

[4] Trachtenberg (1971), 79–81.

[5] I. Toesca (1950), 26; Wundram (1957–9), 207–17.

[6] These probably date from 1330 or earlier. White (1966), 292.

architrave signed by Rosso Pedellaio, who in 1277 had worked on the great basin and perhaps also cast the three nymphs by Giovanni in Perugia.[7] These prominent examples of bronze sculpture may be said to have initiated the revival of bronze on a monumental scale that was to find its fullest realization only in the Renaissance — and of which Andrea's door represents an important episode. It seems very possible that it was in Orvieto that Andrea received the requisite experience — directing the building of wood and plaster supports, preparing models in wax for casting in bronze, filing and polishing the castings, all specialized techniques not normally encountered by the goldsmith or sculptor of monumental reliefs and statues — that prepared him for his first major commission.

Leaving the relatively limited environment of Pisa, then, in the mid-1320s, Andrea would have sought broadening experiences in the richer milieux of Siena and Orvieto. Having acquired proficiency in bronze and/or marble, having participated in or at least witnessed the realization of elaborate facade campaigns, Andrea would have been equipped upon his arrival in Florence to meet the demands of that most sophisticated and ambitious of Tuscan cities — one that, however, found itself momentarily in an artistic vacuum, at least as far as sculpture was concerned. Arnolfo was dead; Tino had already departed for Naples, leaving incomplete the project for a Baptism above the south portal of the Baptistry. The city was poor in native sculptural talent and little remains of significance from the years after Tino's departure.[8] It may very well be that, because no sculptor of consequence appeared on the horizon, the Arte di Calimala (Guild of the Cloth Finishers and overseers of the Baptistry) shrewdly scanned the neighboring artistic strongholds and turned to Siena and Orvieto, perhaps raiding them of their most promising protégé.

Documents place Andrea in Florence between 1330 and ca. 1343. It is possible, even likely, that he appeared there a year or two earlier and completed the Baptism group left unfinished by Tino.[9] The Baptistry doors were in progress from at least 1330 until their installation in time for the Feast of Saint John's Day in 1336 (Doc. 3–32). A reference of 1340 mentions a "magister Andrea maiore magistro dicte opere" as a member of the Council of the Opera (Doc. 36). This remains the only documentary evidence for Andrea's participation in the construction of the Campanile, but a long tradition that reaches back to a contemporary source, Antonio Pucci, informs us that the bell tower begun by Giotto was advanced by Andrea Pisano.[10]

[7] Venturi (1906), 30ff.

[8] Carli (1946), 9–11; I. Toesca (1951), 305f.; Valentiner (1927a), 177–220.

[9] See pp. 54–6ff. On a possible prior trip by Andrea to Venice see chapter 2, n. 3.

[10] Trachtenberg (1971), 4.

Giotto became capomaestro of the Cathedral of Florence in 1334, when work on the Campanile was begun, and remained in that office until his death in 1337.[11] Andrea, having completed the Baptistry doors and already at work on the hexagons for the west facade of the Campanile, was, it would seem, appointed capomaestro upon Giotto's death. The precise contribution of Andrea to the design of the Campanile, and the motivation for the changes he made in Giotto's structure, lie outside the scope of this study.[12] It is likely, however, that Giotto's original conception did not include the elaborate sculptural program that developed after Andrea became capomaestro.[13] The Genesis scenes (Figs. 50–56) on the west side were introduced during Giotto's lifetime;[14] the decision to extend the program with representations of the Labors of Man around the other sides of the Campanile was most likely Andrea's. The inclusion of a niche story was almost surely Andrea's plan with the specific intention of enhancing the iconographic content of the cathedral group and of giving monumental sculpture an important place on the Florentine tower.

In addition to the hexagons, Andrea executed the *Madonna and Child* in the lunette of the upper portal on the north side (Figs. 83, 84), and two (possibly even three) of the eight trecento Sibyls and Prophets that embellish the niche zone (Figs. 74–82); the rest were done in his workshop and by his followers.[15] In 1334 Andrea was commissioned by the Arte dei Baldrigai (the Guild of the Cloth Cutters) to make an iron seal for stamping French textiles (Doc. 35). Although Andrea's name does not appear again in Florentine documents, it has been conjectured with convincing stylistic arguments that he was responsible for the construction of Or San Michele.[16] Also associated with his name in Florence are two statuettes in the Museo dell'Opera del Duomo (Figs. 94–97), almost universally accepted as by the master but actually the work of two different hands: Andrea Pisano and a close imitator of his style.[17]

Documents together with several sculptures that can be connected with them indicate that Andrea returned to the region of his birth ca. 1343 and directed a workshop in Pisa (Doc. 39–56), where he employed, among others, his son Nino.[18] The Saltarelli monument (Fig. 149) in Santa Caterina, Pisa, appears to be a product of this Pisano shop designed shortly after his arrival in Pisa. The master himself executed, perhaps with some assistance, the *Madonna and Child* and closely supervised the design and execution of the angels on the upper and lower levels. Nino and various other

[11] Trachtenberg (1971), 20, 23.

[12] On the building history of the Campanile see Trachtenberg (1971); cf. Kreytenberg (1978), 147–84.

[13] Trachtenberg (1971), 86.

[14] Becherucci (1965), 261. See also p. 40.

[15] See pp. 48–50ff.

[16] Trachtenberg (1971), 76–9.

[17] See p. 56f.

[18] Becherucci (1965). See p. 60.

more or less independent assistants were given the responsibility for the other statues and reliefs.[19] About 1345 a large marble *Madonna and Child* (Figs. 114–116) was executed in Andrea's workshop to replace an earlier one that had fallen from the pinnacle of the Duomo facade in 1322.[20] The *Madonna del Latte* (Figs. 135, 136) and the *Madonna* and two saints in Santa Maria della Spina (Figs. 132–134, 294–296) were also executed in the Pisan workshop: the two Madonnas by Andrea himself, *Saint Peter* by Nino, and *John the Baptist* by Tommaso, the brother of Nino, after a design by Andrea.[21] A Maestà group, comprising a *Madonna and Child* and two angels (Figs. 110–113, 297–300), was begun in Pisa and shipped to Orvieto for completion (Doc. 39–56).[22] By May 1347, Andrea was capomaestro of Orvieto (Doc. 39). A travertine cornice on the exterior of Orvieto Cathedral (Fig. 204) has been attributed to him,[23] as has been, recently, a *Blessing Christ* relief (Fig. 93).[24] With the exception of the Maestà group now in the Museo dell'Opera del Duomo in Orvieto, no other sculptures in that town have been convincingly associated with his name. A reference of October 1349 mentions Nino as capomaestro (Doc. 57); this suggests that Andrea was dead or at least inactive by that date.[25] Vasari records an inscription on a tomb in Florence Cathedral; this inscription, however, is no longer extant and, moreover, postdates the trecento.[26]

Documents, then, establish that Nino succeeded his father as capomaestro of Orvieto in 1349, an appointment he appears to have relinquished by 1350.[27] In 1357 and 1358

---

[19] See pp. 80–90.

[20] Weinberger (1937), 58–91. Becherucci (1965), 246ff. See Doc. 40 and p. 71f.

[21] See p. 92f.

[22] Cellini (1933), 1–20; Lányi (1933a) 204–27. See pp. 69–71, 91–3.

[23] Trachtenberg (1971), 82.

[24] Burresi (1983), 182. See below, p. 53.

[25] The first time Andrea is referred to as "the late master" (Doc. 62) occurs after an almost ten-year gap in the documentation and therefore serves merely as a *terminus ante quem* for the date of Andrea's death. Vasari gives his death date as 1340 in the first edition of his *Lives*, and 1345 in the second; these are obviously errors as Andrea is recorded as capomaestro of Orvieto Cathedral in 1347 (Doc. 39).

[26] The inscription reads as follows: "Ingenti Andreas jacet hic Pisanus in urna / Marmore qui potuit spirantes ducere vultus / Et simulacra

Deum mediis imponere templis / Ex aere, ex auro candenti, et pulcro elephanto"; Milanese (1878), vol. 1, 495. This inscription, as recognized by several writers (see Becherucci [1965], 244, n. 12), postdates Andrea's death by at least a century, but it is very likely a reflection of an earlier inscription or at least refers to a tomb extant at the time it was composed. Becherucci further cites references to the Abbot Moreni, a seventeenth-century scholar, who states that he had found an explicit record of Andrea's tomb in a *Codice Magliabechiano* but could not recall the title of the one consulted; this reference is apparently lost.

[27] A letter of 1350, published in Guglielmo della Valle (1791), 282 (reprinted here, Doc. 61), and noted only by Kosegarten (1967), 235–49 (p. 247, n. 11), indicates that by this date a certain Giovanni Ammannati from Siena was capomaestro. All other scholars take a reference of 1353 to a Maestro Mattheo di Ugolino (Doc. 61) as the

he is recorded as a goldsmith working for the Opera del Duomo and the *comune* of Pisa (Doc. 62–65). A contract of 1362 commissions Nino to execute the tomb of Archbishop Giovanni Scherlatti, who died in March of that year (Doc. 67); the program specified by the contract, however, is not found on the Scherlatti tomb (Fig. 316) in the Camposanto in Pisa but on the tomb of another archbishop, Francesco Moricotti, who died in 1394 (Fig. 317). It has been suggested that when these tombs, originally in the Duomo, were transferred to the Camposanto in the early nineteenth century, the inscriptions were inadvertently reversed.[28] Finally, a document of 1368 records payments made to the sons of Nino, who is now mentioned as deceased, for money owed the sculptor for work on the tomb of the Doge of Pisa, Giovanni Agnello (Doc. 68). The tomb is no longer extant but is known from two prints of the eighteenth and nineteenth centuries.[29]

Thus, with the exception of the problematic Scherlatti monument, no document can be connected with any extant work of art. The basis for establishing a chronology for Nino's oeuvre, then, is purely stylistic. On that basis it can be conjectured that Nino was trained in his father's shop and that his earliest work is the *Bishop Saint* in Oristano (Figs. 130, 131), executed in the Pisan workshop shortly after 1343.[30] In that shop, too, the Venetian *Madonna* (Figs. 118–122) was made.[31] Stylistically more independent from the classicizing ideals of his father are the Detroit and Florentine Madonnas, which therefore were probably executed when Nino was master of his own shop.[32]

Except for his brief tenure as capomaestro of Orvieto, Nino appears to have lived out his life in Pisa where his less talented brother, Tommaso, was also employed – primarily as a goldsmith but with occasional architectural and sculptural commissions. Records concerning Tommaso cover the years 1363–71 (Doc. 69–71). Attributed to Tommaso while engaged in Andrea's Pisan workshop is the figure of Saint Paul for the Cornaro monument and the *John the Baptist* in Santa Maria della Spina (Figs. 128, 294); later, while a member of Nino's workshop, he contributed some figures for the Scherlatti and Moricotti tombs. His major extant work is the signed high altar of San Francesco, Pisa (Figs. 328–337), which shows that he was unequal to the demands of monumental sculpture, a forgotten and sad denouement to the achievements of his great Pisan predecessors.

---

terminus ante quem of Nino's office in Orvieto. Mattheo, however, is already mentioned in a document of 1351 (Doc. 60).

[28] Supino (1904), 230f. See p. 158.

[29] The first is a woodcut of 1783 by Ferdinando Fambrini, a copy of which is in the Gabinetto dei disegni in Pisa (Fig. 327). The second is found in B. Polloni (1835), P. III, T. XI. (Fig. 326).

[30] See p. 63f.

[31] See p. 65f.

[32] See p. 64f.

CHAPTER TWO
The Baptistry Doors

THE PROJECT

The original documents concerning the Florentine Baptistry doors are no longer extant but are known by way of excerpts made in the seventeenth century by Carlo Strozzi and preserved in the Archivio di Stato in Florence.[1] Although a very incomplete, summary, and repetitious compilation, the Strozziane provide the only basis for reconstructing the origin and progress of the project to incorporate metal doors on the Baptistry. From a careful analysis of these documents, the general sequence of events in the execution of the bronze doors may be deduced.[2] The project goes back to 1322 when the Arte di Calimala, which was in charge of the Baptistry, decided to cover the existing wooden doors with metal plates (Doc. 1). But in November of 1329 the officials of the guild altered the plan; instead of the traditional wooden doors clothed in metal, the Baptistry doors were to be made entirely of metal or brass ("metallo o ottone"). Furthermore, the goldsmith Piero di Jacopo was sent to Pisa to sketch the

[1] Florence, Archivio di Stato, Strozziane Serie II, LI, I, and Strozziane, Serie II, LI, II. Specific references are given in Appendix C. On the Strozzi documents see Krautheimer (1970), vol. 2, 362f. Complete references to, and an analysis of, the documents are offered by Falk (1940), 9–13, 40–58. See also Lányi, in Thieme and Becker (1933b), 94–98. Documents concerning the doors are published by Frey (1911), 349–53. The Campanile documents are found in Guasti (1887); excerpts relevant to the construction of the tower are offered by Trachtenberg (1971), 182ff. Most of the documents from published sources are reprinted in Burresi (1983), 202–206.

[2] The reader interested in an analysis of the structure of the doors, a more detailed reading of the documents, and a reconstruction of the process and progress in the execution of the doors is referred to Appendix A.

bronze doors there and then to Venice to find a caster (Doc. 2).[3] Two months later, on 13 January, the "porte di legname" were begun (Doc. 3). This may refer to the laying out and construction of a latticelike skeleton of wooden boards to serve as a kind of scaffold for the wax framework; it may also refer to the making of wood models of the quatrefoil frames to serve as prototypes for the modeling in wax of the framework and as templates for the shaping of the quatrefoil reliefs. From the completed wax model – a prototype of the entire doorframe with its complex of openings for lions' heads, studs, inscription, and quatrefoil reliefs[4] – the bronze framework for each door leaf was to be made. This wax prototype – the "porte di cera" – was completed by 2 April 1330 (Doc. 5). For the next year and nine months Andrea must have been working on the models for the narrative reliefs, for on 9 January 1332 the officials of the Opera met concerning "il fare e fabbricare l'opera delle porte" – presumably the casting process – which was to begin the following day (Doc. 7). Work on the reliefs continued (Doc. 22). From February 1333 until late December 1335 there are references to the cleaning and polishing of the doors, the completion of the lions' heads on the frames, the gilding of the reliefs, and the repair of certain damages or casting flaws (Doc. 20, 22, 26–31). By 20 June 1336 both wings were fully installed on the Baptistry in time for the festival of San Giovanni (Doc. 32).

THE FRAMEWORK

Andrea's Baptistry doors (Fig. 1) impress the viewer as a work belonging to both monumental and "minor" art, the creation of an architect, a sculptor, and a goldsmith. Brilliantly calculated to achieve maximum overall decorative unity, the design

---

[3] Trachtenberg (1971), 55, n. 38, suggests that Andrea was in Venice before coming to Florence and that far from seeking a bronze caster, "un maestro a fondare" (which is *not* the wording of the document), Piero di Jacopo was sent north to seek a *maker*, "un maestro a lavorare la forma," as the reference of 1329 states (Doc. 2), and that it was Andrea himself who was called from Venice. There are good arguments in favor of a Venetian sojourn before Andrea's arrival in Florence. This would explain not only the Venetian character of his new Campanile design and the "Venetian" window on the tower (Trachtenberg [1971], 55f.), but also the similarity of the basic scheme of the Porta di San Clemente of San Marco and the Baptistry doors; see Moskowitz (1983a), 1f. Nevertheless, as we shall demonstrate, it is more likely that Andrea was already in Florence and participated in the designing of the doors while Piero was seeking the services of a bronze worker.

[4] All parts that were to be fire gilt – the reliefs, the lions' heads, and the strips containing the inscription and the stud heads and rosettes – were cast separately and inserted into the framework. A discussion of gilding techniques during the Middle Ages is found in Bearzi's essay in Poggi, Planiscig, and Bearzi (194–).

presents a series of varied geometric shapes that encourage the transition from monumental door to small narrative reliefs that, as we shall see, continually refer back to the shapes and directions of the framing elements. Each valve of the doors is itself framed by a simple rectangular molding that encloses a decorative lattice dividing the doors into twenty-eight rectangular fields disposed vertically in four columns and horizontally in seven rows.[5] This lattice is composed of delicate chains of rosettes alternating with stud-heads and punctuated at the intersections by small lions' heads in quadrilobes. The rectangular fields are delineated further by dentilated moldings that surround not simple quatrefoils, but ones pierced by the angles of rhomboids. These pierced quatrefoils have several functions: They enhance the decorative unity of the doors and at the same time they enliven the grid pattern by reducing its dominating rectangularity. They also serve to reduce and limit the pictorial field, for the action of the narratives rarely extends beyond the limits of an implied inner rectangle whose boundary is defined by the intruding points of the angles and lobes (Fig. 8). As a result of this organization, the viewer is led from the architecture – the door as a whole – through a sequence of progressively smaller geometric configurations involving outer and inner rectangles, quatrefoils and rhomboids, and the smaller unit of the implied innermost rectangle to, finally, the reliefs themselves. Stated in other terms, the eye is led through a series of transitions from the overall, abstract rectilinear pattern to softer, more varied, yet still geometric, configurations, to focus finally on the narratives in which geometrically conceived compositions, decorative rhythms, and naturalistic, organic forms are coordinated. Within this overall unity, the large single figures of Virtues on the two lowest rows – the lateral figures facing toward the center and the inner figures placed frontally – provide a subtly differentiated base for the twenty narrative scenes above which illustrate the life of John the Baptist.

THE RELIEFS: STYLE AND CHRONOLOGY

The quatrefoil, then, serves as a visual transition from monumental door to miniature relief: It enriches the grid pattern of the doors and provides the immediate frame for the individual narratives. The quatrefoil has spatial implications as well. The flat bronze background against which the gilded figures are placed in relief, together with an imaginary "picture plane" in front of the quatrefoil and forward edge of the platform on which the figures are set, delineates, or at least clearly implies, the depth of the space provided for the figures. Neither the front nor the back plane, however, is

[5] On the arithmetical basis for the design of the smaller units, see Zervas (1975).

strictly inviolable but remains fluid to serve the action of the figures and to enhance their impact. The background in *Zacharias and the Elders* (Fig. 7), unfettered by architectural props, appears to expand beyond the material limits of the bronze plane and puts in relief, literally and figuratively, the silent gestures of the stricken priest.[6] Just as the space expands discreetly beyond the material plane of the background, the figures occasionally project forward from the imaginary foreground plane, as when the drapery overlaps the platform on which the figures stand (Fig. 8). In effect, then, the images are situated both in the real, the viewer's world, and in the fictive world of the narrative.[7]

Within the quatrefoil frames the twenty episodes from the life of John the Baptist are related with utmost concentration and focus by means of few figures and the sparing use of props. The austerity of the images, in which strongly projecting figures are set against the broad flat ground, is relieved by the flowing drapery rhythms that enliven the surface of each quatrefoil. Poignant and expressive gestures are often isolated against the flat ground so that the stance of a body, the movement of arms and hands, or the tilt of a head are saturated with significance – as in a pantomime production on a stage. Within these concentrated worlds the figures achieve a monumentality heretofore seen only in large-scale sculpture (Fig. 18). Even when the architectural motifs – fragmentary and sometimes placed obliquely as in Giotto's Arena Chapel frescoes – contribute to the illusion of spatial depth, the impression that there exists a cogent space derives primarily, again as in Giotto's paintings, from the plasticity of the figures themselves. Whether the figures are enveloped by swathes of curvilinear drapery folds that all but mask the body beneath (Fig. 7, right), whether the drapery is conceived architectonically to convey a blocklike ponderous mass (Fig. 7, left), or whether the skeletal structure emerges through the soft, fleshy forms (Fig. 45), Andrea's figures almost without exception have a weight and presence that both demand and create spatial scope.

The drapery style, clearly, is not completely homogeneous: Drapery is employed for structural, decorative, and expressive effects. In some figures there is virtually no play in the rhythms of the garments so that the bulk and weight of the enveloped forms are emphasized. In *Zacharias and the Elders* (Fig. 7) the massive architecture of his form, composed predominantly of verticals and horizontals and surrounded by

---

[6] Falk (1940), 58–64, offers a detailed description and analysis of this relief. Cf. Wundram (1957–9 and 1968), who views the background as a simple, flat, impenetrable plane.

[7] Donatello, a century later, exploited this device of drapery overlapping an element of the real world in his reliquary bust of Saint Rossore. The resulting ambiguities are discussed by I. Lavin (1970), 207–26, and Moskowitz (1981a), 41–8.

a clearly implied volume of space, isolates Zacharias from the more active group on the right. In the latter, the linear play of hemlines and the varied glances and gestures contribute to the expression of powerful consternation experienced by these figures. In contrast to the imposing gravity of Zacharias, other figures have less weight and reveal a search for lightness and grace in keeping with the subject (Fig. 10, right) or to enhance the overall rhythm of the composition (Fig. 13, left). In most of the figures, however, there is a striking balance between the abstract, decorative, or expressive play of drapery, and structural demands. Small in scale yet monumental in conception, the figures act out their destinies with a seriousness of purpose in no way diminished by the ease and grace of their poses and gestures or the lyricism of their drapery patterns.

There are unexpected touches of realism: The censer held by Zacharias in the *Annunciation* resembles a real censer (cf. Figs. 5, 41); the tooling on Zacharias's drapery evokes damasked tapestry; and many individual gestures would seem to be studied from life (Figs. 10, 47). Never stylized, the movements are, however, slow and disciplined. The emotional range of facial expression is limited, as though in reaction to the dramatically expressive figures of Giovanni Pisano and in favor of the restrained expressive content of Giotto's paintings. Nevertheless, upon close examination — and unlike most architectural sculpture these reliefs demand very close scrutiny — the viewer becomes privy to the anxiety of Zacharias, the consternation of his companions, the joyful anticipation of the infirm, and finally the anguish of the disciples (Fig. 7, 19, 47).

The compositions tend to adhere closely to the demands, not of the quatrefoil frame, but of the inner, "invisible" rectangle determined by the intruding points of the angles and lobes. In the *Visitation* (Fig. 8), for example, the companion of Mary provides the left-hand limit of the implied rectangle while the tower delineates its border on the right. The horizontal cornice draws attention to the upper boundary and the lower edge is defined by the platform on which the figures stand.[8] In this manner, and in the majority of reliefs — the main exceptions are the landscapes — the "invisible" inner rectangle provides the actual pictorial field. Also internally, verticals and horizontals predominate as the main compositional vectors. In some cases the central vertical axis, expressed not directly but implied by the points of the angles between the left- and right-hand lobes, functions to isolate, separate, or emphasize an important aspect of the subject or content of the scene. For example, these points provide an invisible barrier that separates the divine and earthly actors in the *Annunciation to Zacharias* (Fig. 5) even though they communicate within a unified space and on a single ground

[8] Kreytenberg (1975), 230.

plane.[9] Similarly, the disparate yet related destinies of Mary and Elizabeth in the *Visitation* (Fig. 8) are expressed by means of the space between their heads, on the one hand, and their intersected arms, on the other, both of which occur in the exact center of the composition.

Despite the predominant rectangularity of the compositions, contrast and balance are the key notes in the internal design as they are in the framework as a whole. Diagonal and circular movements in the architecture, figures, and drapery continually echo the shape of the pierced quatrefoil. The compositional reflections of that shape are strongest, as we shall see, in the earliest reliefs to be designed: the *Annunciation to Zacharias* and the *Birth of the Baptist* (Figs. 5, 6, 9). In the later reliefs, such relationships are more subtle and the dominant references are to the enframing verticals and horizontals. A perfect balance is achieved in the *Funeral of the Baptist* (Fig. 24). The group of disciples in this poignant relief is densely contained within a controlling rectangle. But a strong sense of movement and direction is created by the drapery rhythms that confront this basic shape. The integration of the framing vectors with the internal compositions is responsible, to a large extent, for the extraordinary sense of harmony and balance felt between the narrative and decorative elements of the doors.

The Baptistry reliefs have generally been viewed as homogeneous in style.[10] Close observation reveals, however, a number of subtle changes in composition, in figure style, in the degree of freedom in the handling of landscape elements, and in the conception of the architecture. When viewed against the background of closely related preceding reliefs and of Andrea's own subsequent relief style on the Campanile of Florence, it becomes apparent that the quatrefoils evolve from the more linear and decorative mode of the left-hand wing to the more plastic and monumental relief conception on the right-hand wing. Indeed, the reliefs appear to have been composed more or less (there are exceptions) in the order of the narrative sequence that begins with the *Annunciation to Zacharias* (Fig. 5) on the upper left and ends with the *Entombment of the Baptist* (Fig. 25) on the lower right.

It is, however, the *Birth of the Baptist* (Fig. 9), the fourth relief in the narrative sequence, that appears to have been the first to be designed. It is conspicuously the only relief on the doors in which the figures are arranged in the antiquated manner of superimposed layers that have no coherent spatial relationship to each other. The scene contains, moreover, quotations from Giovanni Pisano's Pisa pulpit, Duccio's Maestà,

[9] Schmarsow (1897), 19.
[10] Cf., however, Wundram (1968), who notes stylistic differences between the left and right valves and argues that the designs on the right are earlier. The discussion on chronology presented here was previously published in Moskowitz (1981b).

and Giotto's Peruzzi Chapel frescoes, and it reveals, more than any other relief, the struggle to adapt previous iconographic patterns to the demands of the difficult – if au courant – quatrefoil frame.[11] Elizabeth's position resembles that seen in Giotto's fresco (Fig. 39) as well as in the possible common source, Nicola's Siena pulpit (Fig. 36). The naturalistic bathing scene, however, would appear to derive from Giovanni's pulpits in which the infant is held in the arms of the midwife who tests the water (Fig. 37). In conformity, however, to Duccio's representation (Fig. 38), the infant is held by the woman to the right rather than the one to the left of the basin and, as in the Maestà, the midwives are seated. Furthermore, the one really novel element in the relief, the ledge on which the midwives sit, may have been suggested to Andrea by Duccio's group, in which the women appear to be seated on a similar horizontal ground plane. Used inconsistently in this relief, it functions with perfect logic in all subsequent scenes in which it appears. Finally, the two women behind Elizabeth are quotations from the Peruzzi Chapel (Fig. 39); in the relief, however, they look distressingly truncated.

The composition of the *Birth of the Baptist* is controlled by rather strong parallelisms between the interior forms and the diagonals and curves of the frame, and by a rather obvious tripartite division in the arrangement of motifs both vertically and horizontally. In the *Birth of the Baptist* – to a far greater extent than in the other quatrefoils – abstract decorative considerations and an insistence on incorporating established iconographic motifs appear to have taken precedence over spatial concerns. This relief remains *retardataire* and is the least successful of the bronze panels. It may have been a demonstration piece presented to the Arte di Calimala, and later incorporated into the fabric of the doors.[12] If so, and despite its conservative features, it is not difficult to understand why the Arte chose Andrea for the execution of this unique commission: The sculptor shows himself intimately acquainted with the work of the great masters past and present, and able to reconcile decorative and iconographic requisites. While paying homage to Giovanni, Andrea remains free from his tense emotionalism, which would have been somewhat alien to the Florentine temperament; while rendering the larger volumes with convincing plasticity – reflecting Giotto's achievement in painting – he executes the minute details such as drapery and damasked textures, hair strands, features, and gestures with a sense of precision and, at the same time, an easy relaxed naturalism.

In the *Annunciation to Zacharias* (Fig. 5), the first episode to be represented on the doors and, quite possibly, the second relief to be designed by Andrea, the spatial contradictions of the *Birth* are not in evidence: Space is delineated quite clearly by the

---

[11] On the history of the quatrefoil frame, see pp. 140–5.

[12] Wundram (1968), 377.

projecting ledge that forms a ground plane, by the depth of the framing elements, and by the planar background. In short, Andrea has created a stagelike space in which the figures can move with relative ease. The internal links to the quatrefoil, however, remain quite strong. Originally, a chain connected the censer to Zacharias's hand in the *Annunciation* (Fig. 6).[13] The diagonal formed by this chain parallels one side of the rhombus, while the curve of Gabriel's bent arm seems a continuation of the swing of the upper left lobe of the quatrefoil. The drapery, as well as Gabriel's wings, parallels or echoes the lines and curves of the pierced quatrefoil while the scalloped edges of the baldacchino both reflect its lobes and connect several of its vertices. This is the only relief on the doors in which a motif, incorporated to unite the interior composition with the surrounding frame, violates the unity of the relief surface; accessories such as the detachable chain of the censer are shunned in all subsequent scenes. In few other reliefs, moreover, does the diagonally oriented rhombus that pierces the quatrefoil play as important a role in the interior composition; the dominant compositional vectors increasingly ignore the diagonals in favor of the verticals and horizontals of the implied inner rectangle.[14]

The composition of the *Annunciation* (Fig. 5) is reminiscent of the *Presentation* (Fig. 42) of 1316 on the Pistoia Silver Altar by Andrea di Jacopo d'Ognabene.[15] The *Visitation* (Fig. 8), too, is very close to a relief in Pistoia (Fig. 43). Despite this possible dependence, the Baptistry *Visitation* introduces a new element in terms of spatial representation. Although the subject lends itself to a symmetrical composition, the strict symmetry of the Pistoia relief and of Andrea's own reliefs illustrating the *Annunciation* and the *Birth* (Figs. 5, 9) is alleviated and an obliquely set architectural element is introduced. This feature recalls the structure in Giotto's *Meeting at the Golden Gate*. From Giotto Andrea has learned that by placing an architectural structure at an angle to the picture plane a more compelling sense of spatial recession can result. Both the *Annunciation to Zacharias* and the *Visitation* (Figs. 5, 8), then, two of the earliest episodes of the narrative, recall compositions on the Pistoia Silver Altar. The latter, although clearly dependent on the traditions of Nicola and Giovanni Pisano, nevertheless diverges from those traditions in ways analogous to the independence shown in Andrea's reliefs a decade and a half later. Especially notable is the muted emotional content, the dampening of the energy of the compositional rhythms, and the more naturalistic rela-

---

[13] This is apparent from the engraving in Lasinio (1821).

[14] Excellent analyses of the relationship of several of the relief compositions to the decorative framework may be found in Kreytenberg (1975), 230;

Schmarsow (1897), 19; and White (1966), 305–8.

[15] Wundram (1957–9), 201. On the Pistoia Silver Altar, see Ragghianti (1954), 423–38; (1955), 102–27; Steingraber (1956), 148–54; Marchini (1966), 135–47.

tionship between figures and architecture in comparison to Giovanni's reliefs. These features suggest that Andrea aligned himself with that current in early fourteenth-century Tuscan sculpture that ran counter to the still dominant influence of Giovanni Pisano and his followers.[16]

Of the first four reliefs on the doors, we have so far omitted discussion of *Zacharias and the Elders* (Fig. 7), the second episode in the narrative. Unlike the other three, which have sources in the Pisani pulpits, in Giotto's paintings, and in the Baptistry mosaics, this relief has no known immediate iconographic precedent and would seem to be inspired primarily by the description of the event in the gospel (Luke I:22).[17] It is the first of several scenes in which there is no indication of setting whatsoever (cf. *Christ Cures the Infirm* and *Funeral of the Baptist*; Figs. 19, 24). Lacking the restricting effects of fragmentary furniture or architecture, the spatial implications in *Zacharias and the Elders* (Fig. 7) are even stronger than in the *Visitation* (Fig. 8). Like the "interior by implication," which Panofsky noted in some early fourteenth-century panels,[18] the background becomes a floating, undefined area suggesting expansion into depth and to either side of the frame. One need only compare *Zacharias and the Elders* (Fig. 7) to Tino di Camaino's Tuscan reliefs to recognize that a conquest of depth in relief sculpture has taken place. On the Petroni monument (Fig. 187), for instance, although the figures in the reliefs are placed against blank backgrounds, the rear planes together with the frames press in on the figures and there is little sense of space expanding beyond the confines of the frames. The first four quatrefoils on the left-hand door leaf, then, suggest a continuing search for a convincing representation of space and would appear to form a plausible chronological sequence, namely, the *Birth*, the *Annunciation*, the *Visitation* and then, very likely, *Zacharias and the Elders* (Figs. 9, 5, 8, 7).

The next relief, the *Naming of the Baptist* (Fig. 10), essentially reverts to the solution seen in the *Annunciation* (Fig. 5), but in it Andrea eschews the more obvious linkages between the quatrefoil and the internal design seen in the first episode. Instead, the emphasis is on the verticals and horizontals that relate to the implied inner rectangle. The last five narratives on the left valve are set in landscapes (Figs. 11–15). Close observation reveals a notable progression from the tight, undifferentiated leaves on the trees of the first landscape scene, to the increasingly freer, more open handling in the subsequent scenes. The compact cluster of leaves in the *Giovannino* panel projects in very shallow relief, and the forms are reminiscent of representations on earlier Pisan

[16] On this anti-Giovannesque current in early fourteenth-century Tuscan sculpture, see Wundram (1957–9), 199f., and chapter 6.

[17] Falk and Lányi (1943), 132–53.
[18] Panofsky (1971), 19.

and Sienese goldsmith work, including those on the Pistoia Silver Altar (Figs. 11, 44).[19] In the second landscape scene, the *Preaching of the Baptist* (Fig. 12), the leaves are handled in a much looser manner, whereas in the last three landscape representations, for instance in *Ecce Agnus Dei* (Fig. 13), the leaves are treated as individual forms with a good deal of space between them. These forms project in higher relief than do the trees in the *Giovannino* panel and anticipate Andrea's treatment of flora in the Campanile Genesis scenes in which there is a good deal of undercutting and a very free handling of leaf forms (Figs. 50, 51). The earliest episode among the landscape scenes, then, indicates Andrea's earlier ties to Tuscan goldsmith work, and the later episodes look forward to the freer handling of his later relief style.

Turning to the right-hand valve, significant changes in architectural representation are evident, and these tend to support the chronology that has been suggested here. We have seen that in the *Annunciation* (Fig. 5), the architecture is completely frontal; its projection in relief, moreover, is very shallow, and the architectural motifs and relationship to the figures recall the *Presentation* on the Pistoia Altar (Fig. 42). The *Visitation* (Fig. 8), on the other hand, is more adventuresome architecturally. On the right-hand valve the prison scenes (Figs. 17, 18, 21) move a step beyond the *Visitation*: The clear implication is that the structures contain space and can enclose figures. Finally, in the *Presentation of the Baptist's Head to Herodias* (Fig. 23), one of the last episodes in which architecture is represented, Andrea abandons the fragmentary architectural motifs of his earlier scenes; here, instead, the figures are contained within a complete three-dimensional building, clearly based on Giotto's Peruzzi Chapel fresco. But just as clearly, the experiment in relief was not entirely successful, for the architecture is too small for the figures, lacking both the height and breadth of the painted prototype.[20] In the final episode, the *Entombment* (Fig. 25), Andrea reverts to a frontal and symbolic architecture – one that, while it nicely balances the opening scene, provides a telling contrast to the very first relief (Fig. 5). Whereas in the *Annunciation* the forms of the tabernacle are extremely flat and essentially decorative, in the *Entombment* the architectural elements project more strongly and seem to enclose the figures behind the bier.

Finally, there are significant if subtle changes in figure style. Compare Andrea's handling of a group of three or more figures on the left and right valves: In *Zacharias and the Elders* (Fig. 7), the pattern of cascading hemlines and small fold forms, remi-

---

[19] Cf. also the Sacra Cintola (Figs. 180, 181) and the reliquary of San Galgano in the Museo dell'Opera del Duomo in Siena. On the relationship of Andrea's sculpture to earlier Pisan goldsmith work, see p. 96f.

[20] In this respect, the architecture recalls the structure in the *Annunciation to Anna* and the *Birth of the Virgin* in the Arena Chapel. The influence of Giotto's Paduan style is explored in chapter 6.

niscent of the agitated linear drapery on the Pistoia altar (Figs. 42, 43), unifies and tends to flatten the group. In the prison scenes on the right valve (Figs. 17, 18, 21), on the other hand, there is less reliance on the decorative effects of curvilinear drapery folds to enliven the compositions. There are fewer curves in the drapery forms and when they do appear, they tend to reflect the broad masses of the bodies beneath – a characteristic of the finest reliefs on the Campanile (Fig. 57). In the left-hand reliefs, the feet are generally obscured by drapery or are tipped down as in Duccio's paintings (Fig. 13), whereas in the right-hand reliefs the feet are more often visible and are firmly planted on the projecting ledge (Figs. 16, 21). One quatrefoil on the doors displays an unprecedented sophistication and monumentality in the manner in which drapery is related to the moving figures. The rearview motif seen in the *Funeral of the Baptist* (Fig. 24) may derive from the similar configuration on the facade of Orvieto Cathedral (Fig. 209), but this possible prototype has been radically transformed by compressing the action into a dense rectangle and emphasizing the drapery rhythms and contrasting movements of the bodies. In this relief, which I suggest was one of the last to be designed, Andrea achieves an extraordinary balance between structural, decorative, and expressive exigencies.

The eight Virtues (Figs. 26–33) are spread across the lowest two registers and are seated symmetrically about the central closure of the doors. It is likely that this series was designed as a group. Their monumental and weighty presence suggests that they too were among the last reliefs to be designed for the doors.

Despite the overall unity of the conception, it would seem that the doors were begun, not by a fully mature, but by a rapidly evolving master who experimented with a variety of solutions to the problems of composition, figure structure, and architectural and landscape environments. The stylistic evolution suggested here is quite remarkable in the work of a medieval sculptor within the short span of little over two and a half years, especially within the confines of a single commission. A detail of the doors and of the Campanile, however, lends support to our chronology. The lions' heads punctuating the framing elements on the left valve of the doors are more linear, less plastic, and in a sense fussier than are those on the right in which, for example, the manes tend to be organized into larger masses of deeply incised and sharply projecting tufts (Fig. 34).[21] These are precisely the characteristics of the lions' heads in lozenges on the Campanile that, moreover, show a greater sensitivity and expressiveness in the modeling of the cheeks, eyes, and foreheads (Fig. 35). It remains to be seen whether the style of the hexagonal reliefs on the Campanile is consonant with that of the doors,

[21] This was noted by Kreytenberg (1975), 230, n.45.

and whether the hexagons represent a continuation of the development observed on the Baptistry.

ICONOGRAPHY AND NARRATIVE MODE

Saint John the Baptist has always been of more than ordinary importance to the citizens of Florence. He is, of course, the patron saint of the Baptistry. Thus the apocalyptic vision of the universe seen in the mosaic vault inside the building might be expected to include some scenes devoted to his life. But the vault contains an unusually large number of scenes – indeed, the most extensive monumental cycle prior to that on Andrea's door – devoted to the Baptist's life.[22] The Baptist is more than the honored patron of the building; he is the patron saint of the city of Florence itself and thus he has always received special reverence. In the 1230s his image appeared on the Florentine silver coin[23] and, toward the end of the century, on the gold florin[24]; it once adorned the city's banner and seal, and it was in his name that contracts were sometimes notarized.[25] In Canto XXXII of Dante's *Paradiso*, the saint is especially honored by being placed opposite the Virgin Mary – higher even than such holy figures as Saints Francis, Benedict, and Augustine. It did not escape the Florentines that even in the Gospels the Baptist is exalted above all other saints, for he is referred to as "more than a prophet" (Luke VII:26). And the Pseudo Bonaventura in his *Meditations on the Life of Christ* goes so far as to call him an angel.[26] No wonder that the Florentines took, and still take, such pride in their patron saint. To this day, the *festa di San Giovanni* remains one of the most important and popular festivals of the year in Florence.

By the early fourteenth century an extensive body of apocryphal literature elaborating the events mentioned in the Bible had achieved tremendous popularity. New episodes and homely details that served to humanize the sacred personages were added to the sparse accounts of the lives of Christ, his family, and his followers. Often, their infancy and childhood were highlighted.[27] These narratives provided the sources for the expanded iconographic content of many of the major monumental cycles of the thirteenth and fourteenth centuries in Italy, such as the Pisani pulpits, Duccio's Maestà,

[22] Falk and Lányi (1943), 133. Portions of the following material appeared in Moskowitz (1985).

[23] Davidsohn (1957), 294.

[24] Goro Dati (1785), 127.

[25] Reference to the seal is found in Zingarelli (1939), 99. Mention of the city's banner and the use of the seal for notarization is found in Braunfels (1953), 145.

[26] Ragusa and Green (1961), 183.

[27] The childhood of Mary, for instance, to which not one word is devoted in the Bible, receives much attention in Jacopo de Voragine's *Golden Legend*.

and Giotto's Arena Chapel frescoes. It is hardly surprising, then, that the precursor of Christ, whose life and passion paralleled and intersected with that of the Savior,[28] should become the subject of such elaboration. Both the Baptistry mosaics, completed in 1325, and Giotto's Peruzzi Chapel frescoes in Santa Croce, dated in the late 1320s or early 1330s, include episodes and motifs that can only be explained on the basis of the popular literary accounts. Among these are Jacopo de Voragine's *Golden Legend*, the Pseudo Bonaventura's *Meditations on the Life of Christ*, and an anonymous life of the Baptist that was in circulation in Italy in the early fourteenth century.[29]

The Baptistry mosaics and Peruzzi Chapel frescoes, in turn, provided the most important and relevant visual sources for many of the compositional schemes on the bronze doors.[30] Nevertheless, several scenes cannot be explained on the basis of these important precedents. For one scene – *Zacharias and the Elders*, which does not appear in the earlier cycles – Andrea confronted the biblical narrative itself; for several other episodes he turned directly to the apocryphal literary accounts. In so doing, he translated the emotional tone of the verbal narratives into a lyrical and at times vividly sequential sculptural narrative mode.

The story of John the Baptist is narrated most extensively in the Gospel according to Luke (I:1–80 III:1–22; VII:18–23), which is the only book to include the first five episodes that appear on the doors: the *Annunciation to Zacharias*, *Zacharias and the Elders*, the *Visitation*, the *Birth of the Baptist*, and the *Naming of the Baptist* (Figs. 5, 7–10). For each of these scenes, with the exception of *Zacharias and the Elders*, a precedent for the general compositional scheme can be found in the Baptistry mosaics, in Giotto's frescoes, or in analogous scenes from the life of Christ (such as the Nativity) in the Pisani pulpits.[31] Lacking a readily available pictorial precedent for the *Elders* (Fig. 7), one of the most expressive scenes on the doors, Andrea turned directly to the gospel account in Luke I:11–22. Here we read that when the angel Gabriel announces to Zacharias that his elderly wife will conceive a son, Zacharias expresses doubts and asks for a sign. As a rebuke for his lack of faith in Gabriel's words, and as a sign of

---

[28] On biblical parallelisms between Christ and the Baptist see Warner (1976), 8f., where the intersecting lives of Christ and John, and Mary and Elizabeth are seen to form a "beautifully wrought double-helix." The parallelism between the lives of Christ and John is apparent in the emphasis on the Baptist's Passion on the doors; the entire right wing is devoted to his martyrdom.

[29] Ragusa and Green (1961), 21–6, 81–4, 174–85; Ryan and Ripperger (1969), 321–7, 502–10. On the anonymous *Vita*, see nn. 35 and 36, this chapter.

chapter.

[30] In her pioneering study of Andrea's Baptistry doors, Ilse Falk (1940), 86–157, offered an exhaustive survey of the history of Baptist cycles in both the literary and visual traditions. On the relationship of the door reliefs to the Baptistry mosaics and the Peruzzi Chapel frescoes see Falk, 157–79, and Falk and Lányi (1943); in the latter, note the diagram on p. 153.

[31] Falk and Lányi (1943). See also p. 12f., this chapter.

their truth, Zacharias's power of speech is taken away until after his son's birth and naming. Outside the temple, the congregation waits for Zacharias to emerge. "And when he came out, he could not speak unto them; and they perceived that he had seen a vision in the temple: for he beckoned unto them and remained speechless." In the relief we see Zacharias on the left, his massive body standing apart from his companions, his right hand pointing to his mouth, his left hand gesturing and isolated against the blank background. Immediately below the hand making signs is the hand of the Elder standing foremost in the group to the right. The isolation of these two hands links Zacharias to the Elders and suggests the role of the central figure as interpreter: Indeed, the latter turns his head toward his companions whose faces and gestures express consternation and astonishment.

For these first two scenes (Figs. 5, 7), Andrea employed a narrative device used earlier by Giotto in the Arena Chapel. The *Annunciation to Zacharias* shows the figures of Gabriel and Zacharias standing before an altar tabernacle. In his office as priest, Zacharias is in the act of swinging a thurible (see Fig. 6), and is caught by surprise by the appearance and astonishing message of Gabriel. Zacharias is seen in left profile. The presence of the altar implies an interior setting, much as the choir enclosure, altar, and pulpit in Giotto's *Expulsion of Joachim* imply an interior. In the following relief, Zacharias is seen in right profile facing the company of Elders. Here there are no props or other indication of setting; the figures are situated against a blank background plane. As the time sequence of the events is very close, the observer can easily imagine Zacharias, who first faces left toward the angel, turning around to exit from the sanctuary and meet his companions outside. This narrative device was probably inspired by Giotto's similar handling of the first two scenes in the Arena Chapel where, however, a continuous sequential movement from left to right (countered in the first scene by the backward turn of Joachim's head) expresses the latter's reluctant departure from the temple precinct and gloomy return to the fields where his shepherds await him.

The third episode on the doors, the *Visitation* (Fig. 8), occurs on the second register of the left-hand door wing. Unlike Bonanus's doors in Pisa (and Ghiberti's two doors), the sequence does not pass across both wings. Instead, one reads from left to right and from top to bottom first on the left-hand and then on the right-hand wing. The reading of the narrative sequence is thus established as analogous to the way one reads the words in an open codex.[32] This also contrasts with the traditional pictorial system (still employed in Ghiberti's two doors) whereby Old Testament scenes are read from top to bottom and New Testament scenes from bottom to top, as for example on Bishop Bernward's doors at Hildesheim, which contain both cycles, one on each

[32] This is observed by Hunisak (1970); see n. 36.

wing.[33] The reading of the narrative sequence on Andrea's doors, so strictly comparable to the way the eye passes across the pages of a codex, is extremely suggestive, as will soon become apparent.

As is true of Giotto in the Arena Chapel – and with as little insistence on rigid adherence to preconceived principles – Andrea established visual and narrative linkages that enrich the meaning, lend thematic unity, and enhance the decorative quality of the Baptistry door reliefs.[34] Just as Giotto, for example, insisted on "unity of place" in the three scenes that occur in front of a temple apse (the *Presentation of the Rods*, the *Watching of the Rods*, and the *Betrothal of the Virgin*, Figs. 215, 216), the three prison scenes on the doors repeat the placement within the composition and the perspective viewpoint of the prison structure (Figs. 17, 18, 21). The five landscape scenes are grouped together as are the two baptism scenes (Fig. 1). Finally, notwithstanding Andrea's evolution from the earlier left-hand door wing to the later right-hand door wing, the first scene in the narrative is echoed in the last: Both the *Annunciation* and the *Entombment* contain decorative Gothic tabernacles that frame the figures (Figs. 5, 25).

The *Visitation* (Fig. 8) is unusual in Baptist cycles, belonging more often to those concerning the life of Mary. But the meeting of Mary and Elizabeth during the latter's sixth month of pregnancy, mentioned briefly in Luke I:36–41, is the focus of much attention in a *Vita* of John the Baptist, formerly attributed to Fra Domenico Cavalca (ca. 1260–1342) but now recognized as the work of an anonymous fourteenth-century writer.[35] Although this *Vita* was probably not the only source for several unusual episodes or details on the doors, the emotional tone of the bronze cycle, the general structure of the narrative sequence and a number of individual motifs find close parallels in this particular literary account.[36]

[33] Hunisak points out that while the events of John the Baptist's life are related in the New Testament, he is considered the last and greatest of the prophets of the Old Testament. See n. 36.

[34] On such linkages in Giotto's frescoes, see Alpatoff (1947), 149–54; reprinted in Stubblebine (1969), 156–69. On the further influences of Giotto on Andrea Pisano, see pp. 109–13.

[35] M. Lavin (1955), 85–101; M. Lavin (1961), 319–26.

[36] Although the *Vita* is mentioned by Falk (1940), 100, in her discussion of the literary tradition concerning the life of the Baptist, it is not specifically related to the Baptistry door narratives. The first to suggest such a connection was Panofsky (1953), 281f. The relationship was further explored, very convincingly, by M. Lavin (1955), 85–101, particularly with regard to the Giovannino panel. Finally, in an unpublished paper based on a seminar report given at the Institute of Fine Arts, New York University, in 1970, John Hunisak established further relationships between episodes in the *Vita* and on the doors. He also noted that the structure of the *Vita* is reflected in that of the Baptistry cycle. The present study was completed when I learned that Dr. Hunisak is indeed publishing his material in a book coauthored with Glenn Andres and A. Richard Turner entitled *The Art of Florence* (Abbeville Press) currently in press. I wish to thank Dr. Hunisak for

The *Vita di San Giovambatista*, contrary to any explicit mention in the Bible, relates that Mary remained with Elizabeth until after the birth of John and, further, that Elizabeth refused to permit the midwives to handle the child, insisting that Mary be the first to touch him.

> Lisabetta comandò alle balie che 'l non toccassono, e rivolsesi inverso da Donna Nostra e reverentemente la pregò che ella il dovesse prima toccare che niun' altra persona . . .[37]

It is Mary herself who wraps the infant in swaddling clothes and brings him to Zacharias to be named. In the *Naming of the Baptist* (Fig. 10) on the doors, Mary presents the infant to Zacharias, a scene unprecedented to my knowledge in the pictorial tradition.[38] There is no doubt about the identity of the person holding out the infant John to Zacharias: With the exception of Christ, only one person wears a halo – Mary in the *Visitation* and in the *Naming* (Figs. 8, 10).[39] In the *Vita*, the loving attention Mary devotes to the infant John serves both to exalt the dignity of the Baptist and to enhance the mood of homely intimacy. This dual aim characterizes the tone of the door relief, as well. While Mary affectionately bends over the miraculous child, she seems to prominently display him to the viewer. The frontality and centrality of the infant Baptist, whose head partially overlaps Mary's halo, expresses clearly that it is indeed a sacred bundle that is displayed to the viewer and presented to Zacharias. At the same time, the Virgin's physical closeness to the child, and the serene expression on the latter's face, may be an allusion to the fact that, according to the *Vita*, she herself wrapped him in a "bellissimo panno bianco" and that "questo benedetto figliuolo, che prima piagneva, istette cheto nel grembo di Madonna."[40]

Turning to the *Young John in the Wilderness*, a scene that has no biblical source, (Fig. 11), one is immediately struck by both the naturalism and the dominance of the landscape elements. The stylized, jagged forms of earlier landscape representations – the Baptistry mosaics, for example, or even the reliefs on Orvieto Cathedral (Figs. 205,

---

generously sharing with me the part of the manuscript that deals with the Baptistry doors. References and page numbers in the present paper are to the earlier unpublished typescript.

[37] The text of the *Vita* of John the Baptist quoted in this paper is from the following undated edition: *Vite de' Santi Padri de frate Domenico Cavalca colle vite di alcuni altri santi*, Milan, edited by B. Sorio and A. Rachelli. On the misattribution of the *Vita* to Cavalca, see M. Lavin (1961).

[38] In the Siena Pinacoteca there is a panel, Byzantine in design, that shows Mary handing the infant John to Elizabeth. This refers to an apocryphal tradition that places Mary in the home of Elizabeth at the time of the Baptist's birth. M. Lavin (1955), 85. In the *Golden Legend* Mary serves as midwife to Elizabeth. Ryan and Ripperger (1969), 323.

[39] Panofsky (1953), 281; M. Lavin (1955), 90.

[40] *Vita*, 405.

214) – are transformed into more naturalistic rock and clifflike features. Furthermore, mountains, trees, and animals have become, to an unprecedented degree, compelling aspects of the representation – not merely symbols or suggestions of place, or space-filling motifs as occur in earlier medieval representations. Rather, these elements create an environment essential not only to the subject but also to the content and meaning of the scene. If the general composition of the bronze relief is based on the Baptistry mosaic, the details of the landscape and the mood of the scene are entirely different. The harsh, barren wasteland of the earlier depiction is replaced by a landscape that appears almost inviting. The young John advances joyfully into the mountains, which are full of plant life, birds, even a lizard. The *Vita* informs us that beginning at the age of five John wandered farther and farther into the woods and stayed away from home for longer and longer periods, to the dismay of his parents.[41] The *bosco* into which he ventured, however, seemed to him to be "quasi . . . un paradiso" full of "gli alberi di sopra freschissimi, e la terra di sotto coperta che pareva un prato pieno di divisati fiori." Andrea has caught the joyful mood of the child as he embarks on his mission as well as the freshness of the surroundings described in the *Vita*.[42]

The Baptist's adult mission in the wilderness, his preaching, and his baptism of the multitude appear in all four gospels (Matthew III:1–17; Mark I:1–11; Luke III:1–18, 21–22; John I:19–34) whereas the baptism of Christ is mentioned only in the first three (Matthew III:13–17; Mark I:9–11; Luke I:21–22). The words, "Behold, the Lamb of God," are quoted twice in the sparsest of the accounts, that of John (I:29, 36). Strangely, two reliefs on the doors are out of sequence: In the gospel of John and in the *Vita* the baptism of the multitude precedes the revelation of Christ to the people with John proclaiming, "Ecce Agnus Dei." On the doors, however, the *Baptism of the Multitude* does not precede, rather it follows the *Ecce Agnus Dei* (Figs. 13, 14). Clearly, Andrea preferred to present a kind of formal and thematic parallel by placing the two scenes of baptism (Figs. 14, 15) on the lowest narrative register.[43] He might, however, have found authority in the Bible for this "artistic license," that is, the juxtaposition of the two baptism scenes. John I:33 narrates a kind of "flashback" *after* the Baptist proclaims the presence of the Lamb of God. We learn that earlier the Baptist had not recognized the Savior: "And I knew him not but he that sent me to baptize with water [i.e.,

[41] M. Lavin (1955), 88. Lavin asserts that a "torrent of water spills down the mountain toward which John is walking" and that this water is the river Jordan near which, according to the *Vita* and other apocryphal accounts, the young John met the Holy Family upon their return from Egypt. Lavin views the presence of this water as an ex-

plicit reference to the episode recounted in the *Vita* but lacking on the doors. After very careful scrutiny of this relief, I am forced to conclude, however, that there is no torrent of water but only a crevice between two rocky cliffs.
[42] *Vita*, 409; M. Lavin (1955), 88.
[43] Falk and Lányi (1943), 141.

the multitude], the same said unto me, Upon whom thou shalt see the Spirit descending and remaining on him [i.e., at the baptism of Christ as explicitly mentioned in Mark I:9–10, Luke III:21–22, and Matthew III:14–16], the same is he who baptizes with the Holy Ghost. And I saw and bare record that this is the Son of God." The "flashback," then, which makes reference to the baptism of the crowd and the baptism of Christ, occurs after the proclamation, "Ecce Agnus Dei." Alternatively – although less likely because the Baptist is represented as a very young child in the wilderness – the positioning of the reliefs may be read as an allusion to an episode recounted in the *Vita* but lacking both in the Gospels and on the doors: the meeting between the twelve-year-old John and the Holy Family in the wilderness.[44] At that time Christ gives John the mandate to preach and to baptize; he then foretells his own baptism by John. Thus, the four scenes showing the adult Baptist in the wilderness – scenes that follow immediately after the Giovannino panel – may be read as adhering to the sequence of Christ's prophecies (Figs. 11–15).

The Passion of John, from the *Feast of Herod* to the *Beheading* and *Burial* seen on the right-hand door leaf, is related in Mark (VI:17–29) and Matthew (XIV:3–12) although the imprisonment and beheading are noted in passing in Luke (III:19–20; VIII:7–9). The story of John in prison sending two of his followers to Christ, who has cured the ill, appears in Luke (III:1–22) and Matthew (IX:2–6). Several details from these Passion scenes have their source in the apocryphal tradition and find close parallels in our anonymous *Vita*. In contrast to the mosaic representation of the *Visit of the Disciples*, in which the figure of the Baptist is seen through the grating, on the doors, more realistically, the disciples peer into a dark vacuum behind the grate (Fig. 18). The figures gesture toward the prison and seem to look at each other in astonishment. The *Vita* relates that when the disciples visited the prison, John was in prayer:

> e S. Giovanni s'era posto in uno de'canti in orazione a non se n'era levato da poich'egli era entrato nella prigione, e non si recordava che dovesse nè mangiare nè bere . . .[45]

The gestures and expression of astonishment of the disciples would seem to be in direct response to the vision of the entranced Baptist, unaware of their presence.[46] A moment later he will approach them with a serene and happy expression on his face.

This relief conflates the visit of the disciples with another incident mentioned in the gospel and elaborated on in the *Vita*, a conflation implied by the immediately following representation, *Christ Cures the Infirm* (Fig. 19). In prison John tells two of his follow-

[44] Hunisak (1970), 16f. But see n. 41, this chapter.   [46] Hunisak (1970), 13f.
[45] *Vita*, 431.

ers to go to where Christ is and to ask, on behalf of John, whether he (Christ) is the one who was promised in the Bible or whether they must wait for another. John, of course, knows that it is the true Savior to whom he has sent his disciples. The two, clearly singled out in the first relief, go to Christ, who, instead of responding directly, performs miracles, curing the ill and infirm. In the relief, Christ, amazingly, wears no halo, an extraordinary iconographic liberty. Andrea, it would seem, chose to represent the moment preceding the miracles – the infirm, as is apparent, are not yet cured – and thus the moment preceding the disciples' recognition of and belief in Christ.[47] Whereas the gestures and expressions seen in the *Visit of the Disciples* suggest that they are responding to the sight of the entranced Baptist, the following scene implies a different preceding episode: the command to the disciples to confront Christ. The two reliefs, then, which are adjacent on the same register, must be read together – another example of internal linkages that enrich the narrative content and aid in its sequential development.

An explicit reference to our *Vita* may be discerned, as well, in the *Beheading of the Baptist* (Fig. 21). The two guards to the left seem to shrink from the sight before them while the executioner, in the very act of striking, turns his head so that his eyes are covered by his left forearm and his nose actually overlaps his arm! Nothing in the Gospels can explain these curious details. But the *Vita* informs us that the guards performed their task very unwillingly, even begging John to forgive them for what they had to do:

> Servo di Dio, perdonami che così ingiusta cosa me conviene fare, e prega Iddio per me che questo faccio molto male volentieri.[48]

John kneels and says that he will pray to God for them.

In the *Baptist's Head Brought to Herod* (Fig. 22), the king, unlike his counterpart in Giotto's fresco, gestures toward Herodias's daughter, who stands defiantly on the left. The *Vita* tells us that the king, at the sight of the bloody head, ordered the official to hand it to the evil daughter:

> e questa pessima figliuola la portò alla più pessima madre, e quando la vide senza misura si rallegrò e recossela in mano . . .[49]

The gesture of Herod in the relief, then, shows his command at that very moment.[50] Immediately following on the same register, we see Salome presenting the head to her mother, who indeed takes it in her hands (Fig. 23).

As is the case with this pair, throughout the cycle whenever possible, scenes adjacent

[47] This observation and insightful interpretation are due to Hunisak (1970), 15.

[48] *Vita*, 434f.

[49] *Vita*, 435.

[50] Hunisak (1970), 16.

on the same register imply cause and effect: Thus, John taken to prison follows John before Herod; the disciples approaching Christ follows their visit to John in prison; the beheading follows the dance; and finally, the funeral immediately precedes the burial. Thus we see the pointed juxtaposition of pairs of reliefs in order to suggest contiguous and related moments.

Given the emphasis on Mary's presence at the Baptist's birth and Elizabeth's refusal to permit anyone but the Virgin to touch, even to wash the child, it is surprising that the nativity scene, which, of course, precedes the naming with Mary holding John, includes the two midwives washing the infant (Fig. 9). The iconographic similarity to a nativity of Christ may have been compelling enough reason to include this motif in a cycle that clearly attempts to foster the parallelisms between the lives of John and Christ.[51] Furthermore, as we have seen, this relief is the most archaic in design, was probably the earliest to be executed, and was very likely a presentation piece later incorporated into the cycle. Thus, it may have been designed before the program as a whole received final definition.

More puzzling is a detail in the *Funeral* and *Entombment of the Baptist* (Figs. 24, 25). The head of John is clearly visible in both reliefs. The *Vita*, however, makes a great point of the inability of the disciples of John to retrieve his head despite strenuous efforts and even intrigues. They finally have to bury the body without the head, lamenting violently this terrible indignity. Two hundred years later, the Baptist reveals the whereabouts of the head to a follower.[52] The fate of the missing head is also recounted in the *Golden Legend*, where, after its discovery, the relic undergoes an incredible series of adventures that carry it across oceans to Constantinople and thence to Poitiers.[53] The Gospels, however, make no mention of the fate of the head nor does the *Meditations on the Life of Christ*, which includes several episodes concerning the life and death of the Baptist.[54] There were, however, two alternative traditions regarding the fate of the head[55] and there must have been a continuing controversy regarding that issue. Whereas the twelfth-century architrave of the Pisa Baptistry and the fifteenth-century embroidery by Pollaiuolo, for example, represent the transportation of the Baptist's body to the sepulcher with the head missing, the mosaics, the Pisano doors, and Masolino's frescoes in Castiglione Olona show the body intact.[56] It would have been easy enough for Andrea to fudge the issue by obscuring the upper part of the Baptist's body with the drapery of

[51] See n. 28.

[52] *Vita*, 435f.

[53] Ryan and Ripperger (1969), 508f.

[54] Ragusa and Green (1961), 21–6; 81–4; 177–85.

[55] Falk (1940), 111–13; Masseron (1957), 137–9.

[56] For the architrave of Pisa see Biehl (1926), Pl. 88b. Pollaiuolo's embroidery is reproduced in Ettlinger (1978), Figs. 63, 64. Masolino's fresco is reproduced in Micheletti (1959), Pl. 78.

one of the disciples. Yet the head is unmistakably present; the tender glances of the Baptist's mourners, full of sadness and love, even lend focus to it, thus explicitly contradicting the account in the *Vita*.[57]

Notwithstanding these divergences from the *Vita*, the general structure of the doors would seem to parallel that of the text.[58] The author of the *Vita* prefaces his work by offering an outline of its contents. It is divided into three parts: (1) from the nativity to John entering the desert; (2) from his preaching to the baptism; (3) from the baptism to the death of John. The first six reliefs on the left-hand door leaf cover the infancy of John to his march into the wilderness. The next four illustrate the preaching of John to the baptism of Christ. Finally, all ten reliefs on the right-hand door leaf concern his Passion and martyrdom. Nowhere is the attempt to foster a parallelism between the life of John and that of Christ more evident than in this distribution, which lends a focus to the Passion of John equal to that usually given in monumental cycles to Christ's corresponding experiences. This parallelism is implicit in the text of the *Vita*, which opens, after some laudatory remarks to God, the Virgin, Christ, and the Baptist with:

> . . . voglio dire della sua vita, meditandola e pensandola, piccolo e grande. E chi legge si ponga mente. Che se la mente fosse divota a meditare la vita di Cristo, e pensare di lui piccolo e grande . . .[59]

Thus, the reader is reminded that contemplation of the life of John will bring to mind the life of Christ.

The *Vita* concludes with a meditation on John's sacred soul and declares that when his soul left his body, it was adorned with all the virtues.[60] *The Golden Legend* quotes John Chrysostom regarding the Baptist: "John is the school of virtues, the guide of life, the model of sanctity, the rule of justice," and so on.[61] The lowest two registers on the doors contain representations of the Virtues: the three theological and the four cardinal virtues together with Humility, traditionally considered the source of all virtues.[62] Nothing could be more expressive of the spirit of the *Vita* than the appearance of these Virtues on the doors. Larger in scale than the figures in the narrative reliefs, and placed

[57] It is tempting to suggest that the inclusion of the head in these last two reliefs indicates that Andrea Pisano, who a few months earlier had created the beautiful sensuous nude Christ in the *Baptism of Christ*, and was shortly to carve one of the most classicizing male nudes of the trecento for the Campanile (see chapter 7), felt something akin to Michelangelo's reluctance to defile, distort, or disrupt the integrity of the human body, and thus anticipates the classical humanism of a later century. On this aspect of Michelangelo, see Hartt (1979), 467.

[58] Noted by Hunisak (1970), 12.

[59] *Vita*, 402.

[60] *Vita*, 436.

[61] *Ryan and Ripperger* (1969), 503; see also Ragusa and Green (1961), 183.

[62] This scheme of eight Virtues was established by Hugh of Saint Victor. See Katzenellenbogen (1964), 80.

symmetrically about the central axis of the doors (Fig. 1), the personifications of the virtues that were the foundation of the Baptist's life and the primary ideals of his spiritual journey serve as a foundation – a subtly differentiated visual socle – for the design of the doors as a whole.[63]

These evident relationships to the apocryphal tradition, and in particular to the *Vita* of John the Baptist take on an added dimension if one considers again the way in which the narrative unfolds on the Baptistry doors – like the reading of words in an open codex. It is as though the momentum of a written verbal account has been literally translated into visual form. One may surmise that to the fourteenth-century observer, word and image, narrative thrust, and pictorial linkages formed an integrated and cross-referential whole, so that the experience of text *or* image took on added resonance.

There is another aspect of the doors that might have been inspired by certain passages in the *Vita*. The decision to create a set of monumental figural bronze doors is anticipated in the bronze doors of the eleventh and twelfth centuries elsewhere in Italy although none of the latter were cast by means of the ancient lost-wax method, the process used for Andrea's doors.[64] An even bolder step, however, one that involved many technical complications, was the decision to gild the figures and settings, leaving the backgrounds as dark foils.[65] The gilding imbues what is essentially a monumental,

[63] The Virtues wear hexagonal halos rather than traditional round nimbi. Acknowledged as an Italian invention (see Didron [1896, 81] and Zucker [1978], 61–77), it may be the invention of Andrea Pisano as no earlier examples are cited in the preceding sources. According to Didron, 83f., the hexagonal nimbus may have symbolic significance, i.e., a reference to twelve, of which the number of sides here is half. There are twelve Virtues on the portals of Paris, Chartres, Amiens, and Reims. Zucker notes that circular nimbi are reserved for the highest rank of sacred figures; square nimbi are for persons who are still living and not of the rank of the highest beings; and polygonal ones are for those in between. This last type of halo most frequently, but not exclusively, is found on Virtues.

It may also be of interest to note that a tradition persisted throughout the Middle Ages of representing Virtues within medallions. Earlier on, the image of a saint or ruler is placed in the center and the associated Virtues are placed at the extremities (in the lobes of a quatrefoil, for instance); later, the Virtues form a series of independent framed figures. The former is characteristic of miniature paintings and church furnishings such as shrines; the latter occurs at Amiens where both Virtues and Vices, enthroned, appear within quatrefoil frames on the west facade. See Katzenellenbogen (1964), 27–44; Sauerlander (1972), 453.

[64] On the casting technique see Bearzi (1980), 219–22. On Italian bronze doors see Boeckler (1953); Matthiae (1971); Leisinger (1957); Pettorelli (1926); Perry (1910); Moskowitz (1983a), 1–4.

[65] The document of 1322, which first records the decision to create new metal doors (Doc. 1), already mentions the possibility of gilding. As the structure of the doors was clearly intended to be the traditional one of metal plates attached to a wooden core, it is possible that each individual plate would have been entirely gilded, somewhat along the lines of Wolvinius's altar frontal in San Ambrosio, Milan. More likely, only certain structural and decorative elements, such as studs or

architectonic structure, with something of the quality of preciousness associated with goldsmith work. But the gilding does more than that: It adds a splendid warmth to the otherwise dark, unreflecting surfaces of the bronze.[66] In the *Vita*, following the baptism of Christ, the author rejoices in the good fortune of the Baptist, whose hand has touched the head of Christ and whose eyes have seen the Holy Ghost from such close proximity that he is able to feel "il dolce calore suo."[67] The Baptist's good luck is compared to that of Peter, James, and John when they saw Christ, "la faccia sua come il sole risplendente,"[68] at the moment of the Transfiguration. Later, when the Baptist returns to the people his own face was "molto isprendiente [sic.]"[69] This is far from the straightforward account that may be read in the Gospels. It may very well be, then, that the decision to create narrative imagery in itself *risplendente* was inspired by the vocabulary and imagery in these and other passages of the *Vita*.[70]

Close as the connections would seem to be between the anonymous *Vita* and the cycle on the Baptistry doors, there may have been other sources, as well. The fourteenth century abounded not only in such narrative accounts but also in Baptist dramas and *laude*, all of which had become part of the collective consciousness and some of which may have provided material for the door reliefs.[71] What is clear is the fact that like

---

rosettes, would have been gilded. In either case, the effect would have been very different from that of Andrea's doors.

[66] For an appreciation of the effect of the gilt on the doors the reader is referred to a set of photographs in the Kunsthistorisches Institut of Florence by photographer Cipriani, which must have been taken very shortly after the doors were cleaned in the 1940s. These photographs were published in Moskowitz (1985).

[67] *Vita*, 422.

[68] *Vita*, 422.

[69] *Vita*, 422.

[70] I should like to express here my profound concern for the highly visible, physical deterioration that the doors undergo year by year due to atmospheric pollution. Studies indicate that short of a total ban on automobile traffic in the center of Florence, only the *complete* isolation of the doors from the atmosphere, either by surrounding them in situ with a hermetically sealed covering or by removing them to a controlled indoor environment, will save them from inevitable further and

irreversible deterioration. See Alessandrini, Dassu, Pedeferri, and Re (1979), 108–24. The reliefs and sculptures of the Campanile have been removed to the Museo dell'Opera del Duomo and replaced by copies. The three bronze doors require similar protection if they are to be preserved for future generations. On the procedures of restoration employed on the Joseph panel of Ghiberti's *Gates of Paradise*, see Baldini (1982), 168–206.

[71] See Falk (1940), 101–4. A listing of Baptist *sacre rappresentazioni* may be found in Cioni (1961). Also of interest is Galante (1935), 14ff., 46ff., 67. The author points out that by the thirteenth and fourteenth centuries one can distinguish between traditional liturgical drama and the new dramatic *laude*. The former were symbolic and were recited in Latin; thus they tended to be inaccessible to the majority of the populace; the latter were realistic and in the vernacular. The former took place in front of an altar and the actors wore clerical garments; the latter occurred generally in a confraternity and the actors wore costumes. The *laude*, which by the fourteenth cen-

Giotto's frescoes in the Arena Chapel, the Baptistry reliefs partake of the same spiritual ethos expressed in such apocryphal accounts as the anonymous "Vita di San Giovambatista": Divine events are interpreted in the most human and down-to-earth terms, without ever sacrificing that sense of the exalted nature of the drama that lifts them into the realm of the spiritual. This classic balance between spiritual idealism and narrative realism informs the art of Andrea Pisano throughout his career.

---

tury were occasionally brought back into the church, were performed on platforms for greater visibility. In the interest of expressive immediacy, simple props to suggest the larger setting were used; furthermore, choreographic movements were stressed. In addition to the *sacre rappresentazioni* and the *laude drammatiche*, there were also *rappresentazioni mimiche*, which must have been something like our present-day pantomimes. Clearly, a possible relationship between the handling of the narratives and their presentation on "platforms" on the Baptistry doors, and the tradition of sacred drama is a subject that deserves further exploration.

CHAPTER THREE
The Campanile

❈

Even before the bronze doors were fully installed on the Baptistry in 1336, Andrea was at work on the hexagonal reliefs for the Campanile of Florence Cathedral (Fig. 49).[1] This magnificent structure was originally designed by Giotto, who served as capomaestro of the Duomo from 1334 until his death in 1337.[2] It is not clear whether Giotto's original conception for the bell tower included any sculptural decoration aside from some pinnacle figures although fairly early on a Genesis cycle was executed on the west facade. Without any doubt it did not include the elaborate program that was to develop after Andrea became capomaestro in 1337.[3]

THE PROGRAM

The series of hexagonal reliefs begins on the west, the main facade, of the Campanile with the Creation of Adam and Eve, their first labors (plowing and spinning), and the inventions of their descendants, Jabal, Jubal, Tubalcain, and Noah (the first shepherd, musician, smith, and vintner, respectively) (Figs. 50–56; Appendix B, Fig. 1). These

[1] By the date of Giotto's death in January 1337, the hexagons on the western facade of the Campanile were already installed. See Becherucci (1965), 261; Trachtenberg (1971), 49; and p. 40, this chapter.

[2] Trachtenberg (1971), 20–48.

[3] A comprehensive interpretation of the program was first proposed by J. von Schlosser (1896), 53–75 and generally has been accepted by later scholars. Cf., however, Trachtenberg (1971), 93, and p. 37f., this chapter.

❈

Genesis scenes on the west facade are followed by representations of the Labors of Mankind distributed across the other three sides of the bell tower (Figs. 57–72; Appendix B, Figs. 2–4). There are representations of the seven *Artes Mechanicae*: Construction, Medicine, Horsemanship, Weaving, Navigation, Agriculture, and Trade. Various contributors to civilization, even pagan figures, find a place. Thus, among the hexagons we find Hercules, who by conquering Cacus cleansed the earth of the monsters of prehistory, thus preparing the way for civilization; Gionitus, the inventor of astronomy; Phoroneus, the founder of law and order; and Daedalus, the inventor of the arts. In addition, a painter and a sculptor are represented. A geometer with compass appears as well, and it is possible that he is intended to represent Architecture, thus completing the triad of the figural arts.[4] Among the five reliefs added to the series in the fifteenth century by Luca della Robbia are representatives of the scholastic or liberal arts.[5] In the row above, seven on each side, are seen the Planets, the Virtues, the Liberal Arts, and the Sacraments. The niches contain Prophets, Sibyls, and Kings who prefigured and heralded the Coming of Christ.

This elaborate program and its sculptural realization is unprecedented on a bell tower.[6] Its appearance is rooted in four separate but related cultural phenomena. First, the Campanile program shares in the scholastic attitude that had swept Europe during the thirteenth century and that is manifested in the encyclopedic content of French Gothic cathedrals. Indeed, to a generation that had fully assimilated the encyclopedic thinking of the medieval Schoolmen and was cognizant of the richly endowed sculptural programs of French Gothic cathedrals, the Campanile program answered to what must have appeared as a notable poverty of iconographic content on the Duomo facade itself. Second, its content represents several stages in the historically complex, organic development of the embellishment of the cathedral group – Baptistry, Duomo, bell tower – in which iconographic schemes of one epoch are richly interwoven with those of later campaigns.[7] Third, it reveals a critical appraisal of formal solutions arrived at in related centers such as Siena and Orvieto. Finally, the Campanile reliefs belong to very specific moments in Florentine history, reflecting in both style and content the changing political, cultural, and economic situation in Florence during the 1330s and 1340s. A discussion of that situation has direct bearing on the chronology and authorship of the Campanile hexagons.[8]

The French thirteenth-century cathedral, in the words of Emile Mâle, can be consid-

---

[4] See n. 23.
[5] On Luca della Robbia's reliefs see Becherucci and Brunetti (1969), 276f., and Pope-Hennessy (1980), 80ff.

[6] A discussion of Italian Campanili is found in Trachtenberg (1971), 151–79.
[7] Trachtenberg (1971), 99ff.
[8] See pp. 46–8 and chapter 7.

ered "the visible counterpart" of the "intellectual edifice" that was being developed by the Scholastic theologians.[9] In its own way, the Gothic cathedral served as a Speculum, a Summa, an Imago Mundi, for its program attempted to encompass the sum total of human knowledge, moral ideals, and God's cosmic plan for the universe. The French cathedral program, if not necessarily derived directly from such schema as Vincent of Beauvais's *Speculum Majus*, is structured in a way that closely parallels the latter.[10] The Speculum is divided into four books: *The Mirror of Nature*, which describes all known natural phenomena; *The Mirror of Instruction*, which reviews the different branches of knowledge (the *Artes Liberales*) and the skills human beings have developed (the *Artes Mechanicae*), *The Mirror of Morals*, which teaches people how to act in accordance with the will of God and offers an exposition of the Virtues and Vices; and *The Mirror of History*, which concentrates on the struggles and progress of mankind as told in the Old and the New Testaments. Pagan antiquity, too, has its limited part in this drama. Together, the four books offer a comprehensive scheme that reveals God's plan for the universe and the central role that man plays in it. This scheme is not only comprehensive, it is harmonious: Every moment in history, every detail of nature, every human act has its place and its relationship to all other elements. For instance, *The Mirror of Instruction* begins with the Fall of Man, the immediate consequence of which is the necessity for toil, and the ultimate consequence of which is the need for redemption. The Mechanical Arts are invented to fulfill our physical needs whereas the Liberal Arts develop our intellectual capacity to distinguish good from evil and assist in making us worthy of grace. The French Gothic cathedral, with its vast program of pictorial and sculptural decoration, and with its tendency toward hierarchical ordering, symmetry, and vertical and horizontal linkages, parallels, then, not only the intellectual scope but also the structure of Vincent of Beauvais's *Speculum Majus*.[11] Italy, though lagging somewhat behind in the development of its arts, was hardly immune from that vision.[12]

The earliest manifestations of the spread of the Scholastic impulse in art are seen in the pulpits of Nicola and Giovanni Pisano where biblical history is augmented by representations of Virtues and Vices, Liberal Arts, and pagan prophetesses of antiquity. The encyclopedic urge expresses itself even more fully on one of the most remarkable secular and civic monuments of the Italian Gothic age: the Fontana Maggiore in Perugia, completed in 1278, with sculptures by Nicola Pisano and extensive contributions

[9] Mâle (1958), 23.

[10] Mâle (1958), 24–6. See also Panofsky (1951), passim, especially 39–41 and 44–9.

[11] Although it may be difficult to prove that any particular cathedral program is based directly on a specific Scholastic text, the theological and philosophical concepts inherent in Vincent of Beauvais's opus belong, as Mâle points out, not to its author alone but to the late Middle Ages as a whole. Mâle (1958), 26.

[12] This is evident, for example, from the writings of Brunetto Latini. See Trachtenberg (1971), 101.

by Giovanni. In addition to scenes from Genesis and an array of prophets and saints, there are several contemporary secular personages, representations of the Labors of the Months, personifications of the Liberal Arts, and various fables and allegorical figures.[13]

It comes as somewhat of a surprise, then, to realize that the two great Tuscan facades that were rising at the turn of the fourteenth century reveal little of this tendency toward an expansion of iconographic content; rather, at Siena and Florence the cathedrals, both dedicated to the Virgin Mary, contain programs that are strictly Mariological. The special reverence and intimacy that the citizens of these two cities felt for the mother of Christ perhaps go far to explain this focus. In Siena she was not only the patron of the cathedral but protector of the city itself; in Simone Martini's fresco in the great council hall of the Palazzo Pubblico she sat enthroned with her court of saints and angels presiding over government deliberations and decisions. Even in Florence, whose patron saint is John the Baptist, she played a special role. It was she who bestowed honor upon the Baptist by her visit to Elizabeth: When the two pregnant women embraced, John jumped for joy in his mother's womb in recognition of the presence of the Savior (Luke I:39–56).[14] But can the personal and intimate relationship that the citizens of these *comunes* felt toward Mary explain fully the concentration on a single theme in the program of the cathedrals?

Two other factors surely come into play both of which militate against the exposition of vast and complex iconographies such as appear on French cathedrals. The first is the Italian predisposition to maintain the autonomy of the figural sculpture in relation to the architecture, and the second is the related tendency to conceive of those figures as individuals rather than as types. On French Gothic facades sculpture and architecture are so closely related – though the former is subordinate to the latter – that the entire fabric of the edifice is virtually equatable with its sculptural and decorative embellishment. The French Gothic cathedral was thus infinitely receptive to the encyclopedic content of Scholastic thinking: Cycles of saints and prophets, angels and elders, virtues and vices, labors and arts could be adequately accommodated by the rows or tiers of columns, socles, lintels, and voussoirs, not to mention the lunettes and niches.

For the Italian sculptor-architect, this architectonic use of sculpture, whereby sculptural form takes on the role of architectural members, could work only in monuments of relatively small scale, and when so used the relationship of sculpture to architecture was inverted. In the pulpits and in the fountain by Nicola and Giovanni Pisano numer-

---

[13] White (1966), 51.

[14] According to the apocryphal tradition, the Virgin Mary was the first to touch the infant John, even before the midwives were permitted to bathe him; and it was she who brought him to Zacharias to be named. See chapter 2.

ous figures substitute for architectural members but, due to the scale, bulk, and in many cases freedom of movement, the individual figures dominate the architecture.[15]

When Giovanni had to apply this thinking to the monumental scale of the Siena Duomo facade he was faced with the problem of maintaining the integrity and individuality of the sculptural components. Clearly, he could neither establish that close affinity between architectural and sculptural scale that was possible on the pulpits, nor permit the almost total integration of architectonic function and sculptural form that was the invention of the French architects. Giovanni found an extraordinary solution. In Siena the architecture serves as backdrop against which the figures perform in dynamic interaction: Both physically and psychologically the figures project out toward the observer and convey a powerful sense of individual character and presence. Arnolfo di Cambio, who was of a completely different artistic temper than Giovanni, was no less insistent on maintaining a strict separation between sculpture and architecture. If the Siena Cathedral facade serves as backdrop for Giovanni's aggressively projecting figures, the Florentine facade provides a stage for Arnolfo's figures. With far more decorum and restraint but no less drama, these figures act out their destinies or communicate their messages as powerful and highly individualized plastic forms. This predilection to give each figure an insistent autonomy necessarily, and quite simply, limited the number of figures that each of these facades could accommodate.

Orvieto Duomo, whose facade was begun ca. 1310, would seem to be a response to (and criticism of) the iconographic paucity that this mode of thinking and design necessitated. Like the cathedrals of Florence and Siena, that of Orvieto is dedicated to the Virgin Mary but its Mariological program is, for the first time, placed within a universal context. The facade includes not only sculptures of Mary enthroned with angels, and scenes from her life, but a Genesis cycle, a Tree of Jesse, a New Testament cycle, and the Last Judgment. On the Genesis pier, in addition, we find representations of the Liberal Arts (e.g., Fig. 214), thus a reference to the mode by which human beings assist themselves toward an understanding of God's plan and make themselves worthy of salvation.[16] At Orvieto, the decision to expand the scope of the illustrative material provoked a highly original solution to the problem of sculptural embellishment: Instead of the niche and pinnacle figures and the lintel or lunette reliefs that abound at Florence and Siena, here all the sculpture (with a few notable exceptions) is concentrated on the four piers of the lower facade. The price paid for the enriched program, however, was a dim-

[15] A possible relationship to Gothic sculpture in Germany, where a similar independence and individuality of sculpture in relation to architecture is often observed, is an issue that deserves investigation.

[16] Carli (1947b), 57; cf. Taylor (1970), 76–8.

inution of the scale of the individual elements so that, unless one is in very close proximity to the surface of the pier, at which point the individual vignettes come into focus, the reliefs tend to merge into a uniform texture – a solution that would have been quite unacceptable to Nicola and Giovanni Pisano. Although the facade as a whole is a masterpiece of design, and the individual reliefs among the most beautiful, powerful, and influential of the trecento, the solution, original as it was, had no successors.[17] The desire to reconcile two conflicting demands – an enrichment of iconographic content and the autonomy of the figural elements with respect to the architecture – clearly called for an entirely different, and unorthodox, approach. That approach was taken in Florence in the 1330s, at which point, one might add, the scheme at Orvieto was essentially fully realized.

The solution to the problem must have struck the planners of the Campanile project with a force and clarity equaled only by the brilliance of the actual execution of the plan, first under Giotto and then under Andrea Pisano. The Scholastic enrichment of the cathedral program could be achieved only by encouraging the spread of iconographic content beyond the confines of the Duomo itself. An organically expanding iconography was already implicit in the historical and cultural topography of Florence: God's universal plan of world history had been magnificently expressed inside the Baptistry in the mosaics, largely executed in the dugento, whereas a Mariological and typological program had been initiated by Arnolfo ca. 1300 on the new facade of Santa Maria del Fiore.[18] Giotto had already introduced the novel idea of including Genesis reliefs on the western face of the bell tower; it was a logical step to continue the band of hexagons around the other sides.[19] The introduction of a second zone of reliefs, the lozenges above the hexagons, resulted in a pointed reference, moreover, not only iconographically but also formally – compare the double row of medallions on the socle of Amiens Cathedral – to French Gothic decorative schemes.[20]

[17] It is true that with the exception of the Campanile of Florence, no new major ecclesiastical constructions were initiated in central Italy for the rest of the century. But even had a new cathedral project come into being, it is doubtful that the Orvieto solution would have been adopted.

[18] Trachtenberg (1971), 99f.

[19] There is some evidence to suggest that initially the north side of the Campanile, overshadowed as its lower zone was in the fourteenth century by a bridge connecting the upper portal to the Duomo, did not contain hexagonal reliefs. At some later date the street portal on the eastern face of the Campanile was enlarged, thus displacing two of Andrea's reliefs; these were either stored or moved to the north side. Then, in the fifteenth century, the decision was made to add five more hexagons to the two trecento ones and to include these on the north side. The commission for the five new reliefs was given to Luca della Robbia. See Trachtenberg (1971), 66f.; also Gilbert (1973), 427–42.

[20] Trachtenberg (1971), 101f. See chapter 8.

Thus to the Genesis scenes were added the Labors of Mankind. In the lozenge-shaped reliefs above are seen the Planets, which influence the course of human life, the Virtues and Liberal Arts through which we develop our potential for good and become worthy of God's gift of grace, and the seven Sacraments through which we attain that grace. The niches in the next zone contain figures of Prophets, Sibyls, and Kings. Prefigurations or heralds of Christ, they address the observer below who awaits His Second Coming.

There is little doubt, then, that the Campanile reliefs and niche figures conform to the general schema of the Scholastic compendia of the thirteenth century. Studied more closely, the Campanile series introduces a peculiarly contemporary and Florentine twist into the conventional program – by omitting one important link in the causal chain from the Creation to the Labors of Man, and also in the particular choice of Labors to be represented. Whereas the medieval Scholastics emphasized the causal relationship of labor to the Fall – in Genesis it is the direct consequence of the Fall – on the Campanile the Creation of Adam and Eve is immediately followed by their first labors and the inventions of their descendants. It can hardly be without significance that the Fall and expulsion of Adam and Eve are omitted; nor is the drama of Cain and Abel represented. Those who planned the program at this early stage suppressed the traditional view of world history in which human toil on earth is the consequence of the fall from grace, and dwelt instead on the concept of manual labor as an achievement.[21]

It is perhaps significant that the scenes on the western face of the Campanile were all conceived and executed during Giotto's lifetime.[22] Even after 1337 when the subsequent reliefs were designed, the program continues its strong emphasis on the creative and productive side of life. Not only are those *Artes Mechanicae* essential for a thriving commercial republic included – Trade, Agriculture, Navigation, for example – but also the arts of Painting and Sculpture. What we would call Architecture appears in its dual aspect: as the art of building (Fig. 69) and, as is the case on the north porch of Chartres, as a mathematical art in the relief representing Geometry (Fig. 71).[23] It would surely be going too far to claim that we are witnessing a precocious elevation of the activities of the painter, sculptor, and architect to the level of the *Artes Liberales*, but the fact remains that out of twenty-one trecento reliefs only one or two belong to the

[21] Trachtenberg (1971), 88–93, observes that Schlosser, in discussing the cathedral program, mistakenly focuses on the causal relationship between the Fall and the necessity for labor – a relationship that is clearly underplayed in the Campanile reliefs. The only reference to the sins of Adam and Eve is the appearance of a bear, an ancient symbol of fornication. See Janson (1952), 66, n. 103.

[22] See p. 40.

[23] According to Mâle, Architecture is sometimes represented by a figure holding a compass and ruler, as at Chartres, or a figure drawing a diagram as at Laon. Mâle (1958), 94.

canonical Liberal Arts,[24] whereas four, and if we include Daedalus, then five, are devoted to the visual arts. The prominence and thus distinction accorded those labors go beyond anything sanctioned by the Scholastic tradition, whether literary or visual, and suggest a nascent perception concerning the dignity of the arts.

In addition to the traditional Labors, of Mankind and in some cases personifications or representatives of those labors,[25] the hexagons include a number of "euhemeristic" heroes – mythological pagan figures who were considered ancient mortal benefactors of mankind, for example, Daedalus, Hercules, and Minerva, the inventor of the art of weaving (Figs. 63, 65, 62).[26] These three reliefs belong to a group that is stylistically the most classicizing of the series and may even, as we shall see, be characterized as protohumanistic in both form and content.[27] Begun during a peak in the civic, economic, and cultural life of the city of Florence, the lowest zone on the Campanile is characterized by a celebrative spirit keenly appreciative of human creative faculties.[28]

Implicit in the program of the second zone is a somewhat altered mood. It has been suggested that the second row of reliefs, which remind us of our limitations and ultimate dependence on the grace of God, was introduced to balance the celebrative and prideful spirit of the hexagons, and thus reflects the developing mood in Florence during the series of crises that preceded and culminated in the Black Death of 1348.[29] The hand of Andrea himself is seen nowhere on the second zone of reliefs suggesting that these were indeed executed after his departure from Florence ca. 1343.

Clearly, the program of the Campanile underwent adjustments with changing times. As we shall see, however, the effects of the changing climate in Florence would seem to be already apparent in several reliefs on the lowest zone.

THE HEXAGONAL RELIEFS

Unlike the bronze reliefs, which may be scrutinized and enjoyed in every pristine detail, the marble hexagons must be read from a considerable distance. This fact alone precluded a design based on geometric subdivisions and subtle internal references to the frame as seen on the doors. Instead, most reliefs on the Campanile employ the full expanse of the available field. In some reliefs the figures and objects adjust to the hex-

---

[24] Astronomy and Geometry; the inclusion of the latter depends on whether one reads Fig. 71 as one of the Liberal Arts or as Architecture. See n. 23.

[25] According to Schlosser (1896), 53ff., the hexagons include Gionitus, the first astronomer, and

Phoroneus, the inventor of law and order.

[26] Seznec (1961), 30f.

[27] See chapter 7.

[28] Trachtenberg (1971), 94, 104f. See chapter 7.

[29] Trachtenberg (1971), 95f.

agonal shape of the frame by bending, leaning, or otherwise taking into account its diagonals (Figs. 50, 51, 53, 54); in others that shape is essentially ignored and the upper and lower angles are left empty or filled in with a decorative pattern (Figs. 55, 57, 68). In either case, the compositions are freed from the insistent rectangularity that permeates the design of the Baptistry reliefs. Instead, a looser symmetry with numerous deviations from the vertical and horizontal, and a concomitant increase in the play of broadly curved forms – for example, the draped tent and curved back in *Jubal* (Fig. 54) – result in a freer, more intuitive compositional organization.

In none of the hexagons is the contrast between plastically developed figures and flat ground as marked as on the doors; indeed, in several Campanile reliefs, particularly the landscape scenes on the west facade, there is a suggestion of spatial continuity from foreground to background that is rare, if not unprecedented, in fourteenth-century relief sculpture (Figs. 50, 51, 56). Moreover, unlike the symbolic architectural props, and either restricted or ambiguous space observed in the bronze reliefs, the hexagons reveal an imagination groping with problems of realistic spatial representation, interior as well as exterior. The depictions of Sculpture and Medicine take place within three-dimensional interiors made credible by means of the oblique placement of furniture and figures, an implied ground plane – not projecting forward as on the doors but inward, behind the hexagonal frame – and a rear wall, the material existence of which is demonstrated by the shelves or tools hung on it (Figs. 57, 68). Movements and gestures are used, not to express emotional or spiritual content, but to convey an activity, human or divine, in a naturalistic way, and this they do with astonishing accomplishment (Figs. 50, 58, 67).

Despite these important differences a common artistic imagination would seem to have controlled the design of the quatrefoils and the conception of the majority of the hexagonal reliefs. On both the Baptistry and the Campanile there may be observed a predisposition to narrative economy rather than iconographic richness. Two or three figures, in general, suffice to convey the content, and these are clothed in fluid, curvilinear draperies that both envelop the figures and suggest the solid presence of the body beneath. Primarily, however, what links the Campanile reliefs to those on the Baptistry is the elevated conception of humanity conveyed through naturalistic and broadly idealized forms, a restrained emotional content, fluid harmonious draperies, and a concentrated focused imagery.

But the style of the reliefs on the Campanile is not homogeneous. In contrast to the minute changes discernible on the doors, which aid in establishing a chronology for the conception and execution of the quatrefoils, on the Campanile there are abrupt changes in style, the significance of which has not been sufficiently recognized. Here we are not dealing with the evolution of a single master as on the doors, an evolution that, it may be remembered, spanned about two and a half years. No one, and rightly so, has ever questioned the essential unity and therefore single authorship of the bronze reliefs. In contrast, although scholars have generally agreed that the twenty-one trecento reliefs (and the niche statues) were executed under Andrea's direction, diverse and contradictory opinions have been continually advanced regarding the authorship of individual reliefs, a problem further complicated by the necessity to distinguish between design and execution.[30] By focusing exclusively on questions of attribution based on individual styles, the broader implications of the diversity to be found among the Campanile reliefs have been missed. There is reason to believe that not all the hexagons were designed under Andrea's direction; the series, in fact, may be divided into three distinct stylistic phases, each of which is connected, at least in part, to the changing cultural and economic climate in Florence.[31]

The first group comprises, as we shall see, all the reliefs on the west face, plus *Sculpture*, *Painting*, and *Medicine* (Appendix B, 5). The seven Genesis reliefs were among the first to be executed; this became apparent when they were removed for installation in the Museo dell'Opera del Duomo and it was observed that they were inserted into the fabric of the wall simultaneously with the incrustation, and therefore before the death of Giotto, who supervised the construction of this section of the Campanile.[32]

In all seven reliefs the entire pictorial field is employed to display and elaborate upon the settings. More so than in subsequent reliefs on the Campanile, the compositions tend to take cognizance of the sloping angles of the hexagons and the implied verticals and horizontals linking their points. Thus, in the first relief Adam appears to lean almost directly on the sloping frame (Fig. 50), the tents in *Jabal* and *Jubal* adjust to the space beneath the upper angle of the hexagon (Figs. 53, 54), and Noah's bowl is situated along the central axis of the composition (Fig. 56). Although never as geometrically controlled as the quatrefoil reliefs, the compositions may be viewed as representing a conscious departure from an earlier canon to which they still adhere more closely than do the reliefs on the other sides of the Campanile.

The figure and drapery style in the Creation scenes (Figs. 50, 51) is identical to that

[30] For example, according to Schlosser (1896), 58, the first three hexagons are by a student of Andrea after sketches by Giotto. I. Toesca (1950), 29, accepts neither Giotto nor Andrea but considers these to be entirely workshop products. In the view of Weinberger (1953), 243–8, the first two are by Andrea and the *Labors of Adam and Eve* is by a Pisan assistant. Becherucci (1965), 242f., on the other hand, ascribes all three to the hand of Andrea. A discussion of the reliefs and a review of the literature is found in Becherucci and Brunetti (1969), 232–9.

[31] See chapter 7. Portions of the material in this chapter and in chapter 7 appear in Moskowitz (1983b).

[32] Becherucci (1965), 261.

in numerous examples on the doors and must be autograph Andrea. Comparing the figure of God the Father with the angel in the *Annunciation to Zacharias* (Figs. 5, 50), one notes in both the same rhythmic series of thin drapery folds breaking up larger flat areas of cloth in curves that converge on the right and spread out to embrace the figures on the left. The relationship of figure to drapery is identical: The pattern of folds, rich as it is, does not overwhelm the figure but allows the subtly swelling forms of the body to show through. Physiognomically, too, Gabriel as well as Christ on the doors is kin to God on the Campanile (Figs. 5, 45, 50). In the *Baptism* the coiffure of Christ, with its locks of hair gently rolling away from the forehead and over the ear, the refined features with small eyes and high cheekbones, and the short straight beard ending in small symmetrical waves find exact counterparts in the Creator on the Campanile (Figs. 45, 50, 51). The treatment of the nude in these reliefs is similar. Especially significant is the handling of contours, which is, as it were, the handwriting of Andrea Pisano: The same subtle transitions from curve to curve and the same nuances in musculature occur in the bronze Christ and the marble Adam (Figs. 45, 50). Such nuances are not easily reproduced by workshop assistants even when following a design of the master. The first panel, then, points to the hand of Andrea Pisano, who, although following a traditional iconography,[33] left his personal imprint on the marble.

The *Creation of Eve* (Fig. 51) is almost identical in style to the preceding relief. In the beautiful figure of Eve one can observe the same sensitivity in the contours as well as a softness and sensuousness in the modeling of the body. The landscape in the two panels is treated similarly with soft, rounded forms for the ground and large flat individualized leaves for the trees.

At the same time, these two panels depart from the style of the doors in a number of significant ways indicating that Andrea is striving toward a more monumental conception of the human figure. The treatment of the nude is freer and more naturalistic. Compare, for instance, the relative proportions of head to body in Christ in the *Baptism* (Fig. 45) and in the *Creation of Adam* (Fig. 50). The taut envelope of skin seen in the bronze contrasts with the softer modeling of the marble relief. The pose in the latter has a kind of classical ease unprecedented in trecento sculpture – or painting, for that matter. There is, moreover, a marked change in the treatment of landscape. Instead of the sharp-edged rocks found in all the landscape scenes on the Baptistry, the marble panels contain softly rounded mounds of earth (Figs. 50, 51, 56). The tightly bunched and undifferentiated masses of leaves that form the trees in the *Young John in the Wilderness* are transformed in the Creation scenes into large, highly individualized leaves, deeply

[33] Cf. Giotto's *Creation of Adam* in a quatrefoil in the Arena Chapel. Stubblebine (1969), Fig. 73.   See also Colombier (1968), 255–8.

undercut (Figs. 11, 50) – a handling of flora already anticipated, as we have seen, in the last three landscapes on the doors. Furthermore, the important distinction between figure and neutral ground in the doors, the effect heightened by the gilding of the figures, has given way to a smoother transition and a sense of continuity between foreground and background.

The remaining reliefs on the west facade – with the exception, perhaps, of *Tubalcain* – were designed by Andrea and executed in whole or in part by assistants. The conception of the *Labors of Adam and Eve* (Fig. 52), the third relief among the Genesis scenes, is Andrea's and the style remains very close to that in the first two reliefs; but the execution degenerates to some extent. The chisel of an assistant is apparent in the torso of Eve, in the landscape elements, and in the drapery, which is less fluid than in the first two hexagons. Another assistant's hand is seen in *Noah* (Fig. 56): The drapery with its tight concentric folds and the stocky proportions of the figure are foreign to Andrea's style, with its more elegant forms, as we know it from the doors and the first two reliefs on the Campanile. The masterful composition, however, recalls Andrea's method of design on the doors: Verticals and horizontals dominate but are interrupted by the curves and angels that lend focus to the "nakedness" of Noah.

In the panel representing *Sculpture* (Figs. 57, 58) we again see an autograph work of Andrea. The seated figure may be compared to the seated Zacharias on the doors (Fig. 10). Not only are such details as the hairstyle and drapery folds similar, but both figures show that sense of easy naturalism that is characteristic of Andrea and that distinguishes him from any other sculptor of the period. Of paramount significance is the nature of the contours in both figures – fluid, subtly changing, approaching geometric regularity yet never stylized – which betray the hand of the same "draftsman." In contrast to Zacharias, however, the Sculptor is turned slightly to a three-quarter view so that the impression of space-displacing bulk is increased in the marble relief. Moreover, there is a radical departure in spatial conception. The furnishings and space are no longer symbolic as in the *Annunciation to Zacharias* (Fig. 5), nor is the space fluid and indefinable as in *Zacharias and the Elders* (Fig. 7). Andrea carries a step further the use of a Giottesque principle from the Arena Chapel already employed on the doors: If objects are placed obliquely, they function as space-creating elements. Thus not only the figure of the sculptor but the bench on which he sits is placed at an angle to the front plane. Yet unlike several interiors in the Arena Chapel, or for that matter in the Peruzzi Chapel frescoes, the scene is not viewed from the outside, as though the spectator were looking into a dollhouse. Furthermore, unlike the backgrounds in the bronze reliefs, here the rear plane functions like a real wall from which objects can be hung. *Sculpture*, then, which is so close to the Baptistry doors in figure style, represents a development away from the latter in the direction of the Renaissance with its concern with naturalistic space. The influences that may have intervened between the doors and the Campanile to produce this marked change in Andrea's conception of pictorial space is the subject, in part, of chapter 4.

This hexagon, indeed, marks a turning point in Andrea's evolution. Compared to the earlier Creation scenes, in *Sculpture* the forms are conceived in broader planes, the drapery folds are less cursive, the composition is simplified and the projection of three-dimensional forms in space is much greater; in short, Andrea has achieved a new level of monumentality. *Sculpture*, as we shall see, is transitional in style and initiates a series of representations conceived *all'antica*; for the sculptor is explicitly represented as an ancient, not a contemporary figure. Significantly, his chisel is set against an "antique" nude figure in-the-round. This is in contrast to the representation of *Medicine* in which both the costumes and the setting belong to the fourteenth century.[34]

Agriculture, too, may be a transitional relief (Fig. 59). Compositionally it is closer to *Noah* than to the classicizing reliefs, and like the earlier series it evidences the sculptor's concern with the representation of figures in space; indeed, it presents a rather daring, if not completely successful, experiment in spatial representation: Whereas the figures are all pressed into the immediate foreground area and the horizon line is visible below, not behind, the figures, three or four layers of space are indicated. At the same time, although related to medieval representations of the Labors of the Months, it strongly recalls antique images of plowmen.[35] Thus, instead of a simple quotation – as for instance the Bacchic figure adapted to Adam and the Nereid transformed into Eve in the Creation scenes[36] – here, a contemporary activity is identified with ancient representations, a process that is even more explicit in *Sculpture*.

Closely associable with *Sculpture* are *Jabal*, *Jubal*, and *Painting* (Figs. 53, 54, 67), in my view, designed but not entirely executed by Andrea. The space-enclosing canopy in *Jubal*, the ingenious device of the open tent flap in *Jabal*, and the astonishing attempt at a perspectival rendering of the easel in *Painting* reveal a mentality experimenting with the naturalistic depiction of objects in space. But close examination of the carving reveals the hands of assistants. *Jubal* and *Painting* differ from *Sculpture* in the static geometry of the curves, especially in the rendering of the backs, and in the tendency to schematize the patterns of the hair (Figs. 54, 57, 67). That the assistant did not precisely follow a sketch or model is indicated by the irrational placement of the easel, which hovers in

[34] See p. 128.
[36] See p. 124ff.
[35] Krautheimer (1970), 345.

midair without support; in contrast, every solid object in *Sculpture* is firmly supported by another one.[37]

At first glance *Tubalcain* would seem to be closely linked to *Sculpture* (Figs. 55, 57). One need only observe, however, the regular, almost geometric curves in the contours of the figure, the mechanical rendering of the hair pattern, and the irrational space and placement of objects to realize that this is the work of another stonemason. The latter closely followed his model, *Sculpture*, to the point almost of copying the drapery style, the pose, and even such details as the form of the bench with its trefoil opening. The balanced composition and realistic depiction of the tools point to a mason of superior talent but one who evidently misunderstood Andrea's aims. Whereas in *Sculpture* an attempt is made to present a coherent space dominated by a simple monumental composition, in *Tubalcain* the organization is controlled by the requirements of abstract design, and the figure and objects are composed into geometric forms. *Geometry* and *Astronomy* (Figs. 71, 72) would also seem to be loosely modeled on *Sculpture*. But as we shall see, these represent a radical retreat from the goals evidenced by the reliefs on the west face and by *Sculpture*. The latter, however, seems to have provided the prototype for a number of subsequent reliefs depicting a seated figure seen in profile.

In contrast to the author of *Tubalcain*, the creator of *Medicine* (Fig. 68) understood the new relief mode in which the illusion of three-dimensional space is created through the use of a platform, obliquely placed objects, and a real, solid wall on which objects, in this case shelves, can be hung. The figure style does not accord with Andrea's; it is likely that the carver of this panel was one of his workshop assistants who later executed some of the reliefs on the upper zone of the Campanile. Similar proportions and a drapery style comparably dependent on Andrea's are seen in *Matrimony* (Fig. 73) from the workshop of Alberto Arnoldi.[38]

[37] The relief representing *Painting* is carved on two pieces of stone, the right portion postdating that on the left. See Gilbert (1973), 427–42, who argues convincingly that the relief was originally on the east wall and that its right half was interrupted by a door, smaller than the present one; when the door was later enlarged this and another relief, *Sculpture*, were removed and stored. When in the fifteenth century the cycle of hexagons was expanded to include Luca della Robbia's reliefs to be placed on the until then empty north face of the Campanile, the two reliefs in storage were taken out and included to make up a total of seven reliefs on the north face. It became necessary, however, to add a right half to *Painting*. It seems very likely that the right half was carved by Luca della Robbia himself; compare the treatment of the perspectivally drawn Gothic triptych with the similarly handled portal serving as backdrop to Luca's relief *Grammar*. Pope-Hennessy (1980), Fig. 29.

[38] On Alberto Arnoldi, see Becherucci (1927), 214–23; (1965), 239–41. The Seven Sacraments on the Campanile have been attributed to Maso di Banco by Kreytenberg (1979b), 72–6. More recently, Kreytenberg (1979a), 31–36, has given the relief representing *Matrimony* to Gino Micheli.

The reliefs on the west facade, then, together with *Sculpture*, *Painting*, and *Medicine*, reveal a unity of aim if not of execution (Appendix B, 5). Of these, only the first two Genesis scenes and *Sculpture* were executed by Andrea himself. In a second and distinct stylistic group (Appendix B, 6), the concern with problems of spatial representation is abandoned in favor of simple, monumental compositions in which the figures, with little indication of setting, are placed against a flat, textured, but neutral, background. No longer are the figures enveloped in concentric, swinging folds and meandering hemlines; indeed, drapery tends to diminish in value as decorative or expressive elements. Furthermore, for the first time classical influence plays a prominent role in the conception of the images. Not only do antique heroes such as Daedalus and Hercules appear in the context of a medieval Christian program – the Labors of Man – but many of the individual figures and motifs are based on ancient prototypes.[39]

The three reliefs among this group on the south side – *Horsemanship*, *Weaving*, and *Daedalus* (Figs. 60–63) – are clearly of superior artistry and there is every reason to believe that they are by the hand of Andrea. The standing figure in *Weaving* (Fig. 62) is reminiscent of numerous female figures on the doors: Compare the companion of Mary in the *Visitation* (Fig. 8), or Salome in the *Dance of Salome* (Fig. 20). As in the latter the arms move freely and gracefully away from the body, a predilection that goes back as far as one of Andrea's earliest works, the Pisan *Annunziata* (Figs. 102, 103).[40] Not even the figure of Salome in the Peruzzi Chapel, from which it would seem the bronze Salome derives, exhibits the naturalistic ease and grace of Andrea's women (Figs. 20, 22). Daedalus may be compared to the figures of Herod on the doors: The intent expression, the features, the configuration of the hair strands are the same. The strikingly original conception of the figure would also lead one to believe that the work was conceived by the master.[41]

These reliefs on the south side are qualitatively superior to those belonging to the same group on the east, which includes *Agriculture* and *Hercules* (Figs. 59, 65). Pressures of time – the need, for example, to direct construction of the upper zone and the niche story, and to begin work on the statues – probably resulted in a certain division of labor that might explain discrepancies such as those seen in *Hercules*: The conception would seem to be Andrea's as well as the execution of the figure, which is treated with supreme mastery; the tree, on the other hand, is clearly inferior to those in the Creation scenes. The upper-right-hand portion of the relief suggests the outlines of a half-completed animal and betrays the hand of an assistant.[42] The seven classicizing

[39] See chapter 7.
[40] On the Pisan *Annunziata*, see p. 51f.
[41] See p. 129.

[42] On the division of labor in a trecento workshop, see White (1959), 254–302.

reliefs on the south and east sides, then, would seem to be for the most part designed by Andrea Pisano but executed with the help of others.

Finally, a third group of reliefs distinguishes itself on the Campanile that betrays an imagination utterly at variance with that of Andrea Pisano's as we have come to know it from the doors and the first two Campanile groups (Appendix B, 7). Nor can we consider this group to belong to a late phase of his development, for the evidence suggests that after Andrea left Florence for Pisa, his style continued to evolve in the classicizing and monumental mode announced in the second group of hexagons. I would suggest that this third group is the product of the members of Andrea's workshop who remained in Florence after Andrea's departure. The Florence of the mid-1340s, however, was very different from that of a decade earlier when Andrea began work on the Campanile reliefs.

Construction and *Law* (Figs. 69, 70) are characterized by symmetrical, hieratic compositions in which a frontal figure dominates. *Geometry* and *Astronomy* (Figs. 71, 72) contain figures placed in strict profile and the furniture is rendered in foreshortened frontal perspective, archaic for this period.[43] The drapery folds are composed of regular geometric curves and the hair patterns are mechanically incised. These characteristics preclude the possibility that Andrea designed or executed any of these reliefs. However much his style changed from the doors to the Campanile, and from the first to the second group on the tower, a profound lyrical humanism and naturalism permeate his style. The Painter and Sculptor are celebrated as individual creators – this at a time when apprenticeship and workshop collaboration were the rule. Even God the Father is presented on a human scale in relation to Adam and Eve, but the Builder is depicted as an emblem of dictatorial authority – frontal, centrally placed, and roughly four times the size of his underlings (Fig. 69). The judge, in *Law*, is seated on a high throne shaped like a mandorla, arms extended as though he were Christ offering the keys to Peter, while the defendants kneel in supplication before him and the jurors humbly attend his words (Fig. 70). *Astronomy* departs still further from the naturalism of the earlier reliefs (Fig. 72). Although the figure is seated at a desk with globe and sextant, the whole image is set, not in a naturalistic space, but within a half-sphere symbolic of the heavens.

The third group of reliefs on the Campanile speaks of a new phase in the development of Tuscan trecento sculpture. The artistic environment in Florence around the middle of the century, as M. Meiss has shown in his study of mid-trecento painting,[44] points to the dominance of the austere, hieratic, and spiritualized mode of representa-

---

[43] On medieval experiments in perspective rendering, see White (1967).

[44] Meiss (1951).

tion of Orcagna – to which these reliefs seem to be allied – rather than the monumental and classicizing conception apparent in the second series of reliefs. The rigidity in the placement of the figures belonging to Group III, the emblematic compositions, and, in the case of *Astronomy*, the reversion to a symbolic rather than realistic conception all suggest a late date for this series.

An observation somewhat difficult to make when studying photographs but quite apparent in front of the reliefs in the Museo dell'Opera del Duomo is that the textures of the backgrounds vary from one series to the next. The differences would seem to support the division into three separate phases and even the chronology suggested here. All the reliefs on the western facade have smooth untextured backgrounds. The representation of *Sculpture*, which I have claimed is transitional between the first and second group, has a *slightly* stippled background texture. Perhaps after the Genesis reliefs were in situ Andrea felt that the motifs would read better and be given added sparkle by enlivening the surfaces of the rear planes. A very similar background texture appears in the representation of *Painting*. Even this seems not to have satisfied Andrea for in *Medicine* and *Agriculture* – reliefs that reveal spatial concerns that link them to the first group – the backgrounds are even more strongly textured. This is the texture that prevails in the entire classicizing group of reliefs in which the figures, simpler and more monumental than in the earlier group, stand out in strong relief. Again, we seem to be witnessing a sculptor who, drawing from earlier experience (especially, perhaps, recalling the effective contrast of gilded figures against a neutral ground on the doors), is experimenting with various modes while work is in progress. The third group of reliefs is quite inconsistent as far as the backgrounds are concerned: The Astronomer is set within a half-sphere that is very lightly, uniformly, and almost mechanically stippled but that is in no way similar to the backgrounds of *Sculpture* and *Painting*; *Building* has a background that, although badly damaged, was originally smooth like the earliest reliefs; and *Law* and *Geometry* have strongly textured backgrounds reminiscent of the second group. *Geometry*, then, although emulating the composition of *Sculpture* or *Tubalcain*, follows the background convention of the middle group of hexagons.

To summarize the sequence of execution on the Campanile, the reliefs on the west face were created between ca. 1334 and ca. 1337, the year of Giotto's death. Although stylistically very close to the Baptistry reliefs, the compositions are freer, the figures more monumental, and the drapery less metallic than on the doors. For reasons that will be explored in chapters 6 and 7, a rather abrupt change of style takes place after Andrea himself takes over the office of capomaestro. Simple, monumental compositions containing few figures, and the integration of classically inspired themes and motifs into a Christian content, characterize these reliefs executed between ca. 1337 and ca. 1343, when it is presumed that Andrea left Florence and established a workshop in Pisa. The third group, then, must have been executed after 1343.

THE NICHE FIGURES AND THE LUNETTE *MADONNA*

After Andrea became capomaestro in 1337, both the design of the bell tower and its sculptural program were altered.[45] One of the abrupt and fundamental changes that Andrea made in Giotto's design for the Campanile was the unprecedented inclusion of monumental niche figures. It has been suggested that the niche story represents a transferral of the Gallery of Kings of High Gothic cathedral facades to a cathedral program that, in the facade of Arnolfo's Duomo, lacked this element of northern Gothic iconography.[46] These changes, which resulted in a much more up-to-date cathedral program, must have been as welcomed by the Arte di Calimala as they were enthusiastically advocated by Andrea who was thereby given the opportunity to expand the sculptural component of the building. Given that the niche story was part of Andrea's plan,[47] we may infer that he designed and probably executed at least some of the figures in the niches. The eight trecento statues are stylistically related, but numerous discrepancies in details of design and conception, and the uneven level of execution, prompt a cautious approach to the question of attribution. Of the four that have commonly been associated with the master's name, the Sibyls alone are of sufficiently high quality in both design and execution to warrant an ascription to Andrea (Figs. 74–77). The Sibyls are characterized by stable but gently swaying poses and drapery that, in the vertical fluting of the lower portions, accents the elongated verticality of both figure and niche design. Gently curving as well as richly cascading drapery rhythms balance and enliven the predominant verticality and at the same time add focus to the prominently displayed scroll held by each Sibyl. In this way the composition of the whole enhances the sense of earnest communication conveyed by the heads with their evocative smiles (Figs. 75, 77). Tilted slightly downward toward the observers below, their heads are composed of smooth, broad faces with small oval eyes and finely chiseled eyebrows; the forms recall those of the Virtues on the doors, in particular, *Charity*, *Temperance*, and *Justice* (Figs. 28, 31, 32).

Andrea's Campanile statues must be viewed in relation to his figure style in the reliefs. In the earlier quatrefoils, there is a greater emphasis on decorative surface patterns in the drapery, whereas in the later narratives and the Virtues, the figures are modeled in

[45] Trachtenberg (1971), 49–56, 85–7.   [47] Trachtenberg (1971), 50f.
[46] Trachtenberg (1971), 98–100.

broader, more volumetric forms; it is this later style that appears in the Genesis scenes on the west face of the Campanile before Andrea shifts to the emphatically classicizing conception seen in the second group of Campanile reliefs. But faced with the task of creating – probably for the first time – monumental stone figures, Andrea returns, in a sense, to an earlier style. Although the impression of stability and weight projected by the Campanile Sibyls would seem to reflect – as in the hexagons – Andrea's keen appreciation of classical sculpture, the calligraphic flourishes and rich surface patterns are closer, in many ways, to the Baptistry than to the Campanile reliefs.

The *Erythrean Sibyl* (Fig. 74) is closest to the Pisan wooden *Annunziata* (Fig. 102) and may be the earlier of the two niche figures. The drapery falls predominantly in vertical folds, and, as though attempting on a monumental scale the freedom seen in the *Annunziata* (the arms of which project into space) and the standing figure in *Weaving* (Fig. 62), one arm is almost completely free from the body. In contrast to the relative severity of the *Erythrean Sibyl*'s drapery, that of the *Tiburtine* (Fig. 76) is composed of a rich pattern of curves and countercurves that more closely anticipates the forms of the Spina *Madonna* (Fig. 133). Also anticipating the latter (and unlike the wooden *Virgin* and the relief representations), the Sibyls display a pronounced Gothic contrapposto. If the resolution of this pose remains somewhat awkward on the Campanile, in the later Spina *Madonna* Andrea exhibits total mastery.[48]

The style of the *Madonna and Child* relief in the lunette from the raised portal of the Campanile (Figs. 83, 84) is inseparable from that of the Sibyls. Once again we find the broad cheekbones, narrow oval eyes, and suggestive smile. The rhythmic, cursive drapery recalls that of the Creator in the first Campanile relief (Fig. 50), but the forms are less linear, more plastic in the lunette; in this respect they come closest to the drapery seen in *Weaving* (Fig. 62). The lunette *Madonna* would seem to belong to Andrea's late Campanile phase, hence to the early 1340s.

The lively expression on the face of the Christ Child is outstanding in its naturalism. The Madonna tickles him under his chin as he laughs and grasps her hand. The gesture of the Madonna, reminiscent of the pointing finger of John the Baptist in the traditional representation of *Ecce Agnus Dei* (see Fig. 13), may be an allusion to the future sacrifice of Christ while the Child's restraining gesture conveys his momentary reluctance. Thus, a very human, everyday gesture and activity is introduced to symbolize deeper theological truths. This device, which becomes common in the fifteenth century, is rather precocious for the 1340s.[49]

The figures of *David* and *Solomon* (Figs. 78, 79) lack even the limited plasticity of

[48] On the attribution of the *Madonna and Child* in Santa Maria della Spina, see pp. 67–9.

[49] Shorr (1954), 168ff.

the Sibyls and display a completely different sense of balance and proportion. Instead of the open, animated silhouettes of the female figures, those of the Kings are closed; their arms are plastered to their bodies; the drapery, especially in the *Solomon*, plunges in strict verticality. The almost total lack of modeling in the chest area and the all too pronounced symmetry of the shoulders lack the more subtle variety of Andrea's surfaces and contours. The carving of the hands is clumsy and the expressions on the faces impassive. Whereas the Sibyls are autograph works of Andrea, the Kings, based probably upon models provided by the master, were executed entirely by members of Andrea's workshop, possibly after Andrea had already left Florence.

The foreboding expressiveness of the four nameless Prophets is far removed from the serenity characteristic of Andrea's figures on the doors and the Campanile discussed so far (Figs. 80–82). Compared to the Sibyls and Kings they exhibit a new psychological aggressiveness that recalls Giovanni's statuary on the facade of the Siena Duomo – tempered, however, by characteristic Florentine restraint.[50] They would seem to reflect the mood of the mid- and late 1340s when Florence found itself plunging into disaster. Of the four, only one figure may plausibly, if with reservations, be attributed to Andrea Pisano, in design if not in execution: the Prophet, possibly Moses, holding a tablet (Fig. 82).[51] The impressive head recalls both Daedalus and Hercules on the Campanile: The hairstyle, though less sensitively modeled, is closer to the former and the beard is closer to the latter. The drapery, with its broad, plastic forms, far less sinuous and linear than in the earlier Campanile statues, seems to be the monumental counterpart of the drapery in *Sculpture* – almost as though the sculptor had suddenly stood up. The other prophets are weaker translations of Andrea's more Gothic style as represented by the Sibyls and the lunette *Madonna*, and were probably executed by members of Andrea's workshop after his departure for Pisa ca. 1343.[52]

---

[50] For an illustration of the fourth Prophet, see Becherucci and Brunetti (1969), Fig. 116. Becherucci (1965), 261, comments that in the more aggressively communicative stance of the Prophet holding a tablet (our Fig. 82), Donatello's Campanile Prophets of the following century are anticipated.

[51] For a review of the literature pertaining to these, see Becherucci and Brunetti (1969), 240–4.

[52] One of the difficulties in inserting the Prophet with tablet into Andrea's oeuvre is the apparent contradiction in an evolution that leads from the Sibyls to the Prophet and ends with the Madonna in Santa Maria della Spina – the latter far less intense and ponderous in its impact and more lyrical and decorative in its forms than the Campanile figure. But the differing subject matter and scale called for different solutions. The Prophet was to be read from a great distance high on the bell tower; it probably benefited from Andrea's experience of the Sibyls, which possibly were not as effective from the ground. (Becherucci, in Becherucci and Brunetti [1969], 242, notes that the Sibyls and Kings received critical consideration only after the use of photography permitted them to be studied in detail.) The Madonna, on the other hand, was intended for the intimacy of an interior space.

CHAPTER FOUR
Andrea Pisano: 1321-1343

Having established Andrea's role in the design and execution of the Campanile hexagons, niche figures, and lunette *Madonna*, it is now our task to examine the isolated statues, statuettes, and fragments in various collections that have been or may be attributed to his hand prior to and after his arrival in Florence. Andrea, as has been noted, is referred to several times in the documents as *orefice*. The scale and workmanship of the bronze reliefs would seem to confirm this; but the demands of small-scale execution and the type of commissions Andrea would have received as a goldsmith do not seem sufficient preparation for the execution of those figures of monumental impact that, as unanimously agreed, are found on the Baptistry doors. The latter presuppose larger scale work in wood or stone, the monumentality of which Andrea, trained as a goldsmith, was capable of reducing to the tiny scale required on the doors.

At least one example of sculpture remains from a period prior to Andrea's appearance in Florence, but it already reveals an astonishing monumentality despite the fact that it is clearly a youthful endeavor: the polychromed wood life-size *Annunciate Virgin* (Figs. 102–104) in the Museo di San Matteo, Pisa.[1] The figure is characterized by a combina-

---

[1] The figure is one of the earliest of a large number of wooden Annunciation figures made in Pisa and Siena during the trecento, most of which, however, more or less derive from the marble *Annunciation* in Santa Caterina in Pisa (Figs. 137, 138, 140–142) traditionally ascribed to Nino. See pp. 74–9. The Pisan wood *Annunziata*, too, had been ascribed to Nino or his school until its restoration in 1946 after which a number of critics, struck by its uniqueness and beauty, recognized it as an early work of Andrea Pisano. The octagonal base bears the date 1321 and the names Agostino

tion of elegance and rigidity. The contours are simple and unbroken but swell slightly to permit the underlying body to assert itself. The weight of the body and the forces of gravity on it are expressed by the long, unyielding, and predominantly vertical folds that break only slightly near the plane of the ground. The resulting columnar form, enlivened, however, by the "entasis" of its contours, is given further potential for movement by the hint of distinction between the engaged and free leg, and by the slight rotation of the body, its spiral movement culminating in the turn of the head. It is perhaps the quality and expression of the head that, more than any other aspect, distinguish this *Annunziata* from others of its type: The face is infused with an inner spiritual and psychological warmth, the expression of which is comparable only to the finest of Giotto's heads, and is seen again in the Sibyls of the Campanile.

Compared to Andrea's subsequent figures, this early work remains relatively static and blocklike. Nevertheless, the hair, physiognomy, and shape of the shoulders are identical to those of the companion of the Virgin in the *Visitation* (Figs. 102, 8). The graceful Salome who dances at the Feast of Herod (Fig. 20) is anticipated in the *Annunziata* whose arms move freely away from the body – a motif rare if not unique in a freestanding figure of this period. The movement of Salome, however, has far greater flexibility and the soft and gently curving drapery folds, resting lightly on the underlying forms, are more elegant.

A life-sized polychromed wood head of an *Annunciate Virgin* (Figs. 105, 106) in the Museo di San Matteo, Pisa, closely resembles the head of the full-length figure and warrants an attribution to Andrea Pisano.[2] It would seem to be slightly earlier than the standing *Annunziata* since the carving of the hair is achieved with less finesse. The pure oval face, the delicate turn of the head asymmetrically poised on the neck, and, in particular, the profile with short straight nose, short upper lip, and hint of a double chin are repeated in the standing Virgin and, much later, in the *Madonna del Latte* (Fig. 107).[3]

---

di Giovanni and Stefano Acolti. The style of the Virgin has nothing to do with that of the Sienese sculptor Agostino di Giovanni and the names belong to no other known sculptors of the period; they refer, most probably, to the painters who colored the surfaces or else to the donors. See Carli (1947a), 47ff.; also Becherucci (1947), 68–70; Valentiner (1947), 163–87. Garzelli (1969), 150f., offers a completely unwarranted attribution to the Sienese sculptor Agostino di Giovanni.

[2] This fragment was exhibited in Pisa in 1947 as belonging to the immediate circle of Andrea Pisano. At that time its damaged and heavily re-painted surfaces revealed little that claimed critical attention. During a reorganization of the Museo di San Matteo in 1970, the fragment came to light again, was identified from museum records, and was restored by removing the later polychromy. In 1972 it was exhibited in the Mostra del Restauro at the Pisan museum. The head was then ascribed to Andrea Pisano by Antonino Caleca, who, in his notes to the catalogue (1972), 89–91, dates the work to Andrea's Pisan period, 1343–47. Soprintendenza ai Monumenti e Gallerie (1922).

[3] On the attribution of the *Madonna del Latte* to Andrea, see pp. 72–4.

The expression, a mere shadow of the original – strangely reminiscent of the ghostly, postrestoration Peruzzi Chapel figures – projects that sense of interior illumination characteristic of Andrea's autograph sculptures.

These two works, the standing *Annunziata* and the fragment in the Museo di San Matteo are, then, the only extant sculptures of Andrea Pisano that date from his early years in Pisa. They already reveal, as will be expanded upon later, Andrea's debt to Giotto and adherence to an artistic current that ran counter to the prevailing style in Pisa during the 1320s, when most sculptors remained under the strong influence of the turbulent, aggressive art of Giovanni Pisano.

In the cathedral museum in Orvieto there is a relief of a blessing Christ who holds a chalice in his left hand, possibly an allusion to the Holy Corporal, revered treasure of the cathedral (Fig. 93).[4] The half-length figure is framed by a trilobe, which in turn is enclosed in a triangular pediment inlaid with colored and gold intarsia. It evidently formed part of a lost tabernacle or tomb. The relief has been attributed to a collaborator of Nino Pisano[5] and, more recently, to Andrea and Nino, and dated 1348–9.[6] These attributions are based in part on the assumption that the work was executed during the years when Andrea and Nino are documented in Orvieto, that is, after 1347. A number of factors, including style, argue against this dating and for an attribution to Andrea alone prior to his appearance in Florence. There is good reason to believe, as we shall see, that Andrea spent some time in Orvieto between his early years in Pisa and his arrival in Florence where he is documented by 1330.[7] The comely, even aristocratic physiognomy with its high cheekbones and neat coiffure, the proportions, and the gestures of the blessing Christ are virtually identical to those of the bronze Christ in the *Baptism*, as well as the *Redeemer* (cf. Figs. 45 and 94). Very close to the latter, too, are the sensitive fingers with their tensile grasp of the object in hand. Not only the style of the figure argues against a dating in the late 1340s or early 1350s, but the aedicula of which it is a fragment must have resembled that on the tomb of Benedict XI (d. 1304) in Perugia, dated early in the century. Andrea, with his early training as a goldsmith, and by now having demonstrated mastery in more than one sculptural technique, may have been called to Florence directly from Orvieto.

By 1330, the date of the inscription on the Baptistry doors, Andrea was working in Florence. It has been unanimously assumed, and never questioned, that he appeared there shortly before January of that year when he is referred to as "maestro delle porte" (Doc. 4). This assumption is based on two considerations: first, the lack of docu-

4 Garzelli (1972), 64.
5 Ibid.

6 Burresi (1983), 182.
7 See pp. 105–8.

mentary reference to Andrea prior to this notice of 1330; and second, the absence of any earlier work in Florence attributable to him. Concerning the documentation, it is necessary to emphasize, once again, the fragmentary nature of the references: Since the Spoglie Strozziane are merely excerpts or summaries from the cathedral records, we may assume that the notice of November 1329 concerning the decision to create metal doors and to send Piero di Jacopo to Pisa and Venice (Doc. 2) represents the culmination, not the beginning, of discussion and debate. The choice of artist must have been based on extremely careful consideration and, likely as not, was based on a demonstration of proficiency and talent. Clearly, the lack of documentary reference is not sufficient evidence to bar Andrea from residency in Florence prior to his known activity in connection with the Baptistry doors. If, on the contrary, one is willing to place Andrea in Florence, say in 1327 or 1328, one may be more willing to find his hand in sculptures heretofore not considered.

One example suggests itself. The Museo dell'Opera del Duomo in Florence possesses a head of John the Baptist, the only fragment remaining from a fourteenth-century statue that was part of a *Baptism of Christ* group (Figs. 86, 87, 91). This group was placed above the south portal of the Baptistry until the sixteenth century, when it was removed as being "tanto goffo" and in ruins; the group was replaced by the statues, still in situ, of Andrea Sansovino.[8] The disposition of the original Baptism group is known from a fifteenth-century *cassone* panel that shows a Gothic tabernacle with three trefoil arches containing a blessing Christ in the center immersed to his waist; to the right of Christ stands John the Baptist in profile with arm raised pouring the holy water, and to the left a third figure presumably holding Christ's garment (Fig. 88). The fragment in the Florentine museum has been identified as the St. John belonging to this group and has been attributed, unconvincingly, both to a hypothetical Master of San Giovanni[9] and to Tino di Camaino.[10] Another fragment, a blessing Christ (Fig. 92) in the same museum, also ascribed to Tino, has been identified as the central figure illustrated in the *cassone*.[11] Tino was working in Florence from

[8] Brunetti, in Becherucci and Brunetti (1969), 228.

[9] Ragghianti (1936), 272–6; Weinberger (1937a), 23–30.

[10] Brunetti (1952), 97–107. Brunetti points out that the iconography is Sienese rather than Florentine. In contrast to the representation in the Baptistry mosaic as well as that in the Arena Chapel fresco, Christ is shown in strict frontality. Christ is similarly posed on the facade of Orvieto and on the baptismal fonts at Rosia and Arezzo,

and a century later, in Ghiberti's relief on the Siena font. See also Brunetti, in Becherucci and Brunetti (1969), 229f.

[11] Brunetti, in Becherucci and Brunetti (1969), 229f. Brunetti's attributions have been accepted by Valentiner (1954), 117–33, who, however, gives an earlier dating, and by Pope-Hennessy (1964), 33. P. Toesca (1951), 264, mentions that the head of the Baptist "rammenta Andrea da Pontedera."

1321 to 1323 and is associated in a document of 1322 with the Baptistry – the same document that first mentions new metal doors (Doc. 1). The blessing Christ is consonant with Tino's Florentine style. The modeling of the head of John the Baptist, on the other hand, with its landscape of hollows and protrusions, is irreconcilable with Tino's blocklike forms that tend to be modeled on the surface alone. Furthermore, the head of the Baptist communicates an intensely expressive inner presence that contrasts strongly with Tino's congenial, moon-faced figures with their more limited projection of energy and animation.

A comparison between the *Saint John the Baptist* – clearly a work of supreme sensitivity – and several figures from the doors and the Campanile reveals a surprising stylistic unity (Figs. 86, 87, 89–91), making an attribution to Andrea highly plausible. The similarity between the marble *Saint John the Baptist* and that in the *Baptism of Christ* (Figs. 86, 89) on the doors is striking. The very shape and structure of the head with its high cheekbones and hollowed-out cheeks, the regulated yet varied rhythm of the hair pattern, the qualified symmetry of the beard seem to derive from the hand of the bronze master. Or compare the figure of the Baptist being led to prison – grave, entranced, lips slightly parted (Fig. 90). Like the prisoner in the relief, the head from the south portal, with its intense gaze and slightly parted lips, projects an image of reserved ardor. Significantly, the Baptist appears to relate to an external figure – clearly, the Christ whom it flanked. This impression of psychological interaction between a statue and its pendant recalls the *Annunziata* in Pisa (Fig. 102), who likewise appears to react, not just physically, but psychologically to another presence, in this case the angel Gabriel. The compelling projection of an interior psychological existence, one that communicates with a second figure, contrasts strongly with the effect of Tino's figures, which always seem self-contained, existing in their own immediate, fictive worlds. The pattern of the hair, however, with its deeply drilled striations would seem to derive from Tino – and beyond Tino, from Giovanni Pisano. As we shall see in a chapter that follows, Andrea had shown himself sympathetic to Tino's art as early as the *Annunziata* in Pisa. And the influence of Tino – qualified as Andrea's reaction is – continues to be felt throughout our sculptor's career.[12]

The *Saint John the Baptist* may have been Andrea's initial testing ground in Florence. The Arte di Calimala must have recognized in Andrea a sculptor who could integrate the avant-garde lyricism of Tino with a more intense, but at the same time restrained, emotional content. These considerations, together with evidence of Andrea's proficiency as a goldsmith and capabilities as a sculptor of large-scale works in wood and stone, must have convinced the Arte that the master from Pisa was equal to the un-

[12] See pp. 98, 102, 105.

paralleled demands of the commission for the bronze doors. Their expectations could not have been more happily fulfilled.

No sooner had the labors of designing and modeling the narratives and Virtues for the doors been completed, when Andrea was called on to execute the series of hexagonal reliefs for the west facade of the Campanile, the cornerstone of which was laid in 1334.[13] It is to this early phase of the Campanile project that several statuettes may also be assigned.

Recent critics are unanimous in ascribing the marble statuettes in the Museo dell'Opera del Duomo, Florence (Figs. 94–97), to Andrea on the basis of their close stylistic affinity to figures on the bronze doors.[14] The head of the *Redeemer* is especially comparable to Christ in the *Baptism of Christ* and in *Ecce Agnus Dei* (Figs. 45, 13), and also recalls God the Father in the Campanile Creation scenes (Fig. 50). The face and hairstyle of the female saint, most likely a figure of Santa Reparata, to whom the Cathedral was originally dedicated,[15] recall the companion of Mary in the *Visitation* and the attendants at the *Birth of the Baptist* (Figs. 8, 9). The pose and drapery, indeed, are so close to the former that one suspects that the relief served as an immediate model. Yet it is almost inconceivable that Andrea would copy his own work so closely.

A detailed examination of the two figures indicates that they are not by the same hand. The drapery of the *Redeemer* is modeled with greater subtlety and fluidity than that of *Santa Reparata*, which by comparison appears somewhat starchy. The edges of her garment are stiffer and the hem lacks the fringe and embroidered pattern seen in the pendant figure. The hands and fingers are more rubbery, lacking the veined and tensile grasp of the *Redeemer*. The carving of the hair is too mechanical, whereas the face appears impassive without the decisive projection of that warm psychological presence we have come to expect from Andrea. The *Santa Reparata*, therefore, is by an assistant or follower of Andrea attempting to emulate his style.

That the two were not conceived and executed contemporaneously is suggested also by the different nature of the carving seen in the back views (Figs. 95, 96): The *Redeemer* was executed as a freestanding figure and the *Santa Reparata* was made to be placed against a wall or in a niche. The Christ figure was probably one of eight marble statuettes – which included the seven planets – commissioned by the *officiali dei mosaici* to be placed on the corners of an octagonal screen surrounding the bap-

[13] Trachtenberg (1971), 21.
[14] I. Toesca (1950), 39f.; Becherucci, in Becherucci and Brunetti (1969), 232f.; Valentiner (1947), 168. Schmarsow (1887), 137–53, was the first to ascribe the statuettes to Andrea.
[15] Guasti (1887), 3.

tismal area in the center of the Baptistry; for unknown reasons work on this project was abandoned.[16] It seems likely that upon suspension of work for the Baptistry screen, a new site had to be found for the *Redeemer* and it was decided to commission a pendant figure. Both were to be placed against a wall or in a niche, thus explaining the lack of finish in the back of the new figure.[17] Stylistically the statuettes belong to the earliest Campanile phase before the master arrived at a more classicizing mode and are thus datable prior to 1337.

The *Madonna and Child* in the Budapest Museum of Fine Arts (Figs. 98–100) has been variously attributed to Andrea or followers, or to Nino.[18] It is extremely close in pose, drapery configuration, and physiognomy to numerous female figures on the doors (Fig. 10) and is executed with far greater refinement and subtlety of modeling and contours than is the *Santa Reparata* (Fig. 97). Andrea's handwriting is evident in the calligraphic linear elements that in no way detract from the stability of the pose. The carving of the hair contrasts strongly with the mechanical and repetitive pattern seen in the *Santa Reparata* and always avoided on the doors. Instead of the impassive expression of the *Santa Reparata*, the Budapest figure projects, as do the Sibyls and lunette *Madonna*, an expression of serene vitality. The figure betrays none of the growing influence of classical sculpture seen on the Campanile and therefore, like the Florentine statuette, probably dates from before 1337, that is, ca. 1335.

Slightly later in date is a headless statue in the Museo dell'Opera del Duomo (Fig. 101) executed by Andrea with the help of assistants. Whereas the relationship of body to drapery and the pattern of folds closely resembles the Budapest *Madonna* (Figs. 98, 99), the bulky classicism anticipates aspects of the Orvieto *Madonna* (Fig. 110); therefore, it probably belongs to the later, more classicizing phase of the Campanile project. The hairpin folds near the chest and in the sleeves are seen in the Campanile lunette *Madonna* and the Sibyls (Figs. 84, 74, 76); the modeling of the hands recalls that of the *Redeemer* (Fig. 94). Only the fact that the drapery folds adhere

[16] Kreytenberg (1980), 3–7.

[17] Kreytenberg (1980), 3–7, believes that the female figure was begun as part of the series of planets, for it, too, "is indeed nearly fully worked" in the back and was thus intended for a free-standing position; when work on the project was suspended, the latter statuette was transformed into the *Santa Reparata*. In my view, the *Santa Reparata* does not lack merely the final modeling and smoothing of the surfaces in the back; rather,

most of the folds, never having been designed as fully developed forms, simply merge into the unmodulated back surface.

[18] Venturi (1905), 126f.; I. Toesca (1950), 56 (by a follower of Nino still subject to the influence of Andrea); Balogh (1953), 71–114 (88ff.). This last, which includes a complete bibliography on the statuette, including several articles in Hungarian journals, argues strongly and persuasively for an attribution to Andrea.

too much to the surface, in contrast to the more integrated and plastic modeling of the *Redeemer* or the Budapest *Madonna*, raises some doubts concerning the execution of the work; we are left with the impression that several hands may have divided up the labor of carving.

The provenance of the headless statue may have been Or San Michele. There is some evidence that Andrea was the architect of the building and that he designed two of the niches in the piers when, in 1339, it was decided that each guild contribute a statue of its patron saint to embellish the grain hall.[19] One of these niches is that of the Arte della Lana, which commissioned a *Saint Stephen* but, a century later, had the figure replaced by a more modern work – the bronze *Saint Stephen* of 1428 by Lorenzo Ghiberti.[20] In his *Commentaries*, Ghiberti mentions that among the sculptures executed by Andrea Pisano there is "una figura di Santo Stefano che fu posta nella faccia dinanzi a Santa Reparata."[21] The wording might be interpreted to imply that the trecento statue was not always to be found at that site. The statue in the Museo dell'Opera del Duomo wears a deacon's collar and it may very well be that this is the figure referred to by Ghiberti.[22]

We have seen that during his Florentine sojourn Andrea does not have total mastery over the problems of monumental stone sculpture in-the-round. In the Sibyls (Figs. 74–77), the conflict between the figure conceived in three dimensions and the surface qualities of relief design has not been completely resolved. The attempt to enhance the monumentality of the figure may explain the somewhat ponderous forms and simplification of drapery seen in the Saint Stephen.[23]

These three figures, then – The *Redeemer*, the Budapest *Madonna*, and the *Saint Stephen* (Figs. 94, 98, 101) – form a fairly unified stylistic group revealing, however, a gradual classicizing amplification of the Gothic mode. The gracious and mellow Gothicism of these figures retained its currency, it should be noted, throughout the trecento even when intermingling with or temporarily interrupted by other currents. Indeed, it is this aspect of Andrea's art that struck a deeply responsive chord in

[19] Trachtenberg (1971), 76–9.

[20] Trachtenberg, 77.

[21] Krautheimer (1970), vol. I, 9.

[22] Valentiner (1954), 131, n. 1, observed that in Ghiberti's bronze statue of Saint Stephen of 1428, made to replace a trecento figure, many of the characteristics of our stone statue would seem to have been retained.

[23] Far more successful in this regard is the Prophet holding a tablet (Fig. 82) from the Campanile, whose attribution to Andrea, however, remains insecure. See p. 50. Conceived with greater plasticity and a more active play of light and dark in the drapery forms, the figure is far more assertive than the *Saint Stephen* and has rightly been viewed as anticipating the plastic and expressive characteristics of Donatello's Campanile figures. Becherucci (1965), 261.

Nino. Stimulated by continuing influences from across the Alps, Nino's mature sculpture anticipates developments of the late trecento, both in Venice and Tuscany, but his roots clearly go back to Andrea's early Florentine style.[24]

By ca. 1343, however, when Andrea left Florence for Pisa, he was in command of a highly sophisticated classicizing style as evidenced by the second group of Campanile reliefs. Just as at an earlier time Andrea had translated his lyrical relief style on the Baptistry doors into a more monumental mode in the Campanile niche figures, now he attempted to apply the classicism of his Campanile hexagons to the problem of a free-standing figure, the *Madonna and Child* for a Maestà in Orvieto, executed in Andrea's Pisan workshop. It is to this workshop that our attention must now turn.[25]

[24] This issue is explored further in the Epilogue.

[25] The most important recent attribution to Andrea Pisano's early period is that of Calderoni Masetti (1978), 1–26, regarding the beautiful silver and copper, partially gilt reliquary cross in the Cathedral of Massa Marittima. Certain details, including the treatment of the drapery, and the emotional tenor of the figure of Christ are, however, alien to Andrea's style as we have come to know it from the doors and the Campanile. Although the master of the Christ figure has attempted to emulate the fluid quality of Andrea's treatment of the hair and beard, there is an emphasis on regular, evenly spaced striations rather than on larger units subdivided into thinner strands as is characteristic of Andrea's work. The conception of the nude finds no counterpart on the doors or Campanile. The nude Christ in the *Baptism of Christ* on the doors (Fig. 45) is composed of subtly modeled flesh and gentle contours, whereas the later nudes on the Campanile are even more classical in conception, and thus quite unlike the Massa Marittima example. The drapery, moreover, is composed of a series of complex, mobile, calligraphic, and thus highly decorative folds and edges strongly reminiscent of Sienese painting and differing markedly from the broader, more classicizing treatment of Andrea's drapery *even* in his earliest reliefs and statues. The Massa Marittima crucifix is, rather, by a Sienese master influenced by both Giovanni Pisano and by Andrea and should be dated in the 1330s. A rejection of the attribution to Andrea, and arguments favoring a Sienese origin of the crucifix, may be found in *Il Gotico a Siena* (1982), 109–12.

A number of crucifixes both large and small, in marble, wood, and bronze, have been attributed to Andrea. See especially Lisner (1970). Although no extant crucifix, in my view, may be ascribed to his hand, it is most probable that Andrea originated a type of crucifix that departed from the canons established by Nicola and Giovanni Pisano. In a study currently in progress, I am exploring the typology of early trecento sculptured crucifixes and attempting to establish which of these may be associated with a probable invention of Andrea Pisano.

CHAPTER FIVE

Andrea's Activity in Pisa and Orvieto and the Problem of Nino Pisano

The last documentary reference to Andrea in Florence is the notice of 1340 (Doc. 36) that he was capomaestro, but the building history of the Campanile strongly suggests that he remained in that city until around 1342 or 1343.[1] From that date until 1347, when he is documented as capomaestro of Orvieto (Doc. 39–56), it is very likely that he was the head of a workshop in Pisa. For one thing, in 1347 and 1348 there are references to payments made to Andrea for several trips he took to Pisa (and Siena), and in March 1348 there is mention of a marble Maestà, including a completed *Madonna and Child* and blocks of stone for two angels, which were brought from Pisa to Orvieto (Doc. 49, 52, 54). On stylistic grounds the *Madonna and Child*, to be discussed later, has been attributed to Andrea.[2] Several works in Pisa, too, plausibly datable to the years between 1343 and 1347, strongly suggest that Andrea was active as a sculptor in his native region during these years.[3] Each of these works, however, also has been attributed to Nino.

This brings us face to face with the thorny problem of distinguishing between the hands of father and son. Before turning, then, to a discussion of Andrea's Pisan workshop, it is necessary to examine Nino's signed sculptures, to determine their salient

[1] Trachtenberg (1971), 50f.

[2] See Cellini (1933), 1–20, Lányi (1933a), 204–27, and Becherucci (1965), 227–63. The Orvieto documents were published by Luzi (1866), 360–2, and Fumi (1891), 60f., 99, 476f.

[3] These include the Saltarelli monument, the *Madonna and Child* on the pinnacle of the Pisa Duomo facade, the *Madonna del Latte*, and the *Madonna* in Santa Maria della Spina.

stylistic characteristics, and to offer a hypothesis (given that none of his extant works are dated) regarding their chronology and thus the course of Nino's stylistic evolution.

The major problem concerning Nino's sculpture was clearly articulated by J. Lányi as early as 1933 when he commented that "le opere di Nino assicurate da inscrizione o da documenti stanno in profonda contraddizione col gruppo delle opere legate al suo nome solo dalla tradizione."[4] Only three statues bear his signature and none is dated; three others were assigned to him by Vasari. The autograph works are the *Madonna and Child* in Santa Maria Novella, Florence (Fig. 109); another on the Cornaro monument in Santi Giovanni e Paolo in Venice (Fig. 119); and the *Bishop Saint* in Oristano, Sardinia (Fig. 130). Vasari, in the second edition of his *Lives*, states that the *Madonna* in Santa Maria Novella was begun by Andrea and completed by Nino, and that it was Nino's first work of art. He assigns to Nino the *Madonna and Child* in Santa Maria della Spina (Fig. 133), the *Madonna del Latte* (now in the Museo di San Matteo) (Fig. 135), and the *Annunciation* group in Santa Caterina (Figs. 137, 138) – all in Pisa.[5] While the three Pisan sculptures that Vasari gives to Nino bear some stylistic relation to each other, any connection to the signed figures in Florence, Venice, and Oristano is remote; for this reason, some writers have rejected the Vasarian tradition and have attributed one or more of these sculptures to Andrea Pisano or others.[6] More often than not, however, scholars have uncritically accepted Vasari's statements and have attempted, often through tortuous reasoning, to postulate chronologies that accommodate the clear visual contradictions. Variations on the theme of style and chronology have been manifold and arbitrary.[7]

The problem is compounded by extreme differences in the perception of the quality of individual works of art; a scholar's assessment of a given sculpture naturally affects his view of its proximity to the master's own hand. Evaluations have ranged from that

[4] Lányi (1933a), 226f.

[5] Milanesi, ed. (1878). Nino is mentioned only in the life of Andrea Pisano despite the fact that Vasari thought that the younger sculptor "fu poi molto miglior maestro che il padre stato non era" (p. 489).

[6] Most notably Lányi and Becherucci.

[7] To cite just a few instances: Carli (1934a), 189–222, accepts all of Vasari's statements and proposes an evolution that leads from the Santa Maria Novella statuette to the Spina *Madonna* and the Santa Caterina *Annunciation* and culminates in the Cornaro *Madonna* in Venice. Weinberger (1937b), 58–91, on the other hand, considers the signed Madonnas to be late works of the 1360s and the Spina *Madonna* a middle work of the mid-1340s. In his view, Nino's early work is independent from the style of Andrea, his middle period betrays the growing influence of the father, whereas the late signed figures reveal a retreat from that influence. I. Toesca (1950), 64f., proposes an evolution that moves from the Florentine group to the Cornaro *Madonna* and ends with the Santa Caterina *Annunciation*. More recently, Vasari's chronology and attributions have been accepted anew by Burresi (1984) in the catalogue for an exhibition of photographs of the Pisani sculptures held in Pisa and Pontedera.

of J. Pope-Hennessy's comment that the *Madonna del Latte* is the work upon which Nino's "claim to be considered a great sculptor must ultimately rest" to that of M. Weinberger's description of the same figure as having a "leaden dullness of expression" with "narrow eyelids looking so much more like dry old sliced parchment than like living skin."[8] The *Bishop* in Oristano has been commended for its "originalità espressiva" by one critic, and by another denied to Nino, despite its signature, because "il modellato . . . e scialbo, l'impostazione della figura assai povera, priva di interesse."[9] Although disparaged by most as unworthy of Nino, the statuette, in fact, is not deprived of merit and its low appeal is due, I believe, to the circumstance that it is known primarily by way of inferior photographs – a situation that, it is hoped, the present study will rectify. Curiously, even the Cornaro *Madonna* has recently been denied to Nino and described as a work of "un collaboratore di Nino con intenzione di imitare il suo stile."[10] Upon which works the conception of "il suo stile" is based, however, is not made clear.

A number of factors limit the credibility of Vasari. In the first edition, only one work of art by Nino is mentioned – the *Madonna* in Santa Maria Novella. As there are, even today, virtually no sculptures in Florence that we may associate with Nino, probably the Santa Maria Novella statuette was the single work by Nino that Vasari knew. Learning from Ghiberti's writings[11] that Nino had executed works in Pisa, Vasari – during his extensive research in Pisa between the first and second editions[12] – must have sought to fill in this gap in his knowledge. In his desire to find some works to attach to the name Nino, he may not have investigated too precisely his sources. Often, moreover, he depended on the help of friends who copied inscriptions for him and checked information.[13]

Given the paucity of useful documents, however, if one chooses to deny one or more of the signed sculptures to Nino and rejects completely the validity of the tradition associating a certain style – however vaguely defined – with Nino, one is led to an art-historical impasse: Nino becomes, in effect, a nonartist known only from a single work of art, the Florentine *Madonna*, never denied to him but also not universally accepted as a masterpiece. Until new documents or signed works are discovered, any attempt to reconstruct an artistic personality seems futile and should be abandoned. This is clearly a valid course. On the other hand, taking a more generous view of the extant sculptures, the documents and the traditional attributions, it is possible to develop a number of hypotheses concerning a sculptor whose style clearly captured the imagination of sub-

---

[8] Pope-Hennessy (1972), 23; Weinberger (1937b), 89.

[9] Burresi (1973), 6–12; I. Toesca (1950), 49.

[10] Wolters (1976), 199.

[11] On Vasari's sources, see Boase (1979), 51f.

[12] Boase, 60, 158.

[13] Boase, 60f.

sequent generations of artists and patrons. Keeping in mind, then, the limitations of further investigations and stylistic analysis, this is, I believe, the more fruitful course.[14]

THE *BISHOP SAINT*

The *Bishop Saint* (Figs. 130, 131) in the Church of San Francesco, Oristano, stands about a meter tall on an octagonal base, the four forward sides of which contain, in beautiful Gothic letters, the following inscription: + NINUS: MAGITRI: ANDREE: DEPISIS: ME FECIT.[15] The statuette fits perfectly with the base, which appears to be made of the same marble as the figure itself.[16] The *Bishop* holds a staff which, however, is broken above and below the right hand, and there are chips missing from the lower ends of the drapery; otherwise, the figure is intact and in good condition. Traces of blue paint are visible on the back of the mantle. The marble retains a polished, luminous quality reminiscent of several sculptures associated with both Andrea and Nino Pisano.

Of the three signed sculptures, the figure in Oristano is closest stylistically to the work of Andrea. Many of Andrea's figures are characterized by a strong impulse toward a graceful Gothic torsion and, concomitantly, by restraints on that impulse so that the forms exhibit a physical as well as psychological *gravitas* that derives from Giotto. This is already apparent in one of the earliest works ascribed to him, the wooden *Annunziata* in Pisa (Fig. 102): Here, as we have seen, Andrea fuses an elegance of movement with a basically Giottesque sense of ponderation.[17] A similar and increasingly more successfully realized search for this synthesis may be observed in his later figures on the doors (Figs. 20, 22) and, as we shall see, in the *Madonna* in Santa Maria della Spina (Fig. 133).

In Nino's *Bishop*, too, one notes the juxtaposition of opposing forces: a balance between a sense of gravity weighing down the figure, the drapery, even the book and the contrasting upward spiral of the body and surge of drapery folds culminating in the turn of the head. The *Bishop*'s facial type, moreover, appears several times on the doors – most notably on the extreme right in the *Entombment of the Baptist* (Fig. 47). At once idealized yet with remarkably realistic details – note the prominent cheekbones, the

[14] Portions of the following discussion appeared previously in Moskowitz (1984).

[15] The Church of San Francesco originally belonged to the Basiliani monks and the statuette traditionally has been considered a representation of Saint Basil. In 1843 the figure was seen in the nave of the church but apparently by 1868 it was forgotten among various ruins in the basement of the convent of San Francesco. See Scano (1900), 133; (1903), 17–30.

[16] Cf. Weinberger (1937b), 85, who states that the base and statuette did not necessarily originally belong together. This doubt seems unwarranted.

[17] See p. 51f.

slightly puffy flesh that descends from nose to mouth, the furrow on the brows — both figures project a similar psychological presence: A tinge of profound anxiety disturbs the otherwise serene and idealized physiognomies. The conception of the human figure seen in the *Bishop*, then, springs from ideals that are fundamental to the art of Andrea Pisano.

THE *MADONNA AND CHILD* IN SANTA MARIA NOVELLA

The *Madonna and Child* (Fig. 109) in Santa Maria Novella, Florence, stands on an octagonal base inscribed with Gothic letters as follows: HOC OPUS FECIT NINUS MAGRI ANDREE DE PISIS. Although there are no visible traces of polychromy, the surface of the statuette is in excellent condition; however, a piece from the back of the Madonna's head and the right index fingers of Christ are missing.[18]

Compared to the other signed works, the Santa Maria Novella *Madonna* is the furthest removed stylistically from Andrea's designs on the doors and the Campanile. Moreover, the classical balance and naturalism that inform the *Bishop* are almost completely abandoned in this work. The *Madonna* slinks, relatively weightlessly, her drapery patterns motivated more by decorative considerations than by posture and gravity. The awkward twist of the *Bishop*'s hand is transformed in the *Madonna* in-

---

[18] Before its present location in the Rucellai Chapel, the group was incorporated into the tomb of Aldobrandino Cavalcanti. Cavalcanti, a Dominican monk, died in 1279 and a tomb was made for him. Nino's statue, however, was not placed on the monument until 1861. See Orlandi (1955), vol. 1, 230–4. Vasari saw the figure near the Minerbetti Chapel in the right aisle (Milanesi [1878], 494). Fra Ugolino Minerbetti died in 1348 (Orlandi [1955], vol. 1, 76) and it is possible that the *Madonna* was made in connection with his tomb or chapel sometime after that date. Becherucci (1965), 257f. It may also be of interest to note that a nephew of Simone Saltarelli was buried in Santa Maria Novella. Orlandi (1955), 374f., n. 1. Simone had been a prior of Santa Maria Novella before becoming archbishop, and he was undoubtedly acquainted with Andrea Pisano. The Pisano workshop executed Saltarelli's tomb in Santa Caterina, Pisa (see below, pp. 80–90), and it may very well be that the connections between the Saltarelli family and the Pisani continued into the next generation. Perhaps the *Madonna* by Nino was made for this later Saltarelli who died in 1361, a date consonant with the style of the statue.

On the other hand, it is possible that the figure was not made for the church at all, for there exists a notice that a certain Lorenzo Ridolfo gave the statuette to the Opera of Santa Maria Novella in 1571 which, in turn, donated it to the clerics. Fineschi, V., *Monumenti di S. Maria Novella*, Tomo I, Parte III. cap. I fol. 4, ms. in Santa Maria Novella, cited in Orlandi (1955), 234.

to an elegant, almost mannered turn. And whereas in the head of the saint (Fig. 131) there is a keenly felt relationship between underlying skeletal (and even cartilaginous, as in the nose) structure and an overlay of soft fleshy forms (characteristic, as well, of Andrea's sculpture), the *Madonna*'s head is composed of more homogeneous, malleable, and sensuous matter (Fig. 108). If the softness of drapery and the facture of the marble surfaces are almost identical with those of the *Bishop Saint*, few works of art associated with Nino's name deserve, to the same degree as does the Florentine *Madonna*, Vasari's praise of Nino's craftsmanship: "si puo dire che Nino cominciasse veramente a cavare la durezza de sassi e ridurgli alla vivezza delle carni."

As is true of the *Bishop*, however, certain characteristic details would seem to have their immediate source in Andrea's sculpture. The ovoid head, broadening smoothly at the cheeks, and the evocative smile, bordering on the sentimental, appear in several figures on the doors (Figs. 8–10). Even the exaggerated contrapposto stance – the S-curve culminating in the downward turn of the head – appears once on the doors in the figure of the violin player in the *Dance of Salome* (Fig. 20). Seen from the rear, the *Madonna*'s projecting elbows pulling the drapery into broad swinging curves recall similar details in the *Funeral of the Baptist* (Figs. 24, 117). This very comparison, however, reveals the distance traversed by Nino away from that balance between structure and decorative elements – virtually a constant in the work of Andrea – in favor of the latter. Whereas in Andrea's figures the drapery reflects the body beneath so that the recessions and projections of the underlying anatomy are clearly indicated, in Nino's *Madonna* these forms are suppressed and the emphasis is, instead, on the abstract, decorative play of drapery curves.

THE *MADONNA AND CHILD* ON THE CORNARO MONUMENT IN VENICE

The third signed figure, the *Madonna and Child* (Figs. 118–122) on the Cornaro monument in the Church of Santi Giovanni e Paolo lies somewhere between the two poles. On the one hand, the emphasis on decorative linear rhythms and the strong S-curve of the pose recall similar features in the Florentine *Madonna*; on the other, the posture of the Venetian figure has less swing, the proportions appear to be less elongated, the turn of the wrists is more naturalistic, and the impression of equilibrium in the structure and pose is far greater than in the Florentine statuette; in short, it displays something of the Giottesque balance and gravity realized in the *Bishop* (Fig. 130).

The pudgy Infant, solidly constructed and broader at the hips than at the shoulders, contrasts with the elongated and slender-hipped Child in Florence.

Compared to the *Bishop*, however, the *Madonna* shows less distinction between the bones of the cheeks and the chin and their fleshy covering (Figs. 120, 122, 131) ; nevertheless, her face has more internal structure than does that of the Florentine *Madonna* with its smoothly continuous surfaces (Fig. 108). Finally, the affectionate gaze of the Venetian *Madonna* is more sober, more restrained than the almost honeyed smile of the Florentine figure.

The socle of the *Madonna* bears a painted inscription, partially obliterated. Reconstructed, it reads: HOC OPUS FECIT NINUS MAGISTRI ANDREE DE PISIS.[19] The hems of the mantles of the *Madonna and Child* are decorated with raised and gilded Gothic letters; these form part of the *Ave Maria* text.[20] The *Madonna* and the flanking saints and angels were not necessarily made for the tomb of Doge Cornaro, which now contains them. Valentiner has observed that the statues are made of Carrara marble, whereas the architectural framing and the figure of the Doge below are composed of Istrian marble; the socles of the statues, moreover, appear to be too large for the niches.[21] It is likely, as we shall see, that the niche statues on the Cornaro monument (Fig. 123) were executed in Pisa and sent to Venice only at the time of the Doge's death in 1368,[22] by which date, however, Nino was already dead.

As the most important sculptor of his day, Andrea Pisano must have exerted a powerful influence on the development of his son, at least during its earlier stages. It seems more than likely that the evolution of Nino moved from a style close to that of Andrea's toward one that increasingly absorbed foreign or other influences.[23] The *Bishop Saint* would seem to be, then, a work created under the close tutelage of Andrea. It reveals the attempt to balance classical weight and repose with Gothic decorative rhythms and expressive content. Although the modeling of the drapery and head is extraordinarily refined, a number of passages – notably both arms and hands – indicate that the author of this work has not yet mastered every detail of his craft. The Venetian and Florentine Madonnas suggest that Nino is moving away from his earlier ideals under the influence of his father, toward a more fluid interpretation of form in which structural equilibrium is not a determining motive. The Venetian *Madonna*, then, is the second and the Florentine *Madonna* the last of Nino's signed sculptures.

---

[19] Valentiner (1926–7), 242f.
[20] See Niero (1971), 45f.
[21] Valentiner (1926–7), 242f.
[22] See pp. 150–2.

[23] Cf. Weinberger (1937b), 66, who sees a growing, rather than a diminishing, influence of Andrea's sculpture on Nino.

THE *MADONNA AND CHILD* IN SANTA MARIA DELLA SPINA

How do the works cited by Vasari fit into this, admittedly skeletal, framework? The *Madonna* in Santa Maria della Spina (Fig. 133) is conceptually closest to the *Bishop* (Fig. 130) in that it demonstrates a clear relationship between body and drapery, a strong distinction between the skeletal structure of the head and its fleshy covering, and a balance between structural and decorative requisites. Thus, one might reasonably suppose that both the *Bishop* and the Spina *Madonna*, if by the same hand, are relatively close in date. Can they *both* be early works? The total mastery of every detail of the *Madonna* in Santa Maria della Spina – from the overall conception to the articulation of each finger (Figs. 132–134) – is virtually impossible to reconcile with the uneven quality of the *Bishop*. This *Madonna* surely represents a peak of achievement, not an early groping for solutions. Suppose we reverse our chronology and say that the Spina figure and the *Bishop* are late works (and that the awkward passages in the *Bishop* are due to the intervention of another hand). Then the inevitable conclusion, which, indeed, one critic maintains,[24] is that in his "early" work (the Florentine *Madonna*, Fig. 109), Nino rejects Andrea's ideals and only later increasingly accepts and assimilates them, creating in the "late" Spina *Madonna* (Fig. 133) a work of art so close conceptually to the sculpture of his father that its attribution has been warmly debated. This presents an evolution, one might even say a youthful rebellion, followed by a conservative return to one's origins, quite difficult to imagine in the fourteenth century.

A third way of accommodating the two sculptures within the evolution of a single master is to consider the *Bishop* an early work and the Pisan *Madonna* a late and mature exemplar of the same ideals that inform the *Bishop*. Then we somehow have to fit the other two signed works between these – which really brings us back to the problem alluded to by Lányi: how to reconcile the style of the *Madonna* in Santa Maria della Spina in which the keynote of every expressive and structural element – the gesture of the hand, the turn of the head, the relationship of the upper to the lower body – is balance and restraint, with the style of the Florentine *Madonna* (Fig. 109), which clearly adheres to contrary ideals.

The contradiction in style between the two Madonnas is evident. First, the equilibrium of the Spina *Madonna* is eschewed in favor of an elegant asymmetry. Second, the structure of the Spina *Madonna*'s face is well defined, the forehead planes sharply set off from those of the eye sockets and the bony projections of the chin clearly felt

---

24 Weinberger (1937b), 66.

beneath the softer substance covering it (Fig. 134); in contrast, the Florentine *Madonna*'s head is smoother, more supple, and far more responsive to the shifting light that glides over its surface (Fig. 108). The extraordinary illusion of the softness of flesh and the silkiness of skin seen in the Santa Maria Novella group is a technical and artistic achievement, indeed, that is virtually unique in the fourteenth century, its true legacy not to be found until the sculpture of Desiderio da Settignano and ultimately Bernini.[25] This surface quality at once enhances the immediacy and accessibility of the figure and reduces its monumentality. By contrast, the incisive carving of the Spina *Madonna* lends a quality of pristine refinement that, far from compromising the grandeur of the image, complements it. Parallels are to be found, not in Nino's work, but in the sculpture of Andrea Pisano.[26]

Finally, the formal means by which the two intimately related figures of Mary and Christ are composed are very different: In the Pisan *Madonna* (Fig. 133), the drapery curves bind the figures inextricably into a compositional unity, for the folds flow continuously and smoothly from one figure to the next; in the Florentine *Madonna* (Fig. 109), the curves tend to halt at the points of juncture between Mary and Christ so that the compositional rhythms do not match, to the same degree as in the Pisan group, the emotional content.

If the Pisan *Madonna* does not fit well into Nino's chronology, it is easily viewed as a work of Andrea, the culmination of his achievements in monumental statuary. The development of his sculpture in-the-round, moreover, has a demonstrable relationship to the more clear-cut evolution of Andrea's relief style. From the relatively austere blocklike forms of the wooden *Annunziata* (Fig. 102) of 1321 (under the influence, as we shall see, of Giotto and Tino di Camaino, whose Pisan work Andrea would have known),[27] the master moved toward a monumental style consonant with the melodious Gothicism seen in the Baptistry reliefs. This occurs in the Campanile Sibyls (Figs. 74, 76), which represent the translation onto a monumental scale of such figures as Christ in *Ecce Agnus Dei* (Fig. 13) or the figure on the far right in the *Naming of the Baptist* (Fig. 10). Here Andrea appears to be grappling — not with total success — with the problem of creating monumental statuary freed from the restrictions of the relief surface yet retaining the linear decorative effects realized in

[25] Possibly in their original state the nudes of the Campanile Genesis scenes had something of this quality; the Orvieto *Madonna* has it to a lesser degree. Technically, there is no question that Nino's achievements have their roots in the training received in his father's shop.

[26] Cf. Becherucci (1965), 35f., who views the Spina *Madonna* (and Orvieto *Madonna*) as a collaborative effort of father and son, i.e., designed, blocked out, and chiseled up to the finishing touches by Andrea, and brought to its final polish by Nino.

[27] See chapter 6.

the quatrefoils. The *Redeemer* and the Budapest *Madonna* (Figs. 94, 98), being small in scale, are more successful translations of Andrea's lyrical relief style into figures conceived in-the-round. In the life-size *Saint Stephen* (Fig. 101), on the other hand, the Gothic contrapposto is more reticent and the calligraphic play of drapery seen in the earlier niche figures is greatly diminished; instead, there is a new amplitude in the underlying mass of the body. Similar characteristics are observed in the later Baptistry reliefs and in the Campanile hexagons. By ca. 1343 when Andrea left Florence apparently to direct the workshop in Pisa, most of the reliefs for the Campanile executed by him or under his direction were complete, the most recent of these in a classicizing style and spirit unsurpassed in the century. It would not be unreasonable to expect that some of the sculptures executed by Andrea in his Pisan shop represent a continuation and development of the classicizing impulse seen in the late hexagons of Florence. The *Madonna and Child* in Orvieto, as we shall see, and the Spina *Madonna* represent successive stages in the sculptor's evolution toward an integration of Gothic and classicizing modes.

The Orvieto statuette (Figs. 110–113) has been convincingly associated (together with angel fragments) with documents of 1348 concerning a Maestà partially completed in Pisa and then sent to Orvieto (Doc. 39–56).[28] The statuette has been attributed to both Andrea and Nino and has even been considered a collaborative effort of father and son, this last a most intriguing hypothesis. Commenting on this figure, Becherucci notes "quella sua ampia e robusta plasticità col trattamento levigato, prezioso della sue superficie."[29] These apparently contradictory qualities impel her to view the *Madonna* as a collaborative effort in which Andrea all but completed the figure, leaving the finishing touches to his son. Similarly, but with a slightly different distribution of labor, Nino's hand is seen in the refined delicate modeling of the *Madonna and Child* in Santa Maria della Spina, the conception and broader execution of which belongs to Andrea.[30]

Collaboration, of course, was common during the Middle Ages. The participation of father and son on a single monument has been noted with regard to the Perugia Fountain, commissioned from Nicola but containing figures that have been attributed to Giovanni.[31] A different kind of cooperative effort took place at Orvieto, where a division of labor from rough to smooth states has been noted.[32] Although it is possible

[28] Cellini (1933), 1–20; Lányi (1933a), 204–27; Weinberger (1937b), 74–79; Pope-Hennessy (1972), 193; and I. Toesca (1950), 53–7, with varying degrees of certainty, give the Orvieto *Madonna* to Nino. Cellini (1933), Lányi (1933), who considers the *Madonna* to be the master's last extant work, Valentiner (1947), and Becherucci (1965) (this last author, with qualifications) ascribe the statuette to Andrea.

[29] Becherucci (1965), 230.

[30] Becherucci (1965), 231ff.

[31] White (1966), 52f.

[32] White (1959), passim.

to imagine that Andrea provided designs or models for statues that were executed by Nino, who imposed his special gift for soft, delicate, and fluid surfaces on the essentially monumental images provided by his father, Becherucci's proposal involves a far more subtle imposition of one sculptor's mode on that of another and is highly conjectural. It should be borne in mind, furthermore, that Nino's gift is inherited from his father; it is not alien to the latter's style. Indeed, were the weatherworn Campanile *Creation* scenes (Figs. 50, 51) still in their original pristine condition, Vasari's description of Nino's art would undoubtedly apply almost as aptly to Andrea's reliefs. Even in their present state, they display a softness and subtlety of modeling quite distinguishable from the work of Andrea's assistants (Fig. 52).

Small in scale but monumental in conception, the Orvieto figure finds its most plausible locus within the framework of Andrea's rather than Nino's evolving style; moreover, the surface modeling and the execution of even the most minute details find strong analogies in Andrea's work. The Orvieto *Madonna* exhibits an articulate contrapposto stance and a naturalistic relationship of drapery to body that not even the most sturdy and Giottesque of Nino's figures, the *Bishop* in Oristano, displays, and this is especially true – in my opinion, very revealing – in the back views. In each of Nino's signed works (Figs. 117–118) the relationship of drapery to underlying form is strongly underplayed in the back views while in the Orvieto *Madonna*, as on the doors and as in the Spina figure (Figs. 24, 112), the elbows push out against the mantles and the folds are disposed to reflect the bodily divisions. Despite the veiled definition of the features, moreover, the structure of the skull is still felt beneath the flesh – certainly far more so than in the Florentine *Madonna* – and the features themselves are very close to those of the Sibyls (Figs. 75, 77). Compare the narrow eyelids, the subtly drawn contours of the broad, smooth faces, and the reserved, evocative smiles. The *Madonna*'s warm serenity is identical in mood not only to the Sibyls but to the lunette *Madonna* as well, and the extraordinary delicacy of her gesture – not characteristic of any of Nino's sculptures – is seen again in the Spina *Madonna* (Fig. 133). In contrast to Andrea's earlier work, however, the Orvieto *Madonna* is almost ponderous in the solidity and stability of the forms.[33] Moreover, the naturalistic relationship between body and drapery, the articulate contrapposto stance, and the pattern of catenary drapery curves would seem to betray an almost vehement de-

[33] It should perhaps be noted that the impression of heaviness conveyed by its present placement (Fig. 110) is significantly diminished when the figure is viewed from below (Fig. 113). Cellini (1933), 14, believes that the Maestà originally stood in a lunette on the Porta di Posterla of Or- vieto Cathedral. The three marbles, however, show not the slightest signs of weathering, making it very unlikely that they were located outdoors; it is more probable that the *Madonna* belonged to an altar and was to be viewed from below eye level.

termination to absorb the lessons of ancient sculpture, examples of which were ample in Pisa. The Orvieto *Madonna*, then, would seem to represent the translation onto a larger scale and more monumental mode of ideals achieved earlier in the Campanile reliefs.

Subsequent to the Orvieto *Madonna*, Andrea strives increasingly to integrate classical composure and stability with Gothic decorative rhythms. He first successfully achieves this in the marble Madonna on the summit of the facade of the Duomo of Pisa, which has also received attributions to Andrea and/or Nino or some other Pisan assistant.[34] The figure was apparently executed to replace an earlier one from the workshop of Giovanni Pisano that fell from its height during an earthquake in 1322.[35] A document of 27 July 1345 refers to payment of ninety-four lire for a block of marble "per fare la nostra donne sopra la porta reale."[36] All earlier scholars have admitted the difficulty of evaluating the work because of its great height; recent new photographs make it possible for the first time to study the work in detail (Figs. 114– 116).

Like the Orvieto *Madonna*, the figure stands solidly in an articulate contrapposto with the Child securely supported by the Madonna's left arm and raised left hip over the engaged leg. The highly plastic drapery, athough conceived in terms of strongly projecting folds that catch the sunlight and create deep shadows, does not overwhelm the underlying forms but rather reflects them; nor do the decorative flourishes of curvilinear hemlines and swinging folds intrude on the sense of mass. The sturdy, robust Christ, sitting squarely on the Madonna's arm with his feet pressing through (though not visible as at Orvieto) the overhanging garment, is twin to the Child in Orvieto. Although the *Madonna* is conceived for a great height with the rear view hardly visible from the ground, the sculptor insists on modeling fully the back of the drapery and expressing its relationship to the underlying forms (Fig. 115). The date 1345 for the document concerning the purchase of marble is perfectly consistent with the place of this extraordinary work in Andrea's development. It is superseded only by the last work attributable to him in Pisa, the *Madonna* in Santa Maria della Spina, in which is achieved an unparalleled integration of diverse stylistic sources: classical composure and stability, Gothic poise and decorative rhythms, and a profound yet exalted sense of

[34] See Supino (1904), 144; Weinberger (1937b), 70; I. Toesca (1950), 57; and Becherucci (1965), 246ff.

[35] I. Toesca (1950), 57; Becherucci (1965), 246.

[36] The document, first published by Bonaini (1846), 125, in the Pisan Duomo archives (Doc. 37), records payment to Bertuccio di Ugolino da Carrara for a piece of marble for a Madonna to be made for the *porta reale*; furthermore, a payment is made to Puccio di Lando of twelve soldi for transport of the said marble to the Opera.

realism. If a new level of sophistication is achieved in the harmonious balance of seemingly opposing elements, the expressive content nevertheless remains unchanged: The Sibyls, lunette relief, Orvieto statuette, Pisa Duomo *Madonna*, and Spina figure each project an identical mood – that balance between gravity and a quiet inner warmth, utterly lacking in the slightest affectations of late Gothic style. One is obliged to regard them all as conceived by a single imagination and executed by a single hand.

By the same token, each manifests a fundamentally different conception in terms of form and psychological content than do Nino's Madonnas. Compare, for example, the rational organization of drapery forms in the Orvieto figure with the unmotivated patterns in the Venetian and Florentine groups. At Orvieto (Fig. 110), for instance, the free leg presses through the drapery and, as in a Roman statue, the drapery disposition appears to be determined by the contrapposto stance; at Venice (Fig. 119), by contrast, the U-shaped fold is retained, but it does not embrace a projecting knee; indeed, the structure of the free leg is not well defined. In the Florentine figure (Fig. 109), on the other hand, the projecting right knee is discernible, but the traditional curved fold has been discarded.[37]

The reasons for assigning the statuette in Orvieto and the over-life-size figure in Santa Maria della Spina to Nino are tenuous at best whereas these figures fit very comfortably into the evolution of Andrea's style. His development as a sculptor of monumental statuary, however, lags somewhat behind his development as a sculptor of reliefs. The Sibyls, as we have seen, may be viewed as large-scale interpretations of figures seen on the doors. The Orvieto *Madonna* represents a stage anticipated in the *Saint Stephen* and successfully achieved in the reliefs on the Campanile. Therefore, it probably dates from relatively early in the span 1343–47. The Duomo facade *Madonna* was executed shortly after 1345 whereas the *Madonna* in Santa Maria della Spina, his most mature extant and complete sculpture, comes at the end of Andrea's sojourn in Pisa.

THE *MADONNA DEL LATTE*

The *Madonna del Latte*, given to Nino by Vasari (Figs. 135, 136), also continues to receive attributions that alternate between Andrea and Nino.[38] As most observers have

[37] One final detail lends support to the attribution of the Spina *Madonna* to Andrea: The lettering along the hems of the garments of both Mother and Child are, like those of Nino's Venetian figures, raised and gilded; but instead of Gothic script, here we find a rare early use of Roman lettering. Andrea's classicizing tendencies, and

Nino's rejection of them, are cogently expressed in these choices. I am indebted to Ms. Christine Sperling, currently at work on a dissertation on Renaissance lettering (Brown University), for these observations.
[38] Becherucci (1965), 255f., assigns the *Madonna del Latte* to Andrea; I. Toesca (1950), 50f., and

agreed, however, the figure is virtually inseparable from the Spina *Madonna* and, if the latter is by Andrea, then the *Madonna del Latte* is, too. As in the standing figure, the intimacy between mother and child is conveyed not only by the obvious means of pose, glance, and physical relationship, but also by way of the curves and countercurves that flow from one to the other, binding the figures into a close unity. In contrast, neither of Nino's signed Madonnas reveals any attempt to employ the curvilinear rhythms of drapery and anatomy for their expressive possibilities. Few of the curves, for instance, in the Santa Maria Novella *Madonna*'s drapery flow *directly* into those of Christ; rather, the linear patterns halt at the points of juncture between Mary and Christ, even changing direction at those points. In the half-length and standing Pisan Madonnas, moreover, the planes of the forehead, nose, and eyelids are subtly set off against each other, resulting in a stronger definition of features.

The half-length of the figure is rare if not unique for sculptures of the period and is clearly a translation into stone of a format that had become very popular for panel paintings. The iconography and composition of the *Madonna del Latte* are based, however, on a type invented by Simone Martini in his lost *Madonna of Humility*.[39] In a copy of that work by Bartolommeo da Camogli in Palermo, dated 1346, the relationship of the Madonna to her son, especially the position of her hands and incline of her head, are so close to that of the marble group as to speak for a common prototype. The delightfully naturalistic motif of the infant's crossed feet seen in the marble group also appears in the painted example and became almost formulaic for nursing Madonnas of Humility throughout the remainder of the trecento. The translation of a painted devotional image into sculpture – polychromed, profoundly naturalistic, and intimate yet life-like in scale – was a highly original invention and supports the authorship of Andrea rather than Nino for this work.

So close is the style to that of the standing *Madonna* in Santa Maria della Spina (Fig. 133) that it must be of approximately the same date, that is, toward the end of the span 1343–47.[40] It dates probably slightly earlier than the Spina *Madonna*, for the smooth

---

Pope-Hennessy (1972), 194, give it to Nino, Weinberger (1937b), 89, denies it to both Andrea and Nino, whereas Burresi (1983), 181, ascribes it to both.

[39] On the origins and meaning of the *Madonna of Humility*, and on the influence of Simone's invention, see Meiss (1936), 435–64; reprinted in Meiss (1951), 132–56.

[40] A *terminus ante quem* of 1343 has been proposed for the *Madonna del Latte* on the basis of a presumed reflection of its iconography and pose

in a dated French work, but this is highly implausible. See Ragghianti (1973), 11–38 (p. 19). The author refers to an alabaster statuette of a nursing Madonna in the church at Muneville le-Bingard (Manche). An inscription on the base states that it was given in 1343 by "Mestre Henri de Dompare clerc de la royne Jeanne d'Evreaux" to the church. Although a full-length figure, the disposition is, in mirror image, quite similar to that of the *Madonna del Latte*. It is more probable, however, that like Andrea's figure the French modeling of the face lacks the subtler modulations of the latter and is closer to the Sibyls and the lunette and Orvieto Madonnas in this regard (Figs. 134, 75, 77, 83, 111). Clearly, however, the *Madonna del Latte* and the Spina *Madonna* represent the culmination of Andrea's experiments with sculpture in-the-round. Throughout the many changes evident in his style, there remains above all a consistency in psychological content, as evident in the warm but serene vitality of the Madonnas and Sibyls as in the tranquil intensity of the Saint John figures in bronze and marble. These aspects, though more difficult to define, are as much a part of an artist's handwriting as are contours, drapery configurations, and physiognomic types.

THE SANTA CATERINA *ANNUNCIATION*

In Vasari's day, the marble *Annunciation* group in Santa Caterina in Pisa (Figs. 137–138) bore an inscription that is quoted in the second edition of his *Lives*: A DI PRIMO FEBBRAIO 1370. QUESTE FIGURE FECE NINO FIGLIUOLO D'ANDREA PISANO.[41] As mentioned earlier, Vasari sometimes engaged others to copy inscriptions for him so that we cannot be certain that he himself transcribed the words on the bases of the Annunciatory pair. The documents for the Agnello tomb indicate that Nino was dead by 1368 (Doc. 68), so the Santa Caterina inscription, if correctly transcribed, proves to be apocryphal. If the work is by Nino, we may simply disregard the date.[42] If not by Nino, we may still take seriously the tradition that had undoubtedly come down to Vasari associating this group with the Pisan artist. It is likely, at the very least, that Nino Pisano conceived a monumental marble Annunciatory pair whose impressive immediacy was achieved by means of lifelike polychromy, expressive gestures, and communicative glances that project exceedingly well across a wide space. In any case, the Santa Caterina *Annunciation* figures or, more likely – as I shall suggest later – their model, became the basis for numerous copies and reflections well into the fifteenth century.

The acceptance of the attribution to Nino generally hinges upon acceptance of the Spina *Madonna* and the *Madonna del Latte* to that artist, attributions that, in the preceding discussion, have been rejected. Even so, the alleged similarities between the *An-*

work was based on Simone's invention. In any case, the provenance of our Madonna in Pisa since at least the sixteenth century, when it is mentioned by Vasari, further argues for a date between ca. 1343 and 1347, and not earlier; for it is unlikely that a masterpiece of this order would have been transported quietly from the city of its origin, which, had it been executed before 1343,

would have been Florence.

[41] Milanesi (1878), 495.

[42] Pope-Hennessy (1972), 195, suggests that the inscription refers, not to the date of execution, but to the installation of the group. As the date is unusually precise (1 February 1370), it does, indeed, suggest the latter.

nunciation and the two *Madonnas* fail, in general and upon close examination, to obtain. Rather, the differences between the *Annunciation* and the Pisan Madonnas on the one hand, and Nino's signed sculptures on the other, are far more telling than the similarities.

It is true that the *Virgin* (Fig. 138) exhibits a Gothic sway that one associates with Nino, that the concentric drapery patterns are similar to configurations seen in the work of both Andrea and Nino, and that the carving of the heads of both Gabriel and Mary (Figs. 143–146) has some of the precision seen in the *Madonna della Spina* and the *Madonna del Latte* (Figs. 134, 135). The slightly projecting lower lip of Gabriel, on the other hand, is not characteristic of these last, but appears in the Madonnas signed by Nino (Fig. 120).

From a stylistic and technical point of view, however, the Santa Caterina *Annunciation* pair has little in common with the signed works of Nino, and has even less to do with Andrea's oeuvre. I would suggest that the author of this compelling and influential work was an independent master who has absorbed influences from Andrea, from Nino, and from yet another important sculptor of the mid-fourteenth century, Alberto Arnoldi.

The *Annunciation* is clearly the work of a mature sculptor capable, as the heads of the two figures reveal, of great subtlety of expression (Figs. 143–146).[43] But in contrast to that impulse toward softness and grace seen in Nino's autograph sculptures, Gabriel (Fig. 137) stands in a relatively rigid pose, his body like a tree trunk about which sharp, linear, and rather stiff folds impose themselves. If the *Virgin* (Fig. 138) exhibits a greater ease of stance, her drapery lacks fluidity, and the large, almost ponderous hands exhibit none of the dainty grace one might expect of a mature Nino. Also contrary to Nino's signed works (and even more so to Andrea's), the relationship of body to drapery in each of the Santa Caterina figures is obscure. In Nino's sculpture, despite the increasing compromise of anatomical equilibrium, the forms of the body – for instance, the projecting knee or the rounded abdomen – are clearly perceived (Fig. 109). Once again, it is difficult to postulate a chronology into which one might plausibly fit the *Virgin* and *Angel of the Annunciation.*

[43] It may be worthwhile to recognize and comment on one of the limitations of our field: the analysis and evaluation of sculptures, especially those that are difficult to see in situ, on the basis of photographs. The Alinari photographs that are commonly available of the Santa Caterina *Annunciation* tend to accent, in the heads, the painted and therefore the superimposed linear rather than the plastic qualities of the figures; hence, the impression of relatively sharp, severe forms rather lacking in charm. Figure 143, a closeup photograph of the Virgin, tends to confirm this impression (perhaps because much of the polychromy, not necessarily original, remains), but Figs. 145, 146 of Gabriel reveal an unexpected subtlety of expression. The carving has some of the precision seen in the head of the Spina *Madonna*, but the smooth planes lack the nuances in surface treatment that was Andrea's legacy to Nino. Both figures in Santa Caterina, moreover, lack that projection of psychological intensity characteristic of Andrea.

Like Andrea and Nino, the author of the *Annunciation* stands in reaction against the hyperenergetic forms and expressionism of Giovanni Pisano and his followers, and it is this, primarily, that connects our three artists. As in the works of Andrea and Nino, the mood of these figures is one of quiet joyfulness. On the other hand, from the stylistic point of view, the sculptor of the Santa Caterina figures adheres to an alternative trend in mid-trecento sculpture — one that makes few concessions to the easy grace of the tradition we must associate with Andrea and Nino. The smooth planes of the faces, which lack the nuances of surface treatment that became Andrea's legacy to Nino, and the sharp, linear quality of the drapery forms recall similar characteristics in Alberto Arnoldi's Bigallo *Madonna* (Fig. 139). This figure stands in a relatively stiff contrapposto. The drapery tends to adhere closely to the trunklike body, occasionally projecting from it in sharp, planar ridges. The drapery of Gabriel is reminiscent of Arnoldi's treatment: Although one of the two major folds on the left side has been flattened through some accident, originally the folds would have looked very similar to the two major drapery projections seen on the left of the Bigallo *Madonna*. Not unsimilar, too, is the manner in which the mantle swings around the upper arm and elbow of the Madonna (seen also in the Bigallo lunette relief). This portion of Gabriel's drapery is damaged, but originally it continued under the forearm to connect with the part around the abdomen; the missing fragments are clearly visible in the Washington *Annunciation* (Fig. 147), a replica of the Pisan marble.[44] The Florentine *Madonna* and the Pisan figures

[44] On the wood replica in the National Gallery, Washington, D.C. (Figs. 147–148), see U. Middeldorf (1976), 85. In February 1979, I examined this group very carefully together with the curator of sculpture, Dr. Douglas Lewis and two museum conservators. Based on external visual data, the figures appeared to me to be authentic fourteenth-century carvings reproducing with almost exact precision, but on a reduced scale, the marble prototypes. However, when they were laid on the ground so that one could peer into the hollows carved into the logs from which the figures were formed, two observations were made that raised some questions concerning their authenticity. (1) Instead of being hollowed out in the back and then closed with another piece, as was commonly done in the fourteenth century, the figures were hollowed out through the center. This is noted by Middeldorf (1976), 8. (On the technique of carving wood sculpture during the Middle Ages and Renaissance, see Strom [1979], 1–29.) (2) The periphery of the bottom of both statues was rather deteriorated by worm holes, but a few inches within these hollows the surfaces were extremely smooth.

Dr. Lewis agreed to remove some chips from the inner core of both figures and to send them to a laboratory for carbon-14 dating. The results of these tests arrived as this book was going to press. The tests have established that the wood from which each figure was carved is old. For the *Gabriel*, using what is referred to as "two standard deviations" (in C-14 dating, 95% of samples fall into this category), the wood is datable from 1100 to 1380 A.D. Under the same assumption, the Virgin was carved from a piece of wood datable from 770 to 1210 A.D. Assuming "three standard deviations" (99.7% of samples fall within this category), the latter figure was carved from a log whose dating range extends into the fourteenth century. It should be noted that the dating of wood based on C-14 tests is likely to differ somewhat exhibit a similar relationship between body and drapery: Broad smooth tubular forms are surrounded by taut passages of drapery accented by strongly projecting planar folds. The differences between Mary and Gabriel are paralleled to some extent by the differences between the left and right angels in the Bigallo: In the former, thin, straight diagonals predominate, whereas in the latter there is relatively greater fluidity introduced by the horizontally drawn curving drapery forms.

The visual evidence suggests, then, that the author of the Santa Caterina *Annunciation* pair is an independent master of considerable ability, strongly indebted to the art of Arnoldi; perhaps he was trained in the latter's workshop and, upon his arrival in Pisa, an initial penchant for severity in the formal as well as psychological aspects of his sculpture became transformed under the moderating influence of the sculpture of Andrea and Nino Pisano. He may even have been required to recreate a model executed by Nino. This model, if we consider the dominant characteristics of the numerous fourteenth-century Ninesque Annunciations (cf., for example, Figs. 140–142) undoubtedly exhibited more subtle nuances in the surface treatment, greater elegance in the gestures, and softer, more fluid drapery forms than is seen in the Santa Caterina *Annunciation*.[45]

---

from the date of actual carving of figures from that wood because the core of a tree trunk (and it is probably from close to the core that our samples were taken) may die long before the tree is cut down. Therefore, the differences in dating between the samples may be explained by the sculptures being carved from logs deriving from trees of different ages. I wish to express my thanks to Alison Luchs of the National Gallery for her cooperation and help in obtaining the information relevant to this discussion and, in particular, for expediting the C-14 results to me in time for this publication.

One cannot discount the possibility – unlikely, in this case – that modern forgeries were made from old wood. In a private communication (telephone conversation, 5 June 1979), Mr. Mario Modestini, who cleaned and restored the group about forty-five years ago in Florence when it was owned by Count Contini-Bonacossi, informed me that at that time the figures were enveloped with seventeenth-century baroque drapery folds in papier-maché. These, together with about ten layers of polychromy, were removed. According to

Modestini, the present polychromy is original and there is no doubt that the pieces are of the fourteenth century and not forgeries; whether by Nino Pisano or not is another question.

[45] Concerning a documented contractual obligation on the part of Francesco Laurana to make copies of a revered original, see chapter 9, n. 20.

In addition to the Santa Caterina group there are over two dozen separate Annunciation figures, some of them still paired, which have been claimed for Nino or his school. In most of these, a pose, a gesture, a drapery form, or a combination of these recall, sometimes rather distantly, elements in the Santa Caterina *Annunciation*. Occasionally, a motif in the Pisan Gabriel appears in a figure of the Virgin, and vice versa. The finest of these Ninesque figures, and the only one to warrant serious consideration as an autograph sculpture, is the wood *Annunziata* in the Museo di San Matteo, Pisa (Fig. 140). The expression of sober humility, however, and the broader, more robust forms of the face suggest that this is the creation of a gifted but independent master. The figure is far more graceful than its counterpart in Santa

It has been claimed that the Santa Caterina *Annunciation* originally came from the Church of San Zenone in Pisa, having been transferred to its present location only in the early fifteenth century. A chronicle dated 16 February 1408 mentions images and statues, including an *Annunciation*, which the Brothers from San Zenone agree to transfer to the church of Santa Caterina.[46] Bonaini, and Supino following him, assume that the *Annunciation* mentioned in the chronicle refers to the marble statues Vasari saw in Santa Caterina with the inscription concerning Nino.[47] Although this is entirely possible, the chronicle may have been referring to some other group. A commemorative plaque, inscribed in Gothic letters and dated 1392, that is at present inserted in the wall of the Seminario of Santa Caterina, states that perpetual masses are to be said for Ginevra Manninghi at the altar of the "new *Annunciation*" (UNA M/ESSA CHE SI DIRA' NELLO/ ALTARE DELLA ANUTIAT/A NUOVA).[48] Perhaps our marble group is the "new" *Annunciation* that, for reasons unknown, replaced an "old" *Annunciation*, namely, a group by Nino Pisano. Possibly the contract for the new group stipulated that it must closely follow the pattern invented by Nino. The association with a lost original became transmuted, by Vasari's time, into a belief that the present group is identical with that lost work. A date of 1370 or slightly earlier is entirely consonant with such developments and even as late as 1392, the date of the Manninghi inscription, the group may have retained its designation as "the new *Annunciation*."

Caterina and the drapery is treated with greater fluidity. Unlike the master of the Santa Caterina *Annunciation*, the creator of the Museo Virgin introduces no formal elements alien to the Andrea/Nino tradition; rather, he remains faithful to the lyrical naturalism and easy grace that remains a constant in the work of both Pisani. One may hypothesize that this figure reflects more closely than does the Santa Caterina Virgin a lost prototype by Nino.

The *Annunziata* in the Louvre (Fig. 141) is superficially the closest to the Virgin in Santa Caterina; here too, however, the gesture and contrapposto are more elegant, and the benign, gentle expression is probably closer to the lost prototype. The almost geometrically regular, ovoid head with its simplified surface treatment, the schematic handling of the drapery forms that lack any strong sense of plasticity, and the tendency to simplify contours and edges betray the hand of a far weaker talent. Exhibiting similar characteristics but less graceful in its pose is a wood figure very recently come to light: the *Annunciata* (Fig. 142) in the Church of Santo Crocifisso, Pontedera. See Burresi (1983), catalogue no. 29. The sensitive head alone compels one to consider this a workshop product with direct intervention by Nino.

[46] Bonaini (1846), 65, 149.

[47] Ibid., 65; Supino (1895), 343–62 (p. 347).

[48] The inscription reads as follows: "AD PERPETUA MEMORIA / NOTA CHE FRATI EL CONVENTO / DI SANTA KATERINA / DI PISA ANO ATTRIBUITO / OGNA DI' I PPETUO UNA M/ESSA CHE SI DIRA' NELLO / ALTARE DELLA ANUTIAT/A NUOVA A MONNA GINEV/RA FIGLIUOLA CHE FU DI LO/RENSO MANNINGO E DONA CHE FU DI MSSER MANFRE/DI BUZZACCHERINO P GRA/TITUDIE DE BENEFICI R/ICEVUTI P L AIA SUA E DE S/UOI A NI MCCCLXXXXII." All inscriptions in the church of Santa Caterina may be found in a mimeographed publication, Corallini (1980). The Manninghi reference is listed as no. 146.

None of the Pisan monuments Vasari added in the second edition of the *Lives* may be convincingly attributed to the hand of Nino.[49] Conceptually and formally, two of these – the *Madonna della Spina* and the *Madonna del Latte* (Figs. 133, 135) – accord very well with the style of Andrea Pisano on the Baptistry doors and the Campanile. Nino's signed sculptures, however, would appear to mark three different points of departure with respect to the work of Andrea. The *Bishop* (Fig. 130) in Oristano is clearly deeply indebted to Andrea's sculpture. Stylistically it shows the influence of the Baptistry doors, whereas technically it recalls the Orvieto *Madonna*, indicating that Nino has absorbed the lessons of craftsmanship by which his father infused some of his marbles with a refined, luminous surface quality. The *Bishop* was probably executed in Andrea's Pisan workshop relatively early in the span 1343–7 during which workshop activity is assumed or recorded, and sent from there to the island of Sardinia.

The Cornaro *Madonna* (Fig. 119) exhibits the same iconographic and compositional formulas as the Orvieto statuette (Fig. 110) by Andrea and may be based on the latter, which, as we have seen, was executed shortly after Andrea departed Florence and arrived in Pisa. The Venetian figure with its dulcet smile, exquisite bend of the wrist, and increased swing of the contrapposto stance indicates that Nino is already moving away from the classical canons established by his father. Although it was probably designed in Andrea's workshop by Nino, its date is relatively late during the span 1343–7. The *Madonna* in Santa Maria Novella (Fig. 109), on the other hand, depends not on the Orvieto statuette, but on Andrea's late *Madonna* in Santa Maria della Spina (Fig. 133). As the last and most personal of Nino's signed sculptures, the Florentine *Madonna* was probably executed after 1350 when Nino established his own workshop in Pisa. A more precise dating must await the discussion of Nino's other late Pisan works.

With this framework in mind, we are now in a position to reevaluate the relationship to the styles of Andrea and Nino of the other major debated attributions. Of primary importance is the Saltarelli monument of ca. 1343 in Santa Caterina, Pisa, in which stylistic characteristics of both Andrea and Nino, as well as of several assistants, are very much in evidence.

---

[49] It is curious that during Vasari's lifetime so little remained or was known of Nino's sculptures that in his first edition (in the life of Andrea Pisano), Vasari mentions only the *Madonna* of Santa Maria Novella. Even in the second edition, not one other work in Florence by Nino is mentioned, although Vasari seems to have felt that Nino surpassed his father in the art of sculpture. In short, no tradition reached Vasari of works executed by Nino in Florence other than the signed *Madonna* made for a Dominican church, Santa Maria Novella with very strong connections to Pisa (see p. 80f). It may be, indeed, that during Andrea's Florentine sojourn Nino was still too young to work independently, perhaps even too young to be counted among the master's assistants.

THE SALTARELLI MONUMENT

The tomb of Archbishop Simone Saltarelli (Figs. 149–156, 158–164) was first attributed to Nino by Da Morrona in 1812 and has since been the subject of contradictory perceptions and attributions.[50] Estimations of the ensemble and its parts have ranged from comments on the "senility" of the Virgin's expression,[51] the "ugliness" of the Christ Child, the "rigidity" of the angels, and the "lack of proportion and unity" of the architectonic parts[52] – to appreciation of the "homogeneity of the conception,"[53] the "liveliness" of the narratives, and the "naturalness" of the effigy[54] in this, Nino's "masterpiece."[55]

This diversity of opinion is due, at least in part, to the fact that the tomb is situated in a relatively dark church and the commercially available and published photographs (usually Brogi) (Fig. 149) create an entirely false impression of the quality of the carving, particularly with respect to the Virgin and flanking angels. Especially disturbing are the dark markings on the Virgin's face, in particular those above the lips (probably caused by a seventeenth-century fire), which, in black and white photographs, do indeed create the impression of a "senile" smile. This impression is false, as Figure 150 indicates. It is essential, then, to begin by discarding older prejudices and viewing the monument afresh with the help of good light and new photographs. These reveal a higher level of execution than had been previously suspected. In addition, the elements of the tomb are distributed with such extraordinarily subtle intelligence – offering a visual and theological demonstration of the journey from life to death to salvation in heaven – that only a master of the very first rank could have been responsible for the design. Details of the design and execution, as we shall see, suggest that the Saltarelli monument was conceived by Andrea Pisano and executed by various members of a rather extensive and complex workshop organization.

Simone Saltarelli was a native of Florence and a prior of the Dominican Church of Santa Maria Novella. His gradual rise to power within the order took him in 1312 to Carcassonne, in 1316 and 1317 to Avignon, in 1318 to Grenoble and, after his promotion to archbishop of Pisa in 1323, he is recorded in Rome in 1324 and again in Avignon in 1328. He was present at the laying of the foundation stone of the Campanile of Florence

---

[50] Da Morrona (1812). Supino (1904), 226, Venturi (1906), 482, P. Toesca (1951), 325, and Carli (1934a), 203ff., with varying degrees of certainty, have tended to accept the attribution – which generally hinges on ascription of the closely allied Spina *Madonna* – to Nino. I. Toesca (1950), 52f. and Weinberger (1937b), 65, assign the tomb to independent workshops. Valentiner (1947), 173, and Becherucci (1965), 248ff., view the monument as conceptually by Andrea with varying degrees of assistance in the execution.

[51] Carli (1934a), 203; Brizio (1943–50), 265–8 (p. 266).

[52] Supino (1904), 226.

[53] Becherucci (1965), 249.

[54] Supino (1904), 226.

[55] Supino, in Thieme and Becker (1933), 103.

in 1334 and thus may have been acquainted with Andrea Pisano, who was then work-ing on the Baptistry doors. He retained very close ties to Florence and to his Church of Santa Maria Novella, where he had private apartments built for his use. Saltarelli appears to have played an important role in the conflict between the pope, Giovanni XXII, and Ludwig of Bavaria, who desired the crown of Italy and the Holy Roman Em-pire. The exact nature of this role is not clear from the records, but he appears to have received the praise of the Florentines and the generous appreciation of the pope. Salta-relli remained archbishop of Pisa until his death at the age of eighty in 1342.[56]

The Saltarelli monument is undocumented, but a *Sepoltuario* of 1620, with addenda postdating 1651, offers the following description: "Il corpo di monsignor Saltarelli, fiorentino, della nostra religione, arcivescovo di questa città, stava in un bellissimo de-posito grande e magnifico, che la sommità arrivava sino al capitello del tetto, ed alto da terra solamente da quattro braccia in circa; era tutto di marmo lavorato con colonnette, angeli e statue, e spostava tutto in fuori sopra quattro capitelli belli e ben lavorati, e tutto aggrappato di ferro, che lo sostenevano in aria."[57]

[56] Orlandi (1955), 230–4.

[57] Supino (1904), 228, transcribed the Sepoltuario entry from a manuscript, entitled *Sepoltuario della Chiesa di Santa Caterina*, Ms., c. 40t, in the Archivio del Capitolo in Pisa. The entry, in its entirety, reads as follows: "Sepoltura Saltarelli. Il corpo di monsignor Saltarelli, fiorentino, della nostra religione, arcivescovo di questa città, stava in un bellissimo deposito grande e magnifico, che la sommità arrivava sino al capitello del tetto, ed alto da terra solamente da quattro braccia in circa; era tutto di marmo lavorato con colonnette, angeli e statue, e spostava tutto in fuori sopra quattro capitelli belli e ben lavorati, e tutto aggrappato di ferro, che lo sostenevano in aria; e stava in mezzo di nostra chiesa, a man manca, per entrare per la porta maggiore, e, per lo scompartimento degli altari fatto di molti anni adreto da'nostri antichi, veniva a essere ai tempi nostri fra l'altare di San Vincenzo e San Tommaso. Ma per l'incendio detto restò tutto concotto, che cascavano pezzi che bisognò levarlo e gettarlo a terra per darli altro luogho, come si dice in questo, a carte 23 tergo; per la qual cosa può ciascuno venire a cognitione della sua grandezza e bella macchina e ricca che era. E si aggiunge di più, che aprendosi la cassa, si trovarono tutte le sue ossa stritulate et in polvere ridotte drento del piviale nel quale fu involto il suo corpo, e pareva che nuovo tanto che era sodo."

Curiously, another published version (from the same manuscript?) is not identical. See Mattei (1772), 81, n. 1. Mattei's version, transcribed from a manuscript dated 1620 entitled, *Ricordo di tutte le Sepolture, che sono in S. Caterina di Pisa scritte soci da me F. Michele Salvetti*, reads as follows: "Sopra l'altare di S. Pietro Martire c'e una sepoltura grande di marmo, nella quale vi è sepolto Monsignor de Saltarelli." Mattei adds that the following passage was written in more modern characters. "La detta Sepoltura era un Sepolcro grande tutto di marmo bello, quale ar-rivava quasi fino al tetto; guastatosi dal fuoco, che abbrugiò tutta la Chiesa l'anno 1651 Pisano la notte della vigilia di tutti i Santi; posto a tempo del P. M. Fra Domenico Amadori Priore del Con-vento nella muraglia in alto, donde in oggi è fatto il Presepio, e per ultimo posto dal P. Priore Padre lettore Fra Aurelio Portigiani nell'uscio di Sagrestia per entrare in Chiesa a mano sinistra nel 1681 Pisano." The latter passage evidently dates from after the fire of 1651 in the church, and thus records the writer's memory of the original disposition of the tomb.

According to Guido Corallini's 1969 pamphlet

From this description, one gathers that the Saltarelli monument was a wall tomb suspended about four braccia above the ground. That it was a grandiose monument is apparent, but that it reached "quasi fino al capitello del tetto" must be taken in the figurative sense, as the Church of Santa Caterina is and was several times the largest conceivable height of the tomb. The phrase "quattro capitelli belli e ben lavorati" probably refers to consoles topped by capital-like elements; these very likely sustained trilobe arches (cf. the Ligo Ammannati tomb in the Camposanto, Pisa) that, in turn, supported the sarcophagus and effigy. The marble colonettes, then, would refer to the twisted colonettes screening the bier; the "angeli e statue" likewise are still part of the tomb. The fact that the structure required additional iron supports, "aggrappato di ferro," suggests that the extant parts were surrounded by a huge superstructure similar to that of several trecento tombs, for example, the monument of Benedict XI in Perugia[58] in which an iron tie-rod above the tall twisted columns helps assure the stability of the structure.

Despite the fragmentary nature of the tomb, and even allowing that some intermediary elements such as consoles are lacking, the extant parts combine into a masterpiece of integration and harmony. The physical and visual base for the composition as a whole is provided by the sarcophagus, which contains three horizontal, rectangular relief fields (Figs. 161–163). Straightforward in style and execution, reflecting none of the advances in relief conception seen on Andrea's door and Campanile, the humble narratives depict important events in the life of the archbishop. The left relief depicts the seated archbishop refusing a sack or purse offered to him (presumably in an effort to induce him to return to Pisa from where he had fled after the excommunicated Ludwig had entered the city with armed forces). In the center he sits on an episcopal seat either receiving a gift of a chalice from a kneeling figure or else giving a gift to his church. To the right he receives the homage of faithful Pisans.[59]

Materially and figuratively, these reliefs are the most earthbound elements of the tomb. Although hardly inventive as individual reliefs, seen as a group they provide a

entitled *La Chiesa di S. Caterina in Pisa*, Pisa, 34, the manuscript, with the additions made in 1651, was formerly in the Archivio Capitolare di Pisa but is no longer extant. A copy of it was made in 1921, however, and deposited in the Library of Santa Caterina. The 1921 copy is no longer in the library; its whereabouts are uncertain.

Before the fire of 1651, the Saltarelli monument was located on the north side of the church but closer to the high altar. After the fire, it was moved in 1656 to the "navatella" and was moved again in 1681 near the door of the sacristy. Finally, in the early nineteenth century it was placed on the north wall near the entrance to the church and after restorations in 1925, again placed along that wall. For a complete and annotated bibliography on the Saltarelli monument, see Ronan (1983), v. II, 154–7.

[58] Brach (1904), 115.

[59] Cf. Venturi (1906), 484.

visual base with predominantly vertical rhythms extending to left and right about a central element, the kneeling figure along the tomb's central axis.

Above the sarcophagus, behind curtain-drawing angels and twisted columns, lies the effigy on a *lit de parade*. As though to dramatize that intermediate stage in the journey of the soul toward heaven,[60] the archbishop, dead and still earthbound, is both revealed by the curtain-drawing angels and obscured by the screen of columns, an invention that was to be repeated, without the same dramatic effect, on at least one later tomb.[61] If the angels lack a totally convincing distribution of weight in their contrapposto stance, they nevertheless function supremely well as part of the rhythm that links them – almost as though by way of a festoon – with the curtains and trefoil arches flowing across the composition. Thus are the vertical elements – the narratives below, the columns, and the angels – balanced by undulating curves that flow horizontally across the visual field.

These curves are echoed in the section above – in the contour of the sarcophagus cover, the garments and wings of the flying angels, and the central field showing the soul carried heavenward. The V-shaped accent of the centrally placed kneeling figure on the sarcophagus is reflected in the upside-down V of the little soul above it. Clearly this level of the tomb represents the next stage in the journey from life to death to heaven. The two saints, Dominic and Peter Martyr, are perhaps the only alien elements from a visual point of view as the tomb now stands – but they are clearly the intercessors. There is no need to show them pleading to the Virgin as does their counterpart in the De Braye monument, for it is evident that the soul, directly below the Virgin herself, will reach its goal.

If the pattern of horizontally flowing curves contributes to the unity of the whole, no less important is the series of interweaving vertical curvilinear elements: the "parenthesis" formed by the curtain-drawing angels, the "reverse parenthesis" of the sarcophagus lid, and the figures flanking the Madonna. The sequence culminates in the S-curve of the Madonna herself. Flanked by ecstatic angels, she gazes lovingly at the Christ Child. The Madonna, as the pinnacle of the composition that ascends upward like the elements of a Gothic cathedral, is the goal and culmination of the impulses – as we are made aware – that determined the course of the life (and death) of Simone Saltarelli.

The conception of the tomb is unusually dramatic: The eschatological components

[60] On the concept of the "journey of the soul" implicit in Gothic as opposed to earlier sepulchral monuments, see s'Jacob (1954), 69, 111, 114ff., 130–5.

[61] Cf. the tomb of Niccolò Acciajuoli (d. 1365) in the Certosa del Galluzzo (Florence). Like the Saltarelli monument, the Acciajuoli tomb has spiral columns, trefoil arches, and a trapezoidal chamber-roof or lid above the effigy. On the Certosa tomb see Ronan, 42–46.

are not simply juxtaposed, but are organized to introduce the element of *time* in the journey to salvation – the movement from life to death to the ascent of the soul, and finally to heaven. This conception is anticipated, as far as I know, only in the tomb of the Duke of Calabria, Charles of Anjou, by Tino di Camaino in Santa Chiara, Naples, dated 1332–33. Here, three of these four stages appear: On a single, continuous field on the sarcophagus, the enthroned monarch is represented, surrounded by his ecclesiastical and secular councillors. On the sarcophagus lies the effigy and high above there are two saints, one of which presents the duke to the Virgin. On the Saltarelli monument, instead of the more traditional emblematic imagery seen on the duke's sarcophagus (appropriate, of course, for a monarch, as in the enthroned emperor on the Henry VII tomb by Tino), there are narrative reliefs vividly portraying events from the bishop's life. The appearance of biographical narrative reliefs, as we shall see, is in itself rather unusual. The sources for the other elements on the tomb are not hard to find. The twisted columns, the curtain-drawing angels, the ascending soul, and the three-part tabernacle all are found on earlier Tuscan tombs: Spiral columns adorn the De Braye monument in Orvieto; curtain-drawing angels also appear on the De Braye monument and on several tombs by Tino; the ascending soul formed part of the monument to Margaret of Luxembourg in Genoa[62] and a tripartite tabernacle surmounts the Petroni monument in Siena and the Benedict XI monument in Perugia (Figs. 173, 174).

The colonettes forming a screen *in front of the effigy*, however, do not appear, to my knowledge, on any earlier Italian tomb although they are found on thirteenth-century French and English tombs.[63] Another rather rare feature of the Saltarelli monument is the appearance of biographical narrative reliefs rather than scenes relating to salvation. During the thirteenth and early fourteenth centuries, biographical narratives are generally found only on saints' tombs.[64] Although Saltarelli is sometimes referred to as *Beato*, he was never canonized.[65]

There is, however, at least one example of an earlier Italian tomb of a noncanonized ecclesiastic with biographical narrative reliefs, that of Bishop Guido Tarlati in the

[62] Cf. also Kreytenberg's reconstruction (1979c), 33–60, of Tino's Orso tomb.

[63] See Roberts (1983), 559–86. From the examples cited by this author, the motif seems to be particularly characteristic of bishops' tombs, an issue that deserves further exploration. (For two later Italian examples, see n. 61.)

[64] An exception, noted by Roberts (1983), is the tomb of Bishop Giles de Bridport (d. 1262) where, however, the biographical reliefs appear not on the sarcophagus but in the spandrels. Saltarelli, as noted earlier, had been to France several times, and it is possible that one or both of these features – colonettes screening the effigy and biographical reliefs – appeared on a French tomb he had seen; according to Roberts (1983), 565, 572, however, there is no earlier extant thirteenth-century tomb with biographical narratives.

[65] See Orlandi (1955), 387.

Duomo of Arezzo by Agostino di Giovanni and Agnolo di Ventura, signed 1330. This has an extensive series of reliefs that celebrate the political and military triumphs of Tarlati, who was made lord of Arezzo in 1321.[66] In 1327 it was he, a Ghibelline expansionist, who crowned Ludwig of Bavaria king of Italy in Milan, an episode depicted in a relief on the tomb. The appearance of biographical narratives on the Saltarelli monument, which seem to refer to Saltarelli's role on the side of Pope Giovanni XXII and against "the accursed Bavarian" as the pope called him,[67] may very well have been justified as a reference to (and criticism of) this imperial alliance so fearful to the Pisans and the Florentines.

Despite some losses and changes of location, the extant components of the Saltarelli tomb were put together, it seems to me, with the same logic that determined the original organization. The monument was conceived by an eclectic but extremely inventive master who has combined elements from the tradition of Tuscan sepulchral monuments in a new and meaningful sequence of visually integrated images.

This master proves to be an artist close to Giotto and, like him, very receptive to architectural and goldsmith design derived from the Gothic north.[68] That he was indeed Andrea Pisano is suggested by several of the sculptural components and by a number of architectural details that refer back to the Florentine Campanile, not only as ultimately executed but as originally conceived by Giotto, who was an important formative influence on Andrea. A reflection of Giotto's design may be seen in the drawing of the Campanile in the Museo dell'Opera del Duomo, Siena.[69] The tabernacle atop the Saltarelli monument is closer, surprisingly, to several of Giotto's architectural designs than it is to analogous elements in earlier Tuscan tombs. In contrast, for instance, to the intricate design but heavy proportions of the tripartite tabernacle on the Petroni monument (Fig. 174), or the much simpler but less elegant tabernacle on Benedict XI's tomb in Perugia (Fig. 173), the Saltarelli tabernacle (Fig. 164) has an airy Gothic delicacy reminiscent of the bifora sections of the Campanile drawing or the framework of the model of the Stefaneschi altarpiece in the painting from Giotto's workshop in the Vatican (Figs. 171, 165). In the latter, as in the Saltarelli monument,

---

[66] White (1966), 287f.

[67] Schevill (1961), 205.

[68] On northern influence on Giotto, see Trachtenberg (1971), 44f.

[69] On the Siena drawing, see Degenhart and Schmitt (1968). Also see chapter 8, n. 28.

Simone Saltarelli probably knew both Giotto and Andrea Pisano personally. It was he who, in 1325, gave permission for the enlargement of the Oratory of Santa Maria della Spina, a building to which, it has been conjectured, Andrea contributed some architectural parts prior to his arrival in Florence (Trachtenberg [1971], 79–81, 79 n. 125). Saltarelli was present at the laying of the cornerstone of the Campanile of Florence in 1334 (Orlandi [1955], 382) at which ceremony Giotto as well as Andrea were surely present.

slender columns are flanked by slim twisted colonettes; below each chamber are three figurated fields, and above, the tripartite vertical impulse continues into the pinnacles. The diagonal projections on the outer flanks of the Saltarelli tabernacle recall the protrusions seen on the spire of the Campanile in the Siena drawing (Figs. 164, 171). The slab on which the curtain-drawing angels and the bier rest, which functions also as a dentilated cornice capping the reliefs, resembles nothing so much as the cornice terminal of the triple bifora zone in the drawing (Figs. 164, 172). On the Campanile itself, several capitals and bases that have convincingly been attributed to Andrea[70] are closely comparable to analogous forms on the Saltarelli tomb (Figs. 164, 166). Although the precision of execution seen in the former is lacking in the Pisan monument, the plastic, sharply delineated, and springy profiles are common to the design of both. Finally, one might add that the angels atop the pinnacles in the Siena drawing, which have eluded reference to any specific sculptor,[71] resemble few figures so closely as they do the lower angels of the Saltarelli tomb (Figs. 149, 154, 168–170).

A single controlling imagination, then, appears to have been responsible for the architectonic and programmatic aspects of the tomb; its individual elements, however, reveal a broad range of styles and quality of execution. The composition of the Saltarelli *Madonna* is very close to that of the *Madonna* in Santa Maria della Spina (Figs. 133, 151). The pose and drapery of the Virgin, and the disposition of the Christ Child, follow the same general scheme. There is, however, a radical simplification of the fold forms, a reduction in the number of cloth layers, and a far more abstract handling of the drapery patterns in relation to the body beneath – at least as regards the Madonna. In the case of the Christ Child, the simplification of the fold forms, if anything, tends to increase the impression of a solidly constructed plastic form; thus, a certain divergence of artistic aims is betrayed. The most notable difference between the Saltarelli and Spina Madonnas is the more dynamic pose of the former in which the classical balance of the Spina group is eschewed in favor of a strong Gothic S-curve. Simone Saltarelli, as mentioned earlier, had been to France on numerous occasions,[72] and it is possible that it was in accordance with his wishes that the author of the tomb project designed a Madonna strongly reminiscent of French models.[73] This apparent concession to French sources does not, however, inform, as we have seen, every aspect of the figure. The heads of Mary and Christ, in particular, are unmistakably Andreesque: Not only are there numerous morphological similarities to Andrea's figures, but more important, the

[70] Trachtenberg (1971), 63.
[71] Trachtenberg, 42f.
[72] See p. 80f.

[73] Cf. Vitry and Briere (1979), Pl. XCIV, 7 (Magny-en-Vexin), and Pl. XCVI, 4 (Troyes).

features palpitate with that reserved vitality characteristic of each of Andrea's statues (Figs. 75, 77, 111, 134). There is, moreover, a similar tendency, despite the more abstract overlay of drapery patterns, to unite the two figures by means of curves that flow from one to the other or echo each other. Thus the curved hemline of the mantle descending across the Virgin's chest continues as a fold of Christ's garment just above her hand, while a broad elongated S-curve sweeps down from the Child's waist to the lowest fold of the Virgin's apron. The corresponding areas in Nino's figures display a change in the direction of the curves resulting in a less unified concordance between the linear play and the emotional content. The persona, if one may use that term, of the Saltarelli *Madonna* differs from that of Nino's two images of Mary: The one in Venice projects a far more spontaneous and direct interaction between Mother and Child, an effect that is intensified in the Florentine version by the scale, the exquisite modeling of the figures, and the heightened expressive content of the features – all of which tend to mitigate what might otherwise be regarded as affectations of pose, gesture, and expression.

The identity of the author of the Saltarelli *Madonna* must perforce remain conjectural, but the figure, as we have seen, is closer in a number of essential aspects to the sculpture of Andrea than to that of Nino. The following hypothesis is offered: If in the Orvieto *Madonna* Andrea displays an almost vehement determination to adopt certain canons of ancient statuary, a similar determination with respect to alternative models may lie behind the conception of the Saltarelli *Madonna*. The sharper, more linear drapery patterns and the insistent Gothic contrapposto reveal the apparent necessity to adhere to foreign models. The first years in Pisa may indeed have been fertile, experimental ones during which Andrea, never dogmatic in his approach to artistic problems, adopted various modes. Gradually he succeeded in synthesizing the contradictory demands of both a Gothic and a classicizing bias – as seen first in the Pisan Duomo *Madonna* and finally in his supreme masterpiece, the *Madonna* in Santa Maria della Spina. Nino, maturing in this climate, clearly found himself increasingly attracted to the more current of these influences, the northern Gothic – without, however, disregarding the classicizing foundations of his own tradition, as any comparison to French Madonnas clearly indicates: Even in comparison to the Saltarelli version, Nino's figures retain a far more articulate relationship of drapery to body. The conclusion seems almost inevitable that the Saltarelli figure represents an almost forced adaptation of an Italian style and model to a French Gothic prototype.

There is no ambivalence of stylistic persuasion in the angels that flank the Madonna (Figs. 151–153): These are unequivocally Giottesque in conception – in their space-displacing forms and gravity-responding drapery that recall those of the *Bishop* in Oristano.[74] As in the latter, both angels display a torsion of the bodies that is accented by the vertically descending drapery folds. The beautiful contrast between the projecting right leg and descending folds of the *Bishop*, however, is eschewed here, very possibly because the plastic and linear elements are subordinated to the total rhythm in which a sequence of curves ascends from the curtain-holding angels below up through the Madonna.

The angel on the right (Fig. 153) is of superior workmanship and is most likely by Nino, designed and executed under the close supervision of Andrea and dated slightly later than the *Bishop* sent to Sardinia. The slightly pursed lips characteristic of the Venetian and Florentine Madonnas appear here as do the half-moon eyes. For the angel on the left (Fig. 152), Nino may have been assisted by another sculptor. To Nino, too, may be assigned the effigy of the archbishop (Fig. 156) on the basis of its similarity to the representation of Scherlatti (Fig. 324), whose tomb was contracted some years later from Nino.[75] Although conventional in pose, both figures are portrayed naturalistically in the serenity of death. Nevertheless, neither displays the insistent realism of Arnolfo's portrait of De Braye, nor the rather generalized features seen on the effigy of Moricotti (Fig. 323) by an assistant of Nino.

The curtain-holding angels (Figs. 149, 154) are by another sculptor, not Nino, but a master unmistakably educated in the Giotto-Andrea Pisano tradition. What the figures lack in that grace and refinement we would expect from even the most classicizing of Andrea's figures (the Orvieto *Madonna*) or even the least elegant of Nino's (the *Bishop* in Oristano), the Saltarelli curtain-holding angels gain in the projection of weight and volume: Broad-boned, robust heads are set on solid, cylindrical necks supported by strong, full-bodied shoulders, and the drapery forms are simple reflections of the volumes they cover. Surveying Tuscan productions from the fourth to the sixth decades of the fourteenth century, only one other group of sculptures comes to mind as being comparably dependent on the art of Giotto and Andrea. Among the generally undistinguished reliefs on the upper zone of the Campanile's western, southern, and eastern sides, several stand out as the products of a superior sculptor closely allied to Andrea. These include the representations of Venus and Arithmetic (Figs. 176, 177), which reveal a more sensitive handling of drapery and facial elements than that seen in most of the other lozenges. Numerous details of morphology, contours, and carving technique in these and several other Campanile lozenges so closely resemble corresponding aspects of the Saltarelli angels as to suggest that the same sculptors are at

[74] These figures too have been the victims of unflattering photographs and should not be judged on the basis of the Alinari or Brogi prints.
[75] See pp. 157–61.

work. Compare, for instance, the lower-right-hand and the lower-left-hand angels on the Saltarelli tomb with the figures of Arithmetic and Faith, respectively, from the Campanile (cf. Figs. 154 and 177; cf. Figs. 149, lower left, and 175). It would not be surprising if Andrea had taken with him, or subsequently called to Pisa, the best of his assistants in Florence.[76]

The reliefs on the front of the sarcophagus with scenes from the life of Simone Saltarelli (Figs. 161–163) are from the hand of yet a fourth member of the workshop whose figure style, if uninspired, derives from Giotto and Andrea Pisano, but whose relief mode exhibits none of the advances toward a coherent, stagelike space seen in the sculpture of the latter; rather, the relationship of figure to frame recalls the less rational handling of Tino di Camaino. Another hand, more strongly influenced by Nino, is apparent in the figures of Saints Dominic and Peter Martyr (Figs. 149, 155), workshop products of competence, but little distinction.[77] The same hand is seen in the representations of Dominican monks standing at lecterns (Fig. 160) on the sides of the sarcophagus. Finally, the reliefs on the lid of the sarcophagus (Figs. 158–159) are by one or two close assistants of Nino (one of which may have been his brother Tommaso), probably executing his designs. The angels carrying the soul of the archbishop closely resemble those flanking the *Man of Sorrows* on the Moricotti tomb (Fig. 318), although they are inferior to the latter in workmanship. The flying angels and the soul appear again on a tomb slab in Cagliari made for a Pisan noblewoman and dated 1345 by inscription (Fig. 157); the style of the relief is very close to that on the sarcophagus lid – further indication, incidentally, of connections between the Pisano workshop and Sardinia.[78]

A picture emerges of a complex workshop organization in which control of the program and overall design of the monument belonged to the head master, namely, Andrea Pisano, but in which a great deal of responsibility and independence was given to several associates – including Nino Pisano, the sculptor from the Campanile in Florence, and the master of the Saltarelli reliefs. Each of these, in turn, supervised a body of workshop assistants. Although the tomb was designed relatively early in the span 1343–7, the execution of its parts probably took several years. Early on, the master himself carved, perhaps with some assistance, the Madonna and Child, and closely supervised the design and execution of the angels on the upper and lower levels. Nothing in the tabernacle angels contradicts an attribution to Nino with a dating some-

[76] A relationship to the Campanile rhomboids is observed by Burresi (1983), 178.

[77] The head of Peter Martyr is a modern replacement in stucco. Supino (1904), 226.

[78] Scano (1903), 23. On the damaged lower edge one can discern part of a date: AD . . . CCCXLV; this places the work in the middle of Andrea's second Pisan period.

what later than that of the *Bishop* sent to Sardinia. The curtain-holding angels, on the other hand, display a style tending more toward the Giottesque than one would expect of Nino during the middle years of the Pisan span when he was engaged in the creation of the Cornaro *Madonna*. The immensity of the project, and the pressures from other commissions, may have necessitated the calling to Pisa of sculptors from elsewhere. Thus, one of Andrea's assistants who had been left behind in Florence was summoned to contribute the curtain-holding angels, and another master was given the responsibility for the reliefs – a master fully capable, if not of great inventiveness, then of designing narrative reliefs that are straightforward in their presentation of the required episodes and that function as part of the balance and structure of the tomb as a whole.

THE SAINT MARTIN LUNETTE IN SAN MARTINO, PISA

That Andrea took with him to Pisa one or more assistants from his Florentine workshop becomes evident again when one examines the lunette relief formerly on the facade of San Martino and now transferred to the interior of the church (Fig. 179).[79] The relief has been much admired for the liveliness of the horse with its taut and springy contours, the subtle surface treatment of the whole, and the expressive relationship, aptly adjusted to the shape of the lunette, between the beggar and the saint. The Church of San Martino was being rebuilt from 1332 until at least 1341, when work is recorded as not yet completed.[80] There is, thus, no obstacle to placing the San Martino relief during the years of work on the Saltarelli monument, that is, during the first few years of Andrea's stay in Pisa. The style of the relief, indeed, is very close to that seen in several reliefs on the Campanile by assistants of Andrea.

As acute as the sculptor's observation is of details of accoutrements and anatomy – note the careful rendering of the bridle, the spurs, even the horseshoe visible under the raised hoof, and the knees, calves, and clavicle – he clearly has difficulty in recreating the structure of the body in the three-quarter views he has chosen. The awkward relationship of right shoulder to neck and torso and of hand to arm in the beggar suggests that this relief was not executed by Andrea, who was perfectly capable of handling the three-quarter view, as seen in *Hope* on the doors, and the *Creation of Adam*, the *Creation of Eve*, and *Sculpture* on the Campanile, among others. Several reliefs on the Campanile are by a stonemason with similar difficulties: the *Labors of Adam and Eve, Agri-*

---

[79] On the San Martino lunette see Supino (1904), 232; Venturi (1906), 485f.; Carli (1934a), 195–7;

[80] Supino (1904), 234; Becherucci (1965), 250.

Becherucci (1965), 250.

culture, and *Trade* (Figs. 52, 59, 66). In each of these the lower portion of the body is shown in a three-quarter view from front or from back, or in profile, whereas the upper portion is pulled parallel to the picture plane; the same holds true for each figure in the San Martino lunette. The figure of the beggar is especially close to Adam in the *Labors of Adam and Eve*. The horse, moreover, resembles the forward horse in *Trade* and differs, in turn, from the representation in *Horsemanship* (Fig. 60), which is autograph Andrea: Compare the shape and contours of the animal, the position of the legs, and the treatment of the mane. Whereas the windblown drapery in *Horsemanship* is justified by the gallop of the steed, it is a mannerism in the Pisan relief in which the animal daintily takes one step toward the beggar. Finally, the evident lack of interest in spatial definition and the emphasis, instead, on linear patterns, add further arguments for giving the relief to an assistant of Andrea's rather than to the master himself. It seems likely that confronted with the complex task of the Saltarelli tomb, Andrea allowed an assistant to design and execute this relief as he did for many of the elements on the Saltarelli monument.

THE ORVIETO ANGELS

The documents of 1348 speak not only of a marble Virgin for the Duomo to be brought from Pisa to Orvieto, but also of two blocks of marble for angels to accompany the Madonna (Doc. 52). Clearly, whereas the latter figure had been executed in Andrea's Pisan workshop, the accompanying angels were to be executed in Orvieto where Andrea had moved his shop. Two fragmentary angels have been convincingly associated with this Maestà (Figs. 297–300).[81] Although both have suffered severe damage as the result of a fall, the remaining surfaces have the same refined, luminous surface quality as the *Madonna* of Orvieto by Andrea Pisano (Fig. 110). Nevertheless, the two figures reveal two different hands. The angel (Fig. 297) which was to the left of the *Madonna* has a more stable pose, broader shoulders, and simpler drapery folds than does the one to the right (Fig. 299) – characteristics equally evident from the back views (Figs. 298, 300). The figure is conceived in terms of firm, rounded underlying forms enveloped by the heavy if sometimes clinging folds of drapery. These drapery forms contrast with the more decorative linear folds seen on the second angel whose proportions, moreover, are slenderer and whose waistline is considerably higher. At the same time, both figures depart from the vehement classicism of the *Madonna*, which, as we have seen, was most likely executed early in the span 1343–7. The left-hand angel comes closer, in its general configuration, to the Spina *Madonna*, which was created toward the end of that time span

[81] Cellini (1933), 1–20; Lányi (1933), 204–27.

when Andrea had succeeded in unifying both his classicizing and Gothicizing impulses in a single work of sculpture. Nothing prevents us from assigning the left-hand angel to the master himself. The right-hand angel, however, with its high-waisted and elongated proportions, swinging drapery folds, and cascading hemlines framing the figures on right and left, strongly recalls the *Madonna* in Santa Maria Novella (Fig. 109). Particularly close are the drapery patterns of the lower half of each figure where, almost fold for fold, the Orvieto angel's mantle repeats the configuration of the Florentine statuette. Thus, either Andrea assigned the second angel to Nino, or the figure was carved by Nino after he himself became capomaestro in 1349.

THE SAINTS PETER AND JOHN THE BAPTIST IN SANTA MARIA DELLA SPINA, PISA

This angel, in turn, is strongly reminiscent of the figure of Saint Peter – here attributed to Nino Pisano – accompanying the *Madonna* in Santa Maria della Spina (Figs. 295, 296). As in the Orvieto angel (Fig. 299), the drapery is conceived as a series of decorative swinging or cascading linear elements moving in directions predominantly parallel to the relief surfaces, not in and out of space. The head, with its melancholic, even anxious expression, and the deeply incised pattern of the hair and beard is, if not identical, at least not inconsistent with that of the *Bishop* in Oristano. In some ways a more accomplished work than the *Bishop*, there is a new emphasis on realistic details such as the wrinkles of the face and the veins of the hands.

The pendant figure of John the Baptist (Fig. 294) is strikingly close to its counterpart on the high altar in San Francesco signed by Nino's brother, Tommaso Pisano (Figs. 331–332). The mechanical carving of the corkscrew curls of hair, the beard, and the fur garment, the stiff poses and graceless gestures, and the flat, overlapping bands of diagonal drapery folds are very similar. The Spina statue is, however, far superior in conception and detail, its proportions are more naturalistic, and the body and drapery are more sensitively articulated. Whereas the San Francesco figurine displays an almost saccharine melancholy – an expression characteristic, as we shall see, of several other works that may be associated with Tommaso – the life-size figure in Santa Maria della Spina has at least a touch of grandeur. All this suggests that the latter was carved by Tommaso while working in his father's Pisan shop and while under his close supervision.

During the years that the brothers were engaged in Andrea's workshop, both Nino and Tommaso tended to subject their own artistic personalities to the controlling force of their father's authority. But whereas Nino's gradual assertion of independence resulted in a highly effective and influential sculptural mode, Tommaso was only able to sustain a relatively high level of accomplishment while under Andrea's watchful eye. As we shall see, when given a commission as an independent master – the San Francesco altarpiece, signed and probably dated ca. 1370, after both Andrea and Nino were dead – Tommaso proved not fully equal to the task.

The angel for the Maestà in Orvieto is the last of Andrea's extant sculptures. At some time after Nino became capomaestro, Andrea appears to have returned to Florence, where he died and was buried.[82] With the death of Andrea, the last of the truly great "primi lumi," who, beginning with Nicola Pisano, had laid the foundations for the Florentine Renaissance of the fifteenth century, was gone. A final brief flowering of the art of sculpture, but of a far more limited nature, makes itself felt with the subsequent development of Nino Pisano.

[82] Becherucci (1965), 244 (referring to Falk [1940], 12; Supino [1933], 103; and Pope-Hennessy [1959]) notes that the Orvieto documents refer to Nino as "magistri Andree" and not "Quondam magistri Andree," the term generally employed if "late master" was intended.

This term was used for Nino himself in 1368. The possibility that Nino became capomaestro while Andrea was still alive is given added weight by Vasari's reference to Andrea's tomb in the Duomo of Florence. See chapter 1, n. 25.

CHAPTER SIX

Andrea Pisano and the Tuscan Gothic Tradition

The revival of an art approaching the standards and ideals of classical antiquity was initiated in Pisa with the arrival of Nicola Pisano from southern Italy. Abandoning what must have appeared to be the static formulas of Italian Romanesque sculpture, Nicola revitalized the ancient narratives, in part, by combining monumental forms and compositions derived from Roman antiquity with the expression of human emotions that were first adequately conveyed in the art of the North. His style evolved from the monumental, if stark, grandeur of his early Pisan reliefs to the rich pictorial images at Siena; it mellowed finally into a more fluid, accessible mode on the Fontana Maggiore in Perugia in which the reliefs are characterized by relatively simple configurations and a freer handling of figures suggestive now of a less hieratic humanity. In Nicola's sculpture the germ of two divergent yet often interweaving currents is found; these provided the source and impetus for the development of his two major assistants. His son, Giovanni, was to develop the emotional current of Nicola's style, in part by transforming the decorative vocabulary of northern art into a very personal and highly charged idiom; whereas Arnolfo's temperament led him in the opposite direction, toward a starkly monumental and classicizing mode. In neither case, however, was the one direction pursued to the exclusion of the other; indeed, the integration of stylistic and spiritual currents from the north with sources in antiquity, achieved with differing degrees of emphasis, characterizes the work of both sculptors and also of Andrea Pisano, a member of the third generation of Tuscan Gothic masters.

Upon his arrival in Florence, Andrea was already the master of a highly developed modeling and goldsmith technique and, as we have seen, had gained some experience in the carving of large-scale sculpture. From where did he arrive in Florence? What evidence is there for his acquaintance with the artistic production of the other major centers of Tuscan Gothic art? In what artistic milieu did he receive his earliest training? A close examination of his oeuvre in relation to earlier and contemporary monuments may reveal to us the itinerary of his career and the sources of influence on his sculpture.

PISA

That Andrea was born and probably grew up in or near Pisa is evident from his signature on the Florentine Baptistry doors as well as from the documentary references to him as Andrea da Pontedera, Andrea da Pisa, or Andrea d'Ugolino da Pisa. Several elements of his style and a number of specific motifs in his sculpture reveal an intimate acquaintance with painting, sculpture, and goldsmith work visible in Pisa prior to 1328 or 1329 when Andrea appeared in Florence.

The relationship of the design of the Baptistry doors to the twelfth-century bronze doors by Bonanus on the Duomo of Pisa was first pointed out by Falk (Figs. 1, 2).[1] Noting that a document of 1329 (Doc. 2) directs the goldsmith Piero di Jacopo to go to Pisa to sketch the doors there, she suggests that the general organization of Andrea's doors derives from Bonanus's Porta di San Ranieri. As in the latter, the Florentine doors comprise a series of figural reliefs surrounded by a decorative chain, and the reliefs are disposed vertically in four columns and horizontally in seven rows. Furthermore, the double row of Virtue reliefs at the base of the Baptistry doors is a transformation of the upper and lower oblong reliefs at Pisa. The result of this transformation is that the Florentine design has a far greater unity and harmony than does that in Pisa; at the same time, the Baptistry doors are provided with a kind of socle that lends a subtle strength to the composition. The framework of Andrea's doors also indicates that the sculptor was aware of other medieval bronze doors extending beyond Tuscany to northern and southern Italy, including doors in Monreale, Trani, and Ravello.[2] These, however, in general show an increase in the number of panels as compared to the Porta di San Ranieri on the Duomo of Pisa (the earliest of the group) so that the individual reliefs tend to be lost in the framing network that dominates the design. Andrea clearly rejects these multipaneled systems (as many as eighty at Ravello), striving instead for a balance between the simple monumentality of Bonanus's early Pisan example and the unified texture of the later doors. In his plastically conceived images clearly projecting from

[1] Falk (1940), 41–3.   [2] Moskowitz (1983a), 1–4.

a neutral background, Andrea further demonstrates his debt to the example closest to home, Bonanus's Porta di San Ranieri in Pisa.

Any sculptor working in or near Pisa – or Siena, for that matter – during the early fourteenth century had to confront the problem of the influence of Giovanni Pisano. Although the Pisa Duomo pulpit had been completed by the end of 1310, that influence continued to dominate Pisan and, to a large extent, Tuscan sculpture well into the second and third decades of the century. The pulpit of San Michele in Borgo, dated after 1310, represents a *popolare* interpretation of Giovanni's style;[3] the early work of Tino di Camaino is often difficult to distinguish from Giovanni's output; the so-called Maestro del Tabernacolo, who executed the *Madonna and Child* on the exterior of San Michele in Borgo,[4] and the equally anonymous author of the tabernacle on the exterior of the Camposanto[5] are examples of the transformation of Giovanni's expressive mode into what has been termed a "manierismo pisano post-giovannesco."[6]

The overwhelming power of Giovanni's turbulent, aggressive art would seem to have left little room for the development of independent talents. Yet almost nothing in the sculpture of Andrea suggests that he was receptive to Giovanni's influence. There was, however, an artistic undercurrent in Pisa and other centers dominated by Giovanni's influence, which tended to conserve the values of Nicola's art with its calmer, more stable compositions and greater emotional restraint. It is this current that may have been important in the formation of Andrea Pisano.

The Sacra Cintola, a singular creation of the late dugento by a follower of Nicola Pisano (Figs. 180, 181), is composed of five miniature silver and enamel reliefs that are all that remain from an extensive series attached to a cloth "belt" that was brought out of the treasury to decorate the exterior of the Duomo on special holidays.[7] Although the figure style recalls that on the pulpits, there is a marked reduction of narrative content resulting in simplified compositions and a rhythmical spacing of the figures to put in relief the gestures and relationships. These characteristics, which parallel developments in the "classical" current of French Gothic sculpture of the second half of the thirteenth century (see chapter 8), are akin to the quiet compositions and measured spacing of the figures in Andrea's Baptistry reliefs. One motif on the doors appears to be a direct quotation: The executioner in the *Beheading of the Baptist* (Fig. 21) is almost identical to that on the Pisan silver relief (Fig. 181).

[3] Carli (1974), 14.
[4] Supino (1905), 51; Carli (1974), 22.
[5] Supino (1905), 60.
[6] Carli (1974), 22.
[7] P. Toesca (1946), 34–6. The Sacra Cintola has been mentioned, in vague terms, in discussions concerning Andrea's style by Salmi (1949–50), 176f., and Castelnuovo (1966). Wundram (1957–9), 203, connects it with the Pistoia workshop of Andrea di Jacopo d'Ognabene.

A rejection of the style and emotional tenor of Giovanni Pisano is seen in the reliefs dated 1316 by Andrea di Jacopo d'Ognabene on the Silver Altar in the Duomo of Pistoia (Figs. 42, 43).[8] Although the reliefs owe much to Giovanni's Pisan pulpit, there are a number of important differences. First, the figures are far more restrained and the compositions more static on the Silver Altar. Second, whereas the *Nativity*, following the example of the Pisani pulpits, is composed of elements distributed throughout the picture field with little attempt to render space naturalistically, the remaining scenes take place in a suggestive space with figures standing on the ground in front of or within architectural or landscape settings. The reliefs on the Silver Altar and on the Baptistry doors have many features in common. In both, the figures are small in relation to the picture field and are not pressed in by background and frame. There is a more naturalistic relationship between figures and architecture than is seen on the pulpits, and the smooth, clearly visible background plane in outdoor scenes implies open air. Finally, each episode – again, with the exception of the most derivative of them, the Pistoia Nativity scene – is self-contained and is revealed through a decorative frame that isolates it from the next scene. It has been conjectured that Andrea Pisano was trained in the workshop of Andrea di Jacopo d'Ognabene[9] and, indeed, the muted emotional content, the dampening of the energy in the compositional rhythms with respect to Giovanni's reliefs, not to speak of the technical training it may have provided, make the Silver Altar a plausible candidate for Andrea's earliest working experience.

The mind and hand of a goldsmith, as noted above, are evident in the architectural motifs and drapery textures seen in the quatrefoil reliefs in Florence. In addition, several apparently insignificant details on the doors hint at Andrea's origins as a goldsmith in or near Pisa. Who but a Pisan goldsmith would have bothered to incise a texture into alternating voussoirs – as appears on the portal in the *Visitation* – in order to convey the light–dark pattern of marble facings ubiquitous on the arches of Pisa (Fig. 182)? Compare, for example, the entrance to the Camposanto (Fig. 183) in which, moreover, the arch with dark and light voussoirs rests, as in the relief, on flat, unadorned pilasters. Who but a Pisan goldsmith would have created a building, the palace of Herodias, capped by an open arcade of countless arches and incorporating an intarsia decoration of quatrefoil and lozenges (Fig. 184)? Pisan architecture abounds with tiers of arcades and also with alternating geometric motifs such as squares, lozenges, and circles, some of which, in turn, contain cloverleaf openings, as in San Cassiano Presso Pisa (Fig. 185). The inclusion of such incised decorative motifs on the Baptistry doors may betray Andrea's deepest affinities.

[8] On the Silver Altar see Ragghianti (1954), 423–38; Steingraber (1956), 148–54; Marchini (1966), 135–47.

[9] Wundram (1957–9), 201.

If certain details on the Baptistry attest to Andrea's origins as a goldsmith, his figure style presupposes experience in the execution of large-scale work in wood or stone, an example of which is found in the Pisan *Annunciate Virgin* (Figs. 102–104). This work clearly pays little homage to the prevailing style in Pisa. The austere and simple forms, barely relieved by a subtle Gothic flow, are characteristic, rather, of Arnolfo's sculpture and Giotto's Paduan style. How could Andrea have become acquainted with the work of Arnolfo and Giotto before his arrival in Florence? Pisa itself would have provided, if not direct examples, at least a few important models that might have encouraged Andrea's anti-Giovannesque stance. The tomb of Henry VII (Fig. 186), commissioned in 1315 from Tino di Camaino, is an extremely independent work of art. Although Tino was presumably trained by Giovanni,[10] the latter's dynamism has been dampened in Tino's sculpture perhaps under the influence of Arnolfo's colder formalism; this too, however, has been transformed by a warmer and less demanding spiritual disposition. The severe blocklike forms, the sharp flat folds, and the restrained emotional content of the figures for the Henry VII tomb are not unlike those that characterize the Pisan *Annunziata*. On the other hand, instead of the limited surface plasticity seen in Tino's figures, Andrea's statue is developed in three dimensions with the arms projecting strongly and the drapery contributing deeply hollowed channels; instead of the awkward contrapposto of Henry's councillors there is, here, a subtle spiraling torsion suggesting the influence, direct or indirect, of French Gothic sculpture. The impact of the Gothic north, of course, is not new to Pisa – Giovanni's ivory statuette of the Madonna and Child in the treasury of Pisa Cathedral is overt evidence of that.[11] But the characteristics of the wooden figure indicate a different intermediary source. It will be recalled that Simone Martini had been in Pisa in 1319 when he painted his famous polyptych for the Church of Santa Caterina.[12] The restrained lyricism of the painted images must have provided an alternative aesthetic standard to an artist predisposed against the hyperenergetic forms of Giovanni. Simone's frescoes in the Saint Martin Chapel at Assisi, considered by some to be rather close in date to his Pisan sojourn,[13] include several figures suggestive of Andrea's sources. Saints Claire and Elizabeth under the entrance arch, for example, exhibit a similar restraint in the translation of the Gothic contrapposto (Fig. 191). The full simple drapery folds and closed contours recall the wooden statue, as do the delicate, even dainty gestures. Perhaps some lost full-length figures by Simone resembling those at Assisi existed in Pisa when Andrea was given the commission for the *Annunziata*. If so, Simone would have been an intermediary, bringing to Andrea reflec-

[10] Pope-Hennessy (1972), 183.

[11] Seidel (1965–6), 171–206.

[12] I. Toesca (1950), 26, related Andrea's style to that of Simone at Pisa and at Assisi.

[13] Paccagnini (1957), 137; Smart (1971), 260.

tions not only of northern Gothic art but, in the space-displaying plasticity and underlying sense of structure in his figures, of Giotto as well.

Around 1323, as noted earlier, Andrea may have been engaged in the project to rebuild the Oratory of Santa Maria della Spina. The few parts of the building that remain from this campaign exhibit a refinement and delicacy that betray the imagination of the goldsmith become architect.[14] Andrea's special liking for pristine moldings set off by sharp dentils, which appear in the rectangular frames around the reliefs on the Florentine doors, is seen earlier on the capitals in the choir of Santa Maria della Spina (Figs. 2, 3). But work seems to have progressed unusually slowly, possibly due to a lack of funds.[15] Andrea, who perhaps considered himself primarily a sculptor anyway, must have found the Pisa of the mid-1320s without potential for his own development. A survey of the extant sculptures produced by followers of Giovanni or by artists who succeeded him strongly suggests that Pisa offered little promise of abundant sculptural activity.[16] It would have been most natural for Andrea at this point to turn his sights to Siena.

SIENA AND ORVIETO

As in Pisa, the style of Giovanni tended to dominate early fourteenth-century sculpture in Siena.[17] In contrast to Pisa, however, during the first few decades of the century Siena offered prolific employment opportunities and a rich cultural environment that stimulated the development of various artistic currents. The sculpture of Andrea Pisano shows strong affinities with several of these alternative modes.

The narrative economy and quiet rhythmic movement seen in a relief in San Francesco, Siena, dated 1298, signal the rejection of Giovanni's rich pictorial style of crowded and complex compositions and strong chiaroscuro effects (Fig. 192).[18] According to the inscription below the relief, the plaque represents the participants in a consecration ceremony for the cemetery of the church. The figures are carved in very low relief and stand

[14] Trachtenberg (1971), 79–81.

[15] Trachtenberg, 79f., n. 125.

[16] Following the departure of Giovanni and then Tino, the office of capomaestro fell to Lupo di Francesco, to whom only a few works, including the Gherardesca tomb, have been given. Several exterior tabernacles containing sculpture have been ascribed to various, usually unknown, followers of Giovanni or Tino. Giovanni di Balduccio, active in the Opera del Duomo under Tino, was probably gone by 1320. Offered an appointment as capomaestro of Pisa in 1349, he refused. On Pisan sculpture of the early trecento, see Carli (1943), 143ff.; (1946), 9–11; (1974); Tolaini (1946), 39–46; Valentiner (1927b), 204ff.; (1935), 8ff.

[17] Carli (1941), 17; Garzelli (1968), 55–65.

[18] On the San Francesco relief see Kosegarten (1965–6), 206–24. See also Carli (1971), 13, and Garzelli (1968), 58.

in parallel rows against the neutral undefined background plane. Since neither the frame nor the background presses in upon the figures – in contrast to many Sienese reliefs of our period – the figures appear to be surrounded by space. Moreover, the volume of the figures is conveyed, not through plastic, but through illusionistic means.[19] Very possibly inspired by antique models,[20] the panel conveys a sense of the sacred and solemn nature of the event depicted.

The style, and especially the technique of the panel with its flattened relief, do not become prevalent in Sienese sculpture. More common are those reliefs characterized by fully plastic figures that dominate the picture field, even overlapping the frame. The compositions are clear and simple; large projecting shapes are set against a blank ground with little or no sense of spatial depth; and the contours often tend to flow in gentle curves (Fig. 174). Tino's reliefs in Siena (and later in Florence) belong to this group. Although, like the author of the San Francesco panel, Tino is predisposed toward relatively simple compositions with few figures set against a smooth, clearly visible background plane, there remains in Tino's reliefs an inherent spatial contradiction. This results from the juxtaposition of figures in high relief that extend to the limits of the picture field, and a flat, impenetrable background plane. Thus, while the Consecration relief represents a solemn contemporary event, taking place within an implied spatial milieu, Tino's reliefs present static images outside of time and space (Figs. 187, 188).

Finally, a group of Sienese reliefs exhibit, in Carli's phrase, the "predella style," which is characterized by an inclination to storytelling and lively description, an absence of drama, a loving attention to detail, and a taste for refined line.[21] Figures are conceived as plastic volumes and often are placed in a three-dimensional space, either real or implied. Examples of this third group of Sienese reliefs include the Tarlati monument of Agostino di Giovanni and Agnolo di Ventura,[22] and the Arca di San Cerbone by Goro di Gregorio (Fig. 193).[23]

During the first three decades of the fourteenth century in Siena, then, a variety of relief styles emerges that would seem to pay little homage to the tradition established by Giovanni Pisano. An alternative to the latter appears, as well, on the Duomo facade. Giovanni had created, in the 1280s and 1290s, a series of powerful figures for the lower facade dynamically relating to each other through gesture and expression across vast architectural spaces. It has been convincingly argued that the sculptural decoration of the upper facade was executed, not as previously assumed in the 1380s after a long in-

---

[19] Unique in these respects for such an early date, the San Francesco relief anticipates Donatello's *schiacciato* relief mode.
[20] Cf. Kosegarten (1965–6), 213f.

[21] Carli (1946), 21.
[22] Carli (1946), 21; Pope-Hennessy (1972), 187f.
[23] Carli (1946), 21.

terruption following Giovanni's death, but during and after the second decade by a workshop reacting against the aggressive and turbulent emotionalism of Giovanni's sculptures on the lower facade.[24] The "Giottesque" *Madonna and Child* above the rose window is manifestly influenced by the sculpture of Arnolfo, as a comparison with his statue from the Florentine Duomo makes clear (Figs. 195, 197). The figures behind balustrades on either side of the Madonna (Fig. 194) recall the kneeling Magus in Arnolfo's Praesepe in Santa Maria Maggiore in Rome (Fig. 196). Although the Sienese predilection for gentle curves and modulated transitions from plane to plane is evident, the relationship of head to body, and the sense of bulk beneath the simplified but by no means schematic drapery on the Duomo figures suggest an awareness of Arnolfo's sculpture in Rome and tend to confirm the early dating of these sculptures. Thus, in addition to its more current local traditions, Siena proffered examples of an Arnolfian–Giottesque tradition, the roots of which go back to the art of Nicola Pisano.

The affinities between these various currents in Sienese sculpture and Andrea's relief conception and figure style are compelling enough to suggest, although they cannot prove, a Sienese sojourn prior to his appearance in Florence.[25] As in Goro's reliefs on the Arca di San Cerbone, Andrea's figures on the doors are conceived as plastic volumes existing in a real three-dimensional space. At the same time, the notational volume of the figures and indeed of the space tends to be considerably greater, as in the Consecration relief, than the actual projections from the back plane – and this is even more true of the Genesis reliefs on the Campanile. In other words, an element of illusionism enters into Andrea's reliefs that is absent in Goro's. In a relief such as *Zacharias Struck Dumb*, which contains no architectural props, the combination and integration of real and illusionistic space is particularly cogent: The shelf supported by consoles tends to limit the spatial depth while the blank background above evokes a sense of expanded space. On the doors, as in the Consecration relief, this blank expanse is analogous to the background in Simone Martini's Uffizi *Annunciation* of 1333, which exhibits that "interior by implication" perceived by Panofsky to be one important phase in the development of Renaissance pictorial space.[26]

[24] Kosegarten (1966), 96–118.

[25] A Sienese period for Andrea has been suggested by Wundram (1957–9), 207–17. Wundram, however, interprets Andrea's relief mode in an unduly restrictive manner, nor does he perceive its development. Thus, in discussing the doors he insists that the figures are placed "innerhalb dieser genau definierten räumlichen Situation" consisting of an inviolable background and ideal foreground plane; elsewhere he notes that Goro's Arca possesses a "Reliefstil, der dem Andrea Pisanos bis in Einzelheiten hinein gleicht." It must be admitted, however, that Wundram's fundamental perception of the affinity of Andrea's style with Sienese art is correct, and his analysis has provided a point of departure for further study.

[26] Panofsky (1953); reprinted (1971), 19.

As is true of the Consecration relief, Andrea's relief surfaces are not activated by busy compositions and picturesque details, but remain relatively unencumbered. The measured spacing of the figures with their gestures isolated against the blank ground further connects the mood of Andrea's reliefs with the Sienese example. The linear harmonies of Andrea's drapery forms, however, are perhaps most closely tied to Tino di Camaino's reliefs in Siena and Florence as is the clarity of the compositions and the Franciscan spirit of the actors. Compare, for example, Tino's *Noli Me Tangere* (Fig. 187) and Andrea's *Ecce Agnus Dei* (Fig. 13). In both, landscape and figural elements are sharply set against the flat back plane of the reliefs, crisp curving drapery folds with meandering hemlines create harmonious surface patterns, and the expressions and gestures convey a sense of rapt sincerity on the part of the protagonists.

Eclectic as he was, Andrea astutely accommodated his sources to his particular task on the doors. Clearly, he was not called upon to represent a solemn contemporary event as on the San Francesco Consecration relief, nor to depict a series of colorful episodes in the life of a beloved local saint as on the Arca di San Cerbone. Neither are his figures intended to be ideal images outside of time and space as on the Petroni monument. Indebted to the Arnolfian–Giottesque tradition, they convince us of their reality by means of the corporeal weight of their forms revealed through the rhythmic but never too abstract hanging of the drapery; they exist in a believable space that does not impinge on that corporeality; and yet the story is raised to a level higher than that of colorful or even solemn everyday life. The projecting shelf, which is so "real" that drapery can hang over it, nevertheless, by its very artificiality within the context of the fictive world of each scene, proclaims the ideality of the images. Gesture becomes ritual; architecture is referred to by symbolic fragments; and the abstract, lyrical rhythms that unify each scene serve to inhibit too immediate a reference to reality. However diverse the sources, on the Baptistry doors form and content are united.

The impact of the Arnolfo–Giotto tradition as seen in Siena is felt in some of the Campanile reliefs where several figures are reminiscent of the Ancestors of the Madonna around the rose window of Siena Cathedral from the late Duomo workshop (Fig. 194). The Sculptor and Painter in the hexagons (Figs. 57, 67), for example, may be compared to the figure to the right of the *Madonna.* In the latter, the sensitive contour of the back – regulated yet varied in its movement, tending toward a geometric curve yet avoiding the schematic – anticipates Andrea's handling of contours. Similar too are the simple yet naturalistic forms draped over corporeal bodies.

Indicative of the complex selection process with respect to the available sources is the fact that, when called upon to create images of the Madonna and Child, it is not to the austere and solemn examples of the Arnolfo–Giotto tradition that Andrea turned, but rather to Sienese examples in painting and sculpture that tended to stress the physical and psychological interaction between mother and son. Every figure of the Virgin by Andrea smiles tenderly toward her Child, her expression suggesting a state of beatitude, and the relationship between the two figures is enhanced by the curves of drapery that tend to bind them together. Andrea's *Madonna del Latte* (Fig. 135) combines the half-length format of Ambrogio Lorenzetti's painting of the same subject[27] with compositional elements derived from Simone Martini's lost *Madonna of Humility*.[28] Consider also the similarities between Goro's *Madonna degli Storpi* (Fig. 198) and Andrea's Pisan half-length group. Stylistically diverse, they are nevertheless created in the same spirit. The intimacy between mother and child is conveyed, not only by means of pose, glance, and physical relationship, but also by way of the series of curves and countercurves that bind the figures together and converge at the mother's breast.

Andrea's treatment of contours, in general, seems closer to Sienese than to Florentine art. Fundamentally characteristic of Florentine painting is the fact that contours, and particularly the contours of drapery, are not primary aesthetic or expressive devices but are descriptive – the extreme edges of the forms depicted. The eye is rarely impelled to follow the course of these edges from beginning to end; the opposite is true of Sienese art. In the earliest reliefs on the doors one notes a "Sienese" attitude toward line: The hem of Gabriel's mantle is pleasing in and of itself; its movement contrasts with the opposing curve of the drapery over the leg. Played against the cascading hemline to the right, the emphatic sweep of the mantle is reminiscent of a similar motif in Duccio's *Deposition* from the Maestà (Fig. 40), where, however, it contributes to the emotional tenor of the scene. Several figures on the left-hand valve are enveloped in drapery that seems to owe as much to Simone's Maestà in the Palazzo Pubblico in Siena as to anything then visible in Florence (Figs. 199, 200). The graceful contours, simple folds, and delicate poise of Salome, indeed, are much closer to the similarly posed figures on the Maestà than to anything in Giotto's frescoes.

One or two unusual iconographic details on the doors can perhaps best be explained only by supposing a prior experience in Siena. Although stylistically superseded by Simone's fresco, the Maestà by Duccio remained the daily and weekly visual joy of the worshippers facing the high altar, or the clergy seated in the choir stalls or walking around the ambulatory of the Duomo of Siena. As an extensive yet small-scale narrative cycle it must have held some interest for Andrea, especially if, as has been generally assumed, he was called to Florence specifically in connection with the commission for the doors. Mention has already been made of the relationship of Andrea's *Nativity* to

[27] White (1966), 245, suggests a dating in the 1320s for Lorenzetti's painting, whereas Borsook (1966), 29, dates it ca. 1340.
[28] See p. 73.

103

that in Duccio's Maestà.[29] Another possible reference to Duccio's painting is found in the bronze *Entombment of the Baptist*, in which two figures are bent over in profile in front of the bier (Fig. 25). This extremely unusual conception has no counterpart in the Pisani pulpits, or to my knowledge, in Florentine monumental painting. Lacking prototypes in the mosaics and frescoes in Florence, the source for Andrea's conception is perhaps seen in Duccio's *Lamentation*, where a single figure in the foreground leans over the bier in the same pose as the two in the bronze panel (Fig. 40).

A few final observations suggest Andrea's presence in Siena. Close as the connection of the bronze reliefs is to the Peruzzi Chapel frescoes in Florence,[30] it is noteworthy that the architectural motifs on the doors are more "modern" than those in Giotto's frescoes. Giotto's architecture recalls the Cosmatesque buildings prevalent in Rome since the thirteenth century,[31] whereas the forms on the doors are distinctly Gothic. Very little monumental architecture in the Florence of ca. 1330 exhibited the motifs that might have inspired Andrea's miniature architecture.[32] Siena, on the other hand, had already witnessed the rise of its Baptistry facade and was producing examples of goldsmith work directly inspired by northern forms.[33] Architectural configurations such as that in the *Entombment of the Baptist* resemble the forms on Ugolino di Vieri's reliquaries and, beyond them, such advanced Gothic examples as Design B of Strasbourg Cathedral (Figs. 25, 167, 201).

Even during his very latest period, when he was capomaestro of the Duomo of Orvieto in 1347, Andrea's decorative language reveals his past contact with Siena. The exterior side aisle travertine cornice of the cathedral has been ascribed to Andrea on the basis of documents and style (Fig. 204).[34] The central motif of this cornice – rosettes in a continuous quatrefoil – appears earlier, at Arezzo, in a carving by the Sienese sculptors Agostino di Giovanni and Agnolo di Ventura (Fig. 203).[35] The transformation of a relatively phlegmatic decorative motif into the "metallically carved rosettes set like jewels in deep quatrefoil frames"[36] is characteristic of the imagination of the goldsmith turned architect.

Finally, Andrea's special interest in landscape would seem to be rooted in the Sienese experience. The concern with pictorial naturalism goes back, to be sure, to the work of Nicola on the Siena pulpit (and later on the Fontana Maggiore in Perugia). But for Sienese sculptors, especially those at Orvieto, landscape elements, rather than remaining minor motifs, become dominant aspects of the representations contributing fully and al-

[29] P. 12f.

[30] Falk and Lányi (1943), 132–53.

[31] Borsook and Tintori (1965), 18f.

[32] Trachtenberg (1971), 44.

[33] Klotz (1965–6), 171–206.

[34] Trachtenberg (1971), 82.

[35] Valentiner (1927b).

[36] Trachtenberg (1971), 82.

most equally with the figures in conveying the essential messages of the biblical stories. We have seen that this holds true, as well, for the Giovannino panel on the doors (Fig. 11), in which, perhaps for the first time in the history of sculpture, the landscape actually encompasses and fills up the entire composition with the figure a relatively small element in one corner.

Several features on the Campanile are anticipated in other Sienese landscape reliefs, for instance, examples coming from Tino di Camaino and his circle. Especially interesting is the landscape in the lunette (Fig. 211) over the funeral chamber of the Tomb of Catherine of Austria in Naples executed by Tino ca. 1324. Tino's relief style seems to have undergone a decisive change at this time: Instead of the flat background plane pressing in against large figures that overlap this plane, as in the Petroni and Delle Torre monuments, in the *Stigmatization of St. Frances* in Naples the landscape elements and architecture are distributed in such a way as to suggest their existence in several planes in depth. Despite the archaism of the mosaic background – which serves, however, to unify the relief with the rest of the tomb – there is a remarkable feeling of spatial continuity that has no counterpart in contemporary sculpture. Naturalistic rocky forms fill the foreground, which contains the figure of the saint; a stepped path leads from him to a chapel set obliquely in the middle ground; and behind this chapel meanders the horizon line. Clearly, there is a groping here for a means to represent landscape with a sense of recession and an evocation of open space – in marked contrast to the crowded reliefs of Giovanni.[37] Similarly, the landscapes on the baptismal font of Arezzo attributed to Giovanni d'Agostino anticipate Andrea's concerns on the Campanile: *Young John in the Wilderness* contains softly modeled landscape forms and a receding architectural structure contributing to a sense of moderate depth (as does the foreshortened foot of John).[38]

The importance given to landscape representation, then, in Andrea's sculpture links him to developments in Siena and related centers. Many attempts have been made to place Andrea's origins in Orvieto itself, but the documentary evidence is lacking to prove any direct connection.[39] The fact remains, however, that in the decades after the construction of the Pisa pulpit and prior to Andrea's doors a major ecclesiastic decorative program was underway, and a veritable army of stonemasons and sculptors was

[37] Valentiner (1935), 92ff.; 152. Giotto headed a workshop in Naples from 1329 to 1333, when he returned to Florence. Shortly thereafter he became capomaestro and initiated the Campanile project. Although Tino's iconography may be based on a lost painting by Giotto (the pose of the saint is similar to that in the Assisi fresco, but the setting is closer to that over the entrance to the Bardi Chapel in Santa Croce), it may be that the great painter, in turn, brought back to Florence Tino's innovations in pictorial relief.

[38] White (1966), Pl. 132b.

[39] For a summary and references, see Wundram (1957–9), 217, n. 53.

105

engaged in that project. The division of labor from masters to assistants was not only extensive but virtually imperceptible in the finished reliefs.[40] The inability of scholars to establish a totally convincing stylistic link between Andrea and Orvieto is not surprising in the light of this. When Andrea was given the commission for the doors, he must have been highly regarded as a bronze sculptor, and he was – or somehow by the mid-1330s, when the Genesis scenes were being carved, had become – a master marble sculptor. Would it not be reasonable to suppose that an ambitious young artist from Pisa – trained as a goldsmith, showing promise as a carver of wood, experienced by now in architecture – would it not be reasonable to suppose that such a person would seek employment in the most prolific and advanced workshop of his day?

The relief of the *Blessing Christ with Chalice* (Fig. 93) strongly suggests Andrea's presence in Orvieto prior to his arrival in Florence.[41] Furthermore, it is clear that the techniques and skills acquired as a goldsmith and a carver of wood and marble are very different from those of a master of bronze. Since Orvieto was the only city in the environs of Tuscany at that time experimenting with monumental bronze sculpture, Andrea may have received the specialized training – the experience of modeling in wax or plaster, and of polishing and refining the cast pieces – at Orvieto.

Finally, the artistic concerns of the sculptors of Orvieto Cathedral had a strong impact on Andrea's Florentine sculpture. In addition to sharing a compelling interest in landscape, Andrea shares with the sculptors of Orvieto (and Siena) a concern for the representation of space. Although many individual scenes on the facade of Orvieto Cathedral are characterized by figures in high relief crowded together with little or no view of the background plane – a relief mode that comes directly out of Giovanni's pulpits – other scenes do, indeed, contain suggestions of deep, almost palpable space (Figs. 208, 212). In one vignette, *Christ Among the Doctors* (Fig. 212), the sense of space is achieved with particular conviction: One can, in fact, imagine a ground plan showing the position of each figure in the circle surrounding Christ, an unthinkable exercise with respect to any of Giovanni's reliefs, notwithstanding the importance of his relief style for Orvieto.[42] *Christ Among the Doctors* may be compared with the Campanile relief, *Medicine* (Fig. 68) with its box space and solid rear wall and its figures disposed in rows diagonally into space. Both at Orvieto and at Florence the figures are conceived as volumes that occupy and displace three-dimensional space. In some panels on the doors, the space-displacing character of the figures is achieved by means of a slight gradation of relief height (Figs. 7, 8, 10, 18), a handling of relief very characteristic of Orvieto

[40] White (1959), passim.

[41] See p. 53f.

[42] Such a plan has been developed for another Sienese relief, the *Baptism* in the Pieve in Arezzo. See Garzelli (1969), 176.

where it is carried out with unequalled subtlety: The angels in the Creation scenes emerge diagonally out of space, a result achieved in part by the difference in the projection between the upper and lower parts of their bodies (Fig. 210).[43]

Andrea also shares with the sculptors of Orvieto an interest in depicting acutely observed objects such as tools and furniture (Fig. 214); this realism goes beyond anything attempted by the Pisani. Finally, a number of iconographic and compositional motifs at Orvieto reappear on the Florentine doors and Campanile. The *Visitation* scenes represented on the Pistoia altar and the Orvieto piers derive from a compositional scheme of Giovanni's Pisa pulpit (Figs. 43, 208). Andrea's version (Fig. 8), especially the position of the arms and hands, is, in fact, closer to that at Orvieto than to the others.[44] Furthermore, although the pose and action of the attendant on the right of the Orvietan scene are different from that in Florence, she regards the event with a sense of quiet contemplation similar to that of the attendant in the bronze relief. The strikingly original conception of the *Funeral of the Baptist* (Fig. 24) is based on a motif that appears several times in Sienese art – at Pistoia, at Volterra,[45] and at Orvieto (Fig. 209). The most immediate source seems to be the latter. The grouping of the figures with three persons seen from behind, between which are glimpsed the heads of the figures facing the viewer, and the rhythmic play of the drapery, which, in the case of the analogous figures on the left, follows the swing of the striding leg, are so close as to argue strongly for Andrea's direct acquaintance with the Orvietan relief.

Compare, too, the *Baptism of Christ* reliefs at Orvieto and at Florence (Figs. 15, 213). Although the figures of the Savior differ in their proportions, the bronze example being more attenuated, the pose and the anatomical divisions are almost identical and, taking into account the fact that the marble carving was never finished,[46] the contours, the shapes, the pattern of the water – transparent so that the form of the legs shows through – are extraordinarily similar.

One final detail links Andrea to Orvieto. The *Madonna and Child* lunette on the Campanile (Fig. 84) is unusual, if not unique, in early trecento architectural sculpture. Half-length Madonna and Child representations in panel paintings are, of course, numerous in the thirteenth and fourteenth centuries, but the only architectural sculpture familiar to me preceding the one on the Campanile is the group by Giovanni in the Camposanto that was made for the tympanum of the west door of the Cathedral of Pisa (Fig. 308). Unlike the Campanile Madonna, it was carved in-the-round (or in very high relief),

---

[43] Was Ghiberti acquainted with the reliefs at Orvieto? A similar use of gradated projections seemed to be so revolutionary in Ghiberti's *Baptism* in Siena. See Krautheimer (1970), 149.

[44] This was noted by Francovich (1927–8), 339–72.

[45] Wundram (1957–9), 216.

[46] White (1959), 254–302.

and the Child is on the Virgin's right rather than on her left. At Orvieto there is a representation of a church; above the side portal can be seen a tiny Gothic lunette containing a half-length Virgin and Child (Fig. 85). As in the Campanile lunette relief, Christ is on Mary's left; furthermore, the relationship of the figures to the lunette shape is extremely close to that at Florence.

The influence of Orvieto on the doors is fairly limited compared to its impact on the Campanile reliefs. Not only do we find in the latter several iconographic adaptations, and a greater interest in naturalistic landscape and space, but the handling of specific motifs such as trees and drapery recalls the treatment of corresponding motifs at Orvieto: Whereas on the doors the tight modeling of trees resembles those on the Pistoia Silver Altar,[47] in the Campanile Genesis scenes the freer, looser treatment and deeper undercutting come close to the representation of trees at Orvieto. Similarly, the drapery on the doors tends toward a metallic hardness that recalls the Silver Altar, whereas the carving on the Campanile – for example, the drapery of God in the Creation scenes – is extremely close to the corresponding scene at Orvieto; in both, soft, concentric folds in thin curves create a linear pattern between broader smooth planes (Figs. 50, 205).

No single group of comparisons among the many put forth here can establish definitively Andrea's presence in Siena or Orvieto before his appearance in Florence. But the cumulative impression is one of a strong and continuous acknowledgment of Sienese achievements. Certainly his contribution to the architecture of the Campanile bears witness to his acquaintance with Sienese forms.[48] And his sculpture – whether we think of Andrea's concern with the naturalistic representation of landscape, his involvement with a relief mode conveying palpable three-dimensionality, whether we consider the lyrical harmonies of his drapery style or the projection of intimacy between mother and child by means of circular flowing compositional rhythms – seems inextricably tied to that of Sienese art. Such pervasive stylistic connections, especially in the face of other strong influences – and we shall see in the following sections the importance of direct acquaintance with Giotto, of the Florentine miniaturist tradition, of classical art and of French Gothic sculpture – can only be explained by the fundamental absorption of Sienese art during a formative phase of development.

FLORENCE

If during the second and third decades of the fourteenth century Florence found itself relatively poor in native sculptors, it was exceedingly rich as far as painting was con-

[47] See p. 15f.   [48] Trachtenberg (1971), 60, 63f.

cerned. The Baptistry mosaics were finally completed in 1325.[49] Major fresco cycles were being initiated or brought to completion in the numerous chapels in Santa Croce. While Giotto's monumental Ognissanti *Madonna* continued to influence numerous lesser masters, Bernardo Daddi was developing a thriving business producing the increasingly popular small devotional panels depicting the Madonna and Child with saints. Also flourishing were the miniaturist workshops such as that of Pacino di Bonaguida. In short, Florence ca. 1330 presented a rich cultural ambiance that, we may be sure, fed the absorbent imagination of Andrea Pisano.

The paintings of Giotto undoubtedly constitute one of the major factors in the formation of Andrea's style. Giotto, indeed, was a formidable contemporary. As White has observed, when Andrea began work on the Baptistry doors he was faced with the following realities:

> Firstly, Giotto's originality in . . . [the Peruzzi Chapel frescoes] lay in their hitherto undreamt of architectural, spatial and descriptive realism. Secondly, on technical, if upon no other grounds, there was not at that date the remotest possibility of matching, much less of surpassing, such pictorial realism in terms of bronze. Thirdly and possibly the most dauntingly, Andrea must have known that whatever his solution, he would inevitably face comparison with Giotto at the hands of the most critical, the most sophisticated, and the most artistically conscious city in Italy.[50]

A lesser artist than Andrea would have succumbed to a servile adaptation of Giotto's inventions. This is precisely what happened with respect to Giovanni Pisano in Pisa, where his followers, with greater or lesser success, continued to imitate the style of their powerful predecessor. Andrea, in contrast, succeeded in integrating the Giottesque aesthetic with sources from the multifarious influences of his earlier years to arrive at utterly original solutions.

We have already touched on the Giottesque current in Sienese art that may have influenced Andrea. Falk and Lányi have demonstrated Andrea's debt to the Peruzzi Chapel frescoes: For those scenes for which Giotto furnished prototypes, Andrea adhered very closely to the examples of the frescoes; and for the many scenes represented on the doors but absent from the frescoes, Andrea turned, if at all possible, to the mosaics in the Baptistry — translating the images, however, into the new pictorial language of Giotto.[51] What these authors fail to observe, however, is that it is in large measure the language of the Arena Chapel, not the Peruzzi Chapel frescoes, that is reflected on

[49] White (1966), 131.

[50] White (1966), 304.

[51] Falk and Lányi (1943), 132–53.

the doors.[52] As is true at Padua, each scene on the doors contains a limited number of protagonists and, except when the intention is to depict a crowd, there is considerable space between and around them. A single, focused image lent significance by means of isolation – by the lack of distracting ancillary themes and motifs – provides the content of each narrative. Architectural props are used sparingly to suggest the setting, to aid in the compositional symmetry or focus, and to provide a limited but nevertheless sufficient spatial scope.

By contrast, Giotto's late Florentine style presents significant differences from the Baptistry reliefs (Figs. 6, 218). Compared to the Peruzzi Chapel frescoes, the bronze panels display a marked reduction in narrative content and in figural action. In almost every comparison, a crowd of people in the paintings is reduced to three or four individuals, a small group to a single figure. In some cases, as in the *Annunciation to Zacharias* (Figs. 6, 218), extraneous figures are eliminated altogether. Invariably, the energetic action of figures in the frescoes (and even more so in the mosaics) is reduced to quiet, concentrated gesture on the doors. Moreover, Giotto displays a stronger interest in classical art than does Andrea on the doors. (It is on the Campanile that the impact of classical art is most evident in the work of Andrea. See chapter 7.) In the frescoed *Annunciation to Zacharias* the stately classicizing figures are dressed in heavy garments that fall in vertical or almost vertical folds. This contrasts strongly with the bronze figures, which recall, in their softer, more swinging rhythms, Sienese and French Gothic art. Even the design of the *baldacchino* in Santa Croce speaks a different language: Nothing intrudes on or softens the insistent rectangularity of Giotto's painted architecture, the columns of which bear classicizing capitals. The woman holding the infant in the *Birth and Naming of the Baptist* (Fig. 39) recalls a Roman matriarch, and the baby John himself resembles ancient sculptures of the nude infant Hercules.[53] In contrast, Andrea portrays the infant tightly swaddled (Fig. 10) (as indeed it is shown in the Baptistry mosaics), and he depicts Mary holding the child close to her bosom, gracefully bending her head toward him. For the most part, he eschews deliberate classical references in the bronze reliefs. What emerges from these observations is the picture of an artist reinterpreting Giottesque values in terms of a new Gothicism (a theme to be elaborated on in chapter 8).

The compelling focus on the essentials of the narrative, with landscape and architectural motifs participating in the concentrated effect, the emphasis on the plasticity of the figures, and the sense of humble dignity evoked by the protagonists of the sacred tale

[52] This is perceived by Kreytenberg (1975), 235. It is very likely that the style of the Paduan frescoes was visible in Florence in the Badia, described by Vasari as Giotto's earliest paintings.

[53] Borsook and Tintori (1965), 18.

clearly reveal Andrea's profound sympathy for the artistic goals of Giotto, particularly his early style as we know it from Padua. By the time of the Peruzzi Chapel frescoes, Giotto himself had already, to some extent, abandoned this aesthetic in favor of an expansion of narrative content and a concomitant enrichment of architectural and drapery motifs. Moreover, Giotto's evolution from the Arena to the Peruzzi Chapel frescoes is characterized by a more coherent disposition of figure groups. At Padua, a crowd is represented by means of two or three individual figures behind which one glimpses a few heads, for example, in the *Watching of the Rods* (Fig. 215) – the same device for depicting a group of people seen on Andrea's doors. By contrast, in Giotto's *Naming of the Baptist* in Florence, the group to the right is composed of several persons standing in rows that move diagonally into space (Fig. 39).

If there is little reflection of the style of the Peruzzi Chapel frescoes on the Baptistry doors, its impact on the Campanile reliefs is notable. Indeed, Andrea's evolution from the doors to the Campanile parallels, in many ways, Giotto's own development. A telling comparison can be made between the *Visit of the Disciples* on the doors and *Medicine* on the Campanile (Figs. 18, 68). In both reliefs a cubic object (architecture or furniture) is seen on the right and a group of people on the left. Compositionally, the two masses in each relief balance each other. But in the bronze panel the space-creating oblique placement of the building is not balanced by the disposition of the figures, which are huddled together into a single mass with no sense of recession. Whenever a crowd is represented on the doors, it is done by means of a few full-length figures between which are thrust several torsoless heads. In the marble relief, by contrast, the chair seen from the right receding toward the left is balanced by the figures, which are arranged in planes receding toward the right. This coherent disposition is similar to that in Giotto's *Naming of the Baptist* in Santa Croce (Figs. 68, 39).

In a single figure, too, the influence of the Florentine frescoes is evident. Similar as the figure of Zacharias on the doors and the Sculptor on the Campanile are (Figs. 10, 57) (the comparison formed the basis for the attribution of the marble to the master's hand), the later figure is no longer seated in profile; rather, it is turned slightly to the three-quarter view so that the hollow of the chest is visible, resulting in a greater emphasis on the solidity of the forms and their projection back in space. The same turn to the three-quarter view is seen in Giotto's figure of Zacharias in the Peruzzi Chapel (Fig. 39). In the marble relief as in the painting, moreover, the spaces are closed off by rear walls, the materiality of which is evidenced in the one case by the nail and tool hung from it, in the other by a small niche that contains a water vase. It is perhaps not coincidental that the statue being carved by the sculptor bears a striking resemblance in pose to the infant Baptist held out by the woman in the painting (Figs. 39, 57).

The representation of space in some of the hexagons not only reflects Giotto's achievements in Florence but in some cases even goes beyond them.[54] The development of spatial representation in the fourteenth century involved a process of bringing a well-defined spatial block – a dollhouse, in effect – closer and closer to the picture plane until its walls extended sufficiently forward of that plane so that the space and figures all appear to be behind it.[55] Like the oblique dollhouse interiors of the Arena Chapel frescoes, Giotto's *Birth of the Baptist* contains a structure that still reveals the forward edges of the architecture. In *Sculpture* and *Medicine* on the Campanile, no fragmentary wall separates the viewer from the interior space. Until the invention of linear perspective in the fifteenth century, there are no significant advances in spatial representation in relief sculpture. Neither Orcagna's *Life of the Virgin* nor Nanni di Banco's *Sculpture* at Or San Michele (Fig. 229) employs devices that go beyond those originated by Andrea.

It seems clear that the Santa Croce cycle had a greater impact on the Campanile reliefs, particularly the early group of hexagons, than on the doors. The marble reliefs reveal a more profound concern with illusionistic space, have more complex compositions, and display a greater emphasis on settings than do the bronze panels. These observations bring to light a curious characteristic of Andrea's creative processes: There is to be noted a rather consistent "time lag" in his assimilation of influences. The impact of recent experiences is rarely felt immediately in his sculpture; it must await experimentation with and assimilation of prior influences before visible references to the more recent events are seen. This would partially explain why the influence of Orvieto appears to be much stronger on the Campanile than on the doors, and why it is on the Campanile and *not* on the Baptistry that we find the strongest reflection of some of Giotto's later achievements in both figural and spatial representation. However, the circumstances of Andrea's Florentine commissions may also explain the variable nature of his relationship to Giotto. During the period when Andrea was designing the reliefs for the doors (presumably between 1330 and 1332), he probably had little contact with the painter, who, after all, was the head of a workshop in Naples between 1328 and 1332. After 1334, when Giotto became capomaestro of Florence Cathedral, Andrea came into the closest possible association with the great painter. Undoubtedly Giotto had a hand in the choice of a sculptor to be given the commission for the Campanile reliefs. He

---

[54] Borsook and Tintori (1965), 8–14, cite evidence that the Baptist cycle, at least, was completed before Giotto left for Naples in 1328. In this case, the designs for the bronze reliefs post- date the frescoes by a few years. The Evangelist cycle, however, may not have been completed until 1335.

[55] White (1967), 39.

must have recognized in Andrea a kindred artistic spirit and a disciple. It is easy to imagine the numerous discussions, the exchange of ideas and fertile consultations between the great aged painter and the younger sculptor when the Campanile reliefs – that is, the hexagons belonging to Group I – were initiated. And Giotto's expectations were surely fulfilled, for the early Campanile reliefs are completely in harmony with his artistic goals.

After his death in 1337, however, the painter's influence diminished to some extent. Having achieved the authority and dignity of the title of capomaestro, it is not surprising that Andrea pursued new goals. In the second group of hexagons, Andrea abandons the three-dimensional mode of representation and returns to one in which there is little or no indication of setting and in which a flat neutral background provides the back plane of the relief. Concomitant with the reduction in peripheral figures and objects in this group of hexagons, and a simplification of compositions, there is an increase in the monumentality of the figures, which no longer display the fluid, calligraphic draperies of Andrea's earlier style. At this point, a new influence makes itself felt, and that is the influence, as we shall see, of classical sculpture. Giotto's impact, of course, has not been negated; it is evident, however, in a general way – in the desire to present idealized, generic images unencumbered by particularized actions or individualized details.[56] The paintings of Giotto were and remained of vital importance to Andrea even after he left Florence. The *Madonna and Child* in Santa Maria della Spina, with its flourish of calligraphic drapery folds and its moderate Gothic sway, reflects stylistic influxes from north of the Alps, but the insistent balance, poise, and sense of weight are deeply indebted to Giotto.

In exploring the milieu into which Andrea was placed upon his arrival in Florence, it is necessary to look beyond monumental painting of the early fourteenth century. Although Giotto's workshop dominates, a second current can be isolated that, while often influenced by Giotto, nevertheless remained independent from his art,[57] and, as we shall see, the stamp of this alternative current is apparent in Andrea's sculpture. Best exemplified by the productions coming from Pacino di Bonaguida's workshop, this activity is the result of a miniaturist taste that prefers lively particulars to austere or dra-

---

[56] An analogous change may be observed at Santa Croce: The figure style, gestures, and compositions on the right-hand wall of the Peruzzi Chapel – the Evangelist cycle – are grander and more monumental than in the Baptist cycle on the opposite wall. Borsook and Tintori (1965), 19f., observe that for this reason the Evangelist cycle had the greater appeal to such painters as Masaccio and Michelangelo. If the Evangelist cycle was the later design, as seems likely (see n. 54), then perhaps the new style, in a very general way, influenced Andrea's second relief group.

[57] Offner (1927a), 3f.; (1927b), 1f.

matic generalizations. Even in a large panel painting such as the *Tree of Life* in the Accademia, a work of the first decade of the fourteenth century, Pacino displays a delicate touch and attention to detail that betrays his principal role as that of illuminator.[58]

In several respects, Andrea's approach to the design of individual reliefs on the doors recalls the art of the small panel painter or miniaturist. One might compare the *Annunciation to Zacharias* with Pacino's tiny medallion representing the Presentation in the Temple from the *Tree of Life* (Figs. 5, 219). In both, the tabernacle is a mere symbol of the larger setting and is used to frame and link the protagonists; in neither are the figures – in contrast to Giotto's fresco in Santa Croce – set within a spatially conceived structure. Not only the architectural form in the background, but the treatment of the altar and the symmetry of the composition in the relief are reminiscent in their precision and delicacy – despite the monumentality of the whole – of the dainty rendering on the panel.

These characteristics belong to the miniaturist tradition as a whole and are not unique to Florence. A more direct connection to Pacino's art can be discerned, however, with regard to the Morgan illuminations of ca. 1320.[59] Paradoxically, while Pacino's large *Tree of Life* takes on the character of a miniature, some of his illuminations have a simplicity of composition and a focus on the essential message of the narrative that results in an unexpected monumentality. Obviously, here we are witnessing the impact of Giotto. Among the most impressive of these leaves is the *Visitation* (Fig. 221). Andrea's corresponding relief on the doors is strikingly close in composition (Fig. 8). Both contain a tall architectural structure with an arched opening and a projection above the arch on the right; from this the figure of Elizabeth emerges. In the center stands the embracing Virgin and to the left a single accompanying figure. Figures and architecture stand on an implied ground plane, the horizon of which, in the illumination, is seen on the lower left. All are placed in front of a blank, unadorned background plane. The iconography and compositional scheme of Andrea's *Visitation* (Fig. 8) are closer to those in Pacino's illustration than to any of the versions seen in Pisa, Pistoia, Orvieto, or in the Baptistry of Florence itself.

Several illuminations in the Morgan manuscript can be compared to representations on the doors (Figs. 220–223). In Pacino's *Noli Me Tangere* and Andrea's *Preaching of the Baptist*, the platforms on which the figures stand develop smoothly and directly into parallel mountain ranges; between these, in each case, a tree juts up into the sky (Figs. 12, 223). The protagonist in each scene is framed by the rocky forms on

[58] On Pacino di Bonaguida, see, in addition to Offner (n. 57), Degenhart and Schmitt (1968), 22; Harrsen and Boyce (1953), 13f.; Smart (1971), 238–42.

[59] Boyce (1953), 13f.

the right. The austerity of the designs in both the Morgan manuscripts and the Baptistry doors goes beyond that sought by Giotto and is relieved only by the decorative embellishment of the framework, the linear scrolls in the one, and the quatrefoil moldings in the other example.[60]

The bronze seated Virtues are among the most monumental of Andrea's figures on the Baptistry doors. And yet they seem to have been inspired by – or at the very least closely resemble – several of the Virtues drawn by Francesco da Barberino for his *Documenti d'Amore* of 1309–13 (cf. Figs. 27, 224).[61] The frontal symmetry, splayed-out arms, the garments broadly draped over the projecting knees, the folds breaking and resting on the platforms below the seat are comparable. Even the device of a curtain hung from a rod in the background, which is seen in the Herod scenes (Figs. 16, 20, 22), occurs earlier in the *Documenti*.

The foregoing comparisons confirm the dualism that we have noted again and again on the doors. The narrative economy, the plasticity of the forms, and the strong idealism of the images reveal Andrea's profound debt to Giotto, whereas the tendency toward symmetry, the decorative linear quality, the attention to detail, and the simplified compositions (these last reinforcing Andrea's Sienese-Gothic tendencies) would seem to owe much to the non-Giottesque current discernible in Florence after the turn of the century.

We have seen that the style of Giovanni's followers persisted in the workshops in Pisa and Siena during the early trecento. But a countercurrent is recognizable in both cities, the roots of which go back to the art of Nicola. Pisan goldsmiths tended to conserve the values of this older art. The brief appearance in Pisa, first of Tino, then of Simone Martini, artists inclined toward a restrained and lyrical aesthetic, lent authority to this countermovement and provided an important influence on the formation of Andrea Pisano.

If the values of Nicola's art persisted as an artistic undercurrent in Pisa, in Siena his sculpture – particularly the richly pictorial style of the Siena pulpit and the more mellow, fluid style of the Perugia fountain – was to be of decisive importance to the development of the relief at the turn of the century. Many aspects of Nicola's art continued to exert an important influence on the sculpture of Andrea, as well. As was true of some of his contemporaries working in Siena, Andrea rejected Giovanni's energetic compositions

[60] To this we might add, however, that something of the linear energy of the mosaic is retained by Andrea in contrast to the more static rhythms of the illumination.

[61] On Francesco da Barberino, see Degenhart and Schmitt (1968), 31–8.

and dramatic emotional content, preferring instead the classical composure and compositional restraint of Nicola's reliefs. Even his treatment of landscape owes much to his predecessor: The naturalistic softening of landscape forms seen on the Campanile – in contrast to the still prevalent Byzantinizing conventions on the facade of Orvieto (Figs. 205, 210) or on the Arca di San Cerbone – was initiated by Nicola in the Perugia fountain (Fig. 189). Andrea and Nicola also share similar responses to antique sculpture as a comparison of the figure *Uxor* on the fountain and the standing woman in *Weaving* on the Campanile indicate (Figs. 61, 238). The graceful contrapposto stance, the rhythmic pattern of the thin, gently curving drapery folds, the transparency of the garment to reveal the beauty of the female form – all these aspects of the Campanile relief speak of a deep absorption of Nicola's late art. One need only compare these examples to any of Giovanni's classicizing female figures with their more angular drapery folds, tense contrapposto stances, and aggressive psychological presences to recognize an alternative response to classical statuary.

Siena, then, provided a rich sculptural milieu essential to Andrea's early development. In that city a variety of styles emerged: Tino di Camaino, Goro di Gregorio, the Orvieto masters, and the sculptors of the upper facade of the Duomo, among others, established independent modes in which were intermingled, with differing emphases, sources not only in the Pisani traditions but in the art of Arnolfo, Giotto, and the Gothic North. The Arnolfian–Giottesque tradition springing from Nicola's early sculpture profoundly affected Andrea's sense of plasticity, figure style, and narrative conception. The calligraphic linear rhythms and the solemn, lyrical mood of Andrea's art, on the other hand, owe a great deal to early trecento painting and sculpture in Siena. This tendency was reinforced, as we shall see, by currents from north of the Alps.

Florence, however, offered a cultural (and, as we shall see in the following chapter, economic and political) environment seemingly calculated to exploit Andrea's potential leading to his greatest achievements in sculpture and architecture. Relatively barren sculpturally, the city was the center of an extraordinarily rich development in the field of painting, and it offered diverse traditions, uniquely suited to Andrea's artistic temperament, from which he could draw. Moreover, a number of projects left incomplete awaited the talents of a master who could match the achievements and integrate the traditions of Italian Gothic art as it had developed up to that time.

The Baptistry doors clearly reveal Andrea's profound knowledge of the decisive achievements of the great masters of late dugento and early trecento Italian art. In his relief conception as well as his figure style, in the details of his ornamentation as well as in the broad architectonic elements of his designs, Andrea was an eclectic artist who drew with sensitivity of purpose and execution from a variety of sources. He inherited from Nicola and Giovanni an attitude, for instance, that permitted the free intermingling of Gothic and classicizing elements.[62] On the Baptistry doors the Gothic quatrefoil is surrounded by classicizing moldings and dentils. The very shape of the quatrefoil, in particular the extremely springy contour of each lobe (which is greater than a half circle), recalls the trefoil arches beneath the relief panels on Nicola's pulpits. At the same time, more in tune with the art of Nicola and Arnolfo than with that of Giovanni, Andrea imposes a clear separation of ornamental elements. Although his design lacks the lushness and dense plasticity of Nicola's forms, each part – quatrefoil, dentil, molding – stands out in pristine clarity. While he abjures the unrelenting geometry of Arnolfo – as seen, for example, in the Ciborium in San Paolo fuori le Mura – the relative economy of the design and details recalls Arnolfo's handling of forms.

Furthermore, the relief mode, compositional devices, and many details are taken over or modified from the painting or sculpture then visible in Pisa, Siena, Orvieto, and Florence. The art of the goldsmith and miniaturist contributed something to the decorative sensibility and the effect of preciousness seen in the Baptistry reliefs. Giotto, on the other hand, inspired the compelling focus on the essentials of the narratives, the broad plasticity of the figures, and the solemn dignity with which they act out their destinies.

Andrea's relationship to Giotto is more complex than has hitherto been perceived. Indirectly, Giotto's painting had played a role in the early formation of Andrea's style. The wooden *Annunziata* is imbued with a restrained and graceful elegance that distantly reflects French Gothic sculpture, but the determining influences would seem to be the architectonic and classicizing approach to the human figure of Arnolfo and Giotto.

In Florence the Baptistry reliefs, although indebted iconographically to the mosaics and the Peruzzi Chapel frescoes, reflect the style and artistic goals of Giotto's Paduan period. Later, when Andrea and Giotto were working together on the Campanile project, direct, daily contact with the painter stimulated the sculptor's development. Anticipating some of the concerns of the Early Renaissance, the first group of hexagons reveals an interest in the representation of interior space and coherent figure groups, manifestly influenced by the Peruzzi Chapel frescoes. In his second group of hexagons, no longer under the direct influence of Giotto, but nevertheless indebted to his example, Andrea pursues a monumental, classicizing style that finds no counterpart (as will become clear in the following chapter) in trecento Tuscany. After his departure from Florence, he continues to evolve a classicizing style integrated, with increasing sophistication, with Gothic forms and rhythms.

[62] On the pulpits we find Gothic capitals on classicizing columns, classical cornices above bundled Gothic columns, and arches with Gothic cusps but with rounded classical profiles.

Trained in or near Pisa, where he received his earliest commissions, Andrea must have spent some time in Siena and Orvieto gaining the expertise that qualified him for his major creations in Florence. His roots are recognizable. But the transformations of his sources result ultimately in a unique and highly personal style. Several aspects of this style, touched upon earlier, still require discussion, particularly the sources of Andrea's art in the classical tradition and in French Gothic sculpture.

CHAPTER SEVEN

Andrea Pisano and Classical Sculpture

According to a notion that has become generally accepted, the interest in classical antiquity on the part of fourteenth-century sculptors retreats from a peak achieved in the dugento to such an extent that the Renaissance, in the words of Panofsky, had to begin "as it were, from zero."[1] One need only compare, however, Ghiberti's Adam and Eve on the Gates of Paradise (Fig. 227) to their fourteenth-century predecessors on the Campanile of Florence (Figs. 50, 51) to recognize that the latter, more than any classical source, provided the initial stimulus for Ghiberti's conceptions. The *Hercules* on the Porta della Mandorla has its precedent on the Campanile (Figs. 65, 228), where he appears, together with several other ancient heroes, as a pagan benefactor of mankind.[2] Nanni di Banco's relief below the *Quattro Coronati* on Or San Michele derives from the Campanile relief representing Sculpture (Figs. 57, 229). And Donatello's freestanding bronze nude *David*, which continues to elude reference to a specific antique source despite its manifest classicism, is prefigured in Andrea Pisano's miniature bronze Christ on the Baptistry doors, and also in the sculpture (significantly, a nude figure in-the-round) being carved by the Sculptor on the Campanile (Figs. 45, 46, 57). Finally, Donatello's conception of the mounted Saint George in the relief from Or

[1] Panofsky (1960), 150, 162; Telpaz (1964), 372–6.

The material in this chapter, together with por-

tions of chapter 2, were combined in Moskowitz (1983b).

[2] Seznec (1961), 30–1.

San Michele derives from *Horsemanship* (Fig. 60).[3] The profound classicism of the Campanile reliefs has been largely overlooked perhaps because it is less archaeological than the classicism of Nicola and Giovanni Pisano, and more modulated by a Gothic poise and a Franciscan spirit than that of Arnolfo di Cambio. Yet not a single figure by Giotto is as evocative of the "classic" phase of Greek sculpture or its derivatives as is the standing figure in *Weaving* (Fig. 62); not a single other nude by a painter or sculptor of the period evinces the Phidian proportions, the feeling for the relationship of bone to flesh, the suggestion of both muscular firmness and sensuous softness as does the Adam on the Campanile of Florence (Fig. 50).[4]

This chapter sets out, first to define classicism as it relates to the Italian Gothic period; second, to provide a preliminary discussion of the limitations inherent in the search for classical sources during this period; and finally, to cite numerous specific examples in Andrea's sculpture of classicizing forms that, with a reasonable degree of plausibility, may be related to antique sculpture.

A common definition of the term classicism, appropriate to a discussion of medieval art, is the use of Greco-Roman motifs to enrich the artist's mode of expression. When Nicola Pisano in his Pisan Baptistry pulpit chose to convey the spiritual attributes of Fortitude (or, as has recently been proposed, Daniel[5]) by means of physical characteristics rather than merely by way of symbolic accoutrements, he chose an antique Hercules for his model. However, although an ancient figure is quoted almost literally, one important aspect of the classical spirit is lacking, an aspect Kenneth Clark calls the "belief in physical beauty that underlies even the squarest athletes of Polycleitus."[6]

A rather different exploitation of antique motifs, thus illustrating a second definition of classicism, occurs in Tuscan painting of the first half of the fourteenth century in which representations of antique sculpture or architectural elements are included for iconographic purposes: A "Trajan" column in a fresco in the upper church at Assisi refers to locale; the statuettes decorating Herod's palace in Giotto's Santa Croce fresco

---

[3] Janson (1963), 30, referring to Schubring (1907), xvii. One might add that even the *schiacciato* technique in that relief may owe something to the landscape scenes on the Campanile with their suggestion of fluid space.

[4] The bibliography on classical revivals in the Middle Ages is too extensive to cite here. It is notable, however, that the following writers who discuss classicism in the work of the Pisani, the Orvieto masters, and Giotto fail to refer to Andrea in this context: Clark (1956), 86–90; Panofsky (1960), 145–56; Rowland (1963), 136–41; Tel-

paz (1964); Vermeule (1964), 27–30. Surprisingly little attention has been paid to classical influence in the sculpture of Andrea Pisano. Even those writers who have observed the sculptor's classicizing tendencies have consistently failed to cite specific sources, writing as though classicism were a self-evident phenomenon; these include Antal (1948), 244; Becherucci and Brunetti (1969), 18; Carli (1969), 50–1; Lányi (1933b), 94–8; I. Toesca (1950), 74, n. 79.

[5] Angiola (1977), 1–17.

[6] Clark (1956), 39.

refer to the pagan culture of King Herod. Panofsky notes that such classical motifs then begin to invade the picture itself; no longer "petrified" into would-be antique sculpture, these now become the living personae of the painted world itself.[7] The figures of Pax and Securitas in Ambrogio Lorenzetti's *Buon Governo* frescoes are examples of such an assimilation, the function of which may have been to convey a political message: In the concept of good government an ancient Roman ideal is revived. These quotations or references generally remain isolated and relatively minor iconographic or decorative elements that do not determine the fundamental character of the styles. If the palace of Herod in Giotto's fresco were decorated with Gothic tabernacles and Gothicizing statuettes, the iconography would be somewhat modified but the essential narrative content and revolutionary style would remain unaltered. Similarly, the figure of Pax in Lorenzetti's fresco could conceivably be replaced by a figure more Gothic in its proportions and drapery style without altering the civic message in any fundamental way.

A third definition of classicism — one derived from the characteristics of the "classic" periods of Greek and Roman art — refers to that desire, in J. J. Pollitt's words, "to find a balance between the representation of the specific and the generic and to make the viewer acutely conscious of both."[8] Finally, the term is sometimes used in a purely formal context: a balance achieved between solids and voids, verticals and horizontals, the sense of movement and stability, etc. Among the unique characteristics of the Arena Chapel frescoes is the fact that they embody these latter manifestations of classicism: Exalted spiritual ideals are harmonized with human emotions; broad generalized drapery forms receive their specific patterns from the pull of gravity and the play of gesture; gestures and poses themselves convey both universal emotions and individual responses. At the same time, Giotto achieves formal harmonies in the relationship of shapes, colors, and values, and these are somehow coordinated with the narrative and psychological content of his paintings. In this extraordinary synthesis, Giotto remains unique for this period.

The artistic scope of Andrea Pisano — or at least the nature of his commissions — was more limited than Giotto's. Nevertheless, during his Campanile period, Andrea, too, achieves a new unity in terms of form and content, both of which embody conscious references to the antique.

The search for classical sources during the Italian Gothic period has, however, a number of obvious limitations. Only in rare cases can one find examples of direct borrowings from ancient remains that can be proven to have been extant and visible in the thirteenth and fourteenth centuries. Among these are the numerous sarcophagi reused

[7] Panofsky (1960), 148. [8] Pollitt (1972), 195.

for Christian tombs throughout the Middle Ages, many of which are still found in the Camposanto in Pisa and elsewhere in Italy. For example, the Phaedra sarcophagus in the Camposanto was reused in 1076 for the burial of Countess Beatrice of Tuscany and stood outside the Duomo in Nicola Pisano's lifetime.[9] In his Pisa Baptistry pulpit, several motifs appear to be quotations from the Phaedra sarcophagus.[10] The historical evidence, in this case, corroborates the assumption, based on visual connections, that the Roman work provided sources for Nicola's pulpit.

Far more numerous than the few examples of verifiable direct borrowings are the countless motifs that resemble classical prototypes but for which we cannot prove that a specific source was available to the Gothic artist. A most useful purpose would be served by attempting to establish a "Handlist of Antiques" known to the Middle Ages comparable to Krautheimer's list of works probably or possibly available to Ghiberti,[11] or comparable to the *Census of Antique Works Known to the Renaissance* (established by the Warburg and Courtauld Institutes and the Institute of Fine Arts, New York University). Lacking such a list, however, we do well to keep in mind that ancient monuments and motifs tend to be stereotypes – that, for example, a reclining male figure with one leg raised and bent, and head leaning on one hand, can be a Bacchus, a fallen warrior, or a river god, and that these figures are repeated innumerable times on Roman sarcophagi scattered throughout the world. Furthermore, much of what is known to have existed during the Gothic period in Italy is either unidentifiable or no longer extant. A manuscript entitled *Libro della composizione del mundo*, written by Ristoro d'Arezzo and dated 1282, speaks of a great quantity of Etruscan vases recently discovered and includes descriptions of painted and sculptured motifs.[12] Even in the fourteenth century there appeared rare individuals with decidedly antiquarian interests. One such personality is Oliviero Forzetto, who, as early as 1335, formed a collection of ancient marbles, bronzes, coins, and engraved gems.[13] Thus, even when a specific prototype is lacking, we are justified in assuming a direct borrowing if the resemblance to some known ancient work is close enough. Both Nicola and Giovanni transformed figures of Hercules, and the latter a Venus Pudica, into Christian symbols. So startling is the resemblance to Roman examples, so innovative the adaptation not only of motif but also of style, that we must assume the borrowings are direct and not through medieval intermediaries.

Finally, there exist figures and compositions that look antique and yet do not resem-

---

[9] Ragusa (1951), 97.

[10] For an extensive examination of the influence of antique sculpture on Nicola Pisano, see Seidel (1975), 307–92.

[11] Krautheimer (1970), 337–52.

[12] Chastel (1959), 165–80.

[13] Weiss (1969), 28.

ble any specific known ancient work. Andrea's standing woman in *Weaving* on the Campanile (Fig. 62) is acclaimed by all observers as astonishingly Attic in flavor. Greek art, however, was practically unknown to the Italians of this period, and no one thus far has been able to find a Roman copy or revival of a Greek prototype that is sufficiently close to the Gothic relief to permit citation as a possible source. And yet, to deny the classicism of the figure, so evocative of Greek classical sculpture or its derivatives, is to disregard visual associations of a primary order.

With the foregoing considerations in mind, we may proceed to search for classical elements and their prototypes in the sculpture of Andrea Pisano.

The bronze reliefs on the Baptistry of Florence contain a number of isolated quotations from or references to antique motifs. The seated Zacharias in the *Naming of the Baptist* depends on ancient Roman patriarch types seen on sarcophagi (Figs. 10, 230).[14] The disciples of the Baptist are given historical authenticity by means of their Roman togas, and the guards wear antique, not medieval, armor (Figs. 17, 18). (This is in contrast to Giotto's Baptist cycle in which the drapery is classicizing without being consistently classical; e.g., the male figures wear mantles but not togas.) The background curtain in the Herod scenes may be a reference to antiquity, for curtains sometimes appear in the background of Roman sarcophagi.[15] One figure on the doors is startling in its classicism: Christ in the *Baptism of Christ* (Fig. 45). This beautiful nude conveys an impression that soft yet taut flesh surrounds an underlying skeletal structure, its geometry revealing itself as the light glides over its surface. Several characteristics of the bronze Christ are seen in some Greek and Roman bronzes of the type to which, for example, the "Idolino" in the Museo Archeologico in Florence belongs: the youthful, slender frame with narrow shoulders, the peculiar swelling of the abdomen, the smooth transitions from plane to plane (as opposed to the hard, linear markings of the Polycleitan canon) and the soft yet taut quality of the modeling. As is true of the makers of the ancient bronzes – particularly those on a small scale – Andrea exploited the possibilities for tactile sensuosity inherent in the process of modeling in wax, a process in which the malleable material responds to the subtlest pressures exerted by the fingers; hence the minute transitions on the light-catching surfaces.[16] As is characteristic of

[14] See n. 28, this chapter.

[15] An example is a sarcophagus, still extant, that stood beside the south portal of the Baptistry in Florence. This sarcophagus is mentioned by Dante and so could have been seen by Andrea. See Seymour (1966), 62 and 229, n. 7, who cites the Roman relief as a source for the curtain symbolism

in Nanni di Banco's *Quattro Coronati*.

[16] It is surprising that in the search for models for Donatello's *David* the Baptistry Christ has never been mentioned as a possible source. Like the *David*, the body of Christ is not that of a muscle-bound athlete (Figs. 45, 46); in this, it contrasts strongly with the exaggerated muscularity and

medieval classicism in general, however, there is little integration or consistent use of classical elements on the doors. If the garments of the disciples are reminiscent of Roman togas, the rhythms of the folds are clearly Gothic; and while the body of Christ evokes ancient sculptures, the head, as has often been noted, recalls the *Beau Dieu* of Amiens.

Compared to the Baptistry reliefs, the Campanile hexagons reveal a more integrated adaptation of antique elements. In the *Creation of Adam* and the *Creation of Eve* (Figs. 50, 51), one may discern a continuing response to the tactile qualities of antique nudes – this time marble rather than bronze sculptures. The treatment here is freer than on the doors. The taut skin that envelops Christ in the *Baptism* (Fig. 45) has become softer in the representation of Adam, whose pose and proportions, moreover, recall numerous figures on sarcophagi, for example, a fallen hunter in Oxford,[17] a figure of Phaeton on a sarcophagus in Florence (which was known in the trecento),[18] and a Bacchic figure in the Camposanto in Pisa (Fig. 231), this last the most likely source for Andrea.[19] Pose and proportions are almost identical, and behind the figure is a form reminiscent of the lowest of the trees in the background of the hexagon.[20] Eve, in the second Campanile relief, is strikingly similar to a figure on a Roman sarcophagus front, of Hellenistic style, in the Museo dell'Opera del Duomo in Siena

antisensual quality of the nudes of Nicola and Giovanni Pisano on the pulpits.

A number of antique small bronzes have been suggested as possible sources for Donatello's figure; as relatively few discoveries of bronze statuettes occurred before 1430 (Krautheimer [1970], 378), it is possible that what was known to the Early Renaissance masters was already known to the fourteenth century. On possible sources for Donatello's *David*, see Janson (1966), 77–103; and for the *Hercules* on the Porta della Mandorla, Krautheimer (1970), 280. See also Trachtenberg's suggestion of an Etruscan bronze source for Donatello's earlier marble *David* (1968), 268–9.

[17] This is cited by Krautheimer (1970), 340, as a possible prototype for a figure in Ghiberti's *Expulsion from the Temple*. In a number of ways, the Roman figure is closer to our Adam than to Ghiberti's figure. The inner contour of the chest and stomach, the turn of the head, the upward thrust of the shoulder and the raised arm (now broken off) find close counterparts in the Florentine marble relief.

[18] Krautheimer (1970), 340.

[19] This *Bacchus* has been suggested as the source for one of the reclining nudes in Nicola's *Last Judgment* at Pisa. See Seidel (1975), 300–90, p. 382.

[20] Another reclining figure on the west face of the Campanile, *Noah* (Fig. 56), also has classical antecedents. But this time the ultimate source, which may have been a drunken figure on a Dionysian relief or a reclining figure on the lid of an Etruscan urn, probably came to Andrea by way of earlier medieval precedents such as those in the Tree of Jesse on the piers of Orvieto Cathedral or in the Baptistry mosaic. See Carli (1947b), Pl. 22, and de Witt (1954), Pl. XXV, respectively. It is noteworthy, however, that the deceased on Etruscan urns often hold libation bowls resembling the upturned vessel held by Noah.

(Fig. 232). According to an old Sienese tradition, the Roman work was found on the site of a temple dedicated to Minerva, the very site on which the Cathedral of Siena was being built. The treatment of Eve's upper torso seen in three-quarter view with one arm raised, the other crossing the body below the breasts, repeats that of the nudes carrying the shell. More important than similarities of motif, however, is the fact that, as in the ancient example, the female nude here is conceived as a lovely, soft, and sensuous form, a conception unequaled in the trecento and speaking clearly for an intense response to Hellenizing classical antecedents. Such a response is prefigured in Nicola's Fontana Maggiore where, in contrast to his monumental nudes, the small figures of Adam and Eve (Fig. 190) seem closer to the spirit of classical nudes. The corresponding figures on the piers of Orvieto, although also to some extent influenced by antique prototypes,[21] are harder, more angular, and less classically proportioned than the Campanile nudes. In the *Creation of Adam* at Orvieto (Fig. 205), the head of Adam is quite large in relation to the torso, the arms are elongated, and the body twisted along opposing axes that remain unintegrated. Moreover, the reclining figure lacks the sense of weight and counterpressure that one feels in the first hexagon in Florence (Fig. 50), in which the disposition of Adam's arm and the thrust of his elbow are in response to the weight of his head and torso. The nudes at Orvieto would seem rather to reflect northern Gothic canons as a comparison, for example, to the figures in the *Last Judgment* at Bourges suggests (Figs. 206, 207).

The Creation scenes, then, point to a new sensitivity to the tactile qualities and proportions of classical nudes. The Genesis reliefs also reveal a new concern with the depiction of landscape (Figs. 50, 51, 56), a concern that, as we have seen, was undoubtedly stimulated by the achievements of early fourteenth-century Sienese painting and sculpture. It is possible, however, that Andrea became acquainted with some examples of ancient Roman landscape reliefs, which are often modeled to suggest atmospheric effects and a gently receding ground. A relief in Berlin contains a number of motifs that are very similar to those in the *Creation of Adam*: a figure reclining or seated on the ground on one side in relationship to a standing figure slightly off center on the other, a ground plane composed of rounded clumps of earth, several trees, and a blank background evocative of space and sky (Figs. 50, 234).[22]

---

[21] Telpaz (1964), 394; Clark (1956), 373.

[22] Cf. also other pictorial reliefs modeled to suggest atmosphere such as a fountain relief in Palestrina and a relief showing an offering to Priapus in Aquileia, illustrated in Bandinelli (1971), Figs. 207 and 96. The composition and landscape treatment of the *Labors of Adam and Eve* (Fig. 52) on the Campanile are particularly close to features in the latter relief. In one significant aspect, Andrea goes beyond his classical sources: It will be noted that in the four landscape settings on the west face of the Campanile, the ground plane appears to recede into the distance. This is achieved partly by means of the soft modeling and the lack of

The adaptation of a reclining figure to an architectural or decorative molding is a frequent device in classical sculpture, one seen, for example, in Trajan's Arch at Benevento and in a medallion on the Arch of Constantine in Rome.[23] In a similar way, the position of the Campanile Adam follows the slope of the hexagonal frame, which provides a comfortable support for the distribution of weight in this particular pose. Also of classical derivation is the device of cutting across the hexagonal frame to provide a horizontal platform for the figures as seen in *Jubal* and *Jubalcain*. This recalls a similar device in the medallions on the Arch of Constantine.[24]

Archaeological evidence has revealed that the hexagons on the west face of the Campanile were inserted into the fabric of the wall simultaneously with the incrustation – that is, during Giotto's tenure as capomaestro, and therefore before his death in 1337. All the other hexagons were inserted after the application of the marble incrustation to the wall.[25] For this reason, and because they embellish the most important side of the bell tower, it is not unreasonable to assume that the Genesis scenes were the first reliefs to be designed and executed. Stylistic considerations tend to support this view: Drapery, figure style, the evident concern with landscape and spatial representation, and the principles of composition are closest among all the hexagons to those of the bronze doors (Appendix B, Fig. 5).

The early reliefs on the west side of the Campanile reveal, then, an interest in the depiction of classicizing figures and an especial concern with the representation of landscape. Elements from ancient art, however, tend to be applied to the medieval iconogra-

---

abrupt transition from ground to sky, and partly by means of a relatively high horizon line. Unlike the classical reliefs, the figures do not stand or lie on a three-dimensional ground plane; the horizon lines can be discerned, for example, above the bodies of Adam and Eve in the Creation scenes, creating the illusion that the ground recedes into the distance. This effect speaks for Andrea's awareness of the developments in Sienese landscape painting where the illusion of great distance and panoramic view is achieved, in part, by means of a high horizon line.

[23] Garger (1945), Pl. XXXIII, and Giuliano (1955), Fig. 54.

[24] It is true that this feature was taken up in medieval reliefs (cf. the quatrefoils at Amiens). But the relationship of figure to frame on the Campanile and the impression that the platform provides a solid ground on which the figures stand are closer to the ancient than to the medieval examples. Furthermore, the medallions along the base of French Gothic cathedrals tend, for the most part, to merge into an overall tapestrylike pattern, whereas the reliefs on the Campanile, like those on the Arch of Constantine, are conceived as self-contained pictorial units separated from the neighboring reliefs; in short, the medallions retain an independence from the architectural monument they adorn.

[25] This became apparent when the hexagons were removed for installation in the Museo dell'Opera del Duomo. Becherucci (1965), 261. Giotto may have been responsible, then, for the earliest phase of the Campanile's program. See Trachtenberg (1971), 86.

phy or, in one way or another, adapted to the Christian context. In contrast, a second group of hexagons exhibits a more integrated relationship between form and content, both of which embody relevant references to the antique.

Following the Genesis cycle on the west face, the program continues around the other sides of the tower with illustrations of the Mechanical Arts.[26] Among these a number of hexagons – *Navigation*, *Hercules*, and *Trade* (Figs. 64–66) on the east face, and *Horsemanship*, *Weaving*, and *Daedalus* (Figs. 60–63) on the south face – are distinguished, for the most part, by their simple, monumental compositions in which the figures, with little indication of setting, are placed against a flat, textured, but neutral background, in strong contrast to the richly pictorial landscapes and interiors of the first group. Only *Hercules*, whose robust yet fluid anatomy reveals an astonishing absorption of classicizing ideals, is placed within a landscape – not the continuous settings seen in the Genesis cycle, but a simplified environment against a textured background – perhaps because the incident chosen demanded a narrative context.[27] In this series, classicizing drapery patterns replace the concentric swinging folds and meandering hemlines reminiscent of the drapery on the doors. For the first time, moreover, the influence of classical sculpture is evident in the very conception of the images.

The representation of *Sculpture* on the north face (Fig. 57) mediates between the first and second group. The figure is not placed against a neutral background, but rather within a coherent interior setting. On the other hand, if one compares the Sculptor to the Creator in the Genesis cycle, one notes that the forms in the first are conceived in broader planes, the drapery folds are less cursive, the figure (and bench) are turned to the three-quarter view (thus increasing its sense of volume in space), and the composition is considerably simplified (Figs. 50, 57). At the same time, *Sculpture* anticipates the fully classicizing style of the second group. The seated figure, like Zacharias on the doors, would seem to derive from an antique prototype such as the patriarch on a Roman sarcophagus in Florence (Fig. 230).[28] Most significant, however, is the conception of the Sculptor: He is depicted as an ancient, not a medieval, artisan and is shown carving an "antique" nude in-the-round (cf. Figs. 58, 233).[29]

---

[26] See chapter 3.

[27] From the late thirteenth century, Hercules had appeared on the seal of the Signoria as protector and symbol of Florence. See Ettlinger (1972), 119–42. Here, however, he is shown as having cleansed from the earth the monsters of prehistory symbolized by Cacus, whose dead body projects from a cave nearby. Schlosser (1896), 53–4. Cf. Dante, *Inferno*, XXV:25.

[28] This, or a similar Roman relief, has been suggested as the source for Giotto's seated *Zacharias* in Santa Croce (Borsook, in Borsook and Tintori [1965], 18).

[29] Egbert (1967), 62. Cf. also Giotto's infant Baptist in the Peruzzi Chapel. Borsook, in Borsook and Tintori (1965), 18, suggests that an infant Hercules may lie behind the frescoed figure.

There is, moreover, a clear reference to an ancient theme: Prometheus Shaping the Body of a Man (Fig. 236).[30] This is in sharp contrast to the iconography of *Medicine* (Fig. 68), which is derived from medieval medical treatises.[31] The personages represented in *Medicine* are wearing contemporary dress,[32] and the physician is distinguished (as physicians were in the trecento) by his beret (which would have been velvet), his hooded cloak, and his gloves.[33] Clearly, with the representation of Sculpture on the Campanile, a different, and possibly a new, interpretation of the theme of the Labors of Mankind is intended.[34]

This interpretation would appear to be carried forward in the hexagons belonging to the second group. The rider (Fig. 60) wears a flowing mantle, rides bareback, and presses his knees firmly against the body of the animal; unlike medieval knights (for example, the San Giorgio in the relief from the Porta San Giorgio, now in the Palazzo Vecchio),[35] this figure is riding in the ancient manner. Andrea has gone directly to an antique prototype; among the examples known in the trecento are a medallion on the Arch of Constantine[36] and a figure on an Early Christian porphyry sarcophagus with a battle relief in the Vatican Museum.[37] Significantly, the latter contains the relatively rare motif of the rider seen from the back. Notwithstanding these possible Roman sources, the flavor of the Florentine relief is undeniably Attic.[38] The same holds true for the standing figure in *Weaving* immediately to the right of *Horsemanship* (Fig. 62). It is true that the costume does not strictly follow classical garments and the intervention of Gothic influence is felt in the meandering flow of the hemline on the right. But the carving in high relief against a neutral background, the pose, and above all, the use of drapery to enhance the rhythms of the female form recall Greek classical sculpture, for example, the figure seen on a fragment from a monumental base, an Attic work of the fourth century in the Fitzwilliam Museum in Cambridge (Fig. 237). The standing figure in *Weaving* has been identified as Minerva, who, according to the mythologies collected by Peter Comestor, belongs to a group of pagan figures that contributed significantly to mankind.[39] In a Roman relief in the Forum of Nerva, the

[30] See Raggio (1958), 44–62.

[31] Cf. a thirteenth-century miniature in the British Museum reproduced in Pedrazzini (1934), 62.

[32] Cf. a Pisan miniature of 1330 in Meiss (1965), 21–34, Fig. 26. Cf. also the procession of citizens in Lorenzetti's *Allegory of Good Government*.

[33] Corsini (1912), 3–6.

[34] On another possibly transitional relief, *Agriculture*, see p. 43.

[35] Salmi (1928), 63–4, Fig. 128.

[36] Giuliano (1955), Fig. 54.

[37] The sarcophagus (Vatican Museum, no. 79) comes from the Lateran and was reused for the tomb of Anastasius IV, who died in 1154; see Ragusa (1951), 158; Fig. 35.

[38] Cf. the tomb stele of Dexileos of the early fourth century B.C. from Athens. Janson (1974), Fig. 2.

[39] Seznec (1961), 16.

different operations of weaving are illustrated while, seated on a dais, Minerva presides over all (Fig. 240).[40] Although the Roman relief cannot be regarded as the visual source for the Campanile hexagon, the clear intention in the latter is the representation *all'antica* of the textile industry (this within the context of the Labors of Man!), that industry, that is to say, on which the outstanding economic power of the republic depended to such a large extent during the period.

The myth of Daedalus and Icarus appears on Roman wall paintings and reliefs and is a favorite theme on gems as well, but I have been unable to find a convincing antique prototype for the conception on the Campanile (Fig. 63). Although neither figure appears, to my knowledge, in medieval figural arts, an inscription on the tomb of Buschetto, architect of the Duomo of Pisa, compares him to Daedalus, the inventor of the arts.[41] Dante mentions the latter – "quello che volando per l'aere il figlio perse" – among various personifications of human activities (*Paradiso*, Canto VIII). But the ambivalence of the medieval position toward one who attempted to deny human limitations is felt in the *Inferno* (Canto XVII), where the terror of Icarus as he perceives that his wings are melting from the sun is compared to Dante's own fear as he descends into the eighth circle on the back of Geryon; by implication, the presumptuous flight of Daedalus and his son is contrasted with the poet's own sacred journey, which ultimately will end in salvation.[42] Only a few decades after the completion of the *Divine Comedy*, Daedalus appears on the Campanile emphatically as a celebration of the invention of the Arts. The conception of the relief is quite extraordinary. The figure is entirely covered with a costume of feathers, complete with two feathered "tails," one behind each leg. A pair of enormous wings is bound to the body at chest and hips, and two convenient handles appear at the upper edges, tightly grasped by Daedalus. The handles may have an antique source,[43] but the feathered costume and the system of straps may well be the imaginative invention of Andrea, who might have asked himself how, exactly, *would* Daedalus have fashioned a workable contraption.

Be that as it may, Daedalus is conceived as a noble, creative benefactor of mankind and, as such, like the figures in *Horsemanship* and *Weaving*, refers to the Labors of Man in terms of antique exponents. The same holds true for *Navigation*, which repeats a motif seen on the tomb of a Roman skipper of the third century A.D. (Figs. 64, 241). *Hercules* (Fig. 65) is comparable to countless representations in ancient times. And *Trade* (Fig. 66) resembles representations on the Column of Marcus Aurelius.[44] It is also very reminiscent of a relief on a funerary stele showing a figure driving a four-wheeled

[40] Picard-Schmitter (1965), 296–321.

[41] d'Ancona (1923), 146–7.

[42] Sinclair (1939), 223–4.

[43] Cf. Reinach (1909), 477, Fig. 5.

[44] Becatti (1957), Fig. 61.

cart filled with wares (Fig. 235).[45] In the latter, as on the Campanile, the driver holds a whip in his right hand and the reins in his left.

Each relief in this series, then, manifests a direct reference to ancient sources in terms of both form and content. There are no minor "invasions" of classical motifs to provide clues to locale as in the frescoes at Assisi or in the Peruzzi Chapel in Florence. There are no symbolically classicizing figures isolated from the narrative context as in the *Effects of Good Government* at Siena. Perhaps for the first time in Italy, moreover, ancient heroes such as Daedalus and Hercules appear in the context of a medieval Christian program with no attempt to transform them into Christian types. Both figures retain their classical identity and, in the case of Hercules, a classical strength and beauty, calling into question Panofsky's "principle of disjunction" by which classical themes, before the Renaissance, are always given nonclassical contemporary forms.[46] The iconography of the Labors of Man, then, would seem to be invested with what can only be described as an overtly protohumanistic character: Contemporary economic and cultural concerns are conceived in terms of ancient representatives or models – a mode of reference we have come to expect in the fifteenth and sixteenth centuries but one that remains rare in the fourteenth.

The reader may well accept the visual evidence for a new response to classical art and yet question the meaning and significance of this "renascence" three quarters of a century before the real Renaissance. We have already suggested that the abrupt change in style between the first and second series of Campanile reliefs may be connected to the fact that Andrea pursued new goals after assuming total control of the Campanile project when he became capomaestro. But the motivation for these changes must be sought beyond the issues of Andrea's personal development as a sculptor. A glance at the cultural and economic climate during the years in which the Campanile project was realized may help explain the circumstances under which Andrea arrived at a classicizing style that finds no counterpart in trecento Tuscany. The bell tower was conceived and its construction initiated during a period of increasing economic prosperity in Florence, a period that, according to Giovanni Villani, reached its peak in the years 1336–8; this has been confirmed by modern scholarship.[47] Villani was a member of that class of merchants who ran the government and directed the Campanile project; his own fortunes rose and declined with the fortunes of Florence itself. If he can be considered a spokesman for Florentine consciousness during the period his *Chronicle* took its final form

[45] Though a provincial work found in Strasbourg, this relief probably reflects more sophisticated Roman models.

[46] Panofsky (1960), 84–5.

[47] Antal (1948), 48; Becker (1967), 89–121; Brucker (1962), 3–4.

(according to L. Green, between 1333 and 1341),[48] then there is some evidence that the members of the upper bourgeoisie who controlled the Campanile project were experiencing a new consciousness of the Roman past of their city. The Florentines, in Villani's words, were "the descendants of a noble progeny and virtuous people such as were the ancient good Trojans and brave and noble Romans,"[49] and in describing Florence during the 1330s he uses terms such as "al modo di Roma." It may very well be that Florentine aspirations at this time demanded a search for an expressive mode that could convey the new sense of confidence, patriotism, and historical pride, particularly for the decoration of a building that had become as much a civic as a religious monument.[50] Andrea's hexagons, most notably the second group, would seem to have met this demand, infused as they are with a classical spirit that reflects a heightened sense of protohumanistic self-consciousness: Contemporary activities, not least among them those symbols of Florence's economic and artistic dominance – the representations of Trade, Weaving, and the Arts – are identified with antique exponents in a style and a relief mode that depend directly on ancient prototypes (Appendix B, Fig. 6).

These reliefs form a unified stylistic and conceptual group quite distinct from those belonging to the third series of hexagons on the Campanile – *Construction*, *Law*, *Geometry* and *Astronomy* (Figs. 69–72). Leaving aside the question of the inferior execution evident here, this series betrays a rejection of the classicizing ideals announced on the western facade and established in the monumental style of the second group. This last group would seem to speak of a new phase in the development of Tuscan trecento sculpture reflecting a mood quite different from that of the first two. By the early 1340s the situation in Florence had begun to deteriorate. One after another, the great banking houses collapsed. Inadequate crops led to undernourishment, which prepared the way for a series of epidemics culminating in the Black Death of 1348.[51] The ouster of the tyrannous Duke of Athens in 1343 was followed by a short period of popular demand for reform; this was superseded, however, by strong oligarchic reaction.[52]

For whatever reasons, and several have been suggested, Andrea left Florence ca. 1343, at which time Francesco Talenti became chief architect.[53] It may be, as suggested earlier, that a new workshop contributed *Astronomy*, *Building*, *Law*, and *Geometry*. The new

---

[48] Green (1972), 9–10, 165–7.
[49] Quoted and translated in Green (1972), 14.
[50] On the Campanile's importance as a civic structure, see Trachtenberg (1971), 174–9. The administration of the Opera del Duomo was entrusted to a group of powerful upper-class merchant guildmen of the Arte della Lana from 1331 on. On the relationship of trecento style to the dictates of this class, see Mustari (1975).
[51] Brucker (1962), 8, 14; Schevill (1961), 224.
[52] Becker (1967), 226–9; Schevill (1961), 265–6.
[53] Trachtenberg (1971), 50–5, 128–50.

emphasis on law and order in Florentine society and an atmosphere that favored religious fanaticism[54] may well account for the appearance of a design in the representation of *Law* that is frontal, emblematic, and hieratic (Fig. 70). The reliefs in this series, which would seem to anticipate the Black Death style observed by Meiss in painting,[55] represent a retreat from the ideals of the earlier hexagons. There is no sign of the sensuous tactile qualities discerned in the Creation scenes on the west face nor of the heroic, classicizing style evident in *Horsemanship* or *Hercules*. Instead, we seem to be witnessing the revival of an anticlassical ideal such as that seen in the fourth-century reliefs on the Arch of Constantine (cf. Figs. 70, 239). The abstract patterns and depersonalized mode of late imperial art may have provided some of the sources for a new style. Contemporary with the establishment of the program for the second tier on the Campanile, then, the last hexagons reflect the mood of an age experiencing the catastrophes that culminated in the Black Death (Appendix B, Fig. 7).

It is apparent that Andrea Pisano's use of classical sources changes as he develops. The doors contain isolated quotations from or references to the antique with no consistent integration of classical motifs into the Gothic idiom. On the Campanile there is an increasing appreciation of the aesthetic qualities of classical sculpture, indeed of Roman sculpture derived from the most classic phases of Greek art. The hexagons reveal interests that anticipate those of the Renaissance: the depiction of naturalistic landscapes, the representation of interior spaces, the portrayal of the nude as an idealized and sensuous form, and the idealization of contemporary, topical concerns by means of their identification with ancient imagery.

The influence of classical art, or rather of classical ideals, is not limited, however, to the direct influence of ancient remains. We have already observed that the classical as opposed to the Gothic current in Tuscan art of the late dugento and early trecento, as seen in the work of Nicola Pisano, Arnolfo di Cambio, and Giotto, resonates in Andrea's sculpture from his earliest to his latest work. In the next chapter we shall find that Andrea was especially responsive to a classicizing current within French Gothic art as well.

If Andrea failed to engender a classicizing following, this may be due, in large measure to the changing circumstances in Florence toward the middle of the century. The hexagons of the post-Andrea period would seem to disclose a sudden break with the earlier response to classical ideals. The needs of the new mood were perhaps best served by adopting the abstract, depersonalized mode of late imperial sculpture. The full realization of Andrea's achievement had to await the vision of the masters of the Early Renaissance. Coming of age during a period of renewed optimism, increasing economic

[54] Becker (1967), 48–9, 226–9.   [55] Meiss (1951).

prosperity, and a deepening consciousness of the republic's ties to its Roman past,[56] Donatello, Ghiberti, and Nanni di Banco turned to the doors and the Campanile as source and background for their own rediscovery of classical antiquity.

[56] As Becker states and amply documents (1967, 237–9), "Despite the hardships of war and the uncertainties of diplomatic maneuver, despite invasion and occupation of Florentine territories, despite plague and famine . . . foreign trade and communal customs receipts remained vigorous and thriving," and there was, moreover, strong Florentine confidence in the fiscal reliability of the republic throughout the first third of the fifteenth century. For a review of the economic forces in operation during this period, see Becker, 235–45. For a discussion of the correlation of economic factors and the flourishing civic humanism in Florence during the first half of the quattrocento, see, especially, 245–50.

CHAPTER EIGHT

Andrea Pisano and French Gothic Art

❖

The extent and importance of northern influence in the art of late dugento and early trecento Italy is an issue that has not yet been resolved. Some writers emphasize the independence of Italian Gothic art, whereas others see it as strongly reflecting developments in the north. In the search for northern links, the art historian is faced with a problem similar to that confronted when seeking classical prototypes and influences: How can one prove that a given motif or work of art conceived during our period is directly, or even indirectly, modeled after or influenced by a particular northern example? We do well to bear in mind that by 1300 a veritable network of Italian commercial and financial interests extended throughout Western Europe, to North Africa, and even to the far reaches of Asia.[1] Tuscan bankers found important positions in the courts of France, and with the establishment of the papacy in Avignon in 1309, a magnetic attraction to that city was felt by many Tuscan tradesmen. So pervasive were the activities of Florentine merchants that they constituted, according to a statement attributed to Pope Boniface VIII, the "fifth element" in the universe, along with earth, air, fire, and water![2] These same tradesmen and bankers were, in the early fourteenth century, the patrons of Giotto and Andrea Pisano.[3] The interests of Guelph Florence, moreover, were intimately connected with those of the French rulers in Naples, who brought with them architects and artisans from the north.[4] There is, indeed, considerable documentary evidence of French artists working in Italy (and of Italian artists

[1] Antal (1948), 12ff.; Larner (1971), 22ff.

[2] Larner (1971), 18.

[3] Antal (1948), 117–29.

[4] Larner (1971), 108ff.; Schevill (1961), 300f.

❖

134

working in the north); in addition, a number of Italian inventories datable to the fourteenth century list French-made objects, some of which are extant in cathedral treasuries.[5] Finally, there were the occasional incursions of major political figures from the north such as Henry VII of Luxembourg, who in 1310 crossed the Alps, passed through Tuscany, and made his way to Rome where he had been promised coronation as the new Holy Roman Emperor.[6] One can easily imagine the accumulation of gifts and acquisitions that clung to the emperor-elect's entourage as he triumphantly entered Italy. Thus, when the formal similarities between two works of art or motifs are visually convincing, one may be justified in presuming a possible direct link. How else explain – to choose an example outside the immediate context of Andrea Pisano – the striking concordance of motif between a thirteenth-century figure from Strasbourg (Fig. 242) and an early fourteenth-century caryatid by Tino di Camaino (Fig. 243)?[7] Now the route taken by Henry VII from Luxembourg to Pisa surely took him through Strasbourg and it is possible that some reflection of the northern figure made its way to Tuscany with Henry. Be that as it may, given the extraordinary development of French architecture and sculpture during the thirteenth century – much of it reflected in small, portable objects – and the commercial and political crosscurrents, especially the international character of Tuscan interests, it is not surprising that a powerful artistic impetus from the north should reach the centers of artistic production in Italy.

Many of Andrea's most impressive achievements are very difficult to explain on the basis of Italian tradition alone, but presuppose an acquaintance with and deep receptivity to developments in the architecture and sculpture north of the Alps. From among the various stylistic threads that make up the rich fabric of French Gothic art, Andrea,

[5] For general discussions on the relationship between French and Italian art, see especially Gnudi (1969), 18–36; (1963), 161–7; (1971). The subject is also taken up by Jullian (1958), 133–46; Reau (1945); Pillion (1906), 354–66; Weise (1956).

In addition, there are numerous articles on the influence of French art on the Pisani, on Giotto, and on Tuscan monuments in general. Among these the following should be noted: Jantzen, (1939–40), 441–54; Klotz (1965–6), 171–206; Middeldorf and Weinberger (1928), 187–90; Seidel (1968–9), 87–151; (1972), 1–50; Trachtenberg (1971), 41f., 44f., 61; Wallace (1953); Weinberger (1963), 203.

The influence of French art on Andrea Pisano is discussed, generally in terms of isolated instances of visual similarities, in the following: Castelnuovo (1966); Pillion (1906), 354–66; Reymond (1897), 121; I. Toesca (1950), 24f.; Trachtenberg (1971), 61, 64, 102; Weinberger (1953), 243–8.

For evidence of French artists or works of art in the fourteenth century in Italy, the following should be noted: Bertaux (1898), 265–76, 369–78; Gnudi (1956), 535–42; Hertlein (1965), 54–70; Middeldorf and Weinberger (1928), 187–90; Ragghianti (1973), 11–38; P. Toesca (1951), 195ff.

[6] Schevill (1961), 184.

[7] A current from Strasbourg to Tuscany, seen in terms of architectural motifs, has been observed by Klotz (1965–6); see also Trachtenberg (1971), 44.

particularly in his early bronze reliefs, assimilated much of the decorative vocabulary of the precious and mannered art originating in Paris around 1300; increasingly, however, he turned back to that current, not surprisingly a "classicizing" current, that appears in Parisian workshops around the middle of the thirteenth century. In his conception of the Madonna and Child, too, Andrea ultimately rejects the courtly style of the mainstream of contemporary French sculpture, responding instead to a more conservative, monumental, and classicizing trend.

His employment of the quatrefoil and other geometric configurations on the Baptistry doors and the Campanile is related to the use of similar motifs on French Gothic cathedrals. This last relationship, however, is a manifestation of a more profound cultural connection than mere taste of artist or patron for motifs, mannerisms, and even general stylistic ideals whose origins may lie in France. We have already observed that with the inclusion of reliefs illustrating scenes from Genesis and the Labors of Mankind the program of the cathedral group was broadened so that its scope began to rival the encyclopedic content of northern cathedrals. The quatrefoil and hexagonal medallions on the Baptistry and Campanile, as we shall see, make the reference to the iconographic and decorative programs of French cathedrals pointed and unambiguous.

BAPTISTRY AND CAMPANILE: RELIEF MODE AND FIGURE STYLE

French reliefs of the thirteenth and early fourteenth centuries in general evolved in two main directions. The choir screen of Notre Dame in Paris (Fig. 245) and the tympanum on the facade of the cathedral of Rouen (Fig. 244) are examples of a relief mode in which the figures are set within clearly defined and real limits: the platform on which they stand, the plane of the background, and the architectural frame that closes the upper and forward limits of this space. In contrast, an alternative relief mode is seen in the quatrefoils of Auxerre Cathedral (Fig. 247) where there is no such spatial box; instead, illusionistic devices, lively figures, and a crowded relief surface animated by the play of light and dark result in a more pictorial relief. The Baptistry panels, clearly, are akin to the first of these approaches. Compare, for instance, the spatial milieu in the *Naming of the Baptist* (Fig. 10) and the *Dance of Salome* (Fig. 244) in Florence and Rouen, respectively: In both reliefs space is defined by the projecting architectural forms above, by the volumes of the figures, and by the depth of the platform on which they stand. Neither Nicola nor Giovanni Pisano employs this kind of boxlike stage; it reappears, however, in Sienese sculpture of the fourteenth century where it is generally employed for the enactment of crowded and lively dramas, as in Goro di Gregorio's Arca di San

Cerbone.[8] In contrast, Andrea adheres to the principles of pictorial restraint seen in the reliefs of Paris and Rouen.

At the same time the bronze panels are more complex than those French reliefs in which all illusionism is absent: The space on the doors is both actual, as in the French box relief, and illusionistic, as in the Consecration relief in Siena (Fig. 192) where the sculptor succeeds in conveying an illimitable background – not solid and impenetrable but fluid and extending beyond the frame.[9] Andrea's contribution to the history of relief sculpture was, in part, to combine the two modes, an achievement that enabled him to create images that hover between narrative realism and ritual drama.

The tendency in the bronze reliefs to poise the figures with an eye for telling gesture and significant pose, combined with a sensitive, rhythmic spacing, compels one to seek further analogies outside the Tuscan tradition. In the altar retable of Saint-Germer-de-Fly and the choir screen of Bourges cathedral (Figs. 250–252), one notes a strongly felt sense of rhythmic balance that results from the sensitive grouping – almost Phidian in character – of solids and voids so that the expanses of ground serve as foils that lend meaning to the gestures and poignancy to the relationships. Similarly, in *Zacharias and the Elders* (Fig. 7), the spatial interval that isolates and separates the figures is the very medium against which, or rather in which, the expressive gestures of the stricken priest take on meaning. Even some individual figures bear comparison: Gabriel in the *Annunciation to Zacharias* closely resembles a figure on this same altar frontal (Figs. 5, 250). In both, soft swinging drapery rhythms on the one hand respond convincingly to the anatomical bulges, and on the other are disposed in parabolic folds that help enliven the surface with lyrical rhythms – without, however, degenerating into purely decorative linear patterns. Again, it becomes apparent that however much indebted Andrea is to Giotto, the sculptor translates the painter's language into a new idiom – though searching equally for a sense of stability and *gravitas*. How different are Andrea's fluid, lyrical forms from Giotto's homogeneous blocks forming body and drapery in the Arena Chapel frescoes. It is Andrea's ability to combine structure and elegance into a harmonious whole that distinguishes the figures on the doors from those of Giotto's paintings and links them closely to tendencies in Parisian art.

The altar retable of Saint-Germer-de-Fly and the choir screen of Bourges represent what several writers have identified as a "classicizing" strain in French thirteenth-century sculpture, one that avoids all decorative flourishes and overexpressive characterizations.[10] This current originated in Paris ca. 1230, reached full flower around the

---

[8] See pp. 100, 101.
[9] See p. 99f.
[10] On Parisian classicism see Gnudi (1963, 1969),

Erlande-Brandenburg (1970), 31–41, and Pillion (1906), 354–66.

middle of the century, and then spread to outlying areas such as Bourges before the ateliers succumbed to the attractions of a second and contemporary stylistic tendency. The latter, which reached its apogee in the famous smiling angel at Reims, is characterized by poses that are less stable, drapery patterns that are more decorative, and faces that express exquisite sensibilities; it is this style that will become germane to the subsequent development of northern Gothic art. Some figures on the doors suggest a qualified response on the part of Andrea Pisano to this more elegant and precious style, particularly as reflected in French goldsmith work. Compare the figures on the left in *Ecce Agnus Dei* (Fig. 13) or, again on the left, in the *Baptism of the Multitude* (Fig. 14) to the angels on the Reliquary of Saint Louis in San Domenico, Bologna (Figs. 253, 254), a work of Parisian goldsmiths. This work, incidentally, came to Italy in the early fourteenth century.[11] Considering that fact, the similarities not only of the drapery style but of certain decorative details are quite suggestive: The crockets and finials embellishing the canopy in the *Annunciation* recall similar motifs on the reliquary; this is true as well of the finials on the *Entombment* (Fig. 25), where, moreover, one finds an embossed diaper pattern reminiscent of the pattern seen on the sides of the French reliquary.

The tension between the current "mannerist" trend and the sculptor's classicizing tendencies is perhaps felt most strongly in the last relief on the left-hand valve. The proportions, the relationship of bone to flesh, and the modeling of the body of Christ in the *Baptism* suggest that Andrea was acquainted with ancient bronzes (see chapter 7). But the physiognomy recalls the *Beau Dieu* of Amiens (Figs. 45, 258). The oval face, thin eyelids, the center part with the hair rolling gently away from the face, the delicate mustache and the beard that parts in opposing symmetrical waves are comparable. But the bronze Christ is not as severe as the *Beau Dieu*; the firmly modeled yet delicate surfaces, the refined and gentle expression suggest, rather, a source in the minor arts, for example, the figure on a reliquary of the late thirteenth century, probably of Parisian origin, which found its way to Assisi and is listed in an inventory of 1338 (Figs. 260, 261).[12] Even closer to our Christ is a bust on a cameo of ca. 1250 from Paris, now in The Hague (Fig. 259).[13] The pattern of the hair and beard, both without the embellishment of curls, the very slight turn of the lips, the thin short nose and delicate planes of the face result in images that remain idealized yet that are softened by a new humanity, still lacking in the austere *Beau Dieu* of Amiens.

Whereas in some reliefs on the left-hand valve of the Baptistry doors one feels the pull of conflicting values, these stylistic tensions disappear almost completely on the

[11] Gnudi (1956), 535–42.

[12] Hertlein (1965), 54–70.

[13] See Wentzel (1975), 31–9.

right-hand valve. There, all exaggerations, all tendencies to overrefinement are held in check by Andrea's classical restraint. On the Campanile Andrea's development is marked by an increase in classical form and content that culminates with his last Florentine reliefs. The monumental and classicizing style of his late hexagons would seem to have satisfied, as we have seen, the growing pride in and consciousness of the Florentine republic's ties to its own Roman past. Is there then a corresponding decrease in French Gothic inspiration in the Campanile hexagons?

In designing the marble reliefs, another aspect of French sculpture seems to have touched a responsive chord. Surprisingly, it is in France, not Italy, that one finds for the first time in medieval art nude figures carved to suggest the softness of flesh, conceived unabashedly as beautiful, sensuous forms – as in a fragment in the Louvre from the choir screen of Notre Dame, Paris (Fig. 262).[14] Compare this on the one hand to a nude by Giovanni Pisano on the Pisa pulpit and on the other to Andrea's Eve in the *Creation of Eve* (Fig. 51) on the Campanile. In the examples from Paris and Florence, the soft, sensuous nudes speak clearly for an intense response to Hellenizing classical antecedents – and contrast strongly with the uncomfortably naked figure by Giovanni. Similarly, the youthful forms and subtly modeled surfaces of Adam on the Campanile (Fig. 50) reveal an attitude toward the representation of the nude figure that is analogous to that seen in the Parisian example. Around the same time, still a few decades before the Campanile relief, we find on the socle of Auxerre Cathedral a languid and sensuous figure of a sleeping Eros (Fig. 263). Another figure from Auxerre, the seated Bathsheba (Fig. 264), is sister to the standing woman in *Weaving* on the Campanile (Fig. 62): Both seem animated by the same ideal of plasticity, easy naturalism, and restrained sensuality. Furthermore, certain reliefs at Auxerre, by the so-called Classical Master, display a concern with classical form and content[15] analogous to that observed on the Campanile. As in the latter, which remains without precedent in Italy, a Christian program is infused with overt references to antiquity (Figs. 263, 265). Not only are there medallions with profile heads *all'antica* as part of the decorative framework surrounding the narrative reliefs (Fig. 246), but in addition to Eros, there is a figure of Hercules, and a satyr. None of these is transformed into a medieval image; rather, their iconography remains frankly pagan, as do their forms. Hercules, for instance, is conceived like a classical statue – anatomically correct, of Phidian proportions, the light playing over subtly shifting planes (cf. Figs. 65, 265). This is in notable contrast to Nicola's muscle-bound and hard-edged Fortitude.[16] The slender forms and softly mod-

[14] Gnudi (1969), 20ff.

[15] Nordstrom (1974), 9.

[16] For an alternative identification of the Pisan Herculean figure, see chapter 7, n. 5.

eled surfaces of the sleeping Adam on the Campanile recall those of the Eros of Auxerre (Figs. 50, 263).[17]

Thus, the classicism of the Campanile hexagons is closer, in many ways, to these currents from the north than to the classicism of Andrea's predecessors in Tuscany – with the sole exception of Nicola Pisano, whose *ultima maniera* on the Fontana Maggiore (Figs. 190, 238) surely is a reflection of that same current.

THE QUATREFOIL

We shall return to the Campanile shortly, but let us now consider the use of the quatrefoil itself on the Baptistry doors and examine its relationship to the history of the quatrefoil medallion in French architecture. In France the quatrefoil shape evolves from simpler to more complex forms; at the same time, the reliefs contained within are part of a more general history of medieval relief sculpture. The quatrefoils of Florence represent an episode in these two related yet independent histories; furthermore, their role in the program of the cathedral group – Duomo, Baptistry, and Campanile – is, as we shall see, analogous to the role of the French quatrefoil in the iconographic and decorative programs of French cathedrals.

It is true that the quatrefoil shape appears earlier in Italian painting, particularly in mural decoration and most notably in the Arena Chapel in the decorative enframing armature of the narratives.[18] For this reason, John White, writing about Andrea's Baptistry doors, comments that "there is no need to search the sculpture of Paris, Bourges and Rouen or to turn to northern metalwork or miniatures for the source of the pierced quadrilobe. Giotto had used it in identical form fully twenty years earlier."[19] But *are* the quatrefoils used in identical form by Giotto? In the Arena Chapel, the frames enclose single figures and small biblical scenes. In either case, the quatrefoil functions essentially like a hole in the wall through which the viewer glimpses a "slice of life." The viewpoint may be quite daring, as in the *Circumcision* (Fig. 225), or the moment chosen rather startling, as in *Jonah* (Fig. 226). The implication here is that the space

---

[17] The classicism at Auxerre, like that in Florence, was not simply an aesthetic device; it expressed a political ideal, though one quite different from that conveyed by the Florentine reliefs. According to Nordstrom (1974), 11–15, 126f., the Auxerre sculptures were created during a period when the royal party was in conflict with the pope and was attempting, ultimately with success, to establish its supremacy by associating the crown with the imperial dignity of the Holy Roman Empire. References to antique motifs, together with a classicizing style, were aids in this imperial propaganda.

[18] See Appendix A, n. 7, for a suggestion by Kreytenberg that the framing design of the doors is based on the pattern on the wall of the Pulci Chapel in Santa Croce, Florence.

[19] White (1966), 304.

and action continue beyond the limits of the frame. On the doors, in contrast, each frame encloses a complete, self-contained image: Never are the figures abruptly cut off or partially concealed by the inner angles of the frame; never is the action imagined as extending beyond the limits of that frame. Giotto's use of the quatrefoil is radically innovative whereas Andrea's is closely tied to the function and appearance of the form on a number of thirteenth-century French Gothic cathedrals.

The earliest quatrefoils embellish the facade of Amiens (Figs. 266–267) (1222–35).[20] Here a double row of reliefs is set above the diaper pattern of the socle walls. The figures stand on the frame itself, on a ledge, or on a rocky mound that cuts across the frame. After Amiens, the quatrefoil enjoys great popularity. It appears, for instance, at Noyon (Fig. 268) (ca. 1240), where a single row of large quatrefoils, this time each one pierced by the angles of a square, is set into a diaper pattern reminiscent of that at Amiens.[21] Henceforth the pierced quatrefoil becomes the preferred shape appearing subsequently on the south transept of Notre Dame, Paris (Fig. 269) (ca. 1260), where, moreover, the shape is inserted into a rectangle.[22] Here there is a new pictorial richness as active, overlapping figures fill not only the quatrefoils, but also the spaces between the lobes and the outer rectangle. This tendency toward increasing pictorial richness and decorative complexity culminates in the quatrefoils on the socle of Auxerre Cathedral (1280–ca. 1310), where two rows of large reliefs at eye level or below support, not the traditional statue columns, but an arcade containing seated figures, perhaps Sibyls and Kings (Fig. 249).[23] The combination of semicircular, ogival, and pointed arches is also new; further, some narratives extend directly from one frame into the next; finally, the rich texture of the reliefs combines with the lively pattern of the surrounding areas and thus the distinction between the medallions themselves and the mural structure becomes blurred, in contrast to the sharp distinction observable, for instance, at Amiens.

This development contrasts with another, a "miniaturist" tendency following the appearance of the first quatrefoils at Amiens. On the transepts of the Cathedral of Rouen (Figs. 248, 270) (1270–1300), there is a radical decrease in size and an increase in the number of reliefs, and rather than sweeping across the facades as at Amiens and Auxerre, they embellish the jambs about the transept portals. More intimate in character, the individual reliefs require very close scrutiny for visibility, tending to lose themselves within the larger decorative scheme. Like the quatrefoils at Noyon and Paris, how-

---

[20] Unless otherwise noted, the dating of French sculpture is that of Sauerländer (1972).

[21] Seymour (1944), 162–82.

[22] The pierced quatrefoil is also seen at Bordeaux and on the exterior of the apsidal chapels at Paris.

[23] The Florentine Baptistry doors contain seated figures, too, but the relationship is reversed: The figures are below and the narratives are above. On the reliefs at Auxerre (with excellent photographs), see Nordstrom (1974).

ever, each quatrefoil here is pierced by the angles of a rhombus, but in contrast to the earlier examples the whole shape is shifted forty-five degrees so that the rhombus stands on one of its corners; further, each quatrefoil is inserted into a rectangular frame. Both of these features – the shift of forty-five degrees and the insertion into a rect- angle, repeated at Lyons Cathedral – herald the form taken up by Andrea on the bronze doors. Further, the relationship of the reliefs to the frame and even several of the com- positions on the doors seem to be anticipated in the Old Testament scenes at Rouen. Here, in a number of reliefs, the figures stand on a platform that cuts across the lower lobes of the quatrefoil just as occurs in Florence (Figs. 271–273). (Note how this dif- fers from Giotto's quatrefoils in which there are never artificial stagelike platforms.) There is, moreover, a similar emphasis at Rouen on verticals and horizontals against which the curves and diagonals of the frame play, and there is a tendency toward com- positional restraint with few props so that the actions and gestures are in sharp focus against the blank, neutral back plane. The *Visitation* on the doors is strikingly close to a relief on the Portail de la Calende at Rouen: In both, a centrally placed figure is flanked by an arched structure on the right that balances a figure on the left (Figs. 8, 272). *Zacharias and the Elders* is comparable to another of the French reliefs where the neutral back plane acts particularly effectively to put the gestures in relief (Figs. 7, 271); other comparisons are equally suggestive.

The Cathedral of Lyons is dedicated to John the Baptist and thus among the many quatrefoil reliefs (ca. 1310) that form a veritable stone tapestry flanking the doors of the facade we find an extensive cycle, sixteen reliefs in all, devoted to the life of the patron saint (Figs. 274–279).[24] Of these, eleven illustrate episodes also represented on the Baptistry doors. Although the style of these reliefs is relatively crude, some of the compositions and iconographic content would seem to be reflected, however distantly, in the Florentine reliefs.

As on the doors, the series begins with the *Annunciation to Zacharias*. The simplicity and symmetry of Andrea's composition is akin to that in the stone relief (Figs. 5, 275). The *Nativity*, the *Naming*, the *Baptism*, and the *Visit of the Disciples* also invite com- parisons with Lyons (Figs. 276, 277). *John Receives His Mission* recalls, in some re- spects, the Giovannino panel on the doors: In both, the bottom lobes of the quatre- foils are filled with rocky forms that develop into mountains on the right; whereas at Lyons a tree fills the upper right lobe and God the upper left, at Florence – due to the somewhat altered iconography, a reflection, of course, of the Baptistry mosaics – we see trees extending into both upper lobes (Figs. 11, 278).

[24] See Pillion (1906), 354–66. The quatrefoils of Lyons had a following that extended from the palace of the popes at Avignon to the choir stalls of Cologne Cathedral. See Jullian (1958), 133–46.

None of these comparisons is intended to assert a French sojourn for Andrea or to suggest any necessarily direct link between the Florence and French designs.[25] They do suggest, however, the creatively eclectic nature of Andrea's approach to artistic problems, as well as the larger context in which the doors must be viewed. For the question naturally arises, Why did Andrea turn to French Gothic art when before his very eyes were the achievements of his formidable contemporaries and predecessors: Giotto, the Sienese, and the Pisani? Is the Tuscan fashion for graceful and linear northern forms, as evident in the increasing incorporation of Gothic motifs in Italian architecture, sufficient to explain this phenomenon? I would argue that in the case of the doors, Andrea selected and assimilated those components of French sculpture that could felicitously contribute to the solution of the specific artistic task at hand: to create a monumental bronze door embellished with a large number of necessarily small-scale reliefs, a door that must satisfy both traditional architectonic and new aesthetic and narrative demands. By employing the French stagelike space in which the protagonists perform with measured yet highly expressive movements, Andrea succeeded in achieving a far greater sense of narrative and spatial realism than that seen in the work of the Pisani, Arnolfo, or Tino. By infusing into the otherwise homogeneous structure of his Giottesque figures something of the fluid, lyrical rhythms found in French sculpture, he succeeded both in linking the internal rhythms of the composition to the curves of the quatrefoil frame and in enlivening the surface pattern of the otherwise rather austere designs of the narratives. Moreover, by confining the actors within the strict limits of the quatrefoil, Andrea maintains the decorative unity and asserts the architectonic function of the door, *as door* – something that is lost, incidentally, in Ghiberti's Gates of Paradise for all its wonderful illusionistic advances and narrative complexities.

But the appearance of quatrefoils on the Baptistry of Florence should be viewed in an even larger context. These quatrefoils are *not* arbitrary transferrals of an Italian decorative frescoed motif to the realm of monumental sculpture, nor can they be understood as mere concessions to the fashion for motifs of French origin. They belong rather to a specifically *cathedral* program. The quatrefoils on French cathedrals contain reliefs that echo or complement the main themes of those cathedrals' programs – and the same holds true in Florence. We have already alluded to the fact that whereas

---

[25] The question, however, deserves further investigation. The configurations of many corresponding scenes are quite similar. Were such compositional schemata transmitted by means of sketchbooks such as that of Villard d'Honnecourt? Or were the configurations diffused by some other means, for example, mystery plays (for which Rouen was famous in the Middle Ages)? The pantomimic character of the Florentine reliefs does indeed bring to mind liturgical drama. Cf. p. 29, n. 71.

in France the apocalyptic and encyclopedic programs that are developed on the façades and in the stained glass windows are encompassed in a single structure, in Florence the iconographic content was realized in a more piecemeal and cumulative way.[26] No less grandiose than those on French cathedrals, the program in Florence was distributed on the three buildings comprising the cathedral group: God's plan of world history appears in the Baptistry mosaics, largely executed in the dugento; an extensive Marian program had been initiated by Arnolfo di Cambio, ca. 1300, on his new façade of Santa Maria del Fiore; and scenes from Genesis, the Labors of Mankind, the Virtues, Planets, Sacraments, and Liberal Arts take their place on the Campanile socle while Prophets and Sibyls proclaim the Coming of Christ from the niches above.

The Baptist cycle on the doors, which includes the *Visitation,* an episode more often seen in the context of the life of Mary or Christ, belongs ultimately to the Marian program of the Duomo group – just as it does at Amiens, Paris, and Reims, all dedicated to the Virgin Mary; indeed, at Amiens scenes from the Baptist's life are found among the quatrefoil medallions. Thus, the Baptistry quatrefoils may be viewed as the counterparts, visually and iconographically, of the medallions incorporated in northern cathedral design (since the design of the Duomo facade lacked these very elements). The Baptistry reliefs, however, are linked not so much to the socle medallions sweeping across the facade of Amiens, nor to the richly pictorial reliefs seen at Auxerre. Rather, it is the multiple strips that form part of the jambs framing the portals at Rouen and Lyons – those quatrefoils of rather restrained compositions and simple, direct expressive content – that provide the most salient antecedents for the appearance of quatrefoils on the Baptistry, significantly on the *porte* themselves.

With this in mind, it becomes evident that the hexagons and lozenges of Andrea's fabric on the Campanile – though they are very un-French, very Italian shapes, if I may say so – also partake of this association, iconographically and as decorative elements.[27] Giotto's original design for the bell tower, as reflected at least in the lower part of the Siena drawing,[28] included a pattern of hexagons extending beyond the base and probably did not carry such associations; they may not even have been conceived for reliefs. Only the decision to embellish the lowest zone with representations of the Creation and Labors of Mankind resulted in a pointed reference to the encyclopedic

[26] Trachtenberg (1971), 99–100, 102, describes the entire cathedral group as belonging to a "collectively iconographic entity" that developed piecemeal due to historical circumstances. The program is encompassed not in a single structure as in France, but by the cathedral facade, the Baptistry mosaics, the doors, and the Campanile.

[27] Trachtenberg (1971), 98–100.

[28] On the Siena drawing, see Degenhart and Schmitt (1968), 89–94, who reject it as from the hand of Giotto and consider it a Sienese adaptation of a Florentine design. Nevertheless, many of the basic elements, as the authors agree, reflect Giotto's design.

program and design of French monuments, a reference enhanced by the subsequent doubling of the relief zones executed when Andrea became capomaestro upon Giotto's death. Here we see the counterparts not of the flanking portal strips of Rouen and Lyons but of the double row of medallions on the socles that belt the lower portions of such French facades as Amiens. From a massive base (Fig. 49) embellished with sculptured medallions rises a giant shaft from whose heights Sibyls and Kings address the population below — figures that, in turn, may be considered the visual and iconographic analogues of the jamb figures on the French monuments. It is perhaps not entirely coincidental that the Genesis scenes on the Campanile tend toward a greater pictorial richness than the austere, simple narratives on the Baptistry, and thus are more in tune with the socle reliefs of Auxerre to which the classicism of the Campanile hexagons also, as we have seen, is linked.

The medallions and niche figures on the Campanile, no less than the quatrefoils on the doors, have no precedents in Italy and are transformations and adaptations from the Gothic north. Andrea's northern sources, then, are at least as important a component in his style and conception of architectural embellishment as anything visible in Tuscany during the early fourteenth century.

THE STATUES

Just as in Andrea's reliefs classical ideals combine with the grace and flowing linearity we associate with French Gothic art, so too do these apparently conflicting modes make their demands on Andrea's sculpture in-the-round. From the early Pisan wood *Annunziata* (Figs. 102–104), with its almost prismatic austerity, erect demeanor, and taut contours to the post-Florentine Saltarelli *Madonna* (Fig. 151), one may discern an increasingly pronounced absorption of French Gothic elements, particularly as regards posture and drapery. Subsequently, however, Andrea succeeds in integrating this Gothic mode with his inherent predilection for monumental classicizing form to arrive at his supreme achievement, the Madonna in Santa Maria della Spina (Figs. 133, 134).

We have earlier connected the style of the *Annunziata* of 1321 with that of Arnolfo di Cambio and Giotto, and have noted that the sculpture of Tino and painting of Simone were the probable vehicles of influence.[29] Subtle influxes from the north, however, permeate the work of all these masters. Many writers have sought to connect Giotto's painted figures with French prototypes. For instance, the figures of Mary in the *Marriage* and the *Wedding Procession* in the Arena Chapel (Figs. 216, 217) have

[29] See p. 98f.

been compared to sculptures on the west portal of Reims Cathedral (Figs. 255, 256).[30] It has been suggested, moreover, that the influence of French monumental sculpture came to Giotto by way of small ivories, for example, an angel in the Metropolitan Museum of Art that recalls the *Queen of Sheba* on the west portal at Reims (Figs. 256, 257).[31] Assuming that a similar source was available to Andrea, it is instructive to compare his with Giotto's response to the French prototype. Giotto has assimilated the rhythm of the drapery folds and the "plain-speaking . . . naturalism"[32] of the ivory but *not* the torsion of the body and the contrasting drapery movements. These last, and the expressive movement of the arms in space, are precisely the elements adopted by Andrea for his *Annunziata*. Clearly, the painter and sculptor exhibit equally sympathetic yet differing interpretations of the French prototype.

The relatively simple, bulky forms and sweeping, unbroken drapery folds of the *Annunziata* are replaced, after Andrea's arrival in Florence, by more fluid postures and richer calligraphic drapery patterns. These characteristics are seen in the figures on the Baptistry doors as well as in the small alabaster *Madonna and Child* in Budapest in which, moreover, an extremely subtle contrapposto is felt in the relationship of the upper to the lower portion of the figure.

In the Saltarelli *Madonna*, the contrapposto sway is much stronger, the drapery folds are developed in a linear rather than in a plastic manner, and there is relatively little to convince an observer that the drapery hangs over a solidly constructed form. These are the very characteristics that one finds in the vast majority of early fourteenth-century French Madonnas by which date a strong *hanchement* had become virtually de rigueur. In contrast to the idealized and monumental images of the great trumeau figures of the thirteenth century, when the Madonna descended from cathedral facades to be reproduced almost ad infinitum in statues and statuettes, in gold, silver, stone, alabaster, ivory, and wood, she lost her monumental grandeur, and her form became more abstract and weightless as the drapery, seemingly unsupported by a solid structure beneath, took on a rhythmic life of its own.[33]

The apparent necessity to incorporate such French mannerisms, however, would seem to have come into conflict with the sculptor's inherent tendencies toward a restrained, classicizing naturalism. The sharp linearism of the Saltarelli *Madonna*, the diminished

[30] Jantzen (1939/40), 441ff.; White (1966), 217, and Pl. 93.

[31] White (1966), 217, 410, n. 14. The ivory statuette, however, has more recently been dated to the late fourteenth century. See *Les Fastes du Gothique, le siècle de Charles V*, Exhibition Catalogue, Paris (1981), 198.

[32] White (1966), 217.

[33] On the subject, see Koechlin (1924), 490–6; Lefrançois-Pillion (1925), 129–49; Schaefer (1954); Suckale (1971).

plasticity of the Virgin's garments, and the limited expression of an anatomical structure beneath do not characterize Andrea's last Madonnas on the Pisa Duomo facade and in Santa Maria della Spina. These would seem to reflect rather an earlier or at least an alternative stylistic tendency observable in France. Around the turn of the century, in reaction to the worldly elegance and preciosity of Parisian productions, a new type of Virgin was born in Burgundy, the center of the Cistercian order (which previously had frowned upon sculpture of any type).[34] The Abbey of Fontenay possesses a beautiful and much underappreciated *Virgin and Child* that is astonishingly classical in the relationship of drapery to body, in the balanced and controlled rhythms of the folds, in the equilibrium of the stance and broad plasticity of the modeling (Figs. 280, 281).[35] No other French statue offers itself so compellingly as a possible source of inspiration for Andrea's conception in the Spina *Madonna* (Fig. 133). The stance and physiognomy of the French Virgin, the angle at which she turns her head toward Christ, the manner in which she holds him and the expression, with its tender glance and loving smile – uncharacteristic of the period – seem reflected in the Tuscan example. The crowns decorated with fleur-de-lys are similar as are the folds of the mantle and dress, which combine into single tubular forms. In both, the mantle is draped over the right arm and is pulled up in a series of concentric folds toward the left. Both statues are carved fully in-the-round and the pattern of folds in the back, especially the veils, is similar. The *Virgin* of the Abbey of Fontenay represents the fusion of older ideals that emphasize broad plastic values and compositional balance with a new, more humanized image of the Virgin, one that was currently being publicized by the descriptions of Cistercian writers.[36] This image seems reflected in the *Madonna and Child* of Santa Maria della Spina.

Tuscan Madonnas, indeed, from the time of Nicola to Andrea and Nino Pisano, follow a development parallel to, but later than, that of French Virgins of the thirteenth and fourteenth centuries. The classicizing tendencies of Italian sculptors, however, determined that their figures never lose their sense of solid underlying structure and that the drapery rhythms never degenerate into purely abstract linear forms. Andrea clearly rejected the predominant style of French fourteenth-century Madonnas. It remained to the generation of Andrea's son Nino to absorb the ideals of the mainstream of early fourteenth-century French sculpture, which when fused with the indigenous classical tradition prepared the way and may have been an important source for the great movement of the late trecento and early quattrocento, the International Gothic style.

[34] Schaefer (1954), 48f.

[35] I am indebted to the Abbot Aynard of Fontenay for permission to study and photograph the *Virgin and Child*.

[36] Schaefer (1954), 48f.

In summary, the highly refined, precious and mannered art emanating from Paris around 1300 leaves its strongest mark on Andrea's early reliefs for the Baptistry of Florence. But his native classical bias and his pictorial restraint as a disciple of Giotto gain ascendancy in the later bronze reliefs. From this point on, his receptivity to the "classical" tendency in French Gothic art, a tendency manifested in such examples as the altar retable of Saint-Germer and the jubé of Bourges, is affirmed in compositions in which action and repose, structure and elegance, figure and surrounding space are harmoniously balanced. These are the values expressed in the Campanile hexagons, which, although created in an artistic climate anticipated at Auxerre, develop in a direction far removed from the episodic and richly pictorial reliefs seen on the facade of the French cathedral. The Madonna and Child in Pisa reveals, once again, that Andrea, in looking to the north, rejected the courtly style of the mainstream of contemporary French sculpture, responding instead to those examples that conserve the values of an older, more monumental, and classicizing tradition.

CHAPTER NINE
Nino Pisano

Nino Pisano began his career in Andrea's Pisan bottega, which was active between the years 1343 and 1347. We have already outlined the development of his style from one adhering to the classicizing principles of his father toward one that increasingly assimilated northern Gothic influences. Although it would be unwise to attempt too precise a dating of Nino's sculptures, a general chronology based on the few documents, the signed works, and the relationship of attributed works to the signed examples may now be attempted.

The *Bishop Saint* in Oristano (Fig. 130) and the upper angels of the Saltarelli monument (Figs. 152, 153), still Giottesque in their ponderation, belong to the early phase of this first Pisan period. The two saints atop the sarcophagus (Figs. 149, 155), though somewhat less distinguished in their design and facture, were undoubtedly executed under Nino's immediate direction. He also contributed the effigy of the deceased (Fig. 156). One figure not previously discussed also belongs to this early phase of Nino's career: a statuette of Saint Francis in the depository of the Opera del Duomo in Pisa (Figs. 282–284). This work has been associated with the Scherlatti monument.[1] Although it is almost exactly the same size as two other figures more plausibly connected with that tomb (78 cm as opposed to 80 cm for the Saint Peter and Saint Paul [Figs. 285–288]), on stylistic grounds it can hardly date from 1362 when Scherlatti died and

[1] Burresi (1973), 6–12. The attribution to Nino is due to Papini (1912), 159f. Cf. Burresi (1983), 187.

a contract for the tomb was drawn up between Nino and the executors of the archbishop's will. Unlike Nino's later work, *Saint Francis* combines a strong sense of weight and gravity with a restrained elegance in the contrapposto stance and the fall of the drapery, the very characteristics that distinguish the early *Bishop* of Oristano and the slightly later angels from the Saltarelli tomb. Several details look ahead to Nino's style in a later work, the *Saint Peter* on the Cornaro monument (Figs. 125, 126), in particular, the carving of the hair and beard, and the structure of the head with the plane of the brow bending sharply at the temples and creating deep shadows beneath the eyebrows. The figure of Saint Francis, then, must have been made, not for the Scherlatti tomb, but for some other monument, possibly even the holy water stoup upon which it stood in the Baptistry of Pisa until the early seventeenth century.[2]

During the middle of this period, that is ca. 1345, Nino executed the *Madonna and Child* (Figs. 118–122) in Venice – not necessarily for the Cornaro monument – that combines elements from both the Orvieto and the Saltarelli Madonnas by Andrea. The pose, gesture, and disposition of the *Madonna*'s drapery are modeled after the Orvieto statuette (Fig. 110) as is the position and four-square huskiness of the Christ Child. In contrast to the Orvieto figure, however, the Venetian *Madonna* displays a pronounced Gothic sway and the tilt of the Madonna's head toward the Child resembles, and is even at a sharper angle than, that of the Saltarelli *Madonna* (Fig. 151).

It is, in fact, very unlikely that the figures of Mary, Saint Peter, and Saint Paul on the Cornaro monument were made for the tomb.[3] In his last will and testament, dated 10 January 1367, Doge Marco Cornaro stated his desire to be buried in the Church of Santi Giovanni e Paolo (and if that was not possible, then in the Church of Santa Maria of the minor friars) and that an "honorable tomb" should be constructed in the place where he was to be buried (Doc. 38). The implication would seem to be that up to that point, at least, no tomb had been commissioned. As from a stylistic point of view the Venetian *Madonna* cannot have been made between the date of the last will and 5 December 1368, the *terminus ante quem* for Nino's death (Doc. 68), clearly the *Madonna* must have been executed prior to any consideration for the Cornaro monument – executed, that is, either for another tomb or altar, or for no particular monument but to be sold as needed. Nothing prevents us, then, from placing the *Madonna* within the period when Nino was his father's assistant in Pisa. The accompanying saints on the Cornaro tomb also belong to these years. Every detail of the Saint Peter (Fig. 125) suggests that

[2] Papini (1912), 159f.

[3] Valentiner (1926–7), 242f., observed that the statues are made of Carrara marble whereas the architectural framing and the figure of the doge below are composed of Venetian marble; the socles of the statues, moreover, appear to be too large for the niches.

it must be placed between the *Bishop* of Oristano (and consequently the Saltarelli angels and the figure of San Francesco) and that other Saint Peter in Santa Maria della Spina (Figs. 295, 296). The heavy voluminous drapery with calligraphic hemlines in the two figures of Peter marks a radical departure from the soft, clinging, gravity-drawn drapery seen in the earlier sculptures. At the same time, from the Cornaro to the Spina figure there is a markedly greater linearity in the treatment of anatomical details and drapery. The accompanying saint on the Cornaro monument, on the other hand – *Saint Paul* (Fig. 128) – whose body movements are less free, whose drapery is less naturalistic, and whose hair and beard display a mechanical symmetry of design, betrays the hand of Tommaso Pisano, who was also an assistant in Andrea's workshop. Although the over-all conception is far superior to that of the saints on the San Francesco altar signed by Tommaso, *Saint Paul* may be compared to the saint on the extreme left of the altarpiece (Figs. 330, 334). Especially comparable are the facial features and expression, the me-chanical carving and pattern of the beard, and the very narrow sloping shoulders. Tom-maso shows an increasing tendency to accentuate the furrows of the brow and lines of the cheeks in his search for expressiveness. This tendency is seen again in the statuette of Saint Paul (Fig. 287) in the Museo di San Matteo, Pisa, here attributed to Tommaso. The head of the Venetian Saint Paul is not lacking in a certain nobility, a quality Tom-maso evidently was able to sustain in works executed while in his father's shop but that may be seen to diminish in works produced during his collaboration with Nino or after he became an independent master (see chapter 10).

If the Madonna and two saints were executed by Nino and Tommaso working in An-drea's Pisan shop, it is inconceivable that the angels at the far ends of the tomb (Figs. 123, 124, 129) also came from this workshop. Nothing in the oeuvre of Andrea, Nino, or Tommaso resembles the quasi-geometric simplification of forms seen in the angels, although the sculptor probably had in mind the upper angels of the Saltarelli monument.

The Cornaro angels were designed at a later date (probably after the death of the Doge in 1368) by a Tuscan sculptor, perhaps a former assistant of Nino who, upon the latter's death, was called on to execute peripheral figures for Cornaro's tomb to be added to the three already available. The rather drastic simplifications of form suggest that these angels were executed with some haste. The sculptor combines elements that may be associated with several Tuscan masters. The blocky, simplified forms of the drapery are reminiscent of those of the attendants of *Henry VII* (Fig. 186) by Tino and also re-call the angels holding candelabra on Orcagna's tabernacle in Or San Michele. The chubby faces with their excessively elongated eyes and broad smiles recall some faces by Giovanni di Balduccio. The execution, however, belongs to two different hands: The intent of the sculptor of the left-hand angel was to emulate as closely as possible the face and expression of the Cornaro *Madonna* herself as comparisons of the front and profile views make clear (Figs. 120, 122, 124). The right-hand angel, by a lesser talent, has more schematized hair patterns, the smile is transformed into a grimace, and the figure indicates less understanding of the contrapposto pose (Figs. 123, 129).

Toward the end of the bracket 1343–7, Nino enters a new phase in his development. Undoubtedly stimulated, in part, by Andrea, whose Saltarelli *Madonna* would seem to be based on a French model, Nino's work now shows an increasing assimilation of northern Gothic elements. To this phase belongs the *Saint Peter* accompanying the *Madonna* in Santa Maria della Spina and, a few years later when he must have followed his father to Orvieto, the right-hand angel of the Maestà (Figs. 295, 299, 300). By October 1349 Nino was capomaestro of Orvieto Cathedral but no other work in that city may be attributed to him.

Nothing is known of Nino's activity between the end of his tenure as capomaestro of Orvieto in 1350[4] and 1358–9 when documents refer to goldsmith work done for the *comune* of Pisa (Doc. 62–5). No extant examples of such work have been attributed to him. As most of the remaining works associated with Nino (the major exception being the Florentine *Madonna)* are in Pisa or may be related to a Pisan commission, it is probable that at the end of his stay in Orvieto Nino returned to Pisa to establish a workshop there.

Nino's second Pisan period, then, extends from ca. 1350 until, at the latest, 5 December 1368. Probably datable to the late 1350s and early 1360s are two Madonna and Child figures, one in the Detroit Institute of Arts and the other in Santa Maria Novella, Florence (Figs. 301, 303, 108, 109). The tendency noted in the figures of Saint Peter in Santa Maria della Spina and the angel in Orvieto (Figs. 296, 299) may be observed in these Madonna groups, too. In contrast to his earlier, more classicizing style, there is a continuing shift toward more elongated proportions, a stronger Gothic contrapposto stance, and swinging drapery rhythms played against vertically cascading hemlines.

The beautiful marble statuette (76.2 cm) in Detroit, which retains traces of gilt and polychromy, has received attributions that alternate between Andrea and Nino (Figs. 301–303).[5] The figure, however, is so close in conception and execution to the *Madonna* in Santa Maria Novella that it is surely by the same hand. The elegant Gothic

---

[4] See chapter 1, n. 27.

[5] First published as a work of Nino by Valentiner (1927a), 195–216, and Heil (1927), 62, this attribution was reaffirmed (1930) by the latter and then (1938) by the former. About a decade later, however, Valentiner changed his mind and ascribed the statuette to Andrea (1947), 163–84. Subsequently, I. Toesca (1950) published the marble figure as "Workshop Nino Pisano (?)." The discussion that follows is adapted from Moskowitz (1984).

contrapposto of the Detroit *Madonna* represents a clear break with the more stable postures seen in Andrea's figures (Figs. 110, 133). The soft modeling of the face, in which the sense of underlying bone structure is deemphasized (Fig. 303), is akin to Nino's treatment in the Florentine *Madonna* as is the sweet, almost honeyed smile, less subtle than the restrained expressions characterizing all of Andrea's figures (see Figs. 111, 134, 135). The Christ Child with his narrow temples, puffy cheeks, and open mouth is almost identical to the Florentine Christ. Other details further reveal the correspondences between the Florentine and Detroit sculptures. The carving of the Madonna's hair in regular waves forming a pattern of striations on the surface contrasts with the variegated, far more plastic handling apparent in all of Andrea's figures, but is similar to that seen in the Venetian and Florentine Madonnas (Figs. 108, 120). Each of Nino's statuettes strives for an almost artificial elegance; a clue is to be discovered in the mannered turn of the wrists, discernible in the Detroit figure as well. Such unmotivated bends or twists do not appear in Andrea's sculpture. Compared to the Florentine *Madonna*, however, the figure in Detroit places a greater emphasis on the articulation of the body beneath the drapery, and the displacement of the hips and shoulders is less pronounced.[6] Therefore, like the Venetian figure, the Detroit statuette probably stands somewhere between the earlier Pisan figures (Fig. 130) whose style still betrays the Giottesque and classicizing *gravitas* of his father and the Florentine *Madonna* (Fig. 109), which reveals Nino's strong response to early fourteenth-century French Gothic style. The Detroit *Madonna* shows particular closeness to a group of Madonna and Child statuettes coming from an influential Parisian atelier active during the second quarter of the fourteenth century.[7] Pose, gesture (especially the downward bend of the right hand), and drapery configuration unify this entire group, and a description of one of these figures – the *Virgin and Child* from the parish church in Bouée (Loire-Atlantique) (Fig. 305) – applies equally well to our statuette: "Elégante sans excès, d'afféterie sereine sans sévérité, la Vierge atteint à une sorte d'équilibre classique entre naturel et préciosité."[8] Equally suggestive is a comparison of the Detroit *Madonna* with an ivory seated *Virgin and Child* (Fig. 304) made in Paris between 1320 and 1330; it is of more than passing interest that this object is listed in an inventory in San Francesco, Assisi, dated 1370.[9] The physiognomic type of the French Virgin with her small

[6] The back is modeled with greater plasticity and in greater detail than is the case with either the Cornaro or the Santa Maria Novella *Madonna*. These two, however, though considerably under life-size (125 cm and 135 cm, respectively), were intended for tombs or altars in public places rather than for more intimate settings. The De-troit *Madonna*, only 76.2 cm, is exquisitely modeled in the back and was clearly designed for close viewing and private devotion.

[7] Cf. *Les Fastes du Gothique*, catalogue nos. 8, 31, 32, 33, 34, and 35.

[8] Ibid., 89.

[9] Ibid., 181f.

narrow eyes, slender nose, and tiny, V-shaped mouth seems reflected in the Tuscan example.

Not only does the Detroit statuette accord much better in style with Nino's oeuvre than with Andrea's, but when it is viewed in the context of the general evolution of Tuscan Gothic Madonna and Child images, it clearly fits into a development subsequent to that of Andrea's figures; indeed, the Madonna statues by Andrea and Nino Pisano may be said to form the penultimate and final chapters, respectively, in the history of Tuscan Gothic Madonnas preceding the great developments at the turn of the fifteenth century. As is true of its counterpart in France, the *Madonna and Child* in Tuscany evolves from an austere iconic image toward one increasingly infused with a sense of humanity and intimacy. In Nicola Pisano's Arca di San Domenico *Virgin and Child* of ca. 1265 (Fig. 306), the Madonna is rigid and columnar with closed contours, prismatic drapery folds, and compact forms. She looks straight ahead and the Child's glance is perpendicular to hers. On the Siena Duomo pulpit (1265–8), the Virgin and Child still direct their glances across each other, but the drapery folds are less angular and the Christ Child is not as stiff (Fig. 307).

The image of the Madonna and Child undergoes a radical development in the sculpture of Giovanni Pisano. His earlier figures of ca. 1300 – the Pisa Baptistry tympanum *Madonna*[10] and the ivory statuette[11] – are characterized, as were Nicola's Madonnas, by mother and child without closeness – physical or emotional. Only in a later work, the half-length *Madonna* for the Pisa Duomo of ca. 1302 (Fig. 308),[12] can one speak for the first time of a mother–child bonding, a relationship that characterizes all of Giovanni's subsequent Madonnas.[13] Here Christ and Mary turn toward each other and their intimacy is emphasized by the curve of Mary's veil, which is continued in the line of Christ's arm and mantle. In the Arena Chapel statue of ca. 1305,[14] the Child has lost all rigidity and leans toward Mary, his arm resting on her shoulder. Finally, in the Prato statuette of ca. 1312 (Fig. 309), the pitch of the relationship intensifies. Christ touches Mary's crown as she leans her head downward to direct her smiling gaze at Him. No longer a Roman matron with regular and planar features – characteristics of Nicola's early Madonnas – Giovanni's Prato *Madonna* presents delicate transitions in the soft

[10] White (1966), Pl. 37b.

[11] Ibid., Pl. 37a.

[12] Although generally considered an early work by Giovanni (c. 1280), a document of 1302 concerning a block of marble for a Madonna and Child group to be made for the *maiori ecclesia* may be connected with this half-length figure. See Barsotti (1957), 47–56. As indicated by Barsotti, the style of the figure is consonant with a later date; its iconography, in my opinion, supports this thesis.

[13] See Seidel (1972), 181–92.

[14] Pope-Hennessy (1972), Fig. 19.

planes and the contours of the face. This softening of the features and increase in the sense of intimacy between the two figures are the points of departure for Andrea's conception. As a disciple of Giotto, however, and because of his profound classical stance, Andrea rejects the extreme emotionalism of Giovanni, just as he rejects the extravagances of fourteenth-century French sculpture. These latter ideals are absorbed, rather, by Nino as is evident in his Detroit and Florentine Madonnas. In these, he wholeheartedly incorporates some of the mannerisms found in early fourteenth-century French sculpture, particularly the exaggerated Gothic S-curve in the stance, the idiosyncratic turn of the wrists, the winsome smiles, and the melodious drapery patterns (cf. Figs. 302, 305). Nino's Madonnas, in turn, were to inspire dozens of lithe, svelte, smiling Marys gazing lovingly at Christ with an unprecedented intimacy of expression.[15]

Among such figures may be counted an alabaster statuette (35 cm) of exquisite workmanship in the Staatliche Museen, Berlin (Figs. 310, 311) by a very close follower of Nino, probably one trained in his workshop.[16] The figure is closely modeled on, though is not identical to, that in Santa Maria Novella (Fig. 109). Like the Detroit *Madonna*, however, the back is carved with a precision and finish that are fully equal to the front view.[17] On the other hand, the Christ Child's ears are out of proportion to his head and the carving of the hair is somewhat cruder than one would expect from a work by Nino.

Somewhat further removed, yet still very close to the master's style, is the polychromed marble *Madonna and Child* (60 cm) (Fig. 312) formerly in the church at Mantignano, now stored in the palace of the archbishop of Florence.[18] It, too, depends icono-

[15] The sculpture of Nino Pisano and his followers, even those works that date from the decade or two after the Black Death, seem to belie the notion of a return to iconic and inaccessible images in the representation of sacred personages following that great catastrophe. Although this is an issue that deserves further investigation, it is possible that the hieratic, pessimistic art of the mid-trecento (which is the focus of Meiss's provocative study [1951]), and the intimate evocative style of Nino are opposite sides of the same coin. Perhaps each reveals an attempt to deal with catastrophic reality — one by means of pietistic discipline, the other by means of sentiment and sensibility. There is some evidence, moreover, that the apocryphal literature that contributed so much to the new direct relationship between worshipper and the holy personages during the earlier part of the fourteenth century continued to find strong following even after the Black Death. The *Meditations on the Life of Christ* by the Pseudo Bonaventura, dating from the late thirteenth century, was copied hundreds of times during the following centuries and continued to exert an influence on the visual arts. See Ragusa and Green (1961), xxii. Even so stern a mystic as the Dominican preacher Jacopo Passavanti (1302–57) insisted on the humanity of Mary, who remains "tutta piena di pietade e di misericordia" — the very image preferred by Nino and his followers. On Passavanti, see Petrocchi (1978), 65–7.

[16] Volbach (1930), 91, attributes the figure to Nino and states that it comes from Tuscany. See also Valentiner (1927b), 195ff.; I. Toesca (1950), 56.

[17] See n. 6.

[18] This work is attributed to Nino by Carli (1934a) and to a follower by I. Toesca (1950), 56.

graphically and stylistically on the Santa Maria Novella *Madonna* (Fig. 109), although its nearest antecedent from all viewpoints is the statuette in Berlin (Fig. 310). The sculptor is somewhat less adept at handling the contrapposto stance than was Nino, and other details such as the round peasant face and short, thick neck of the Madonna betray the hand of a follower rather than Nino himself. Like the Berlin statuette, the work shows close study of Nino's technique, especially his ability to bring out the luminosity of the marble surfaces.

The last Madonna that deserves serious consideration is the over life-size (172 cm) figure in Santissima Annunziata in Trapani, Sicily (Figs. 313–315), a masterpiece that epitomizes that development of intimacy and tenderness in the relationship of mother and child with which the late thirteenth and fourteenth centuries concerned themselves so fervently.[19] By means of touch and glance, the colloquy between the two personages has an emotional intensity that is perhaps not found again until the baroque period. There can be no doubt that the work is not by Nino although there is an indirect connection between the sculptor of this superb marble and the Ninesque tradition. I would ascribe this work to the master of the Santa Caterina *Annunciation* pair (Figs. 137, 138). The robust, handsome face of the Madonna recalls the figure of Mary in Pisa, and the drapery exhibits that combination of fluidity and rigidity that we have observed in the Pisan group. The comparison to the Pisan *Angel* (Fig. 137) would be even closer were not parts of two strongly projecting folds in the latter broken off; this is apparent from a glance at the Washington replica (Figs. 147, 148). The strong neck, cylindrical arms with strongly projecting elbows, the large hands, and the folds in the back of the mantle that merge into the smooth planes of the otherwise unembellished rear view resemble comparable details in the Santa Caterina group. Finally, the author of both groups is clearly concerned with the effective display of life-size and over-life-size figures communicating

---

[19] On the Trapani *Madonna*, see especially Bottari (1969–70), 297–332. According to local legend, the figure originally came from the "east." On its way to Pisa, it was thrown into the sea near Sicily during a storm and later found by fishermen of Trapani. A seventeenth-century source notes that the mantle of the Madonna contained an inscription in Arabic but in "Syriac" letters. The inscription is not extant; it included the date 730 and stated that the figure was made for a priest in Endithet, Cyprus. Kruft, 302, translates this Muslim date as 1352. He notes, further, that the alabasterlike marble has characteristics that indicate a Greek origin, and proposes the extremely

interesting hypothesis that the Trapani *Madonna* was made by a Pisan sculptor working in Cyprus.

The figure, which is considered to have miraculous properties, had tremendous appeal during the fifteenth and sixteenth centuries, and was copied numerous times. On at least two occasions, a sculptor — Francesco Laurana — was specifically obliged by contract to execute marble copies of the Trapani *Madonna*. See Kruft, 297f. Copies and adaptations of the figure are to be found in the Louvre; in the Museo di Arte di Catalona, Barcelona; in the Duomo of Palermo; in a church in Erice; in the Detroit Institute of the Arts (an ivory statuette), and elsewhere.

with each other; and it is difficult to think of another fourteenth-century sculpture that achieves this so successfully.[20]

In considering Nino's activity as an independent master after 1350, one is confronted with the problem of the Scherlatti and Moricotti monuments (Figs. 316–318, 320–324) now in the Camposanto, Pisa. A contract between the executors of Giovanni Scherlatti's will and Nino Pisano (Doc. 67) stipulates that Nino make and install in the Duomo of Pisa a wall tomb of Carrara marble to include a reclining effigy of the archbishop flanked by marble angels. The sepulcher is to be surmounted by a polylobed arch also of Carrara marble. The front of the sepulcher should contain in the middle a Pietà flanked by angels and the side compartments should contain the Virgin Mary and John the Evangelist, each flanked by two angels. There should also be figures of Saints Peter and Paul flanking the monument. The sarcophagus was apparently to be supported by consoles surmounted by three polyfoil arches, all done according to a drawing that Nino had supplied to the executors. Payment is to be made for the purchase of gold leaf.

In the sixteenth century, the marble tombs of Archbishop Scherlatti (d. 1362) and Archbishop Moricotti (d. 1395) were seen on the wall of the sacristy opposite the doorway. In the eighteenth century, the tombs were still there and were described as similar.

[20] The attributions of Madonna and Child figures to Andrea and Nino are numerous and for the most part unwarranted. The following is a list of rejected attributions with brief comments on their relationship to our sculptors:

1. Berlin (Dahlem), formerly Simon Collection. I. Toesca (1950), Pl. 152. By a late trecento/early quattrocento follower of Andrea Pisano.

2. Binghamton, University Art Gallery (State University of New York at Binghamton). Published in sale catalogue, American Art Galleries, *Order of Sale* (1968), catalogue no. 119. By an early fifteenth-century follower of Nino Pisano.

3. Cleveland Museum of Art (see Wixom [1972], 263–83), by a late trecento follower of Andrea Pisano.

4. Fiesole, Museo Bandini. Viani (1981), no. 21. Late trecento follower of Nino Pisano.

5. Florence, Horne Museum. Provincial follower of Nino.

6. Florence, San Frediano. Polychromed wood. Follower of Nino Pisano, second half trecento.

7. London, Victoria and Albert Museum. Gilt bronze figurine, 9.3 cm high (not including head,

which is not original). Attributed to Nino by Weinberger (1937b), 69. By mid-fourteenth century follower of Andrea Pisano.

8. Palaia, San Andrea. Procacci (1933), 238. I had considered this to be by a late trecento follower of Nino. The intriguing possibility that the follower is Francesco di Valdambrino is suggested by the recent discovery of an inscription with date made during restorations on the sculpture by Dottoressa M. Burresi. According to a brief notice in *La Nazione*, 16 January 1984, the inscription on the base reads: "Fatta fare dalla compagnia dei Bianchi di Palaia 1403. Magister *Francisco de Senis sculpsit.*"

9. Pisa, Museo di San Matteo, formerly on the spire of Santa Maria della Spina. Carli (1934a), 197; Carli (1974), 25f.; Weinberger (1937b), 86, and Fig. 37. Mid-trecento follower of Andrea Pisano, close to author of London gilt bronze figurine.

10. Pisa, San Nicola, wood Madonna and Child. Carli (1960), 56; Burresi (1973), 9f. By close follower of Nino Pisano, third quarter of the fourteenth century.

By 1833 the two tombs were in a chapel of the Camposanto, most likely the same chapel where they are today and where they were seen in 1837.[21] The tomb that contains, on the face of the sarcophagus, the program specified in the contract is labeled by an inscription (of later date) on the lower ledge as the tomb of Moricotti (Fig. 317), whereas the tomb opposite has an entirely different program although in a similar format (Fig. 316). For this reason, Supino suggested that when the tombs were transferred from the Duomo to the Camposanto in the early nineteenth century, the sarcophagi were inadvertently switched so that the sarcophagus now identified as that of Moricotti actually belongs to Scherlatti and is the one executed by Nino.[22]

Some scholars have rejected the attribution to Nino, despite the correspondence between the contract and the program of the reliefs, on the grounds that the reliefs are too advanced for the 1360s and are more consonant with the later dating of Moricotti's death in the 1390s. According to one view, the abundant drapery foreshadows the style of Sluter; according to another, the exuberant ornamental effect of the drapery forms rounded out at the bottom connect the tomb to the International Gothic style.[23]

Before considering the attribution of each tomb, it is worth examining the relationship between the two. Evidently, one of them was intended to be an almost exact replica of the other. Although the programs of the reliefs differ, in each case the sarcophagus front is divided into three fields, each of which contains a large figure in the center flanked by smaller angels. As to the effigies, fold for fold, contour for contour, the disposition of the drapery is identical, down to the detail of the garment tucked under and around the feet. Close examination reveals, however, that the figure on the tomb labeled Scherlatti is more sensitively carved and, moreover, represents an older man (Fig. 324). The wrinkles on the brow, the crow's-feet about the eyes, the folds of skin from the nose toward the chin, and the open mouth revealing a row of upper teeth are all lacking in the figure above the Moricotti tomb in which the carving is smoother and more generalized (Fig. 323). The difference in quality between the two effigies is small but noticeable. Curiously, this difference is inverted with regard to the sarcophagus fronts. The reliefs on the tomb labeled Moricotti (Fig. 317) are unquestionably of higher quality than those on the tomb opposite (Fig. 316): The handling of drapery is more sensitive, the faces more expressive, and the modeling both more subtle and more precise.

Without regard to any external evidence, if one may assume that the prototypes in each case are of higher quality, it seems clear that although the effigy above the tomb labeled Moricotti was intended to replicate that labeled Scherlatti, the reliefs of the lat-

[21] Ronan (1982), 138ff.

[22] Supino (1904), 229f.

[23] The attribution is rejected by Salmi (1930), 175–91; Weinberger (1937b), 85f.; I. Toesca (1950), 49; Kosegarten (1967), 235–49, p. 244.

ter were carved in emulation of those of the former. Thus, it seems probable that in both cases the effigy of one belongs to the sarcophagus front of the tomb on the opposite wall. The conclusion seems inevitable that Nino Pisano executed the effigy above the Scherlatti inscription and the sarcophagus front of the tomb opposite in fulfillment of his contract obligations to the Scherlatti family.

Other factors tend to support this view. With the exception of the open mouth and teeth (a predilection of Nino's),[24] the realistic details of the figure of Scherlatti are found on the effigy of Archbishop Saltarelli in Santa Caterina, Pisa, which, as we have seen, was executed in Andrea's shop probably by Nino. The reliefs on the so-called Moricotti tomb – which we shall henceforth refer to as the "Moricotti" tomb – are also not inconsistent with the style of Nino despite the objections referred to above. The execution is uneven, probably due to workshop intervention, but the head of Christ (Fig. 318) has a refinement and a sensitivity of expression, and the carving of hair and beard a richness of texture, that recall the *Bishop Saint* in Oristano (Fig. 131). Furthermore, although it is true that the decorative exuberance of the rounded-off drapery forms of Mary and John foreshadow aspects of the International Gothic style, the same may be said for the voluminous and richly cascading drapery forms seen in the earlier figures of Saint Peter and the Orvieto angel (Figs. 296, 299). Indeed, as has already been suggested, Nino may be considered an important link between the courtly Gothic of early fourteenth-century European art and the International Gothic style as it developed in Italy. Finally, a great deal of weight must be given to the fact that a contract exists stipulating a specific program, and a sarcophagus plausibly connected with Giovanni Scherlatti is extant with that very same program. It seems extremely unlikely that Nino would have changed the program having signed a contract for the commission.[25]

Francesco Moricotti was appointed Archbishop of Pisa in 1363. He died, probably at a ripe old age, in 1395.[26] The effigy above the "Moricotti" monument represents a rather young man (Fig. 323), suggesting that the figure was executed at a time considerably before the death of its intended occupant. As Moricotti's tomb was conceived to closely follow that of his predecessor, it seems rather unlikely that it would have been designed and executed over three decades later; rather, it is more probable that Moricotti ordered his tomb shortly after his appointment as archbishop in 1363 and that he ordered it

---

[24] Cf. the *Man of Sorrows* from Santa Cecilia in the Museo di San Matteo (Fig. 319) and the *Christ Child* of the Cornaro monument (Fig. 121).

[25] Similar conclusions have been reached independently by Burresi (1983), 186f.

The reliefs on the "Moricotti" sarcophagus (i.e., that made for Scherlatti) still have traces of gold leaf, but on the tomb opposite no such traces are visible to the naked eye. The Scherlatti contract mentions payment for gold leaf. These observations do not, of course, rule out the possibility that the later tomb was also embellished with gold leaf.

[26] See n. 21.

from the very same workshop that had executed the monument of his predecessor Scherlatti. Thus, it could have been made any time between 1363 and 1368, the *terminus ante quem* for the death of Nino Pisano. Although undistinguished, the tomb is clearly Ninesque and was probably executed by assistants following the general design of the earlier monument. Nino himself may have been busy with a far more pressing commission from a powerful and demanding patron – Giovanni dell'Agnello, Doge of Pisa, a subject to which we shall return shortly.

There are extant at least five other sculptures that may belong to either the Scherlatti or Moricotti monuments: two angels (Figs. 290–293) and a figure of Saint Peter (Figs. 285, 286) in the Opera del Duomo, and figures of Saint Paul (Figs. 287, 288) and a *Bishop Saint* (Fig. 289) in the Museo di San Matteo. As the contract for the Scherlatti tomb calls for two saints and two angels, and the Moricotti monument was evidently a replica of the former, there must have been at least one more saint and two more angels; these are lost or unidentified.

One of the angels (Figs. 290, 291), with its graceful garment subtly reflecting the columnar torso beneath, is extremely close in style to the angels in relief on the "Moricotti" tomb, particularly the angel to the right of Christ (Fig. 318). The second (Figs. 292, 293), although evidently designed by the same hand, is somewhat harder and more mechanical in its execution, particularly in the carving of the features and hair. That these two angels are not from the same monument is suggested by their differing sizes (61 cm and 50 cm) and by the fact that the first is left rough in back whereas the second is carved fully in-the-round. The pose of the 60-cm-high angel (Fig. 290) and the expression on its face as though holding back tears clearly indicate that it belonged to a tomb and flanked the effigy. The other figure (Fig. 292), whose face and arms are damaged and whose expression is less identifiable, may also, however, belong to a tomb. If these may be associated with the Scherlatti and Moricotti tombs, as seems very plausible, there is no way to determine which angel belonged to which tomb although, again, one may hypothesize that the one of superior quality (Fig. 290) is closer to Nino's own hand and belongs to the monument for Scherlatti.

The three extant saints (Figs. 285–289) are each 80 cm high; two of them, however, are carved only in the front with the back left in a rough state. Only the figure of Saint Peter (Fig. 286) is carved fully in-the-round. The Scherlatti contract calls for representations of Saints Peter and Paul. It is not likely, however, that both of these extant figures come from the same tomb since they would have been symmetrically disposed on the tomb and so either both would have been carved fully in the back, or neither would have been. As is the case with the angels, probably one of these belongs to the Scherlatti and the other to the Moricotti tomb.

The style of all three saints is closer to that of Tommaso than to Nino Pisano. The resemblance between Saint Paul (Fig. 287) and its counterpart on the Cornaro monument (Fig. 128), as well as several figures on the altar in San Francesco (Figs. 330–334), has already been pointed out. That same resemblance obtains with respect to Saint Peter (Fig. 285), which may be compared to the second saint from the left (Fig. 330) on the altar in San Francesco. Especially close is the handling of the drapery and the awkwardly realized contrapposto stance. As is true of the figure of Saint Paul, the right hand of the *Bishop Saint* (Figs. 287, 289) is grossly distorted. The facial features, hair, and beard are twin to those of Saint Francis on the extreme right of the San Francesco altar (Fig. 334). The phlegmatic drapery and inarticulate contrapposto stance further suggest that the *Bishop Saint* is by Tommaso.

On the basis of the central panel of the "Moricotti" tomb (Fig. 318), a half-length *Man of Sorrows* (Fig 319), formerly in the Church of Santa Cecilia and now in the Museo di San Matteo, may also be attributed to Nino.[27] The narrow shoulders, delicate features, and rich hair pattern are almost identical; the partially open mouth showing a row of teeth is also characteristic of Nino. The relief has been identified with "una bella e devota Pietà di marmo con l'armi dei Gherardeschi e Upezzinghi," which was once in San Francesco de'Ferri and was made to honor a marriage between members of the two families bringing peace to the former rival groups.[28] An inventory of 1833 refers to a relief with the Gherardeschi and Upezzinghi arms that stood under a Pietà; the relief is extant in the Camposanto (Fig. 325). This relief has been attributed, without cogent reasons in my opinion, to Tommaso Pisano.[29] Although the Pietà under discussion may be that which was made for the Gherardeschi and Upezzinghi families, there is at present no evidence to support this.

Sometime after 13 August 1364 when Giovanni dell'Agnello, a wealthy and powerful merchant of Pisa, assumed the title of Doge and initiated his tyrannous regime, Nino was commissioned to make the Doge's tomb.[30] A document of 5 December 1368 (Doc. 68) refers to a payment of twenty gold florins (obviously a *final* payment) to be made to the heirs of Nino for money owed by Giovanni dell'Agnello for the latter's tomb. According to the document, the monument stood near the Church of San Francesco by the door through which one enters the first cloister. The facade of San Francesco was destroyed and rebuilt in the nineteenth century, but a woodcut of 1783 by Ferdinando Fambrini (Fig. 327) and an engraving by B. Polloni in his *Vedute Esterne di Chiese Antiche di Pisa*, 1835 (Fig. 326) show the facade and the adjoining

---

[27] Supino (1904), 239; Supino (1933), 103.
[28] Supino (1904), 239.
[29] Supino (1904), 239; Venturi (1906), 517.

[30] On the life of Giovanni dell'Agnello, see Caturegli (1921); also Bonaini (1846), 59–61.

cloister with its doorway flanked by two trecento monuments. Which one is that of the Doge? According to Bonaini, Giovanni dell'Agnello was a vain man who liked to display himself with a great deal of pomp (but who was recalcitrant in paying the wages owed to artists such as Nino and Tommaso Pisano).[31] It seems likely that the more elaborate of the trecento monuments flanking the doorway is the tomb commissioned from Nino. No extant fragments have been convincingly identified with this monument. The Agnello tomb is the last known work of Nino Pisano. Undoubtedly, the family workshop continued to be active, now under the direction of Tommaso.

[31] Bonaini (1846), 59.

CHAPTER TEN
Tommaso Pisano

Tommaso Pisano seems to have been known primarily as a goldsmith, although, like Andrea and Nino, he was called on to design architectural and sculptural projects as well. The first record of him is in a document of 1363 when he is mentioned, together with several other goldsmiths, as participating in the war between Pisa and Florence, a war that lasted until 1364.[1] Between 1364 and 1368 he was engaged by the Doge of Pisa, Giovanni dell'Agnello, in various capacities: Among other things he designed a new palace (only the foundations were built, undoubtedly because work was halted after the expulsion of the doge), he executed a marble throne for the tyrant that was placed in the main tribune of the cathedral, and he built a tomb for the doge's wife, Margharita (Doc. 68), destroyed in a fire of 1596.[2] An inventory of 1368 (Doc. 70) for which Tommaso was a witness refers to him as *aurifice*.[3] The marble altar in San Francesco (Figs. 328–337) is the only signed work by Tommaso and bears the inscription TOMASO FIGLIUOLO . . . STRO ANDREA . . . F . . . ESTO LAVORO ET FU PISANO. Considering the weakness of the design and execution, it is likely that the work dates from after Nino's death when the vacuum left by the latter was filled by Tommaso; thus, we may date the high altar to the late 1360s or early 1370s. A reference of 28 September 1368 mentions Tommaso in connection with some angels for the Opera del Duomo (Doc. 71); these have not been identified. There are three more references to Tommaso, one in 1370 and two in 1371, but no mention of any work of art is made.

[1] Supino (1904), 245.
[2] Bonaini (1846), 60f.; Supino (1904), 236–45; Milanesi (1848), vol. 1, 493.
[3] Bonaini (1846), 60; Milanesi (1848), vol. 1, 493.

The marble altar of San Francesco (Figs. 328–337) is an elaborately sculptured and polychromed polyptych that contains in the center a Virgin and Child flanked by four angels, two of which are flying and holding a cloth of honor over her head.[4] To left and right in individual niches there are standing saints, three to each side. The background of the niches is painted with a variety of patterns in gold and color. The San Francesco altarpiece was evidently the prototype for Jacopo della Quercia's Trenta altarpiece of 1416–22, also an elaborate marble polyptych,[5] and this fact may indeed be Tommaso's most important claim to a place in the history of art. Tommaso's figures, however, could hardly have proved inspiring to Jacopo for they are stiff and awkward and the drapery lacks fluidity. The stance of the Virgin (Fig. 329) is an inept attempt to reproduce a contrapposto pose. Only the reliefs in the predella below have a certain homely charm – as in the Annunciation (Fig. 335) in which a curious servant peers over the shoulder of Gabriel in order to be privy to the message, or in the Baptism of Christ (Fig. 336) in which the Savior stands waist high in the water in a relaxed pose with one leg crossed over the other, or again in the Resurrection (Fig. 337) in which an angel appears just in time to prevent the lid of the sarcophagus, pushed up by the omnipotent Christ, from falling on the ground and breaking (or perhaps it is the angel who has kindly lifted the lid to avoid harm to Christ's head as he resurrects). The "predella style" of earlier Sienese sculpture has its last fling in these reliefs.

As we have seen, Tommaso Pisano was a competent enough sculptor during the years that he worked in close collaboration with Andrea or Nino. He was responsible for the *Saint Paul* (Fig. 128) made in Andrea's workshop between 1343 and 1347 which was later sent to Venice for the Cornaro monument. He also may have executed, under the direct supervision of Andrea, the figure of John the Baptist (Fig. 294) in Santa Maria della Spina. In Nino's workshop in the 1360s he collaborated on some figures for the Scherlatti and Moricotti tombs (Figs. 285–289), and finally, as an independent master he executed the altar in San Francesco (Fig. 328). Rather than an evolution toward increasing mastery, one may discern in the work of Tommaso a devolution from his earlier works executed under the watchful eye of his father to his middle period in collaboration with the apparently less stringent Nino to his late independent work. With the San Francesco altar, the so-called Pisan school, so brilliantly initiated by Nicola Pisano over a century earlier, effectively reaches its demise.[6]

---

[4] The Christ Child's head is not original.

[5] Pope-Hennessy (1972), 212.

[6] It hardly seems possible that anything might linger from this tradition to feed into the great flowering of sculpture that was to take place at the turn of the quattrocento. Yet there are tantalizing indications that younger talents who were eventually to rise above the level of their masters were nurtured in the late Pisan workshops of both Nino and Tommaso Pisano, a subject to which we shall return in the Epilogue.

CHAPTER ELEVEN
Summary and Conclusions

Andrea d'Ugolino signed the upper edge of the framework of the bronze doors and in so doing identified himself as a Pisan. The visible signature of even a major artist on a monument was a rather rare occurrence in the Middle Ages. By prominently signing the doors, Andrea does more than inform the world of his place of origin. He makes a statement about his artistic tradition, and with an understated objectivity he confronts the viewer with a pointed reference to the aggressive, turbulent art and signature of his great predecessor, Giovanni Pisano.[1] Like Andrea's art, this inscription represents both a reaction against the style of Giovanni and an affirmation of the Pisan heritage shared by both.

The evidence points to Andrea's initial training in a Pisan goldsmith shop where he would have learned to work on a tiny scale developing an eye and a hand for minute decorative details. The miniature and at the same time monumental figures on the Baptistry doors, however, presuppose experience in a broader handling of plastic masses than was within the range of the medieval goldsmith. Evidence for this experience is seen in the wooden *Annunziata* of 1321. In Pisa Andrea found himself aligned to that

---

[1] Two long inscriptions on Giovanni's Pisa pulpit inform the viewer that Giovanni comes from Pisa and "is endowed above all others with command of the pure art of sculpture, sculpting splendid things in stone, wood and gold." Reference is made to "hostile injuries" he has experienced, the cause of which is envy, but, the wording goes on to say, "He proves himself unworthy who condemns him who is worthy of the diadem." For a complete transcription and translation of the inscriptions, see Pope-Hennessy (1972), 177f.

undercurrent of artistic activity that ran counter to the dominant mode of expression influenced by the sculpture of Giovanni Pisano. But the situation in Pisa was not favorable to Andrea's development; employment opportunities must have been extremely limited as there were no major sculptural projects under way, and even the plan to rebuild Santa Maria della Spina had withered by ca. 1325. Compared to the huge undertakings at Siena and Orvieto, Pisa must have seemed a dead end.

Andrea's relief style on the doors and on the Campanile, as well as many aspects of his contribution to the architecture of the Campanile, speak for an intimate acquaintance with, and the decisive impact of, Sienese art. That the environment in Siena stimulated artists to seek independent and personal modes of expression is clear from the variety of styles that developed during the first three decades of the fourteenth century. Sienese painters and sculptors avidly and visibly absorbed influences from the north and thus represented to the rest of Italy, as the far-reaching commissions during these decades indicate, *the* "avant-garde"; only Giotto rivals the Sienese in the cosmopolitan nature of his commissions.

Indeed, Sienese art and the painting of Giotto represent the two important artistic phenomena, both rooted in the sculpture of Nicola Pisano, that most profoundly affected Andrea's oeuvre. Predisposed against the intense emotional content and hyperenergetic forms of Giovanni's art, Andrea succeeded in combining and integrating elements from the rich and varied artistic modes that the climate in Siena encouraged. The clarity of the compositions, the linear harmonies of the draperies, and the humble idealism of the figures are indebted to the aesthetic of Tino di Camaino. The realist impulse, with its insistence on a palpable spatial environment, suggests Andrea's appreciation of such lesser Sienese masters as Goro di Gregorio. A number of specific motifs on the doors and Campanile would seem to depend directly on reliefs in Orvieto. The subtle draftsmanship and plastic definition of Andrea's carved contours lead, by way of the marble figures surrounding the rose window of Siena Cathedral, to Arnolfo – the softer, more mellow Arnolfo of the *Praesepe* in Rome. Finally, Andrea's sympathetic response to French art, already apparent in his earliest reliefs, would seem to have been stimulated by those elements in Sienese painting and sculpture that reflect the courtly elegance of French forms at the turn of the century. In short, Siena served as a fulcrum of divergent impulses that stimulated and provided sources for Andrea's receptive imagination. The sculpture of Nicola Pisano lies at the root of many of these Sienese developments; thus Sienese art, in its complex and variegated manifestations, may be seen to provide the most salient connecting link between Andrea's sculpture of the 1330s and the revolution that began three quarters of a century earlier.

In Florence, the sculptural embellishment of the Duomo came to an abrupt halt with the death of Arnolfo in 1302. Even the brief appearance of Tino did not alter the artistic momentum that had shifted from sculpture to painting – until the blatant gaps, decoratively and iconographically within the cathedral group became all too apparent, as it must have to anyone aware of the rich sculptural programs that had burst forth on northern cathedrals and even in Siena and Orvieto. By 1330 talk, if not plans, must already have been underway for the construction of a new Campanile. But there was unfinished business to attend to. Although the Baptistry mosaics had recently been completed, the statues begun by Tino for the portals were still unfinished and the plans for new metal doors remained dormant. If interest and money were not lacking during these years when the Florentine economy was approaching its peak, a sculptor equal to the tasks at hand was not to be seen within the city walls. Arnolfo and Tino had been trained in Siena; it was to Siena that the Operai probably turned. It seems likely that Andrea Pisano emerged from the Sienese-related workshop of Orvieto to take up the challenge of the Florentine projects.

Arriving in Florence, Andrea took up the work left unfinished by Tino, and executed the *Baptist* above the south portal of the Baptistry. His proven experience in monumental sculpture and his training as a goldsmith made him the logical choice for the execution of the Baptistry doors. The duality inherent in this background expresses itself artistically in Andrea's absorption of both traditions that were flourishing in early-trecento Florence: Giotto and the miniaturist schools.

We have seen, however, that despite the essential unity of the style of the reliefs, the bronze doors represent a watershed of many diverse influences, in addition to those of Giotto and the miniaturist schools. Tuscan monumental sculpture, goldsmith work, Sienese painting, and French art also played important roles. The almost miraculous integration of these disparate elements accounts for the decorative unity of the doors despite subtle changes in composition, figure style, and the handling of landscape and architectural motifs. These changes form the basis for the chronology that has been suggested regarding the conception and execution of the individual quatrefoils, a chronology more or less following the narrative sequence. In the earliest reliefs, the designs are determined to a large extent by abstract compositional considerations and established iconographic motifs. The later narratives reveal a willingness to experiment both spatially and compositionally. Furthermore, from the agitated linear patterns and small fold forms on the left valve, elements that contribute to the overall decorative effect of these reliefs, the style shifts to the more restrained and plastically conceived forms on the right valve.

The influence of Giotto is not limited to Andrea's Florentine period; it extends back in time to the Pisan *Annunziata* and forward to Andrea's late Pisan style. Whereas the wooden *Virgin* and the bronze reliefs reflect the impact of Giotto's Paduan style, the early Campanile hexagons, executed during the years when Andrea and Giotto were in direct, daily contact, are deeply indebted to the Peruzzi Chapel frescoes in their concern with the representation of interior space and coherent figure groups. In his second group of hexagons, no longer under the direct influence of Giotto, Andrea pursues a monumental, classicizing style that nevertheless remains indebted to the great painter's example. The idealized images, in which an imposing psychological and physical presence is achieved by means of the plasticity of the forms unencumbered by extraneous gestures or details, reveal Andrea as a true disciple of Giotto.

Deeply receptive to northern influence, Andrea's Florentine art reflects both the "mannerist" trend that had dominated Parisian workshops, and the classicizing current in Gothic sculpture. In addition, he was nourished by his native tradition: Classicism becomes a dominant element in his Campanile reliefs. The twenty-one reliefs on the lowest zone of the bell tower fall into three groups (Appendix B, 5–7), each of which may be connected in part to Andrea's changing role vis-à-vis the Campanile projects and in part to the changing cultural and economic climate of Florence. Those on the west side of the Campanile are stylistically and conceptually closest to the Baptistry reliefs. They reveal a similar interest in landscape representation but a more sophisticated handling of landscape and spatial elements. These early hexagons were created by Andrea Pisano with the help of assistants during the years when the sculptor was closely associated with Giotto, the capomaestro of Florence Cathedral.

The representation of *Sculpture* marks a turning point in Andrea's development. Markedly more monumental than the preceding reliefs, and conceived *all'antica*, *Sculpture* anticipates the "classical" reliefs of the east and south sides of the Campanile. In this second series of hexagons the concern with three-dimensional space is abandoned in favor of simple, monumental compositions in which the figures are placed against a flat, textured but neutral background. Iconography, figure and drapery style, and relief mode are clearly based on antique models. Each relief belonging to this group can be compared, either in terms of individual details or in its entirety, to an ancient prototype. This new style, which I have associated with the years following Giotto's death when Andrea became capomaestro of the Cathedral of Florence, may be connected in part with Andrea's new position in the Opera. With the overwhelming influence of Giotto's immediate presence gone, Andrea may have gained a new freedom to develop a classicizing impulse, announced earlier but achieving full expression only after 1337. The style of this group of reliefs, moreover, reflects a cultural climate highly receptive to the development of a classicizing mode of expression.

The Campanile project presented new problems requiring solutions quite different from those of the bronze doors. But in the two groups of hexagons associated with Andrea Pisano, the preference for compositional restraint and fluid draperies remains consistent. And the Giottesque idealism, in which an elevated concept of humanity is conveyed through broad naturalistic forms, a restrained emotional content and concentrated imagery is little altered.

A third series of hexagons, however, betrays a retreat from the protohumanistic ideals of the preceding group and anticipates the style that has been associated in Tuscan painting with the years following the Black Death. These were created by a new workshop called in after Andrea's departure for Pisa ca. 1343.

Having established a workshop in Pisa, Andrea found himself struggling between two modes, and in the process prepared the ground for future developments in Tuscan sculpture. The Orvieto *Madonna*, though infused with a gracious Gothic spirituality, is relatively stocky in its proportions whereas the stance and the rhythm and plasticity of the fold formations would seem to emulate some ancient prototype; in contrast, the Saltarelli *Madonna*, round-faced and carrying a full-bodied Giottesque Child, sways in an exaggerated Gothic pose and wears drapery almost totally lacking in body, the folds defined almost entirely by a series of linear curves on a planar surface. This tension between an impulse on the one hand toward decorative calligraphic rhythms, and on the other toward classical composure and stability, is wholly resolved in his late great *Madonna* in Santa Maria della Spina, datable toward the end of his Pisan sojourn, ca. 1347.

The Pisano workshop, the most active in Tuscany at the time, produced a number of distinct personalities. Andrea's assistants on the Saltarelli monument included one or two sculptors called from Florence who had worked on the Campanile, and his two sons Tommaso and Nino. Tommaso was the more malleable and lesser talent; closely following designs of Andrea (and later of Nino), he was able to produce some statues of note that essentially follow the canons established by his superiors. Nino, on the other hand, was a far more independent sculptor. He, too, however, experienced the conflict felt earlier and much more sharply by Andrea between the demands of two apparently opposing ideals (a conflict that, in one way or another, is characteristic of all Italian art of the fourteenth and fifteenth centuries).[2] His earlier figures – the *Bishop* in Oristano, the upper angels on the Saltarelli monument, and the *Saint Francis* in the Pisan Opera del Duomo – each turn slightly in a graceful, gentle torsion, but the gravity-drawn drapery descends in soft, predominantly vertical folds. The magnetic pull toward the decorative complications of contemporary French Gothic currents is felt in the

[2] The interweaving of opposing currents is implicit in the chapter headings in Hartt (1979), and is explicit in the organization of Beck (1981). Note also Pope-Hennessy's inclusion of Ghiberti, Jacopo della Quercia, and Nanni di Banco in his book on Italian Gothic sculpture (1972).

figures of Saint Peter in Santa Maria della Spina and the second angel in Orvieto. In these, Nino abandons that careful adjustment of decorative effects to anatomical structure seen, for example, in Andrea's Spina *Madonna* in favor of an emphasis on the surface rhythms of swinging curves and falling arabesques – anticipating the stylistic components of a Ciuffagni or a Niccolò Lamberti by half a century. By the time of the Santa Maria Novella *Madonna*, the attraction of the courtly ideal of French art with its mannered exaggerations prevails, and Nino's conception of the Madonna and Child and of the Annunciation became paradigms for almost a countless number of subsquent representations extending well into the fifteenth century.

Although nothing extant coming from his workshop indicates that Nino was capable of the orchestration and execution of complex programs such as Andrea achieved on the Baptistry doors or the Saltarelli monument, nevertheless, Nino proffered an aesthetic ideal that has much in common with, and may very well have prepared the ground for the reception of, the International Gothic style in Italy. Furthermore, it is clear that the workshops of Nino and Tommaso Pisano provided the technical training that enabled a few later masters to produce sculptures of superior quality. Inspired by the palpitating forms of Andrea and the engaging sentiments and *sfumato* surfaces of Nino, the master of the Santa Caterina *Annunciation* and the Trapani *Madonna*, and the sculptor of the Berlin *Madonna*, are the heirs of the exceptional technique of carving and polishing that we have noted in the work of Andrea and Nino; thus a tradition of technical mastery was kept alive. Can there be any doubt, indeed, that the Pisano workshop provided for the continuity of a tradition of mastery in goldsmith work and stone carving that would prove extremely important at the turn of the century? It was surely this tradition that was responsible, in part, for the fact that when new programs and patrons emerged in the early fifteenth century, younger and more inventive talents were ready, and able, to take on the new challenges.

Some Thoughts on the Pisano Legacy

The great flowering of Tuscan sculpture that began with the earlier Pisani concludes with the work of Nino for, as is generally acknowledged, little sculpture of note was produced after his death. Executed to satisfy the increased demand for both large and small devotional images, the host of Madonna and Child statuettes and Annunciation groups by the followers of Nino are derivative in style and iconography. As we have seen, however, even during the fallow decades the works of a few masters shine through the generally mediocre productions of the latter part of the century. Nevertheless, the momentum of the earlier period in terms of patronage and communal enthusiasm seems to have been spent; the productions of the period are stylistically heterogeneous to the point of confusion; and clearly, no sculptor was able to approach the stature of any of the major masters of the earlier Tuscan Gothic period. Yet suddenly, or so it seems, four giants appeared on the scene: Lorenzo Ghiberti, Nanni di Banco, Jacopo della Quercia, and Donatello. This anomaly has provoked a continuing, but not entirely fruitful, search for the roots of these sculptors' styles in the work of any number of immediately preceding masters who, in turn, have been viewed as the generally feeble descendants of the tradition that began with Nicola and was still thriving during Nino's lifetime.

A recurrent theme in Early Renaissance art-historical literature – one that is more often expressed by way of suggestion than by way of assertion – concerns a possible stylistic thread that connects early quattrocento sculpture with the sculpture of Andrea and Nino Pisano. The lack of a coherent view of the oeuvre of these earlier masters has, however, hindered attempts to find demonstrable links. Even more important is the fact that the last few decades of the trecento comprise a period not yet well defined in the literature, especially as far as sculpture is concerned. Although it is not within the scope of this study to attempt such a definition it may be possible to indicate some of the connecting threads – fragile as they undoubtedly are – between the achievements of the second and third quarter of the trecento and those of the Early Renaissance. In the case of Tuscan workshops separated by only a few decades it should be possible to trace such links on technical, no less than on stylistic, grounds.

One of the most pervasive, yet understated, lines of thought concerns a possible relationship between the sculpture of the Pisani, especially Nino, and that of the young Jacopo della Quercia. There is as little agreement, however, on attributions to the young Jacopo as there is regarding the intermediate links in the chain that connect him to our Pisani. Jacopo's origins have been sought, for example, in the workshop of the Dalle Masegna brothers, and it has been suggested that his early style can be imagined as being very close to that of the sculptor who executed the Annunciation on the high altar of San Francesco, Bologna.[1] Closely related in style to the Annunciation group in Bologna – related in iconography, however, to trecento Sienese painting – is the *Madonna of Humility* (Figs. 349, 350) in the National Gallery in Washington, D.C., which has received various attributions including one to the young Jacopo.[2] Also considered an early Jacopo, although difficult to reconcile with the style of the Washington *Madonna*, is the standing *Madonna and Child* now on the Piccolomini altar in the Siena Duomo.[3] Each of these works – the Bologna altarpiece, the *Madonna of Humility*, and the Piccolomini *Madonna* – in turn, has been related to earlier trecento sculpture.

These figures do exhibit characteristics that recall the work of Nino. One might compare the type of the *Virgin Annunciate* in Bologna with several of Nino's Madonnas (e.g., Figs. 119, 302), or the Gabriel with the angels on the Saltarelli monument (Figs. 152, 153). The aristocratic Christ in the Coronation of the Virgin on the Bologna altarpiece, however, resembles the *Redeemer* in Florence (Fig. 94) by Andrea, whereas the altarpiece itself, conceived like a giant sculptured polyptych, derives from Tommaso's Pisan marble altarpiece (Fig. 328).[4] The influence of Tuscan sculpture, and

[1] Seymour (1973), 26.
[2] Seymour and Swarzenski (1946), 129–52; Seymour (1973), 26f. Opinions concerning the attribution of the Madonna have varied; for a bibliography see Middeldorf (1976), 66f. Strom (1980), 17–23, reaffirms its attribution to Jacopo.
[3] The work has been seen as an example of a particular current in late trecento sculpture – a

neo-pisanismo – which, in this example, reveals an enthusiasm not just for Nicola and Giovanni Pisano, but also for Andrea and Nino. Carli (1949), 19.
[4] It is not without significance, incidentally, that the latter eventually served as the model for Jacopo della Quercia's Trenta Altar. See Pope-Hennessy (1972), 212.

especially of Nino's sculpture, on developments in Venice has indeed often been noted and has been held to be the catalyst that liberated the Dalle Masegna brothers from the conservatism that characterizes Venetian and Emilian sculpture until the 1380s.[5]

Likewise, the *Madonna of Humility* reveals close study of the *Madonna del Latte* by Andrea (Figs. 349–350; 135–136). Reminiscent of the latter is the pose of the Christ Child – note especially the position of the legs and feet – and the way the veil frames the Madonna's face and then folds over itself in a broad curve to reveal the undersurface. The insistent continuity of curves binding the figures together also seems inspired by Andrea's example. Finally, the rear view, where the folds diverge in broad diagonal curves toward the slightly projecting elbows, translates the crisp and polished forms of the Pisan example into broader, more monumental terms. The sculptured *Madonna of Humility* has been noted for the originality of its invention, that is, the translation into marble of a subject and iconography that had had a long tradition in painting, going back to Simone Martini. In this regard too Andrea anticipates the author of the *Madonna of Humility* for the marble nursing *Madonna* by Andrea is itself based on Simone's lost prototype.[6]

The cathedral workshop in Lucca, too, where Jacopo's father's presence is known from 1394, has been conjectured as Jacopo's training ground. It has been claimed that Jacopo worked under Antonio Pardini of Pietra Santa, capomaestro of the cathedral who is documented in Lucca from 1395 to 1419.[7] Antonio, according to this view, was trained in Nino Pisano's workshop and executed a number of the late trecento wood figures generally associated with the latter.[8] Although Antonio Pardini remains a shadowy figure to whom attributions rest on conjecture alone – there are no signed or documented sculptures from his hand – there are a number of works from Lucca Cathedral (whether by Pardini or not) that reveal the continuity of that tradition of lightly swaying poses and gently swinging drapery rhythms[9] that we see in the Madonnas and the Annunciations by Nino and his followers. All these hypothetical connections between Jacopo and late trecento sculpture deserve further investigation.

The issue of Jacopo's connection to Lucca is raised once again by two reliefs belonging to the circle of Nino and Tommaso but not attributable to the hand of either of these sculptors. The first, in a parish church near Lucca, is a relatively undistinguished and little-known relief of a Madonna and Child flanked by two angels that has been

[5] On Nino's influence in Venice see Bettini (1932), 347–59; Mariacher (1947), 140–9; Fiocco (1947), 134–6; Gnudi (1950), 48–55; Wolters (1976), 66f., 70, 108, 214.
[6] See p. 73.
[7] Baracchini and Caleca (1973), 33, 38–41.

[8] Baracchini and Caleca (1973), 36. These authors even ascribe the "Scherlatti" monument to Pardini; p. 138.
[9] See Baracchini and Caleca (1973), Figs. 254–258.

attributed, on insufficient grounds in my opinion, to Nino and assistants (Figs. 338, 339).[10] The style of the relief is far from unified, indicating that at least two hands were involved. The drapery and stance of the Virgin immediately call to mind the central figure in Tommaso's San Francesco altarpiece (Fig. 329) and yet in some ways this figure is closer to the Santa Caterina *Annunciation* (Figs. 137, 138) and other sculptures that may be associated with it. One might compare, for instance, the large drapery folds forming "shelves" that swing diagonally from left to right in the Santa Caterina *Gabriel* and in the *Madonna* of Trapani. The angels, on the other hand, closely parallel the entire series of flanking angels found on the Scherlatti and Moricotti tombs (Figs. 316, 317). Yet in the Lucchese example, the structure of the underlying bodies is more carefully studied and the drapery more strongly differentiated from the underlying forms. Instead of illogically merging into the framework as occurs on the Pisano tombs, the full length of the angels is visible as they hover slightly above the ground. Whoever designed and executed these angels, he must have been trained in the shop that was responsible for the Scherlatti and Moricotti monuments. The same or possibly a third hand may be discerned in the figure of the Christ Child. Although earlier prototypes were followed in the carving of the hair, the face reveals a new robust naturalism in the subtle differentiation of the fleshy parts and is closer to some early heads by Jacopo della Quercia than to the examples by Andrea and Nino (cf. Figs. 339, 346).

Far more intriguing and suggestive is the series of reliefs with a Pietà and flanking saints in the Cappella del Sacramento in San Martino, Lucca (Figs. 340–345).[11] Perhaps due to its diminutive size and unfortunate location, as well as to the poor photographs that have been available until recently, the relief has received neither the attention nor the assessment it deserves. As is the case with the *Madonna* relief discussed earlier (Fig. 338), the angels flanking the figure of Christ are so close to those in Nino's tombs in the Camposanto as to warrant an attribution to a sculptor trained in that workshop; furthermore, the *Man of Sorrows* as well as the flanking figures of Mary and John are directly inspired by their counterparts on the "Moricotti" tomb (i.e., the tomb front made for Scherlatti's sarcophagus). The Christ also resembles the *Man of Sorrows* in the Museo di San Matteo, Pisa (Fig. 319). So close are these connections that the relief has even been attributed to Nino himself.[12]

This attribution fails to take note of several extraordinary departures from the prototype. The handling of the relief in which the arms of Christ are detached from the background and carved fully in-the-round to connect again at the lower edge of the relief (Fig. 344) has no parallel in Nino's oeuvre. Furthermore, although it is evident

[10] Ragghianti (1960), 63, n. 37; Baracchini (1981), 179f. Burresi (1983), 189.

[11] See *Jacopo della Quercia* (1975), 30–9.

[12] Burresi (1983), 189.

that the central group is patterned after the Pisan Pietà, it is equally clear that the sculptor is searching for contrary effects: Instead of the crisp pattern of wavy striations in hair and beard, here there are soft shadowy undulations, more plastic and less linear than in the prototype. The poses, drapery, and heads of Mary and John are modeled closely on their counterparts in Pisa, and yet the faces have a depth of expression unequaled in the work of Nino; this expressive quality is enhanced, if not determined, by the facture of the surfaces suggesting, rather than defining, the forms (Figs. 342, 343). The sculptor replaces the swirling decorative effects of the Pisan examples with a few large and simple planes resulting in an increased monumentality that belies the tiny scale of the reliefs (27.5 cm in height). Finally, in place of the narrow shoulders, cylindrical arms, and planar surfaces of the Pisan *Man of Sorrows*, one finds in the Lucchese relief a powerful, muscular body in which chest, rib cage, and soft fleshy stomach are clearly differentiated, resulting in a far more classicizing interpretation of the male body. At least one observer has attributed this relief to the youthful Jacopo della Quercia,[13] but the attribution has been rejected by most other scholars.[14] It is, to be sure, difficult to find convincing comparisons between the acknowledged work of Jacopo and this relief. Nevertheless, whoever the author of this extraordinary series of fragments may be,[15] he represents an important link between the workshop of Nino Pisano and the artistic milieu immediately preceding the great developments of the early quattrocento.

Less problematic is the influence of Andrea and Nino on Florentine sculpture at the turn of the fifteenth century. The Silver Altar for the Baptistry of Florence adapts to a rectangular format the relief mode of the doors with its stagelike interior spaces and landscapes with rocky outcroppings that support the figures.[16] The emphasis on surface rhythms through fluid drapery forms and the serene idealization of many of the figures (although this is mingled with a new emphasis on realism of details), as well as numerous elements of its iconography (cf. the enthusiastic stride of the young John marching into the wilderness), derive from the Baptistry doors.

Several masters of the late trecento cathedral workshop seem to have been especially receptive to the art of Andrea and Nino, transforming their gently swaying figures and curvilinear drapery rhythms into formulas for a more or less uniform army of saints and apostles.[17] Piero di Giovanni Tedesco's Duomo saints and music-making angels (Fig.

---

[13] Salmi (1930), 175–91.

[14] See *Jacopo della Quercia* (1975), 30f.

[15] The present disposition is not original and five separate pieces have been incorporated into a more modern structure. The two small sections at the ends (Fig. 340) are earlier and do not come from the same workshop.

[16] On the Silver Altar, see Brunetti in Becherucci and Brunetti, vol. 2 (1969), 215–24.

[17] See Becherucci and Brunetti, vol. 1, Figs. 123–129.

348), in particular, pay distant tribute to Andrea's Florentine statues and statuettes,[18] and even a figure that has been tentatively attributed to Nanni di Banco[19] seems inspired by one of Andrea's Duomo statues: the *Saint Stephen* (cf. Figs. 348 center, and 101).

The International Gothic phase of Early Renaissance sculpture – and even painting – may very well owe a strong, if largely unacknowledged, debt to Andrea and Nino. Who could deny that the hipshot poses – often exaggerated beyond anatomical plausibility – the slender proportions, the dainty gestures, and swinging or cascading drapery folds seen in the paintings of Lorenzo Monaco and the early work of Ghiberti are anticipated in some of the Madonnas by Nino and his followers? Even as late as ca. 1440 a figure by the Sienese "Maestro dell'Osservanza" would seem to bear an unmistakable relationship to Nino's Detroit *Madonna* (Fig. 302).[20] The similarity between the exaggerated stance of Nanni di Banco's prophet for the Porta della Mandorla and Nino's Florentine *Madonna* becomes evident when the two are confronted (Figs. 109, 347), as do the similarity of proportion and the handling of the garments – the swinging concave "shelves" of drapery – between Ghiberti's *Saint Stephen* and Nino's *Saint Peter* (Fig. 296). Needless to say, Ghiberti's first set of bronze doors is directly inspired by Andrea's, not only in its general format and in its relief mode with projecting platforms on consoles defining the space, but also in the search (eventually abandoned by Andrea but a continuing feature in the north doors) for decorative unity by means of uniting the curves and diagonal rhythms of the quatrefoil frame with the compositional patterns of the narratives within.

The more fundamental revolution of Early Renaissance sculpture, however, derives from the reintegration of classical form with classically oriented content. In the sculpture of Andrea Pisano, we witness not only a precocious appreciation of the aesthetic qualities of classical sculpture, but also the first step toward that reintegration – one that ultimately led, in the early fifteenth century, to the creation of a population of stone and bronze that could serve as symbols, as definitions, and as sources of inspiration for the ideal of *virtù* propagated by the Italian humanists.

[18] Becherucci and Brunetti (1969), Figs. 122–129.
[19] Brunetti in Becherucci and Brunetti (1969), p. 251, Fig. 122.
[20] See *Il Gotico a Siena* (1982), 398.

APPENDIX A

The Execution of the Baptistry Doors

Andrea Pisano's Baptistry doors represent an outstanding technical achievement in their structure and construction.[1] The latticelike framework of each door was cast in one single piece.[2] This framework, which includes the rectangular denti-

[1] Very little technical information on the doors has been published. Unpublished communications by Bruno Bearzi, who directed the cleaning of the three Baptistry doors in 1945, to Kreytenberg (1975, 220f.) inform us that the doors are made of brass alloy (76 percent copper, 22 percent zinc, and 2 percent tin) and that the framework of each valve is cast in one piece except for the parts to be fire gilt. The even thickness of 1 cm of the cast framework indicates the high technical competence of the caster; Ghiberti's first doors do not have an even thickness throughout, thus resulting in considerable waste of metal. All other information set forth in this appendix concerning the structure and casting of the doors derives from a careful examination of the doors themselves, from a letter to me from Bearzi dated 26 October 1977 in answer to my questions, and from discussions held in front of the doors with Signor Roberto Salvestrini, who was an assistant to Bearzi during the cleaning of the doors after the war and who also worked on repairs made following the 1966 flood. I am deeply grateful to Signor Salvestrini for his patience and cooperation in helping me understand the processes involved. A discussion of the casting technique and structure of Ghiberti's doors is found in Bearzi (1980), vol. 1, 219–22, where it is stated that the structure of Ghiberti's first door is the same as that of Andrea's. See also Krautheimer (1970), 113, 115, n. 2, 116, n. 6, 190f. Gilding techniques are discussed in Bearzi's essay in Poggi, Planiscig, and Bearzi (194–).

[2] Although it is generally assumed that the framework was cast according to the lost-wax method (Falk [1940], 44f.; White [1966], 303), there apparently lingers some doubt. Pope-Hennessy (1972), 191, writes, "The door was cast not, like the caryatids of the Fontana Maggiore at Perugia and the bronze doors of Ghiberti, by the *cire perdue* method, but on another system." In answer to my queries on the subject of the method of casting

lated moldings, and the quatrefoil moldings together with a backing for the reliefs, contains a series of twenty-eight round openings to aid in the adjustment of the reliefs and also to make for better aeration in the casting process (see Fig. 48). The framework also contains small openings at the intersection of the grid for the insertion of lions' heads as well as openings between the rectangular moldings to contain the strips with stud heads, rosettes, and the inscription. The unframed quatrefoil reliefs, the strips with the inscription, the stud heads and the rosettes, and the lions' heads in tiny framed quatrefoils – all parts, in short, that were to be fire gilded – were cast separately.[3] The separately cast and gilt portions were then inserted into the framework from the front, the parts having been modeled and cast so carefully that they could be inserted into the respective openings with only minor chiseling, filing down, and other adjustments. Careful examination reveals that the inner edges of the quatrefoil moldings do not merely dovetail, but in most cases slightly overlap the quatrefoil ground of the reliefs; this was achieved by hammering the inner edges of the moldings with a metal tool, thus slightly flattening them to overlap by half a centimeter or so. The alloy used for the bronze doors[4] made for a fairly elastic substance that permitted these adjustments.

The figures, platforms on consoles, and architectural and landscape elements were modeled in solid wax, attached to a wax quatrefoil slab, and then cast in a solid piece. For the lions' heads Andrea modeled a small number in wax – some facing front, others to the right, and others to the left. These were then cast in solid bronze. The latter, however, then served as models for new molds to be made that, when filled with wax and cast, resulted in hollow lions' heads. At ground level it is possible to identify a few hollow-cast lions' heads. The circular openings in the back of the door frame are closed off with bronze cylindrical plugs.

A careful analysis of the documents yields, at best, only the most general sequence of

---

the doors, Bearzi wrote, "Certamente la porta e state fusa col sistema della cera perduta, *almeno per i panelli*" [italics mine]. To cast the framework by this means in one piece, Bearzi added, is "una cosa assai difficile per quei tempi ed anche per oggi." This would seem to leave open the possibility that the framework was cast according to some other method. The document of 2 April 1330, however, which refers to the completion of *le porte di cera* is almost unassailable evidence that the framework was modeled in wax as it is hardly possible that the modeling of all the reliefs could have been finished by that early date. See Falk (1940), 44f. An excellent discussion of the lost-wax method may be found in Stone (1982), 87–116.

[3] These parts had to be cast separately because in the process of fire gilding they had to be placed *in* a furnace – unlike the frame itself. Had they been cast as part and parcel of the frame, the entire frame would have had to be placed in the furnace, at that date a technical and constructional impossibility (Bearzi [1980], 221).

[4] See n. 1.

events in the execution of the bronze doors (see chronology at end of appendix).[5] On 13 January 1330, the *porte di legname* were begun (Doc. 3). This does not necessarily refer, as has previously been thought, to negative wood molds for the framework into which the wax was poured or pressed,[6] but may refer either to a wood scaffolding for the entire wax framework or to positive models for the wax framework. The woodworkers, for instance, probably made wood quatrefoil frames looking very much like the modern ones that now surround the Competition reliefs by Brunelleschi and Ghiberti in the Bargello. It is likely that only a few were constructed to serve first as models for the framing elements and then as templates for the flat quatrefoil slabs in wax to which the figures and landscape elements would be attached. The models were carved by carpenters or cabinetmakers to Andrea's specifications, after which (Doc. 4) Andrea and his assistants proceeded to model the wax framework based on the wooden prototypes.[7] This must have been a delicate and time-consuming labor for the entire framework, with its complex of openings, and its rectangular and quatrefoil moldings and dentils had to be modeled so as to result in a single, homogeneous structure before being swathed in plaster of Paris. This work took until 2 April 1330, when *le porte di cera* were completed (Doc. 5). One may assume that by now, Leonardo quondam Avanzi, the bell-caster from Venice (Doc. 2, 12), was on the scene and the casting of the first door

[5] Such an analysis, somewhat difficult to follow, and with slightly different results is found in Falk ([1940], 9–13, 40–58). See also Kreytenberg (1975), 222–4.

[6] Falk (1940), 55f.; Kreytenberg (1975), 222.

[7] This explains why there is only a nine-day gap between the dates work on the wood framework and work on the wax models was begun and why, moreover, it is in connection with the latter that Andrea is first mentioned as beginning work on the doors (Doc. 4); i.e., at that time he literally begins the labor of modeling in wax. It has been argued that Andrea appeared in Florence as the sculptor of the reliefs, not the designer of the door frame, and that the design was adapted wholesale from the format of the walls of the Pulci Chapel of 1300–10 in Santa Croce. See Kreytenberg (1975), 226–8, who points out that Andrea's name appears for the first time, not on 13 January 1330, when the wooden framework for the doors was begun, but on 22 January as "maestro delle porte." This difference of one week can hardly be used as the basis for negative conclusions concerning Andrea's participation in the design of the doors. It is true that the general pattern on the Pulci Chapel wall appears on the doors, translated, however, from quatrefoil-in-square to quatrefoil-in-rectangle. But the details of the design on the doors — the style of the moldings with their crisp profiles, the precise geometry of the curves of each lobe, the relationship of quatrefoil to rectangle, the appearance of dentils, etc. — are in their clarity of organization and in their vigorous plasticity so in harmony with the reliefs as to speak for a common origin, a single imagination. Even if the basic unit of the design — quatrefoil within rectangles — were predetermined, the details would perforce be relegated to the master. It seems, however, more reasonable to assume that the design was worked out by the master in consultation with the patron, the Arte di Calimala, and that the signature, placed on the frame itself, refers to the door as a whole.

leaf was soon to begin. One may assume further that for the next year and a half (for which period there are no documents) Andrea was at work designing and modeling in wax a number of reliefs for the first door leaf employing, as indicated earlier, the *porte di legname* as templates for the individual quatrefoil backgrounds. Lippo Dini and Piero di Donato were either assisting Andrea or, more likely, helping with the casting and finishing of the framework (Doc. 6).

On 9 January 1332 the officials of the Opera meet with Andrea concerning "il fare e fabbricare l'opera delle porte," which is to begin the following day (Doc. 7). Andrea has probably presented one or more completed models for the reliefs and discussion is taking place regarding technical procedures and problems in casting the miniature figures and props in bronze; undoubtedly the bell caster (Doc. 2, 12) is also present at this meeting.

For the rest of 1332, Andrea is engaged in making some reliefs – *alcune storie* – and twenty-four lions' heads (Doc. 9), presumably still for the first door leaf. By 27 April 1332, a final payment is made to the Venetian bell caster (Doc. 12). Surely both door frames and perhaps even some of the reliefs Andrea had executed are cast and are in their rough state. The Venetian bronze caster had remained on the scene for two years. Working in close contact with and under the supervision of this master, Andrea, his assistants (especially Piero di Donato [Doc. 8]), and other workers must have learned a great deal about the operation of a foundry. The documents make clear that some of the reliefs and at least half of the lions' heads were not yet cast by the time the Venetian left the scene in April of 1332.

The next important document, dated 27 February 1333, is ambiguous (Doc. 15), but could be explained by a slip of the pen on the part of Strozzi (or his source).[8] Here it is stated that Piero di Donato agrees to clean and polish the door that is "nella chiesa di San Giovanni" and to raise and adjust it like the one already in the church – "rizzarla e aggiustarla come è la detta porta che è nella detta chiesa." Since the cleaning and polishing surely took place in the Opera, not in the church, if we substitute *Opera* for the word *chiesa* in the first reference, it becomes apparent that the first door leaf is already installed and the second is ready for chasing; indeed, a payment has (probably) recently been made to Pasquino for erecting scaffolding for the installation of the first door leaf; this payment, however, could have taken place any time between 25 March 1332 and 24 March 1333 (Doc. 10). Another possible interpretation of the document is that after the first door frame had been installed adjustments were found to be necessary; these were made and the door was replaced on the Baptistry. Subsequently, a trial installation of the second door frame was effected while it was at its lightest shortly after casting

[8] Falk (1940), 51.

and before the reliefs were inserted in the frame. It was this trial installation that revealed a casting flaw resulting in a misalignment.[9] This would explain why both door leafs at this point are found in the church (Doc. 15). If this hypothesis is correct, then the second door leaf was subsequently removed and brought back to the Opera and Piero di Donato entrusted with the task of straightening it (Doc. 16). By 25 March 1333 (of unspecified date but clearly after 27 February), Piero is *paid* for cleaning, polishing, and installing the "porta ch'è nell'Opera di S. Giovanni . . . come l'altra ch'è in S. Giovanni" (Doc. 17). As we shall see, however, the doors are still not well aligned.

In any case, it seems evident that the first door wing was satisfactorily installed by 27 February 1333. This may be further adduced from the fact that at various times in 1332 and up to, at the latest, 24 March 1333, Andrea is paid and acknowledges receipt of the 98 florins agreed upon for the narratives (Doc. 14, 18–21).

Andrea is now at work on the reliefs for the second door leaf. On 24 July 1333, he agrees to make another twenty-four lions' heads by 1 December, and to gild and install them as he had done on the first door – "quella porta di metallo che è nella detta chiesa di S. Giovanni" – and to do these things on the door that is now in the Opera – "quella porta di metallo che adesso è nell'Opera di S. Giovanni." He further agrees to gild the narratives as he had done for the first door, and he is to be paid 40 florins (Doc. 22). It is clear that all the reliefs for the second door (but not the lions) have been cast; indeed, two weeks later he receives final payment for the reliefs (Doc. 23). Thus, the design and execution of the reliefs took approximately two years and ten months (April 1330–February 1333). Ten months later, all casting and gilding must have been completed and the foundry ready to be dismantled. In May 1334, the house or shed that had been built for the foundry is torn down (Doc. 24).

There is a hiatus in the records of progress on the doors between the summer of 1333 and January 1335 when the doors, to the exasperation of the officials, are still not fully installed (Doc. 25). Falk points out that work probably was delayed due to the terrible flood of November 1333, which devastated parts of the Baptistry.[10] Also accounting for the delay may be the fact that by January 1335 the Campanile was already being constructed and Andrea was at work designing and executing the first series of reliefs for the western facade. He is called back to the door project and argues for more funds.

[9] After the 1966 flood, this second casting error came to light. The molten bronze had been poured into the mold of the framework from openings at two corners of the long sides. The bronze did not fuse properly after flowing toward the center of the framework so that in the shrinkage caused by the cooling process, a diagonal break about one third of the way down the door developed. This was repaired (by Andrea as we shall see) by riveting a small piece of metal across the crack (Kreytenberg [1975], 222; Bearzi, communication of 1977, see n. 2).

[10] Falk (1940), 53.

In the meantime, Piero di Donato cleans, polishes, and attempts to straighten the second door leaf, which, it is discovered, is twisted (Doc. 27). But he finds that he has not the courage to do so – "non glie ne dava l'animo" – and so Andrea agrees to take on the task (Doc. 28, 30); Piero is relieved of his obligation (Doc. 29). Although one can see today that the two door leafs are not perfectly aligned, Andrea achieved a fair degree of success. By 20 June 1336 both door leafs are fully installed on the Baptistry, four days before the Festival of San Giovanni. The metal debris resulting from these labors is weighed and totals 3,315 pounds (Doc. 32).

A ring familiar to modern ears is sounded by the evidence of cost overrun in the project. In fact, however, Andrea's estimate of 500 gold florins (as indicated in Doc. 25) was fairly close to the mark, at least compared to Ghiberti's for his first door on the north side.[11] Andrea received 98 gold florins for the set of quatrefoil reliefs on each door leaf (Doc. 14, 20), thus 196 florins. (The documents do not make clear whether this includes the eight Virtues, although, as no separate mention of these is made, it is probable that these were included in the designation *storie*.) Forty florins was the agreed-upon price for the making of the lions' heads and for the gilding of these as well as the quatrefoil reliefs for each door wing (Doc. 22); of this sum, 20 florins were for the lions' heads alone as can be seen from a subsequent notice (Doc. 26). Piero di Jacopo received at least 70 florins for unspecified work on the door (Doc. 13). This rather high amount indicates that he was the major assistant goldsmith to Andrea. This is a final payment made in November 1332 and can hardly refer to his trips to Pisa and Venice, which took place in November 1329.[12] Piero di Donato, who was entrusted with the job of polishing, cleaning, and installing the doors received 48 florins for one leaf (Doc. 15). A similar amount must have been estimated for the second leaf. A subsequent reference mentions only 28 florins for cleaning, polishing, and straightening that leaf; as we have seen, however, it was never successfully installed by Piero (Doc. 27). So far, the labor expenses total 422 gold florins. Another goldsmith, Lippo Dini, is mentioned twice early in the project (Doc. 6, 7). His wages are not given but if they, together with miscellaneous expenses such as payments to laborers for building scaffolding and for installation, etc., totaled 78 florins or more, then the estimated expenditure of 500 florins would have been reached as, indeed, is indicated by the document of 30 January 1335 (Doc. 25). Another 10 florins is agreed upon for Andrea to straighten the misaligned doors. Finally, 17 florins come to Andrea for arranging for the marble doorsill; this is paid sometime before 24 March 1337.

[11] This estimate, and the recorded payments, are for labor alone, not materials. On the estimated and final costs of Ghiberti's north doors, see Krautheimer (1970), 46, 105.

[12] Cf. Falk (1940), 50.

Appendix A: The Baptistry Doors

Square brackets indicate my interpretation of work referred to.

	FRAMEWORK	RELIEFS	LIONS' HEADS	GILDING	HANGING, POLISHING, ETC.
29 Nov. 1322	Decision to cover doors with metal. Doc. 1.				
6 Nov. 1329	Decision to make metal doors. Piero di Jacopo sent to Pisa and Venice. Doc. 2.				
13 Jan. 1330	Wooden framework begun. Doc. 3.				
22 Jan. 1330	Maestro Andrea begins work on doors. Doc. 4.				
2 April 1330	Wax framework is completed. Doc. 5.				
14 Oct. 1331	Lippo Dini and Piero di Donato work on doors. Doc. 6.				[Possibly they are polishing and finishing first framework.]
9 Jan. 1332		Officials meet with Andrea and Lippo re the making of the reliefs. These are begun next day. Doc. 7.			
1332 (i.e., 25 March 1332–24 March 1333)	Piero di Jacopo and Piero di Donato work on door. Doc. 8.				
1332 (i.e., 25 March 1332–24 March 1333)		Andrea makes some narratives and 24 lions' heads [for left-hand valve]. Doc. 9.			
1332 (i.e., 25 March 1332–24 March 1333)					Pasquino is paid for scaffolding, etc., for installing the door [left-hand leaf]. Doc. 10.
23 April 1332	Officials review Piero di Jacopo's bill. Doc. 11.				
27 April 1332	Final payment to Venetian bell caster. [Both frames and perhaps some reliefs are cast.] Doc. 12.				
17 Nov. 1332	Final payment of 70 florins to Piero di Jacopo for work on doors. Doc. 13.				

	FRAMEWORK	RELIEFS	LIONS' HEADS	GILDING	HANGING, POLISHING, ETC.
27 Feb. 1333		Andrea acknowledges receipt of 50 of the 98 florins he should receive; also acknowledges receipt of 12 florins. Doc. 14.			Piero Donato agrees to clean, polish, erect, and adjust door like the other by June for 48 florins. [First door already installed.] Doc. 15.
1332 (i.e., 25 Mar. 1332—24 Mar. 1333)		Series of payments to Andrea for reliefs. Doc. 18.			Piero Donato cleans, polishes and erects the door. Doc. 16.
		Andrea is paid 50 florins for work on the doors [reliefs, lions' heads, etc., for left door leaf]. Doc. 19.			
1332 (i.e., 25 Mar. 1332—24 Mar. 1333)		Andrea is paid 12 of the 98 florins for narratives [for left leaf]. Doc. 20.			Piero Donato paid 20 florins for work on door in Opera: cleaning, polishing, installing, like the one in S. Giovanni. Doc. 17.
24 July 1333		Andrea agrees to make 24 lions' heads by 1 Dec.; to gild them (like lions on first door); to assemble them on door that is in Opera; to gild the reliefs of that door as was done on first door. For 40 florins. Doc. 22.			
9 Aug. 1333		Andrea receives 36 florins remaining of his wages for the reliefs of door now in Opera. Doc. 23.			
19 May 1334	(Foundry building is torn down. [Therefore, everything is cast and fire gilt.]) Doc. 24.				
30 Jan. 1335	(Officials push to get doors finished and installed by next June. Andrea claims 500 florins is not sufficient to get the job done.) Doc. 25.				
7 Mar. 1335		Andrea is paid 20 florins for 24 lions' heads. Doc. 26.			Piero di Donato is paid 28 florins for cleaning, smoothing, and straightening doors. Doc. 27.

	FRAMEWORK	RELIEFS	LIONS' HEADS	GILDING	HANGING, POLISHING, ETC.
8 Aug. 1335					Piero fails, and Andrea agrees to straighten twisted doors. Doc. 28.
25 Oct. 1335					Piero is relieved of obligation to straighten doors. Doc. 29.
27 Dec. 1335					Andrea agrees to straighten doors in Opera in one month for 10 florins. Doc. 30.
15 March 1336				Agreements and contracts made with Andrea to gild and adjust bronze door of S. Giovanni, etc. [A resume of previous contracts?] Doc. 31.	
20 June 1336					Metal scraps and dust from doors weigh 3,315 pounds. Doc. 32.
1336 (i.e., 25 Mar. 1336–24 Mar. 1337)					Andrea paid 17 florins to bring slab of marble to Florence. Doc. 33.
6 Feb. 1338					Marble doorsill is placed under bronze door. Doc. 34.

The Disposition and Chronology of the Campanile Hexagons

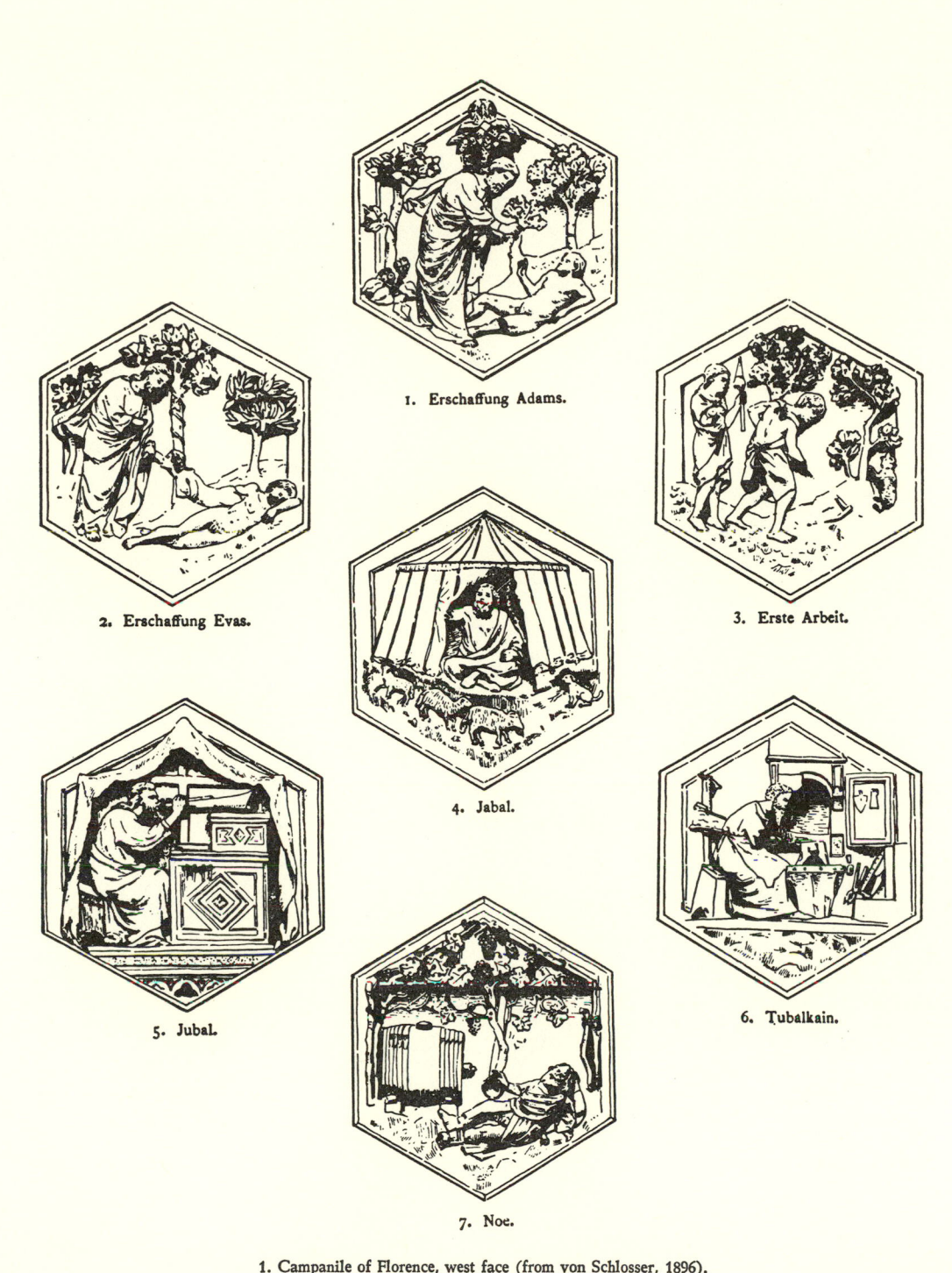

1. Erschaffung Adams.

2. Erschaffung Evas.

3. Erste Arbeit.

4. Jabal.

5. Jubal.

6. Tubalkain.

7. Noe.

1. Campanile of Florence, west face (from von Schlosser, 1896).

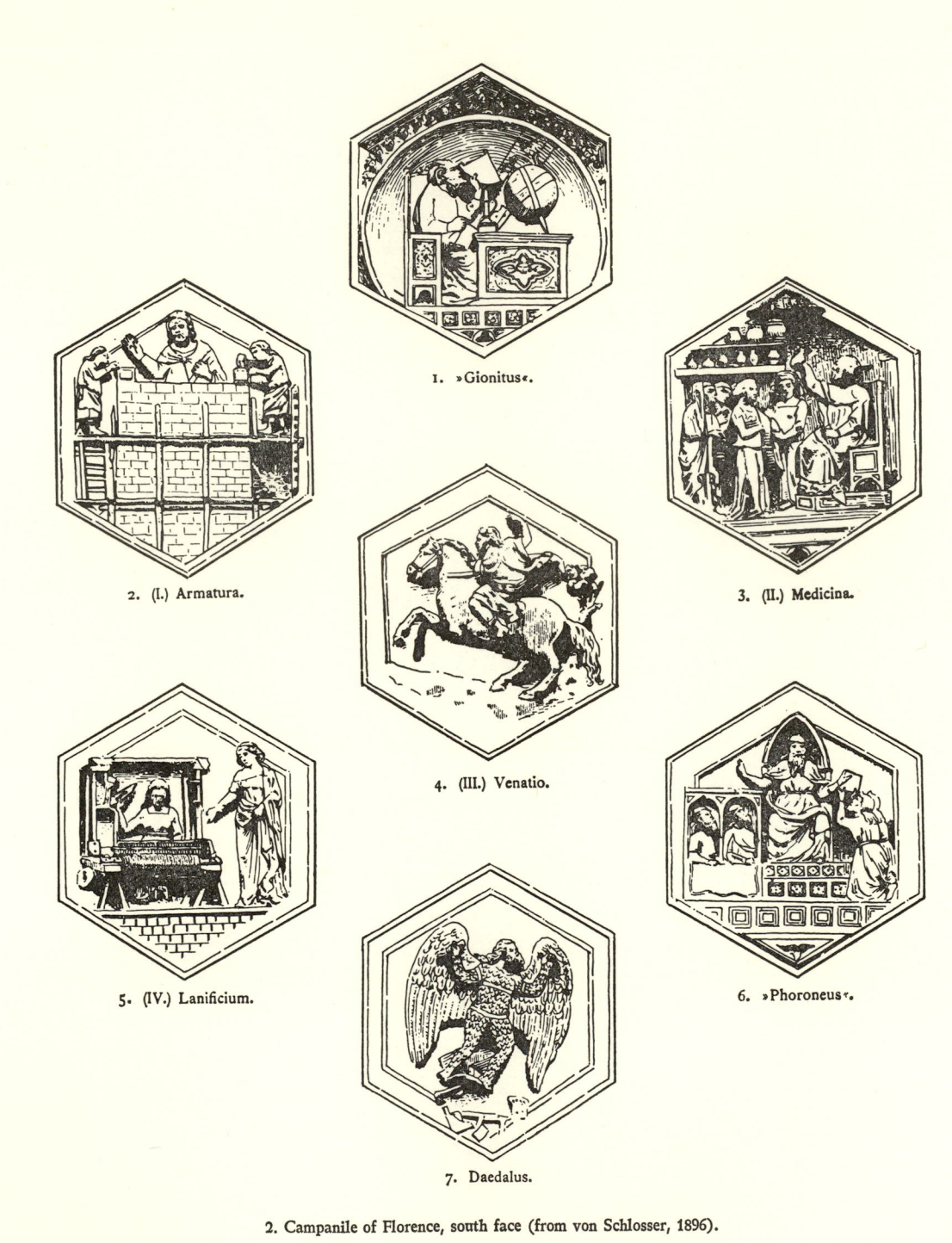

1. »Gionitus«.

2. (I.) Armatura.

3. (II.) Medicina.

4. (III.) Venatio.

5. (IV.) Lanificium.

6. »Phoroneus«.

7. Daedalus.

2. Campanile of Florence, south face (from von Schlosser, 1896).

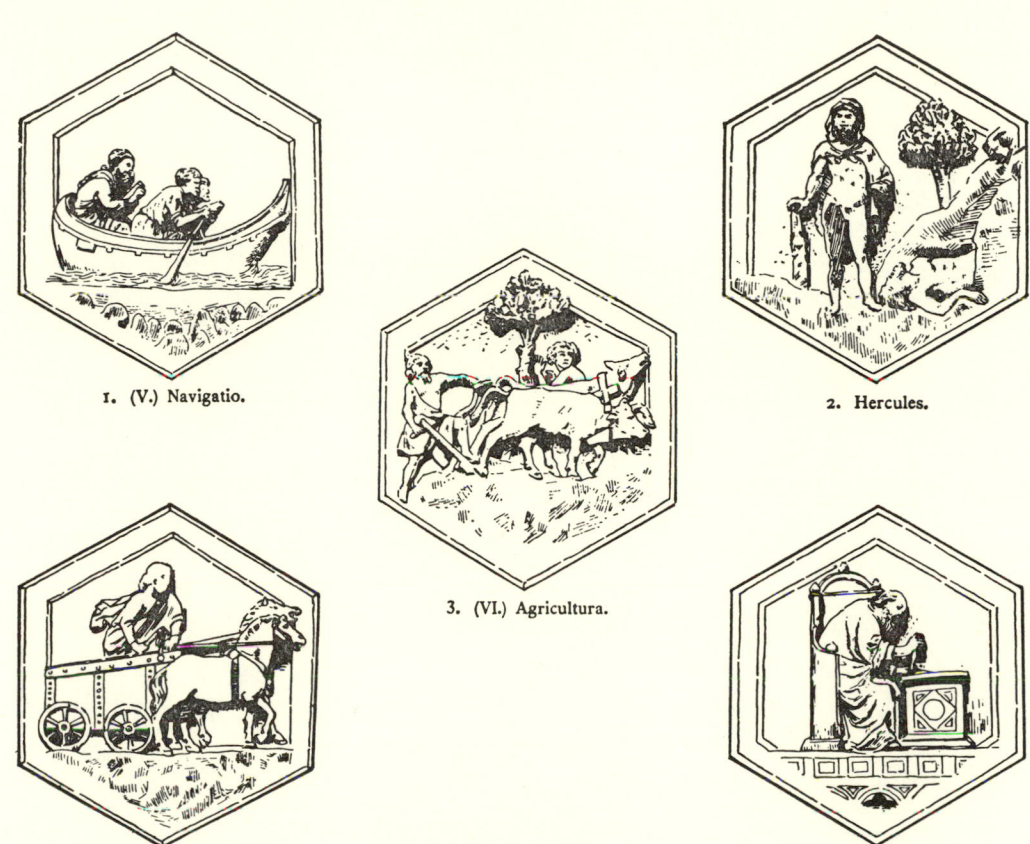

1. (V.) Navigatio.

2. Hercules.

3. (VI.) Agricultura.

4. (VII.) Theatrica.

5. Architektur.

3. Campanile of Florence, east face (from von Schlosser, 1896).

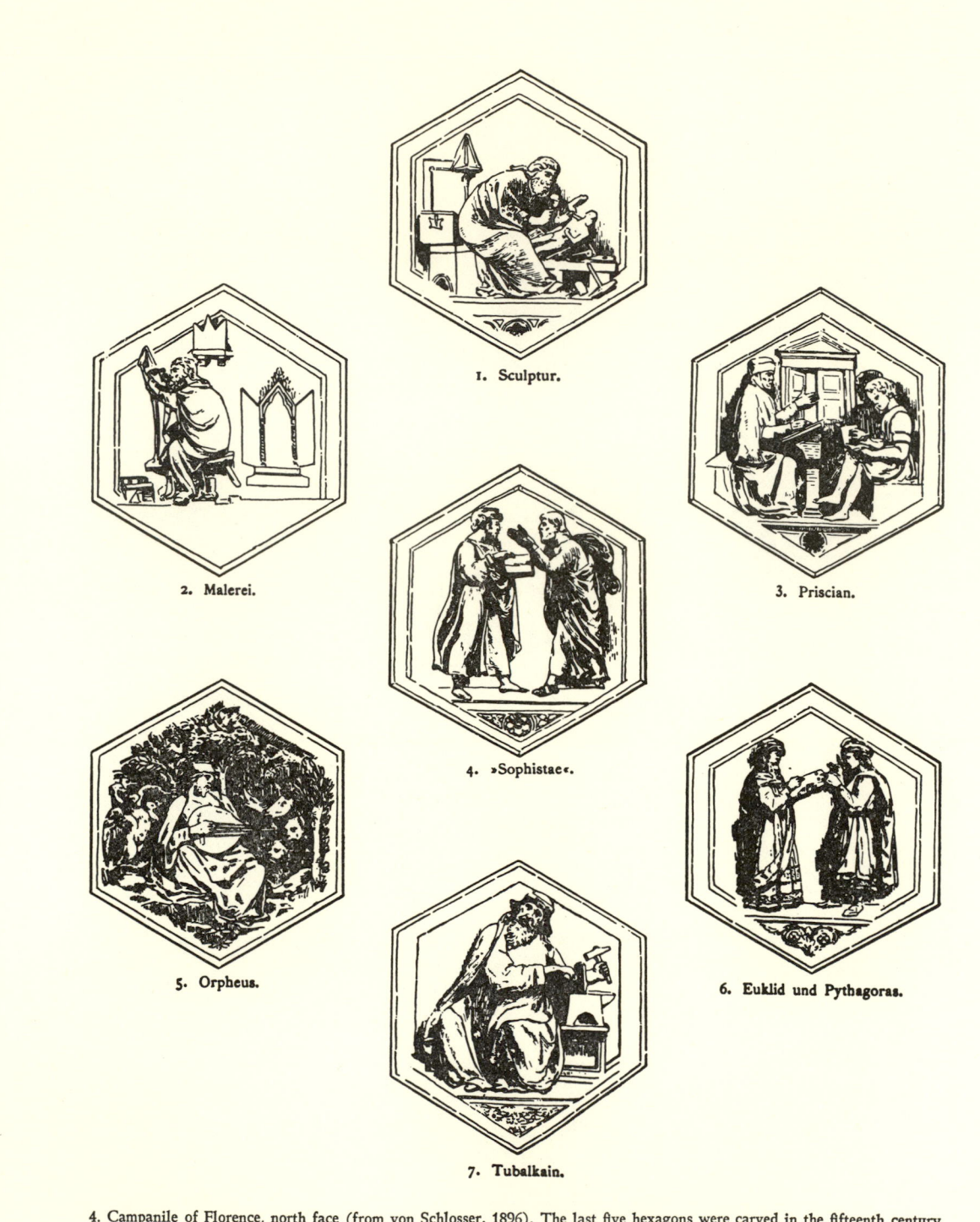

1. Sculptur.

2. Malerei.

3. Priscian.

4. »Sophistae«.

5. Orpheus.

6. Euklid und Pythagoras.

7. Tubalkain.

4. Campanile of Florence, north face (from von Schlosser, 1896). The last five hexagons were carved in the fifteenth century by Luca della Robbia.

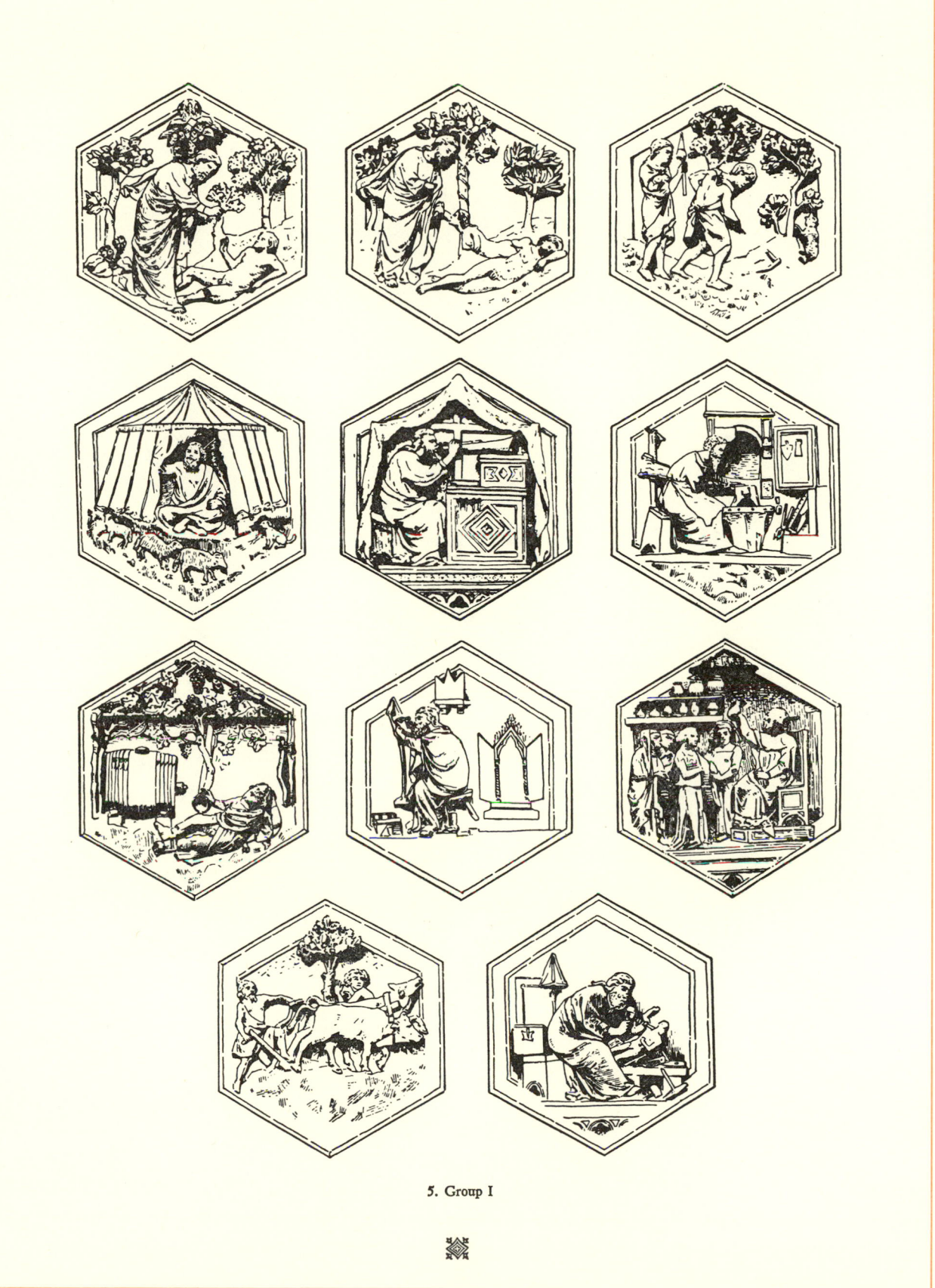

5. Group I

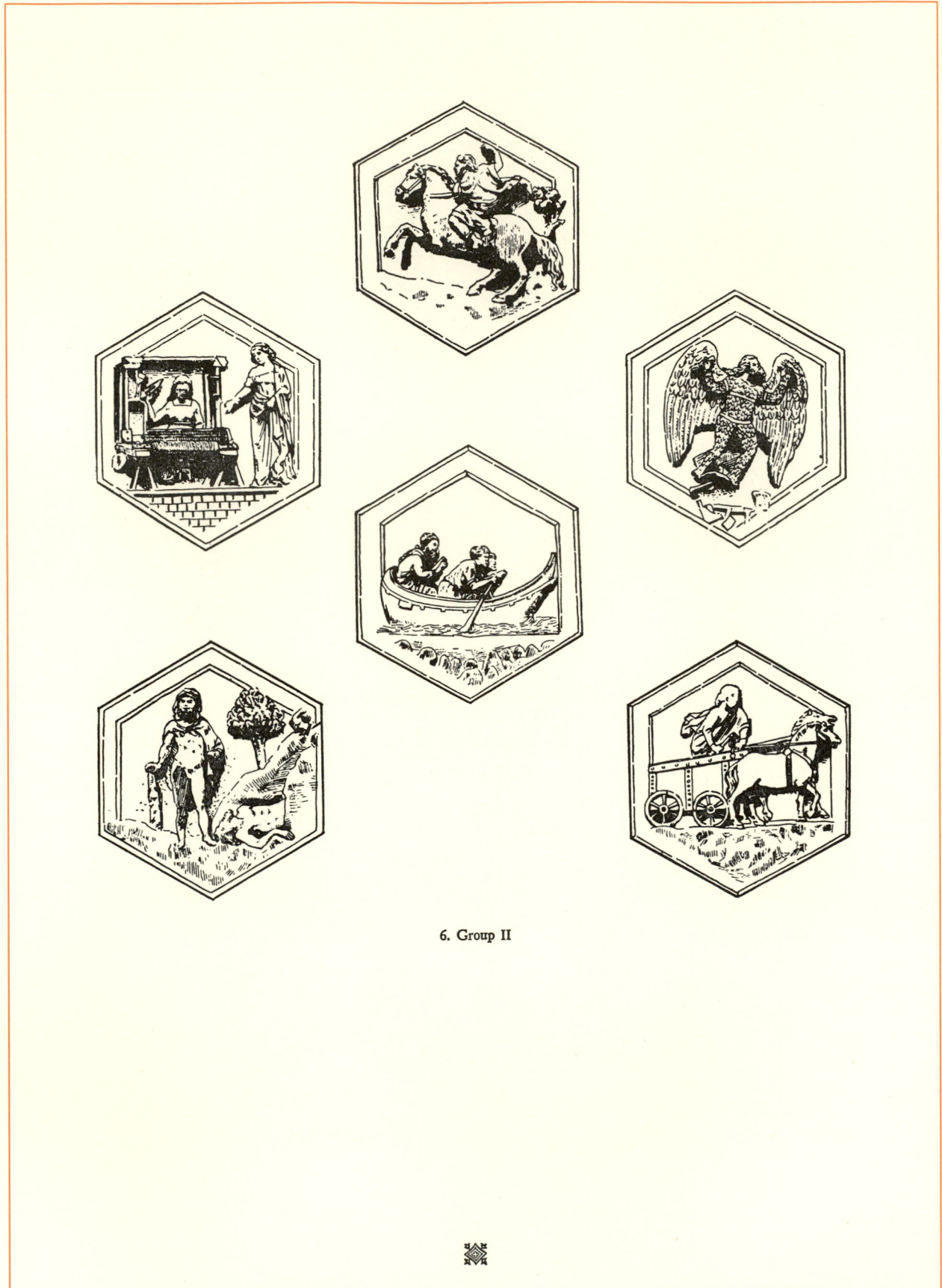

6. Group II

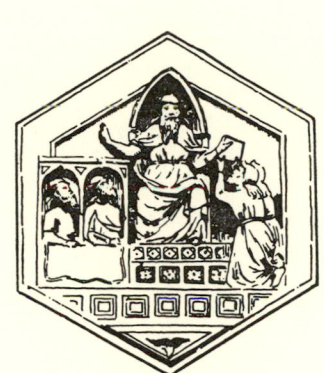

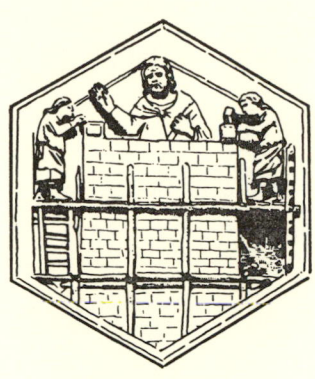

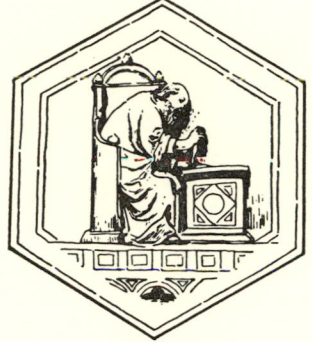

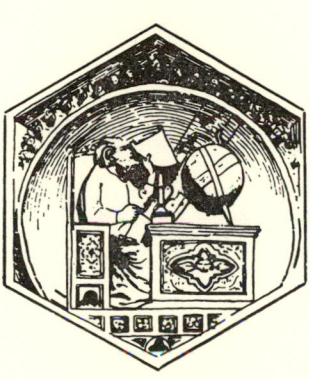

7. Group III

APPENDIX C
Documents

❖

I. THE BAPTISTRY DOORS OF FLORENCE

The documents of the Arte di Calimala, the Guild of the Cloth Finishers, which was in charge of the Baptistry, are not extant but are known from excerpts and copies made in the seventeenth century by Carlo Strozzi and preserved in the Florentine Archives as Strozziane, Serie II, Vol. LI, I and Strozziane, Serie II, Vol. LI, II. With the exception of a few minor errors and three omissions, these have been carefully transcribed by Frey (1911), 349–53. They are reproduced here with corrections or new transcriptions by Gino Corti and exact references to their locations in the Strozziane. It is important to emphasize the summary nature of Strozzi's compilations. It is very likely that not all the documents were extant in the seventeenth century; and even if they were, Carlo Strozzi may have failed to record all of them. Not mentioned in previous discussions of Strozzi's compilations concerning Andrea's doors is the fact that the references are interspersed with notices that have nothing to do with the doors and that those concerning the doors are not always transcribed chronologically so that when not specifically dated, interpretation is made more difficult. Furthermore, several times Strozzi summarized the same document twice, apparently forgetting that he had already made reference to it. In those cases where the same document is excerpted twice, usually with a slight change in wording or with the addition or omission of an exact date or reference to his source, the more informative of the two will be transcribed here; reference to the location of the alternative excerpt will, however, be given as well as any additional information provided by the latter. Another problem in the interpretation of these documents is that payment

❖

for work often seems to lag far behind the actual labors; furthermore, a record of labors does not always have a corresponding payment recorded by Strozzi, and vice versa.

Dates here are given in modern style when possible, followed by Florentine-style dating in parenthesis, which are those found in the Strozzi excerpts. It is important to remember that a date given as "(1332)" means, in modern dating, any time between 25 March 1332 and 24 March 1333. The folios contain pagination in pen and pencil; the first given here is the one in pen; the second, the one in pencil.

Doc. 1. 29 Nov. 1322 Porte di S. Giovanni si cuoprino di rame dorato o di metallo. Maestro Tino Camaini da Siena si conduca a lavorare nell'opera di S. Giovanni ne'lavori da farsi quivi come parrà a'Consoli e Officiali. (LI, I, fol. 160r./169r. See also LI, II, fol. 118r./122r.: Liber reformationum dal 1320 al 1322.)

Doc. 2. 6 Nov. 1329 Si delibera che le porte della chiesa di S. Giovanni si faccino di metallo o ottone, più belle che si può, e che Piero d'Iacopo vadia a Pisa a vedere quelle che sono in detta città e le ritragga, e dipoi vadia a Venezia a cercare di maestro che le faccia, e trovandolo, che lui deva essere il maestro a lavorare la forma di detta porta di metallo etc. (Ex libro reformationum, etc. Artis Calismare, 1327–1331; 5 novembre [1329] [LI, I, fol. 150r./159r.]. See also LI, II, fol. 117v./121v.)

Doc. 3. 13 Jan. 1330 (1329) A dì 13 Gennaio furno cominciate le porte di legname. Libro detto (i.e., Liber reformationum dal 1327 al 1331). (LI, II, fol. 117v./121v. See also LI, II, fol. 150r./159r.)

Doc. 4. 22 Jan. 1330 (1329) Maestro Andrea d'Ugolino, maestro delle porte, cominciò a lavorare a dette porte il dì 22 Gennaio 1329. Libro detto. (LI, II, fol. 117v./121v. See also LI, I, fol. 150r./159r.)

Doc. 5. 2 Apr. 1330 A dì 2 Aprile 1330 furono finite le porte di cera. (LI, I, fol. 150r./159r. Ex libro reformationum, etc. Artis Calismare 1327–1331.)

Doc. 6. 14 Oct. 1331 Lippo Dini e Pietro di Donato lavorano alla porta del metallo. (Libro reformationum dal 1327 al 1331.) (LI, I, fol. 150v./159v. See also LI, II, fol. 117v./121v.)

Doc. 7. 9 Jan. 1332 (1331) Ufficiali sopra il mosaico conducono sopra il fare e fabbricare l'opera delle porte della chiesa di S. Giovanni, Andrea d'Ugolino e Lippo Dini orefice, il dì 9 Gennaio 1331, i quali il giorno doppo cominciorno a lavorare. (Liber reformationum dal 1331 al 1342.) (LI, II, fol. 118r./122r. See also LI, I, fol. 167r./176r.: Requisizioni e reformazioni dall'anno 1331 al 1332.)

The following two excerpts, which appear consecutively in Strozzi's notes, have not (to my knowledge) been previously published. No day or month is given. As Document 8 contains the first mention of Piero di Jacopo actually working *on* the doors (previous references concerned his trip to Pisa and Venice), it must precede that concerning his bill of 23 April, Doc. 11.

Doc. 8. (1332) Piero d'Iacopo, orefice da Firenze [e] Piero di Donato, orefice del popolo di S. Felice di Firenze, lavorano alla porta di bronzo di S. Giovanni, 1332. (Libro d'Inquisitioni, etc., 1332 e 1333.) (LI, II, fol. 114r./118r.)

Doc. 9. Maestro Andrea di ser Ugolino da Pisa fa alcune storie e 24 teste di lione per la porta del metallo che si fabbricava 1332 e 1333, Libro detto. (LI, II, fol. 114r./118r.)

Doc. 10. (1332)   A Pasquino Telli ferraiuolo si paga lire 18 s. 8 per fune, taglie e canapi e carrucole che prestò alla coperta [sic, = Opera] di S. Giovanni, e per ferramenti che prestò e vendé, quando si rizzò la porta di S. Giovanni, c. 16. (LI, I, fol. 94v./103v.)

Doc. 11. 23 Apr. 1332   Officiali eletti a rivedere il conto a Piero d'Jacopo, orefice, per il tempo che fu a lavorare nelle porti [sic] di bronzo della chiesa di S. Giovanni etc., c.16, c.22, 23 aprile. (LI, I, fol. 168r./177r.)

Doc. 12. 27 Apr. 1332   Maestro Lunardo quondam Avanzi campanarii de Venetiis, de cappella S. Salvatoris, fa fine all'Arte et Opera di S. Giovanni per resto di tutto il salario dovutoli per la detta Arte e Opera per le porte e per cagione delle porte di bronzo della chiesa di S. Giovanni Battista di Firenze. Il salario di detto maestro Lunardo fu lire 600 di bagattini, e per il vitto suo e di due suoi compagni per 6 mesi, oltre il tempo che stette alle spese dell'Opera, doveva havere soldi 16 il giorno, etc., c.16, c.17. (LI, I, fol. 168r./177r. See also LI, II, fol. 118r./122r.: Liber reformationum dal 1331 al 1342 c.6, c.17.)

Doc. 13. 15 Nov. 1332   Piero d'Iacopo, orefice da Firenze, fa fine all'Opera di S. Giovanni di fiorini 70 che doveva havere per il lavoro fatto per lui nelle porte della chiesa di S. Giovanni, c.49. Libro d'Inquisizioni, Giuramenti e altri atti dell'Arte de' Mercatanti delgi anni 1332 e 1333. (LI, I, fol. 72r./83r.)

Doc. 14. 27 Feb. 1333 (1332)   Maestro Andrea di ser Ugolino da Pisa fa fine all'Opera e confessa havere ricevuto fiorini 50 a conto de' fiorini 98 che doveva havere dall'Opera di S. Giovanni per il lavoro della porta di metallo nelle quali [sic] lavora il detto maestro Andrea. Item confessa havere ricevuto fiorini 12. (LI, I, fol. 72r./83r.)

The following three documents concern the cleaning, polishing, and installation of the second door by Piero di Donato. The first refers to an agreement, the second to the actual labor, and the third to payment for this labor.

Doc. 15. 27 Feb. 1333 (1332)   27 febbraio. Piero di Donato, orefice del popolo di S. Felice di Firenze, piglia a pulire e nettare quella porta di metallo che è nella chiesa di S. Giovanni, e dirizzarla e aggiustarla come è la detta porta che è nella detta chiesa, a tutte spese di detto Piero, per prezzo di fiorini 48 d'oro, e doveva tutto haver finito a giugno prossimo. (LI, I, fol. 72r./83r.)

Doc. 16. 1332/1333   Piero Donati orafo pulisce e forbisce e rizza la porta di S. Giovanni, c.14. (LI, II, fol. 115v./119v.)

Doc. 17. (1332)   A Piero Donati orefice si paga lire 29 per lavorio che de'fare nella porta ch'è nell'Opera di S. Giovanni, che la de' pulire e forbire e rizzare come l'altra ch'è in S. Giovanni, c.14. (LI, I, fol. 94v./103v.)

The following four documents refer to payments for reliefs and lions' heads for the first door leaf. Thus, although the payments may have been made any time between 25 March 1332 and 24 March 1333, they refer to work that must have been completed before 27 February 1333, because by that date the first door was already installed (Doc. 15).
Document 18 (to my knowledge) has not previously been published.

Doc. 18. (1332)   Maestro Andrea di Ugolino da Pisa fece le stoire della porta di S. Giovanni e però se li paga più danari. (Uscita di S. Giovanni e S.to Eusebio, 1332 e 1333, c.7, c.15, c.16.) (LI, II, fol. 115v./119v.)

Doc. 19. (1332)   A maestro Andrea d'Ugolino da Pisa si paga lire 72 s. 10 per lo lavorio che de'fare nelle porte di S. Giovanni, c.14. (LI, I, fol. 94v./103v.)

Doc. 20. (1332) A maestro Andrea da Pisa si paga lire 17 s. 8 i quali danari doveva havere della somma di fiorini 98 d'oro per le storie che fece nelle porte di S. Giovanni, c.15. (LI, I, fol. 94v./103v.)

Doc. 21. A maestro Andrea da Pisa si paga lire 52 s. 4 per componimento del suo salario dell'edificamento delle storie della porta di S. Giovanni, c.16. (LI, I, fol. 94v./103v.)
Andrea is now beginning work on the second set of lions' heads:

Doc. 22. 24 July 1333 Maestro Andrea di ser Ugolino da Pisa convenne con gl'officiali di mosaico edificare e fare ventiquattro teste di leone, di metallo, da detto giorno al primo di Dicembre e indorarle, come sono edificate e indorate quelle teste di leoni che sono in quella porta di metallo che è nella detta chiesa di S. Giovanni, a tutte spese di detto maestro Andrea fuorché d'oro e di metallo, e quelle così edificate e indorate commettere bene in quella porta di metallo che adesso è nell'Opera di S. Giovanni, e indorare le storie della detta porta bene e sufficientemente come sono l'altre dell'altra porta con i patti soprascritti, e tutto promette fare per prezzo di fiorini 40. (LI, I, fol. 72r./83r.)

Doc. 23. 9 Aug. 1333 Maestro Andrea di ser Ugolino da Pisa riceve dall'Opera di S. Giovanni fiorini 36 per resto del suo salario dell'edificio delle storie di metallo di quella porta che adesso si fabbrica nella detta Opera. (LI, L, fol. 72v./83v.)

Doc. 24. 19 May 1334 Casa che fu fatta a S. Eusebio per gettare le porti [sic] di metallo fatte per la chiesa di S. Giovanni, si rovini, c.41. (LI, I, fol. 168v./177v.)

Doc. 25. 30 Jan. 1335 (1334) Porte di metallo di S. Giovanni essendovisi già molto tempo

lavorato e non essendo ancora finite et havendo gl'officiali di mosaico trattato quanto bisognasse per finire detto lavoro da farsi in dette porte con maestro Andrea da Pisa, disse non bastare fiorini 500. È deliberato che gl'officiali di mosaico faccino finire le dette porte siché sieno finite e messe su per la festa di S. Giovanni prossima futura. (Inquisizioni e riformagioni dell'Arte de'Mercatanti, 1334 e 1335.) (LI, I, fol. 163r./172r.)

Doc. 26. 7 Mar. 1335 Maestro Andrea da Pisa se gli paghi fiorini 20 per 24 teste di lione d'ottone, fatte da lui per operare alle porte del metallo che si fanno alla chiesa di S. Giovanni. (LI, I, fol. 163v./172v.)

Doc. 27. 7 Mar. 1335 (1334) A Piero di Donato, orefice, se gli paga fiorini 28 per nettatura, limatura e dirizzatura delle suddette porte di bronzo. (LI, I, fol. 163v./172v.)

Doc. 28. 8 Aug. 1335 Maestro Andrea da Pisa piglia a dirizzare, a rischio dell'Arte, le porte di metallo che erano così torte che non si portevano adoperare, che già maestro Piero disse volere dirizzare lui e poi non gl[i]e ne dava l'animo. (LI, I, fol. 163v./172v. See also LI, II, fol. 118r./122r.: Liber reformationum, 1334 e 1335.)

Doc. 29. 25 Oct. 1335 Havendo Piero del quondam maestro Donato pigliato a dirizzare le porte di metallo di S. Giovanni, che una parte di essa [sic] era torta, et a pulirle, e non bastandoli dipoi l'animo di farlo, viene dall'Arte disobbligato, 1335, 25 ottobre. Liber reformationum, 1335 e 1336. (LI, II, fol. 118r./122r. See also LI, I, fol. 165r./174r.)

Doc. 30. 27 Dec. 1335 Andrea orefice, figliuolo del quondam ser Ugolino notaio da Pisa, piglia per fiorini 10 a dirizzare la porta di metallo esistente nell'Opera di S. Giovanni, in termine d'un mese, c.71. (LI, I, fol. 170v./ 179v. See also LI, II, fol. 118r./122r.: Liber

reformationum dal 1331 al 1341, c.71.)
The following appears to be a resume of agreements and contracts between Andrea and the Opera:

Doc. 31. 15 Mar. 1336 (1335)   Patti e convenzioni fatte con Andrea d'Ugolino orefice, per indorare et accomodare la porta di bronzo di S. Giovanni, etc., c.80. (LI, I, fol. 170v./ 179v. See also LI, II, fol. 118r./122r.: Liber detto, c.80.)

Doc. 32. 20 June 1336   Scarpellatura, ritagli e polvere delle porte di metallo di S. Giovanni pesorno libbre 3315. (LI, I, fol. 165r./174r. See also LI, II, fol. 118r./122r.)

Doc. 33. (1336)   Si paga lire 25 a maestro Andrea Pisano perché faccia recare marmo delle parti di Lunigiana a Firenze per ponere alla porta della detta chiesa per solliazi [*sic*]. (Uscita di S. Giovanni 3 di S. Eusebio, 1336.) (LI, I, fol. 95r./104r.)

Doc. 34. 6 Feb. 1338 (1337)   Soglia di marmo si pone alla porta di bronzo di S. Giovanni, c.111. (LI, I, fol. 171r./180r.)

II. *Concerning an iron stamp for marking imported cloth made by Andrea for the Arte de' Baldrigai, the Cloth Cutters' Guild*

Doc. 35. May 1334   Florence, Archivio di Stato. Strozziane, Ser. II, vol. LI, I.
Diedi al maestro Andrea di ser Ugolino da Pisa soldi 56 di piccioli per un marco di ferro che haveva l' Arte de' Baldrigai, da marcare panni per bollarne i panni francesi, c.18. Uscita dell' Arte, 1333 e. 1334. (Fol. 96r./105r.)

III. *Mention of Andrea as capo-maestro of cathedral works of Florence*

Doc. 36. (26 Apr. 1340)   Florence, Archivio

di Stato, Capitoli del Comune di Firenze, Registri #17 (1336–1386). Fol. 77r.
In Dei nomine amen. Anno sue salutifere incarnationis millesimo trecentesimo quadragesimo inditione viiiᵃ die vigesimosexto mensis aprilis. Actum Florentie apud ecclesiam Sancte Reparate, presentibus testibus Vannuccio ser Cini de Sancto Miniate et Francia Nuccii de Sancto Ieminiano ad hec vocatis et rogatis.
Pateat evidenter quod sapientes et discreti viri dominus Bartholomeus de Chastro Florentino, Naddus de Bucellis, Iohannes Guidonis de Antilla, Vannes Donnini, Guido Guaze, Cennes Nardi, Forese Ferrantini, Iohannes Geri del Bello, Fuccius Magistri, Coppus Borghesis, Chele de Agugl[i]one et Vannes Armati, cives honorabiles florentini populares, habito prius colloquio consilio et trac[ta]tu super infrascriptis cum reverendo in Christo patre et domino, domino Francischo episcopo florentino et calonacis et cappellanis dicte ecclesie, ac etiam cum consulibus Artis lane et operariis dicte ecclesie, ac etiam cum magistro Andrea maiore magistro dicte opere; facto prius et obtento partito inter eos ad fabas nigras et albas; providerunt et deliberaverunt quod chalonecha et habitatio chalonachorum dicte ecclesie fiat et construatur iusta dictam ecclesiam versus meridiem et versus plateam de Bonizis. Rogantes me Locterium notarium infrascriptum ut de predictis publicum conficerem instrumentum.
(In margin: De calonaca S. Reparate.)

IV. *Concerning payment for a marble block on which is to be carved a Madonna to be placed above the main portal of the Cathedral of Pisa*

Doc. 37. 27 July 1345   Pisa, Archivio di Stato, Opera del Duomo di Pisa, 88 (Libro d'Entrata e Uscita, 1346), c. 86v.
Bertuccio quondam Ugolino da Charara ebe adì XXVII di Lugl[i]o, per pregio di marmo per

fare la Nostra Donna sopra la porta reale, dela soma di libre XCIII e soldi X.   Lire XLVI, s. X.

E arechatura lo soprascritto marmo dala legatia a chasa del'Opra, diedi a Paccio di Lando da Limiti.   s. XII.

V. *Last will and testament of Doge Marco Cornaro*

Doc. 38. 10 Jan. 1367   Venice, Archivio di Stato. Procuratori de citra, b. VI, 439: testamento del doge Marco Corner (10 gennaio 1367, m.v.)

Item volumus, si aliud Omnipotens de nobis disponeret, corpus nostrum sepelliri in loco Sanctorum Iohannis et Pauli fratrum Predicatorum, si ibi locus habebitur conveniens nobis et statui nostro. Verum si huiusmodi locus ibi non posset haberi, tunc corpus meum sepelliatur in loco fratrum Minorum Sancte Marie. Volumus autem quod in illo dictorum duorum locorum ubi sepelliemur, fiat una archa honorabilis, in qua corpus nostrum solum sit et non alterius. Vero corpus domine ducisse uxoris nostre, quando Dominus illam ad se vocabit, ponatur iuxta nos in archa predicta.

VI. *Orvieto: Andrea as capomaestro of Opera del Duomo*

Orvieto, Archivio dell'Opera del Duomo. Camerlinga, Libro III.

Doc. 39. 14 May 1347   Die XIV mensis Maii 1347, solvit et dedit dictus camerarius Luce magistri Johannis clavario pro pretio unius catorci tondi, et clavis cum sera, pro domo quam mag. Andreas de Pisis caputmagister Operis nove Ecclesie majoris Urbisveteris, habitat pro dicto Opere, VIX sold. (Fol. 138v.)

Doc. 40. 24 May 1347   Die XXIIII mensis Maii.
VI soldos, VI denarios solvit et dedit dictus

camerarius magistro Meo magistri Andree, fabro, pro pretio unius virghe acciarii, quam fabricavit pro quadam gravinella et II scalpellis pro magistro Andrea de Pisis, capudmagistro dicti Operis. (Fol. 141v.)

Doc. 41. 1 Aug. 1347   VII soldos, X denarios solvit magistro Andree de Pisis pro cenabro, biacca et cera colla pro pignendo. (Fol. 160r.)

Doc. 42. 4 Aug. 1347   Die IIII mensis Augusti [1347].
VII soldos, X denaros solvit magistro Andree de Pisis, pro cenabro biacca et cera colla pro pignendo. (Fol. 160r.)

Doc. 43. 6 Aug. 1347   XII soldos solvit et dedit camerarius Nuccio Benci mercianti, pro pretio folearum pro ornamento figure Virginis Marie. (Fol. 160r.)

Doc. 44. 6 Aug. 1347   Die VI mensis Augusti.
III soldos solvit Nuccio Butii pro pretio coloris mordentis pro auro mictendo in vestimentis Virginis Marie (Fol. 160r.)

Doc. 45. Aug. 1347   The upper part of the page has been torn away so the day of the month is missing; according to Fumi (1891), 99, the document refers to 9 August; therefore, the two immediately following it are also of that date.
. . . solvit et dedit dictus Stephanus camerarius dicti Operis, Christiano magistri Landi pro [pre]tio duorum petiorum lapidum de marmo albo, exstimatos per magistros dicti Operis.

Doc. 46. Aug. 1347   . . . soldos, VI denarios solvit et dedit dictus camerarius Iohanni Butii Lonardelli, pro pretio quorumdam petiorum panni lini veteris pro Angelis impannandis.

Doc. 47. Aug. 1347   III soldos solvit et dedit dictus camerarius Vannutio Cecchi Carsie pro hovis pro clara fienda pro coloribus liquefaciendis figura seu imagine Virginis Sancte Marie et Angelorum troni.

The following is published in Fumi (1891), p. 99; I was unable to locate the documents in the Archives. The first, however, seems to combine our Documents 41 and 46.

Doc. 48. VIJ sol. et X den. – Magistro Andree de Pisis pro cenabro, biacca et cera colla, 1 libra et IIJ den. – pro pretio quorumdam petiorum panni lini veteris pro angelis impanandis.
Nallo Barthi pro duabus unciis azzurri ad rationem VJ sol. pro uncia et pro modico cerosse et pro XIJ foliis auri ad rationem VJ den. pro quolibet folio pro Maiestate pulcra de marmore ornanda.

Doc. 49. 26 Sept. 1347 [Die XXVI Septembris 1347,] Vannutio Cecchi pro XI diebus quibus extra Operi servivit in eo quod ivit cum magistro Andrea caputmagistro dicti Operis dum ivit Senas pro facto marmoris, et etiam Pisas, ad rationem VI soldorum pro quolibet die; lib. III et VI sold. (Fol. 178v.)

Doc. 50. 6 Feb. 1348 Die Mercurii, sexta mensis Februarii [1348]. Magistro Nicole magistri Dominici, campanario, pro pretio unius campanelle parve ponende apud locum Maiestatis porte Pusterule, de metallo, et pro ferris mozzi et pro ipso mozzo parvo, et pro corda pro eadem campanella. XXIIII soldos. (Fol. LXv.)
Nallo Barthi, mercianti, pro duabus unciis azuri, ad rationem VII soldorum pro uncia, et pro modico cerosse, et pro XII foliis auri, ad rationem Vi denariorum pro qualibet folia, pro Maiestate pulcra de marmore ornanda, XXI soldos, Vi denarios. (Fol. LXv.)

Doc. 51. 25 Feb. 1348 Die Lune, XXV mensis Februarii [1348]. Vannutio Cecchi Carsie pro XXXVII diebus quibus servivit Operi extra, apud Pisas et Senas pro facto marmoris et pro magistro Andrea capitemagistro, inter duas vices, in eundo stando et reddeundo, ad

rationem VI soldorum pro die, secundum conventionem secum factam. Undecim libras et II soldos. (Fol. LXXIr.)

Doc. 52. 3 Mar. 1348 Die Lune, tertio mensis Martii [1348]. Monaldus camerarius suprascriptus dedit et solvit Dominico Vannis victurali, pro apportatione duarum salmarum et vectura mulorum deferentium de marmore a civitate Pisarum ad Urbemveterem, et Maiestatem cum lapidibus de marmore pro Angelis fiendis circa honorem dicte Maiestatis, et pro pedagiis et gabellis totius itineris: in totum XXIIII libras et XVIII soldos. (Fol. LXXVr.)

Doc. 53. 3 Mar. 1348 Vicho numptio Episcopatus Urbisveteris, qui ivit Romam cum litteris Operis ad dictum Episcopum, pro commissione generali habenda nomine ipsius Episcopi super facto Operis, et qui tulit litteras fulcitas, secundum commissionem sibi factam circa necessaria Operis et pro facto marmoris de Roma trahendi. Quatuor libras. (Fol. LXXVr.)

Doc. 54. 21 Mar. 1348 Die Veneris, XXI mensis Martii [1348]. Nerino Iannuccii, pro victura sui ronzini per eum prestiti ad rationem VIII soldorum pro die, quando magister Andreas ivit Senas pro facto marmoris, pro XII diebus. Quatuor libras et XVI soldos. (Fol. LXXXIIv.)

Doc. 55. 1 Apr. 1348 Nallo Barti mercianti pro media libra masticis pro colla pro lapidibus ponendis in facie anteriori dicte Ecclesie et pro modica cere albe. XVII sol. (Fol. LXXXVIIIIr.)

Doc. 56. 26 Apr. 1348 Die Sabati, XXVI mensis Aprelis [1348]. Magistro Andree Capitimagistro dedit et restituit, quos ipse suo verbo expenderat, pro duabus limis de acciario et pro una salma carbonis et pro modica burrace pro gallis de ramine saldandis. XXV soldos. (Fol. LXXXIIv.)

VII. *Nino as capomaestro of Orvieto*

Orvieto, Archivio dell'Opera del Duomo. Cabine II, Libro III.

Doc. 57. 22 Oct. 1349   Die XXII Octubris [1349]. Item dedit et solvit magistro Nino magistri Andree pro duobus corregiis pro trapano.   V soldos.
Item dedit et solvit dicturs camerarius magistro Nino magistri Andree, capiti magistrorum Operis predicte [*sic*], pro suo salario trium mensium incipiendorum a XVIIII diebus Iulii proxime preteritis, ad rationem CXXX florenorum in anno, XXXII florenos et medium auri. (Fol. LXXXIIv.)

Doc. 58. 17 Nov. 1349   Die XVII dicti mensis [Novembris, 1349]. Item dedit et solvit magistro Nini magistri Andree, pro suo salario pro pluribus diebus quibus servivit in Opere.
VI florenos, III libras et VII soldos. (No pagination, verso.)

Doc. 59. 1350   The following is a letter dated 1350 from Donadio Malavolti, Bishop of Siena from 1317–50, addressed to the Commune of Orvieto. It is published in Guglielmo della Valle, *Storia del Duomo di Orvieto*, Rome (1791), and refers to a Giovanni di Maestro Ammannato as capomaestro of Orvieto Cathedral. I have been unable to locate this letter.
Nobilibus et prudentibus viris Prioribus Settem, et ipsis Settem Gubernatoribus et Defensoribus Communis et Populi de Civitate Urbeveteris amicis carissimis. Donos Deus, Dei Gratia Episcopus Senensis, salutem et dispositam ad beneplacitum voluntatem. Imposuimus experto viro Magistro Vanni olim Magistri Ammannati Civi Senarum generali operario et capiti Magistrorum Operis vestre majoris Ecclesie Urbeveteris, quod ex parte nostra vobis super facto certi vestri lignaminis loqueretur. Super quo facto

est de nostra intentione et beneplacito plenarie informatus. Unde etc. Datum in Cassaro nostro de S. Innocentia, die ultimo Februarii indictione prima.

By January 1351 Matteo Ugolini was capomaestro:

Doc. 60. 14 Jan. 1351   Eodem die [sabati XIIII Ianuarii 1351]. Item dedit et solvit magistro Mactheo Ugolini pro pensione domus ser Savini domini Petri, in qua idem magister Ugolinus [*sic: Mactheus Ugolini*] inhabitabat pro tribus mensibus [elapssis].   Viginti soldos.
Item expendit pro vino et carnibus, quod et quas dedit certis magistris dicti Operis qui iverunt cum magistro Mactheo ad videndum lapidem altaris et concam baptismatis pro eas duci faciendo ad Urbemveterem.   Trigintasex soldos et sex denarios. (Camarlinghi, 1350–7. Fol. 39v.)

Doc. 61. 9 Mar. 1353   Die Sabati nona mensis martii 1353.
Magistro Matheo Ugolini, caputmagistro dicti Operis, recipienti pro infrascriptis magistris et manualibus laborantibus extra terram. (Fol. 13r.)

VIII. *Nino as goldsmith working for Opera del Duomo and Comune of Pisa*

(Regarding making and installing a silver altarpiece and making an enameled insignia for the Opera.)

Doc. 62. April 1358   Florence, Archivio di Stato, Notarile antecosimiano, No. F569 (1353–60), fol. 127r.–128v.
Coscius condam Gaddi de cappella Sancti Felicis, Ninus condam magistri Andree de cappella Sancti Laurentii de Rivolta, et Simon dictus Baschiera de Cappella Sancte Cecilie, aurifices coram me Francischo notario supra-

scripto et testibus infrascriptis, habuerunt et receperunt a domino Bonaiu[n]cta Maschani operario opere Sancte Marie maioris ecclesie, existente in presentia dominorum anthianorum pisani populi, videlicet ser Coli Scarsi lucum tenentis ser Pieri de Sancto Casiano prioris dominorum anthianorum, Gabrielli Iacobi Melani, Andree Scarsi, Perii cestarii, magistri Nicolini di Corno, Iohanni Maggiulini, Andree ser Averardi de Montefoschuli et Perii vinarii, anthianorum pisani populi et eorum mandato, sequentes formam consilii senatus et credentie dominorum anthianorum pisani populi et aliorum ordinum pisane civitatis celebrati Pisis in sala dictorum dominorum anthianorum Dominice incarnationis anno mccclviij, indictione xjᵃ, tertio kalendas martii, vel alio tempore vel datali, et retificati per consilium pisani populi die suprascripta, libbras quinquaginta una et uncias tres argenti, videlicet libbras quadragintaocto et uncias novem dicti argenti in virgis battutis ad modum cintule argentee que consueverat circumdari [sic] pisanam maiorem ecclesiam, et non clavate, et libbras duas et uncias sex dicti argenti in virgis, quod argentum Gaddus olim pater dicti Coscii aurifex, Meus aurifex de cappella sancti Gregorii et Francischus aurifex condam Coli de cappella sancti Christofori Kinthice habuerunt et receperunt a domino Iohanne Coccho olim operario dicte opere, antecessori dicti domini Bonaiuncte, pro ipsa opera dante pro faciendo inde per dictos Gaddum, Meu[m], Francischum, aurifices, cintulam unam de argento planam et albi coloris ad modum cintule que esse consuevit et poni consuevit in festivitatibus circumcirca pisanam maiorem ecclesiam, per cartam rogatam inde et scriptam in actis dicte opere a Francischo condam Franciscii sellarii notario mccxlvij, indictione xiij, nonas may, vel alio tempore vel datali. Et quod argentum in dicto pondere predictus dominus Bonaiuncta [habuit] a suprascripto Francischo auri-

fice et a suprascripto Coscio filio condam et heredum [sic] suprascripti Gaddi, dantibus et consignantibus pro se ipsis et heredibus suprascripti Mei, videlicet libbras quadragintaocto uncias novem dicti argenti in virgiis battutis, et libbras duas et uncias sex dicti argenti de argento in suprascripta carta comprehenso per cartam inde rogatam et scriptam a Blasio Clavelli notario in actis dicte opere Dominice incarnationis anno mccccl, indictione tertiadecima tertiodecimo Kalendas decembris. vel alio tempore vel datali. Quam dactionem idem dominus Bonaiuncta operarius, volens liberari et absolvi a receptione suprascripti argenti, quod iam ante habuerat a suprascriptis Coscio et Francischo aurificibus, et exinde deceterum non teneri, fecit predictis Coscio, Nino et Simoni aurificibus secundum formam dicti consilii, videlicet cuilibet eorum pro tertia parte dicti argenti pro faciendo inde tabulam unam argenteam ab altari et ponendum ad altarem pisane maiorem [sic] ecclesie. De quibus libbris quinquaginta una et unciis tribus dicti argenti predicti Coscius, Ninus et Simon, videlicet quilibet eorum pro tertia parte, dicti argenti in dicto pondere vocaverunt se a dicto domino Bonaiuncta operario, dante et consignante operariatus nomine pro dicta opera, bene quietos [et] contentos, et inde dictum dominum Bonaiunctam eiusque heredes et bona liberaverunt et absolverunt. Insuper predicti Coscius, Ninus et Simon aurifices ex certa scientia et non per errorem volen[te]s ad infrascripta teneri et obligari ipsi et quilibet eorum, non obstante quod hec facere non tenea[n]tur, per sollemnem stipulationem, convenerunt et promiserunt suprascripto domino Bonaiuncte operario, operariatus nomine pro dicta opera recipienti, facere et ponere super ipsa tabula argentea fienda, intus et extra dictam tabulam, signata [sic: signa] opere sancte Marie maioris ecclesie suprascripte, ismaltata et magna et bene confissa et firmata et apparente firmate [sic] et sufficien[ti] modo, ad beneplacitum suprascripti domini Bonaiuncte operarii, et eo numero signorum ut sibi videbitur convenienti et in locis ipsium tabule ut ei videbitur convenientibus; et nulla alia signa vel lictere super ipsa tabula adponi vel fieri possint nec debeant super ipsa tabula, numquam removenda inde vel elevanda, ad penam librarum centum denariorum pisanorum a quolibet predictorum Coscii, Nini et Simonis in solidum auferendam ad opus et utilitate [sic] dicte opere, se et quemlibet eorum in solidum et suos et cuiusque eorum in solidum heredes et bona dicto operario pro dicta opera obligando, et renuntiando beneficio epistole etc. et omni alii iuris etc. Insuper predicti domini anthiani mandaverunt quod nulli liceat actentare quod dicta signa vel aliquid eorum dicte tabule super ipsa tabula fienda et exmaltanda, cassare vel removere aut destruere, sive cassari, destrui vel removeri facere aut permictere, et quicunque contra predicta venerit vel fecerit, incurrat indignactione Pisani Comunis, et nichilominus dicta signa et lictere opere reficiantur et apponantur super dicta tabula expensis et sumptibus cui[us]cumque contrafacientis. Actum Pisis in sala palatii dominorum anthianorum Pisani populi, presentibus ser Bartholomeo Henrigi de Montefoschuli tunc existente cancellario dominorum anthianorum predictorum et Iacobo Bernardi Forretanei notario nunc dominorum anthianorum Pisani populi, testibus ad hec rogatis Dominice incarnationis anno mcclviiij, indictione xj, sexto kalendas may.

Doc. 63. 15 May 1358   Regarding repair of silver trumpet belonging to Comune of Pisa. Pisa, Archivio Capitolare. B5, Vetustissima Pisanae Civitatis Monumenta, F. (Fol. 11r.) [Ydus May, XI° indictionis (1358)]. Nino aurifici quondam magistri Andree, de cappella Sancti Laurenti de Rivolta, florenum unum de auro, vel eius valentiam, pro actatura

quam fecit de una tuba de argento Pisani Comunis.

Doc. 64. 26 Apr. 1359   Pisa, Archivio di Stato, Comune, A, 128, fol. 112v.–114v. The following is probably an extract of Doc. 41 and was made for the Commune of Pisa, which had ultimate authority in these matters. Suprascripto die (sexto kalendas may, xi indictione [1359]). Providerunt domini Anthiani Pisani populi, partitu facto inter eos ad denarios albos et giallos secundum formam brevis Pisani populi. [omissis] Et quod super tabula argentea que fieri debet ad presens per Coscium condam Gaddi, Simonem dictum Baschieram et Ninum condam magistri Andree aurifices, ponenda ad altare pisane maioris ecclesie, fiant et fieri debeant per ipsos aurifices signa opere Sancte Marie maioris ecclesie, intus et extra ysmaltata, apparentia, sufficientia et bene confissa ipsi tabule, videlicet tria ex parte interiori et tria ex parte exteriori, in locis de quibus operario maioris ecclesie videbitur convenire, ad penam librarum quinquaginta denariorum pisanorum pro quolibet suprascriptorum Coscii, Simonis et Nini auferendam ad opus dicte opere, et super ipsa tabula permansura firma. Et si inde tollerentur vel elevarentur aut destruerentur ipsa vel aliquid eorum, incontinenti debeant refici sumptibus et expensis contrafacientis. Et quicumque contrafecerit incurrat indignationem Pisarum Comunis, et nicchilominus dicta signa sic remota reficiantur et fiant de novo a capite super ipsa tabula.

Doc. 65. (15 May 1358)   Regarding silver altarpiece with figures to be made by Nino and other goldsmiths. This document was published by Francesco Bonaini in the *Annali delle Università Toscane*, vol. 1, Pisa (1846a), 554–5, as in the Archivio Capitolare della Primaziale di Pisa. I was unable to locate Filza E containing this document in the Cathedral Chapter archives; it has apparently been lost. Below is Bonaini's transcription.

MCCCLVIIII, Octavo decimo Kalendas Iunii. XI. Indictione.

Providerunt domini Antiani pisani populi partitu facto inter eos ad denarios albos et giallos secundum formam brevis pisani populi et providendo commisserunt.

Ser Rozello de Aritio vicario etc. Quatenus viribus sui officij et presentis commissionis ad petitionem et instantiam Domini Bonaiuncte Mascarj operarj opere Sancte Marie Majoris ecclesie pisane civitatis cogat et cogere possit et debeat Coscium quondam Gaddi aurificem de cappella sancti felicis et Ninum quondam magistri Andree de ponthere aurificem de cappella sancti Laurentii de Rivolta et simonem dictum baschiera aurificem de cappella sancte Cecilie pisanos cives quibus ipse operarius dedit et consignavit libbras quinquagintaunam et uncias tres argenti ad pondus per cartam rogatam a francischo verij de vico notario et scriba publico dicte opere de mense Martij proxime preteriti pro faciendo una cum alio argento quod Canonici pisani capituli dare et expendere offerebant quandam tabulam argenteam cum figuris schultis tenendam certis temporibus super altari majoris ecclesie nullo termino assignato dictis aurificibus de infra quem dictam tabulam debeant perfecisse realiter et personaliter videlicet quemlibet ipsorum aurificum per se ad dandum et prestandum dicto domino Bonaiuncte Operario pro dicta Opera recipienti ydoneam causionem et securitatem de conservando predictum argentum pro dicta opera. Et si dictam tabulam infra terminum octo mensium proxime venturorum dictis aurificibus assignandum a dicto domino Bonaiuncta operario infra quem promictant dictam tabulam perfecisse totaliter et perfecte non perfecerint laudabiliter et complete dicti aurifices dictum argentum totum in lega argenti sufficientis boni et puri elapso termino suprascripto incontinenti ipsi domino Bonaiuncte operario dicto nomine recipienti debeant restituere et consignare. Et predicta faciant et facere teneantur cartis publicis intervenientibus in laudem convenientis sapientis dicti operarij cum promissionibus et obligationibus et penalibus stipulationibus et opportunis quibuslibet roboratis que de jure bene valeant et teneant. Et quod terminus dictorum octo mensium prorogari non possit.

IX. *The Scherlatti monument*

Doc. 66. (16 Feb. 1362)   Last will of Giovanni, archbishop of Pisa, 16 February 1362. Florence, Archivio di Stato. Notarile antecosimiano. L 384 (1359–63), fol. 88r.

In primiis quidem iudico corpus meum sepelliendum in Pisana maiori ecclesia, subtus scalas lapideas seu marmoreas ex latere dextro ipsius ecclesie, in quadam arca marmorea ibi fienda et ponenda, super qua arca ego volo et mando me sculpi in forma et ymagine archiepiscopali, et ibi meam eligo sepulturam ...

Doc. 67. (15 Mar. 1362)   Contract for the Scherlatti monument.

Florence, Archivio di Stato. Notarile antecosimiano. L 384 (1359–63), fol. 103v.–104v.

Magister Ninus filius quondam magistri Andree de Pontehere, de Capella sancti Laurentii de Rivolta, aurifex et magister et sculptor lapidum, per solemnem stipulationem convenit et promisit venerabilibus viris dominis Gualterio Abbati monasterii Sancti Michaelis de Burgo, Silvestro magistro et rectori hospitalis novi Misericordie de Pisis, Francisco ser Puccii canonico pisano et magistro Simoni de Paniccijs de Bulgaro fideicommissariis et executoribus testamenti et ultime voluntatis

Reverendi in Christo patris et domini, domini Johannis olim pisani archiepiscopi, facere fabricare sculpere ponere ordinare laborare et murare ac solidare in pisana maiori ecclesia, subtus scalas marmoreas seu lapideas ipsius ecclesie ex latere dextro ipsius ecclesie, tumbam et sepulturam ipsius domini Archiepiscopi in hunc modum factam, videlicet sepulturam unam de marmore de Carraria, in qua ponatur corpus ipsius domini Archiepiscopi, et super qua tumba seu sepultura sit sculpta relevata ymago ipsius domini Archiepiscopi in forma Archiepiscopali cum plumaccio de marmoro sculpto subtus capite, et cum uno angelo de marmore a quolibet latere ipsius. Et super ipsam tumbam seu sepulturam sit unus arcus de marmore supradicto cum archettis inginocchiatis, et in facie ipsius tumbe in medio sit Pietas cum uno angelo a quolibet latere, et ab una latere sit ymago beate Virginis Marie cum duobus angelis, et ab alio latere sit ymago beati Johannis evangeliste cum duobus angelis, et a latere uno ipsius sepulture sit ymago sancti Petri et ab alio sancti Pauli; et omnia sint de marmore supradicto. Et subtus dictam tumbam sit unus arcus cum tribus archettis inginocchiatis, et ab utroque latere ipsius sepulture sint sculpta arma ipsius domini Archiepiscopi et prout et sicut et eo modo et forma ut in quadam pictura per eundem magistrum Ninum data dictis fideicommissariis per omnia continetur. Omnibus suis ipsius magistri Nini sumptibus et expensis hinc ad quindecim menses proxime venturos pro infrascripto pretio inde percipiendo ut infra dicetur, sine briga molestia reclamatione curie et ullis expensis, alioquin pena dupli florenorum ducentorum decem auri solemni stipulatione. Et omnes expensas que inde fierent, eisdem fideicommissariis dare solvere et resarcire promisit, obligando inde se et suos heredes et bona omnia dictis fideicommissariis et mihi notario suprascripto tanquam persone publice agenti stipulanti et recipienti

pro omnibus quorum interest et intererit. Renuntiando omni iuri canonico et civili et omni alii iuri unde se a predictis vel aliquo predictorum posset defendere vel tueri. Quod opus laudari debeat per suprascriptum dominum Gualterium Abbatem Sancti Michaelis et per dominum Ranerium priorem Sancti Sisti Pisani. Quare suprascripti domini fideicommissarii superius nominati, fideicommissariatus nomine, presente et consentiente venerabili viro domino Rayneiro priore Sancti Sisti Pisani, subcollectore Camere Apostolice, et presentibus et consentientibus fratribus Simone et Ieronimo, monacis monasterii Sancti Ieronimi de Agnano et eiusdem monasterii sindicis et procuratoribus [omissis] per solemnem stipulationem convenerunt et promiserunt suprascripto magistro Nino dare et solvere vel dari et solvi facere eidem magistro Nino vel suis heredibus vel eius certo nuntio vel cui ipse preceperit, pro predictis omnibus et singulis fiendis, ut supra dicta sunt et promissa, florenos ducentos decem auri bonos et iusti ponderis, et totum aurum necessarium ad ornaturam dicti laborerii, hinc ad suprascriptum terminum, sine briga molestia reclamatione Curie et ullis expensis, alioquin pena dupli suprascriptorum florenorum ducentorum decem auri, solemni stipulatione promissa; et omnes expensas que inde fierent, eidem magistro Nino dare solvere et resarcire promiserunt, obligando inde se et quemlibet eorum, dicto fideicommissariatus nomine, et bona hereditatis dicti domini Archiepiscopi dicto magistro Nino et eius heredibus. Renuntiando omni iuri etc. Et etiam actum inter dictos contrahentes, dictis nominibus, ex pacto expresso habito et apposito inter eos, quod solutio dicte quantitatis florenorum vel alicuius sue partis, vel absolutio, seu aliqua compensatio vel exceptio seu aliquid aliud huic contractui contrarium vel nocivum, non possit probari mostrari vel opponi per testes vel alia presumptione nisi per hanc cartam cassam vel alia contracartam factam a bono et legali notario.

Actum Pisis, in camera habitationis domini Iohannis de Barba, Pisani canonici, posita intra claustrum nove canonice, presentibus venerabili viro domino Antonio de Scribanis, Pisano canonico, domino Guillielmo monaco monasterii Sancti Michaelis de Burgo, et aliis testibus ad hoc vocatis et rogatis, suprascriptis anno et indictione, die quintadecima Martii.

X. *The Agnello tomb*

Doc. 68. 5 Dec. 1368   Pisa, Archivio di Stato. Comune, A, 142 (Provvisioni degli Anziani), fol. 18v.

Nonas Decembris, septime Indictionis. Providerunt dominj Antianj pisani populi Imperiales vicarij etc. partitu facto inter eos ad denarios albos et giallos secundum formam brevis pisani populi, Quod Thomasus filius olim magistri Andree de Pontehere et Andreas filius condam et heres Nini condam suprascripti magistri Andree habeant et habere possint et debeant de bonis domini Johannis de Agnello olim ducis Pisarum, venditis vel vendendis, in una parte florenos viginti aurj quos dictus Ninus olim pater dicti Andree recipere habebat et sibi restitit solvi a dicto domino Johanne de summa pretij magisterij sepulcrj marmorej ipsius dominj Johannis scultj et fabricati per ipsum Ninum ad petitionem dicti dominj Johannis apud ecclesiam Sancti Francisci juxta portam qua itur in primum claustrum dicte ecclesie. Et in alia parte florenos triginta aurj suprascripto Thomaso debitos a suprascripto domino Johanne, pro designatura certorum designamentorum sepulcrj marmorei quod dictus dominus Johannes fierj volebat in pisana maiori ecclesia in loco in quo domina Macthea, olim eius uxor, sepulta est. Et quorumdam aliorum designamentorum palatij quod idem dominus Johannes volebat sibi con-

struj debere in loco ubi domus erant quas destruj fecit. Et pro designatione cuiusdam sedis more tronj regij, quam idem dominus Johannes volebat fierj de marmore politissimo in coro maioris ecclesie in qua resideret in apparatu ducali. Et pro factura cimerij ipsius dominj Johannis de gesso, et pro pittura coloratura et ornatura ipsius cimerij. Et quod Laurentius Bindacchj et Opisus Falconis cives pisani, officiales electj a Comunj Pisarum super faciendo devenire in Comune Pisarum bona prefati dominj Johannis vel eorum successorum possint teneantur et debeant per se vel alios dare et solvere vel dari et solvi facere suprascriptis Thomaso et Andree vel dicto Thomaso recipienti pro se et dicto Andrea eius nepote, suprascriptos florenos quinquaginta aurj debitos eis occasionibus suprascriptis. Et quod exactor suprascriptorum officialium vel eius successor, de pecunia suprascripta ab eis habita vel habenda de bonis dictj dominj Johannis venditis nel vendendis, possit teneatur et debeat dare et solvere suprascriptis Thomaso et Andree vel suprascripto Thomaso recipientj pro se et dicto Andrea, suprascriptos florenos quinquaginta aurj in auro absque solutione cabelle [*canc.*; vel alterius dirictus]. Et quod notarius ipsorum officialium possit et sibi liceat inde facere quaslibet scripturas utiles et opportunas virtute presentis provisionis, nullo obstante.

XI. *Tommaso Pisano*

See also Doc. 68.

Doc. 69. 15 Feb. 1368   Pisa, Archivio di Stato, Opera del Duomo di Pisa, 18 (Inventario dei beni dell'Opera, 1368), fol. 63v.

Actum Pisis, in domo dicte Opere posita in Cappella S. Maria maioris Pisane ecclesie, in cancelleria dicte Opere, presentibus Henrico quondam Pilistri de S. Pietro, de Cappella suprascripta S. Marie, factore dicti Operarii, et

Tomaso aurifice quondam magistri Andree de Ponte Here, scruptore [*sic*] lapidum de Cappella S. Laurentii de Rivolta, et Iacobo quondam Pieri, archimagistro magistrorum dicte Opere, de Cappella S. Marie maioris Pisane ecclesie, testibus ad hec rogatis, Dominice Incarnationis anno millesimo trecentesimo sexagesimo octavo, indictione sexta, quartodecimo Kalendas Martii.

Doc. 70. 15 Feb. 1368   Pisa, Archivio di Stato, Opera del Duomo, 18, fol. 2r. Actum Pisis in Cancellaria sive apotheca in qua tenentur libri et acta dicte opere, posita in cappella S. Marie maioris ecclesie pisane civitatis, presentibus Henrico quondam Pilistri de Sancto Pietro et Tomaso aurifice condam magistri Andree de Pontehere de cappella Sancti Laurentii de Rivolta etc., testibus ad hec rogatis et vocatis dominice Incarnationis anno MCCCLXVIII, indictione sexta, quarto decimo Kalendas Martii.

Doc. 71. 28 Sept. 1368   Pisa, Archivio di Stato. Opera del Duomo, 92 (Entrata e Uscita del'anno 1368), c. 130r.
Tomasus magistri Andree de Pontehere, aurifex, pro diebus tredecim quibus laboravit ad opus dicte Opere in faciendo angiulos marmoreos, ad rationem solidorum viginti quinque per diem, lib. sedecim et sol. quinque.

BIBLIOGRAPHY

Alessandrini, G., G. Dassu, P. Pedeferri, and G. Re. "On the Conservation of the Baptistry Doors in Florence." *Studies in Conservation* 24 (1979) : 108–24.

Alpatoff, M. "The Parallelism of Giotto's Paduan Frescoes." *Art Bulletin* (1947) : 149–54; reprinted in J. Stubblebine, ed., *Giotto: The Arena Chapel Frescoes*. New York, 1969.

Andres, G., J. Hunisak, and A. R. Turner. *The Art of Florence*. In press.

Angiola, E. M. "Nicola Pisano, Federigo Visconti, and the Classical Style in Pisa." *Art Bulletin* 59 (1977) : 1–27.

Antal, F. *Florentine Painting and Its Social Background*. London, 1948.

Baldini, U. *Metodo e Scienze Operatività e Ricerca nel Restaure* (exhibition catalogue). Florence, 1982.

Balogh, J. "Etudes sur la collection des sculptures anciennes du Musée des Beaux-Arts." III. *Acta Historiae Artium* I (1953) : 71–114.

Baracchini, C. *Il Secolo di Castruccio, Fonti e documenti di storia Lucchese* (exhibition catalogue). Lucca, 1981.

Baracchini, C., and A. Caleca. *Il Duomo di Lucca*. Lucca, 1973.

Barsotti, R. "Nuovi studi sulla Madonna eburnea di Giovanni Pisano." *Critica d'Arte* n.s. 4 (1957) : 47–56.

Bearzi, B. "La technica usata dal Ghiberti per le porte del Battistero." *Lorenzo Ghiberti nel suo tempo* (Atti del Convegno Internazionale di Studi, Firenze, 1978) 2 vol. Florence, 1980.

Becatti, G. *Colonna de Marco Aurelio*. Milan, 1957.

Becherucci, L. "I rilievi dei Sacramenti nel Campanile del Duomo di Firenze." *L'Arte* 30 (1927) : 214–23.

– "Exhibition of Pisan Trecento Sculpture." *Burlington Magazine* 89 (March 1947) : 68–70.

– "La bottega pisana di Andrea da Pontedera." *Mitteilungen des Kunsthistorischen Instituts in Florenz* (1965) : 227–63.

Becherucci, L., and G. Brunetti. *Il Museo dell'Opera del Duomo a Firenze*, 2 vols. Florence, 1969.

Beck , J. *Italian Renaissance Painting*. New York, 1981.

Becker, M. *Florence in Transition*, vol. I. Baltimore, 1967.

Biehl, W. *Toskanische Plastik des Frühen und Hohen Mittelalters*. Leipzig, 1926.

Bertaux, E. "Le tombeau d'une Reine de France à Cosenza en Calabre." *Gazette des Beaux-Arts* 19 (1898) : April, 265–76; May, 369–78.

Bettini, S. "L'ultima e la più bella opera di Jacopo e Pier Paolo dalle Masegne." *Dedalo* 12 (1932) : 347–59.

Bianchi Bandinelli, R. *Rome: The Late Empire*. New York, 1971.

Boase, T. S. R. *Giorgio Vasari, the Man and the Book*. Princeton, 1979.

Boeckler, A. *Die Bronzetüren des Bonanus von Pisa und des Barisanus von Trani*. Berlin, 1953.

Bonani, F., "Memorie inedite di disegno," *Annali delle Università Toscane*, vol. 1, Pisa. (1846a) : 429–592.

― *Memorie Inedite intorno alla vita e ai dipinti di Francesco Traini e ad altre opere di disegno dei secoli XI, XIV, e XV*. Pisa, 1846b.

Borsook, E. *Ambrogio Lorenzetti*. Florence, 1966.

Borsook, E., and L. Tintori. *Giotto: The Peruzzi Chapel*. New York, 1965.

Bottari, S. "Una scultura di Nino Pisano a Trapani." *Critica d'Arte* n.s. 3 (1956) : 555–7.

Boyce, G. K. *Italian Manuscripts in the Pierpont Morgan Library*. New York, 1953.

Brach, A. *Nicola and Giovanni Pisano*. Strasbourg, 1904.

Braunfels, W. *Die Stadtbaukunst in der Toskana*. Berlin, 1953.

Brizio, A. M. "Nota su Andrea Pisano." *Studio Medioevale* 16 (1949–50) : 265–8.

Brucker, G. *Florentine Politics and Society, 1343–1378*. Princeton, 1962.

Brunetti, G. "Note sul soggiorno Fiorentino di Tino." *Commentari* 3 (1952) : 97–107.

Burresi, M. "Per l'identificazione di Nino Pisano." *Critica d'Arte* n.s. 20 (1973) : 6–12.

― *Andrea, Nino, Tommaso. Scultori Pisani*. Pisa, 1983.

Calderoni Masetti, A. R. "Il Reliquiario della Croce di Massa Marittima." *Mitteilungen des Kunsthistorischen Instituts in Florenz* 22 (1978) : 1–26.

Carli, E. "Il problema di Nino Pisano." *L'Arte* 37 (1934a) : 189–222.

― *Tino di Camaino Scultore*. Florence, 1934b.

― *Sculture del Duomo di Siena*. Torino, 1941.

― "Sculture pisane de Giovanni di Balduccio." *Emporium* 97 (1943) : 143–54.

― *Goro di Gregorio*. Florence, 1946.

― "La mostra dell'antica scultura pisana." *Emporium* 105 (1947a) : 47–57.

― *Le Sculture del Duomo di Orvieto*. Bergamo, 1947b.

― "Una primizia di Jacopo della Quercia." *Critica d'Arte* I, fasc. 27 (May 1949) : 17–24.

― *La Scultura lignea Italiana*. Milan, 1960.

― *Scultura Italiana, II, Il Gotico*. Milan 1969.

― *L'Arte nella Basilica di S. Francesco a Siena*. Siena, 1971.

― *Il Museo di Pisa*. Pisa, 1974.

Castelnuovo, E. *Andrea Pisano (I Maestri del Colore)*. Milan, 1966.

Caturegli, N. *La Signoria di Giovanni dell'Agnello in Pisa e in Lucca e le sue relazioni con Firenze e Milano (1364–68)*. Pisa, 1921.

Cellini, P. "Appunti Orvietani per Andrea e Nino Pisano." *Rivista D'Arte* (1933) : 1–20.

Chastel, A. "L' 'Etruscan Revival' du XV° Siècle." *Revue Archéologique* 1 (1959) : 165–80.

Cioni, A. *Bibliografia delle sacre rappresentazioni*. Florence, 1961.

Clark, Sir K. *The Nude*. Garden City, N. Y., 1956.

Cohn-Goerke, W. "Giovanni d'Agostino." *Burlington Magazine* 75 (1939) : 180–94.

Colombier, P. du, "Sur la transmission des schemas des compositions au moyen âge." *Gazette des Beaux-Arts* 72 (1968) : 255–8.

Corallini, G. *Le Iscrizioni Tombali e Commemorative della Chiesa di S. Caterina in Pisa* (1980) (mimeographed pamphlet).

– *La Chiesa di S. Caterina in Pisa*. Pisa, n.d.

Corsini, A. *Il Costume del Medico nelle Pitture Fiorentine del Rinascimento*. Florence, 1912.

Da Morrona, A. *Pisa illustrata*, Pisa vol. III, (1812).

d'Ancona, P. *L'uomo e le sue opere nelle figurazioni italiane del medioevo*. Florence, 1923.

Dati, G. *Istoria di Firenze*. Florence, 1785.

Davidsohn, R. *Storia di Firenze*, vol. II, part 2. Florence, 1957.

Degenhart, B., and A. Schmitt. *Corpus der Italienischen Zeichnungen, 1300–1450*, vol. 1, part 1. Berlin, 1968.

della Valle, G. *Storia del Duomo di Orvieto*. Rome, 1791.

de Witt, A. *I Mosaici del Battistero di Firenze*, vol. II Florence, 1954.

Didron, N. *Christian Iconography*. London, 1896.

Egbert, V. W. *The Medieval Artist at Work*. Princeton, 1967.

Erlande-Brandenburg, A. "La Sculpture à Paris au Milieu du XIII° Siècle." *Bulletin de la Société de l'histoire de Paris et de l'Ile-de-France* (1970) : 31–41.

Ettlinger, L. "Hercules Florentinus." *Mitteilungen des Kunsthistorischen Instituts in Florenz* 1 (1972) : 119–42.

– *Antonio and Piero Pollaiuolo*. New York, 1978.

Falk, I. *Studien zu Andrea Pisano*. Hamburg, 1940.

Falk, I., and J. Lányi. "The Genesis of Andrea Pisano's Bronze Doors." *Art Bulletin* 25 (1943) : 132–53.

Fiocco, G. "Fatti Veneti alla Mostra della Scultura Pisano del Trecento." *Arte Veneta* 1 (1947) : 134–6.

Francovich, G. de. "Lorenzo Maitani scultore e i bassorilievi della facciata del Duomo di Orvieto." *Bolletino d'Arte* 7 (1927–8) : 339–72.

Frey, K., ed. *Scritte di M. Giorgio Vasari*. Munich, 1911.

Fumi, L. *Il Duomo di Orvieto*. Rome, 1891.

Galante, V. G. *L'apparato scenico del dramma sacro in Italia*. Turin, 1935.

Garger, E. von. *Der Trajansbogen in Benevent*. Berlin, 1945.

Garzelli, A. "Scultura del Trecento a Siena e fuori Siena." *Critica d'Arte*, 15, n.s. 94 1968 : 55–65.

– *Sculture Toscane nel Dugento e nel Trecento*. Florence, 1969.

– *Museo di Orvieto*. Bologna, 1972.

Gilbert, C. Review of Trachtenberg, *Campanile*, in *Art Quarterly* 35 (1972) : 427–32.

Giuliano, A. *Arca di Costantino*. Milan, 1955.

Gnudi, C. *Nicolo, Arnolfo, Lapo*. Florence, 1949.

– "Nuovi appunti sui fratelli Dalle Masegne." *Proporzioni* 3 (1950) : 48–55.

– "Il Reliquiario di San Luigi Re di Francia in S. Domenico a Bologna." *Critica d'Arte* n.s. 3 (1956) : 535–39.

– "Relations between French and Italian Sculpture of the Gothic Period." *Introduction to Romanesque and Gothic Art. Acts*

of the 20th International Congress of the History of Art, Vol. 1. Princeton, 1963.

– "Le Jubé de Bourges et l'Apogée du 'Classicisme' dans la Sculpture de l'Ile de France au milieu du XIII° Siècle." *Revue de l'Art* 3 (1969) : 18–36.

– et al. "Su inizi di Giotto e i suoi rapporti col mondo gotico." *Giotto e il suo tempo*. Rome, 1971.

Green, L. *Chronicle into History*. Cambridge, Mass. 1972.

Guasti, C. *Santa Maria del Fiore*. Florence, 1887.

Hahnloser, H. R. "Urkunden zur Bedeutung des Türrings." *Festschrift für Erich Mayer zum sechzigsten Geburtstag*. Hamburg, 1959.

Harrsen, M., and G. K. Boyce. *Italian Manuscripts in the Pierpont Morgan Library*. New York, 1953.

Hartt, F. *History of Italian Renaissance Art*. Englewood Cliffs, N. J., 1979.

Heil, W. "A Madonna and Child by Nino Pisano." *Bulletin of the Detroit Institute of Arts* 8 (March 1927) : 62.

– "Italian Sculpture in Detroit." *Parnassus* 2 (1930) : 15–17.

Hertlein, E. "Capolavori Francesi in San Francesco d'Assisi." *Antichità Viva* 4 (1965) : 54–70.

Horn, W. "Romanesque Churches in Florence." *Art Bulletin* 25 (1943) : 112–31.

Hunisak, J. "Andrea Pisano's Bronze Doors." Unpublished seminar paper presented at the Institute of Fine Arts, New York University, 1970.

Il Gotico a Siena (exhibition catalogue). Siena, 1982.

Jacopo della Quercia nell'arte del suo tempo (exhibition catalogue). Siena, 1975.

Janson, H. W. *Apes and Ape Lore*. London, 1952.

– *The Sculpture of Donatello*. Princeton, 1963.

– "The Image of Man in Renaissance Art: From Donatello to Michelangelo." In B. O'Kelly, ed., *The Renaissance Image of Man and the World*. Columbus, Ohio, 1966.

– "The Equestrian Monument from Cangrande della Scala to Peter the Great." In Janson, *Sixteen Studies*. New York, 1974.

Jantzen, H. "Giotto und der Gotische Stil." *Das Werk des Künstlers* 1 (1939/40) : 441–54.

Jullian, R. "Lyons et l'Italie au moyen âge." *Revue des Etudes Italiennes* 5 (1958) : 133–46.

Katzenellenbogen, A. *Allegories of the Virtues and Vices in Medieval Art*. New York, 1964.

Klotz, H. "Deutsche und Italienische Baukunst im Trecento." *Mitteilungen des Kunsthistorischen Instituts in Florenz* 12 (1965–6) : 171–206.

Koechlin, R. "Essai de classement chronologique d'après la forme de leur manteau des Vièrges du XIVe siècle debout, portant l'Enfant." *Actes du Congrès d'Histoire de l'Art* (1924) : 490–6.

Kosegarten, A. "Beiträge zur Sienesischen Reliefkunst des Trecento." *Mitteilungen des Kunsthistorischen Instituts in Florenz* 12 (1965–6) : 207–24.

– "Einige Sienesische Darstellungen der Muttergottes aus dem frühen Trecento." *Jahrbuch der Berliner Museen* 8 (1966) : 96–118.

– "Aus dem Umkreis Nino Pisanos." *Pantheon* 25 (1967) : 235–49.

Krautheimer, R. *Lorenzo Ghiberti*. 2 vols. Princeton, 1970.

Kreytenberg, G. "Zu Andrea Pisanos Türe am Florentiner Baptisterium." *Das Münster* 28 (1975) : 220–35.

– "Der Campanile von Giotto." *Mitteilungen des Kunsthistorischen Instituts in Florenz* 20 (1978) : 147–84.

— "MCCCXLI: Gino Micheli: Da Ch(a)stello." *Antichità Viva* 18 (1979a): 31–6.

— "The Sculpture of Maso di Banco." *Burlington Magazine* 121 (Feb. 1979b): 72–8.

— "Tino di Camainos Grabmäler in Florenz." *Städel–Jahrbuch* 7 (1979c): 33–60.

— "Andrea Pisano's Earliest Works in Marble." *Burlington Magazine* 122 (Jan. 1980): 3–7.

— * *Andrea Pisano und die Toskanische Skulptur des Vierzehnten Jahrhunderts*. Munich, 1984.

Kruft, H. W. "Die Madonna von Trapani und ihre Kopien. Studien zur Madonnen-Typologie und zum Begriff der Kopie in der Sizilianischen Skulptur des Quattrocento." *Mitteilungen des Kunsthistorischen Instituts in Florenz* 14 (1969–70): 297–332.

Lányi, J. "L'ultima opera di Andrea Pisano." *L'Arte* 36 (1933a): 204–27.

— "Pisano, Andrea." In U. Thieme and F. Becker, eds., *Allgemeines Lexikon der bildenden Künstler*, vol. 27. Leipzig, 1933b.

Larner, J. *Culture and Society in Italy, 1290–1420*. New York, 1971.

Lasinio, G. P. *Le tre porte del Battistero di San Giovanni di Firenze*. Florence, 1821.

Lavin, I. "On the Sources and Meaning of the Renaissance Portrait Bust." *Art Quarterly* 33 (1970): 207–26.

Lavin, M. "Giovannino Battista: A Study in Renaissance Religious Symbolism." *Art Bulletin* 37 (June 1955): 85–101.

— "Giovannino Battista: A Supplement." *Art Bulletin* 43 (1961): 319–26.

Lefrançois-Pillion, L. "Les Statues de la Vièrge à l'Enfant dans la sculpture française au XIVᵉ siècle." *Gazette des Beaux-Arts* 77 (1935): 129–49, 204–27.

Leisinger, H. *Romanesque Bronzes: Church*

Portals in Medieval Europe. New York, 1957.

Les Fastes du Gothique, le siècle de Charles V (exhibition catalogue). Paris, 1981.

Lisner, M. *Holzkruzifixe in Florenz und in der Toskana*. Munich, 1970.

Luzi, L. *Il Duomo di Orvieto*. Florence, 1866.

Mâle, E. *The Gothic Image. Religious Art in France of the Thirteenth Century*, trans. D. Nussey. New York, 1958.

Marchini, G. "L'altare argenteo di S. Jacopo e l'oreficeria gotica a Pistoia." *Il Gotico a Pistoia nei suoi Rapporti con l'Arte Gotica Italiana*. Pistoia, 1966: 135–47.

Mariacher, G. "Note su Nino Pisano e la scultura gotica Veneziana." *Belle Arti* I, 3–4 (1947): 140–9.

Masseron, A. *Saint Jean Baptiste dans l'art*. Vichy, 1957.

Mattei, A. *Ecclesiae Pisanae Historia*. Lucca, 1772.

Matthiae, G. *Le porte bronzee byzantine in Italia*. Rome, 1971.

Meiss, M. "The Madonna of Humility." *Art Bulletin* 18 (1936): 435–66.

— *Painting in Florence and Siena After the Black Death*. Princeton, 1951.

— "An Illuminated Inferno and Trecento Painting in Pisa." *Art Bulletin* 47 (1965): 21–34.

Micheletti, E. *Masolino da Panicale*. Milan, 1959.

Middeldorf, U. *Sculptures from the Samuel H. Kress Collection*. London, 1976.

Middeldorf, U., and M. Weinberger. "Französische Figuren des Frühen 14. Jahrhunderts in Toskana." *Pantheon* 1 (1928): 187–90.

Milanesi, G., ed. *Le vite de' piu eccellenti pittori, scultori ed architettori, scritte di Giorgio Vasari*, vol. 1. Florence, 1878.

Moskowitz, A. "Donatello's Reliquary Bust of Saint Rossore." *Art Bulletin* 63 (1981a): 41–8.

* The present volume was already in press before I was able to obtain access to this recent publication by Kreytenberg.

– "Osservazioni sulla Porta del Battistero di Andrea Pisano." *Antichità Viva* 22 (Jan./Feb. 1981b) : 28–39.

– "The Framework of Andrea Pisano's Bronze Doors: Some Possible Non-Tuscan Sources." *Source* 2 (1983a) : 1–4.

– "Trecento Classicism and the Campanile Hexagons." *Gesta* 22 (1983b) : 49–65.

– "A Madonna and Child Statue: Reversing a Reattribution." *Bulletin of the Detroit Institute of Arts* 61 (1984) : 34–47.

– "Some notes on narrative mode and iconography in Andrea Pisano's bronze doors." *Renaissance Studies in Honor of Craig Hugh Smyth*. Florence, 1985.

Mustari, F. L. "The Sculptor in the Fourteenth Century Florentine Opera del Duomo." Ph.D. diss., University of Iowa, 1975.

Niero, A. "Un' arcaica formula di 'Ave Maria' nella statua Veneziana di Nino Pisano." *Bollettino dei Musei Civici Veneziani* 16 (1971) : 45–6.

Nordstrom, F. *The Auxerre Reliefs, a Harbinger of the Renaissance in France During the Reign of Philip le Bel*. Stockholm, 1974.

Offner, R. *Italian Primitives at Yale University*. New Haven, 1927a.

– *Studies in Florentine Painting, the 14th Century*. New York, 1927.

Orlandi, S. *"Necrologio" di Sta. Maria Novella*, vol. 1. Florence, 1955.

Paccagnini, G. *Simone Martini*. Milan, 1957.

Panofsky, E. *Gothic Architecture and Scholasticism*. London, 1951.

– *Early Netherlandish Painting*. Cambridge, Mass., 1953. Reprint ed., New York, 1971.

– *Renaissance and Renascences in Western Art*. New York, 1960.

Papini, R. *Catalogo delle Cose d'Arte e di Antichità d'Italia*. Pisa, Rome, 1912.

Pedrazzini, C. *La farmacia storica ed artistica Italiana*. Milan, 1934.

Petrocchi, M. *Storia della Spiritualità Italiana*, vol. 1. Rome, 1978.

Pettorelli, A. *Il Bronzo e il Rame nell'Arte Decorative Italiana*. Milan, 1926.

Picard-Schmitter, M.-Th. "Recherches sur les métiers à tesser antiques: à propos de la frise du Forum de Nerva, à Rome." *Latomus, Revue d'études latines* 24 (1965) : 296–321.

Pillion, L. (Lefrançois-Pillion). "La sculpture italienne du XIVème siècle." *Revue de l'Art* 19 (1906) : 241–54; 354–66.

Poggi, G., L. Planiscig, and Bearzi. *Donatello: San Ludovico*. Trans. E. Vaquer and S. M. Abernathy. New York, 194–.

Pollitt, J. J. *Art and Experience in Classical Greece*. Cambridge, 1972.

Polloni, B. *XII Vedute Esterne di Chiese Antiche di Pisa*. Pisa, 1835.

Pope-Hennessy, Sir J. "Pisano, Andrea." *Enciclopedia Universale dell'Arte*, vol. 1. Rome, Venice, 1959. col. 383–7.

– *Catalogue of Italian Sculpture in the Victoria and Albert Museum*, vol. 1. London, 1964.

– *Italian Gothic Sculpture*. New York, 1972.

– *Luca della Robbia*. Ithaca, N.Y., 1980.

Proccacci, U. "Ignote sculture lignee nel Pisano." *Miscellanea in onore di I. B. Supino*. Florence, 1933 : 233–45.

Ragghianti, C. L. "Opere sconosciute di Tino di Camaino." *Critica d'Arte* 1 (1936) : 272–6.

– "Aenigmata Pistoriensia." I. *Critica d'Arte* n.s. 1 (1954) : 423–38; n.s. 2 (1955) : 102–28.

– "Arte a Lucca – Spicilegio." *Critica d'Arte*, n.s. 7 (1960) : 57–83.

– "Il maestro mosano di carrara e bilinguismi pisano-francesi." *Critica d'Arte* n.s. 20 (1973) : 11–38.

Raggio, Olga. "The myth of Prometheus, Its Survival and Metamorphosis up to the Eighteenth Century." *Journal of the Warburg and Courtauld Institutes* 21 (1958) : 44–62.

Ragusa, I. "The Re-use and Public Exhibition of Roman Sarcophagi during the Middle Ages and the Early Renaissance." M.A. thesis, Institute of Fine Arts, 1951.

Ragusa, I., and R. Green. *Meditations on the Life of Christ.* Princeton, 1961.

Reau, L. *Les Sculpteurs Français en Italie.* Paris, 1945.

Reinach, S. *Répertoire de la statuaire grecque et romaine,* vol. II. Paris, 1909.

Reymond, M. *La Sculpture Florentine.* Florence, 1897.

Roberts, M. E. "The Tomb of Giles de Bridport in Salisbury Cathedral." *Art Bulletin* 65 (1983) : 559–86.

Ronan, H. "The Tuscan Wall Tomb 1250–1400." Ph.D. dissertation, Indiana University, 1982.

Rowland, B. *The Classical Tradition in Western Art.* Cambridge, Mass., 1963.

Ryan, E. G., and H. Ripperger, trans., *The Golden Legend of Jacobus de Voragine.* New York, 1969.

Salmi, M. *Romanesque Sculpture in Tuscany.* Florence, 1928.

– "La giovinezza di Jacopo della Quercia." *Rivista d'Arte* 12 (1930) : 175–91.

– *Lezioni di storia dell'arte medievale.* Rome, 1949–50.

Sauerländer, W. *Gothic Sculpture in France, 1140–1270.* New York, 1972.

Scano, D. "Una statua di Nino Pisano." *Arte e Storia* 19 (1900) : 133.

– "Scoperte artistiche in Oristano." *L'Arte* 6 (1903) : 15–30.

Schaefer, C. *La Sculpture en Ronde-Bosse au XIVᵉ Siècle dans la Duché de Bourgogne.* Paris, 1954.

Schevill, F. *History of Florence.* New York, 1961.

Schlosser, J. von. "Giusto's Fresken in Padua und die Vorläufer der Stanza della Segnatura." *Jahrbuch der Kunsthistorischen Sammlungen des Allerhöchsten Kaiserhauses* 17 (Vienna) (1896) : 53–75.

Schmarsow, A. "Vier Statuetten in der Domopera zu Florenz." *Jahrbuch der Königlich Preussischen Kunstsammlungen* 8 (1887) : 137–53.

– "Andrea Pisano." *Festschrift zu Ehren des Kunsthistorischen Instituts in Florenz.* Leipzig, 1897.

Schubring, P. *Donatello (Klassiker der Kunst).* Stuttgart, Leipzig, 1907.

Seidel, M. "Die Elfenbeinmadonna im Domschatz zu Pisa." *Mitteilungen des Kunsthistorischen Instituts in Florenz* 12 (1965–6) : 171–206.

– "Die Rankensäulen der Sieneser Domfassade." *Jahrbuch der Berliner Museen* n.s. 11 1969) : 81–160.

– "Die Berliner Madonna des Giovanni Pisano." *Pantheon* 30 (1972) : 181–92.

– "Studien zur Antikenrezeption Nicola Pisanos." *Mitteilungen des Kunsthistorischen Instituts in Florenz* 19 (1975) : 307–392.

Seymour, C., Jr. "XIII Century Sculpture at Noyon and the Development of the Gothic Caryatid." *Gazette des Beaux-Arts* 6th ser. v. 26 (1944) : 162–82.

– *Sculpture in Italy, 1400–1500.* Baltimore, 1966.

– *Jacopo della Quercia.* New Haven, 1973.

Seymour, C., Jr., and J. Swarzenski. "A Madonna of Humility and Quercia's early style." *Gazette des Beaux-Arts* 6th ser. v. 30 (1946) : 129–52.

Seznec, J. *The Survival of the Pagan Gods,* 2d ed. New York, 1961.

Shorr, Dorothy. *The Christ Child in Devotional Images in Italy in the Fourteenth Century.* New York, 1954.

Sinclair, J. D. *Dante's Inferno.* New York, 1939.

s'Jacob, H. *Idealism and Realism, A Study of Sepulchral Symbolism*. Leiden, 1954.

Smart, A. *The Assisi Problem*. Oxford, 1971.

Soprintendenza ai Monumenti e Gallerie per le Province di Pisa, Lucca, Livorno e Massa-Carrara. *Mostra del Restauro*, Pisa, Museo di San Matteo (26 Sept.–5 Nov. 1972).

Steingraber, E. "The Pistoia Silver Altar: A Re-examination." *Connoisseur* 138 (1956): 148–54.

Stone, R. "Antico and the Development of Bronze Casting in Italy at the End of the Quattrocento." *Metropolitan Museum Journal* 16 (1982): 87–116.

Strom, D. "Studies in Quattrocento Tuscan Wooden Sculpture." Ph.D. dissertation, Princeton University, 1979.

– "A New Look at Jacopo della Quercia's Madonna of Humility." *Antichità Viva* 19 (1980): 17–23.

Stubblebine, J., ed. *Giotto: The Arena Chapel Frescoes*. New York, 1969.

Suckale, R. *Studien zu Stilbildung und Stilwandel der Madonnenstatuen der Ile-de-France zwischen 1230 und 1300*. Munich, 1971.

Supino, I. "Nino e Tommaso Pisano." *Archivio storico dell'Arte* I, 5 (1895): 343–62.

– *Arte Pisano*. Florence, 1904.

– *Pisa*. Bergamo, 1905.

– "Pisano, Nino." In U. Thieme and F. Becker, *Allgemeines Lexikon der Bildenden Künstler*, vol. 27. Leipzig, 1933.

Taylor, M. D. *The Iconography of the Facade Decoration of the Cathedral of Orvieto*. Ann Arbor, University Microfilms, 1970.

Telpaz, A. Markham. "Some Antique Motifs in Trecento Art." *Art Bulletin* 46 (1964): 372–6.

Toesca, I. *Andrea e Nino Pisani*. Florence, 1950.

Toesca, P. "Oreficerie della Scuola di Nicola Pisano." *Arti Figurative* 2 (1946): 34–6.

– *Il Trecento*. Turin, 1951.

Tolaini, E. "Su alcune statue dell'Oratorio di Santa Maria della Spina." *Belle Arti* 1 (1946): 39–46.

Trachtenberg, M. "An Antique Model for Donatello's Marble *David*." *Art Bulletin* 50 (1968): 268–9.

– *The Campanile of Florence Cathedral*. New York, 1971.

Valentiner, W. R. "Die Sculpturen Nino Pisanos in Venedig." *Zeitschrift für Bildende Kunst* 60 (1926–7): 242–3.

– "Nino Pisano." *Art in America* 15 (1927a): 195–216.

– "Observations on Sienese and Pisan Trecento Sculpture." *Art Bulletin* 9 (March 1927b): 177–220.

– *Tino di Camaino: A Sienese Sculptor of the Fourteenth Century*. Paris, 1935.

– *Catalogue of an Exhibition of Italian Gothic and Early Renaissance Sculpture*. Detroit Institute of Arts, 1938.

– "Andrea Pisano as Marble Sculptor." *Art Quarterly* 10 (1947): 163–87.

– "Tino di Camaino in Florence." *Art Quarterly* 17 (1954): 116–33.

Venturi, A. "La scuola di Nicola di Apulia." *L'Arte* 7 (1904): 1–7.

– "Una Madonna di Nino Pisano nel Museo Nazionale di Budapest." *L'Arte* 8 (1905): 126–7.

– *Storia dell'arte Italiana*, vol. IV. Milan, 1906.

Vermeule, C. *European Art and the Classical Past*. Cambridge, Mass., 1964.

Viani, M. *Fiesole (Museo Bandini)*. Fiesole, 1981.

Vite de' Santi Padri de frate Domenico Cavalca colle vite di alcuni altri santi, Milan, ed. B. Sorio and A. Rachelli. n.d.

Vitry, P., and G. Brière. *Documents da Sculpture Française*. New York, 1969.

Volbach, W. F. *Mittelalterliche Bildwerke aus Italien und Byzanz* (Bildwerke des Kaiser Friedrich Museums). Berlin, Leipzig, 1930.

Wallace, R. "L'influence de la France gothique sur deux des précurseurs de la Renaissance Italienne: Nicola et Giovanni Pisano." Ph.D. thesis, University of Geneva, 1953.

Warner, M. *Alone of All Her Sex*. London, 1976.

Weinberger, M. "The Master of S. Giovanni." *Burlington Magazine* 70 (1937a): 24–30.

– "Nino Pisano." *Art Bulletin* 19 (1937b): 58–91.

– "Review of Toesca, *Pisani*." *Art Bulletin* 35 (1953): 243–8.

– "Remarks on the Role of French Models within the Evolution of Gothic Tuscan Sculpture." *Acts of the 20th International Congress of the History of Art*, vol. I. Princeton, 1963.

Weise, G. *L'Italia e il Mondo Gotico*. Florence, 1956.

Weiss, R. *The Renaissance Discovery of Classical Antiquity*. Oxford, 1969.

Wentzel, H. "Eine Pariser Kamee des 13. Jahrhunderts in byzantinischem Stil." *Études d'art Français Offertes à Charles Sterling*. Paris, 1975.

White, J. "The Reliefs on the Facade of the Duomo at Orvieto." *Journal of the Warburg and Courtauld Institutes* 32 (1959): 254–302.

– *Art and Architecture in Italy, 1250–1400*. Baltimore, 1966.

– *The Birth and Rebirth of Pictorial Space*, 2d ed. Boston, 1967.

Wixom, W. "A Masterpiece Attributed to Andrea Pisano." *Bulletin of the Cleveland Museum of Art* 40 n. 10 (Dec. 1972): 263–83.

Wolters, W. *La Scultura Veneziana Gotica*. Venice, 1976.

Wundram, M. von "Studien zur Künstlerischen Herkunft Andrea Pisanos." *Mitteilungen des Kunsthistorischen Instituts in Florenz* 8 (1957–9): 199–222.

– "Stileinheit und künstlerische Entwicklung in der Bronzetür Andrea Pisanos." *Kunstchronik* 21 (1968): 375–7.

Zervas, D. F. "The *Trattato dell'Abbaco* and Andrea Pisano's Design for the Florentine Baptistry Door." *Renaissance Quarterly* 38 (Winter 1975): 483–503.

Zingarelli, N. *La Vita, I Tempi e le Opere di Dante*, vol. I. Milan, 1939.

Zucker, M. S. "The Polygonal Halo in Italian and Spanish Art." *Studies in Iconography* 4 (1978): 61–77.

LIST OF ILLUSTRATIONS

INDEX

Index

Index

ILLUSTRATIONS

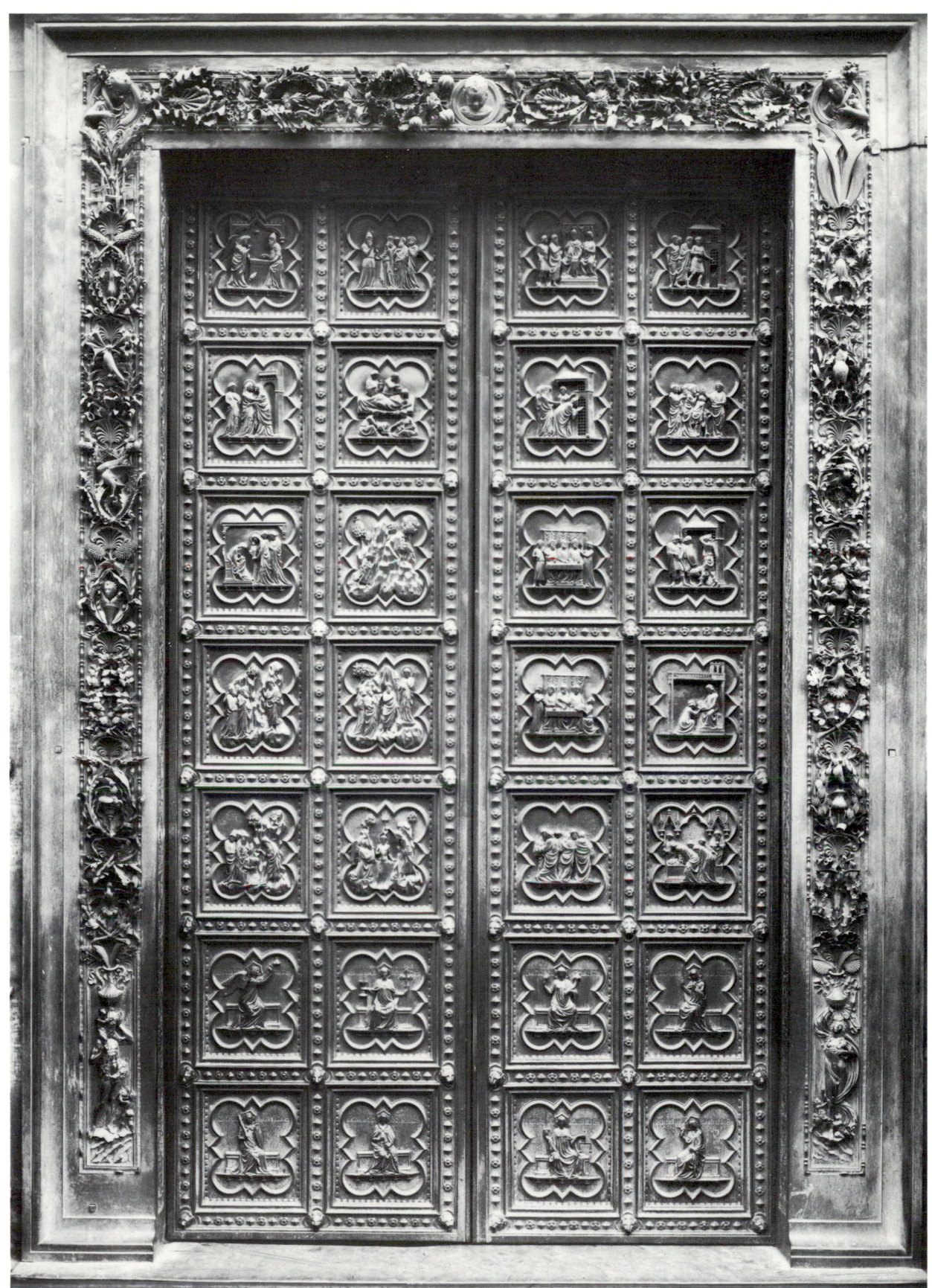

1. Andrea Pisano: Bronze doors (ht 486.2 cm, width 280.25 cm). Florence, Baptistry

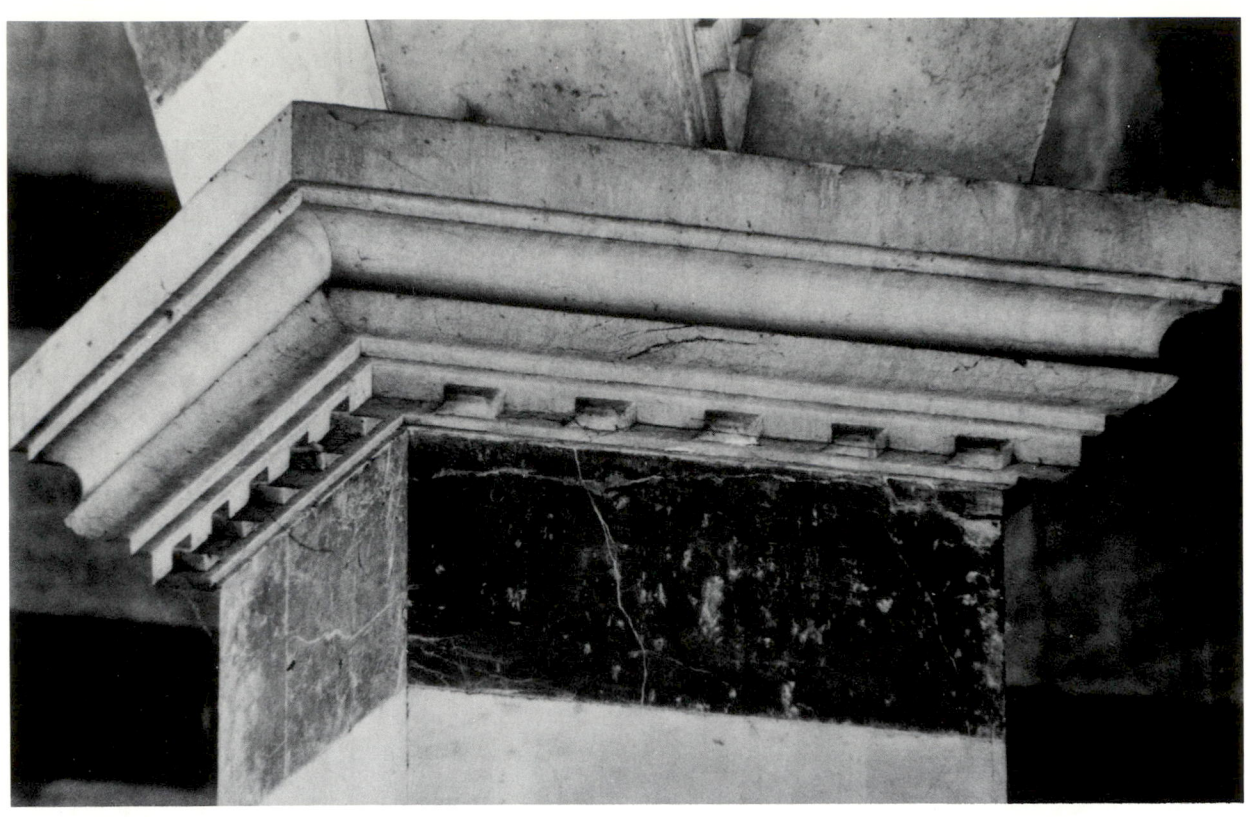

2. Andrea Pisano (?): Interior capital. Pisa, Sta. Maria della Spina

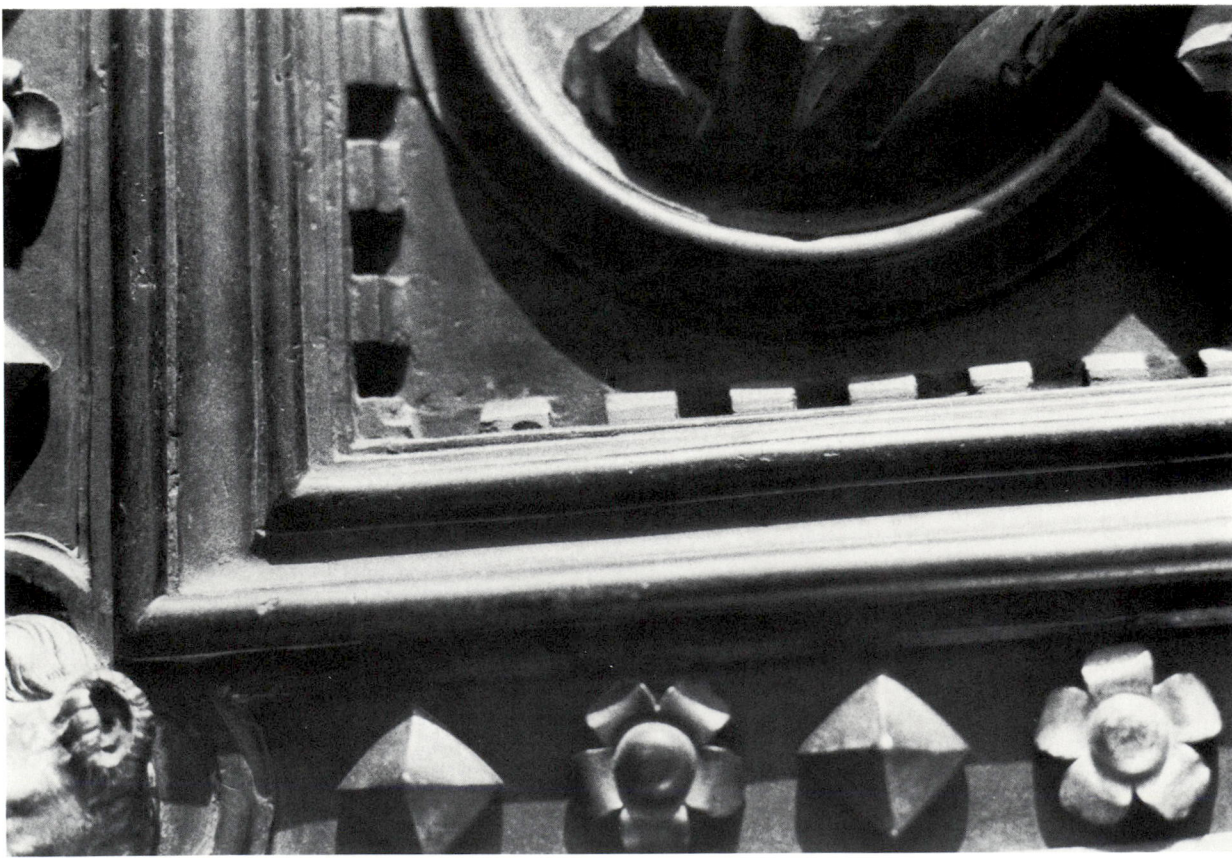

3. Andrea Pisano: Baptistry doors, detail. Florence, Baptistry

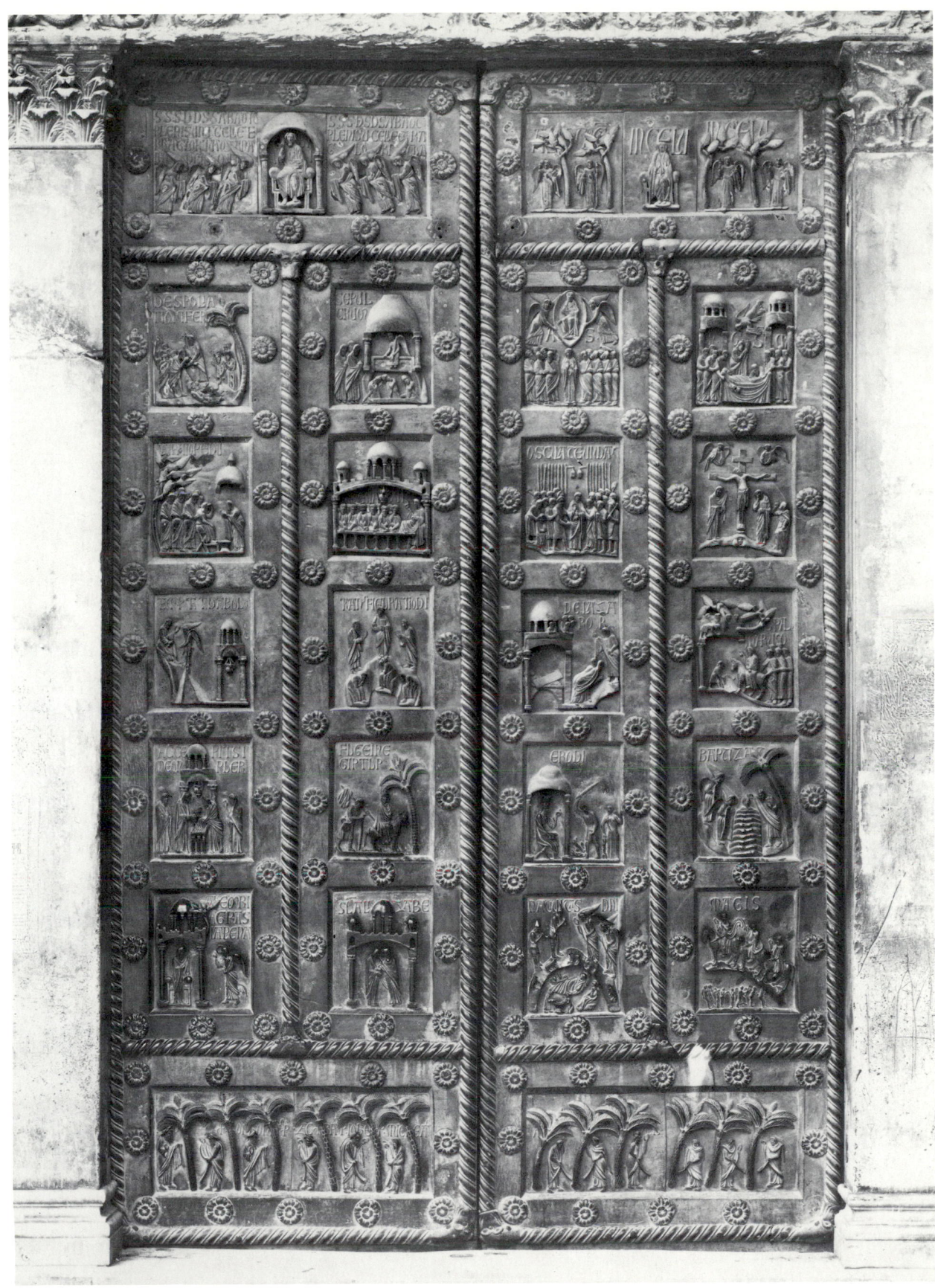

4. Bonanus: Bronze doors. Pisa Cathedral

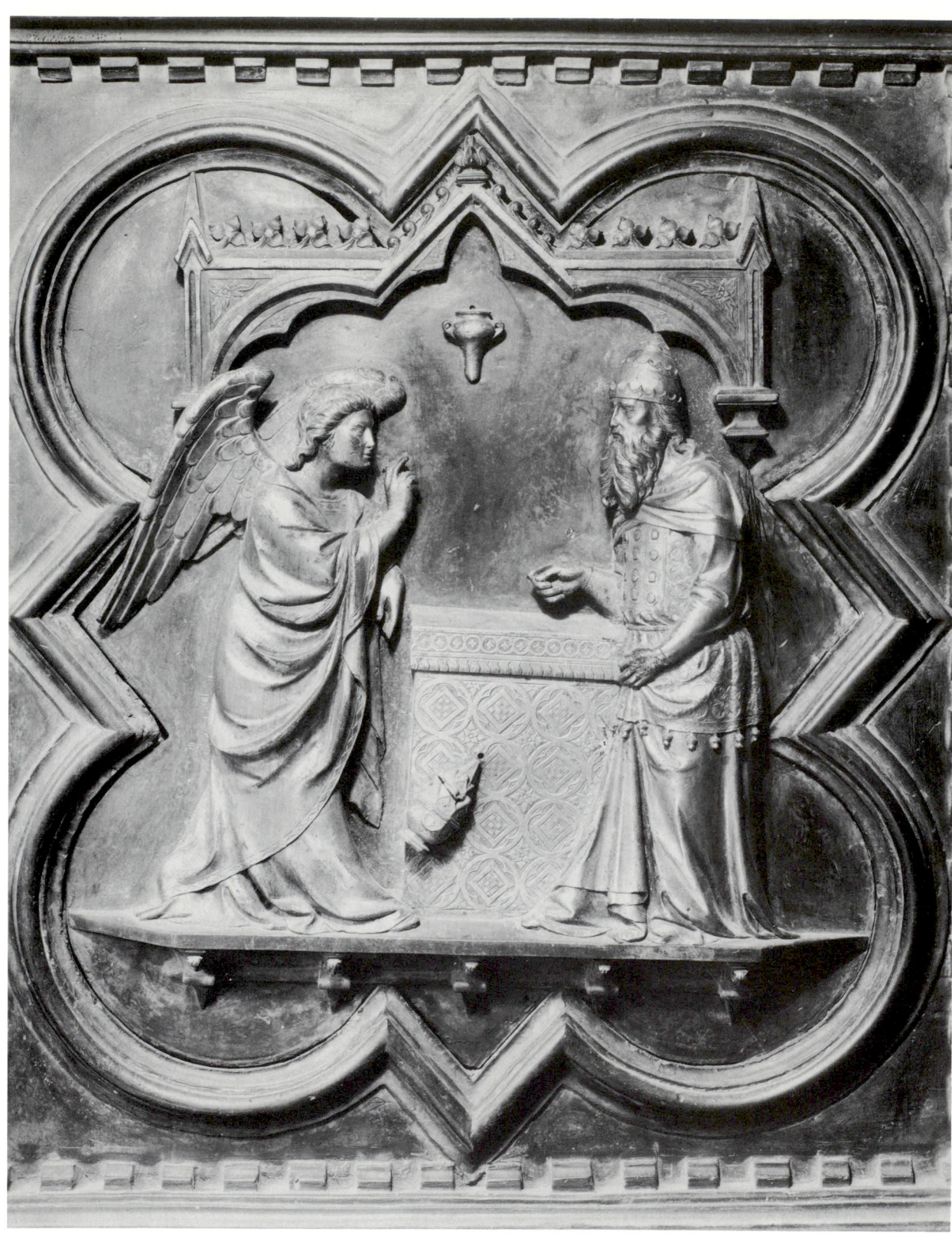

5. Andrea Pisano: *Annunciation to Zacharias*. Florence, Baptistry doors

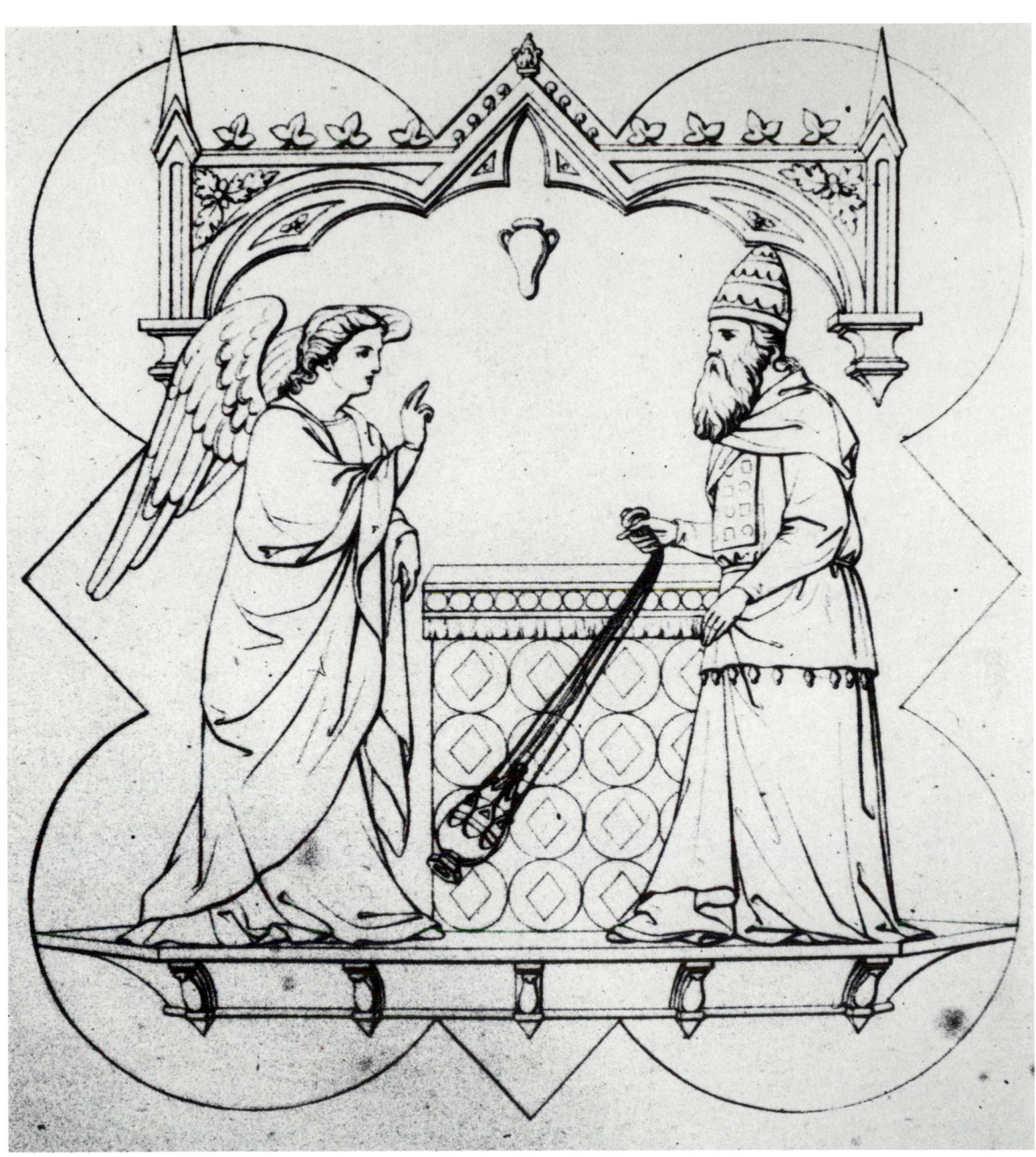

6. G. P. Lasinio: *Annunciation to Zacharias*

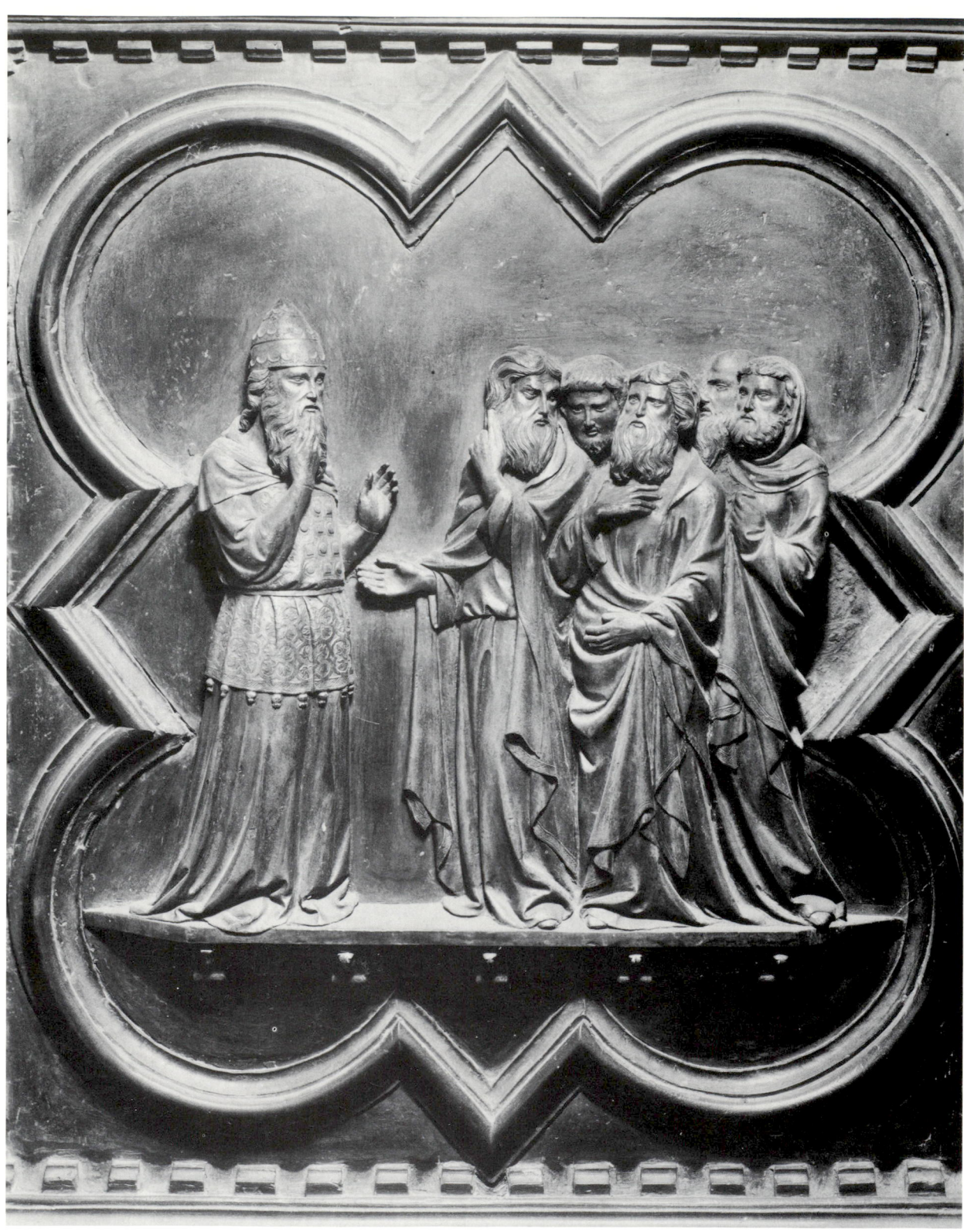

7. Andrea Pisano: *Zacharias and the Elders*. Florence, Baptistry doors

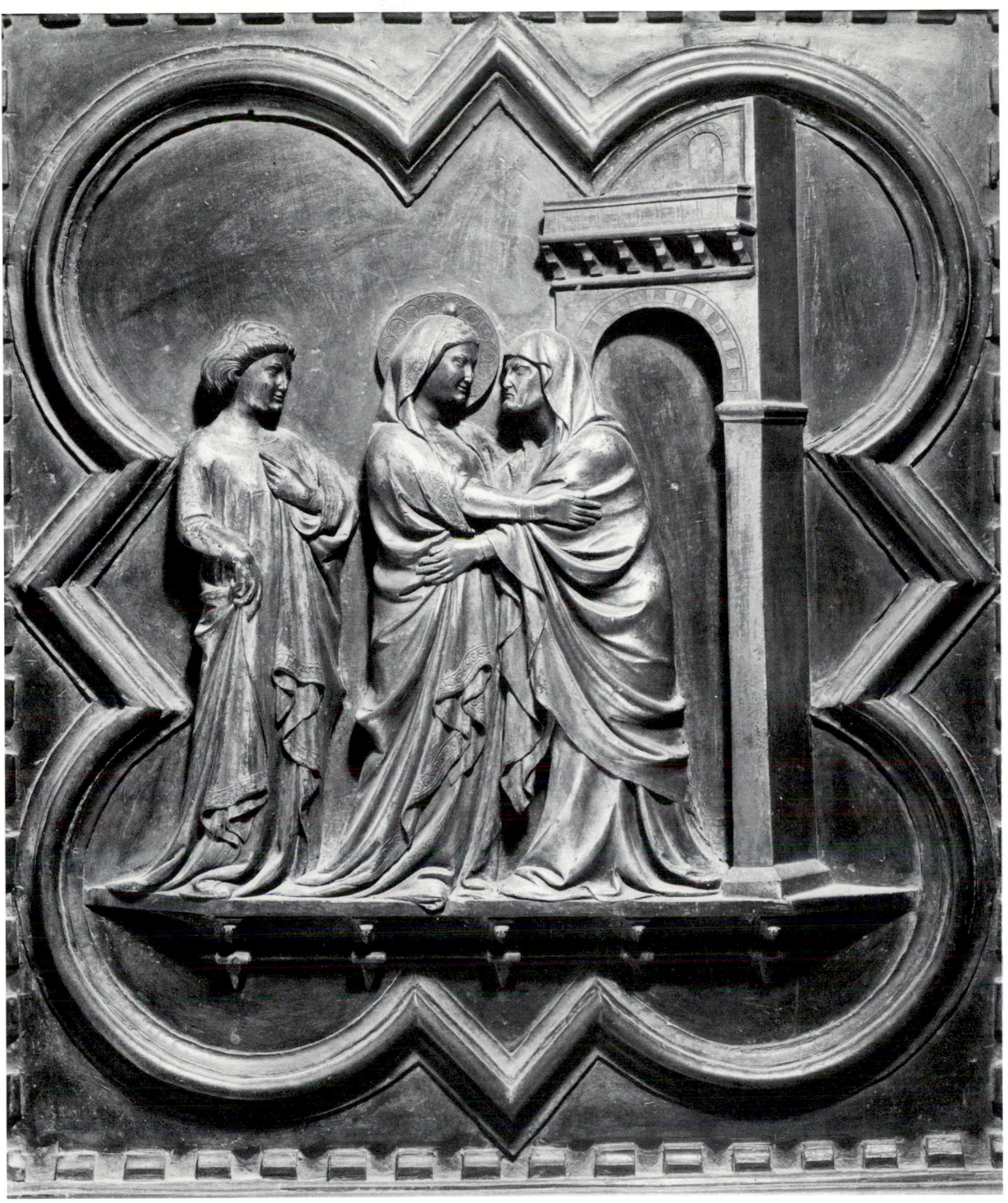

8. Andrea Pisano: *The Visitation*. Florence, Baptistry doors

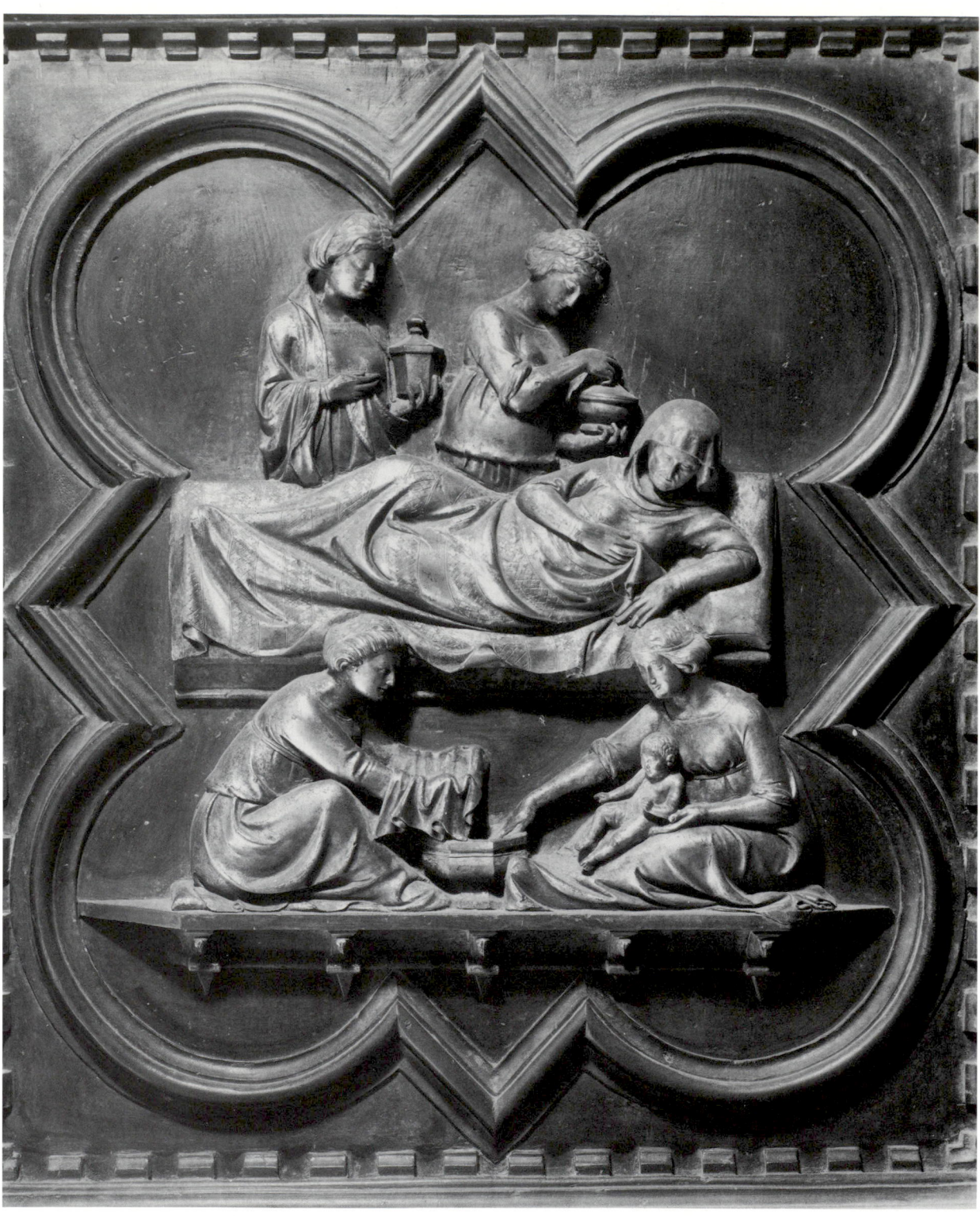

9. Andrea Pisano: *Birth of the Baptist*. Florence, Baptistry doors

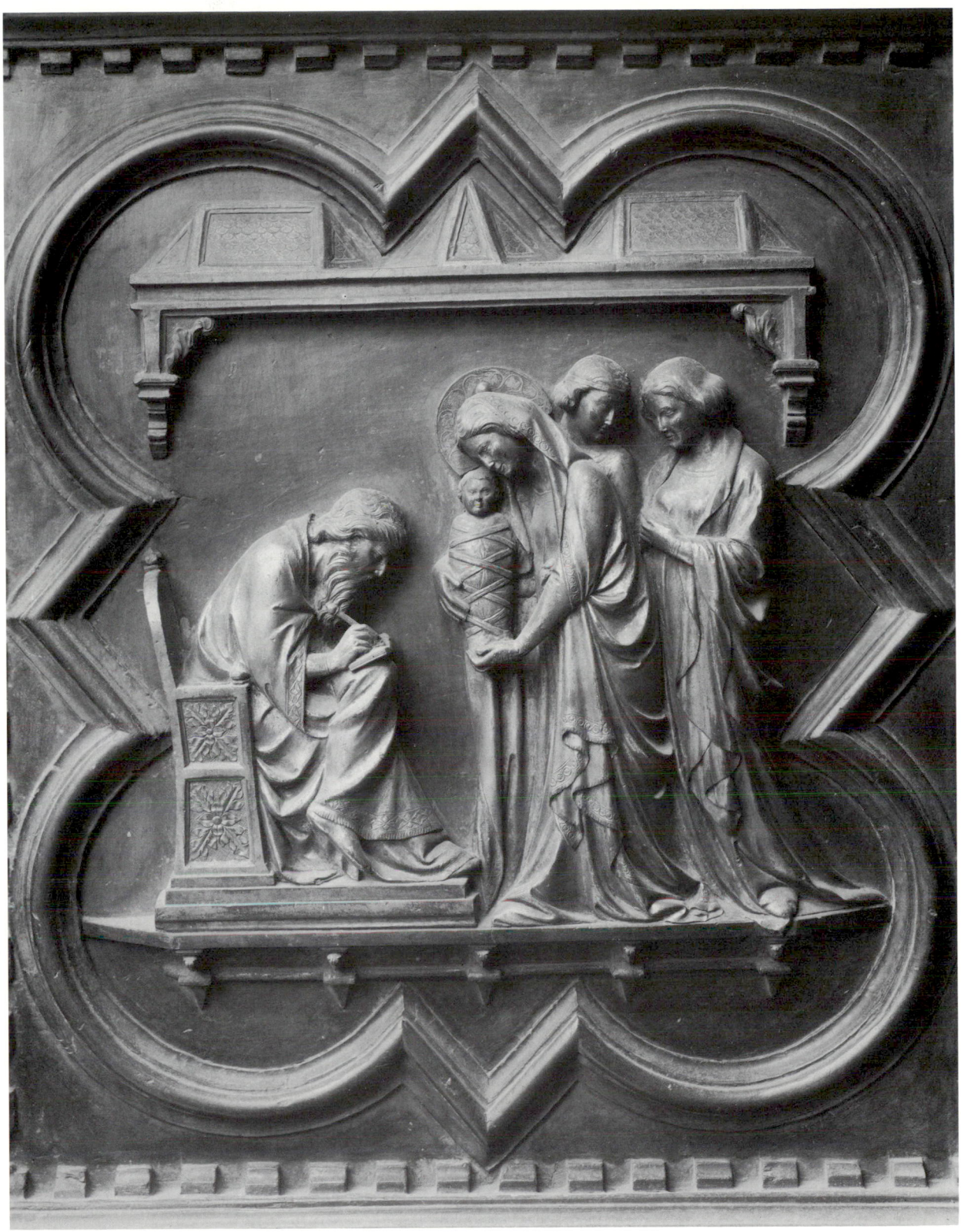

10. Andrea Pisano: *Naming of the Baptist*. Florence, Baptistry doors

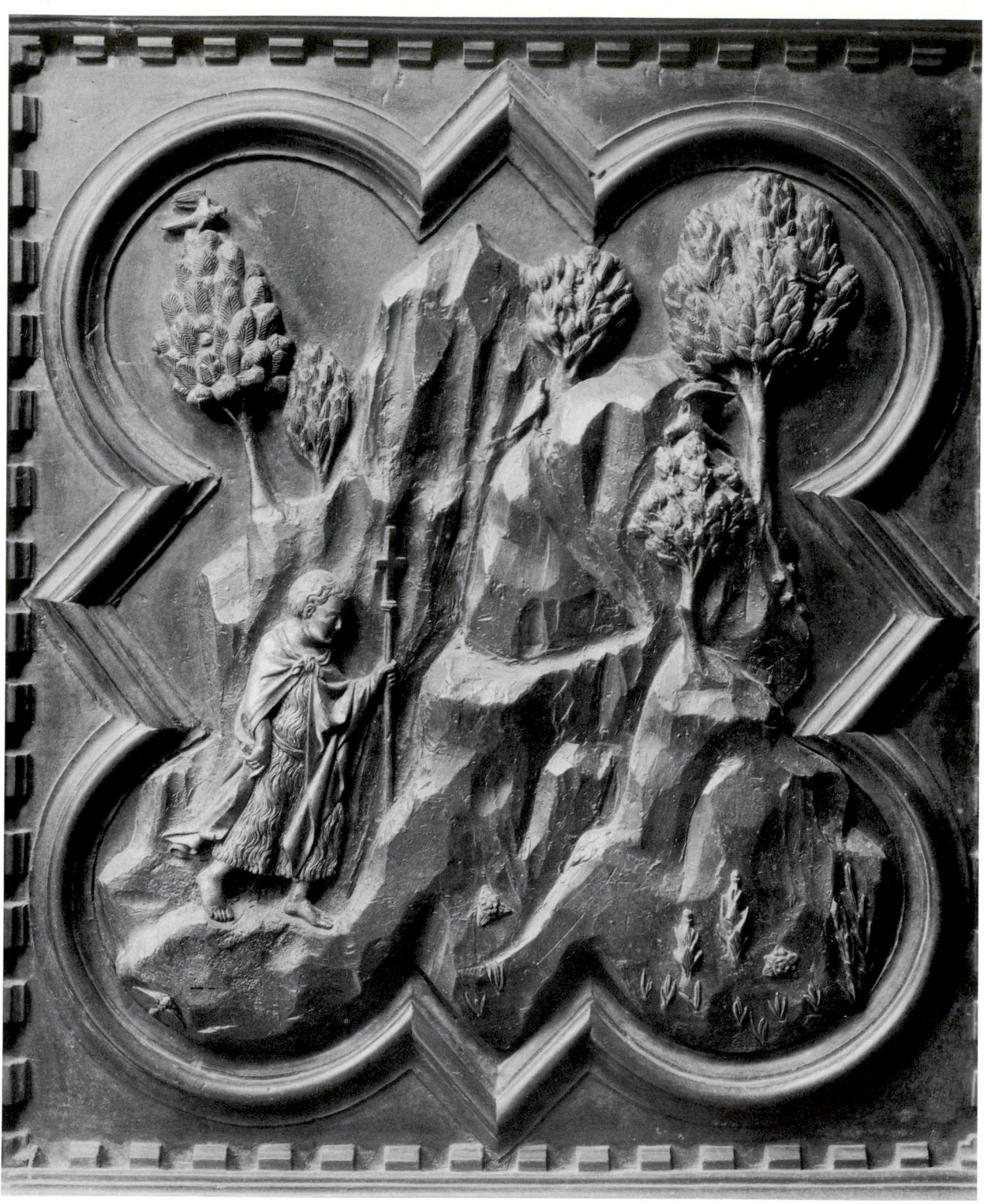

11. Andrea Pisano: *Young John in the Wilderness*. Florence, Baptistry doors

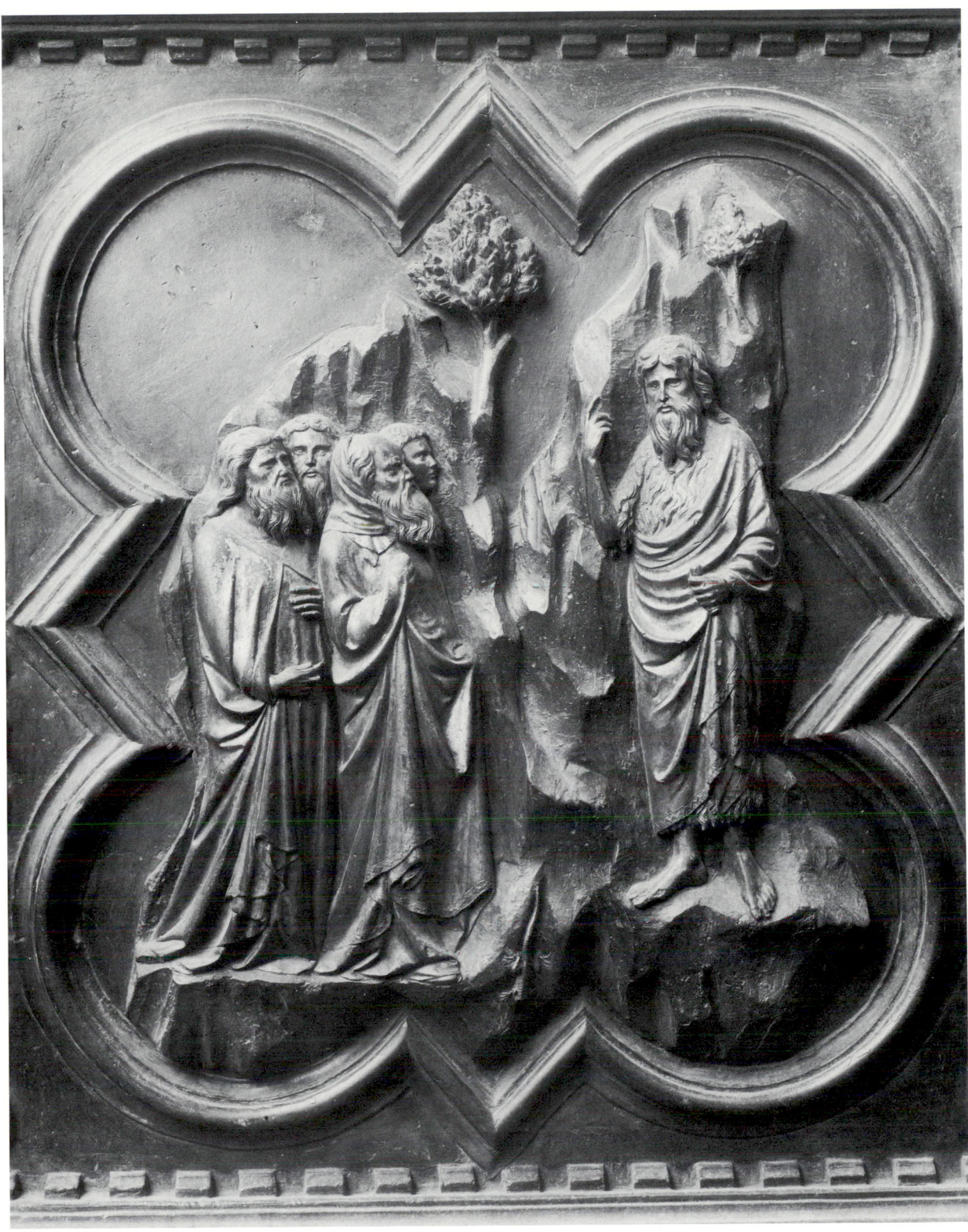

12. Andrea Pisano: *Preaching of the Baptist*. Florence, Baptistry doors

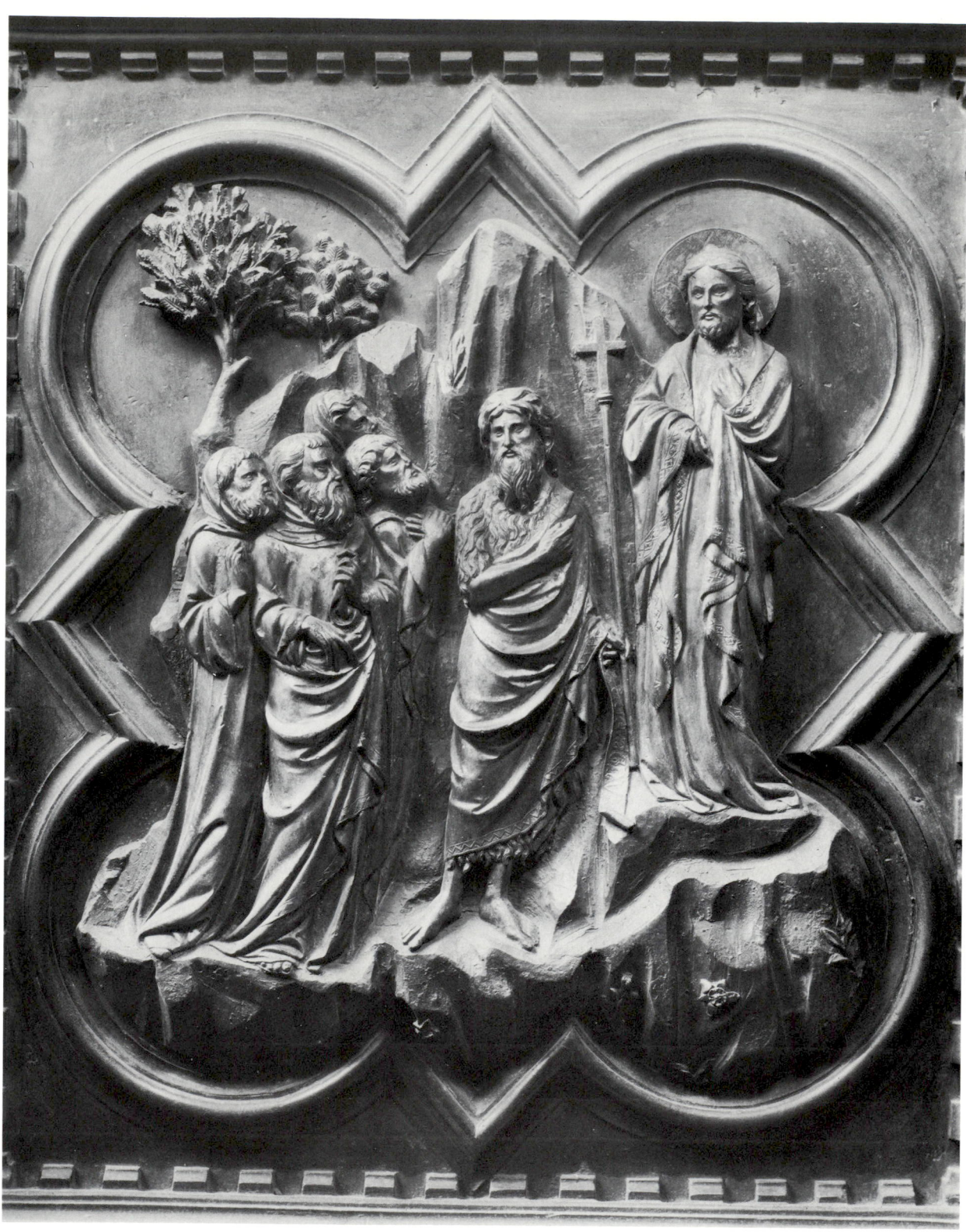

13. Andrea Pisano: *Ecce Agnus Dei*. Florence, Baptistry doors

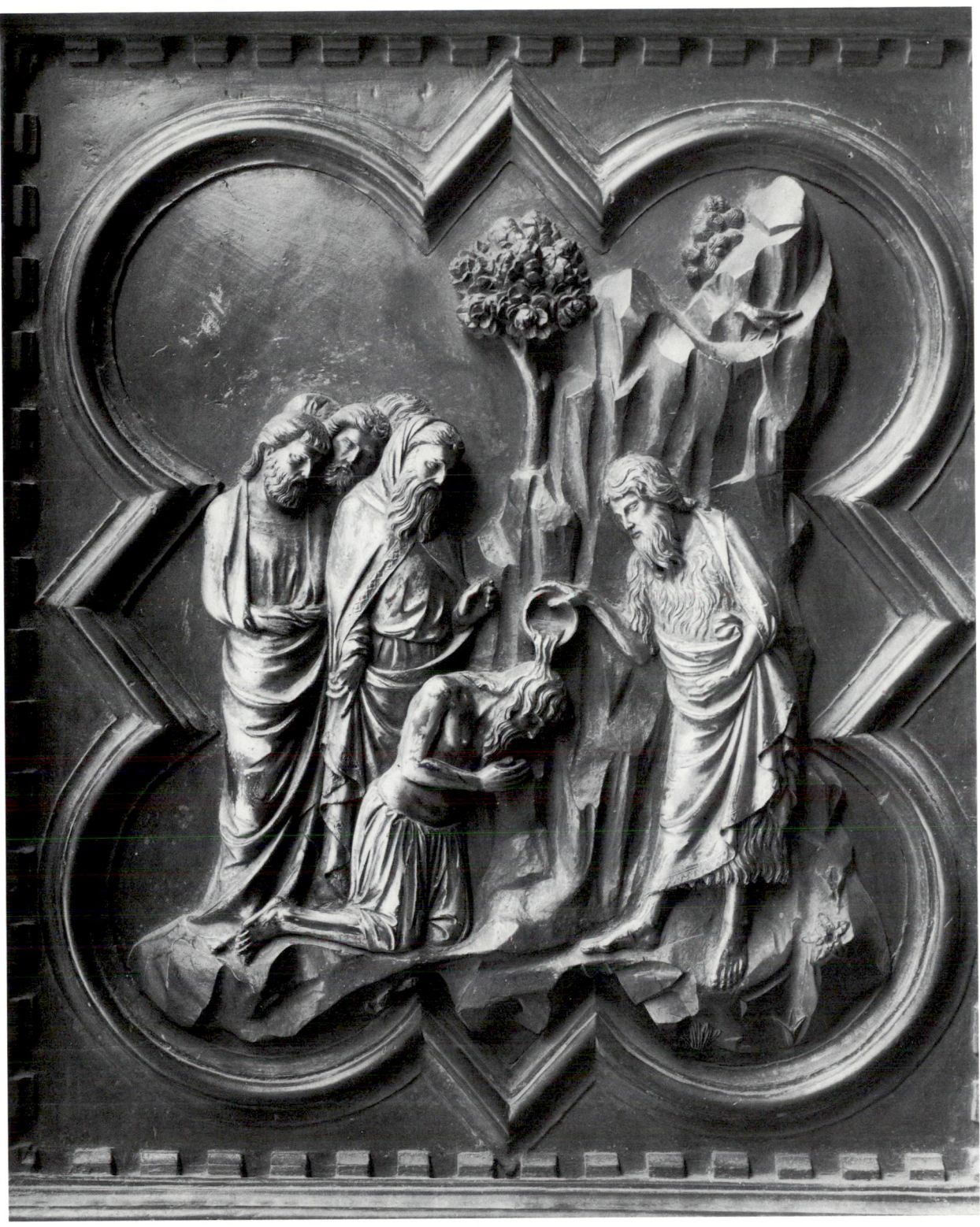

14. Andrea Pisano: *Baptism of the Multitude*. Florence, Baptistry doors

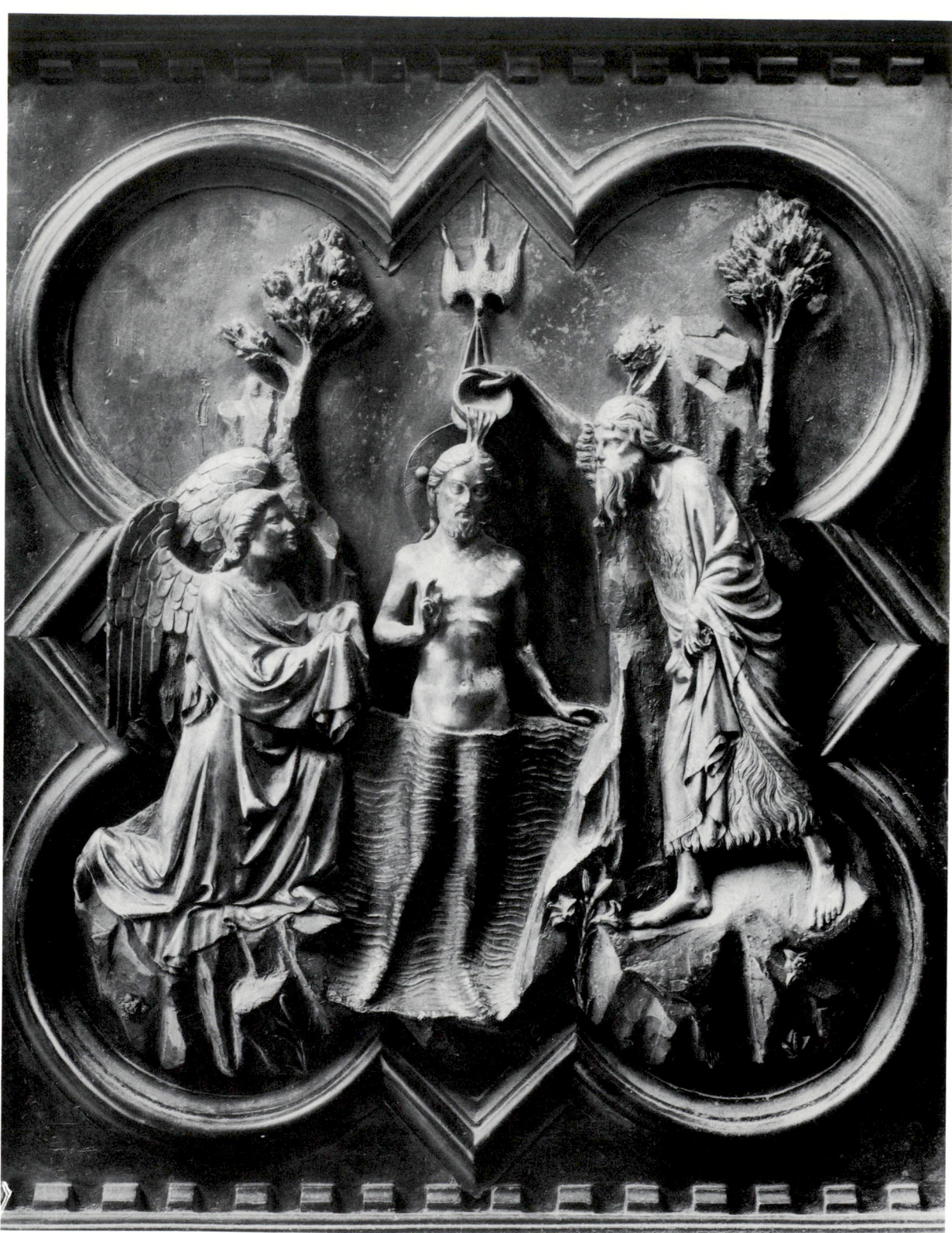

15. Andrea Pisano: *Baptism of Christ*. Florence, Baptistry doors

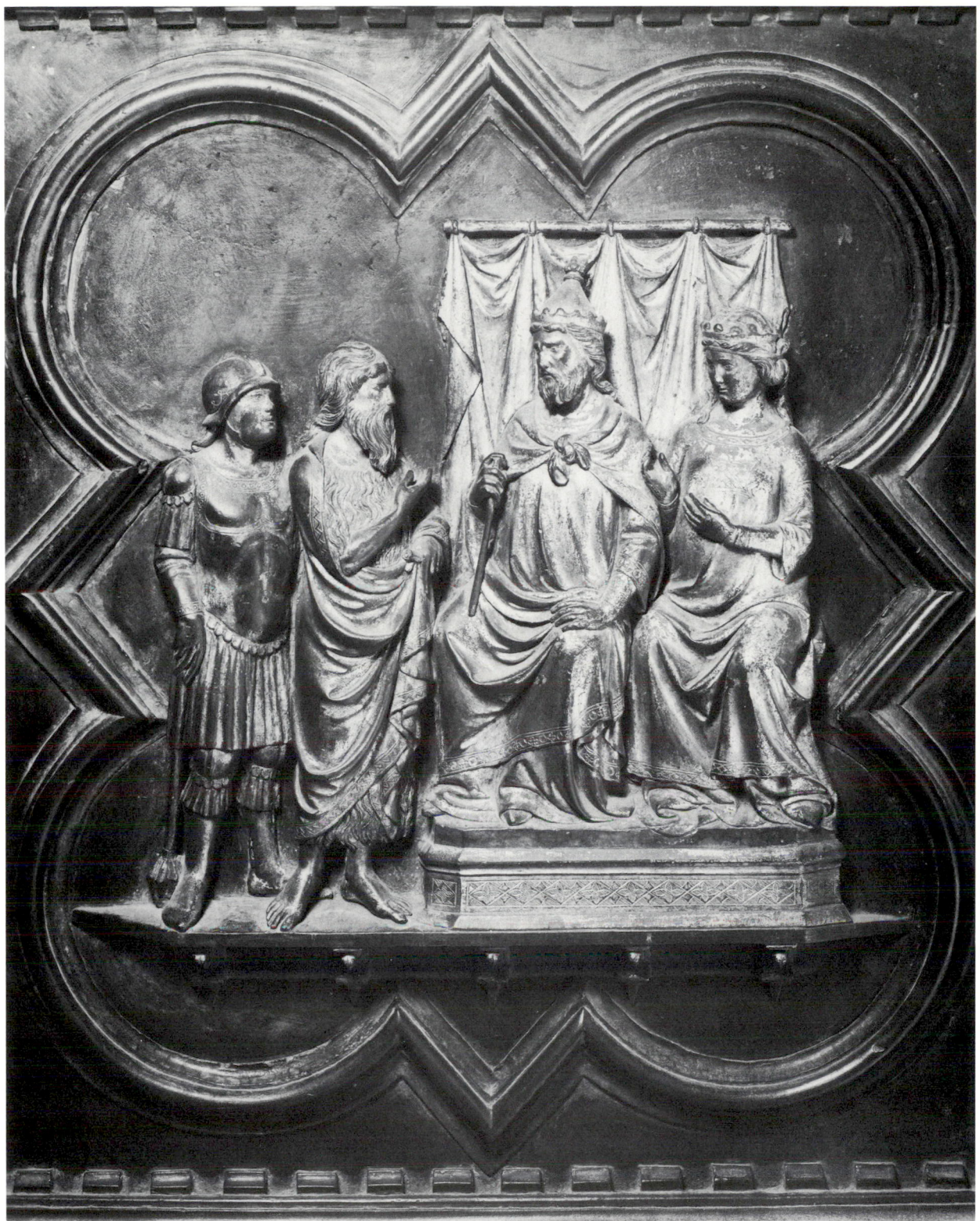

16. Andrea Pisano: *Baptist Before Herod*. Florence, Baptistry doors

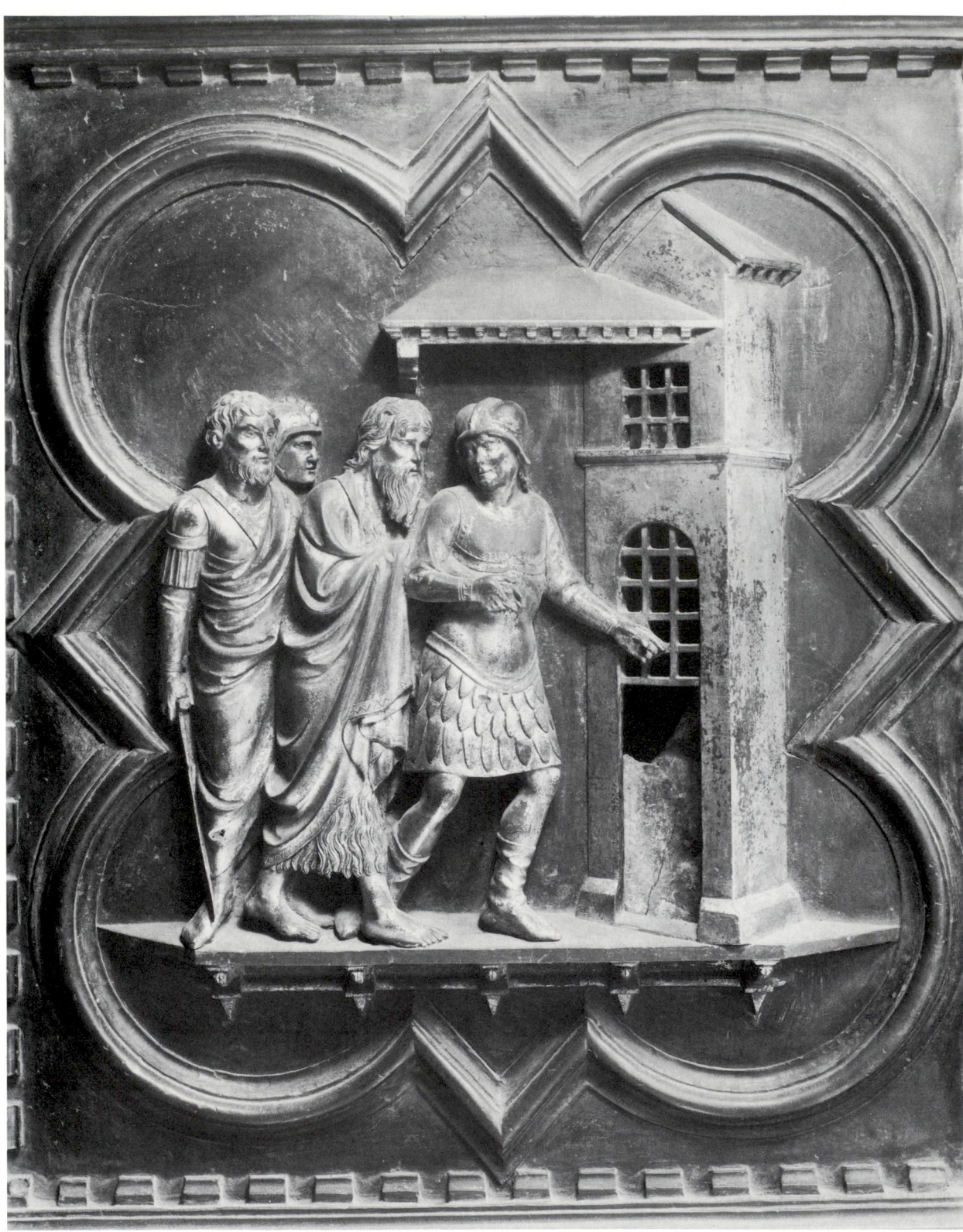

17. Andrea Pisano: *Baptist Led to Prison*. Florence, Baptistry doors

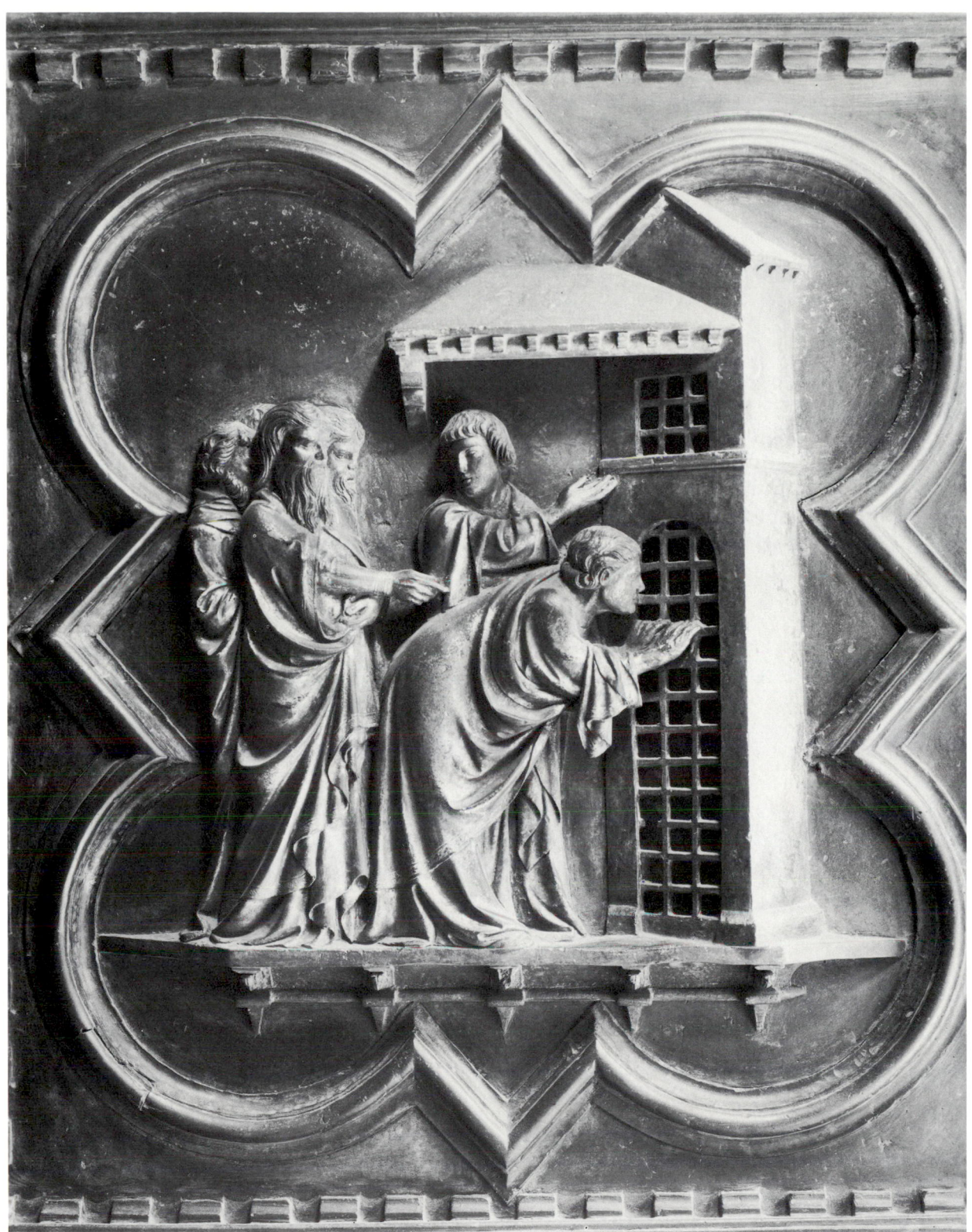

18. Andrea Pisano: *Visit of the Disciples*. Florence, Baptistry doors

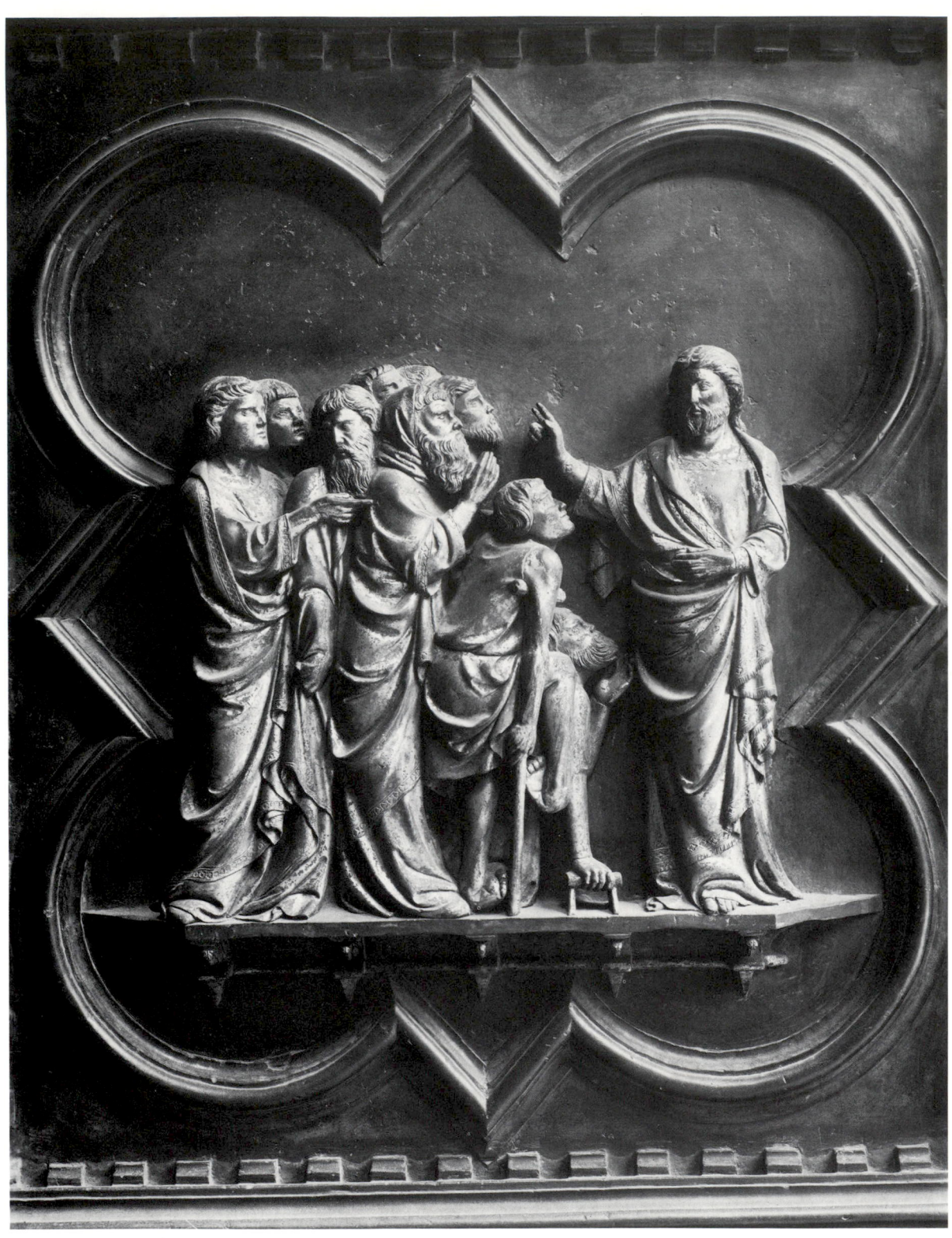

19. Andrea Pisano: *Christ Cures the Infirm*. Florence, Baptistry doors

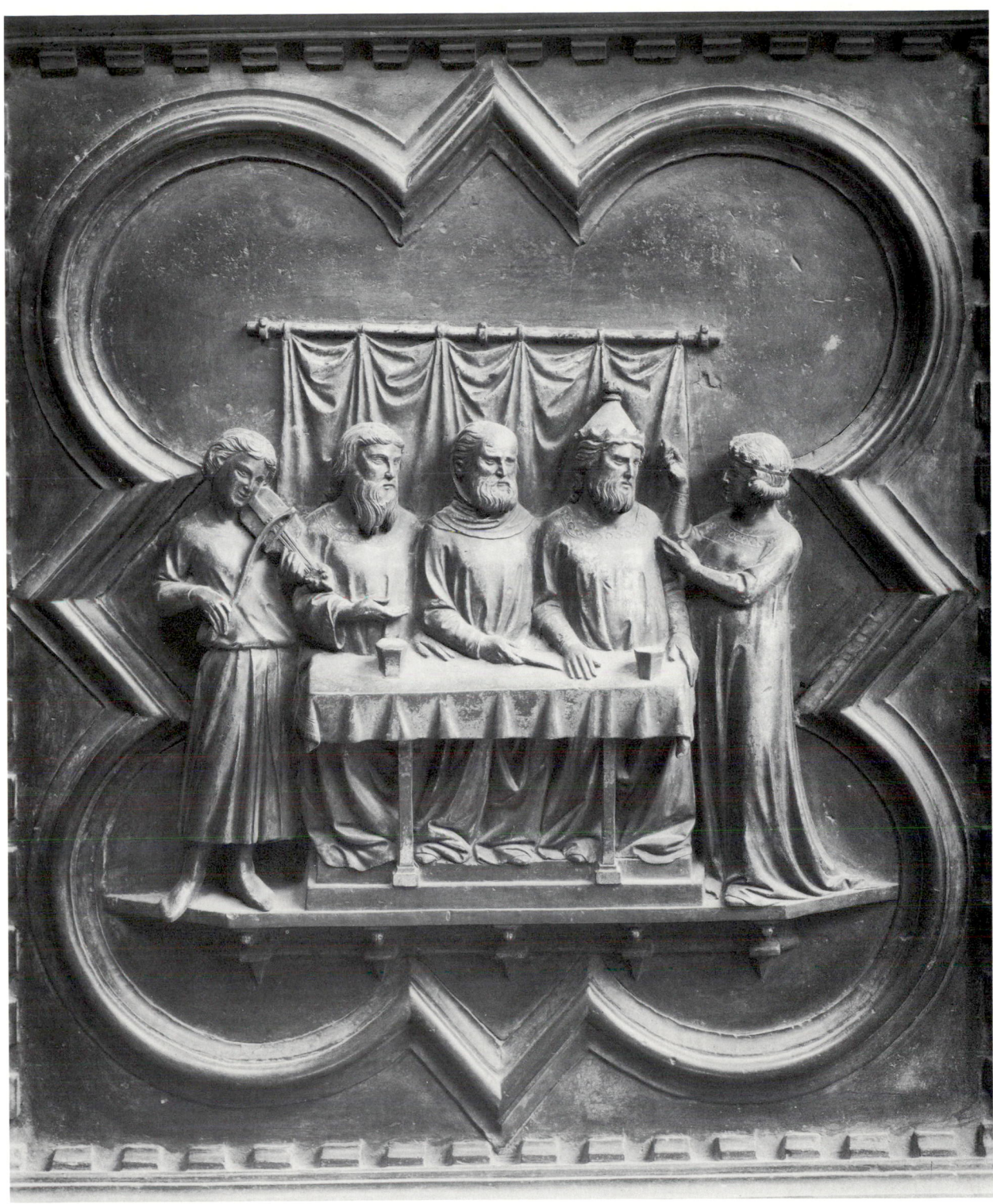

20. Andrea Pisano: *Dance of Salome*. Florence, Baptistry doors

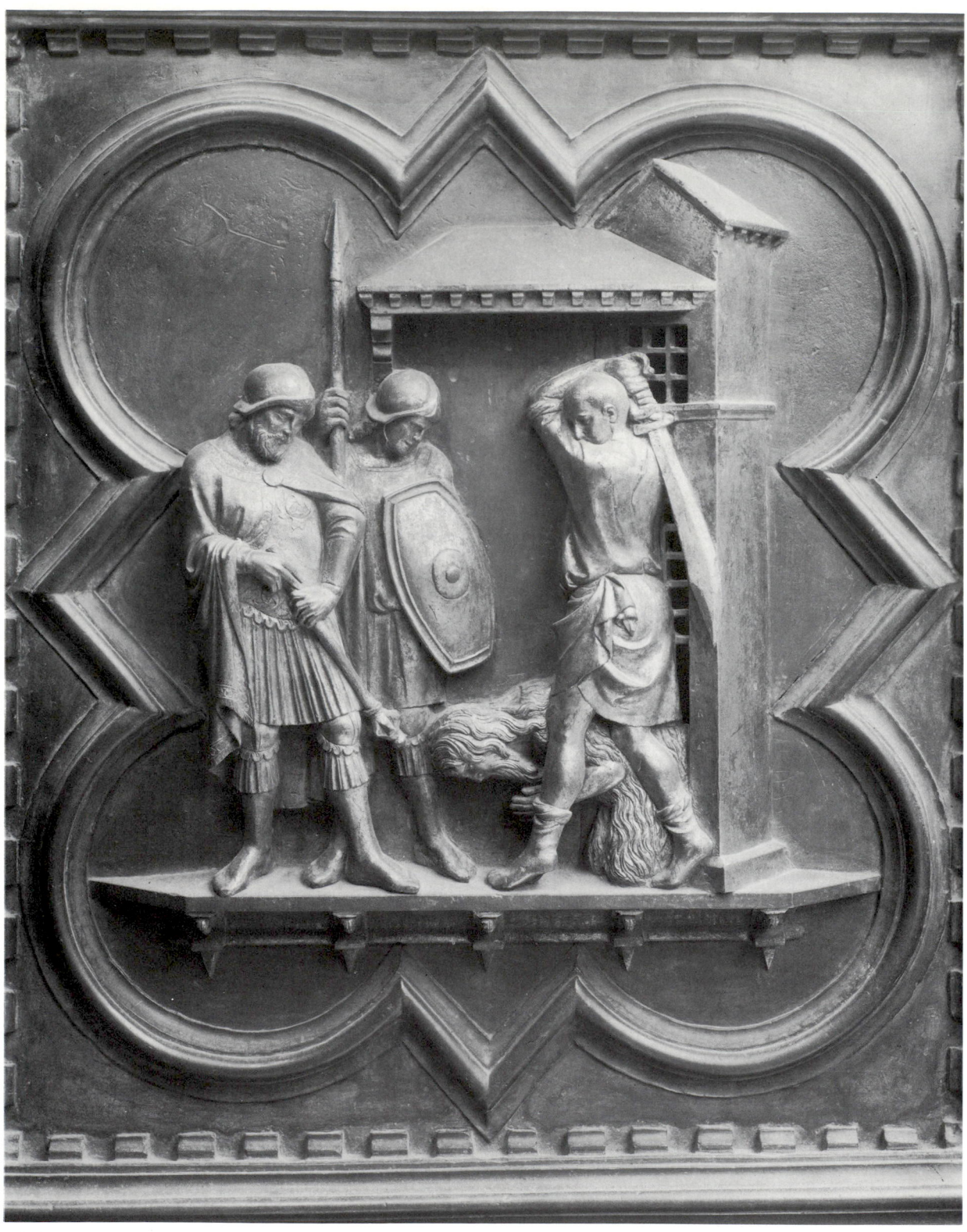

21. Andrea Pisano: *Beheading of the Baptist*. Florence, Baptistry doors

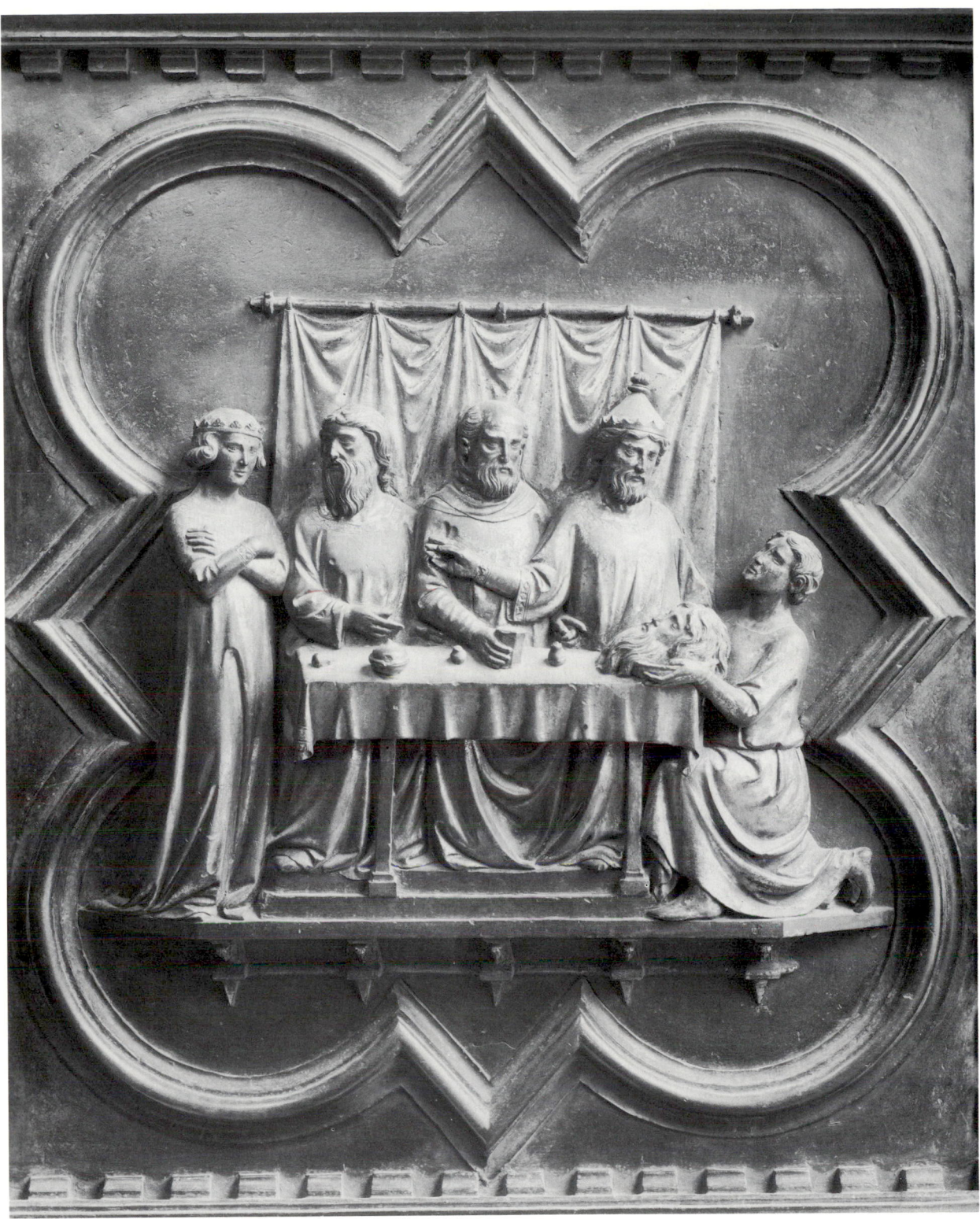

22. Andrea Pisano: *Baptist's Head Brought to Herod*. Florence, Baptistry doors

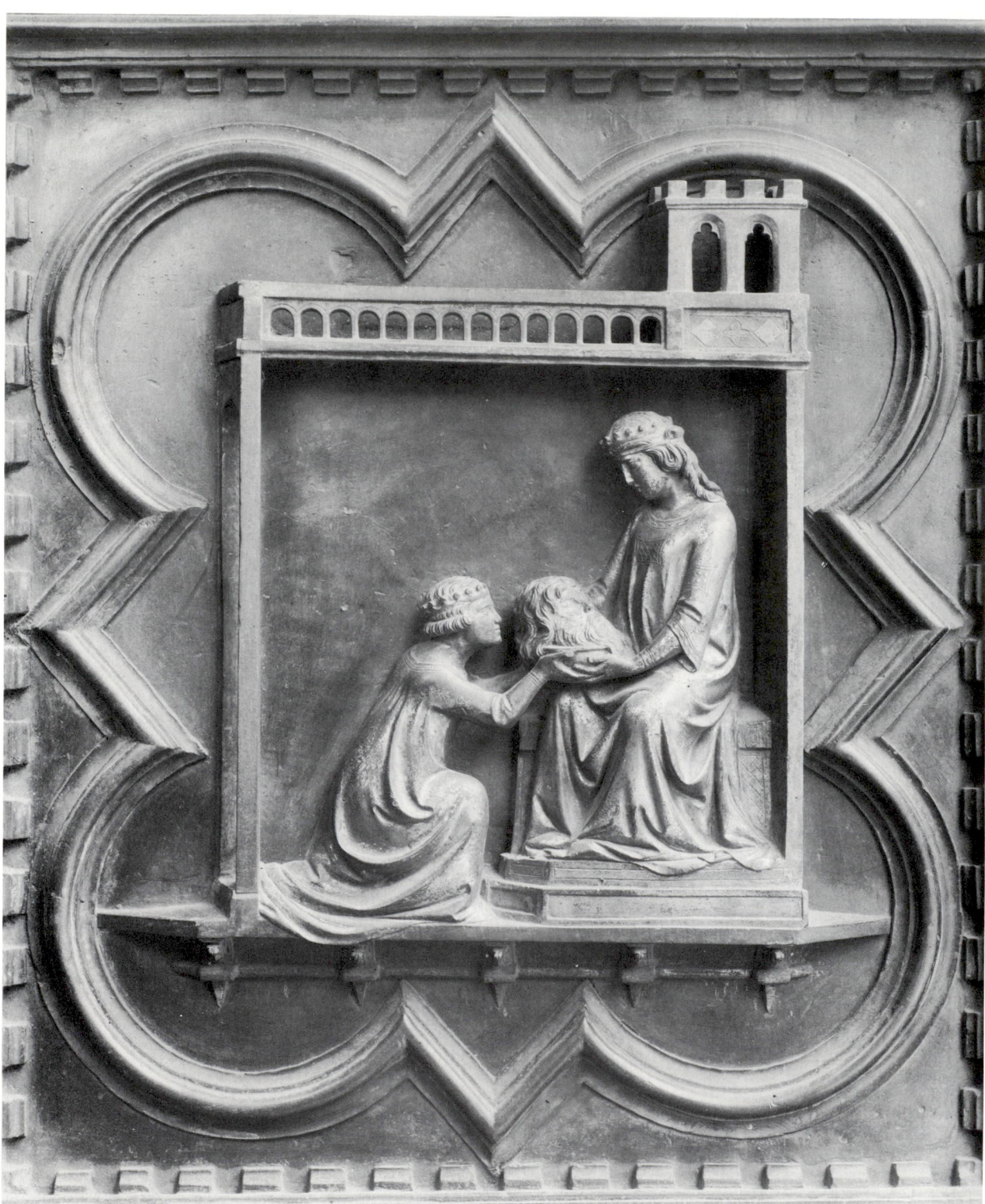

23. Andrea Pisano: *Presentation of the Baptist's Head to Herodias*. Florence, Baptistry doors

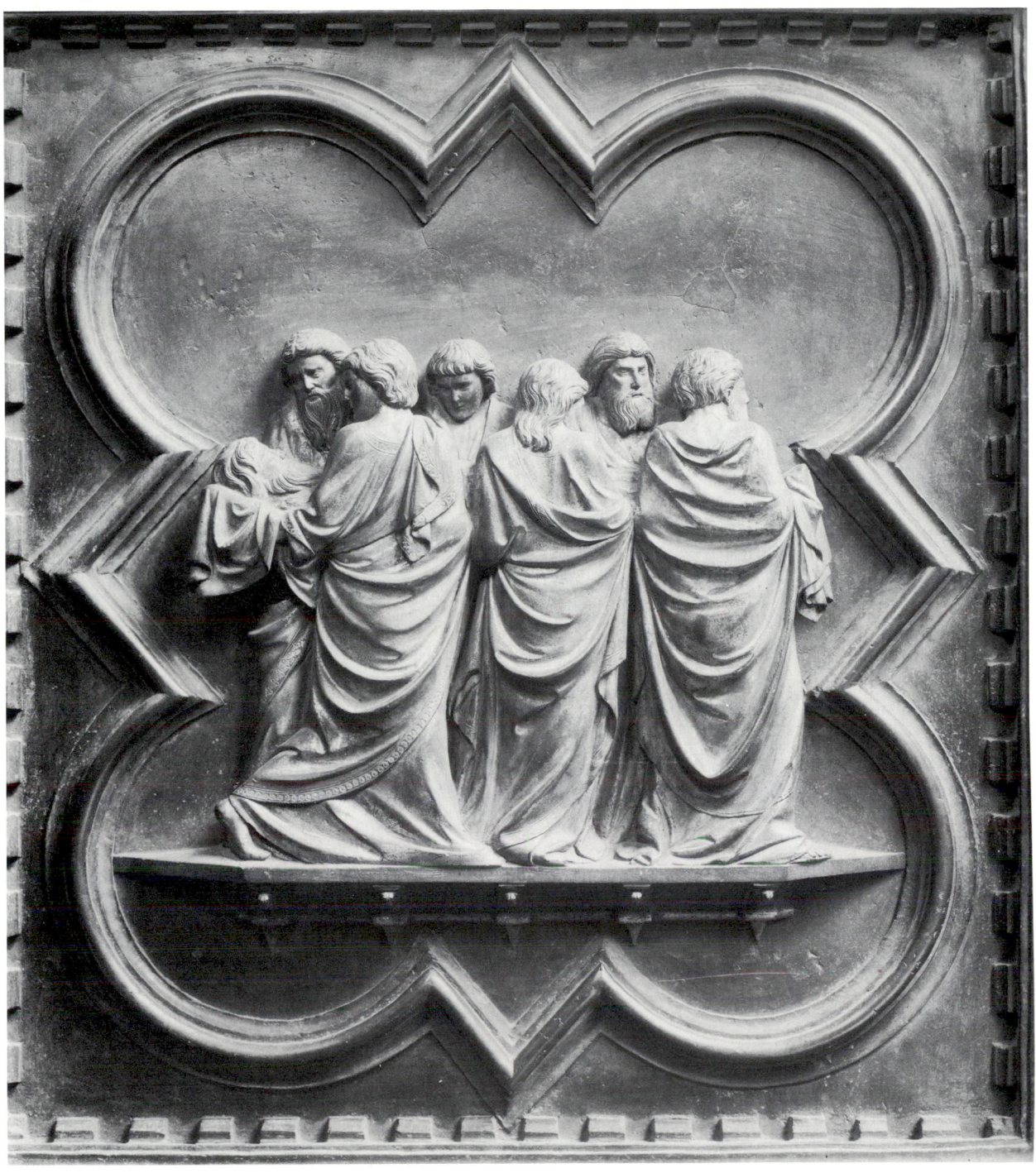

24. Andrea Pisano: *Funeral of the Baptist*. Florence, Baptistry doors

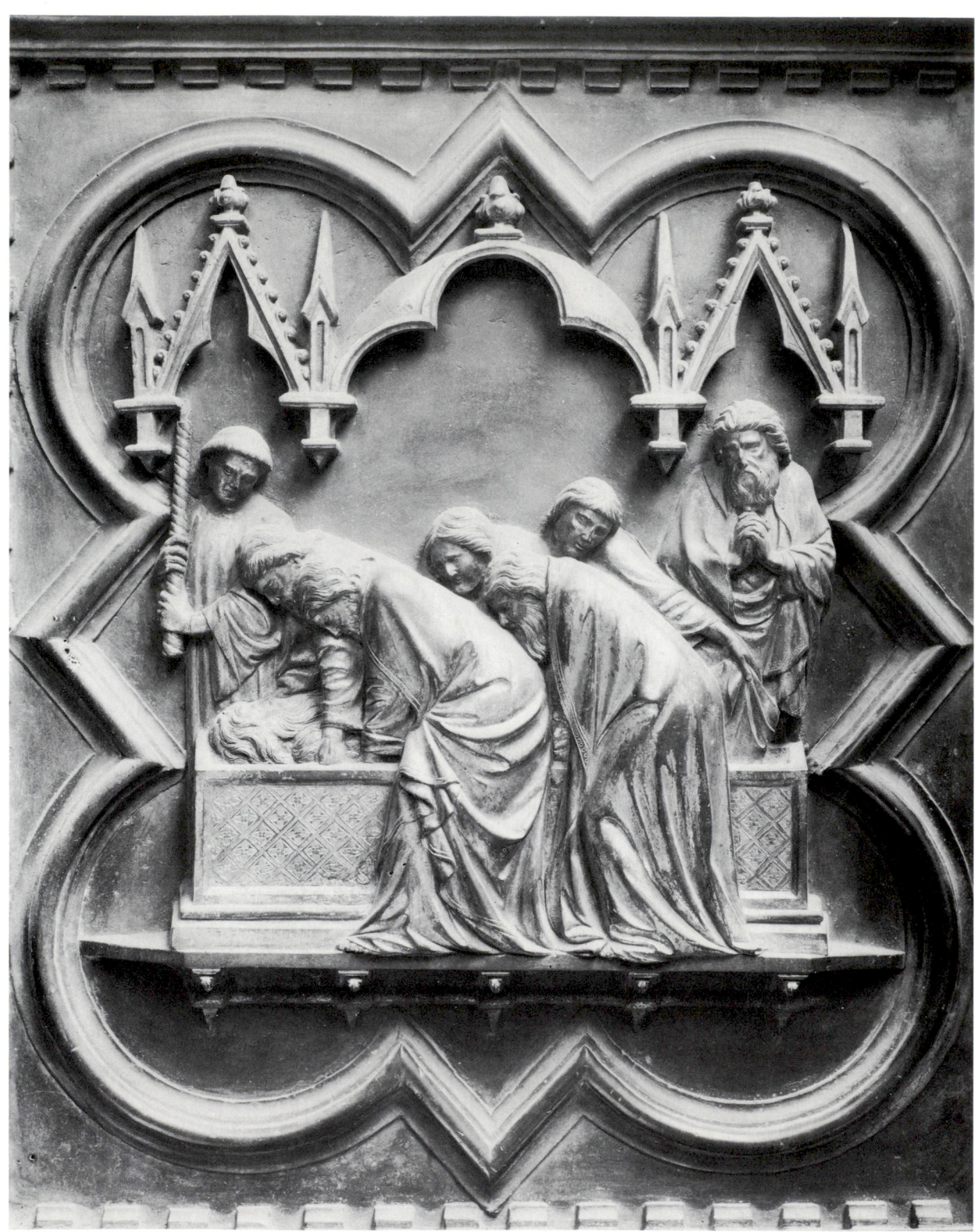

25. Andrea Pisano: *Entombment of the Baptist*. Florence, Baptistry doors

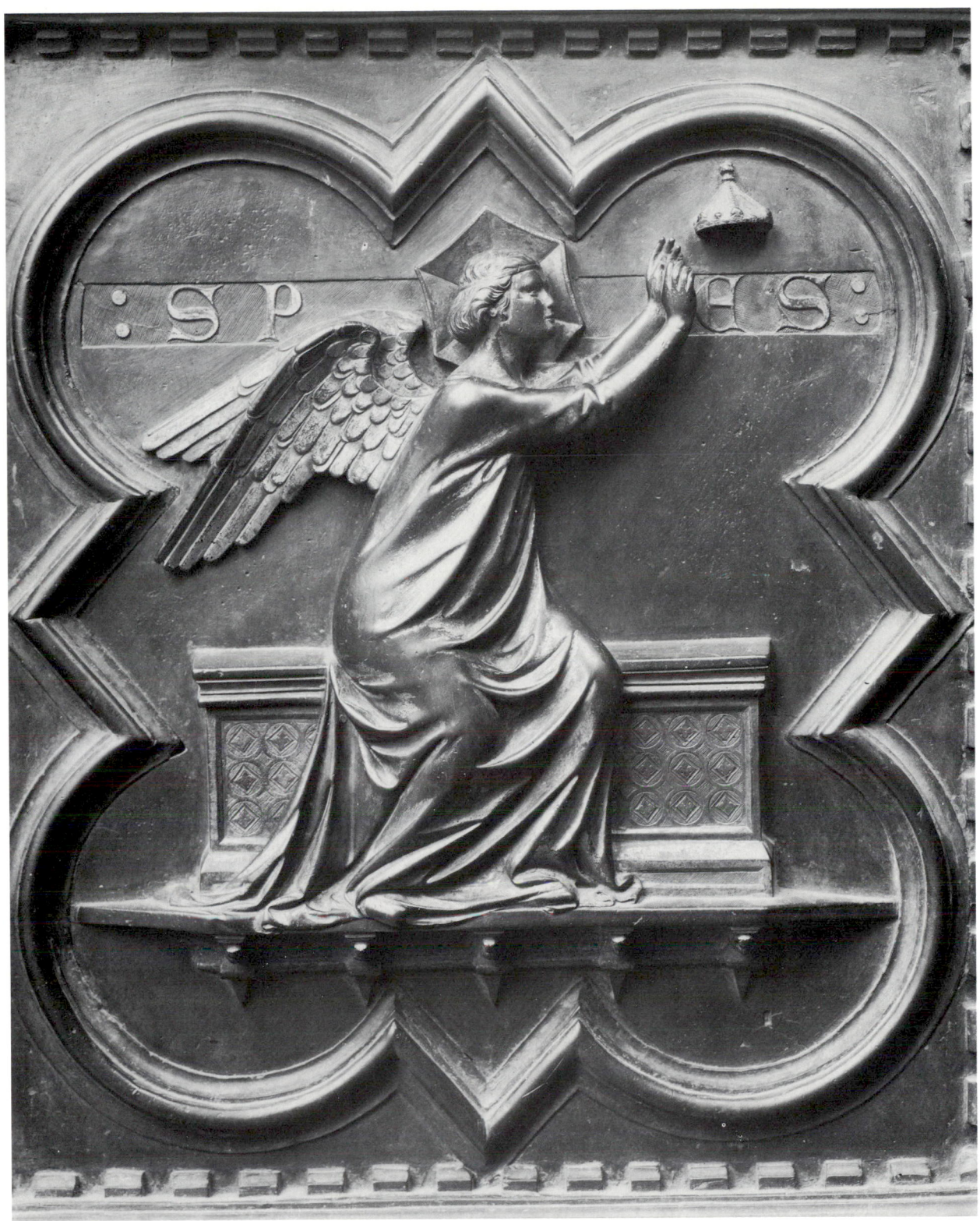

26. Andrea Pisano: *Hope*. Florence, Baptistry doors

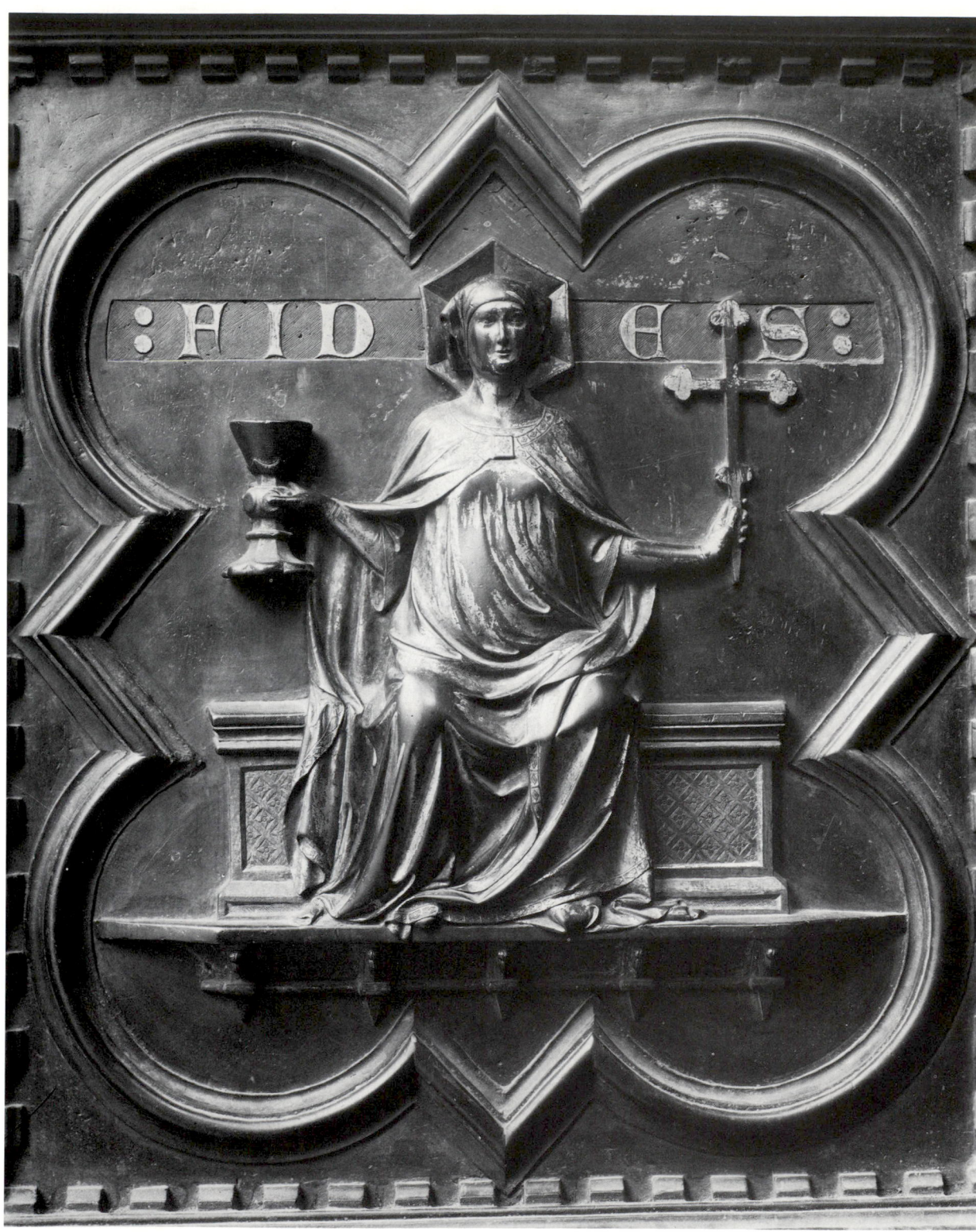

27. Andrea Pisano: *Faith*. Florence, Baptistry doors

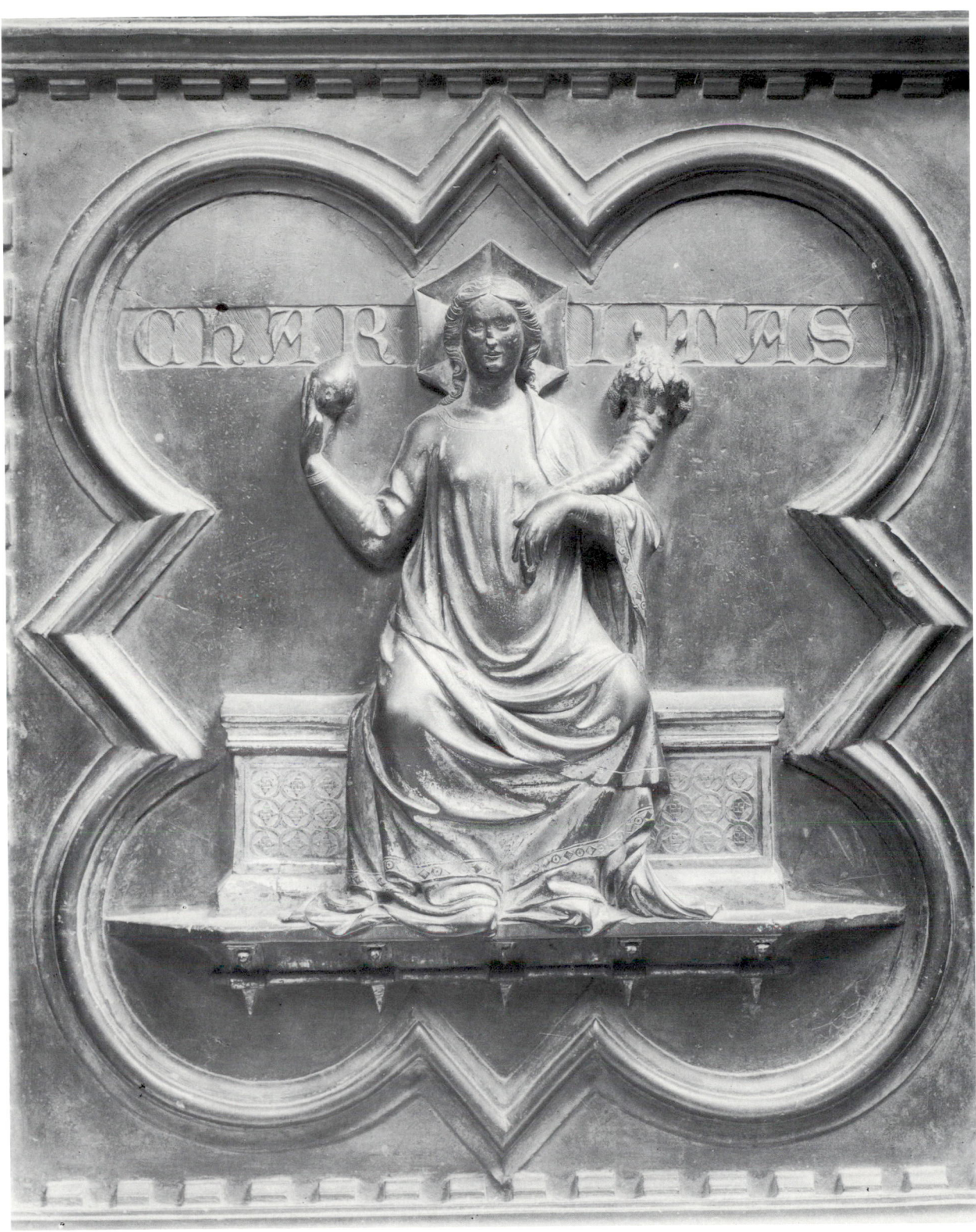

28. Andrea Pisano: *Charity*. Florence, Baptistry doors

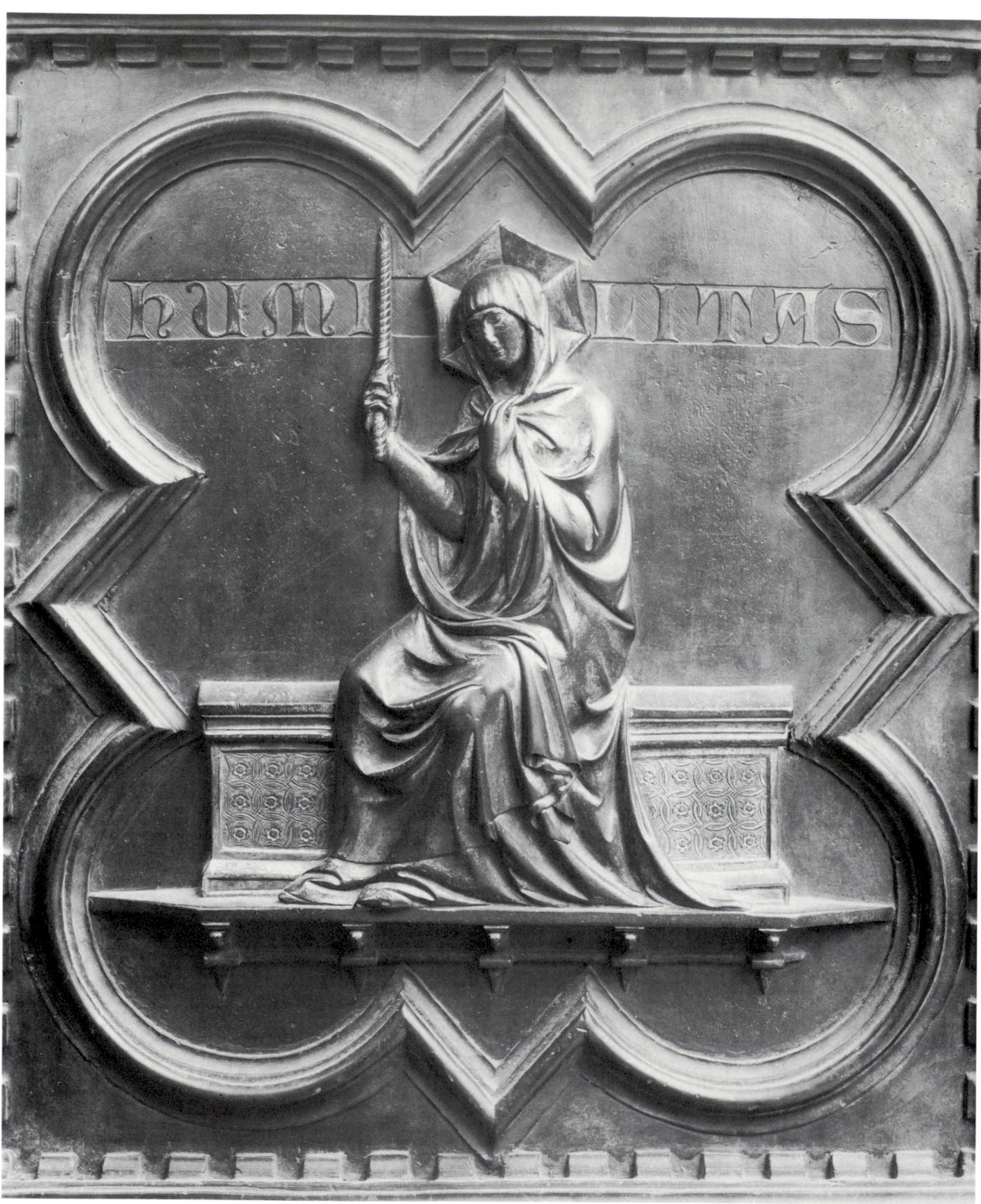

29. Andrea Pisano: *Humility*. Florence, Baptistry doors

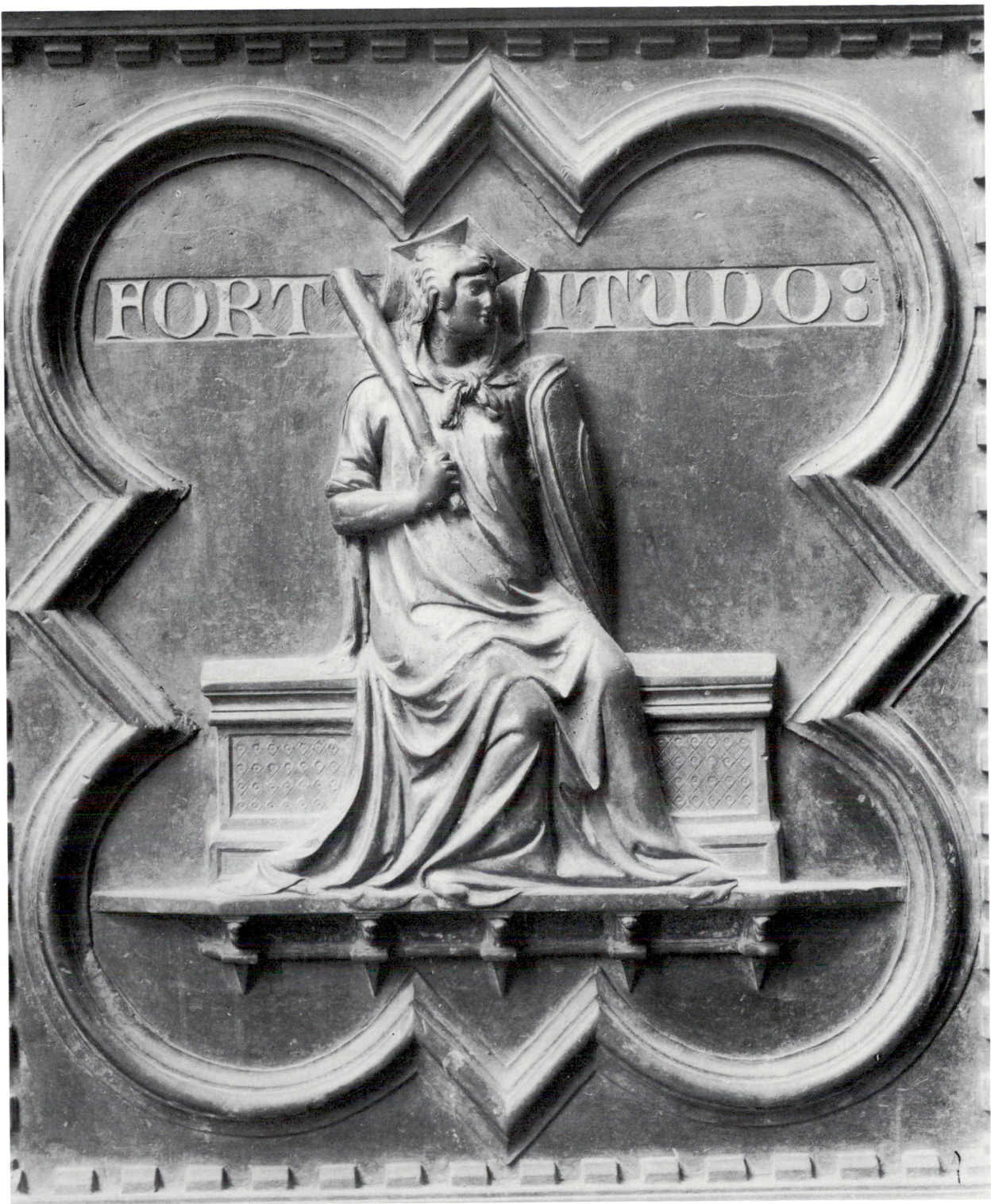

30. Andrea Pisano: *Fortitude*. Florence, Baptistry doors

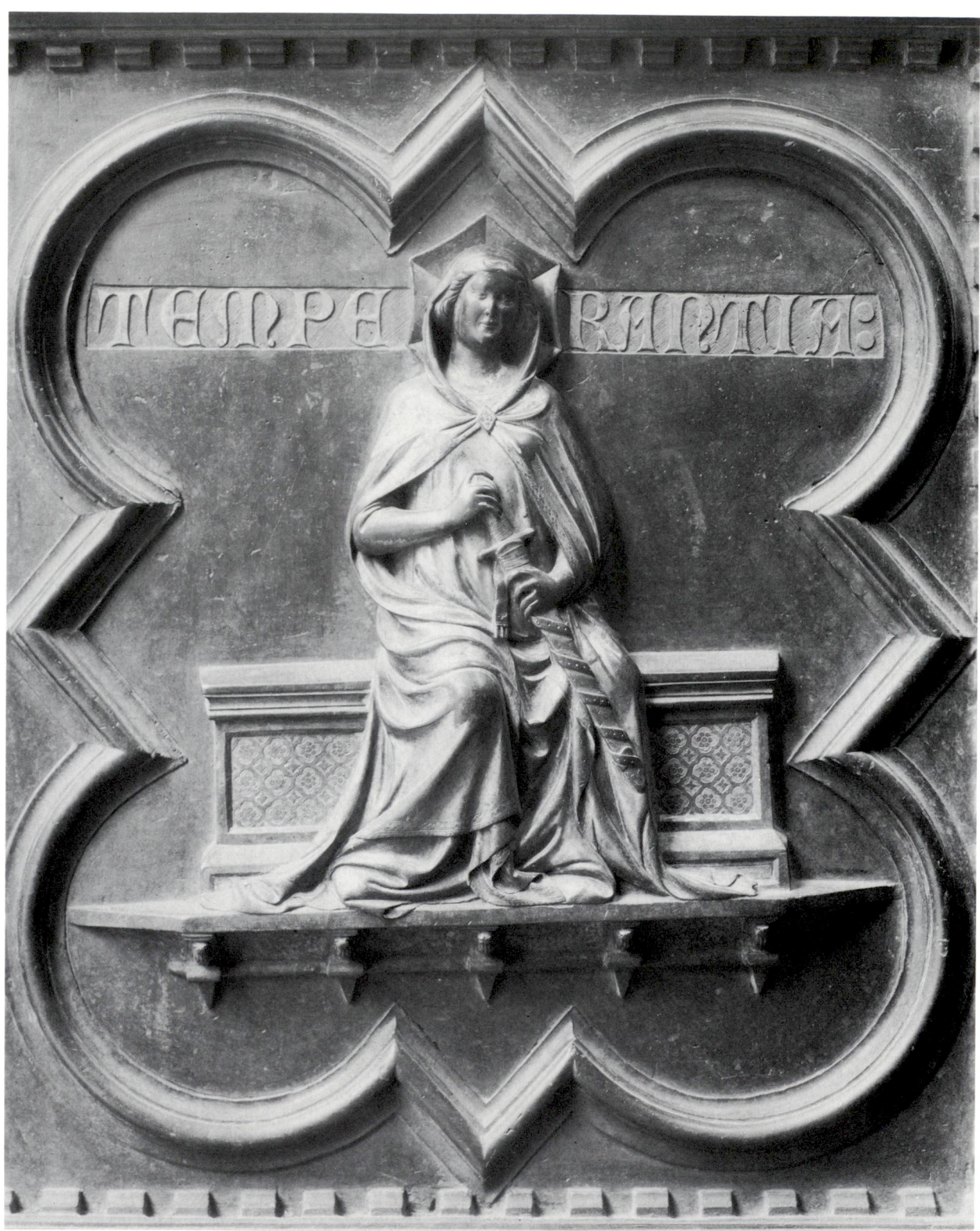

31. Andrea Pisano: *Temperance*. Florence, Baptistry doors

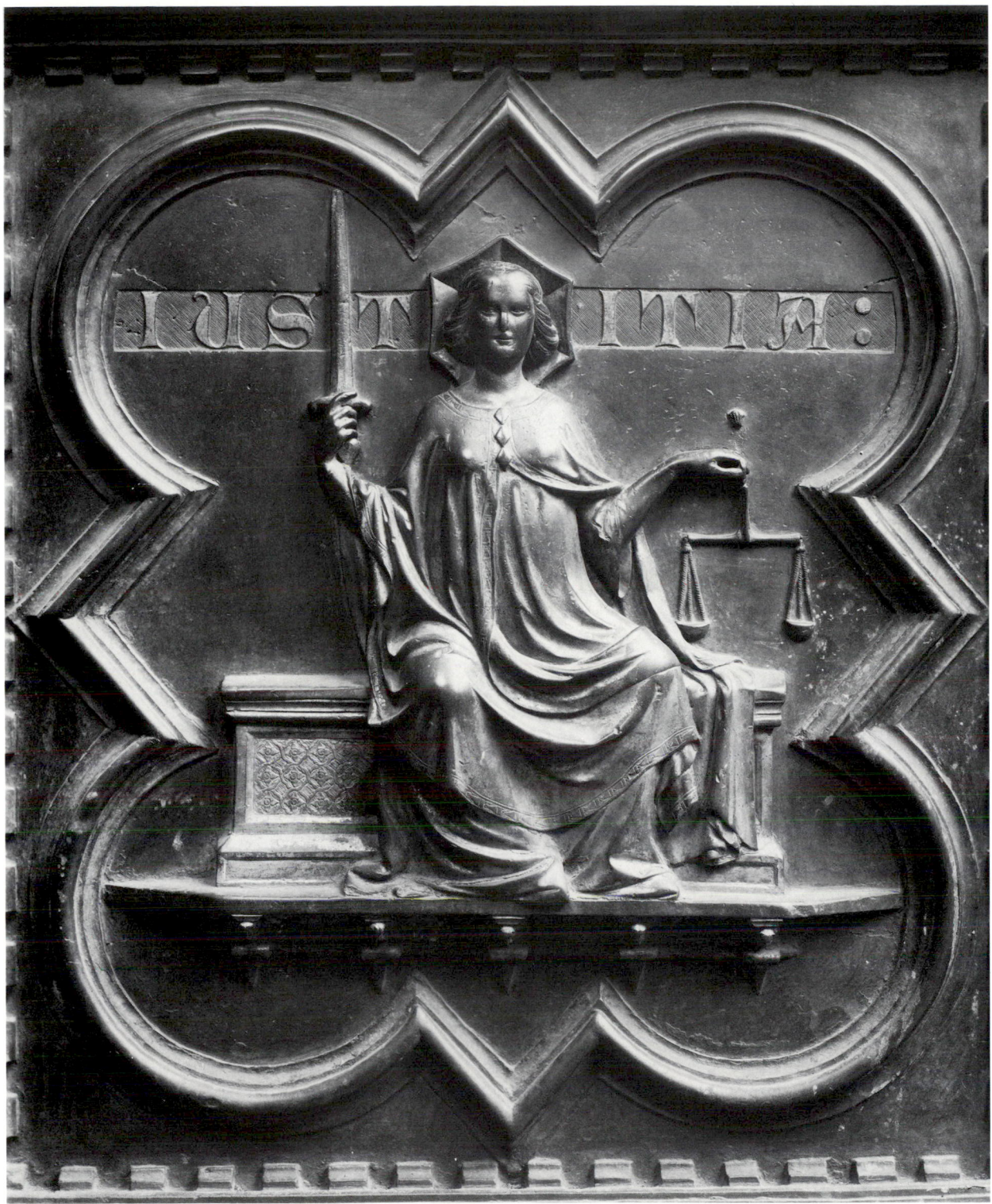

32. Andrea Pisano: *Justice*. Florence, Baptistry doors

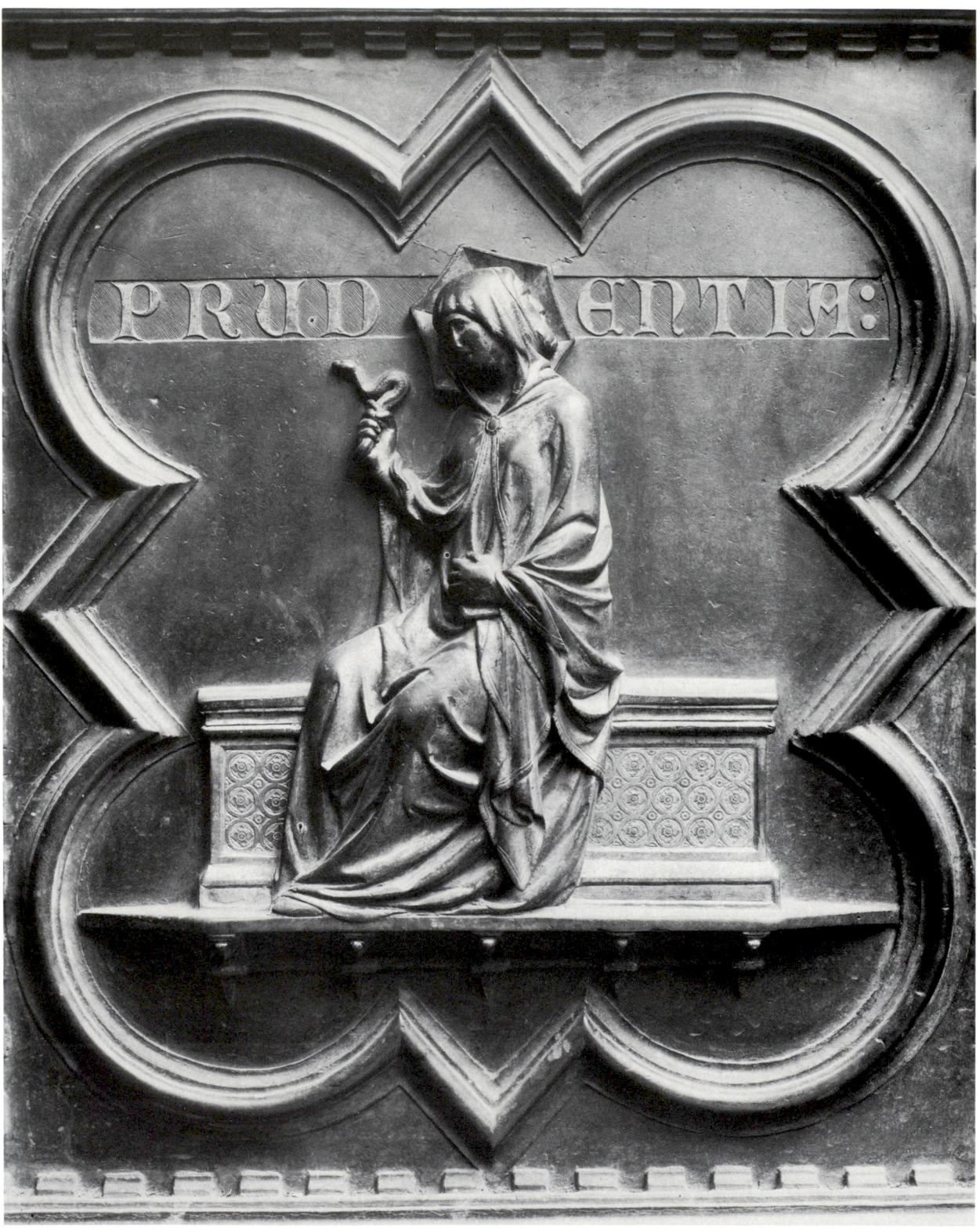

33. Andrea Pisano: *Prudence*. Florence, Baptistry doors

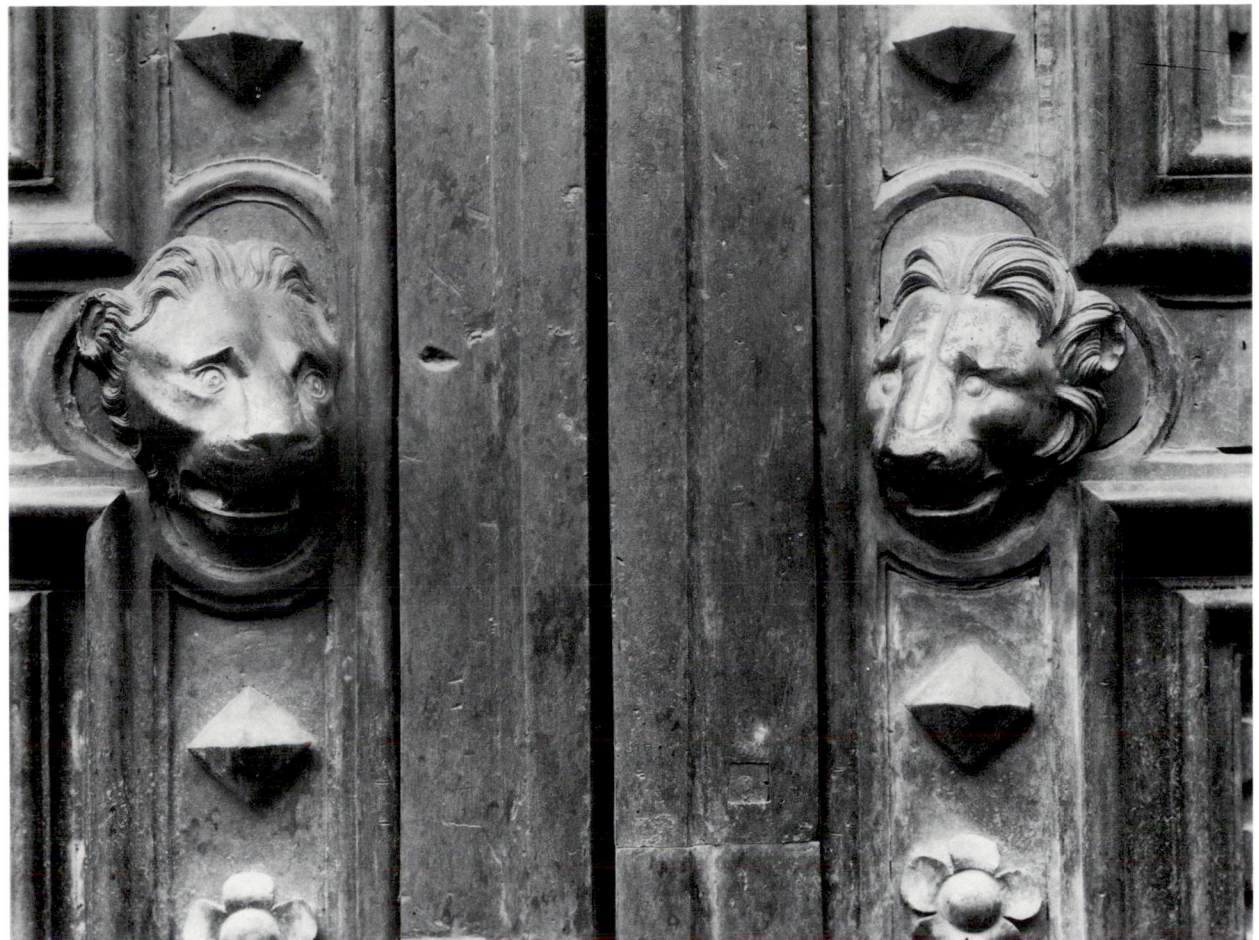

34. Andrea Pisano: Lions' heads. Florence Baptistry doors

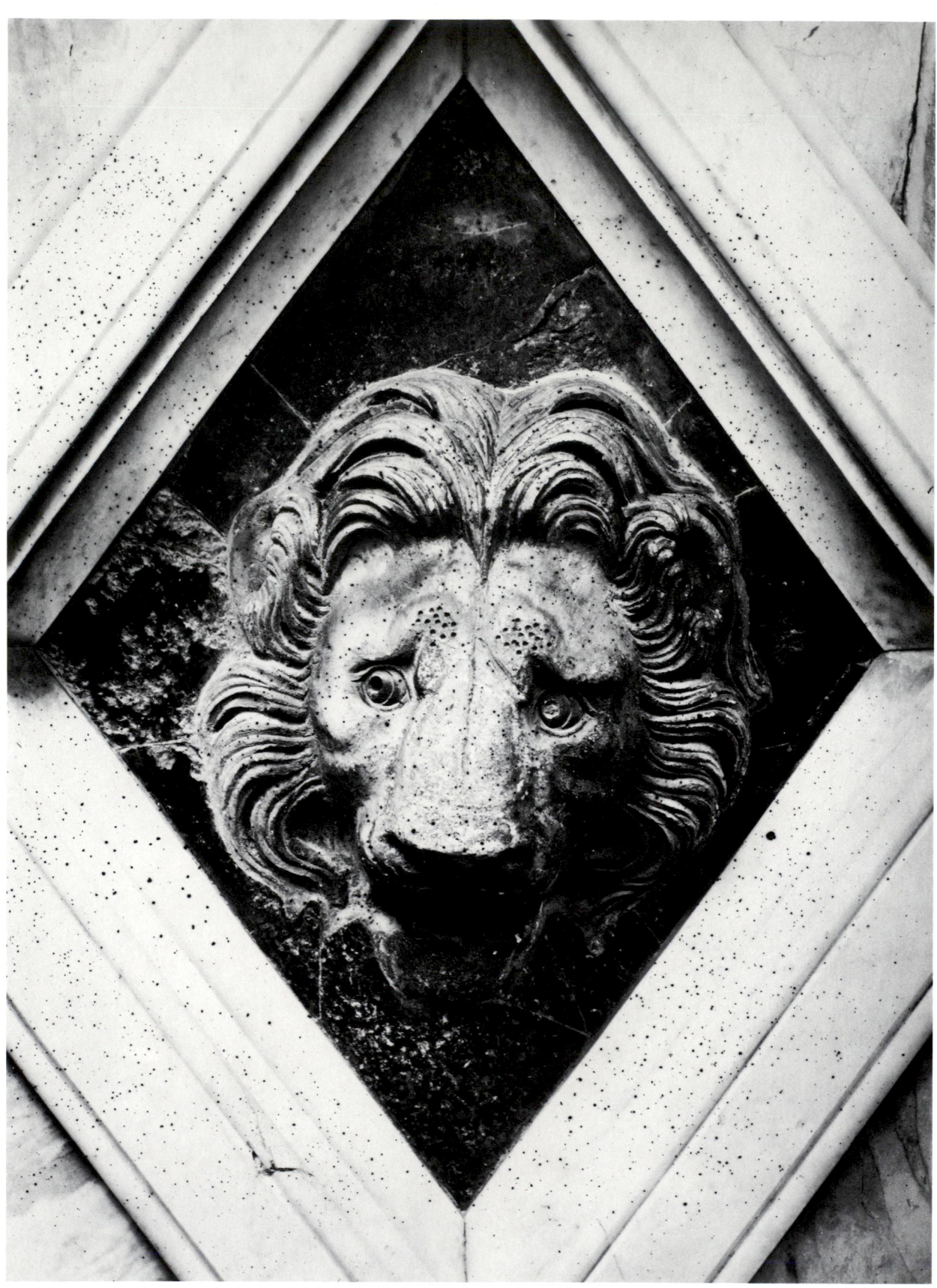

35. Andrea Pisano: Lion's head. Florence, Campanile

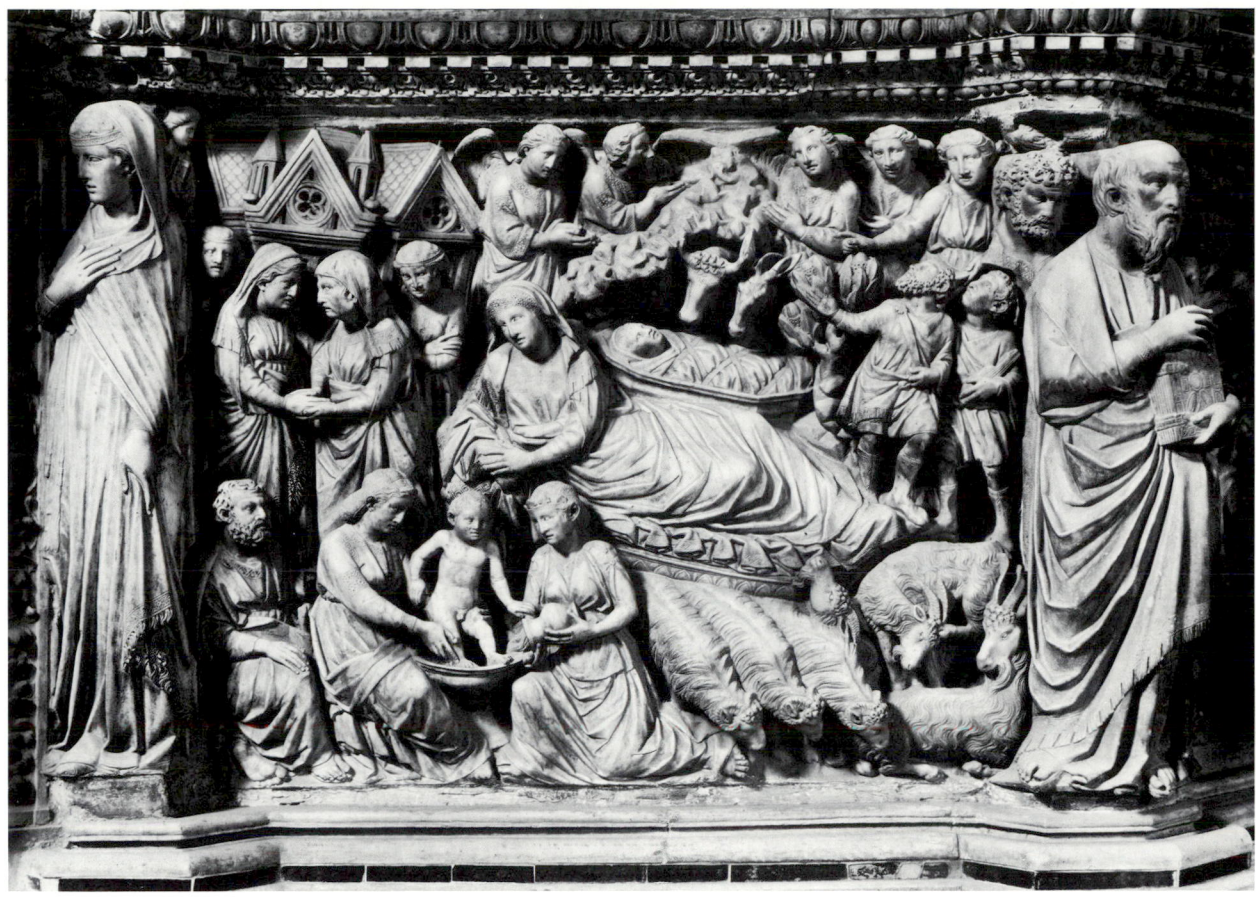

36. Nicola Pisano: *Nativity*. Pulpit. Siena Cathedral

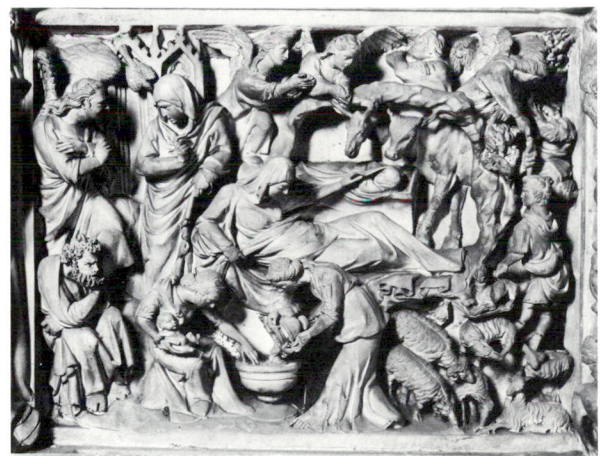

37. Giovanni Pisano: *Nativity*. Pulpit. Pistoia, San Andrea

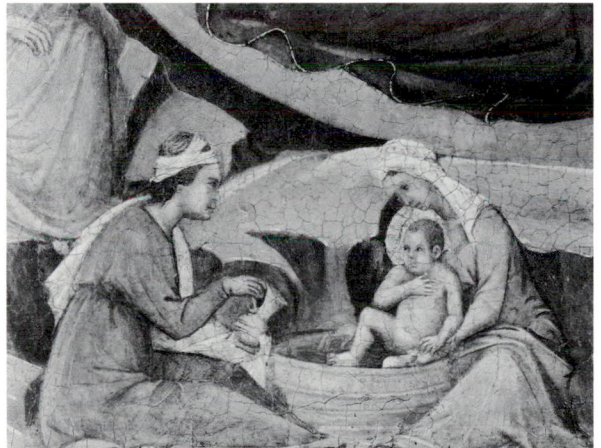

38. Duccio: *Nativity*, detail. Washington, D.C. National Gallery

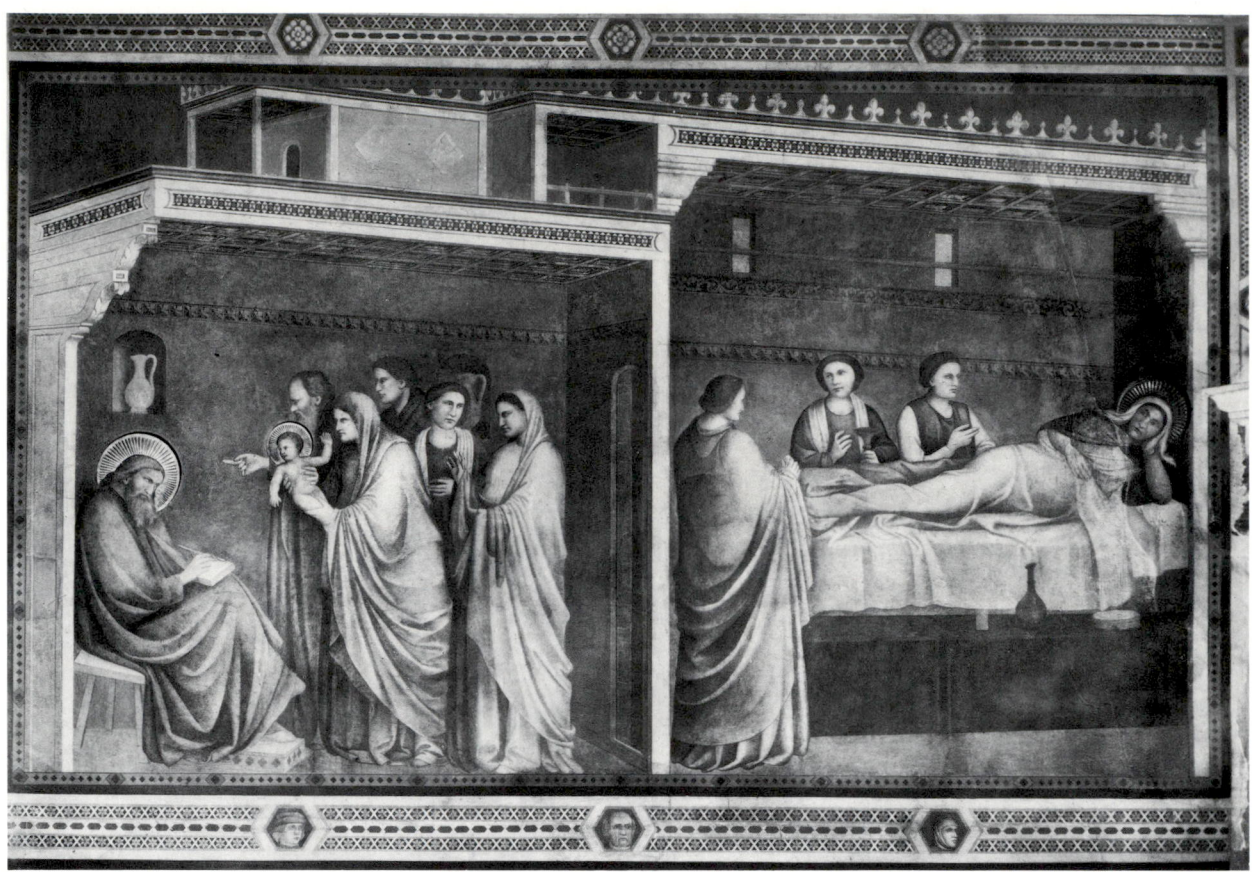

39. Giotto: *Birth and Naming of the Baptist.* Florence, Sta. Croce

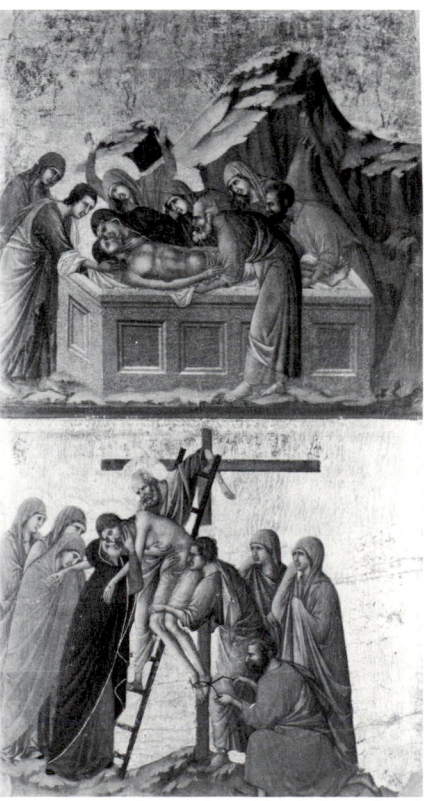

40. Duccio: *Lamentation* and *Deposition.* Siena, Museo dell'Opera del Duomo

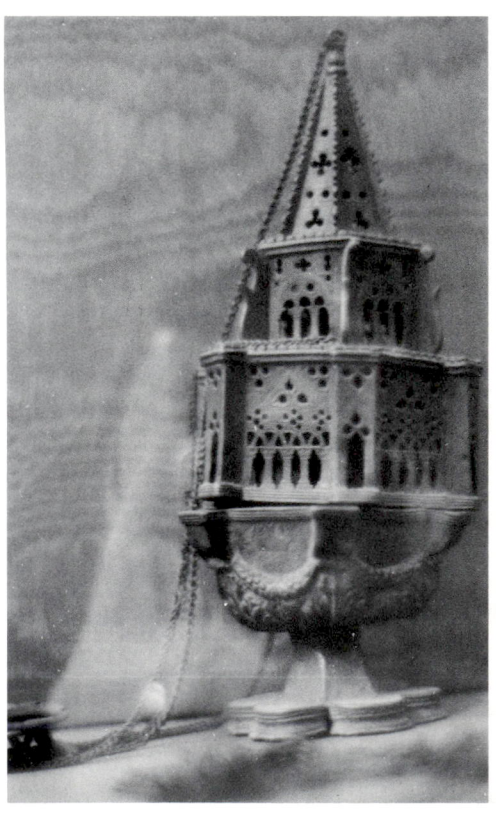

41. Censer. Pisa, Museo di San Matteo

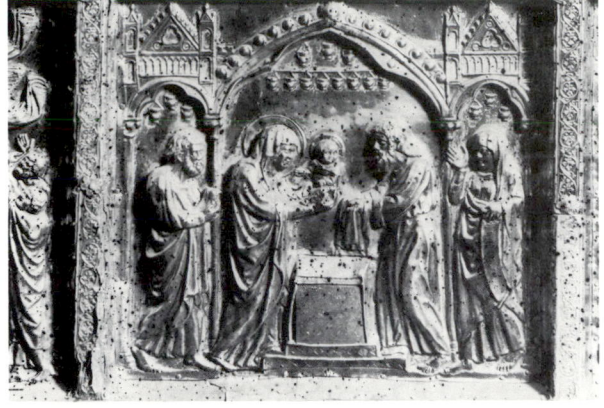

42. Andrea da Jacopo d'Ognabene: *Presentation*. Silver Altar. Pistoia Cathedral

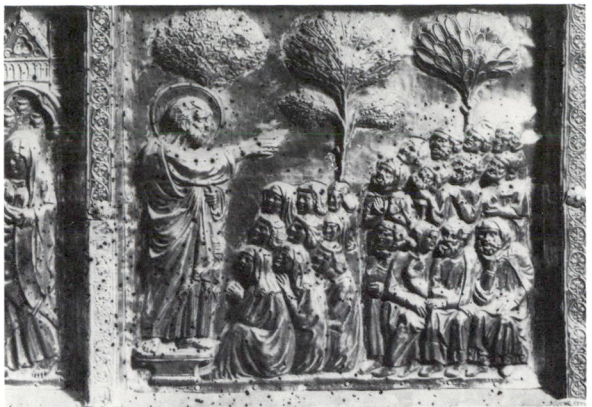

44. Andrea da Jacopo d'Ognabene: *Preaching of San Jacopo*. Silver Altar. Pistoia Cathedral

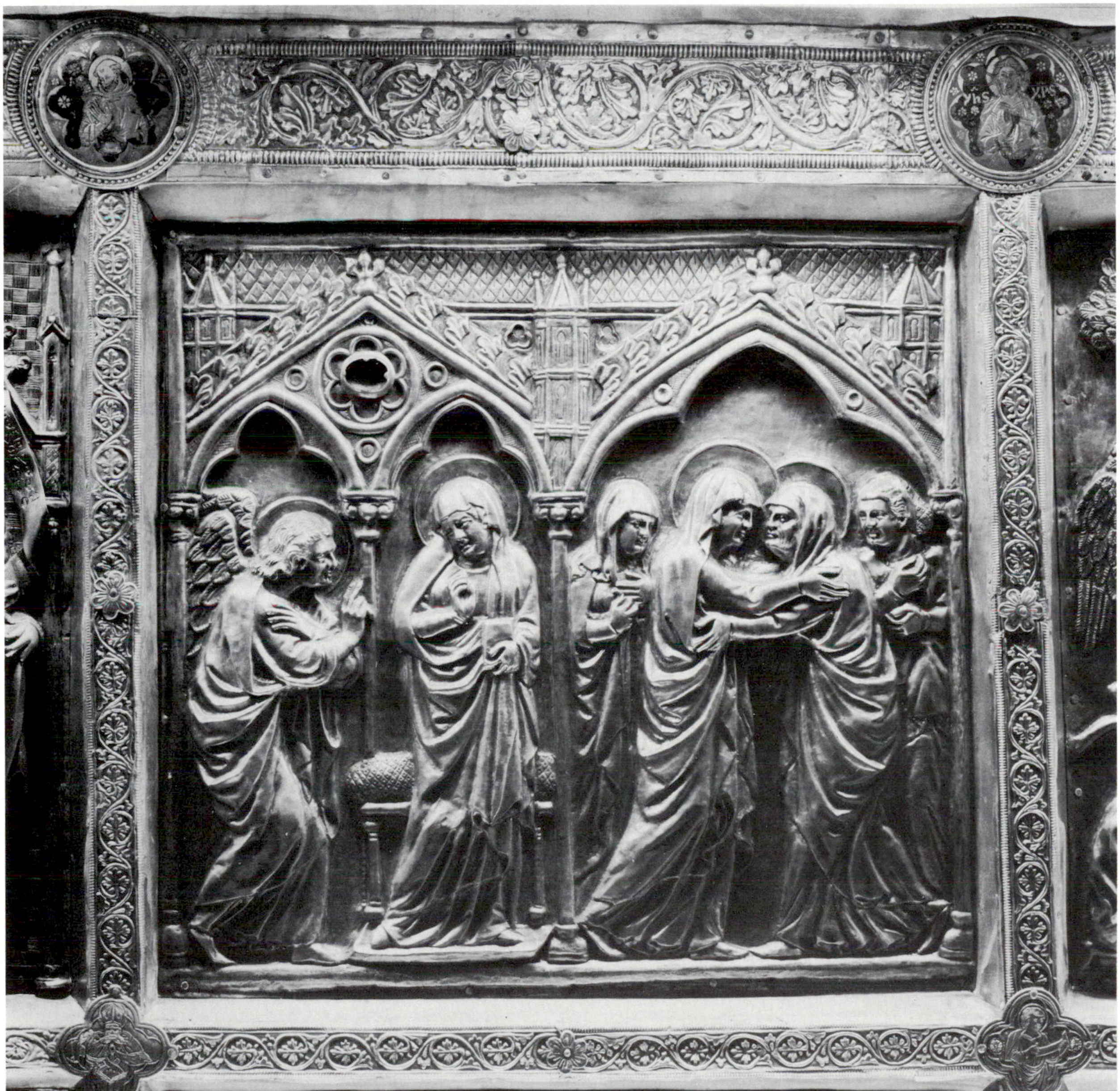

43. Andrea da Jacopo d'Ognabene: *Annunciation and Visitation*. Silver Altar. Pistoia Cathedral

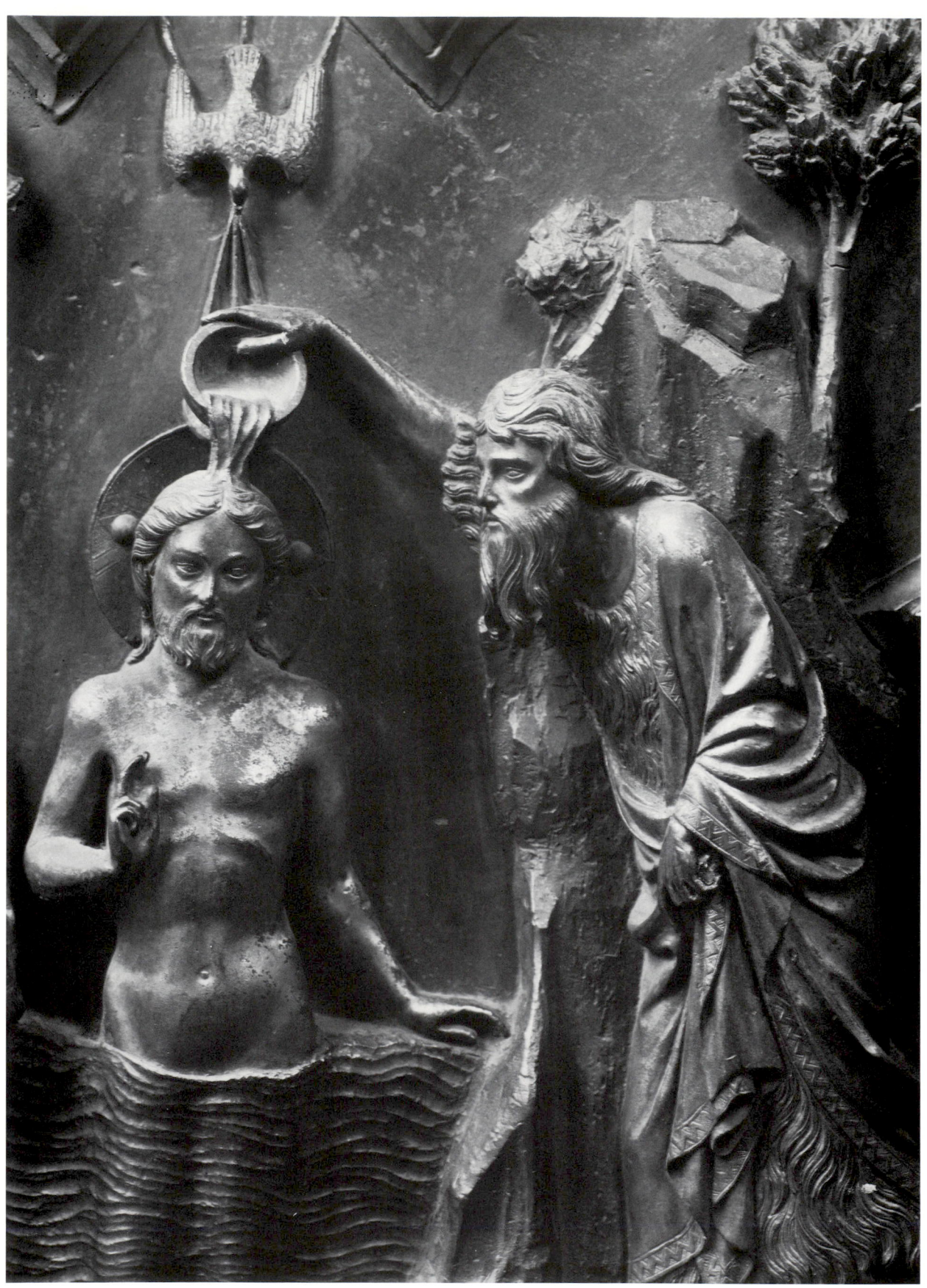

45. Andrea Pisano: *Baptism of Christ*, detail. Florence, Baptistry doors

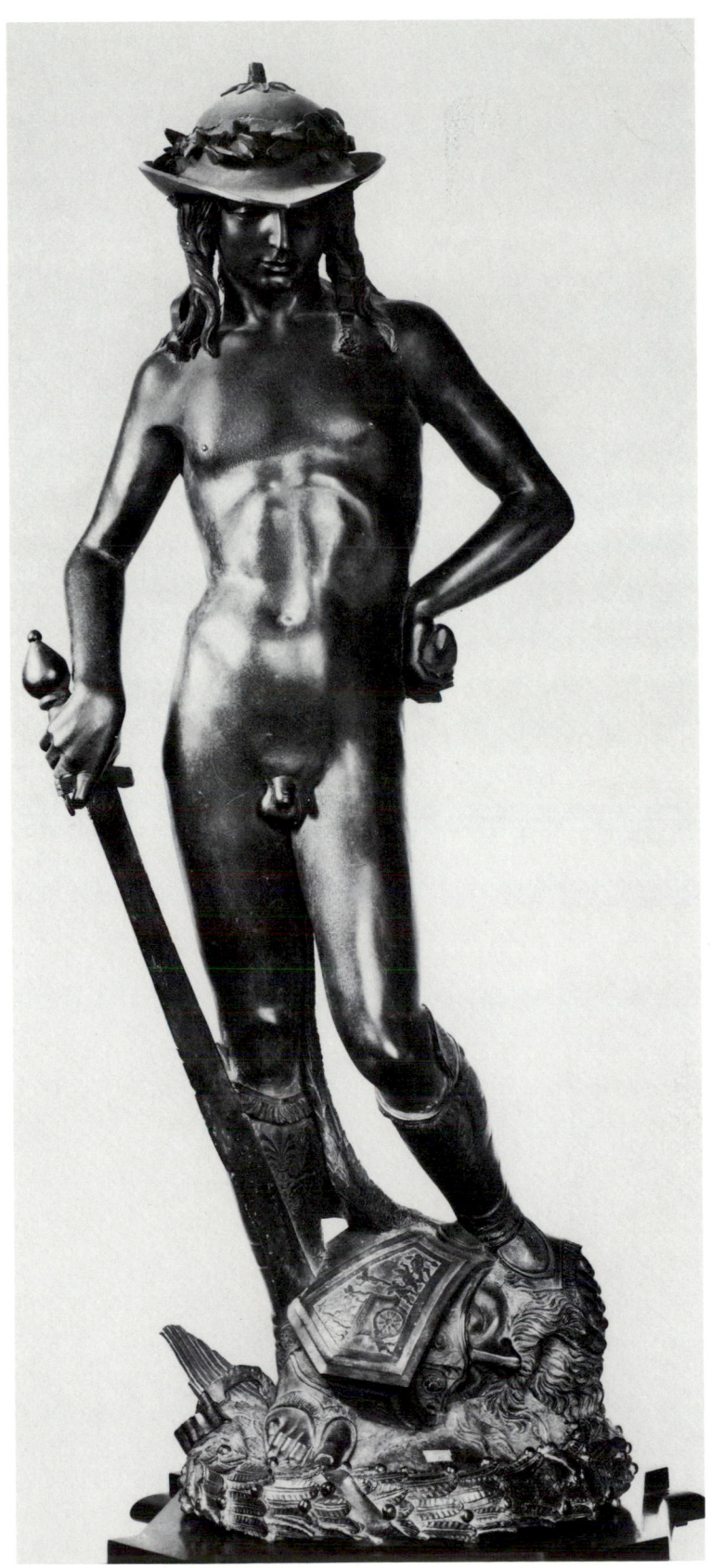

46. Donatello: *David*. Florence, Museo Nazionale

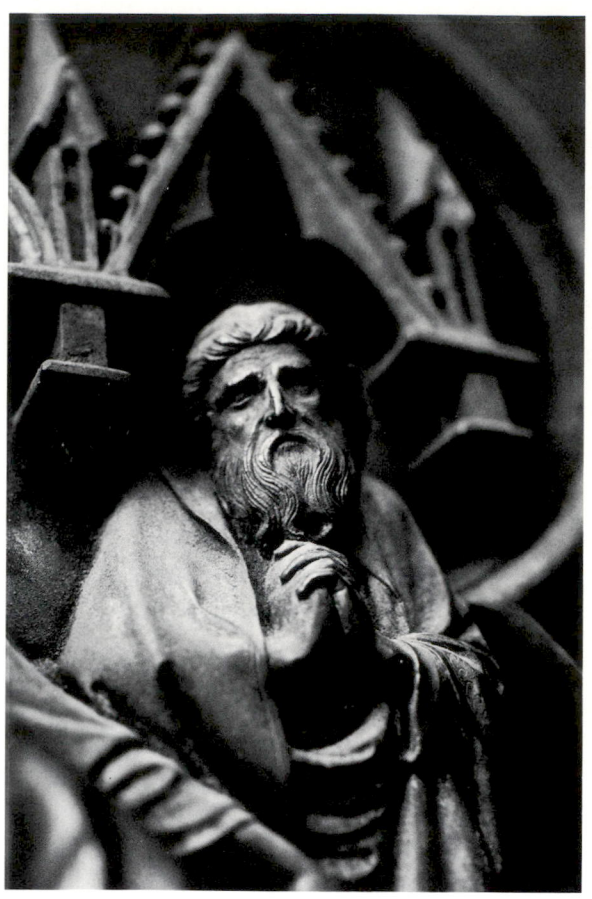

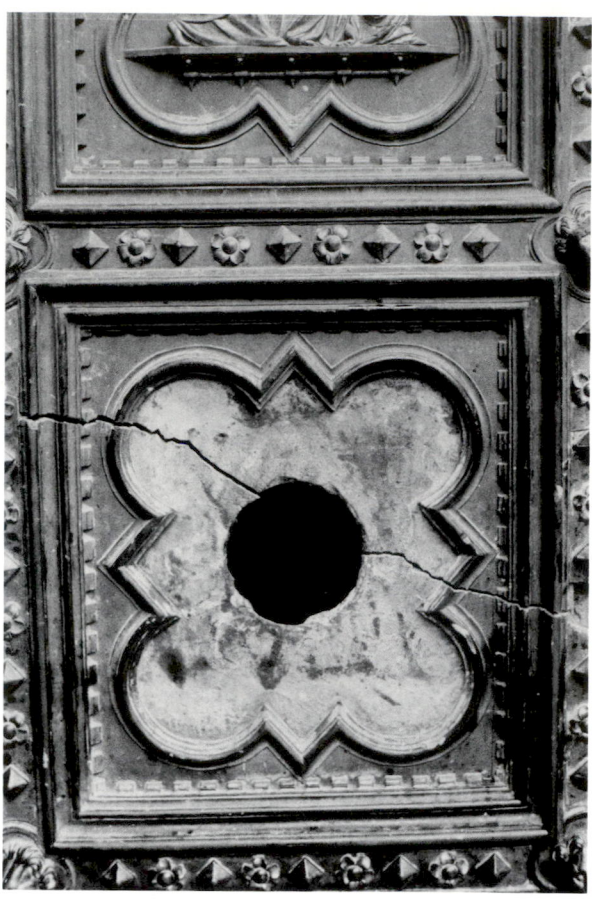

47. Andrea Pisano: *Entombment*, detail. Florence, Baptistry doors

48. Florence Baptistry doors. Framework, detail (*Charity* removed)

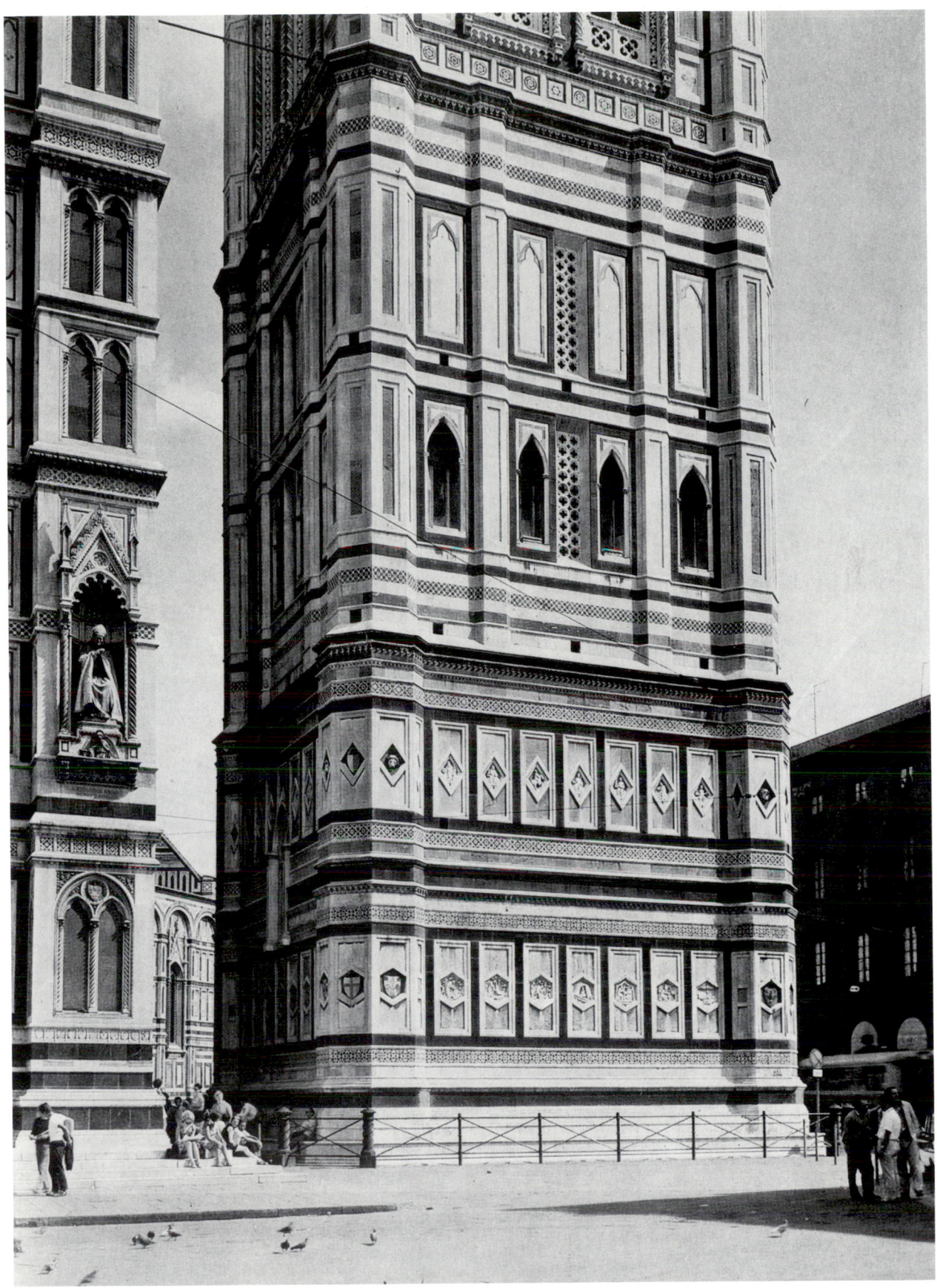

49. Florence Campanile

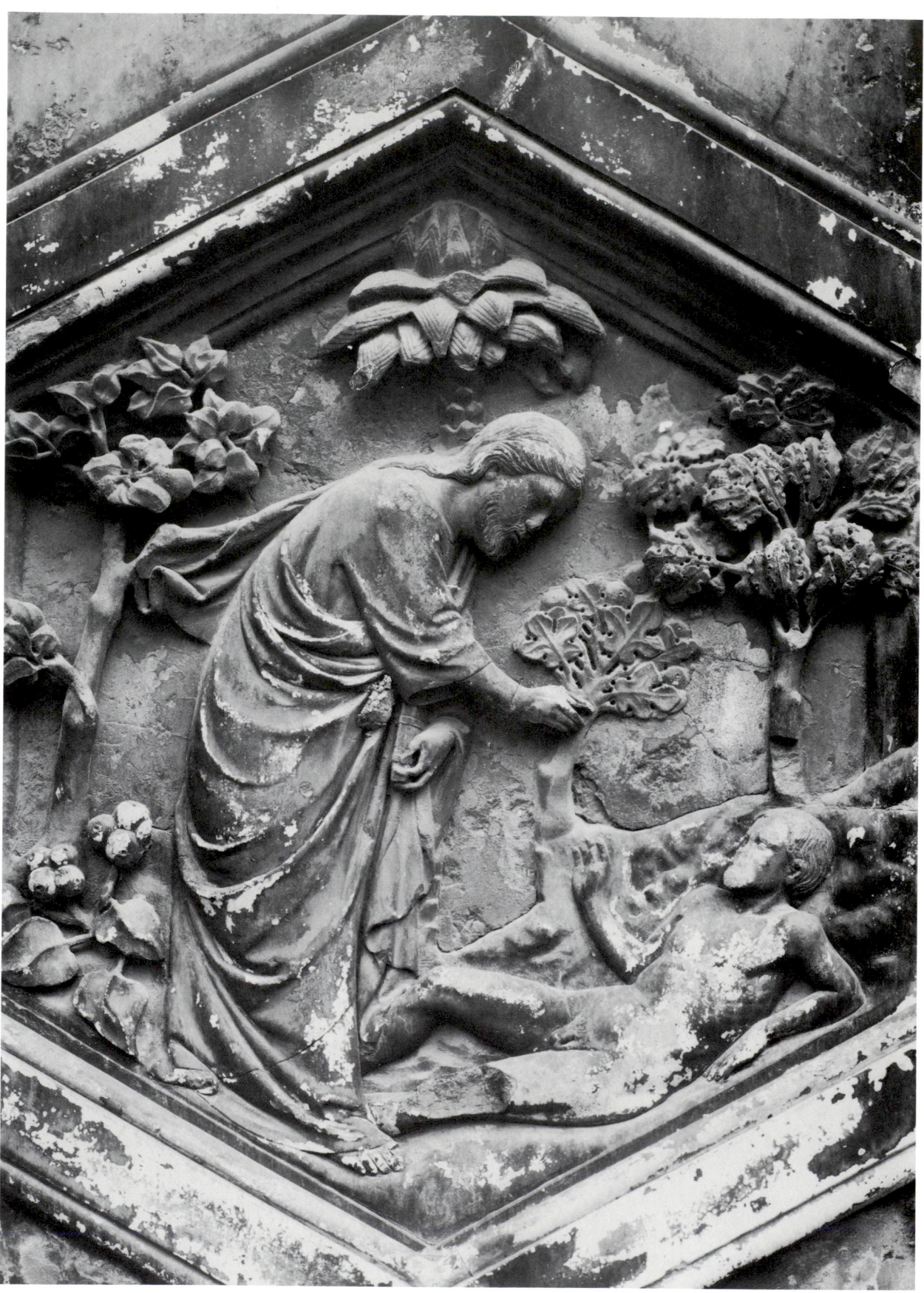

50. Andrea Pisano: *Creation of Adam* (ht 83 cm, width 69 cm). Florence, Museo dell'Opera del Duomo

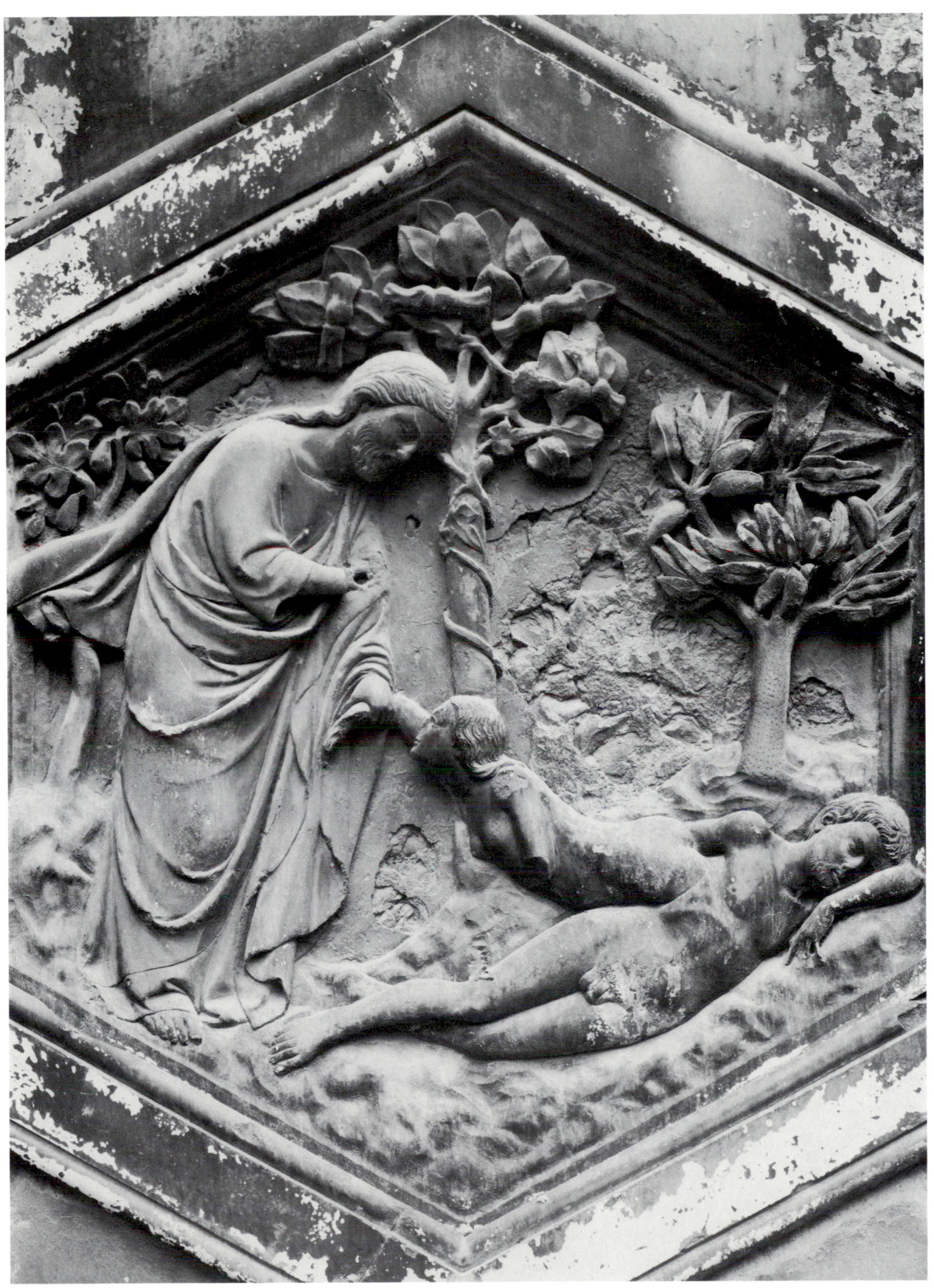

51. Andrea Pisano: *Creation of Eve* (ht 83 cm, width 69 cm). Florence, Museo dell'Opera del Duomo

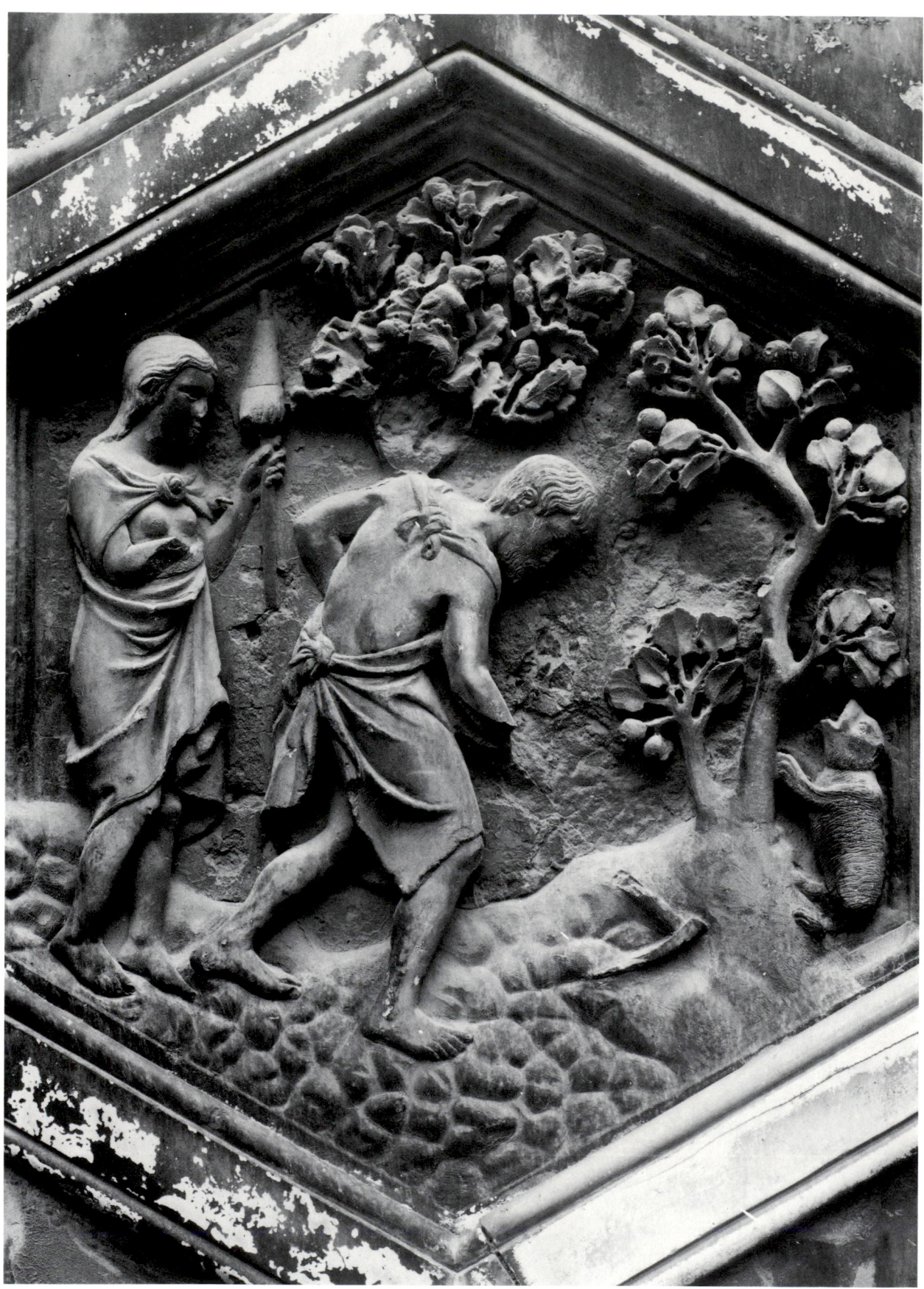

52. Andrea Pisano workshop: *Labors of Adam and Eve* (ht 83 cm, width 69 cm). Florence, Museo dell'Opera del Duomo

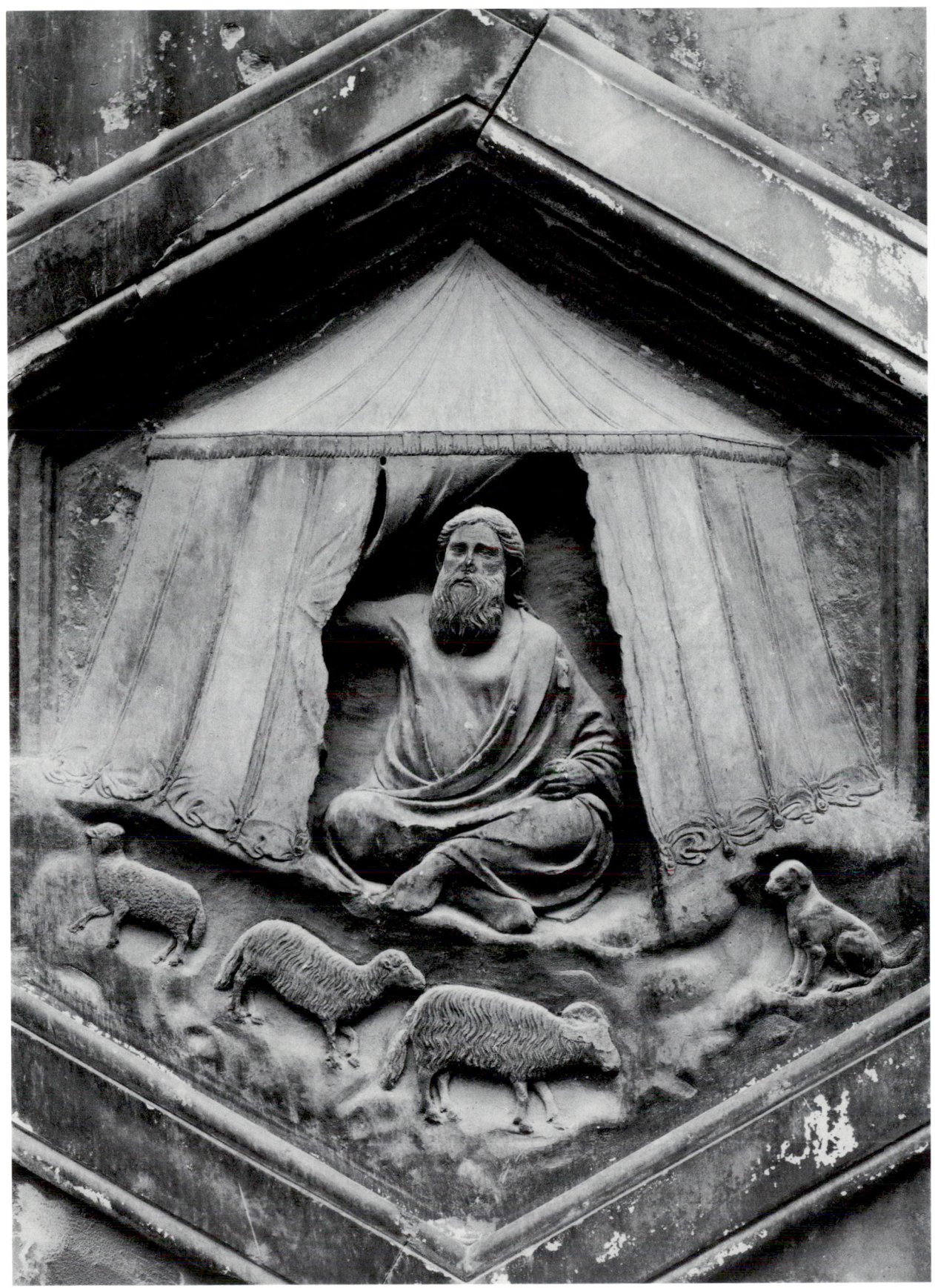

53. Andrea Pisano workshop: *Jabal* (ht 83 cm, width 69 cm). Florence, Museo dell'Opera del Duomo

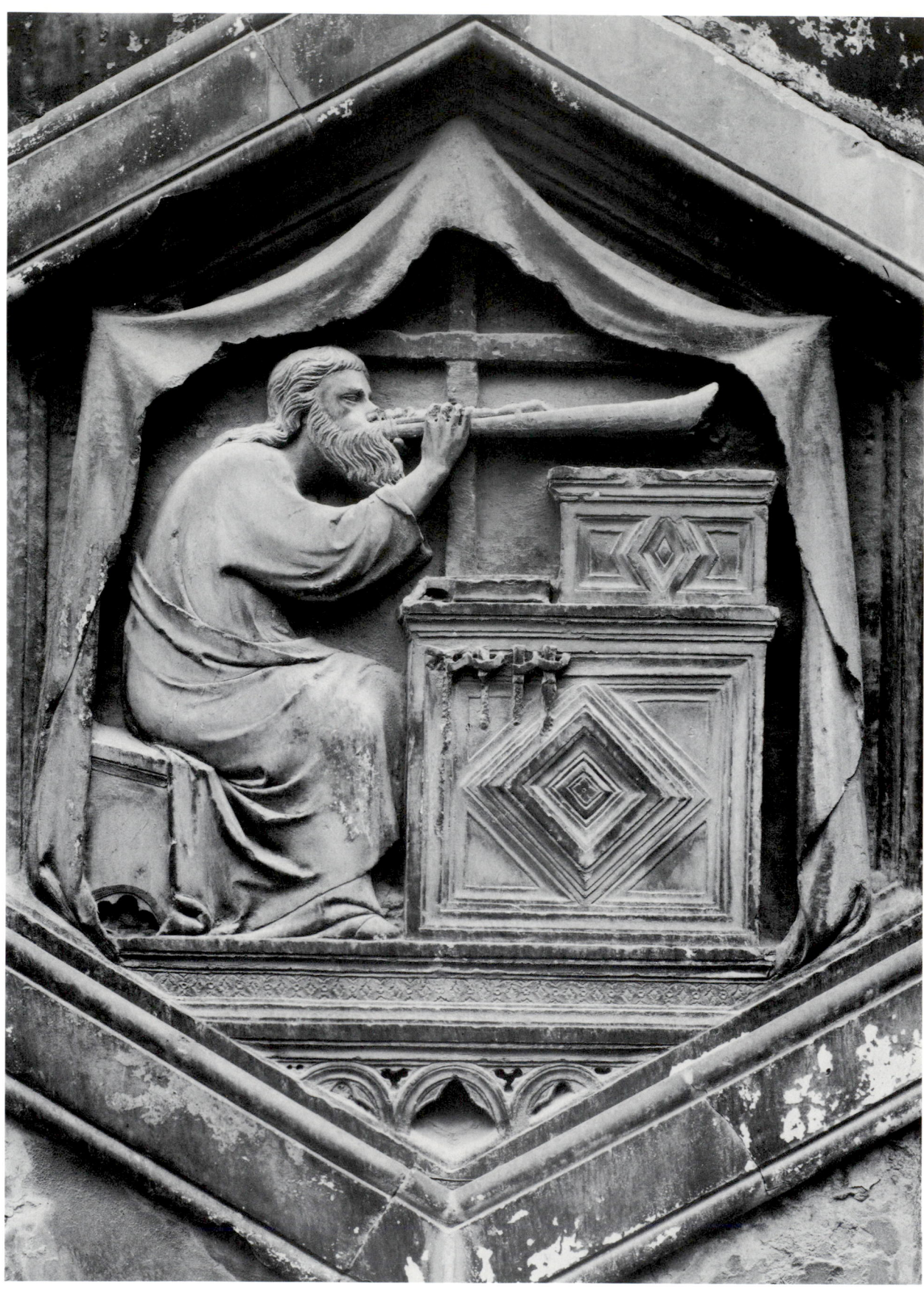

54. Andrea Pisano workshop: *Jubal* (ht 83 cm, width 69 cm). Florence, Museo dell'Opera del Duomo

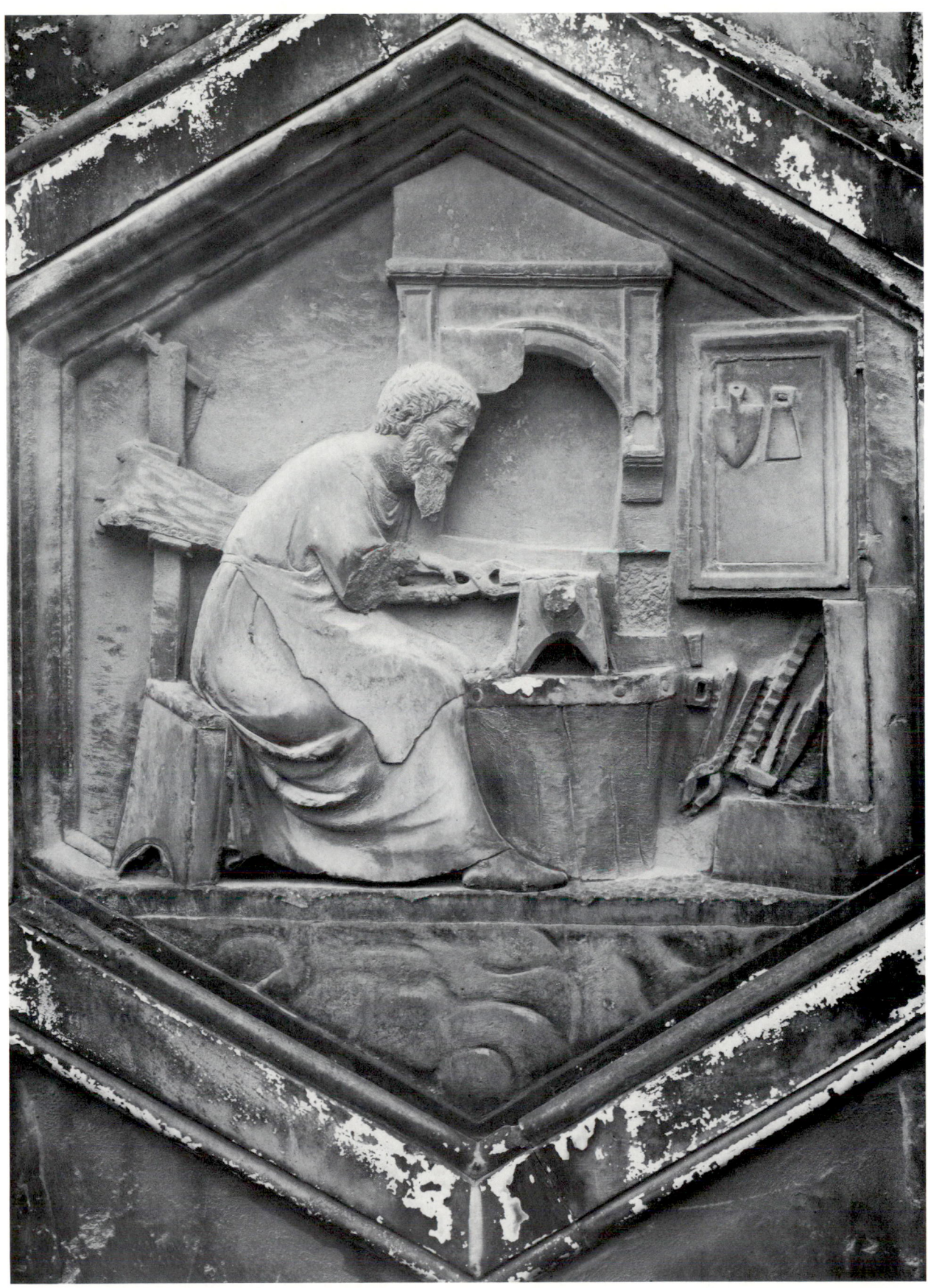

55. Andrea Pisano workshop: *Tubalcain* (ht 83 cm, width 69 cm). Florence, Museo dell'Opera del Duomo

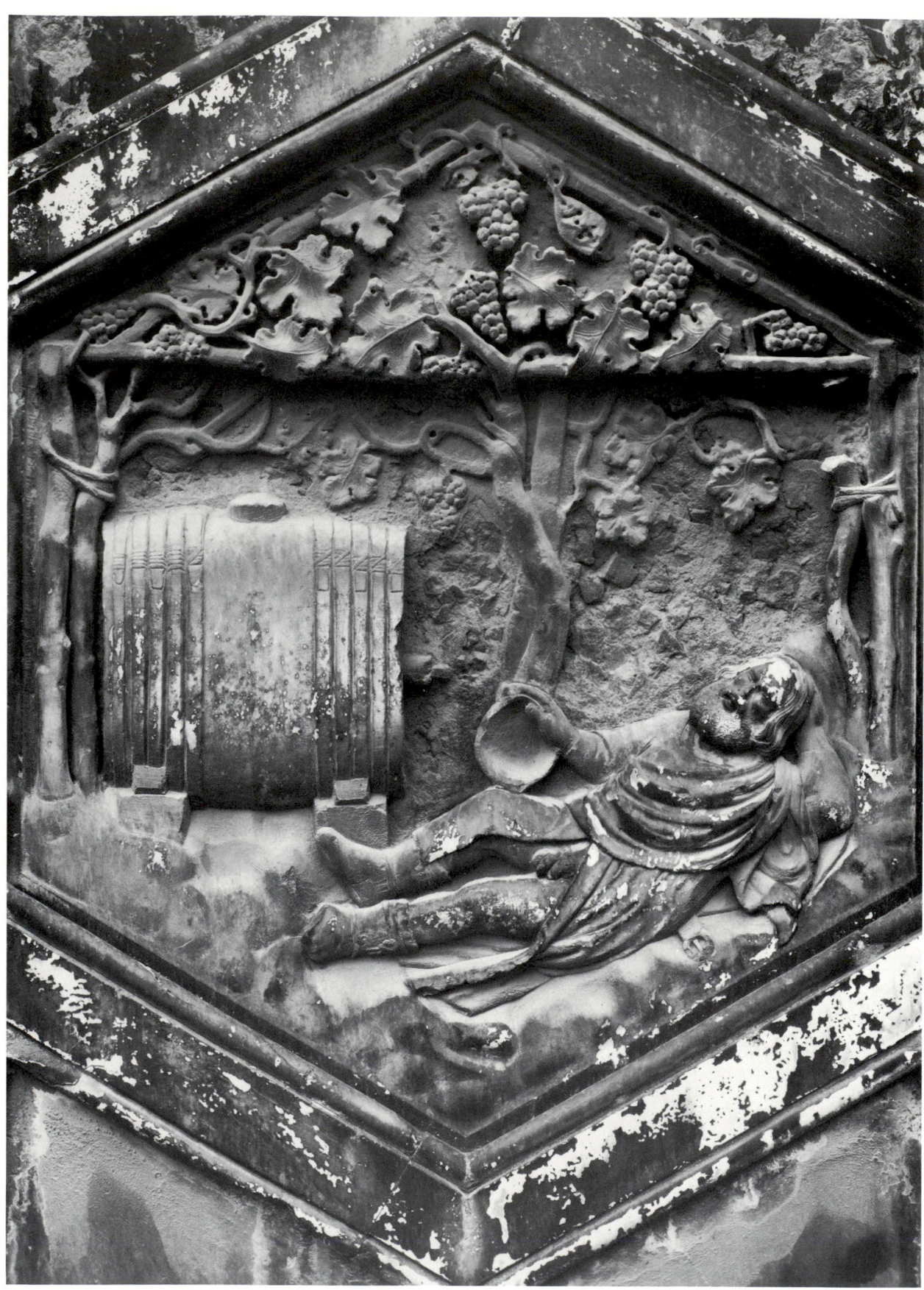

56. Andrea Pisano workshop: *Noah* (ht 83 cm, width 69 cm). Florence, Museo dell'Opera del Duomo

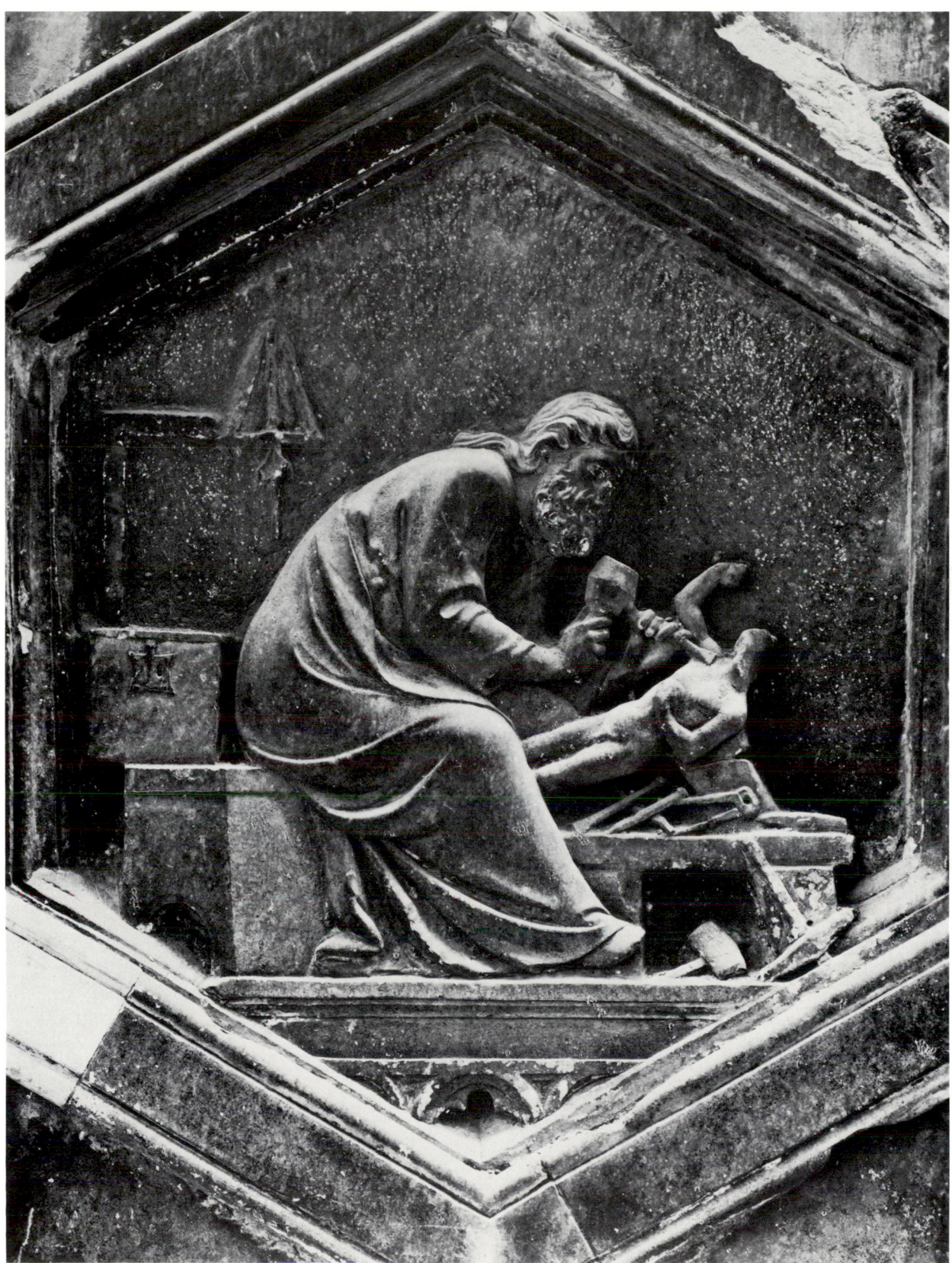

57. Andrea Pisano: *Sculpture* (ht 83 cm, width 69 cm). Florence, Museo dell'Opera del Duomo

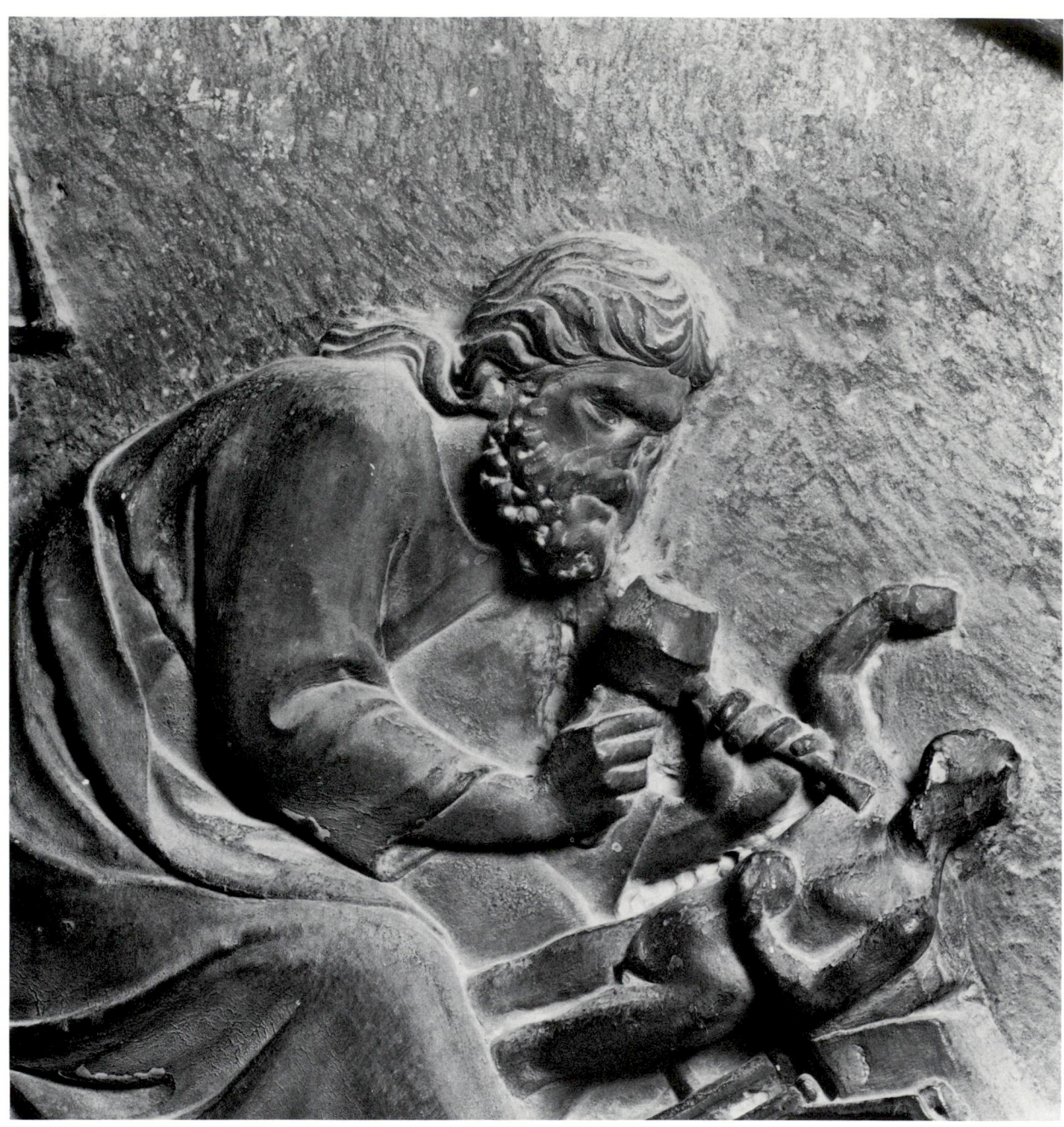

58. Andrea Pisano: *Sculpture*, detail. Florence, Museo dell'Opera del Duomo

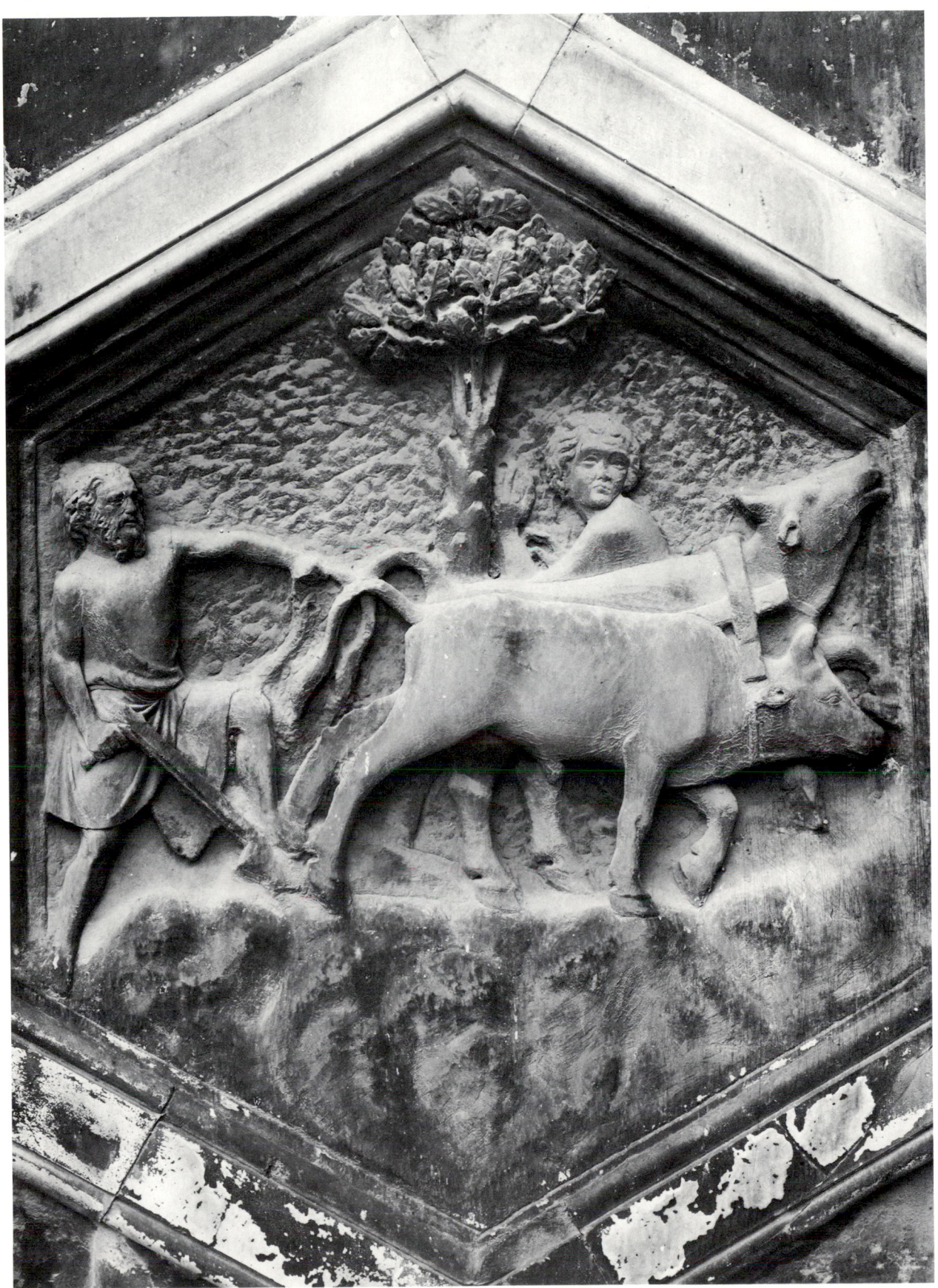

59. Andrea Pisano workshop: *Agriculture* (ht 83 cm, width 69 cm). Florence, Museo dell'Opera del Duomo

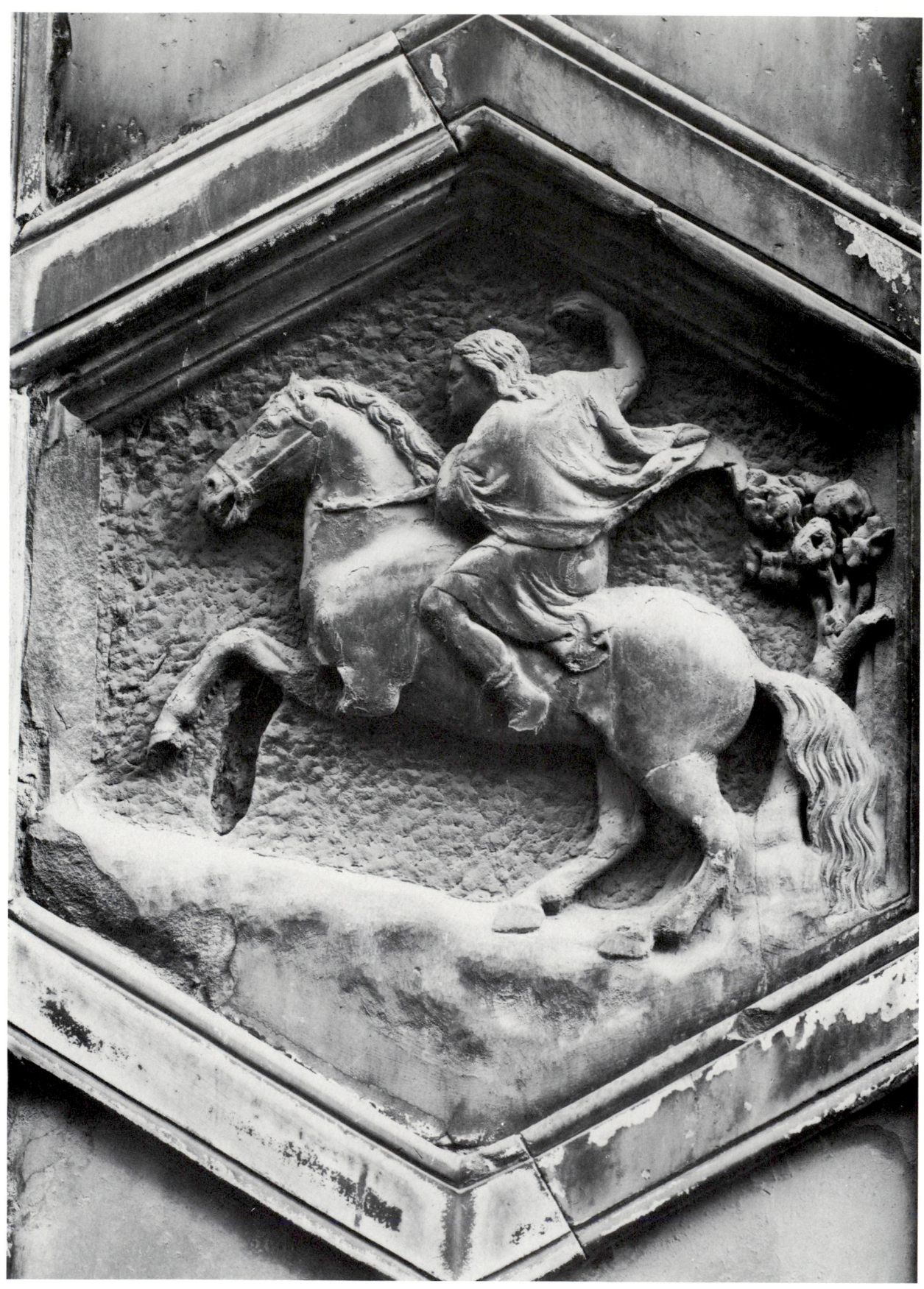

60. Andrea Pisano: *Horsemanship* (ht 83 cm, width 69 cm). Florence, Museo dell'Opera del Duomo

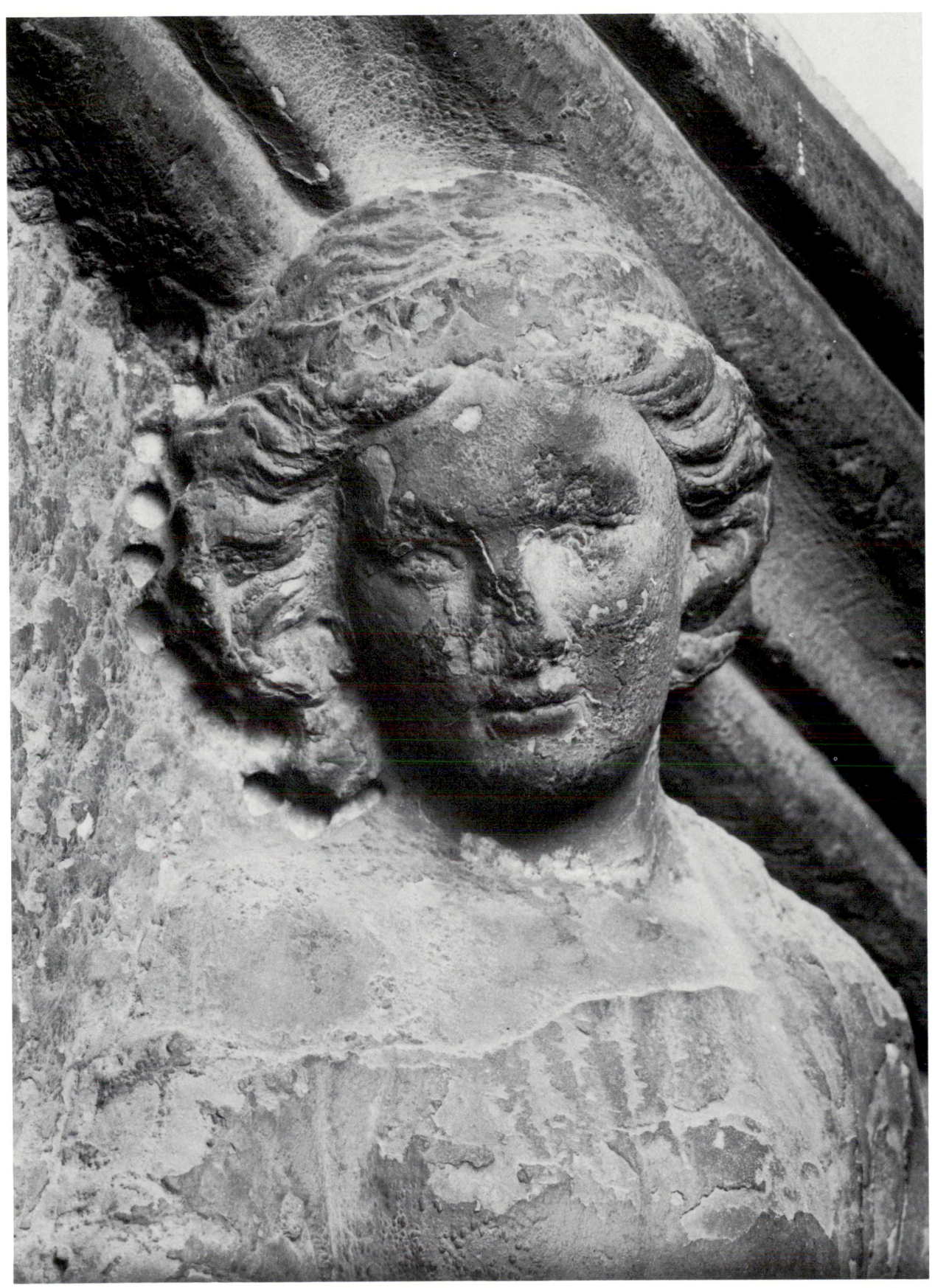

61. Andrea Pisano: *Weaving*, detail. Florence, Museo dell'Opera del Duomo

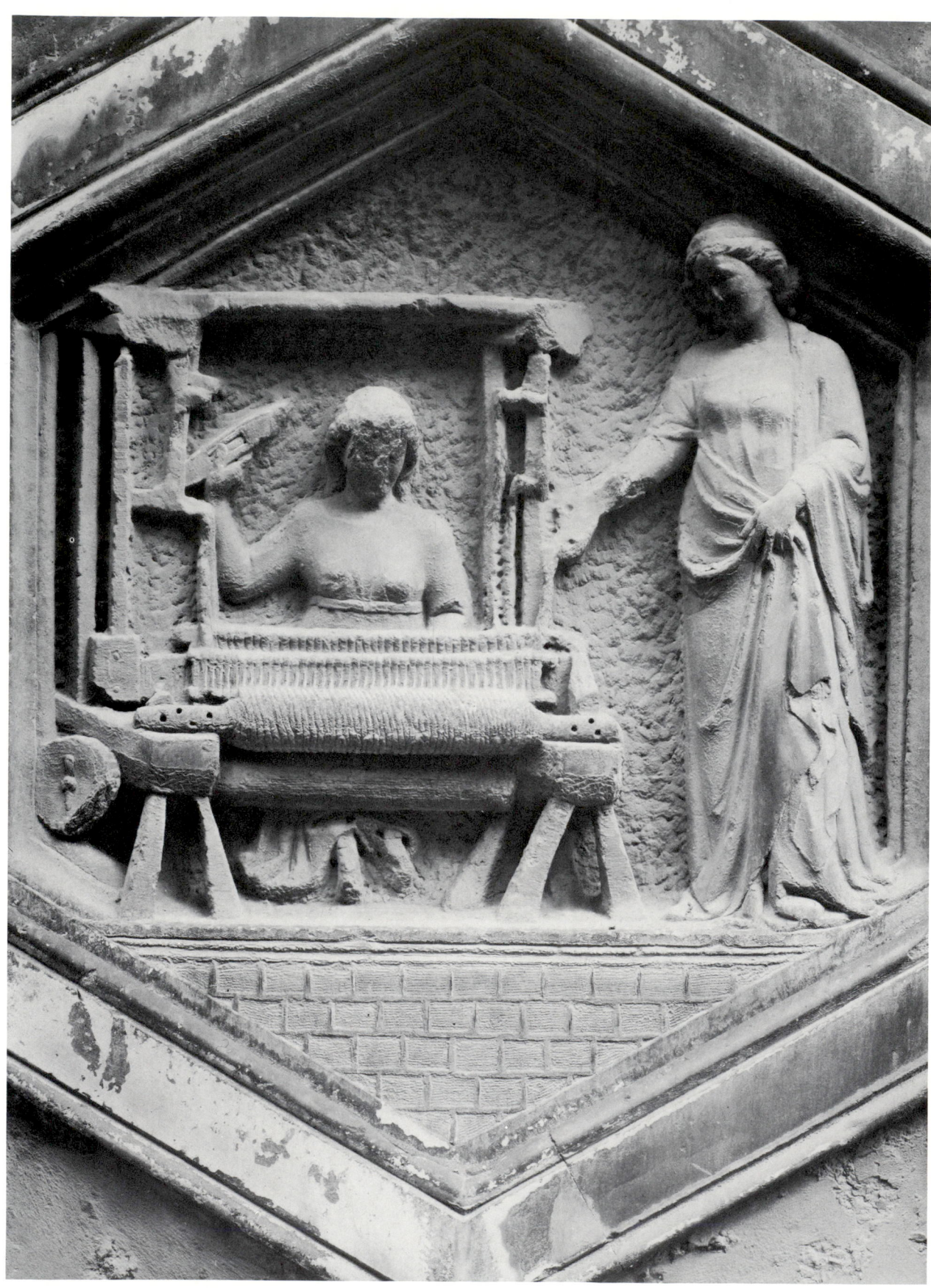

62. Andrea Pisano: *Weaving* (ht 83 cm, width 69 cm). Florence, Museo dell'Opera del Duomo

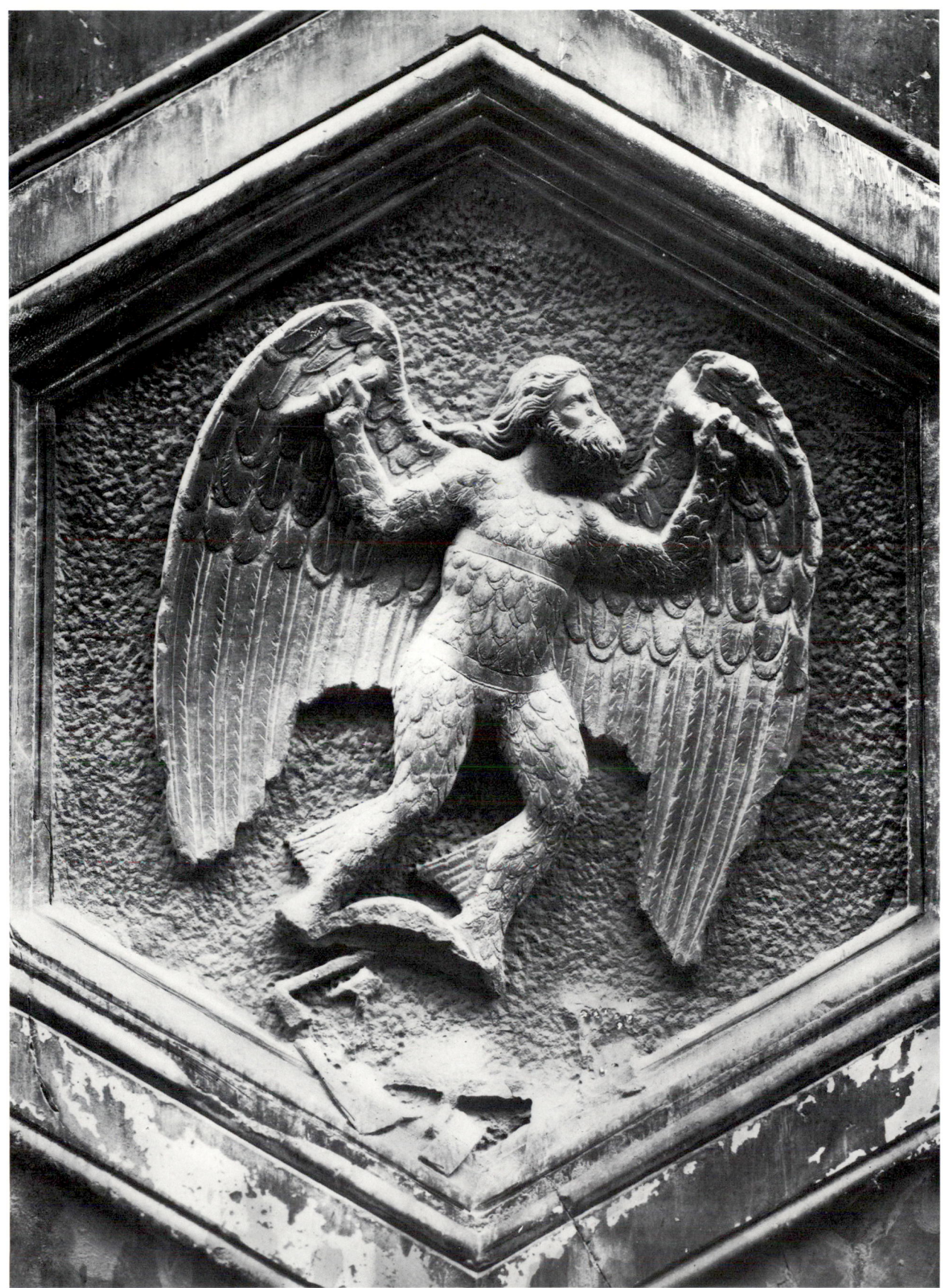

63. Andrea Pisano: *Daedalus* (ht 83 cm, width 69 cm). Florence, Museo dell'Opera del Duomo

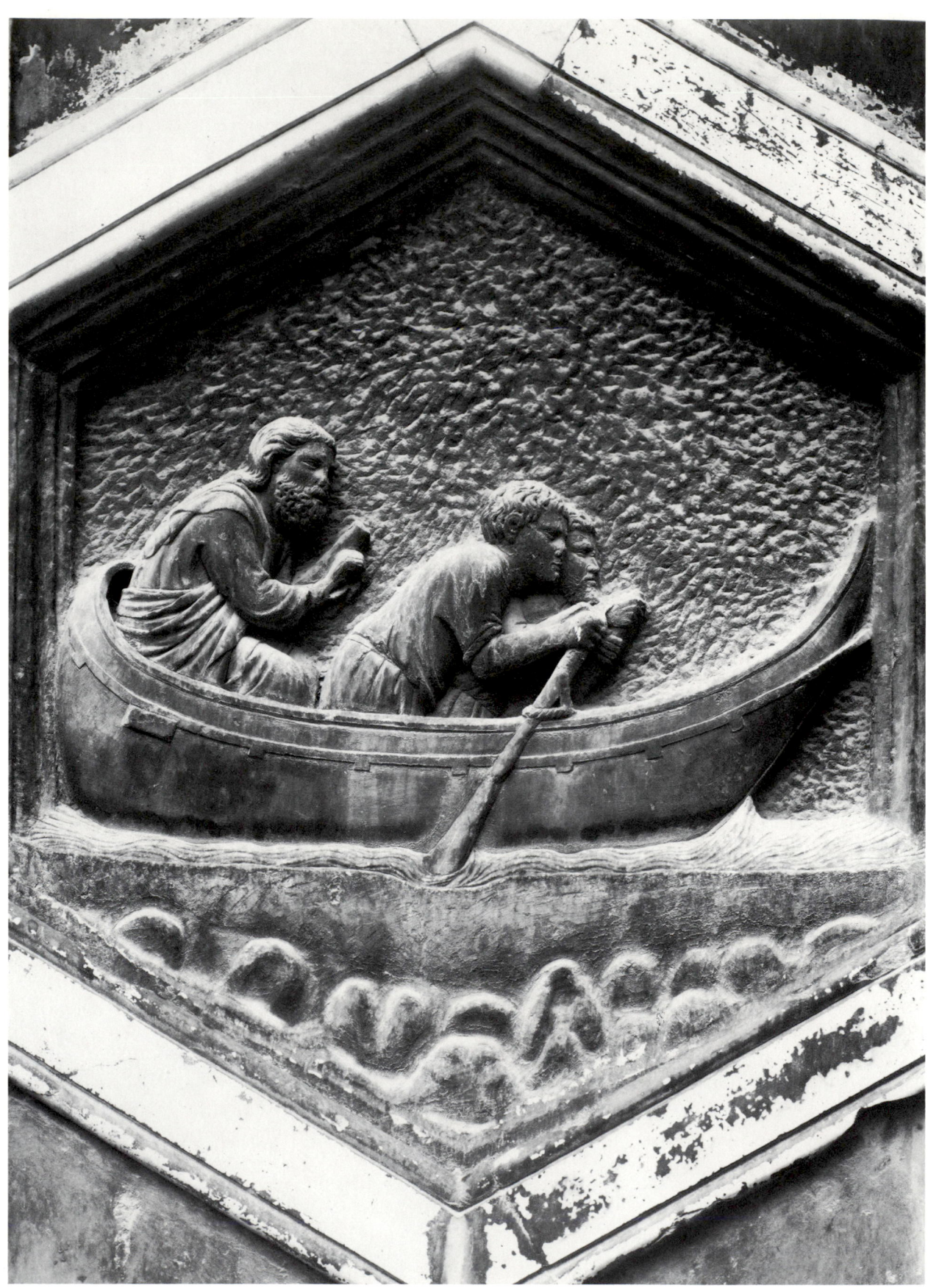

64. Andrea Pisano workshop: *Navigation* (ht 83 cm, width 69 cm). Florence, Museo dell'Opera del Duomo

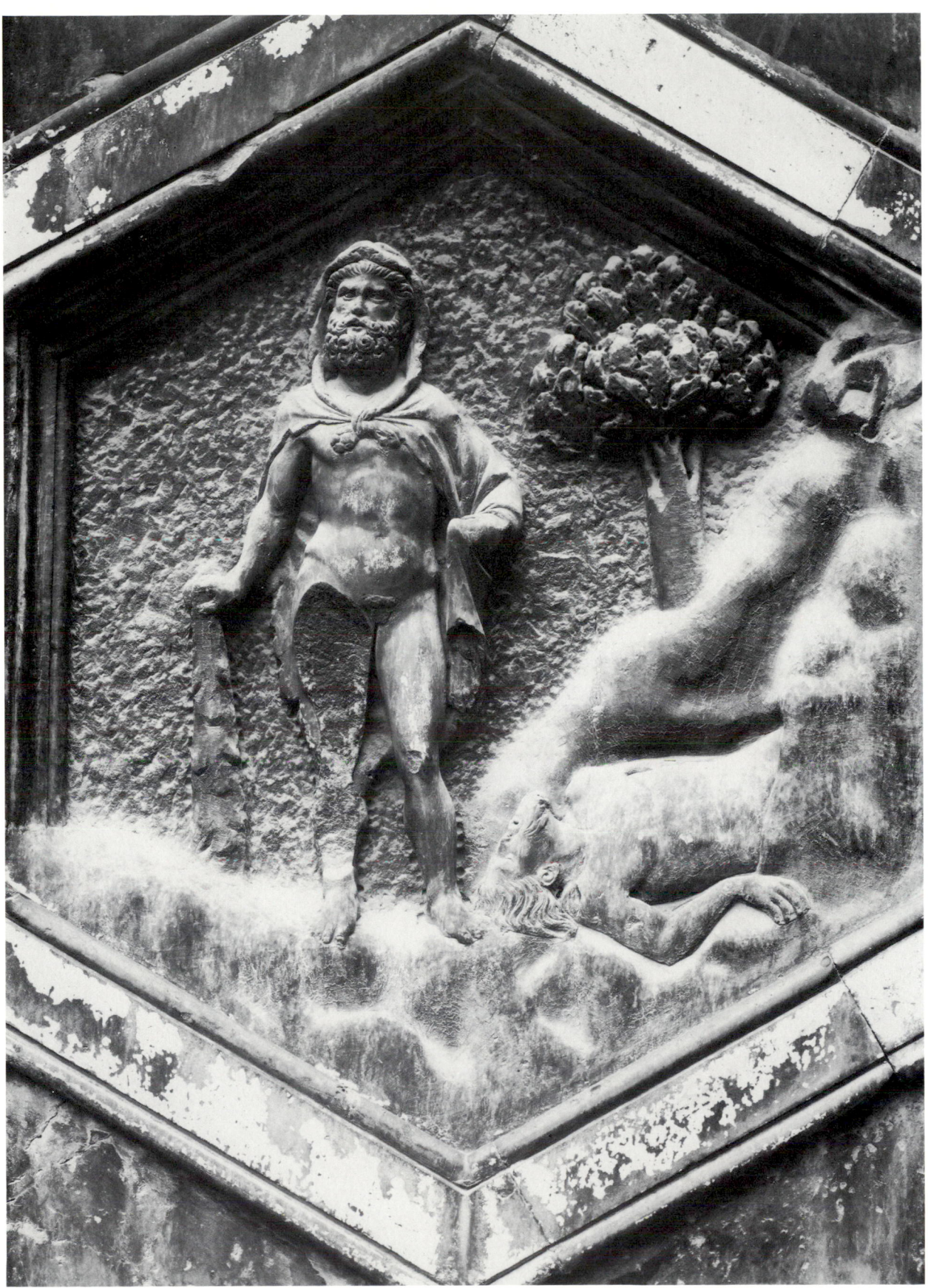

65. Andrea Pisano workshop: *Hercules* (ht 83 cm, width 69 cm). Florence, Museo dell'Opera del Duomo

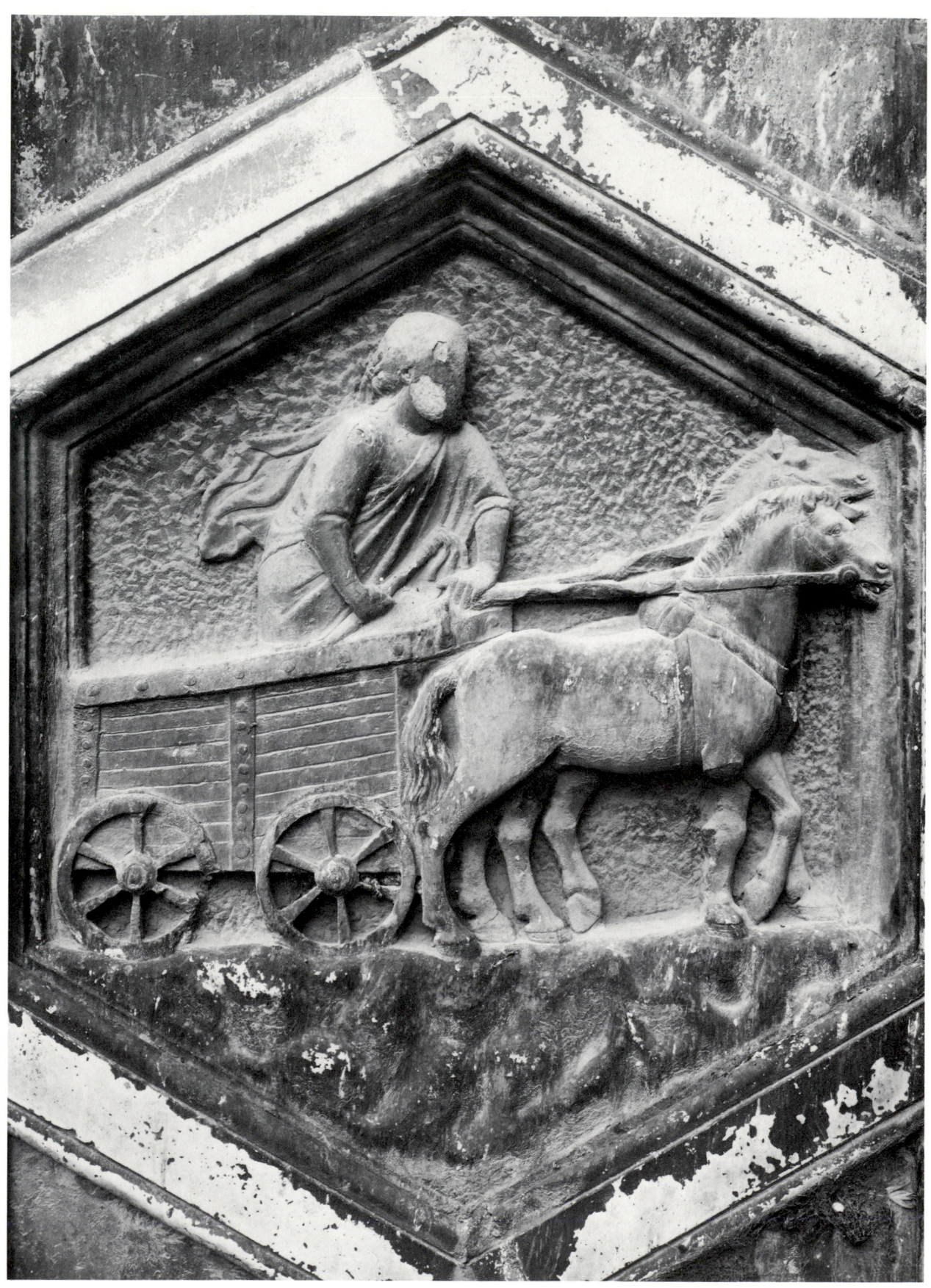

66. Andrea Pisano workshop: *Trade* (ht 83 cm, width 69 cm). Florence, Museo dell'Opera del Duomo

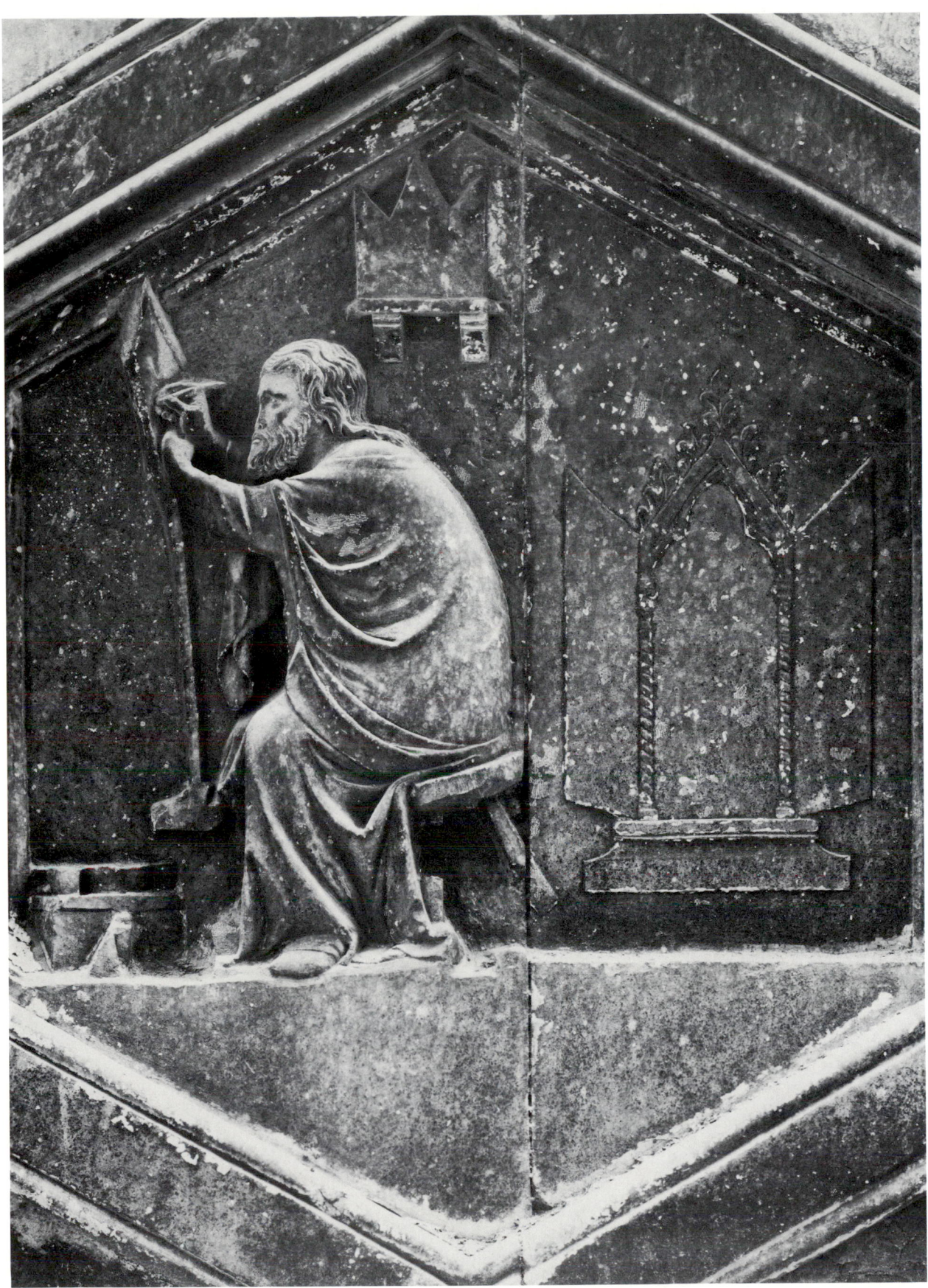

67. Andrea Pisano workshop: *Painting* (ht 83 cm, width 69 cm). Florence, Museo dell'Opera del Duomo

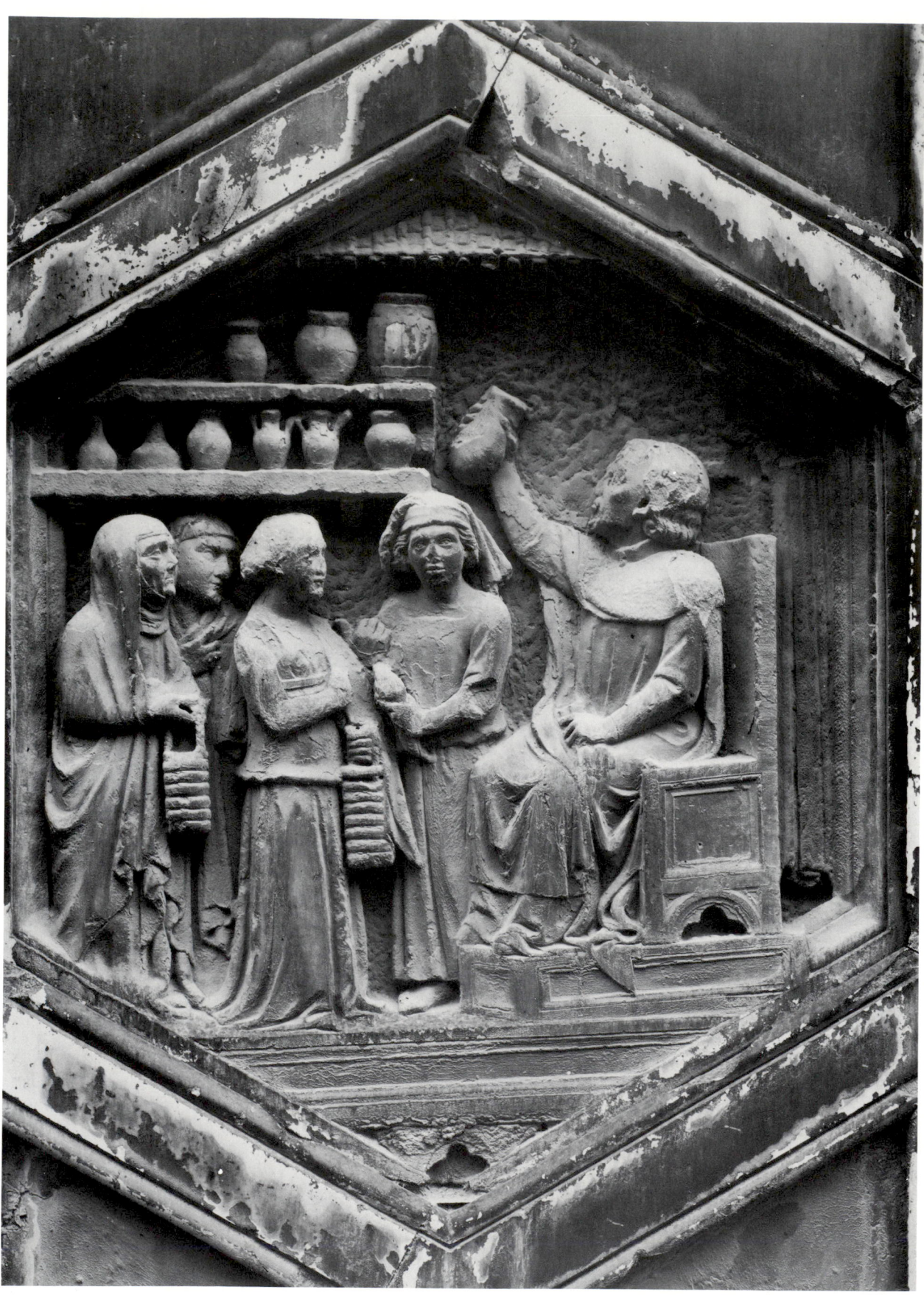

68. Andrea Pisano workshop: *Medicine* (ht 83 cm, width 69 cm). Florence, Museo dell'Opera del Duomo

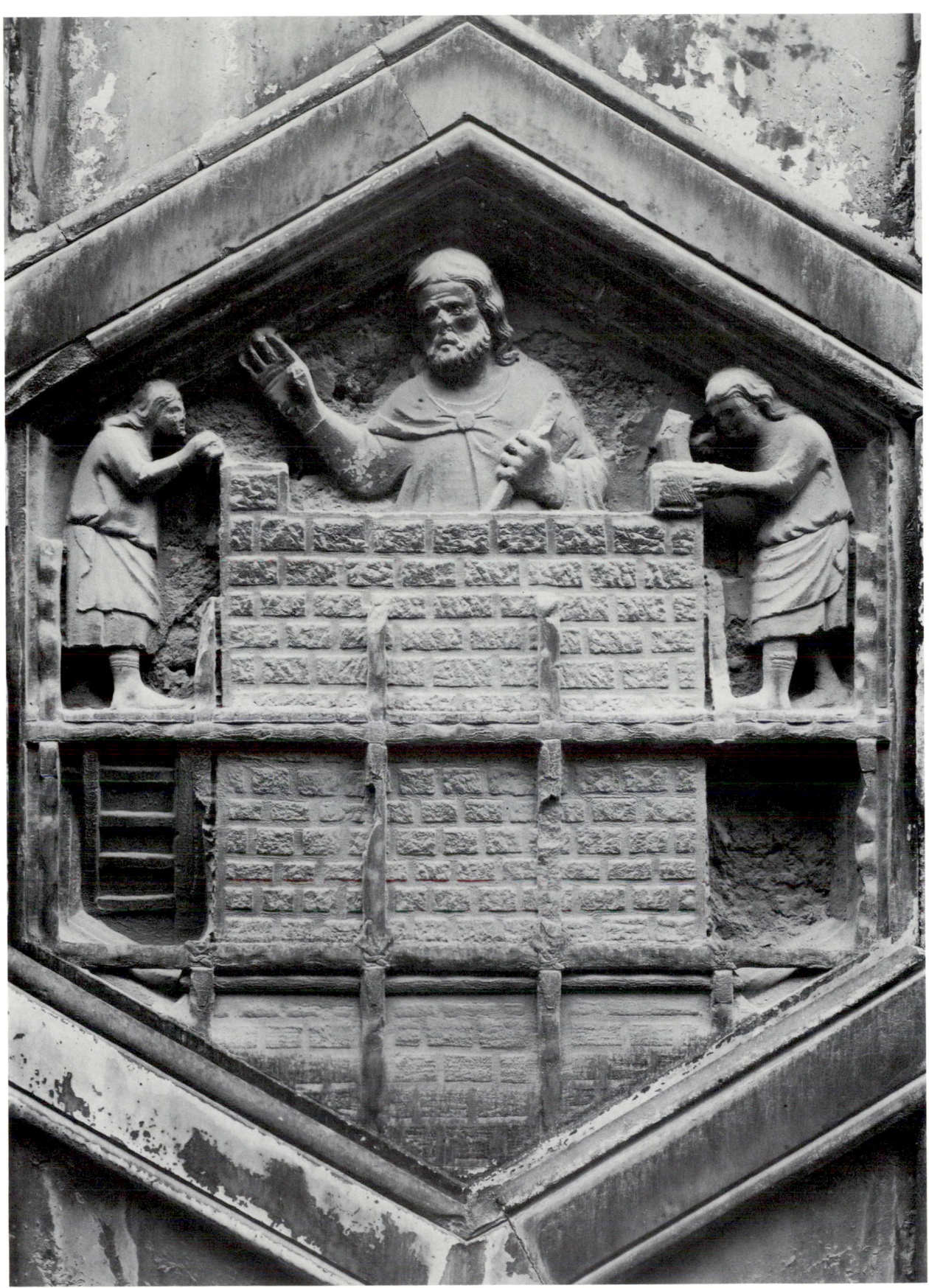

69. Campanile workshop, after 1343: *Construction* (ht 83 cm, width 69 cm). Florence, Museo dell'Opera del Duomo

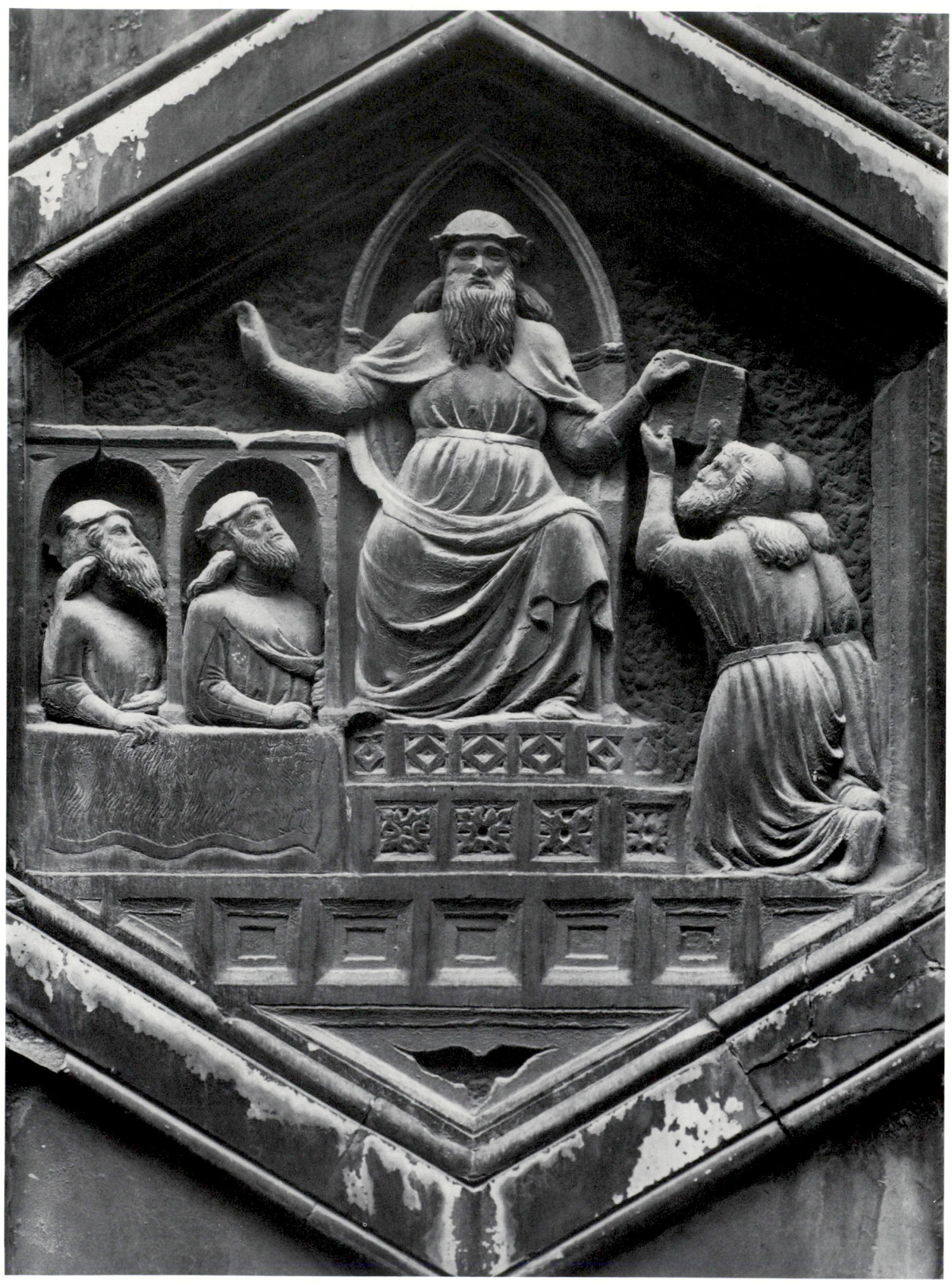

70. Campanile workshop, after 1343: *Law* (ht 83 cm, width 69 cm). Florence, Museo dell'Opera del Duomo

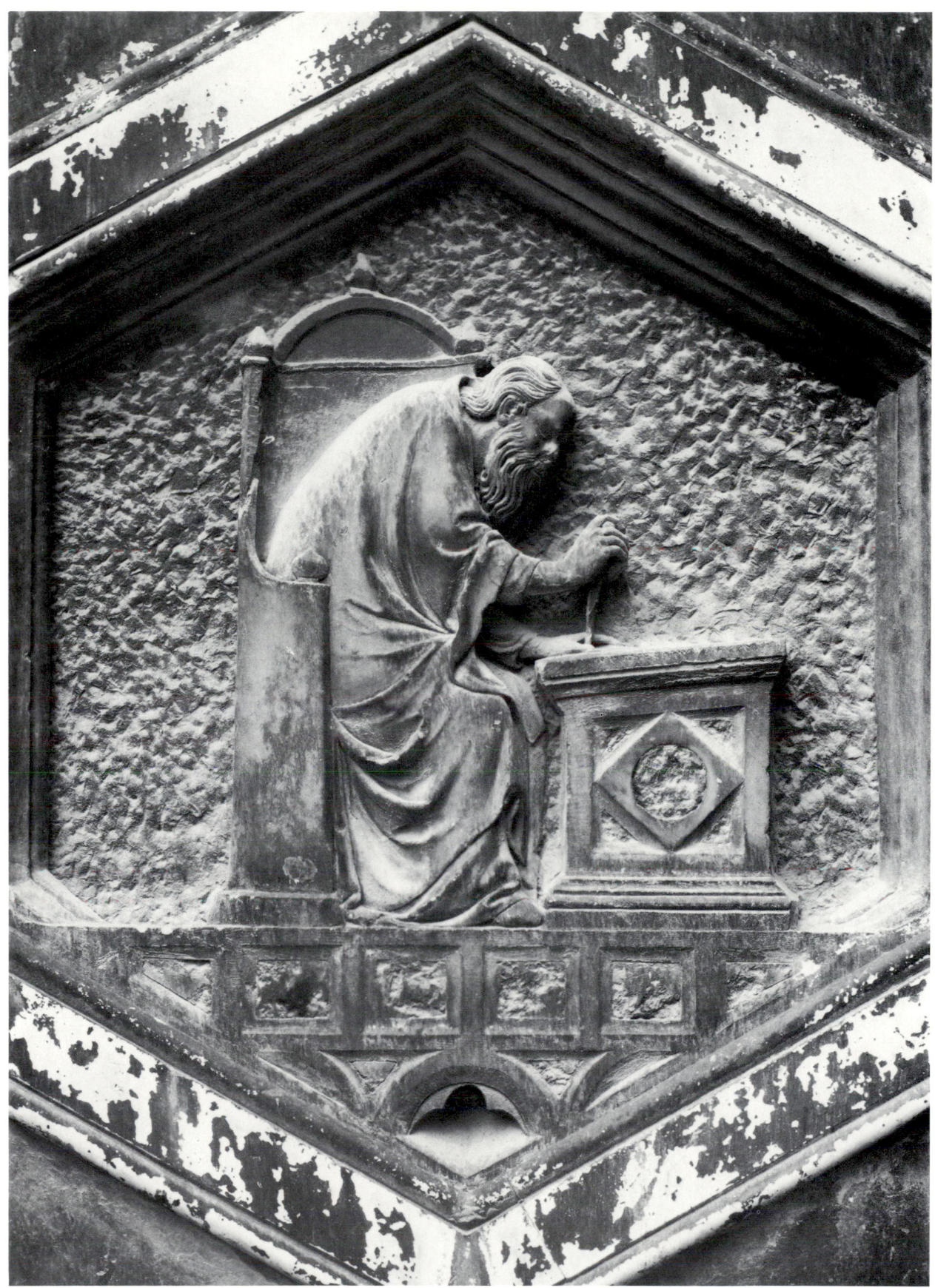

71. Campanile workshop, after 1343: *Geometry* (ht 83 cm, width 69 cm). Florence, Museo dell'Opera del Duomo

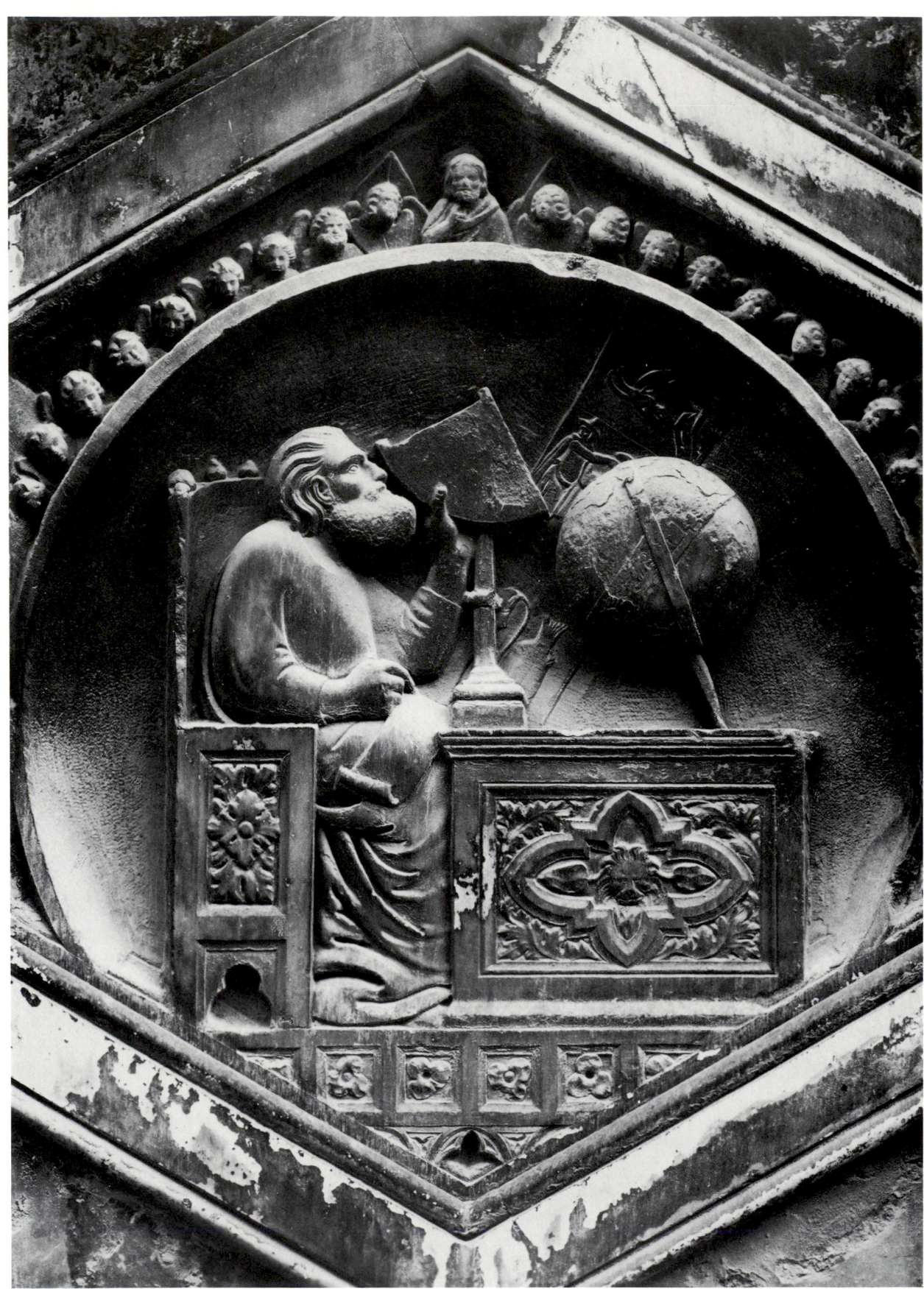

72. Campanile workshop, after 1343: *Astronomy* (ht 83 cm, width 69 cm). Florence, Museo dell'Opera del Duomo

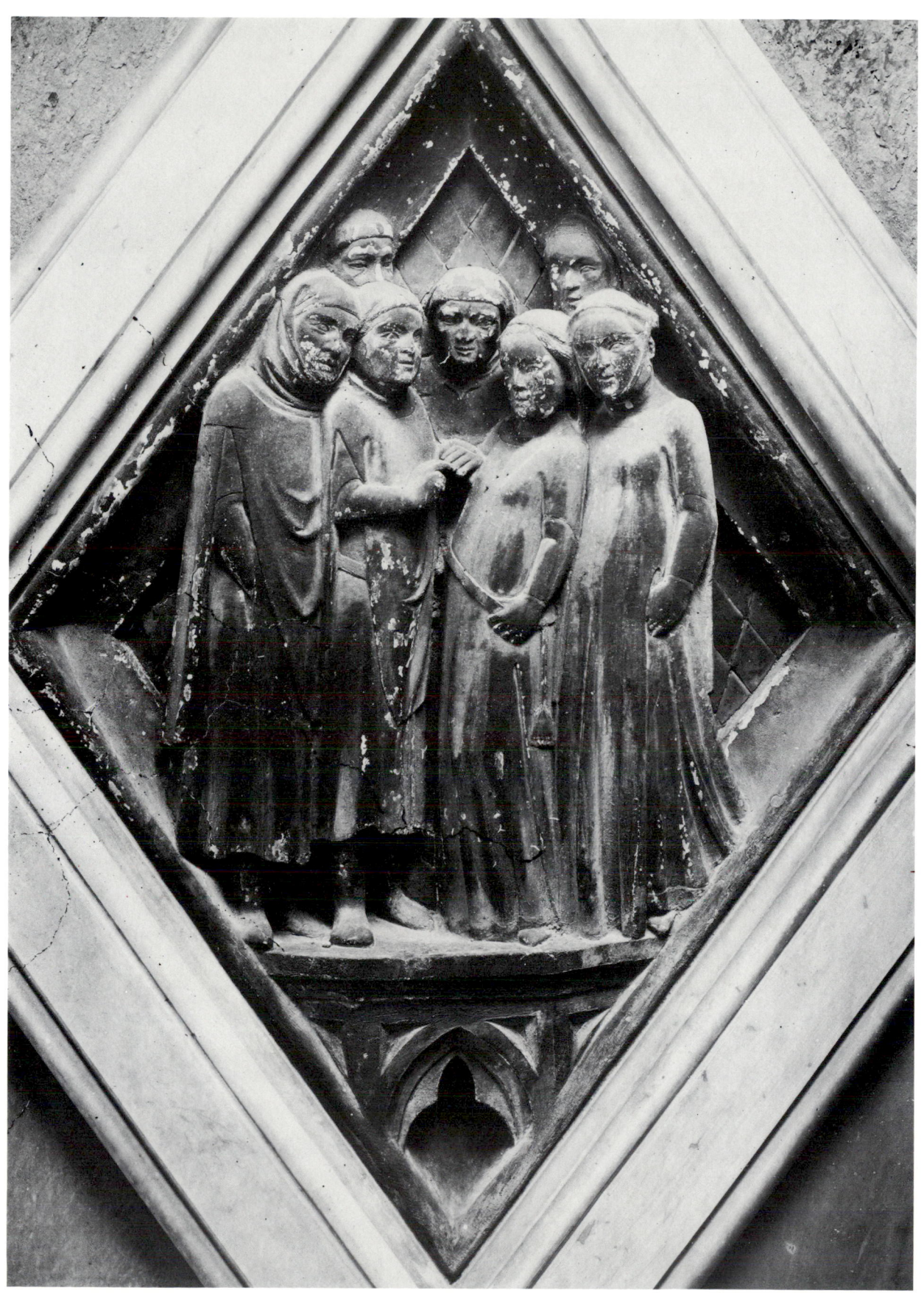

73. Alberto Arnoldi workshop: *Matrimony* (ht 87 cm, width 63.5 cm). Florence, Museo dell'Opera del Duomo

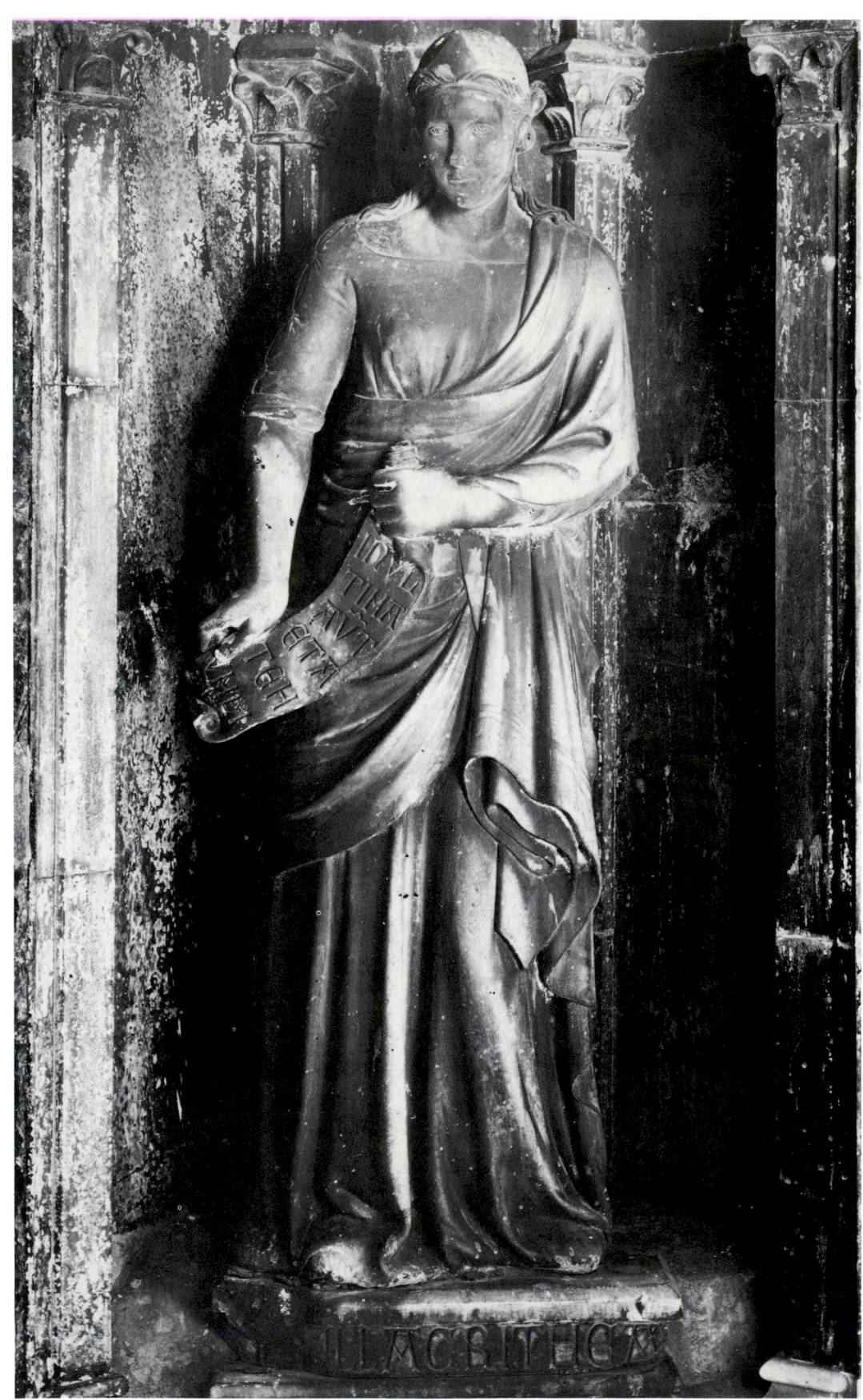

74. Andrea Pisano: *Erythrean Sibyl* (ht 176 cm). Florence, Museo dell'Opera del Duomo

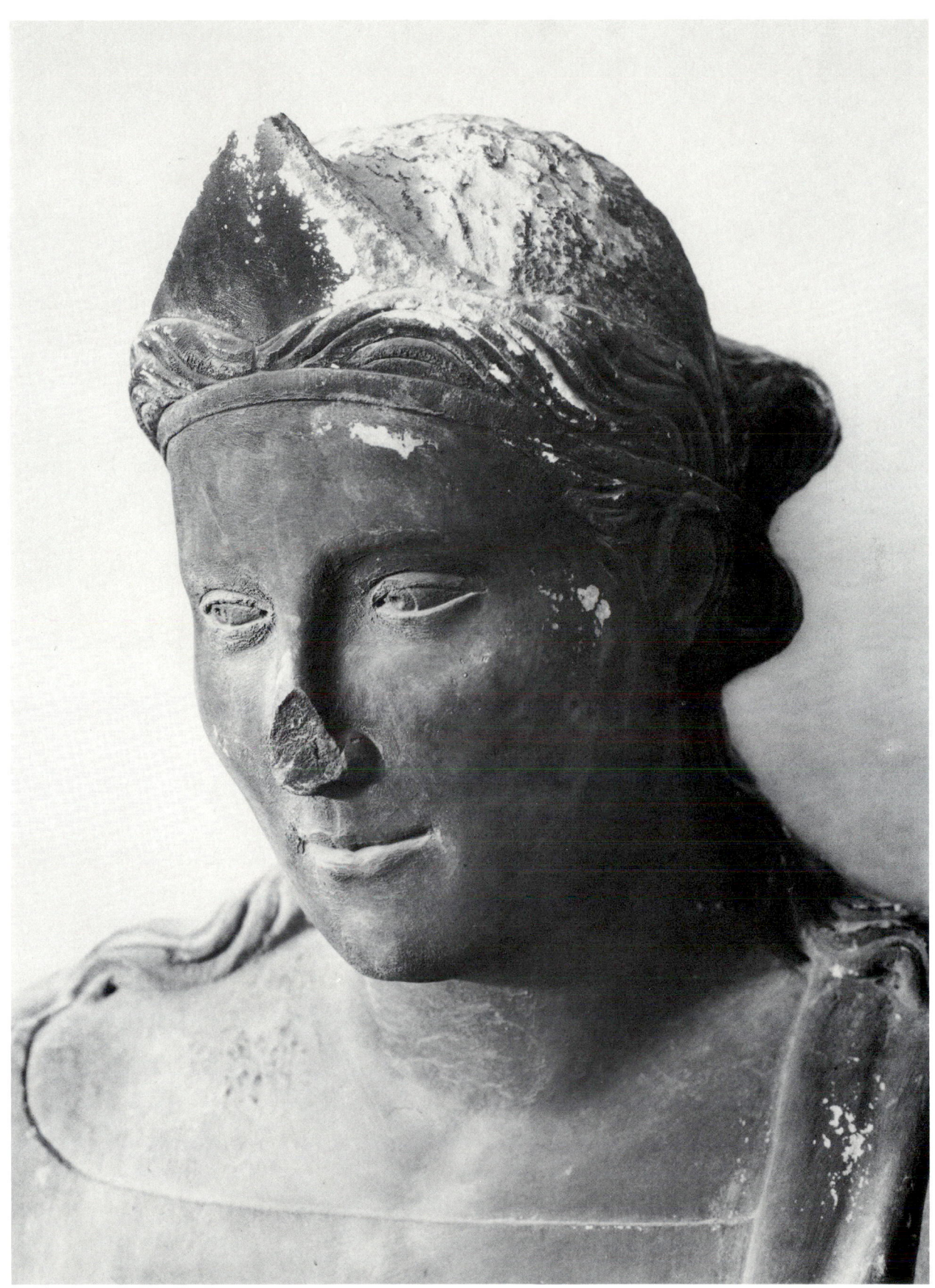

75. Andrea Pisano: *Erythrean Sibyl*, detail. Florence, Museo dell'Opera del Duomo

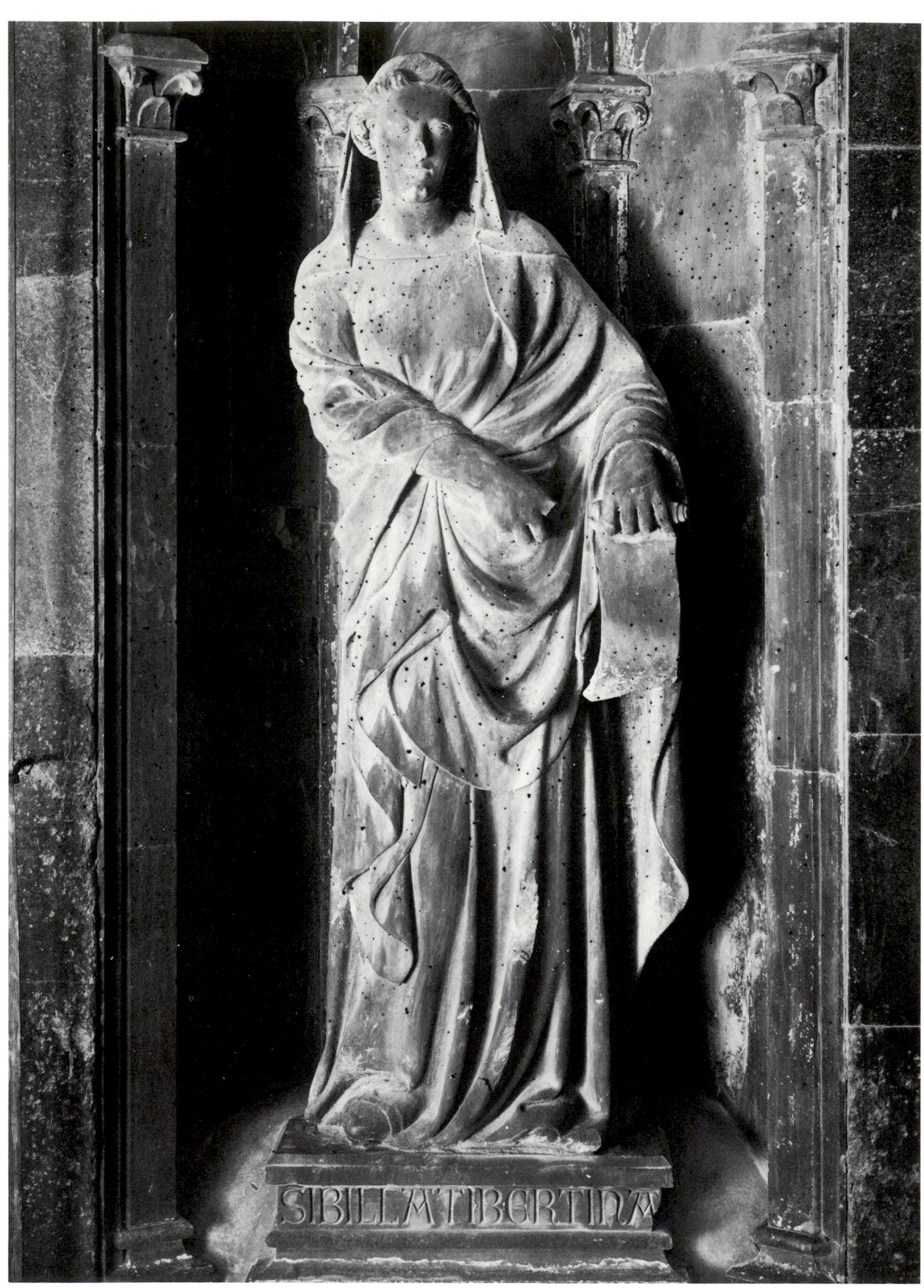

76. Andrea Pisano: *Tiburtine Sibyl* (ht 180 cm). Florence, Museo dell'Opera del Duomo

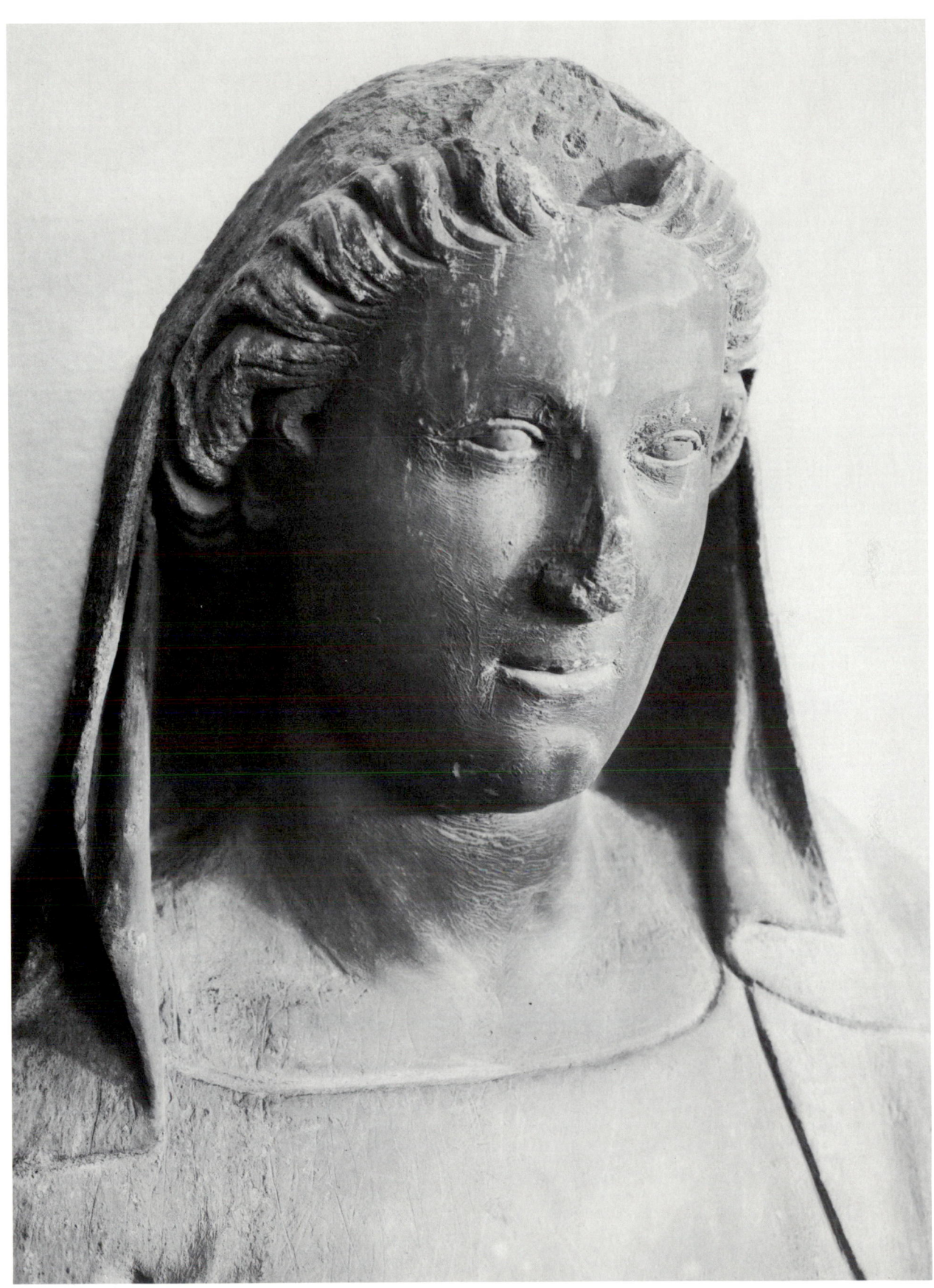

77. Andrea Pisano: *Tiburtine Sibyl*, detail. Florence, Museo dell'Opera del Duomo

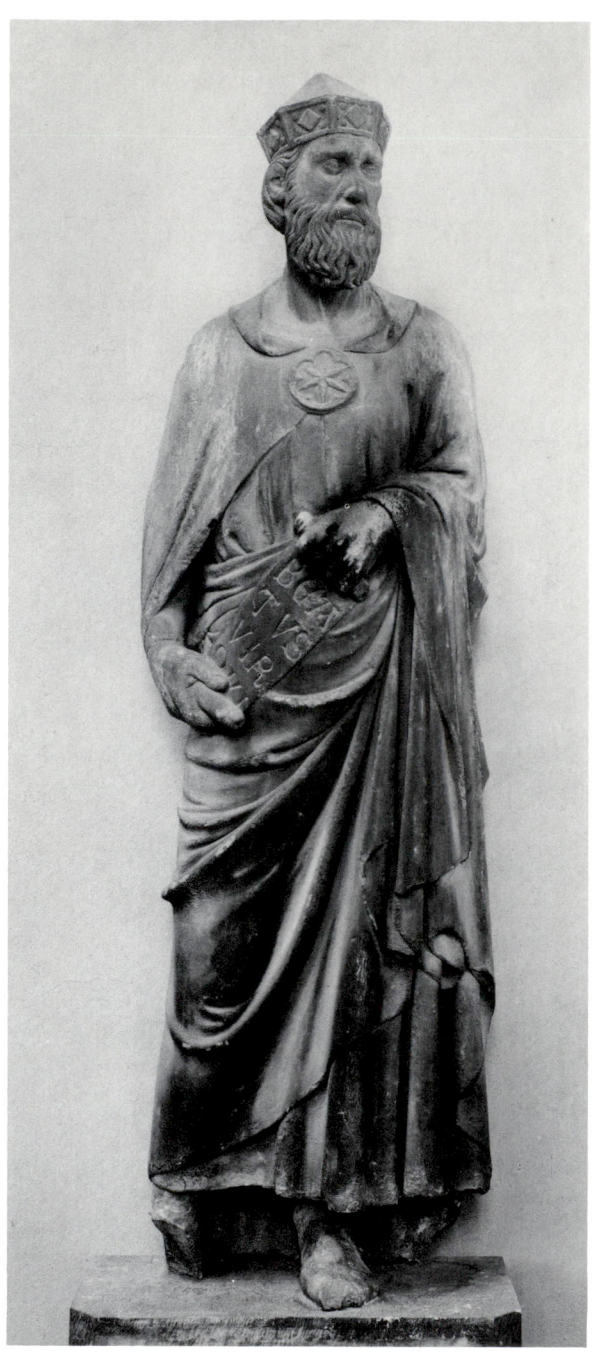

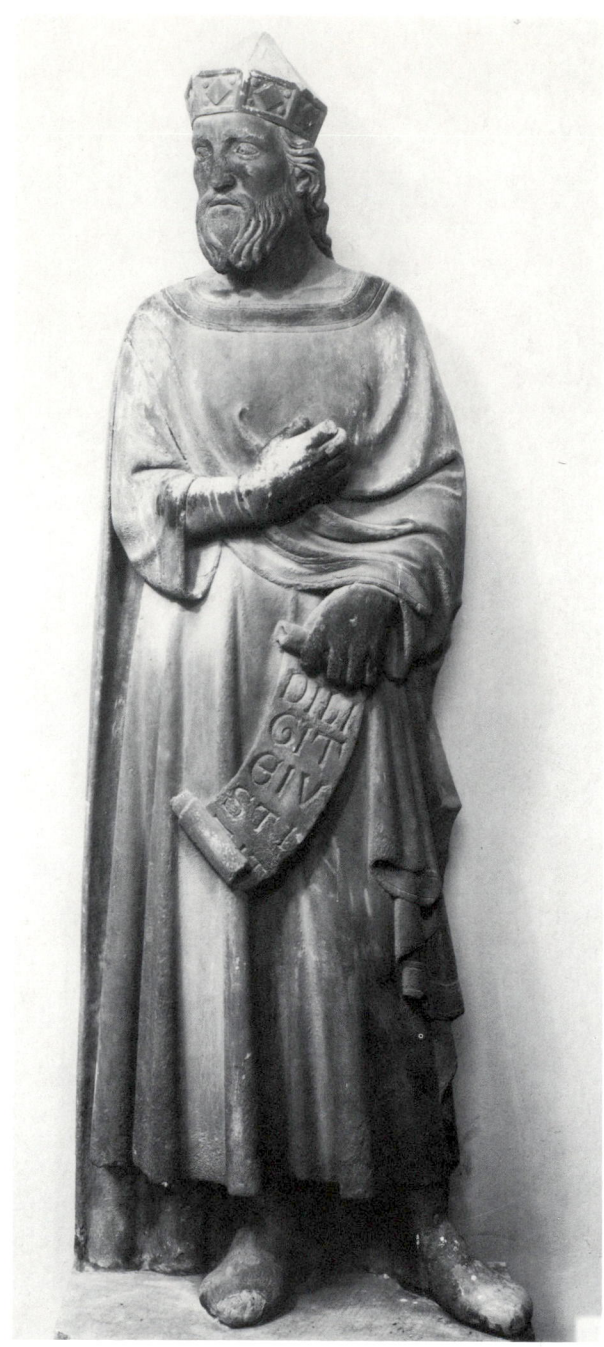

78. Andrea Pisano follower: *David* (ht 188 cm). Florence, Museo dell'Opera del Duomo

79. Andrea Pisano follower: *Solomon* (ht 191 cm). Florence, Museo dell'Opera del Duomo

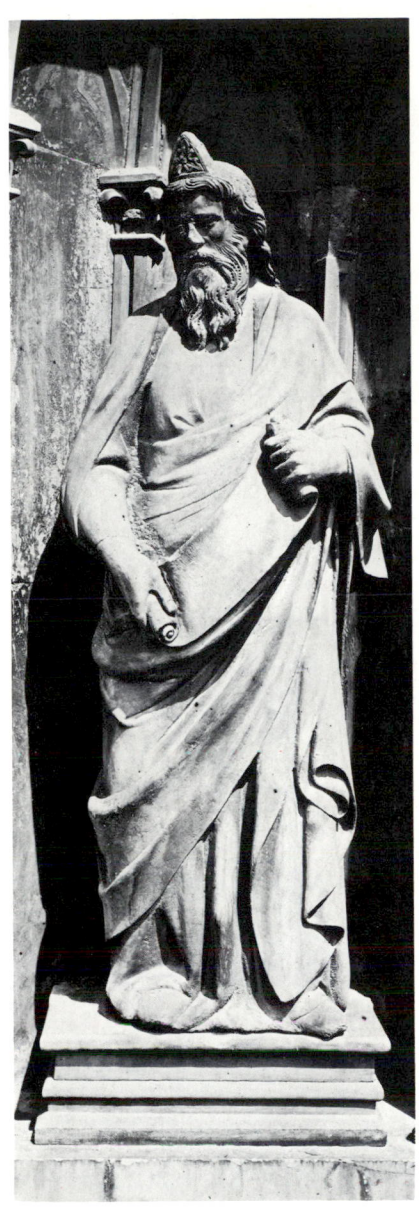 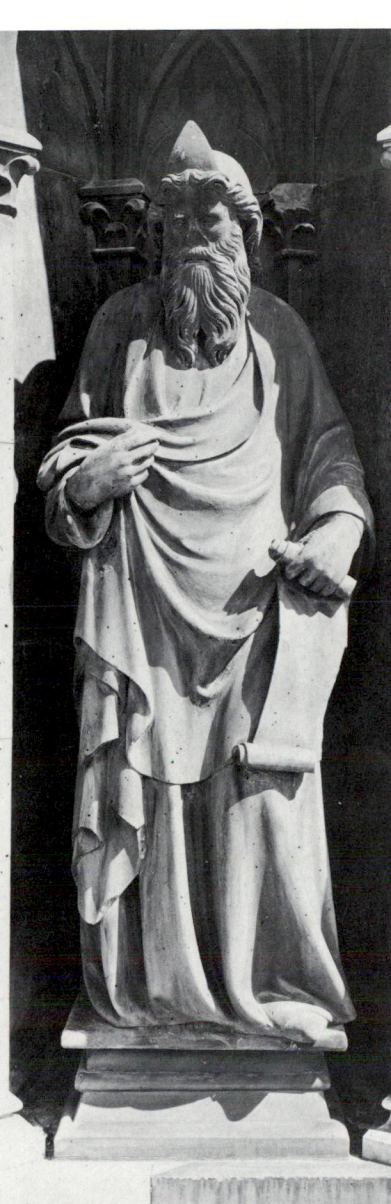 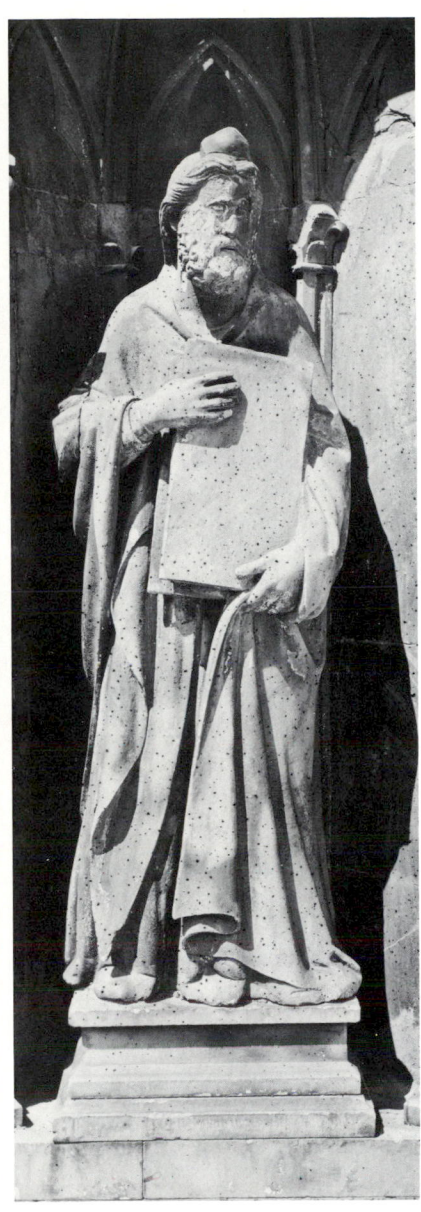

80. Andrea Pisano follower: *Prophet* (ht 178 cm). Florence, Museo dell'Opera del Duomo

81. Andrea Pisano follower: *Prophet* (ht 178 cm). Florence, Museo dell'Opera del Duomo

82. Andrea Pisano follower: *Prophet* (ht 182 cm). Florence, Museo dell'Opera del Duomo

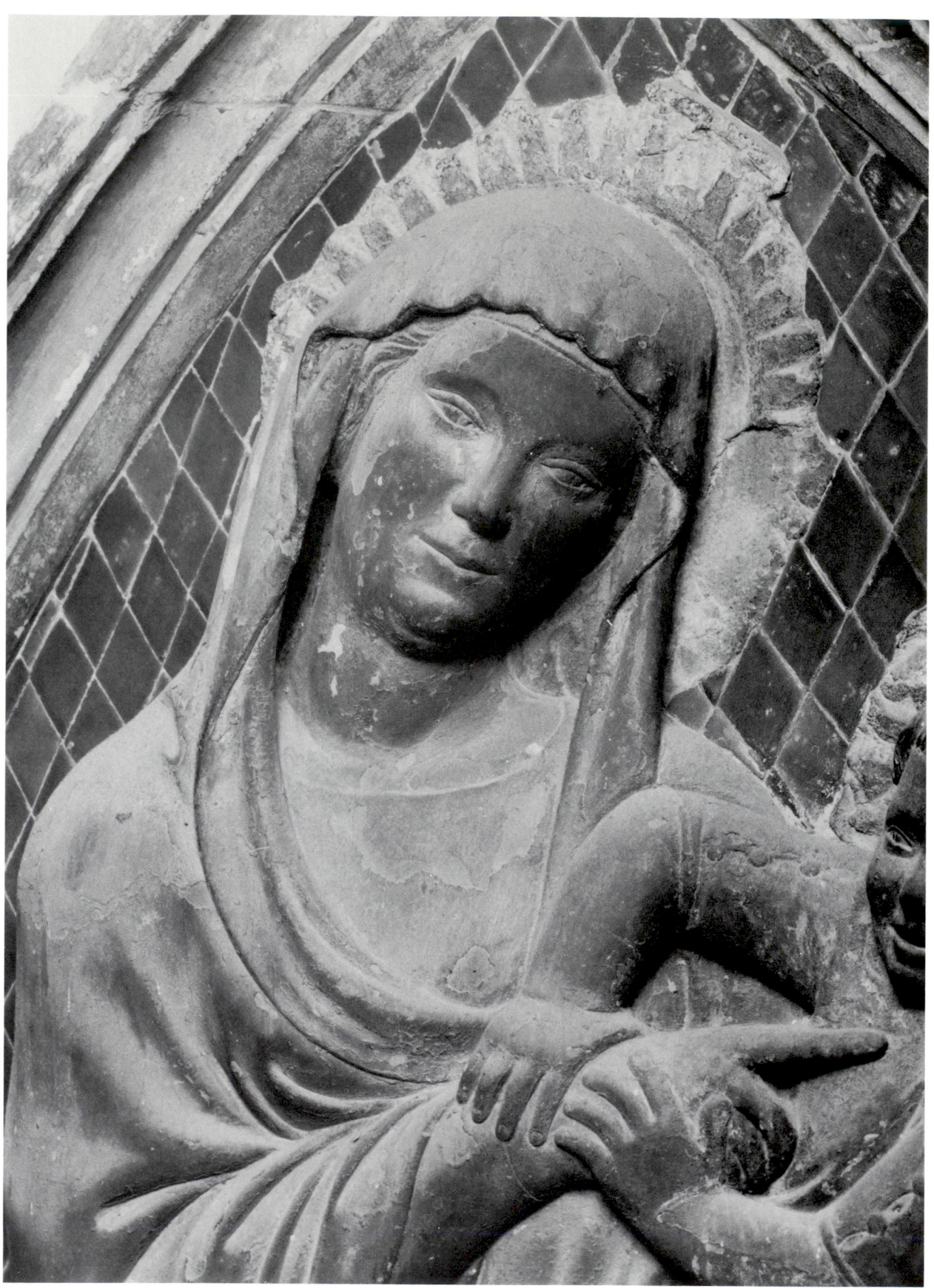

83. Andrea Pisano: *Madonna and Child*, detail, lunette relief. Florence, Museo dell'Opera del Duomo

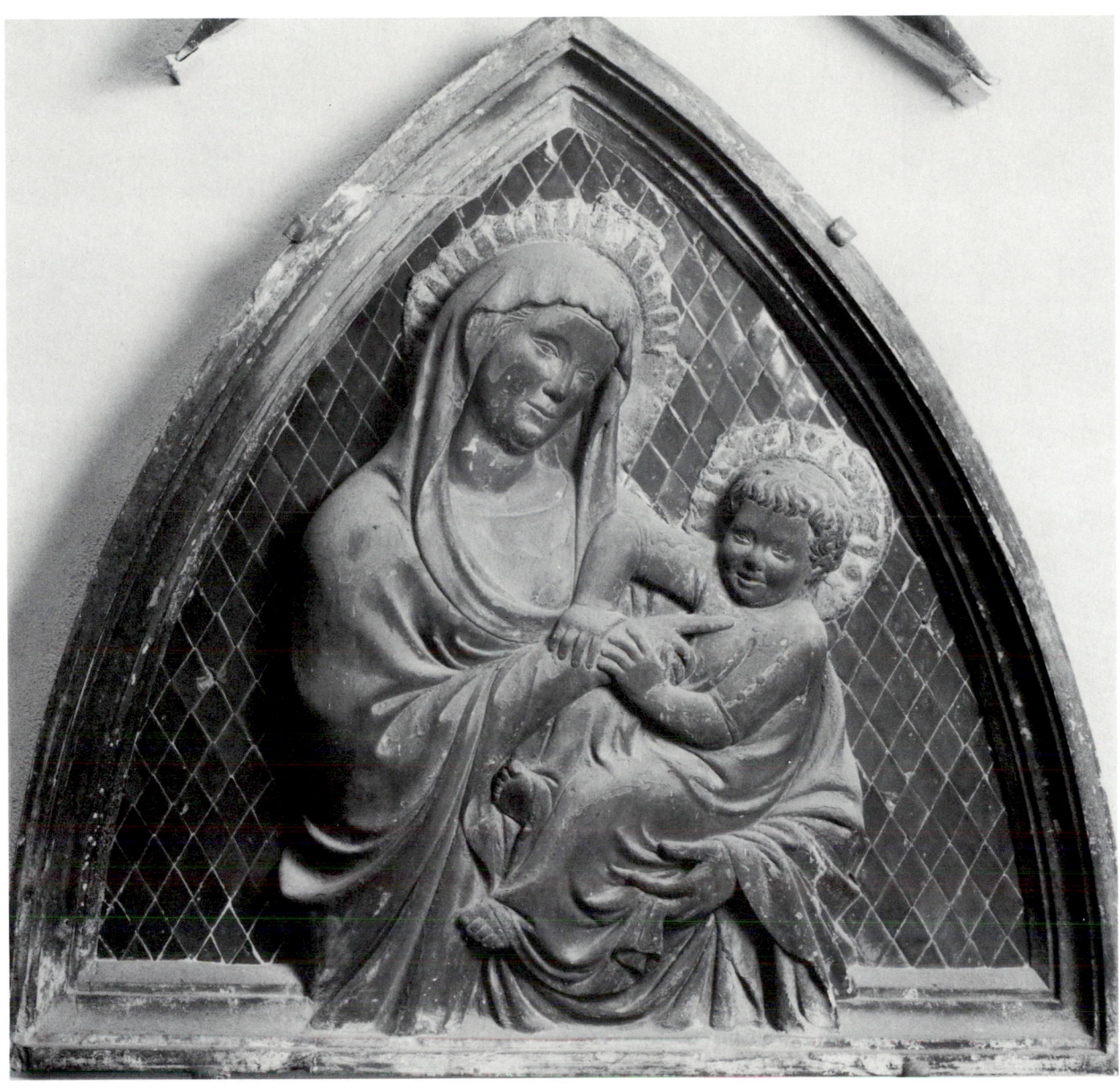

84. Andrea Pisano: *Madonna and Child*, lunette relief (ht 83.5 cm, width 88 cm). Florence, Museo dell'Opera del Duomo

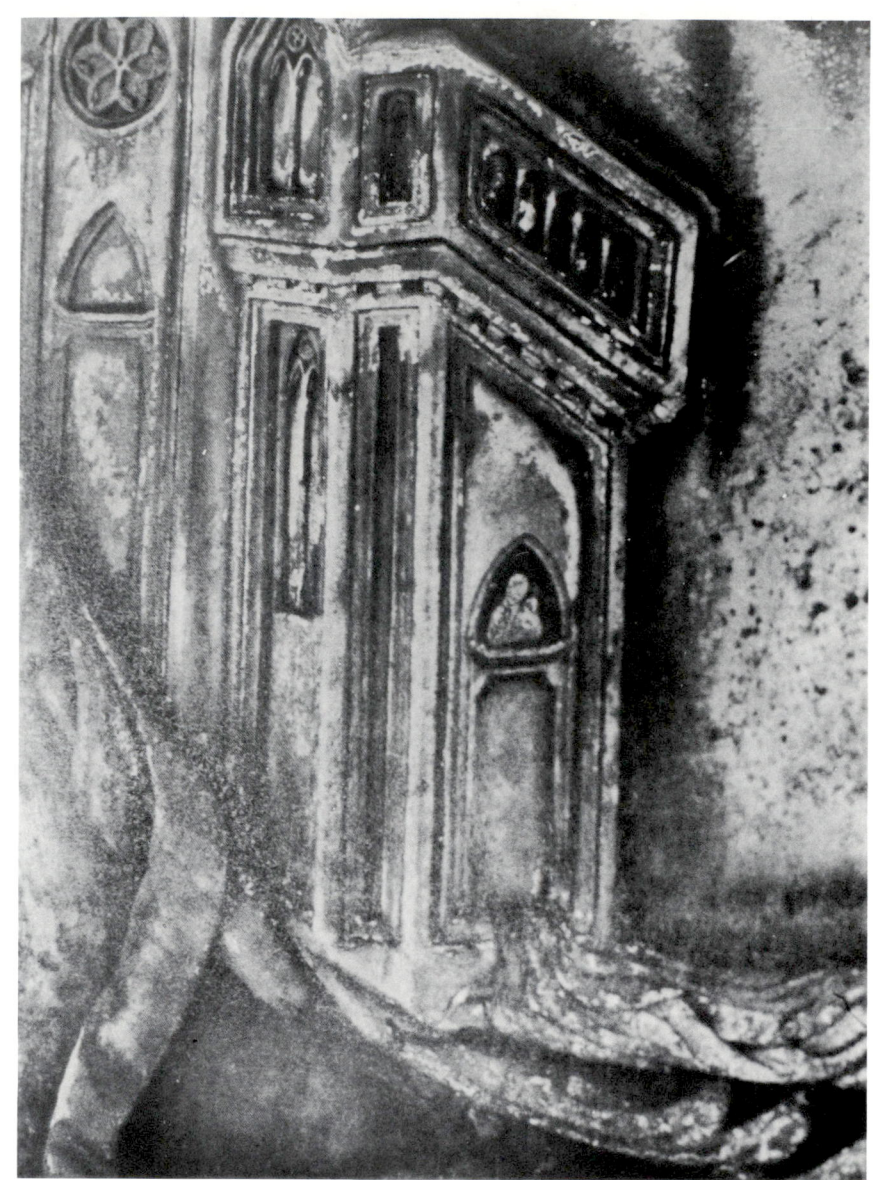

85. Orvieto Cathedral, facade relief

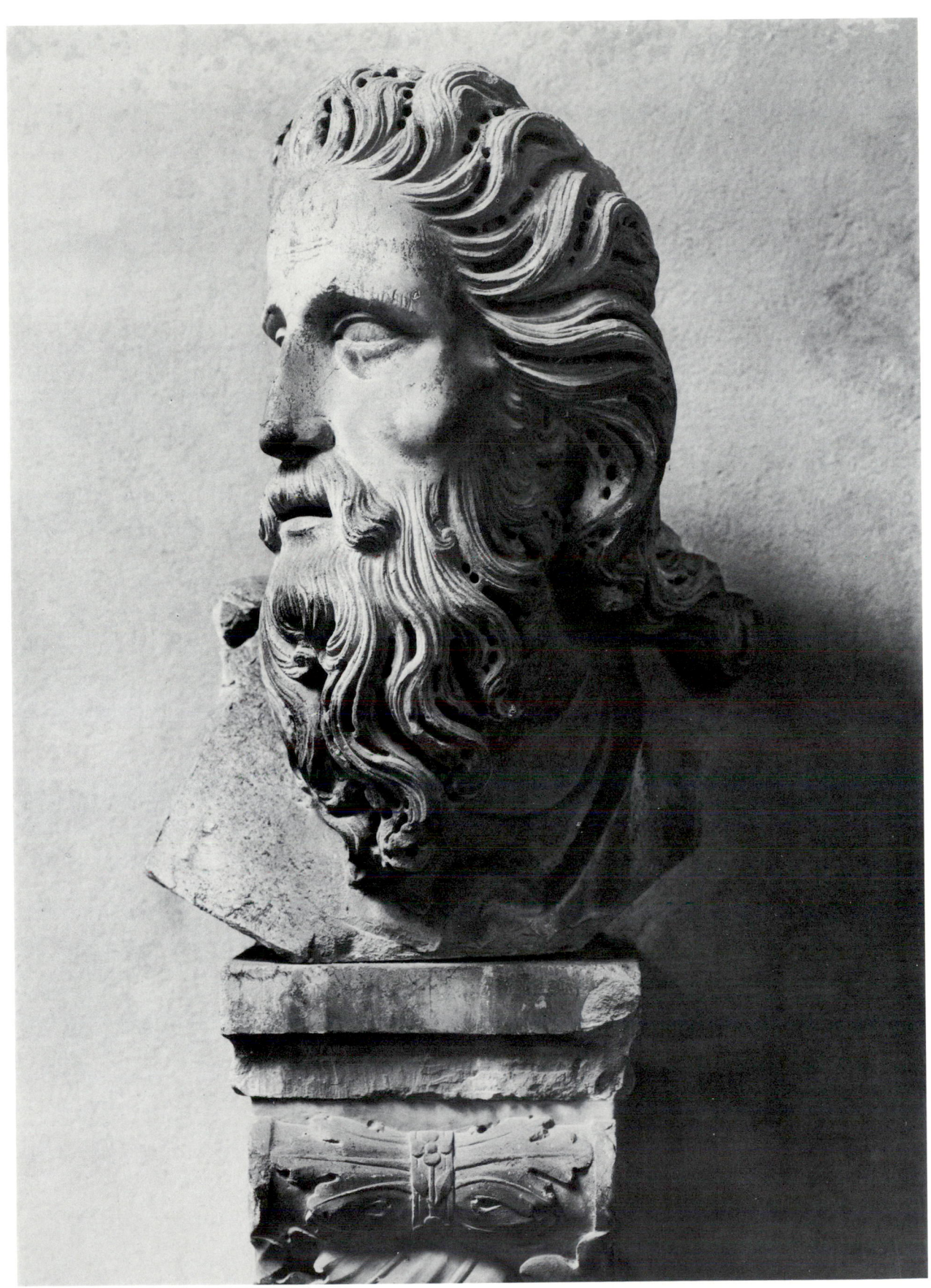

86. Andrea Pisano: *St. John the Baptist*, fragment (ht 55 cm, width 41 cm, depth 25 cm). Florence, Museo dell'Opera del Duomo

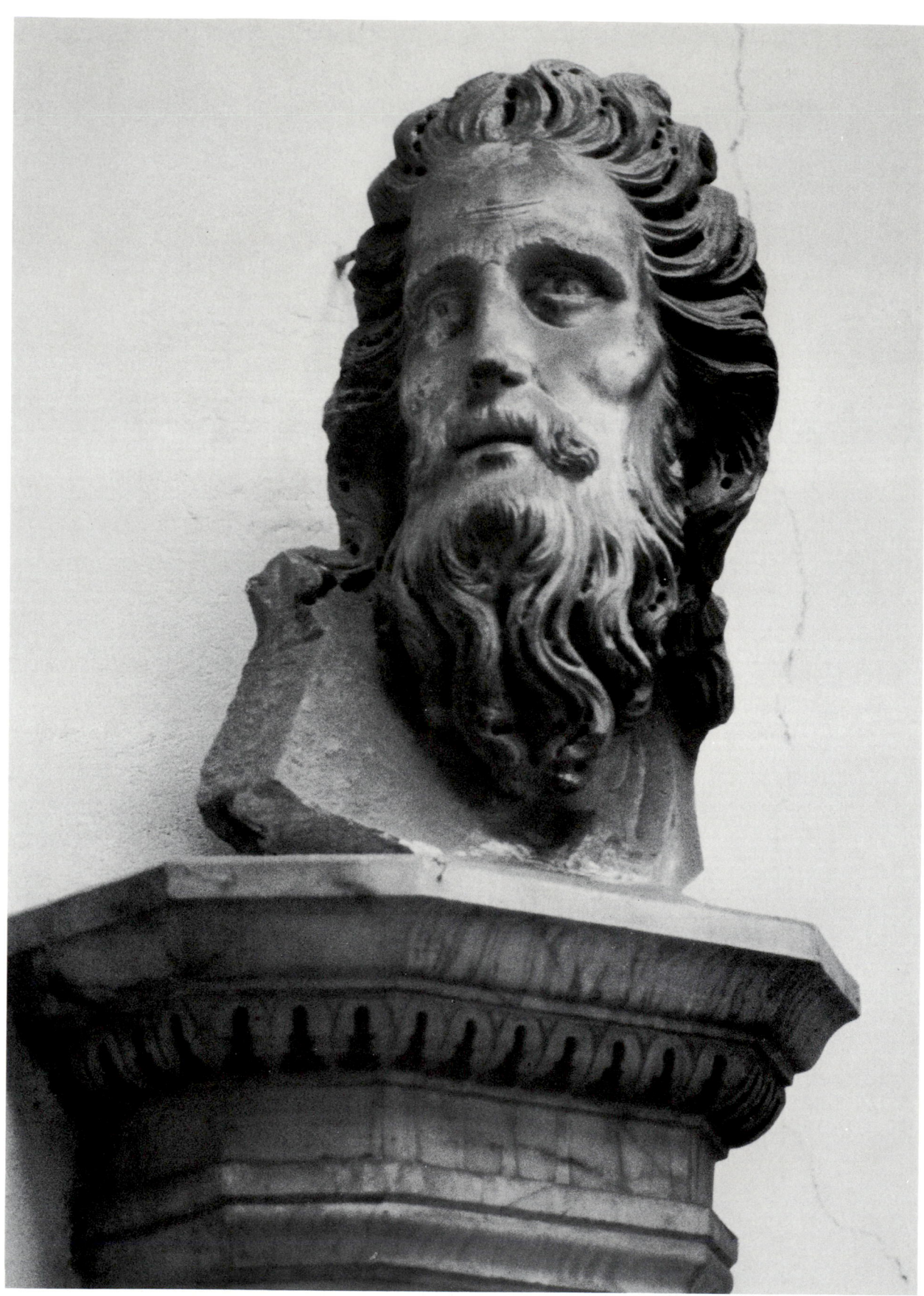

87. Andrea Pisano: *St. John the Baptist*, fragment. Florence, Museo dell'Opera del Duomo

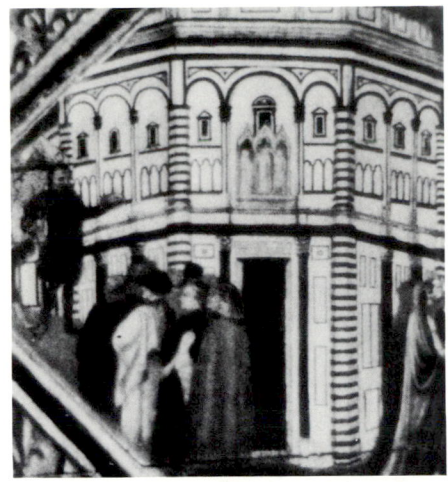

88. Cassone panel, detail. Florence, Museo Nazionale

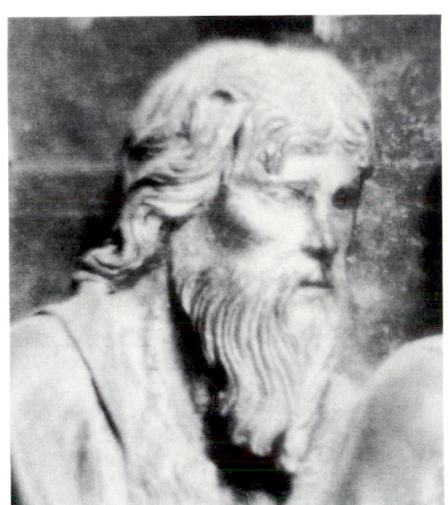

90. Andrea Pisano: *Baptist Led to Prison*, detail. Florence, Baptistry doors

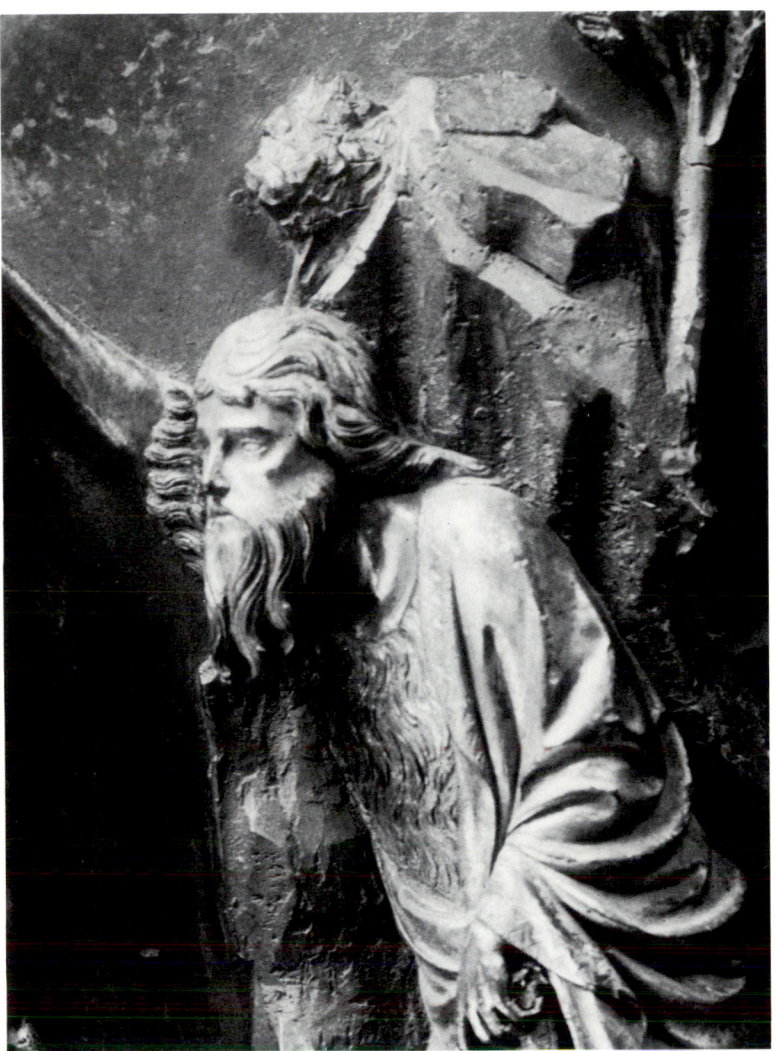

89. Andrea Pisano: *Baptism of Christ*, detail. Florence, Baptistry doors

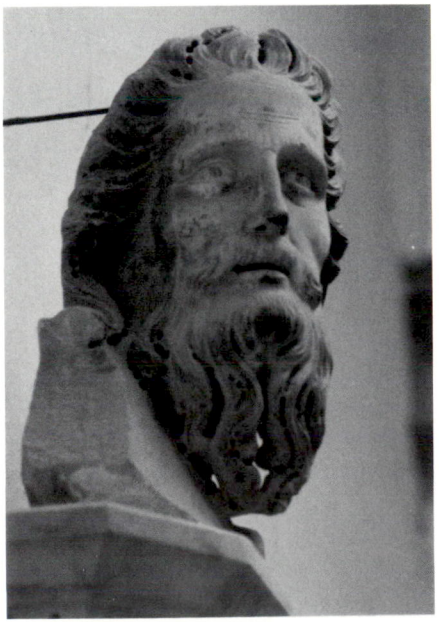

91. Andrea Pisano: *St. John the Baptist*, fragment. Florence, Museo dell'Opera del Duomo

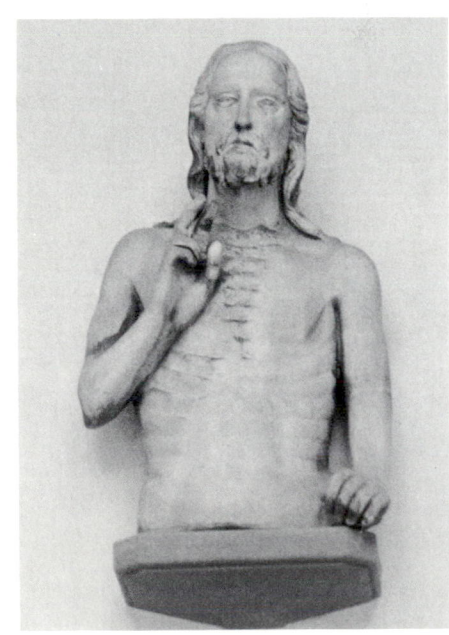

92. Tino di Camaino (?): *Christ*, fragment (ht 105 cm). Florence, Museo dell'Opera del Duomo

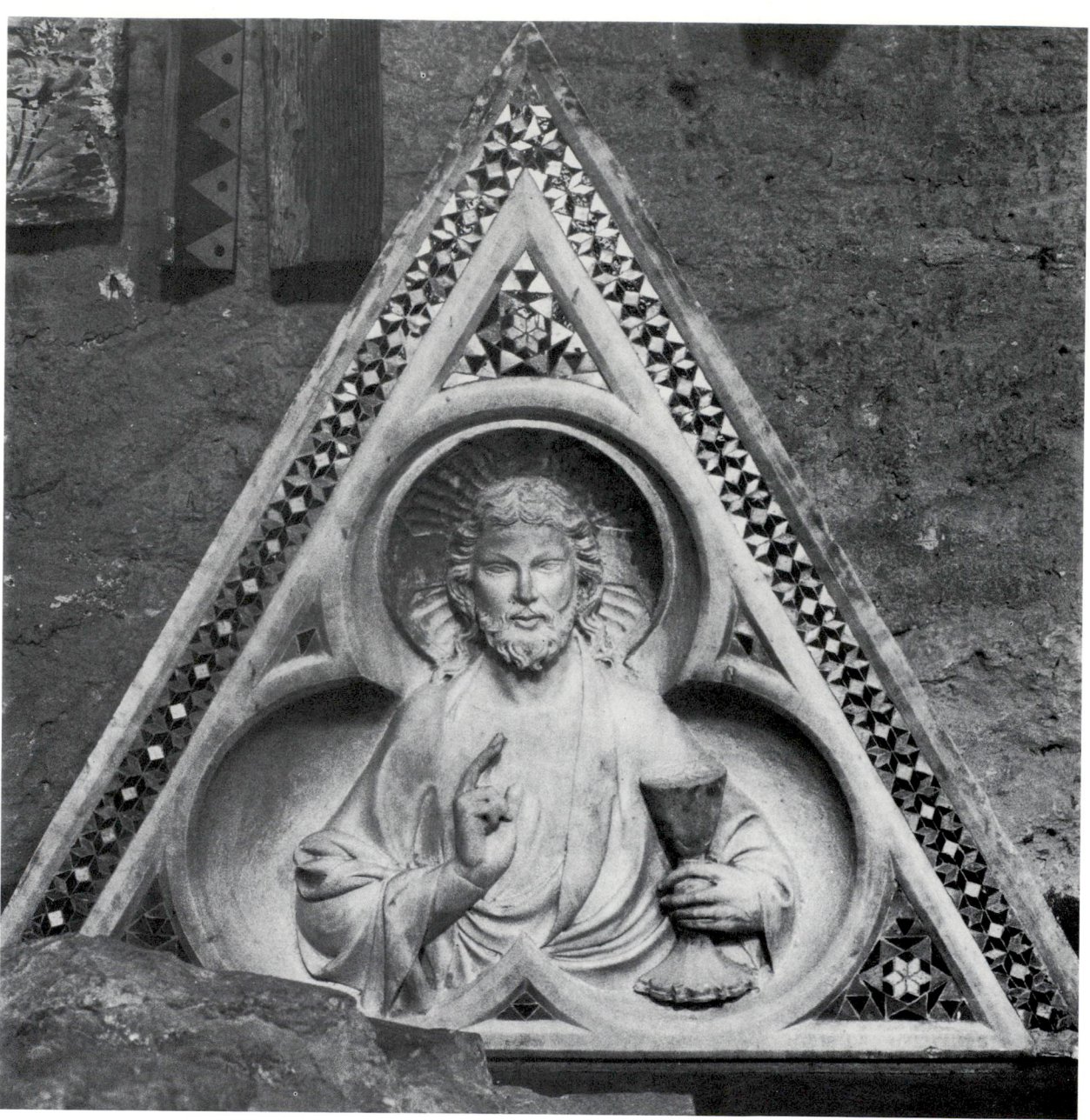

93. Andrea Pisano: *Blessing Christ*, relief (ht 98 cm, width 95 cm). Orvieto, Museo dell'Opera del Duomo

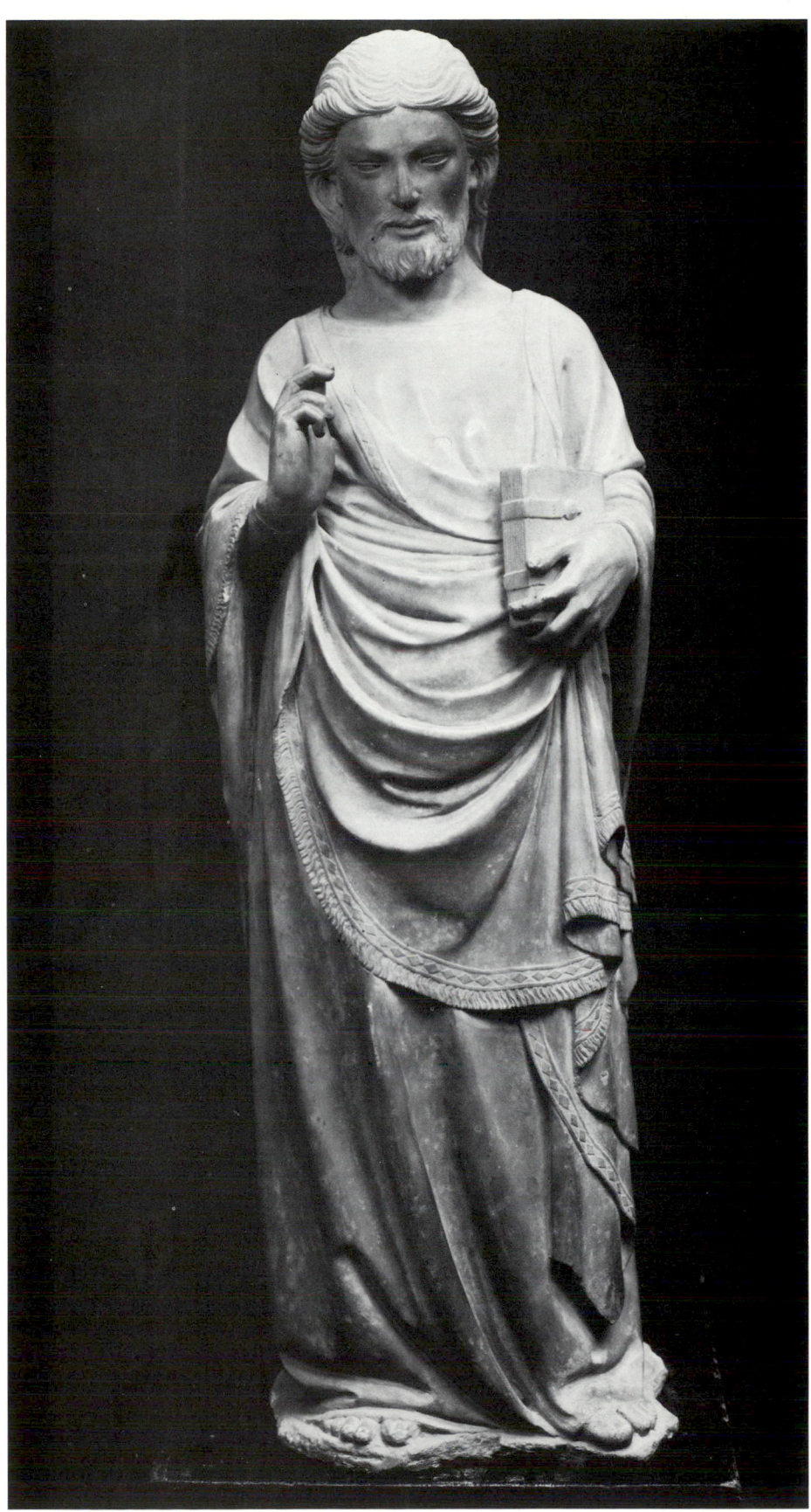

94. Andrea Pisano: *The Redeemer* (ht 75 cm, width 24 cm, depth 19.5 cm). Florence, Museo dell'Opera del Duomo

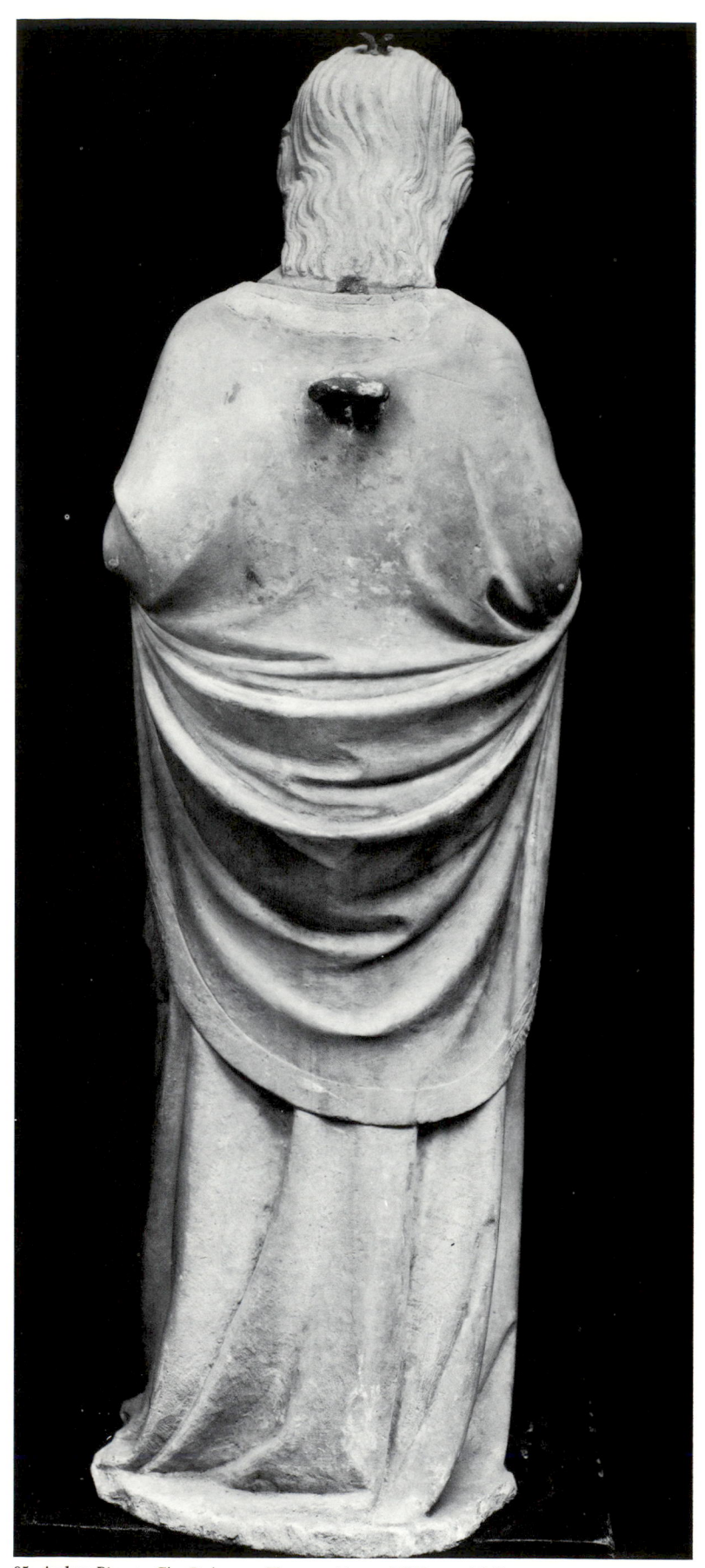

95. Andrea Pisano: *The Redeemer*. Florence, Museo dell'Opera del Duomo

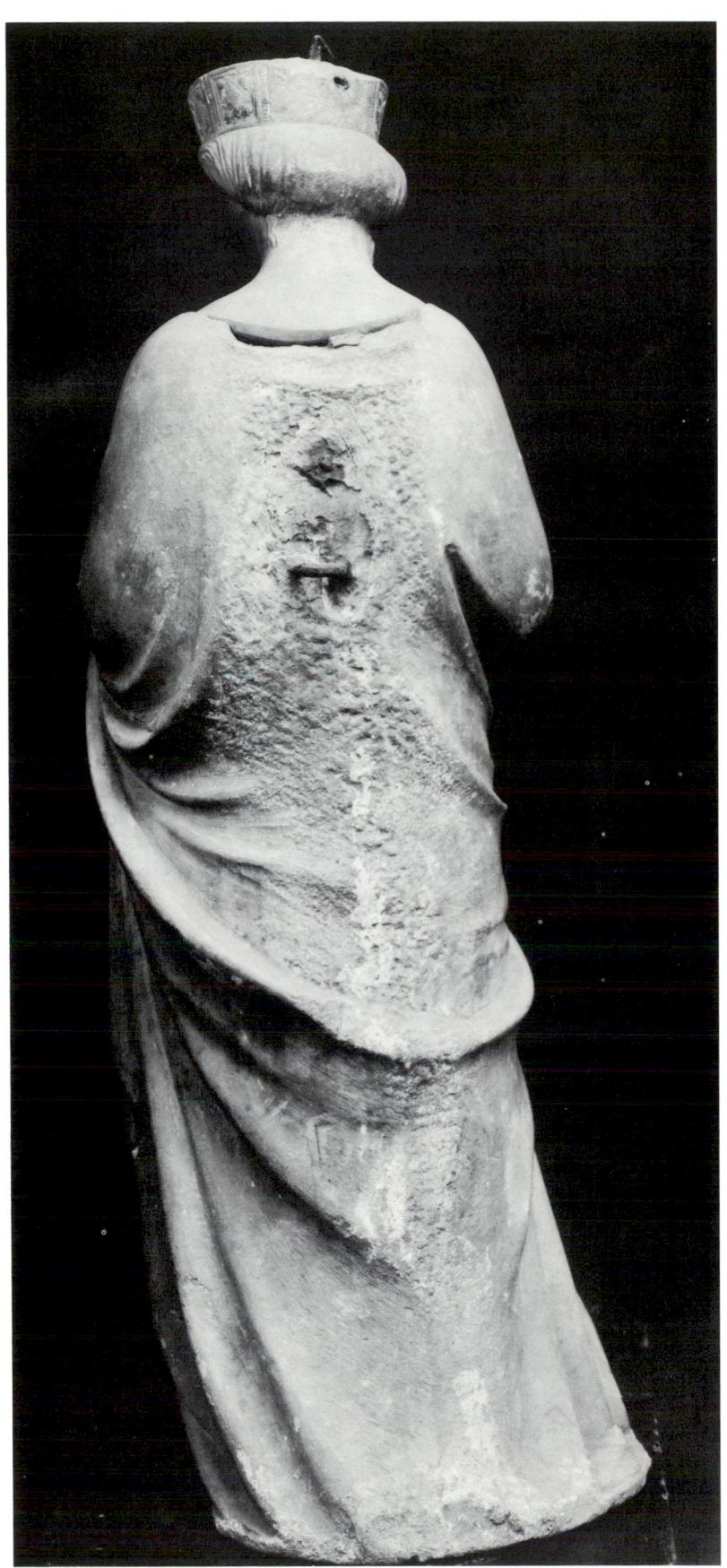

96. Andrea Pisano workshop: *Saint* (Sta. Reparata?). Florence, Museo dell'Opera del Duomo

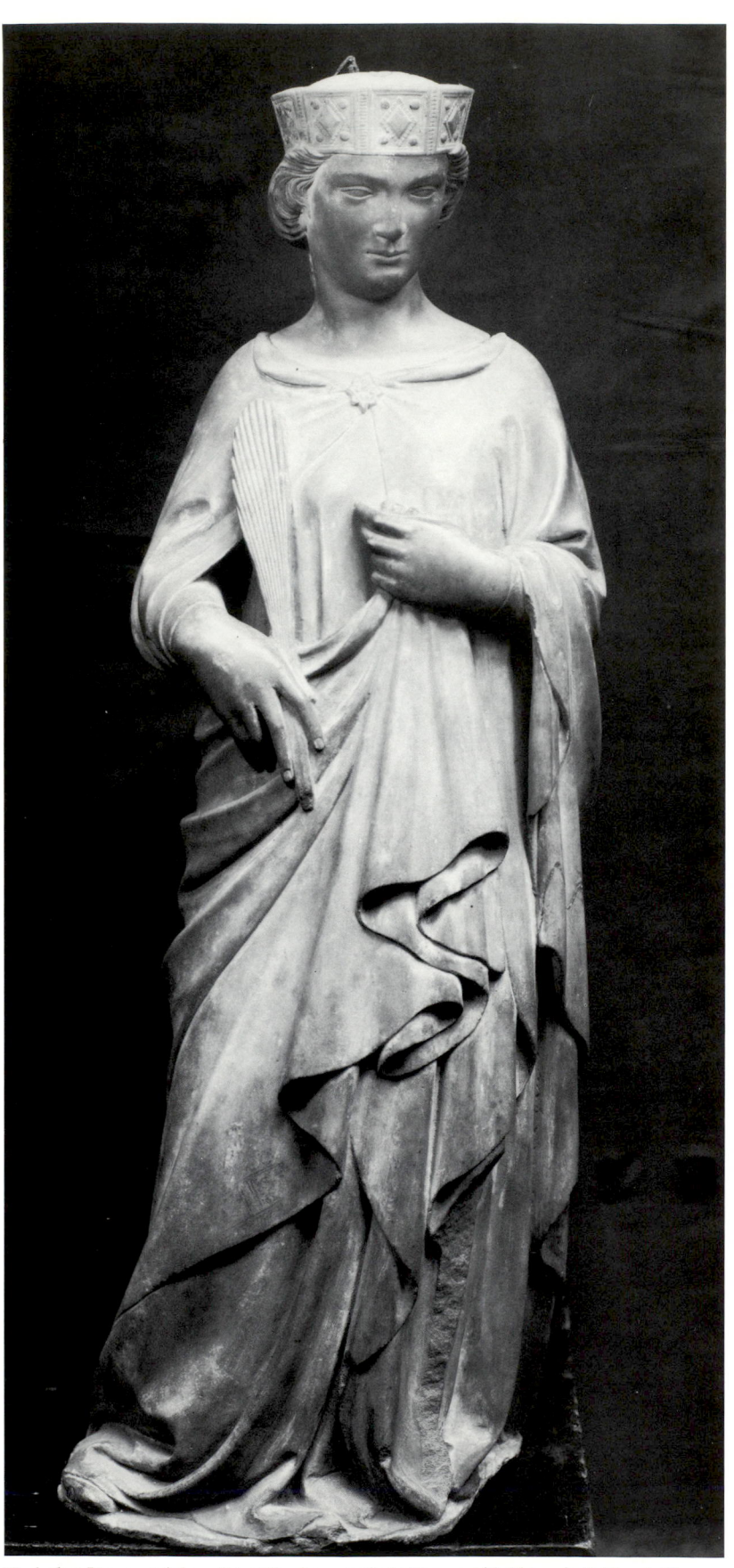

97. Andrea Pisano workshop: *Saint* (Sta. Reparata?) (ht 70 cm, width 25 cm, depth 20 cm). Florence, Museo dell'Opera del Duomo

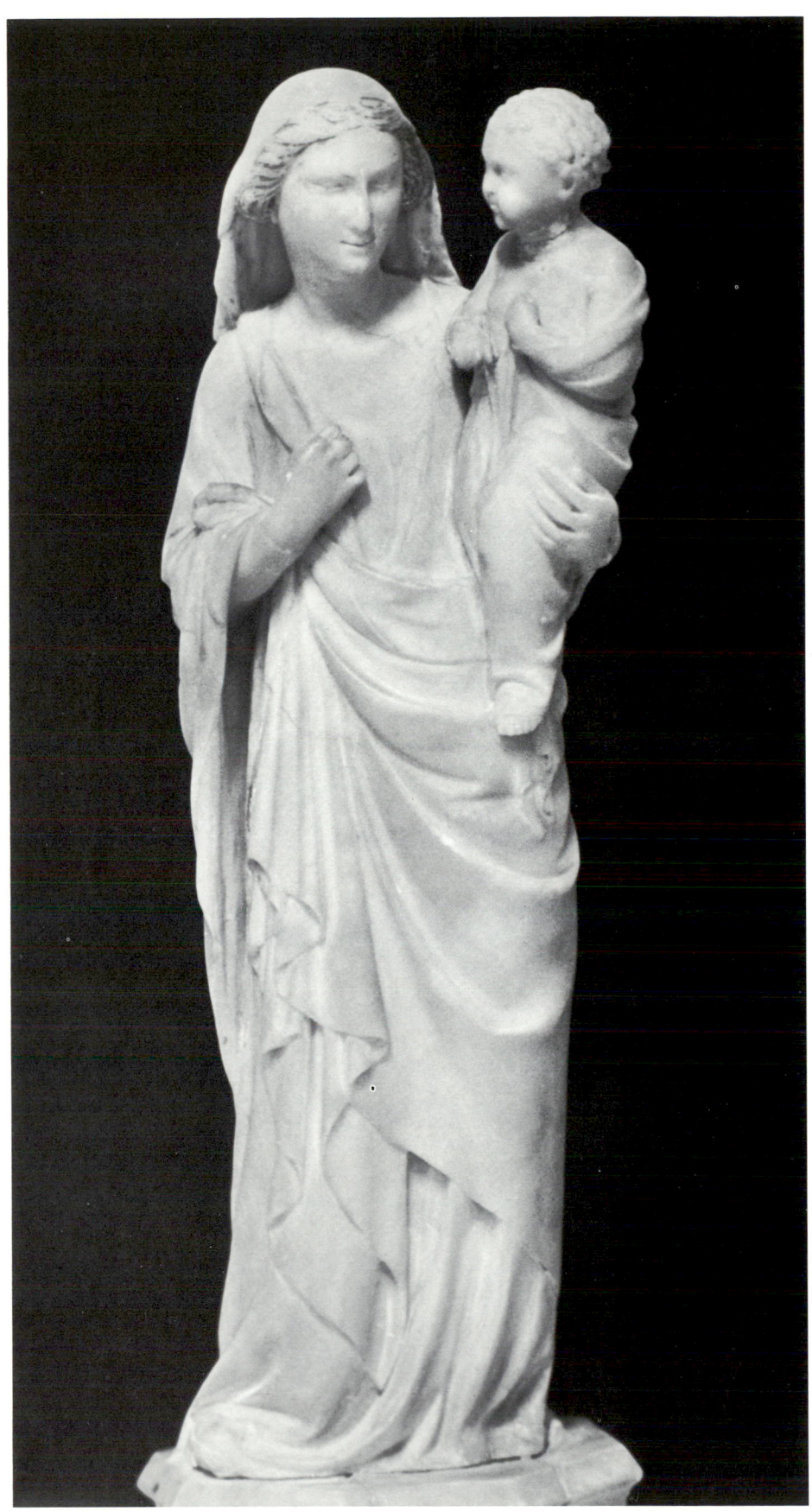

98. Andrea Pisano: *Madonna and Child* (ht without plinth 31 cm). Budapest, Museum of Fine Arts

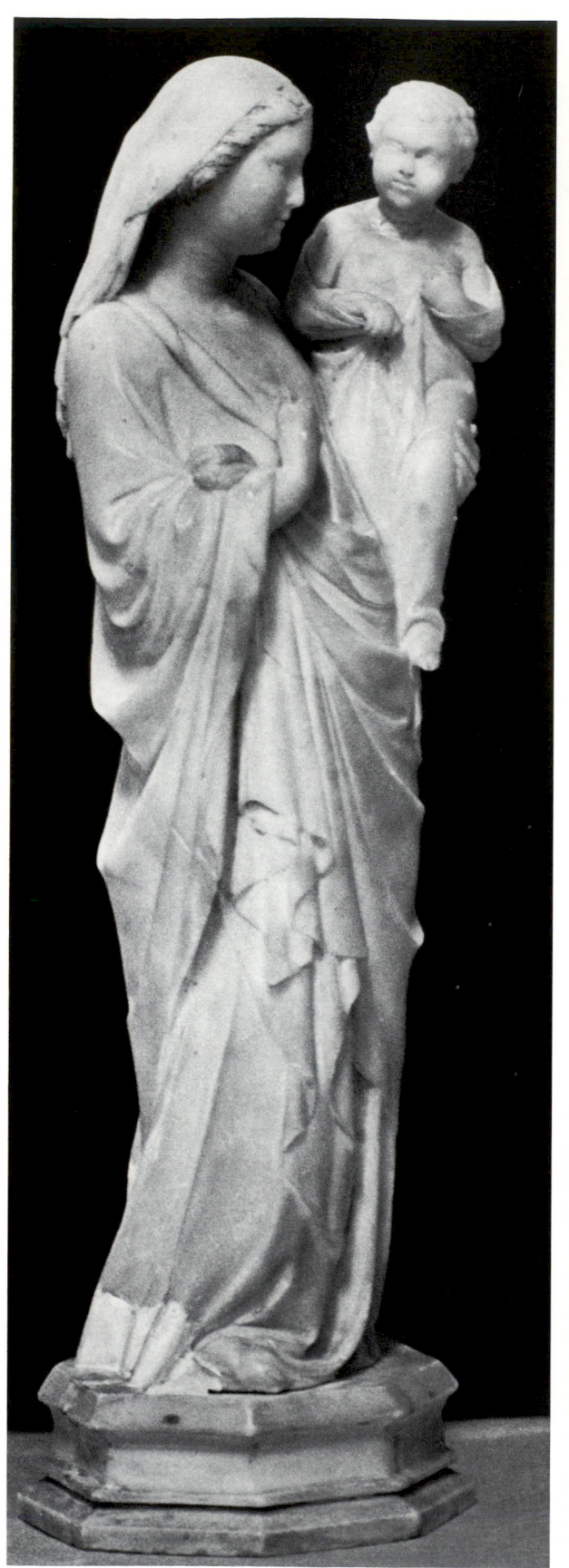 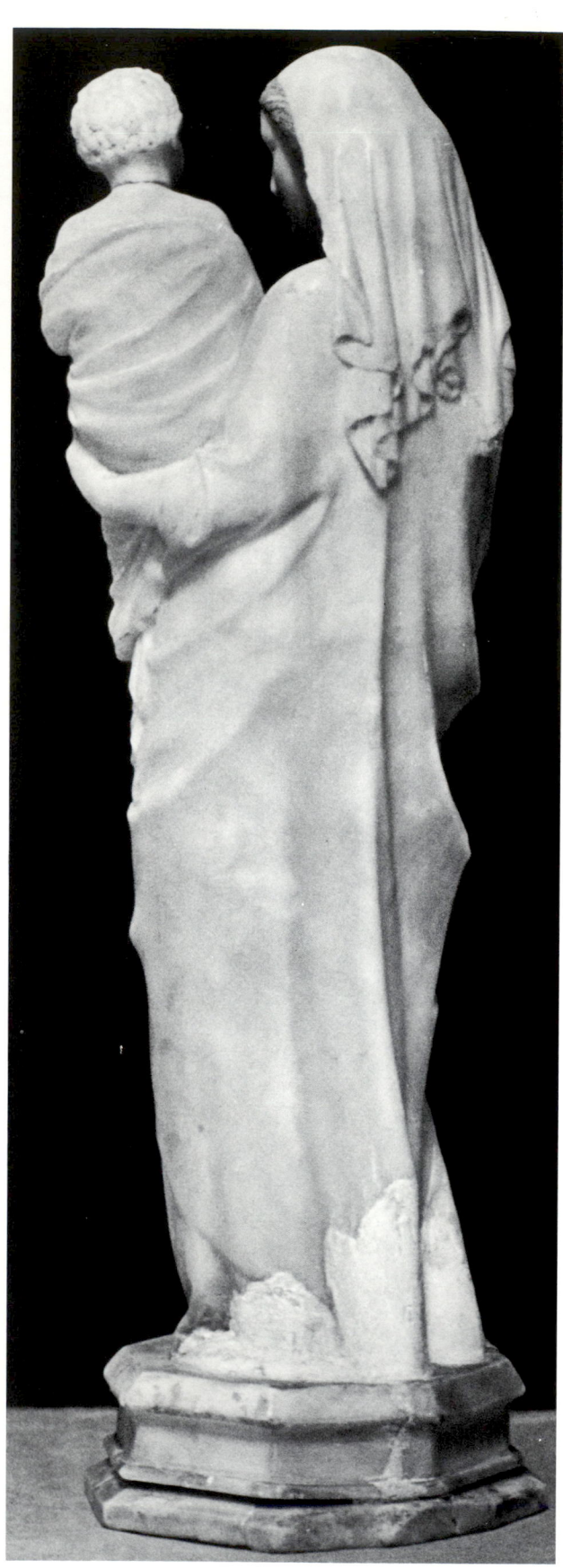

99. Andrea Pisano: *Madonna and Child*. Budapest, Museum of Fine Arts

100. Andrea Pisano: *Madonna and Child*. Budapest, Museum of Fine Arts

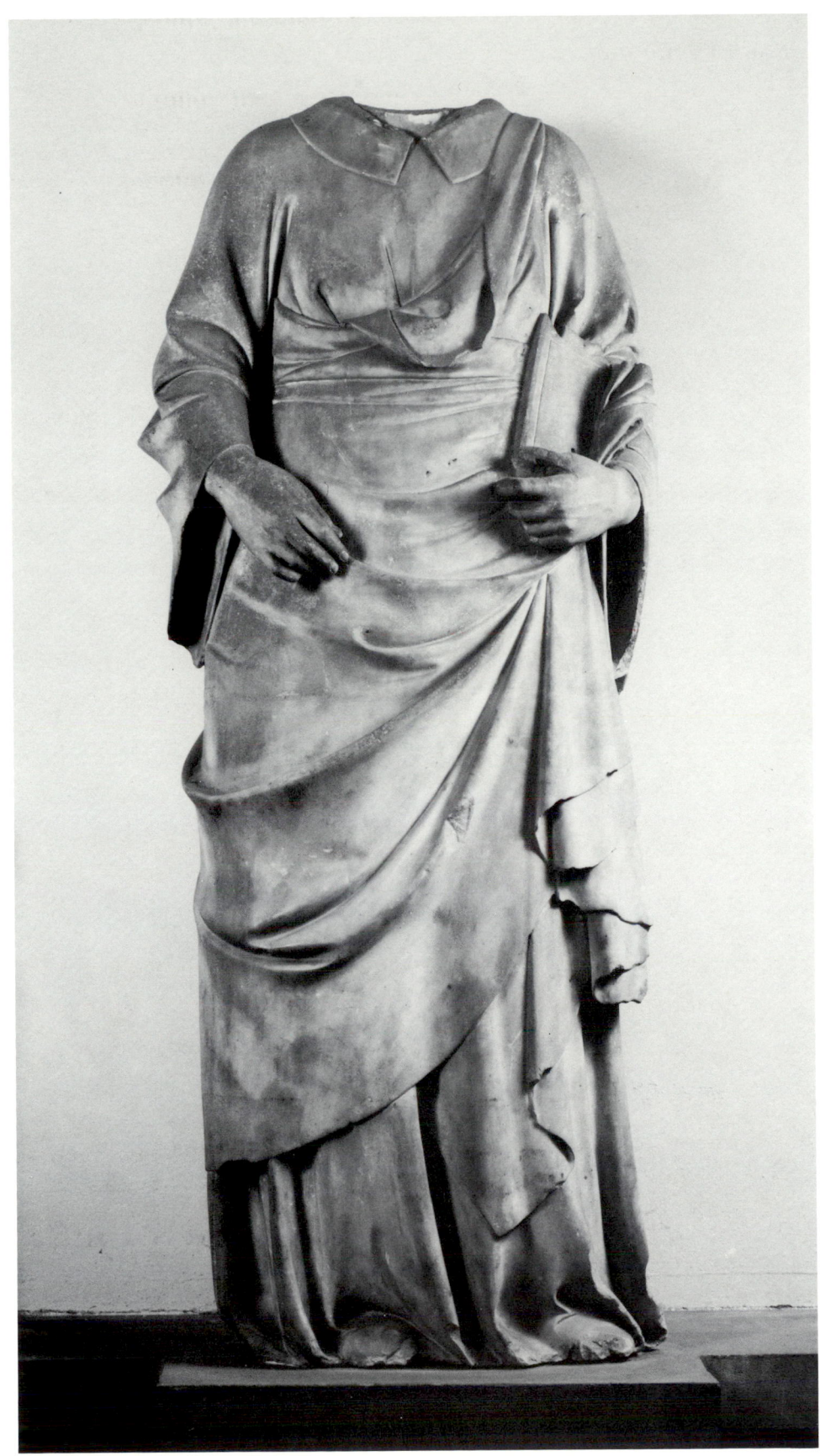

101. Andrea Pisano(?): *St. Stephen* (ht 177 cm). Florence, Museo dell'Opera del Duomo

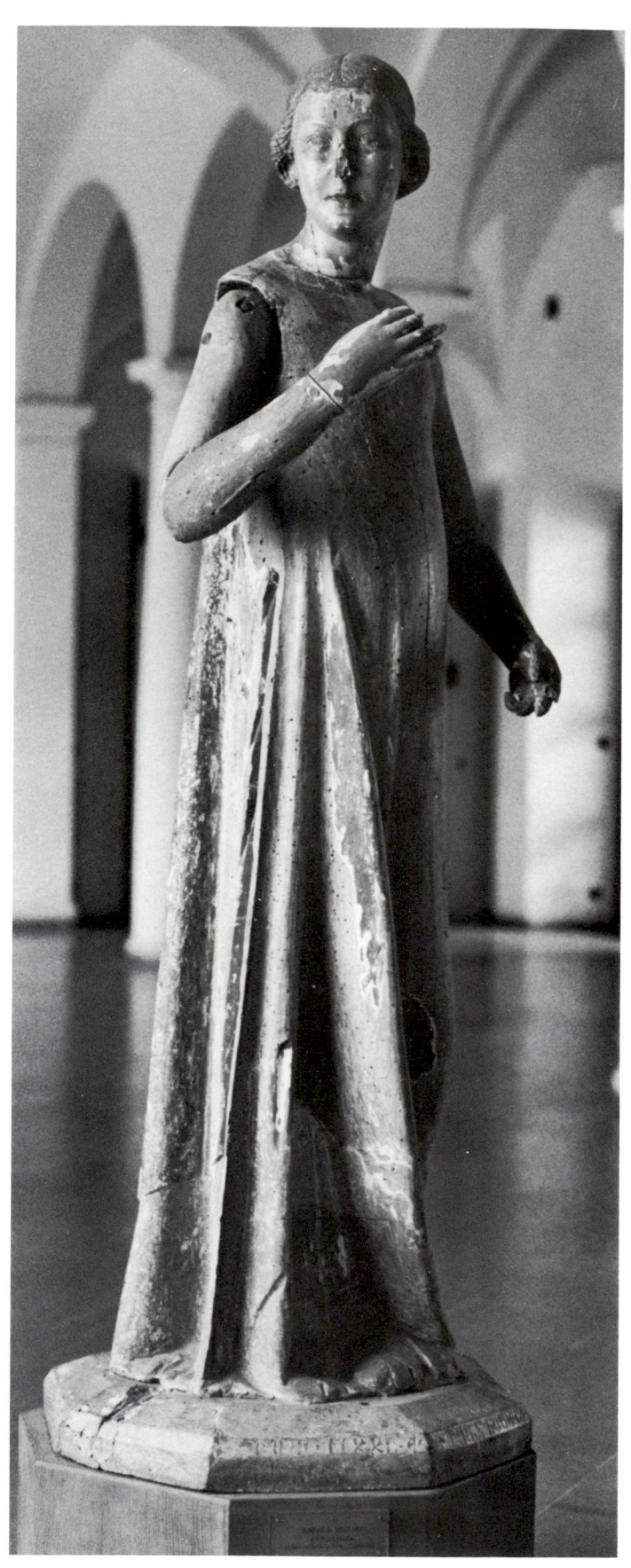

102. Andrea Pisano: *Virgin Annunciate* (ht 110 cm). Pisa, Museo di San Matteo

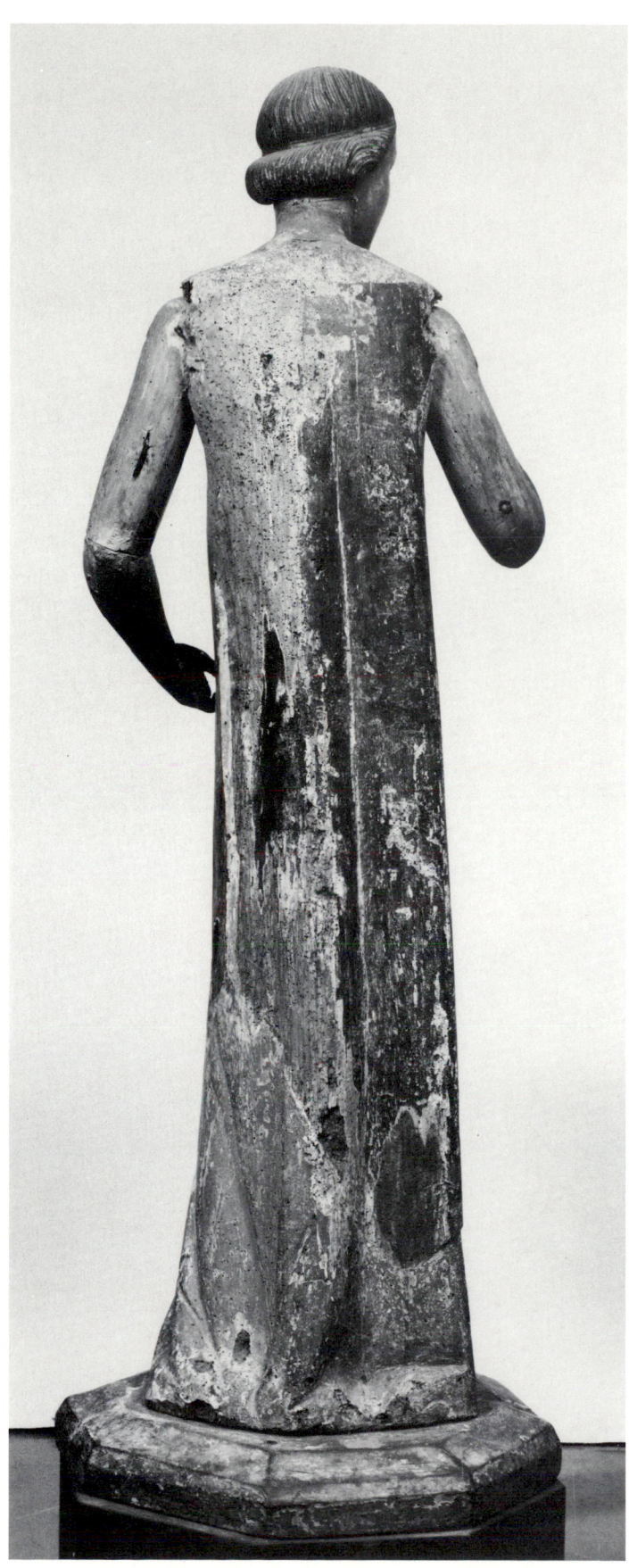

103. Andrea Pisano: *Virgin Annunciate*. Pisa, Museo di San Matteo

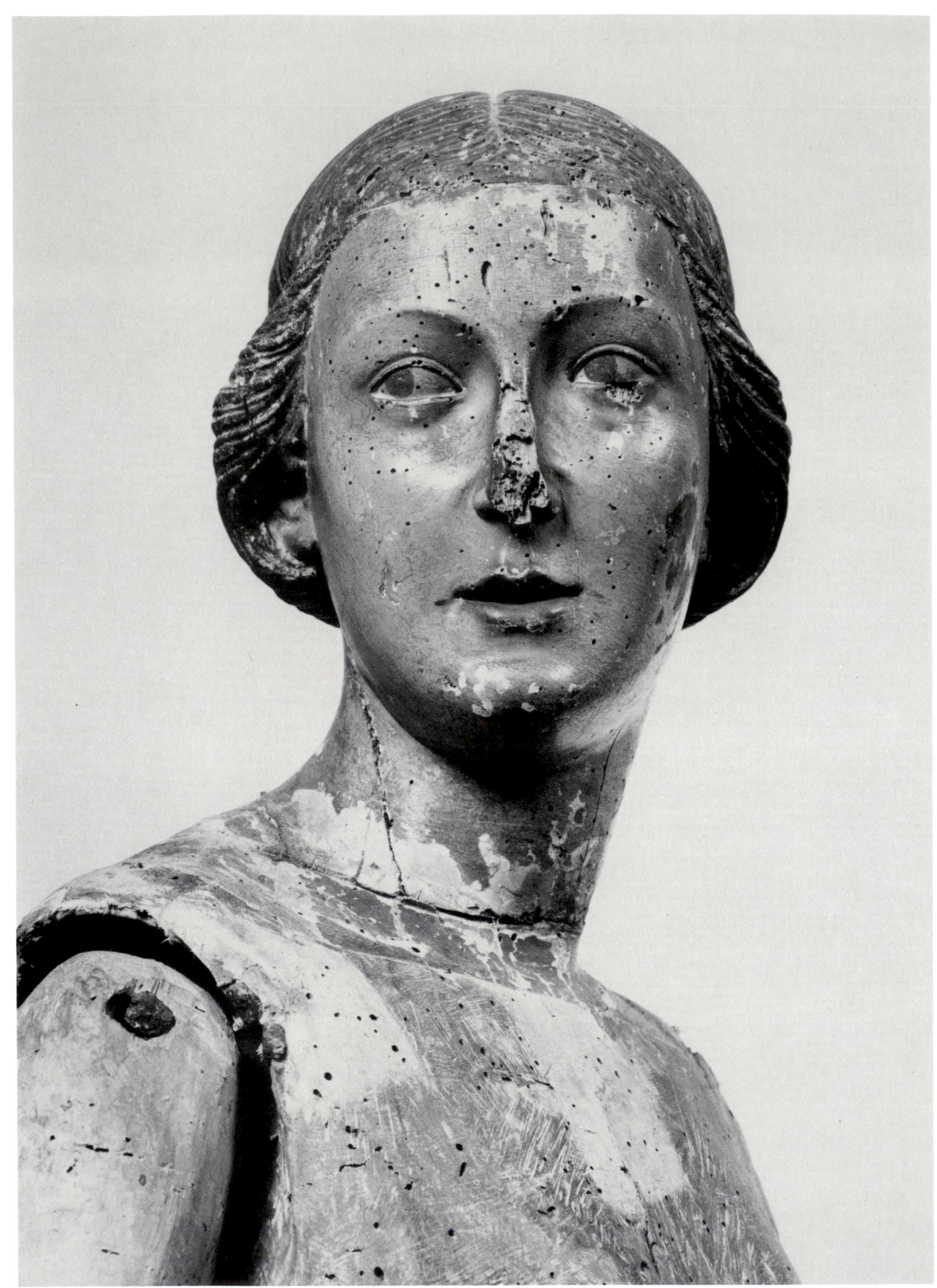

104. Andrea Pisano: *Virgin Annunciate*, detail. Pisa, Museo di San Matteo

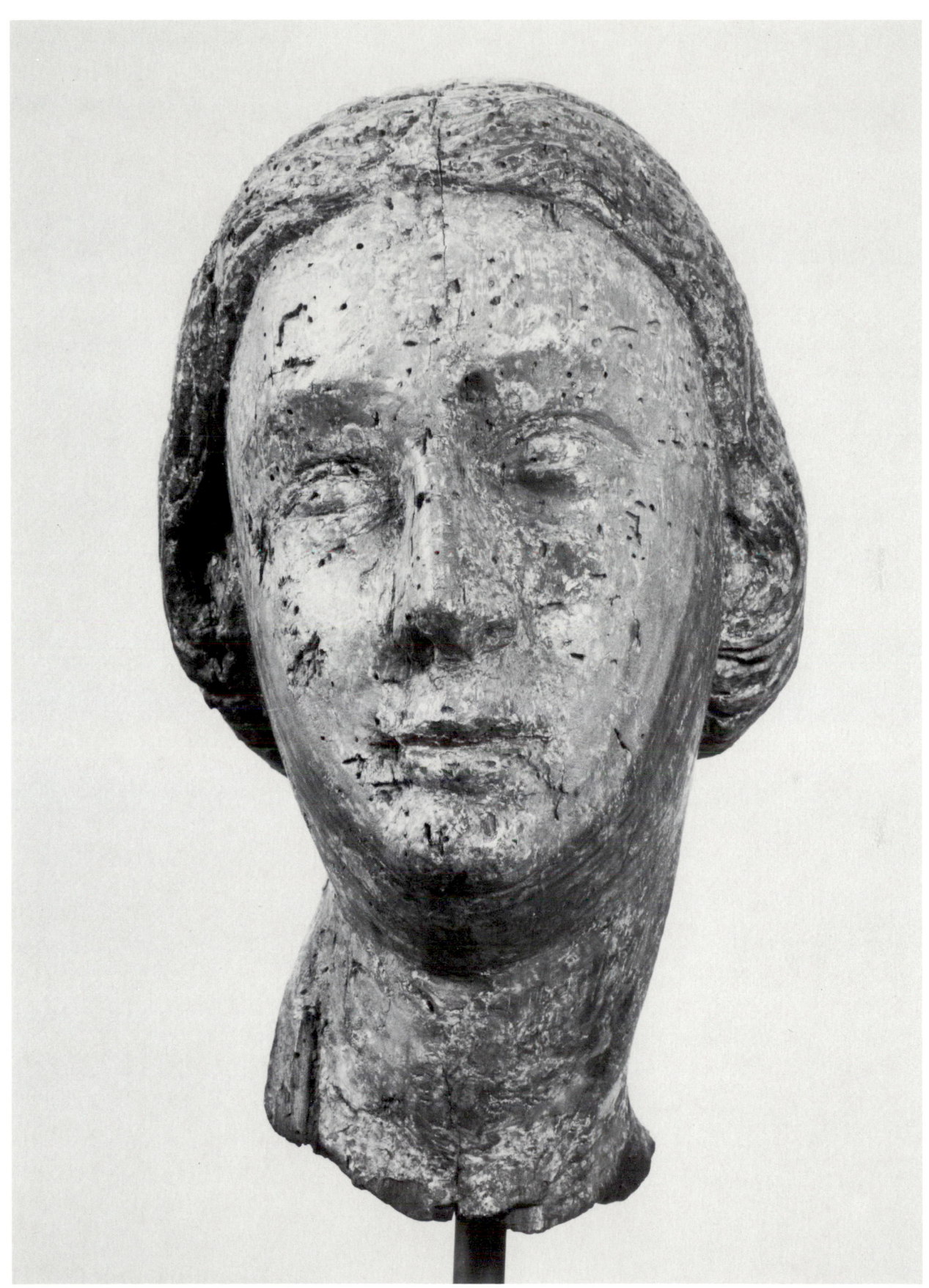

105. Andrea Pisano: *Virgin Annunciate*, fragment (ht 33 cm). Pisa, Museo di San Matteo

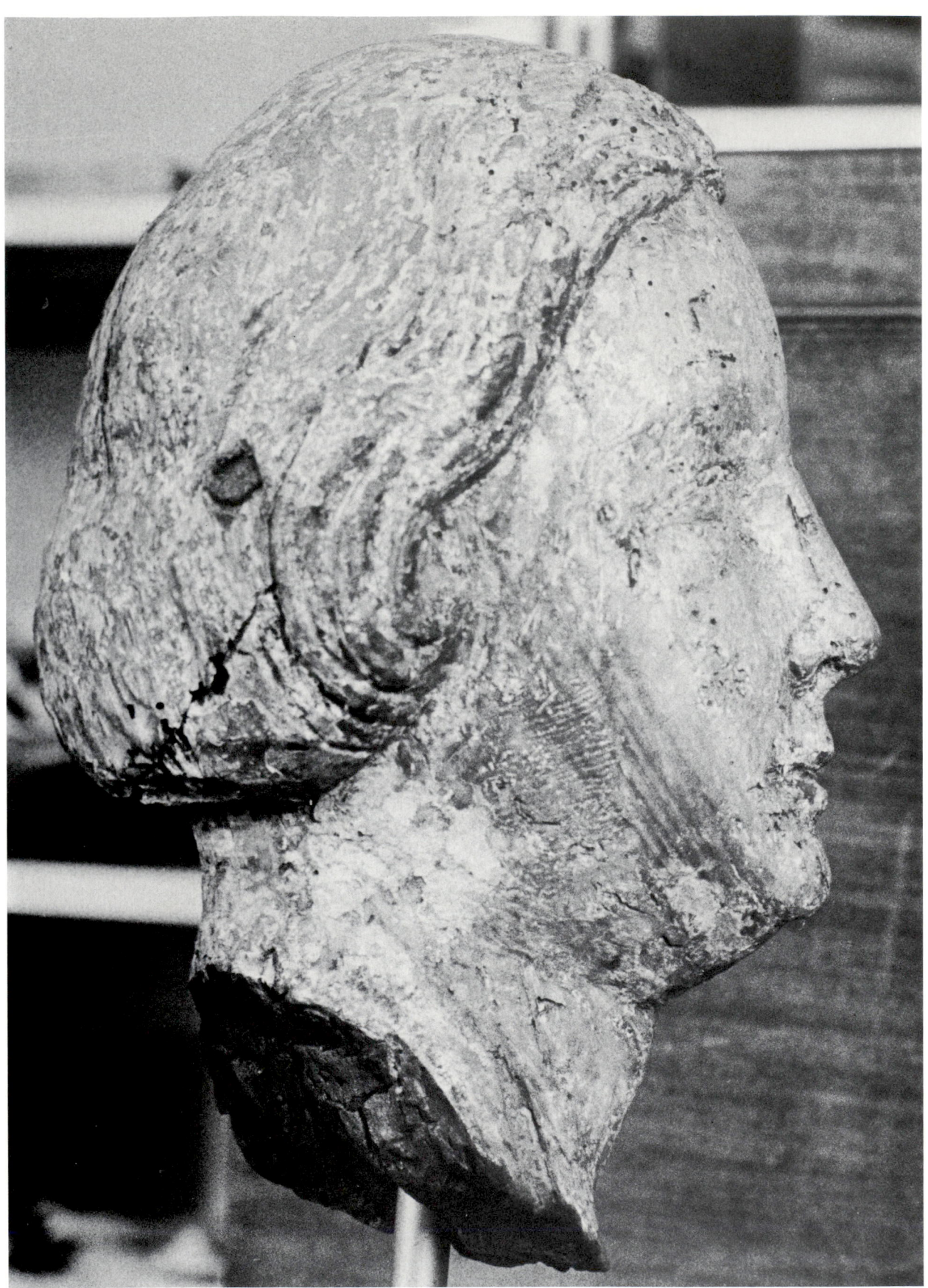

106. Andrea Pisano: *Virgin Annunciate*, fragment. Pisa, Museo di San Matteo

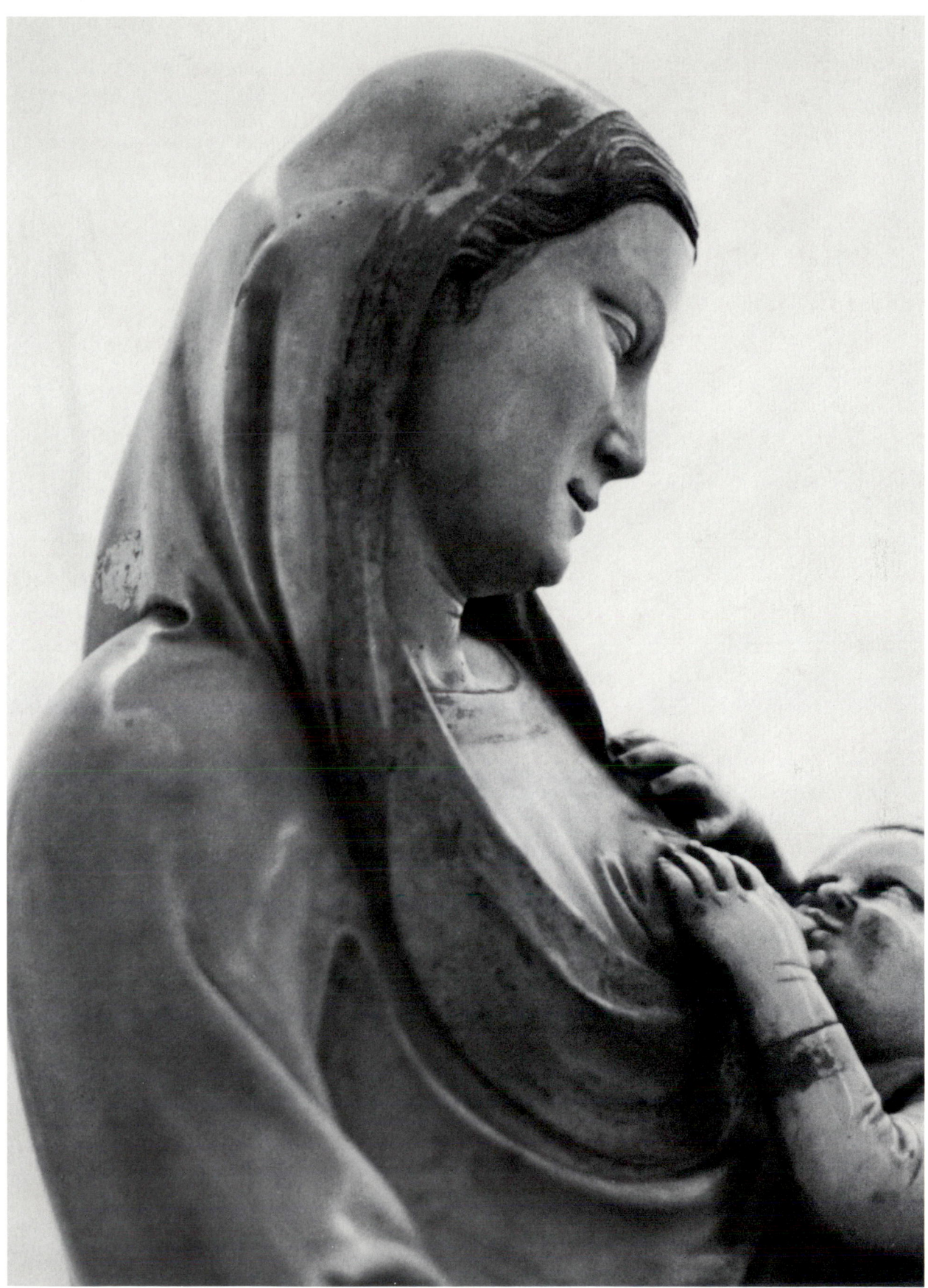

107. Andrea Pisano: *Madonna del Latte*, detail. Pisa, Museo di San Matteo

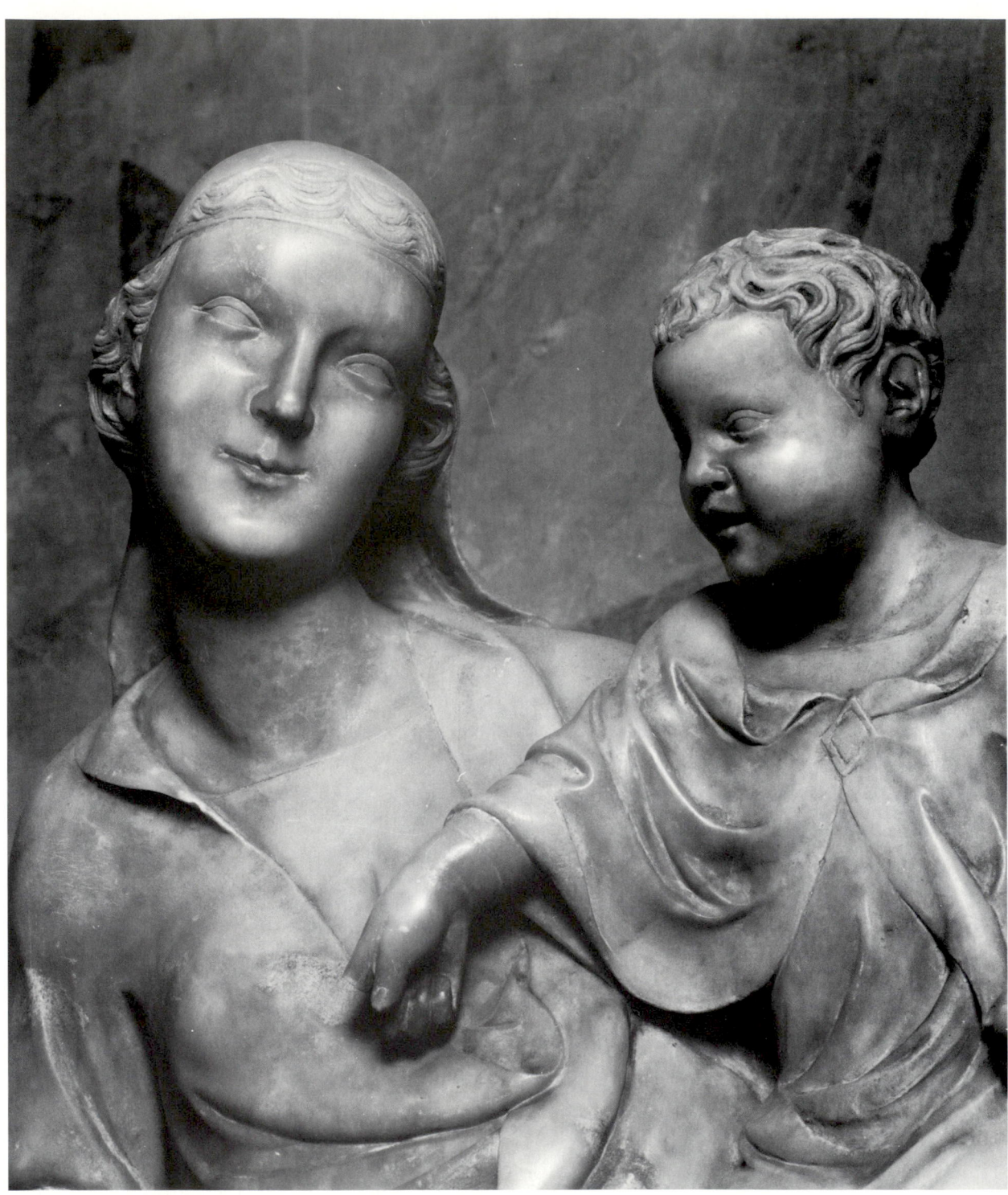

108. Nino Pisano: *Madonna and Child*, detail. Florence, Sta. Maria Novella

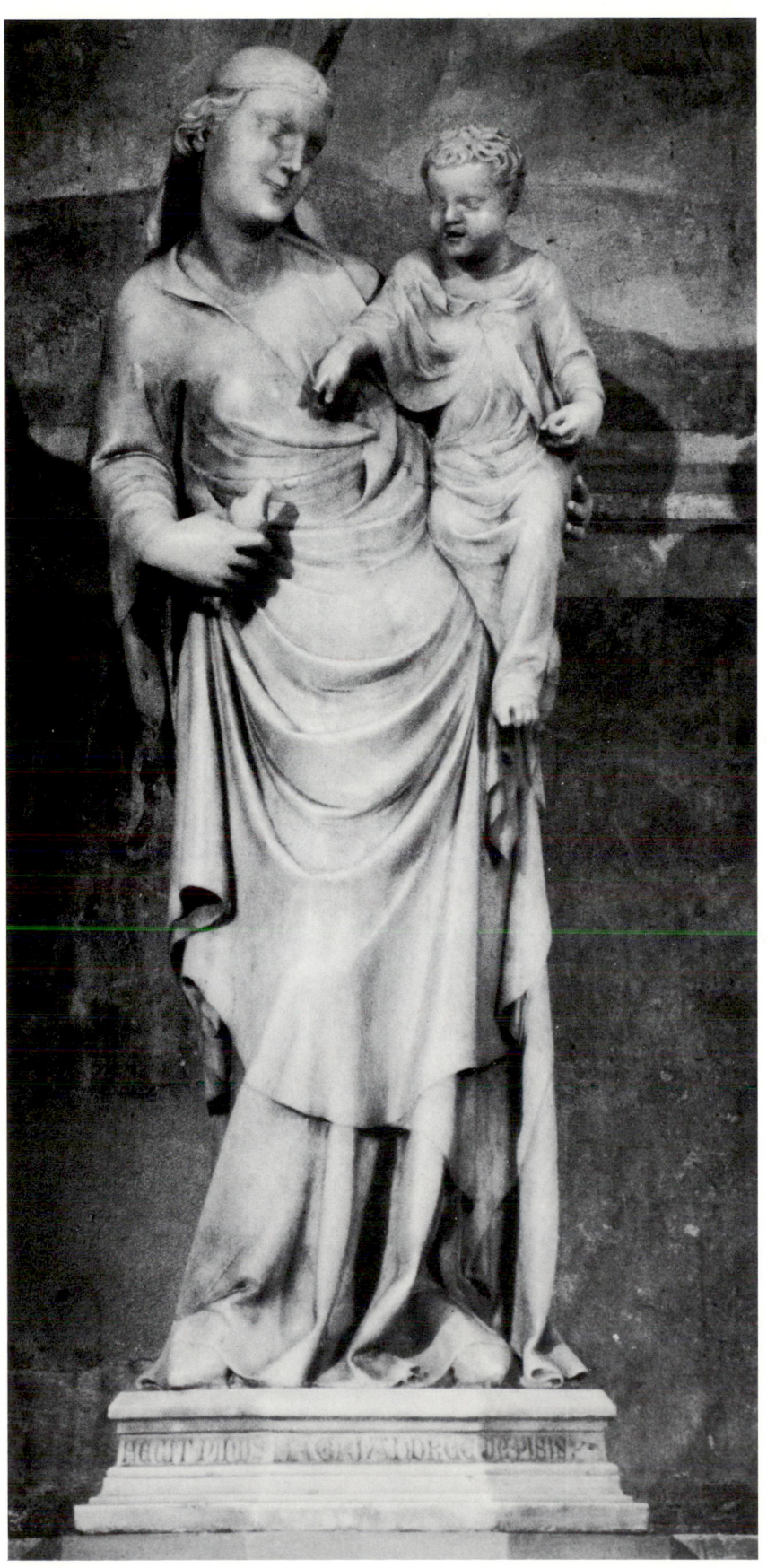

109. Nino Pisano: *Madonna and Child*. Florence, Sta. Maria Novella (ht 135 cm)

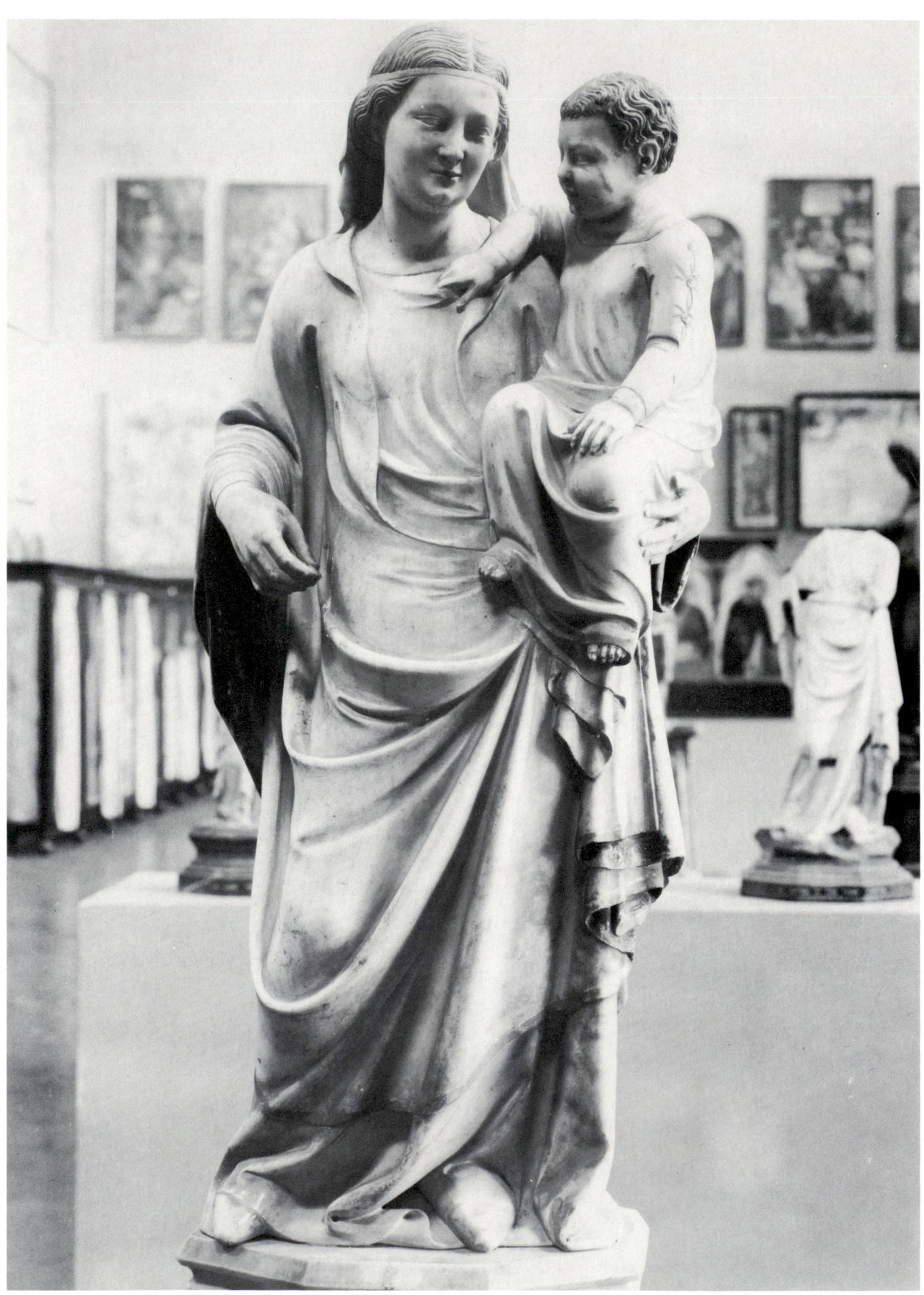

110. Andrea Pisano: *Madonna and Child* (ht 86 cm). Orvieto, Museo dell'Opera del Duomo

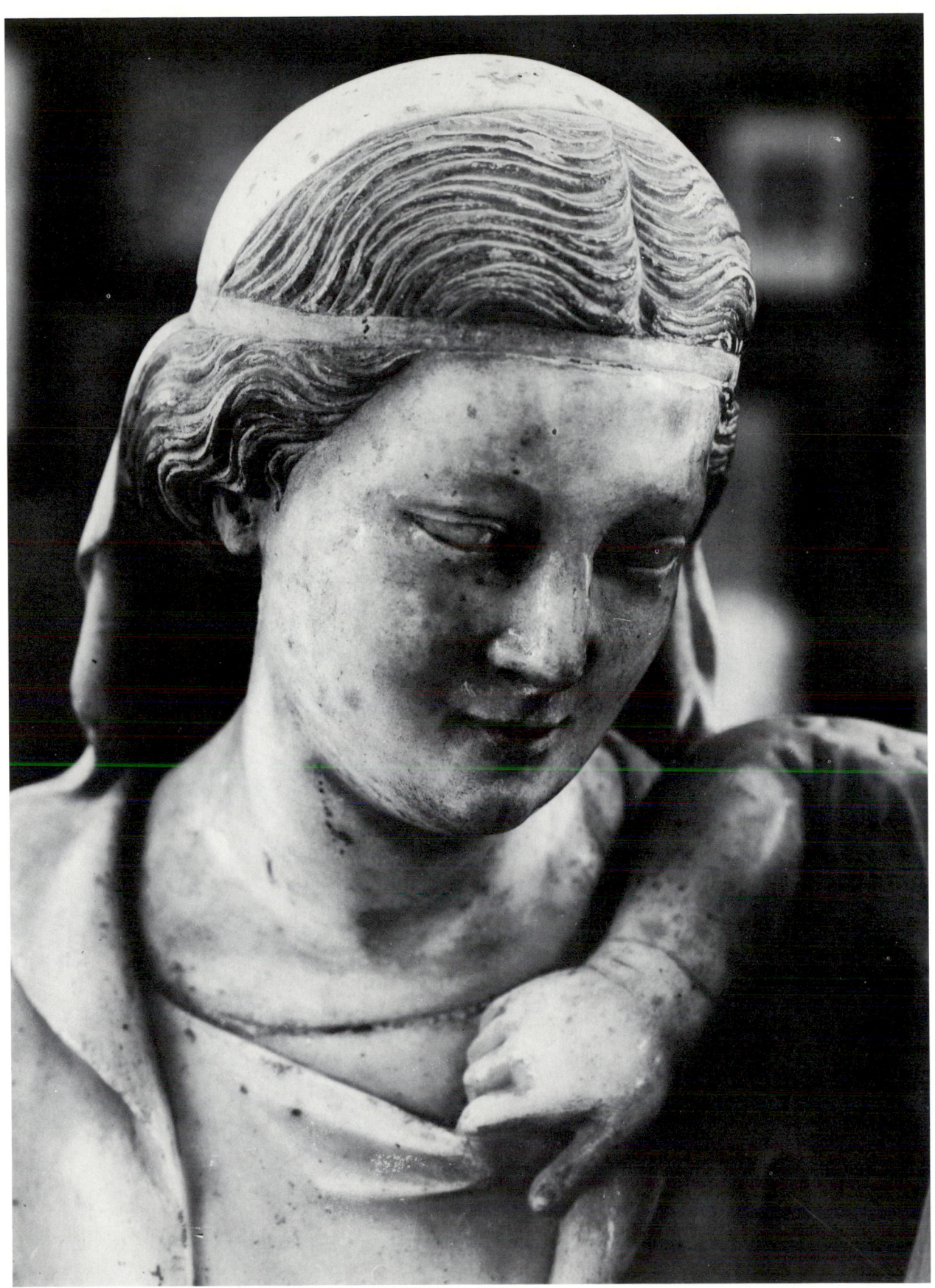

111. Andrea Pisano: *Madonna and Child*, detail. Orvieto, Museo dell'Opera del Duomo

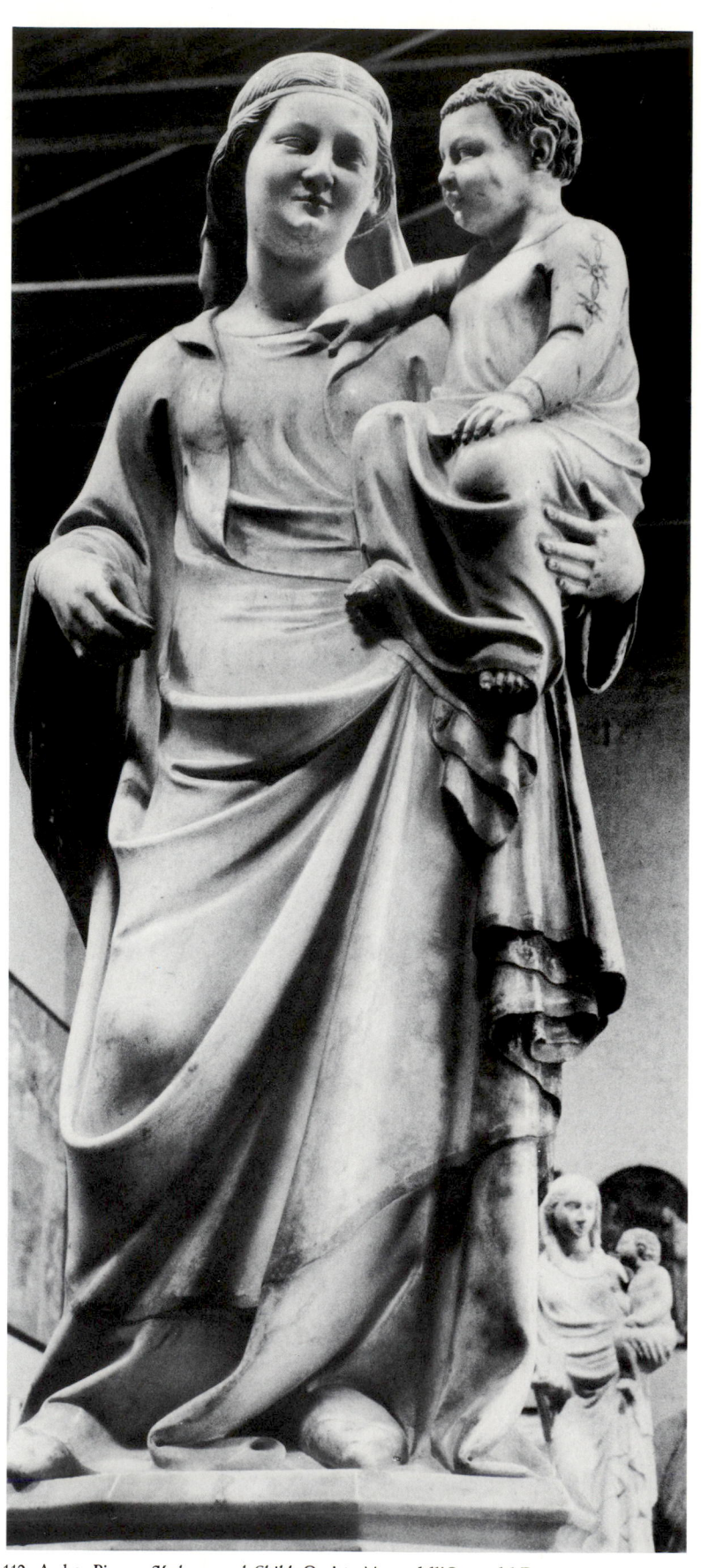

112. Andrea Pisano: *Madonna and Child*. Orvieto Museo dell'Opera del Duomo

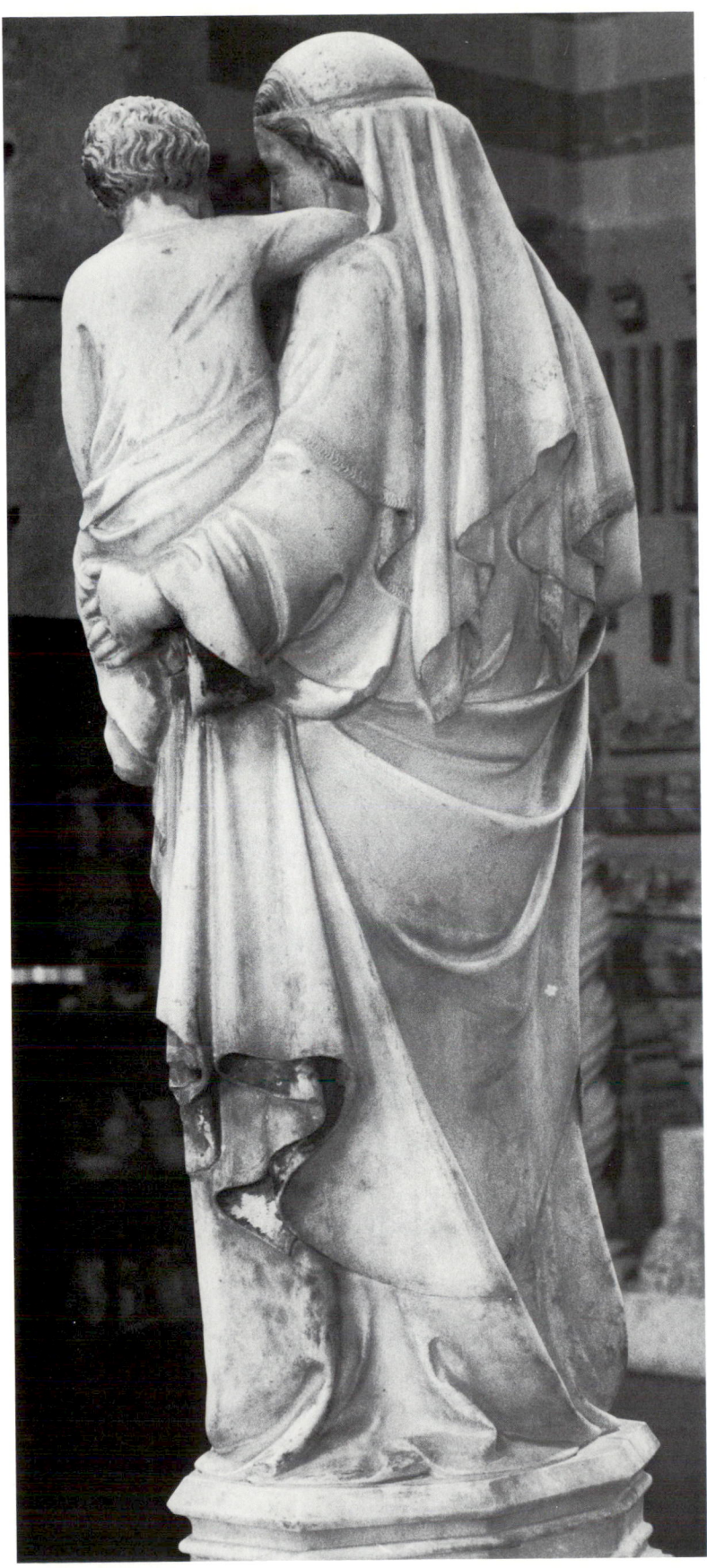

113. Andrea Pisano: *Madonna and Child*. Orvieto, Museo dell'Opera del Duomo

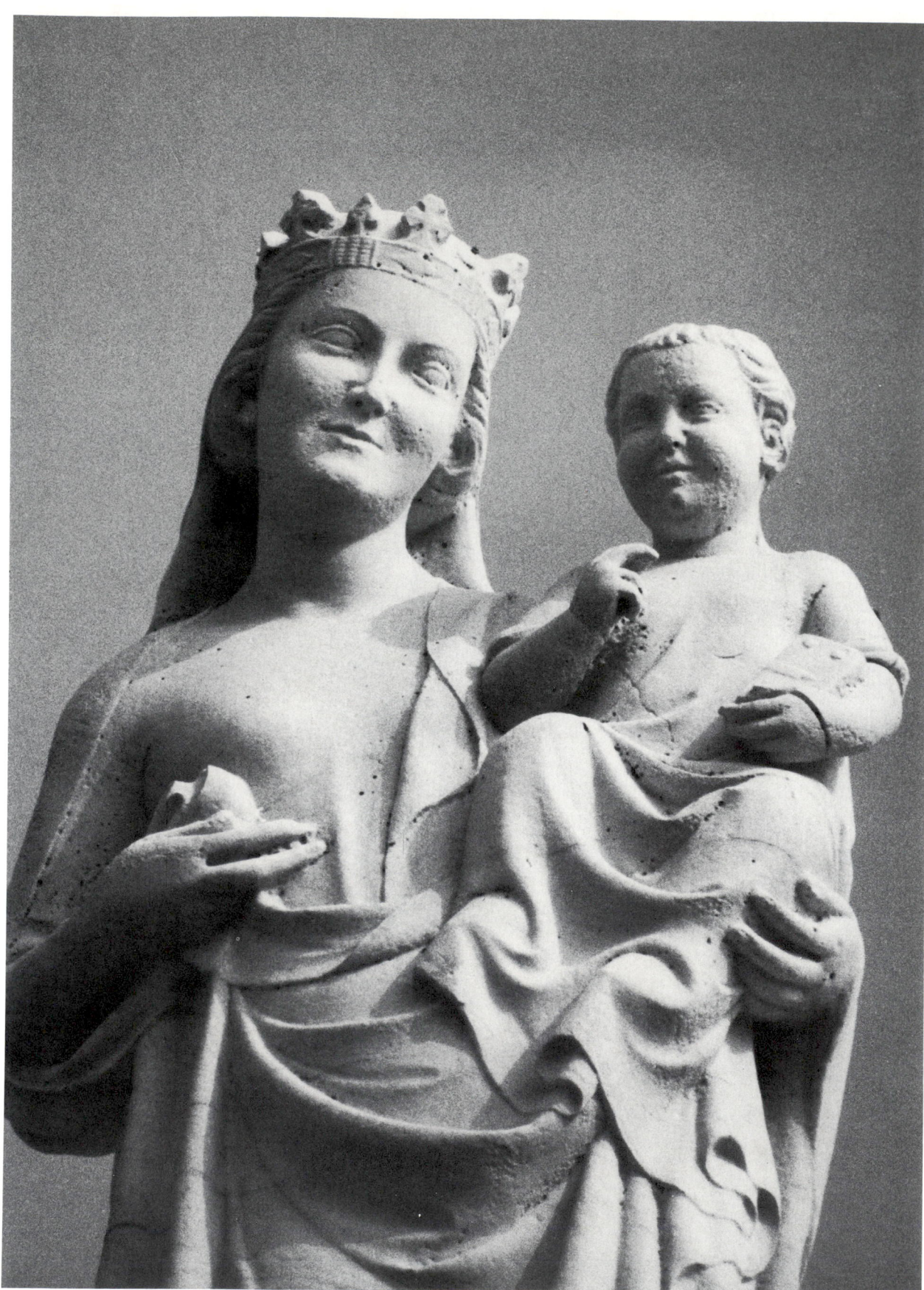

114. Andrea Pisano: *Madonna and Child*. Pisa Cathedral

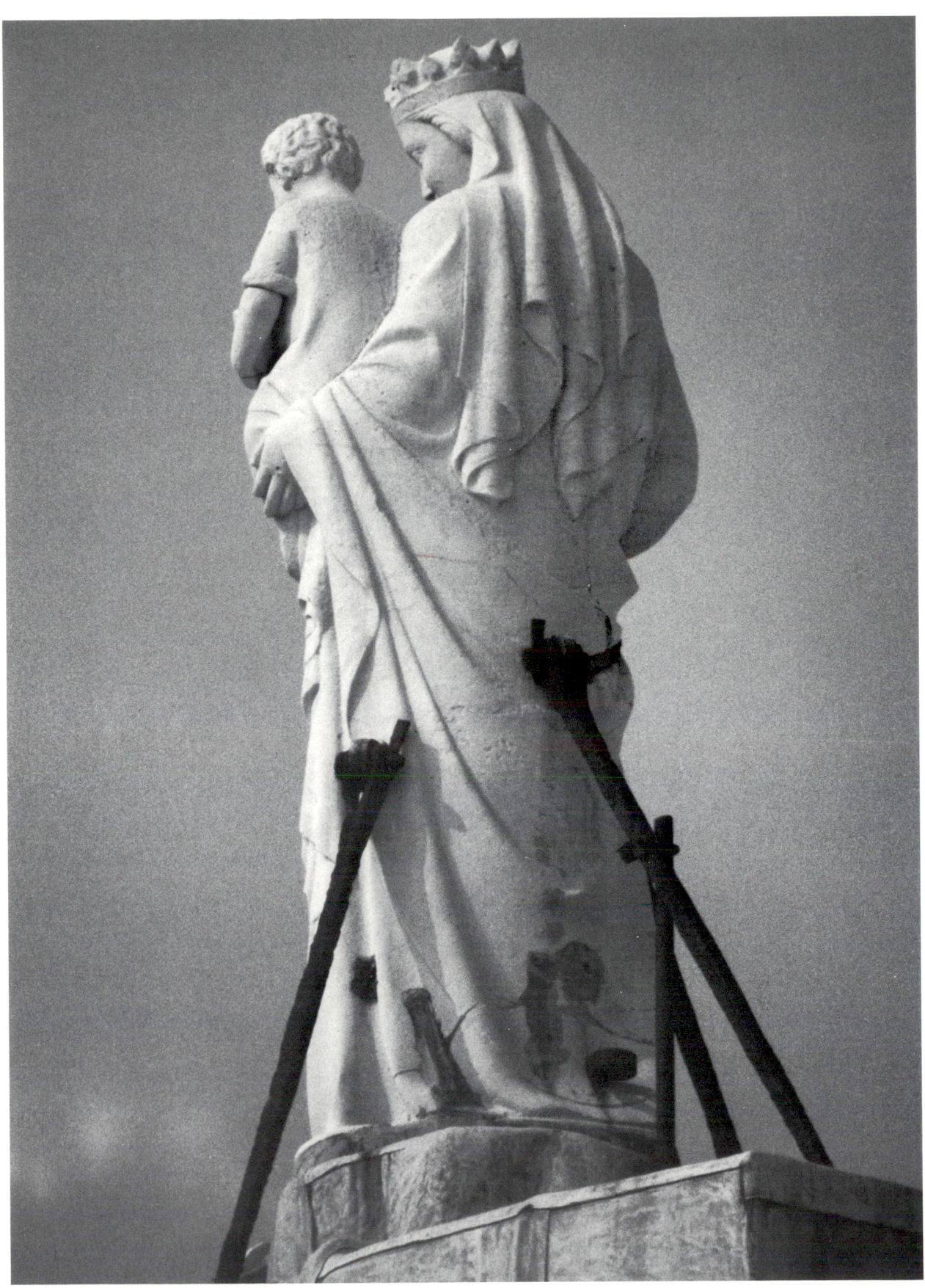

115. Andrea Pisano: *Madonna and Child*. Pisa Cathedral

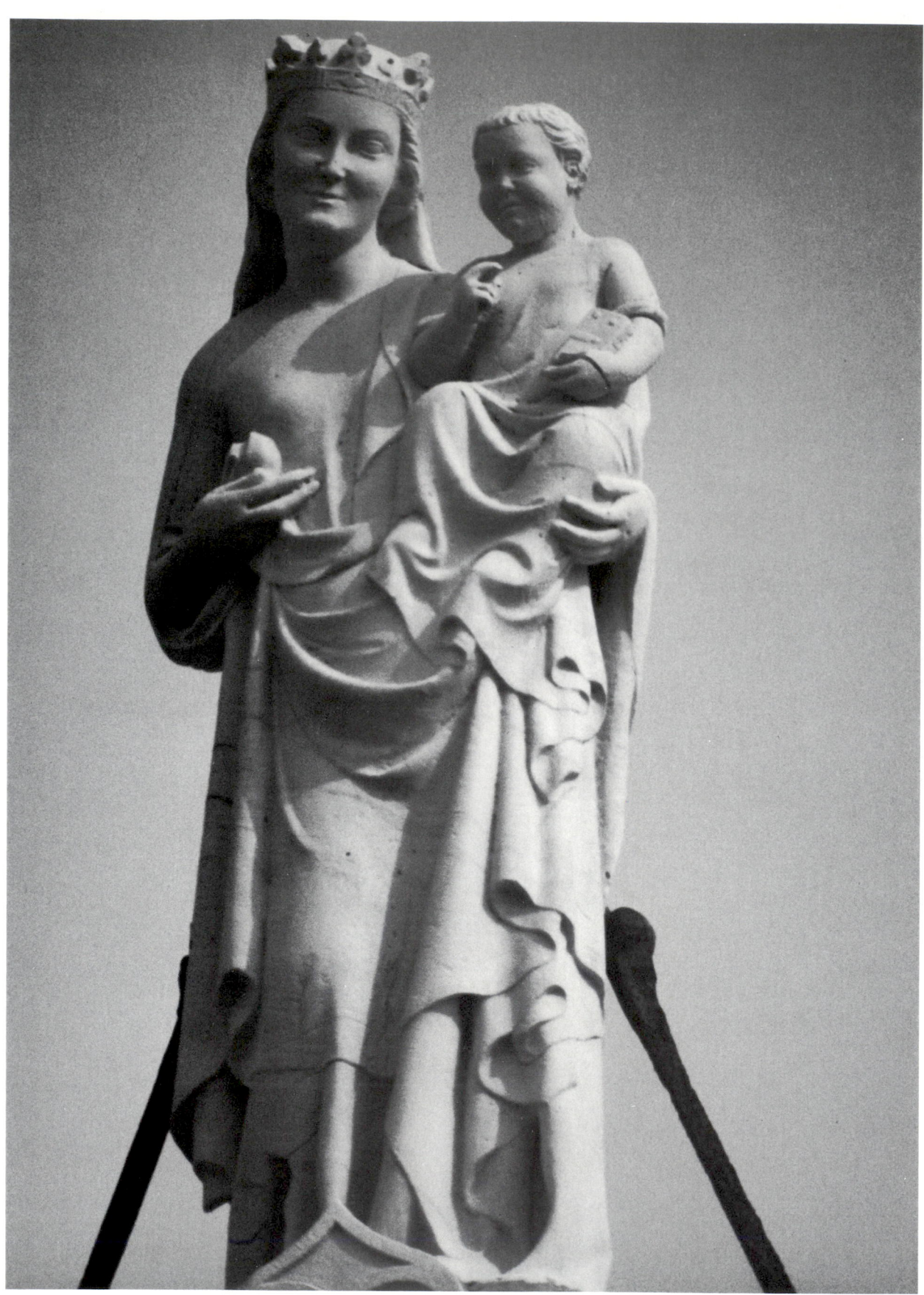

116. Andrea Pisano: *Madonna and Child*. Pisa Cathedral

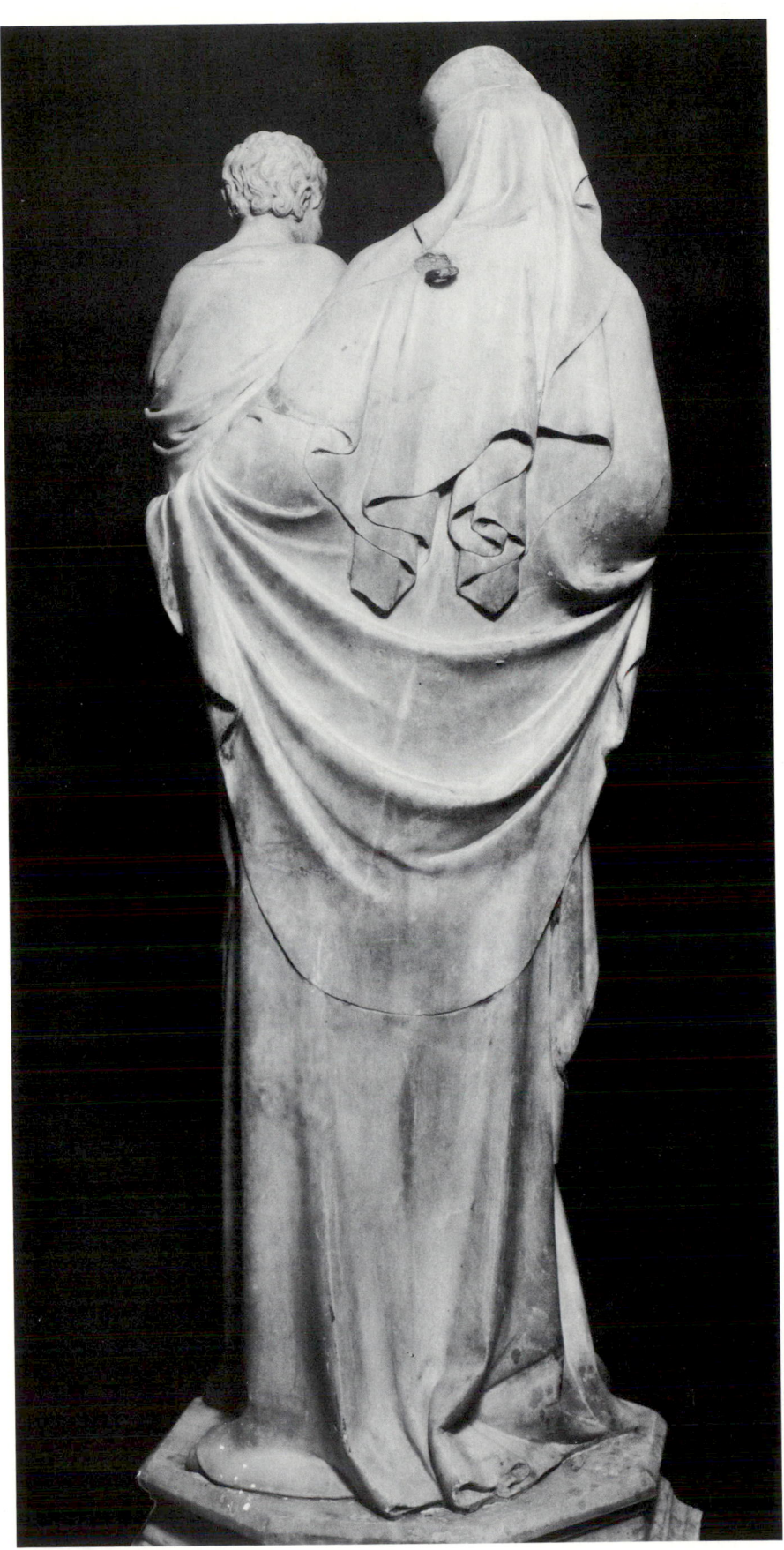

117. Nino Pisano: *Madonna and Child*. Florence, Sta. Maria Novella

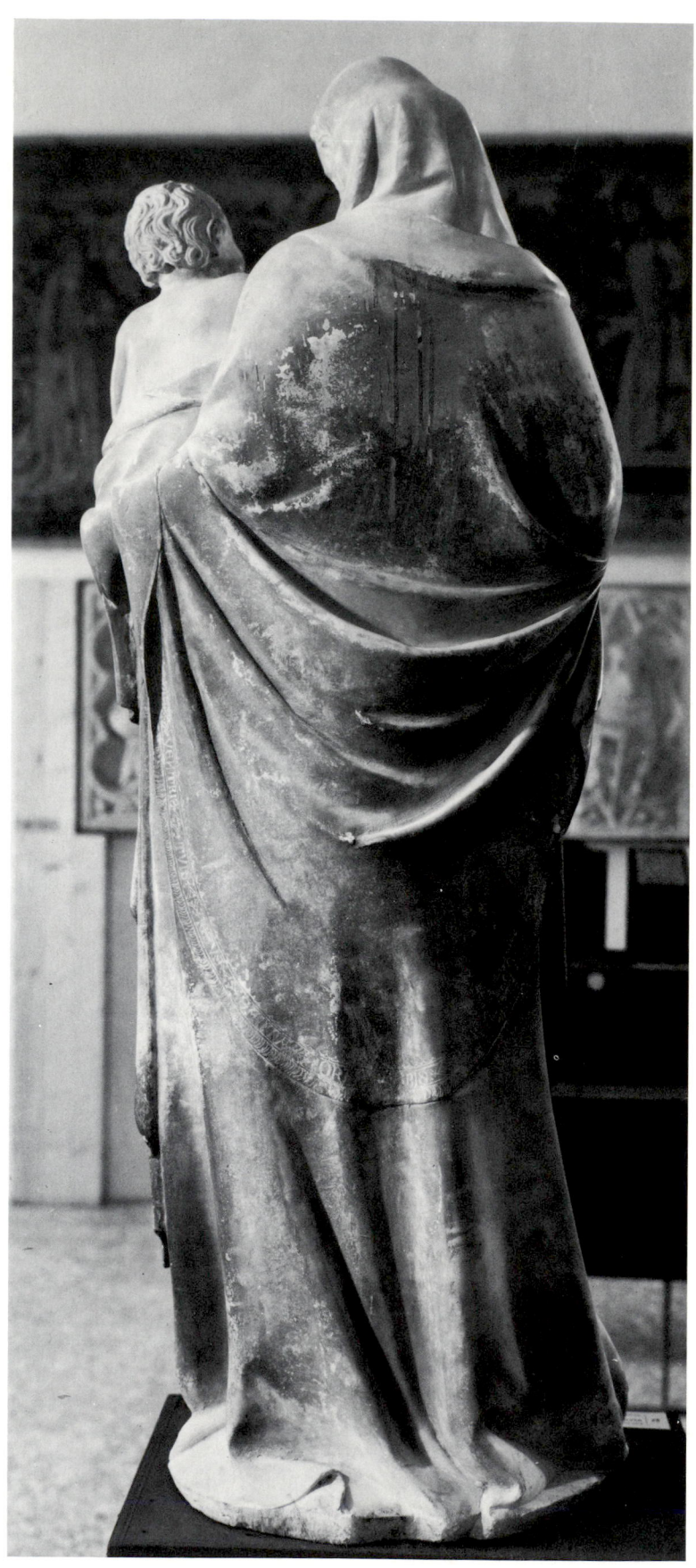

118. Nino Pisano: *Madonna and Child*. Venice, Santi Giovanni e Paolo

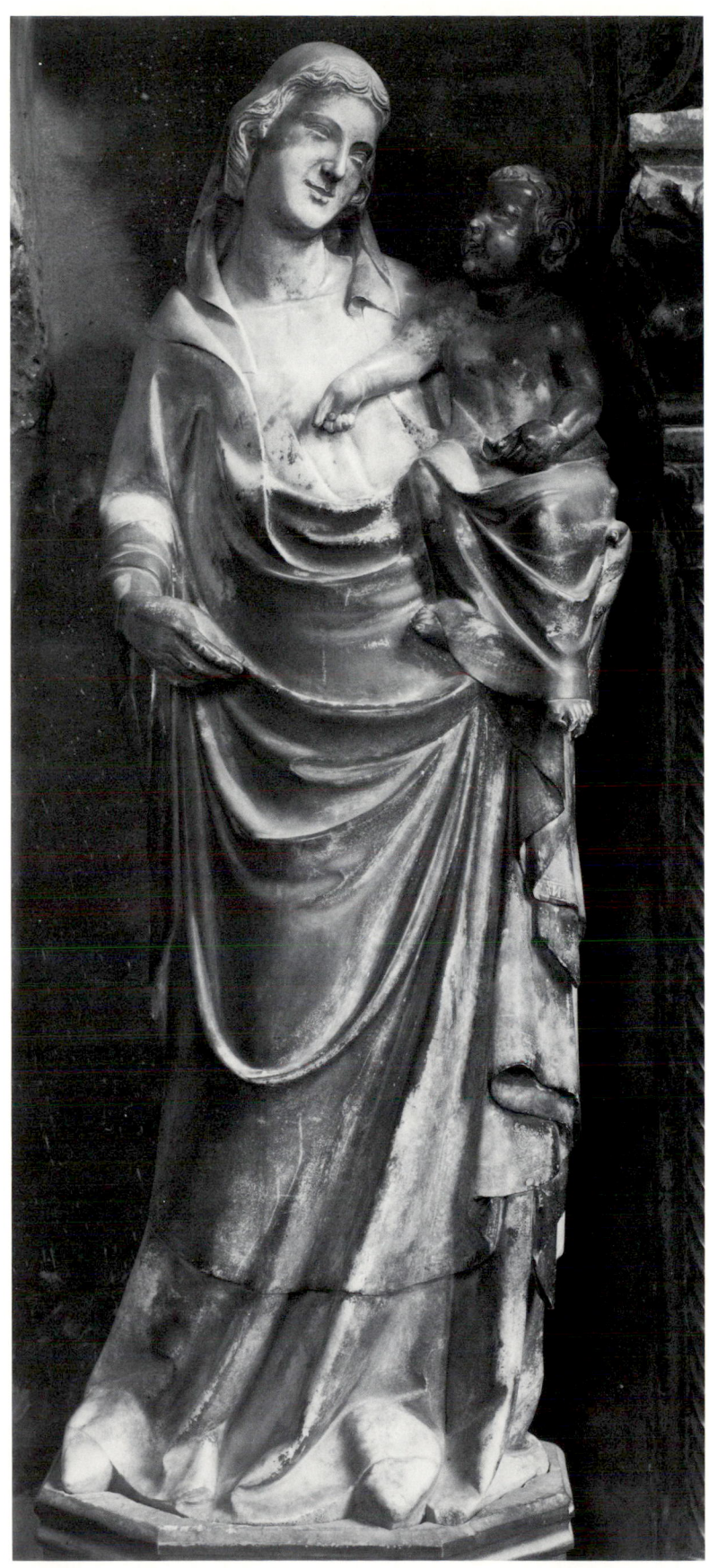

119. Nino Pisano: *Madonna and Child* (ht 125 cm). Venice, Santi Giovanni e Paolo

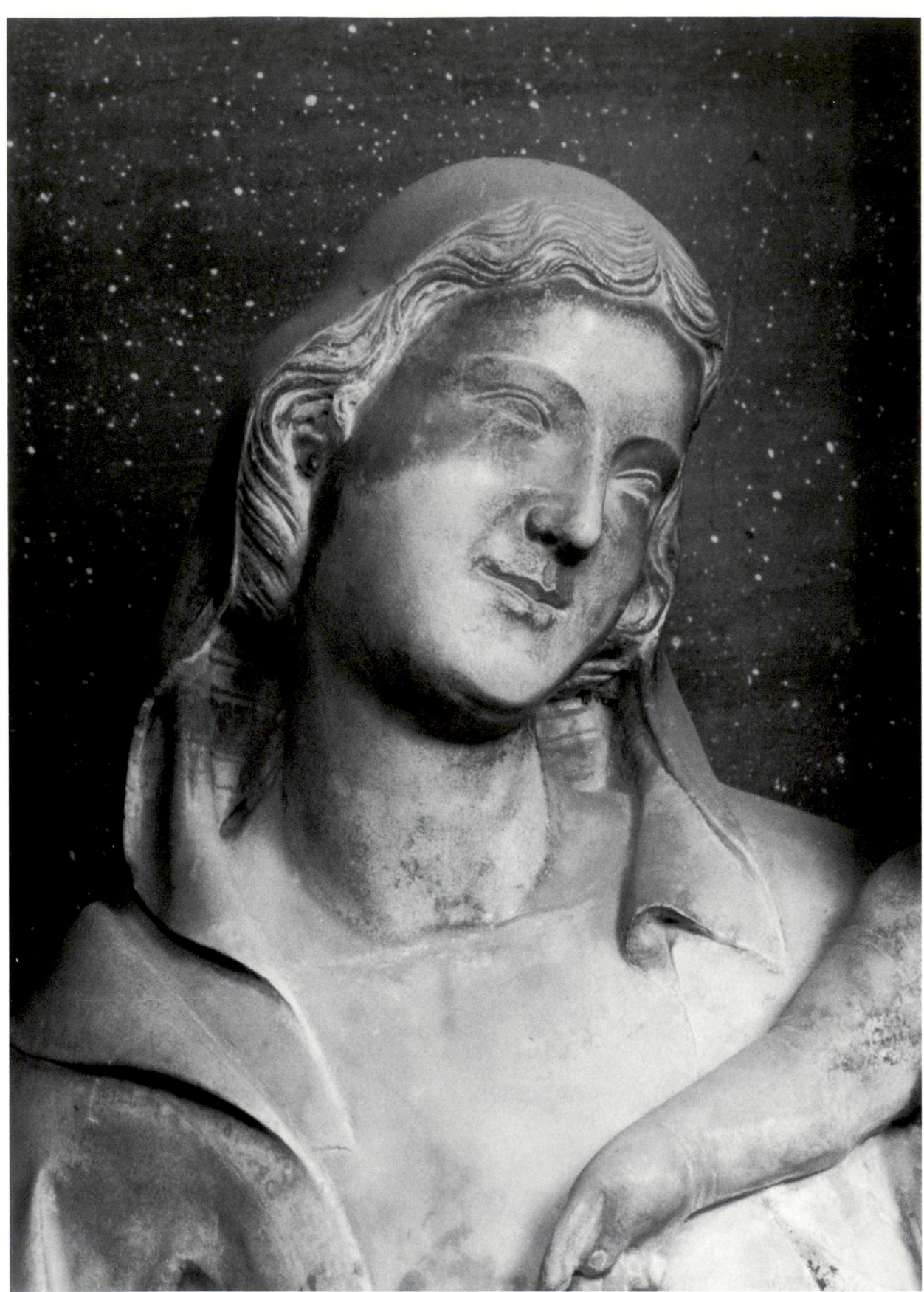

120. Nino Pisano: *Madonna and Child*, detail. Venice, Santi Giovanni e Paolo

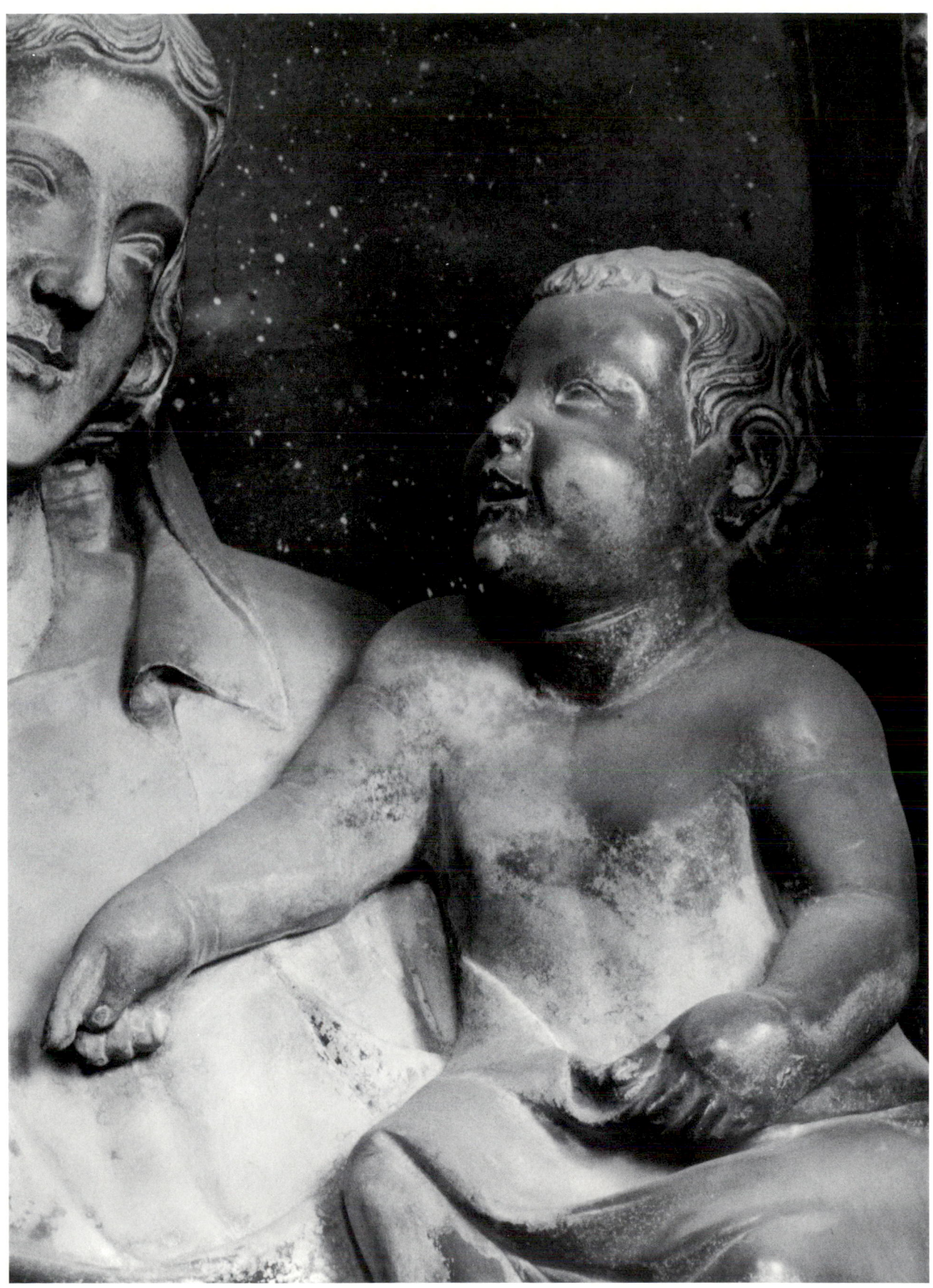

121. Nino Pisano: *Madonna and Child*, detail. Venice, Santi Giovanni e Paolo

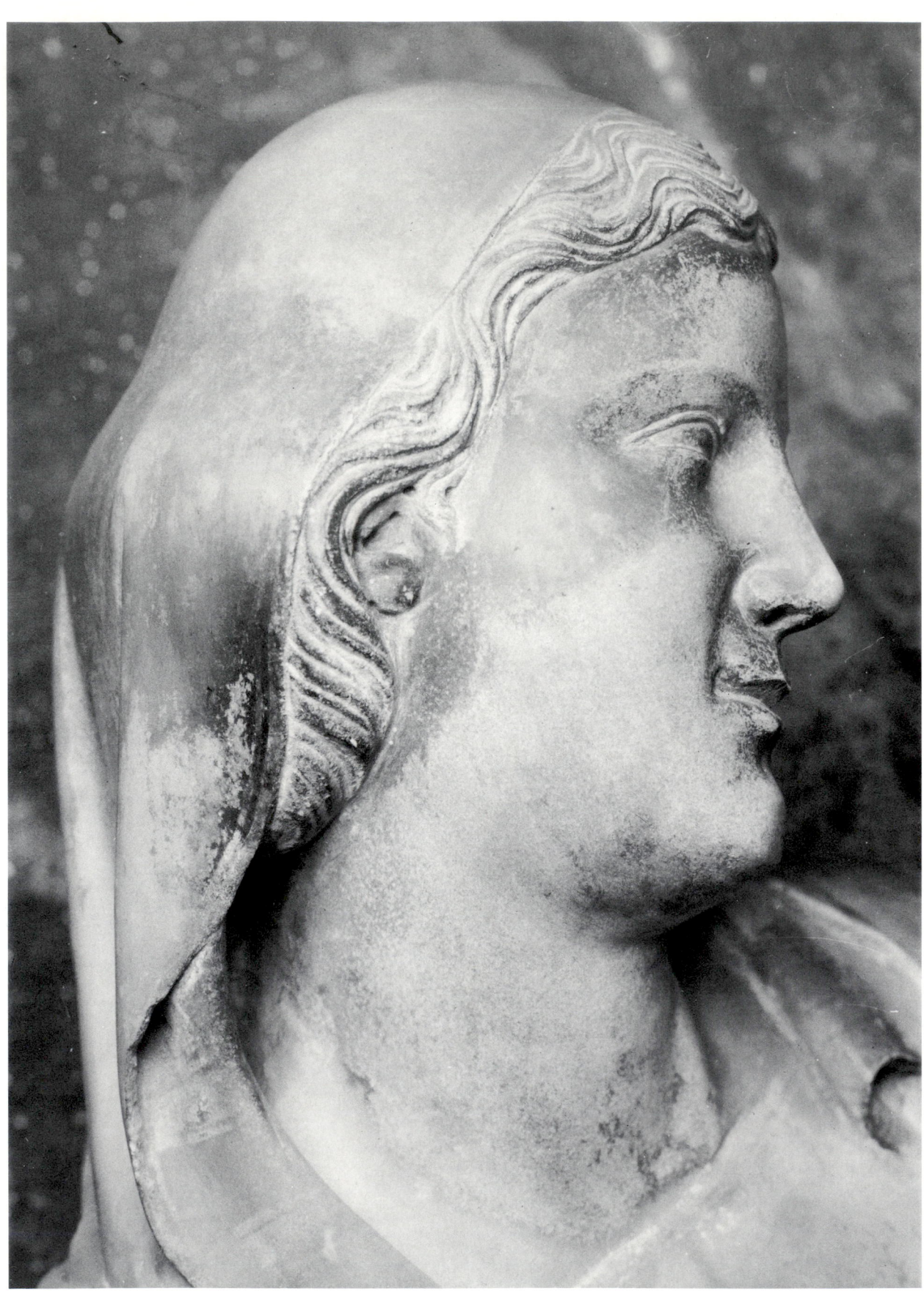

122. Nino Pisano: *Madonna and Child*, detail. Venice, Santi Giovanni e Paolo

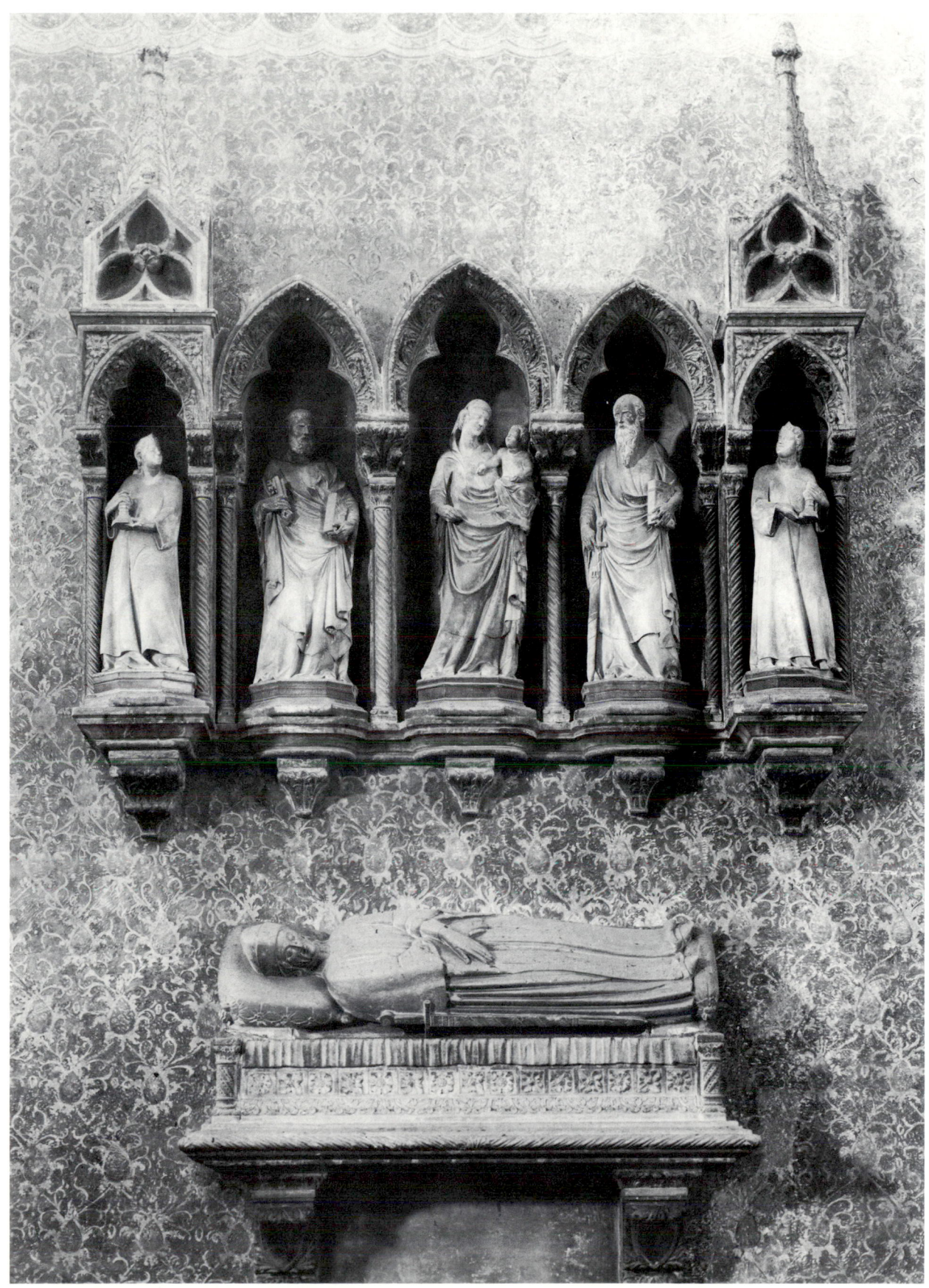

123. Cornaro Monument. Venice, Santi Giovanni e Paolo

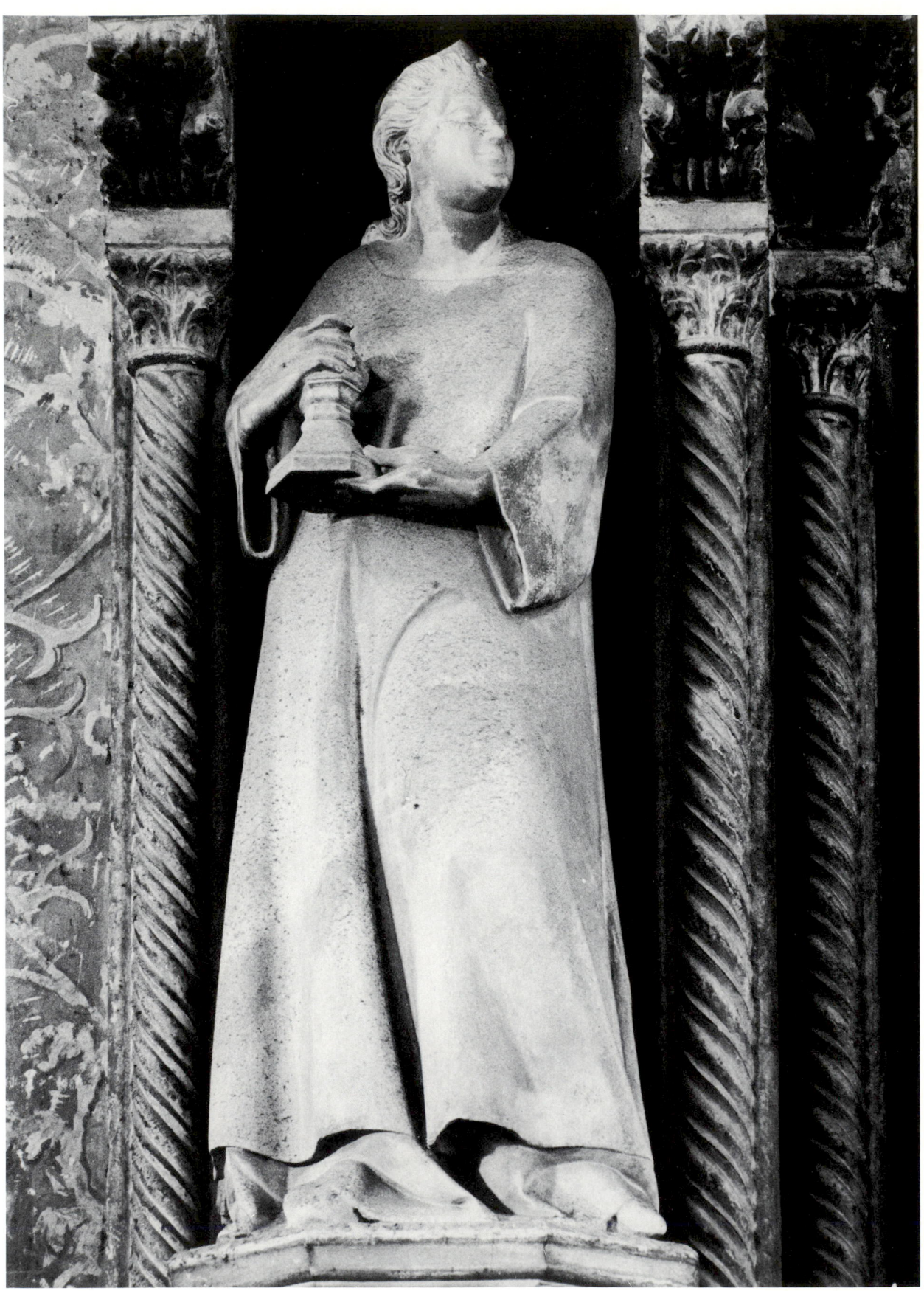

124. Tuscan workshop: *Angel* (ht 108 cm). Venice, Santi Giovanni e Paolo

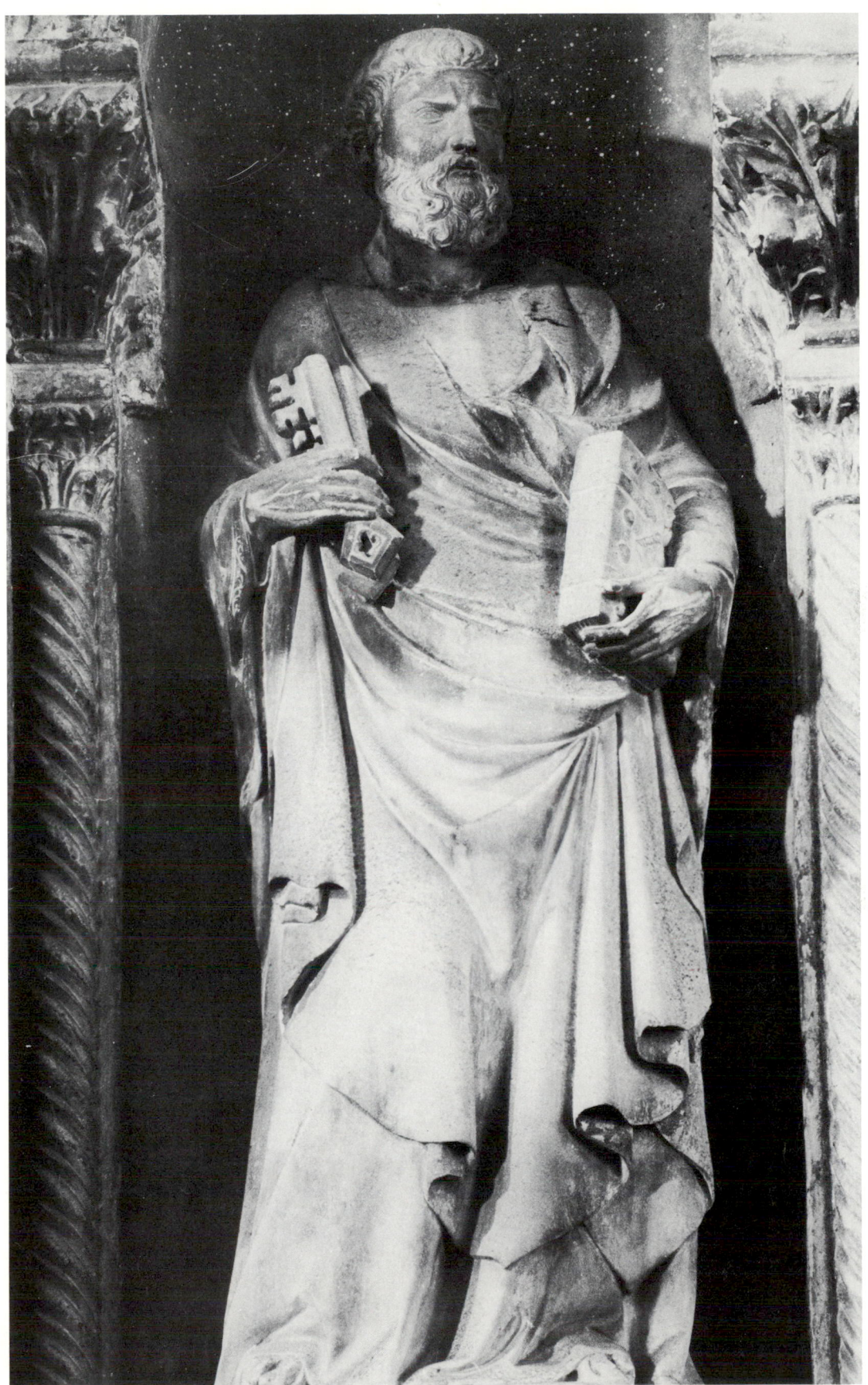

125. Nino Pisano: *St. Peter* (ht 123 cm). Venice, Santi Giovanni e Paolo

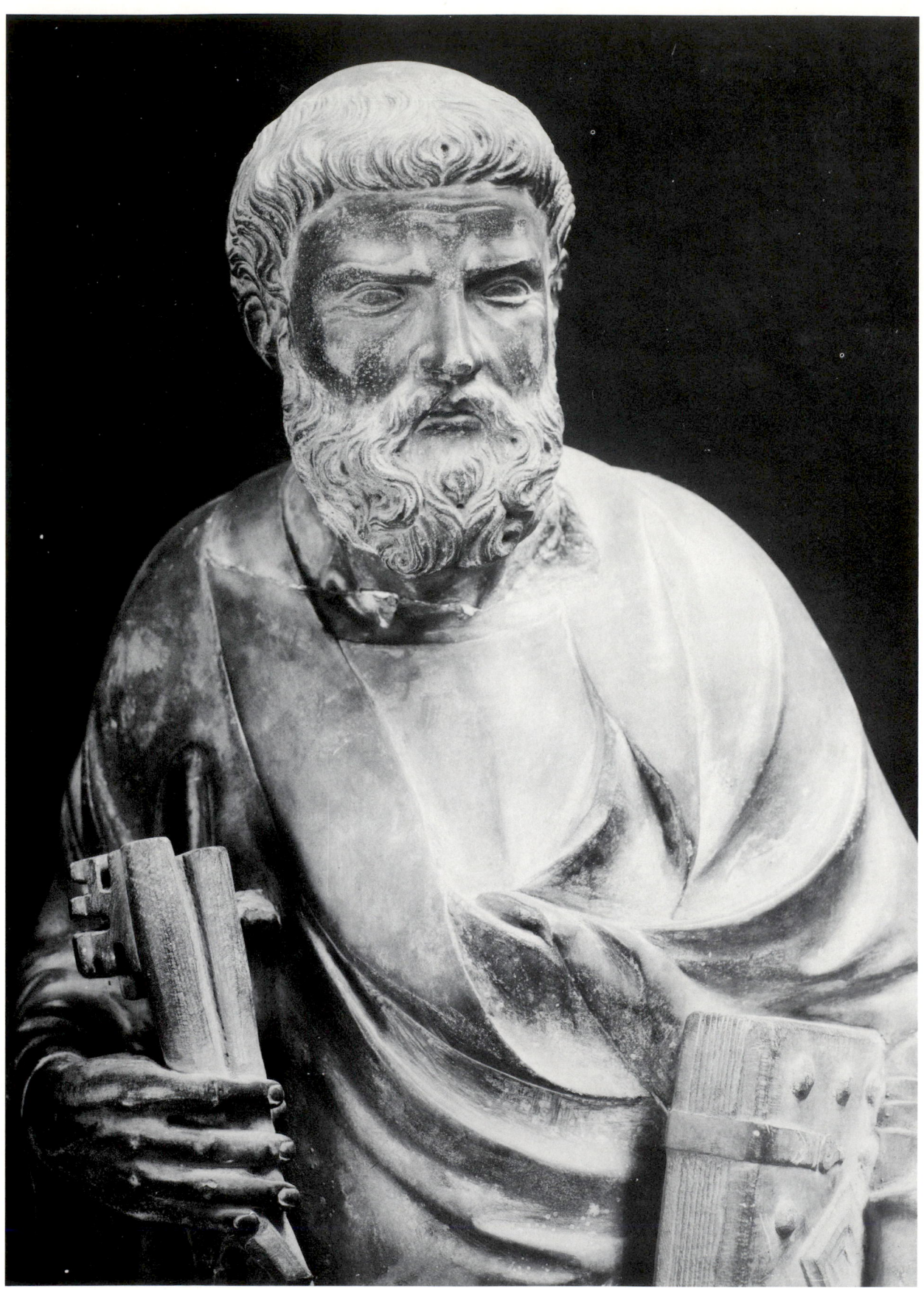

126. Nino Pisano: *St. Peter*, detail. Venice, Santi Giovanni e Paolo

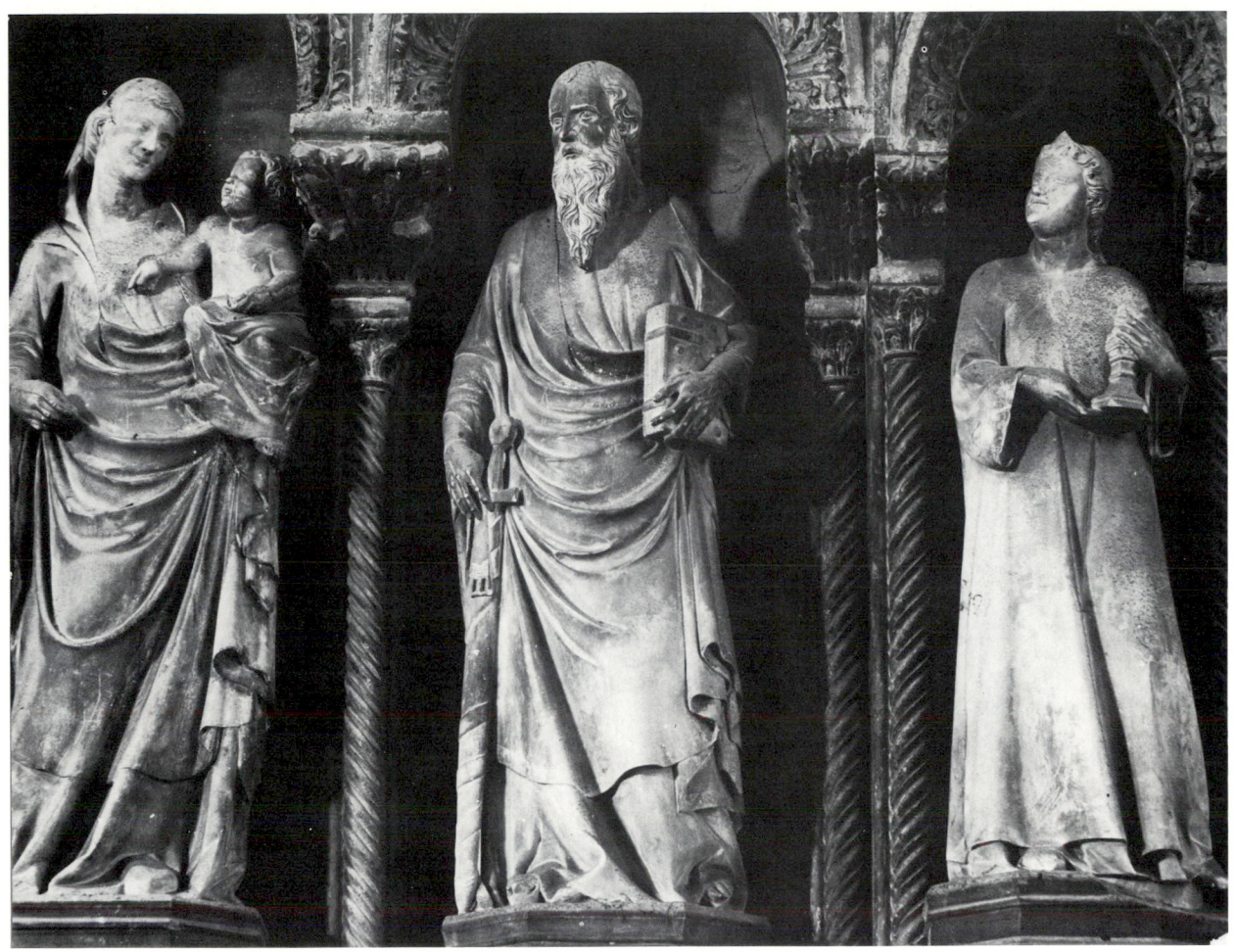

127. Cornaro Monument, detail. Venice, Santi Giovanni e Paolo

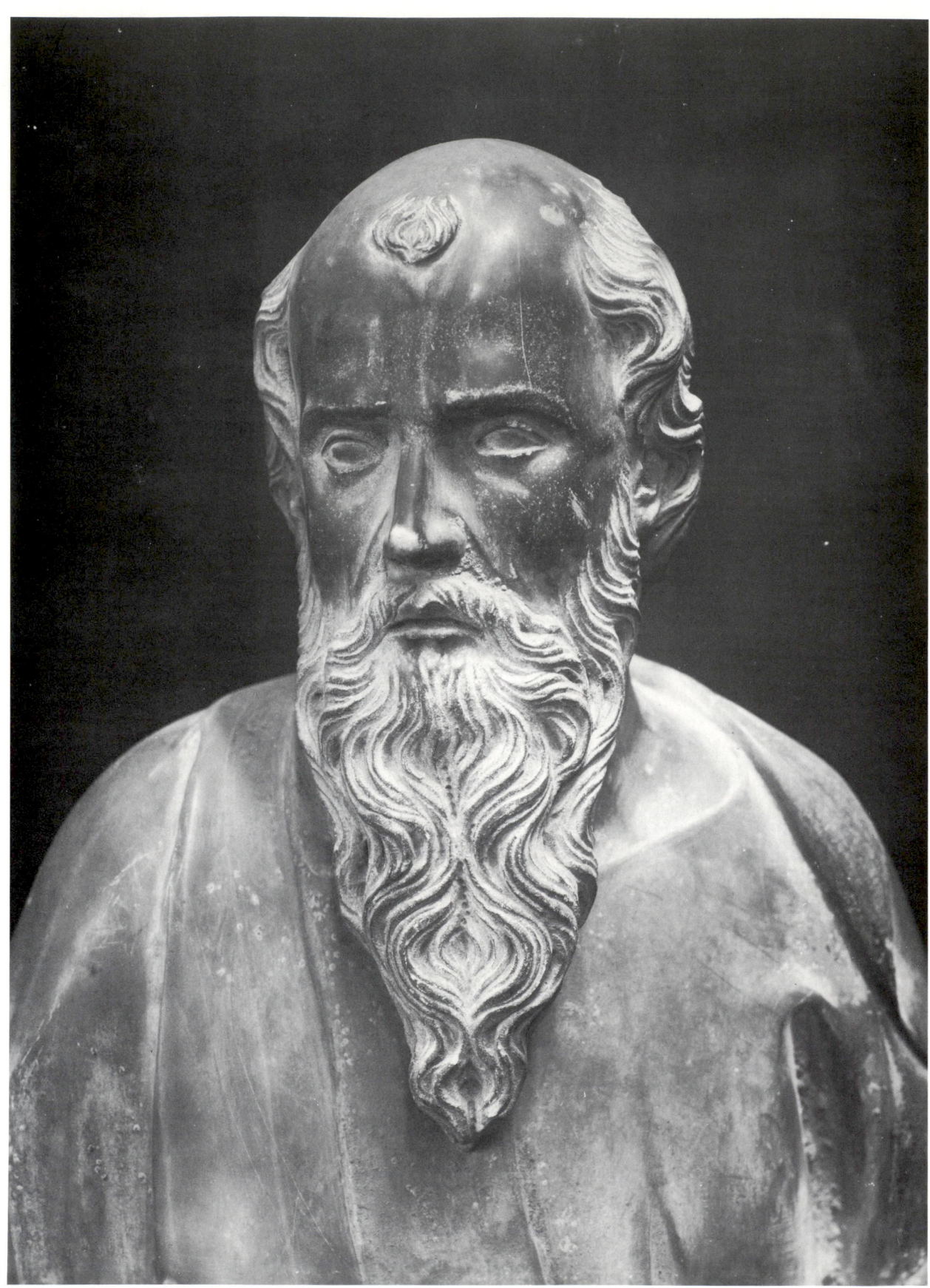

128. Tommaso Pisano: *St. Paul*. Venice, Santi Giovanni e Paolo

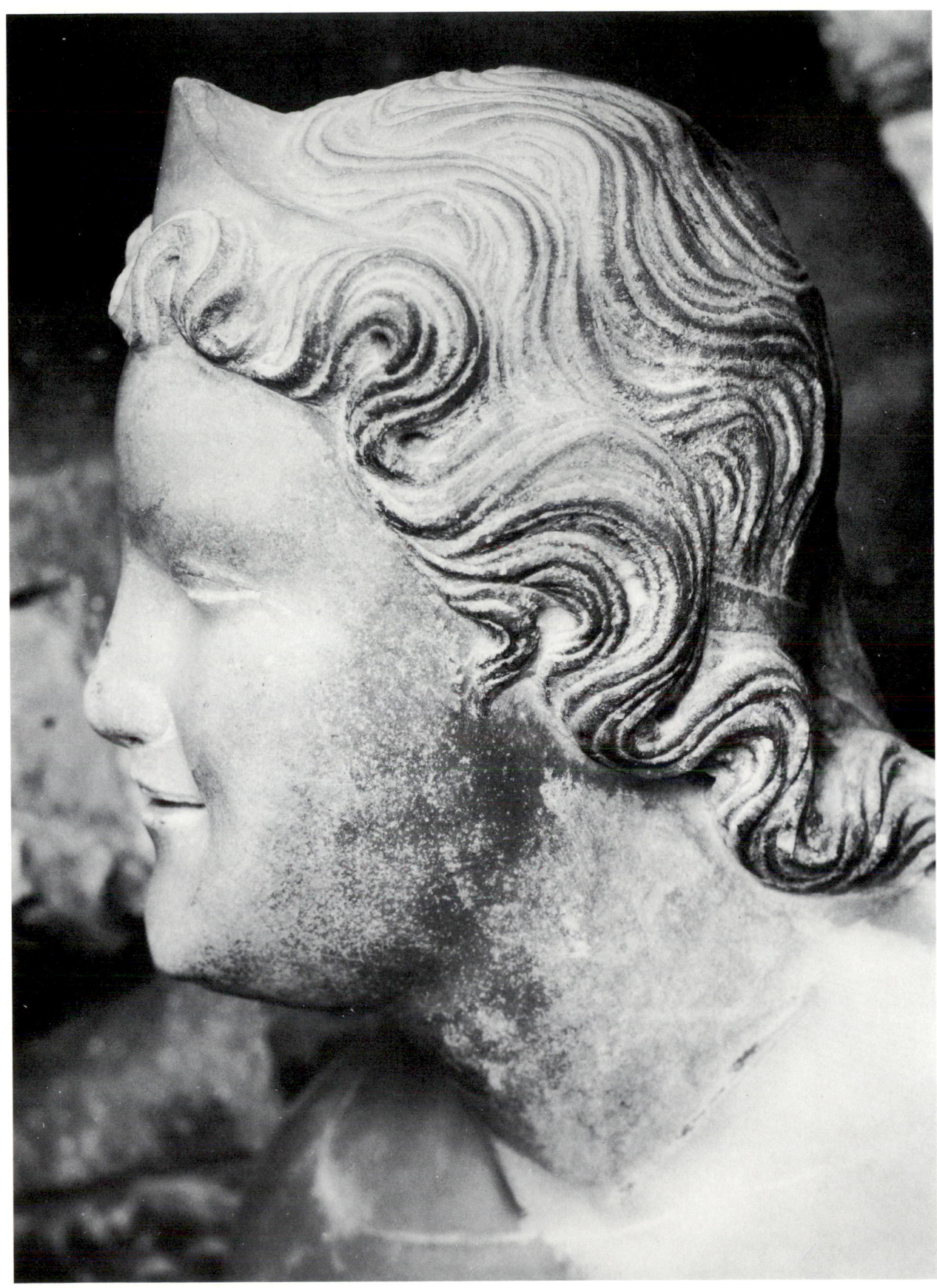

129. Tuscan workshop: *Angel*. Venice, Santi Giovanni e Paolo

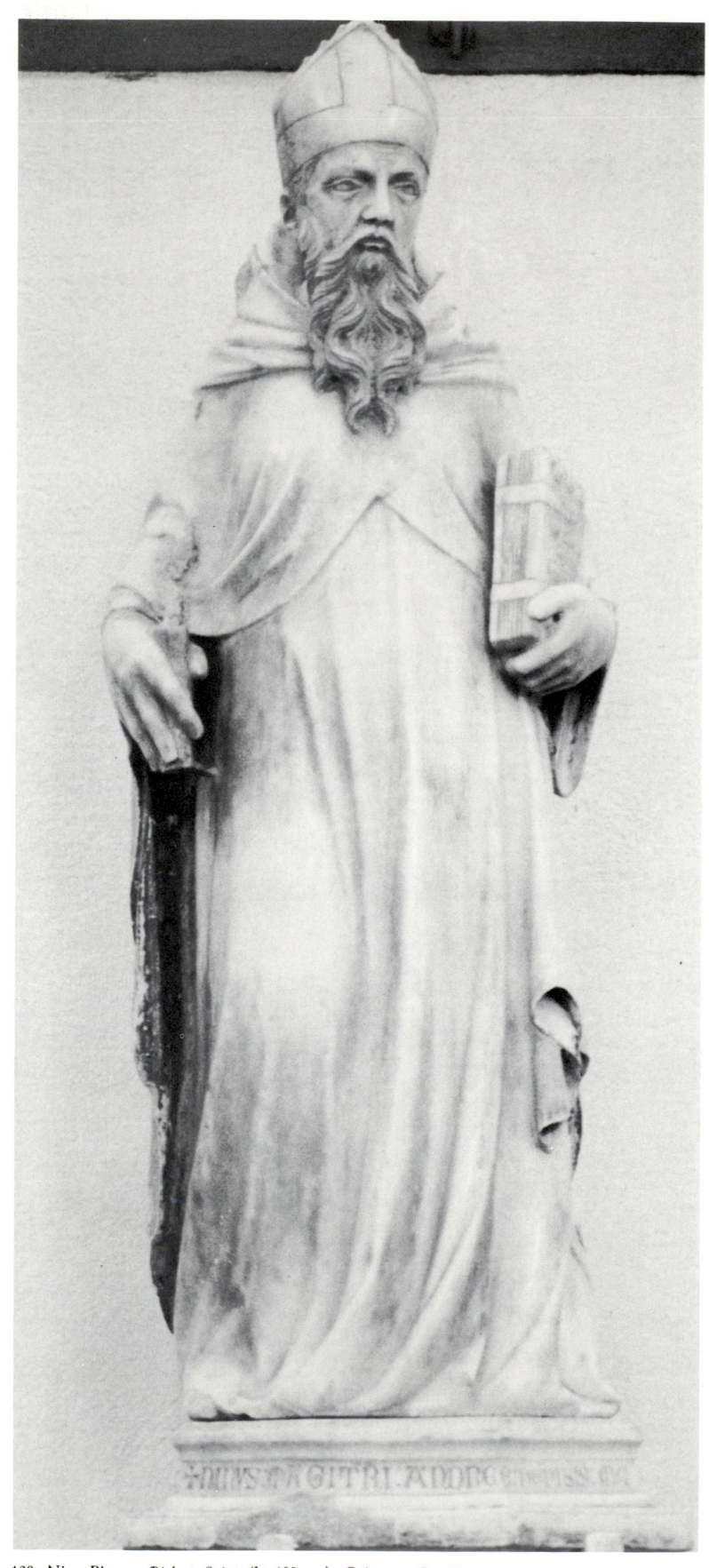

130. Nino Pisano: *Bishop Saint* (ht 100 cm). Oristano, San Francesco

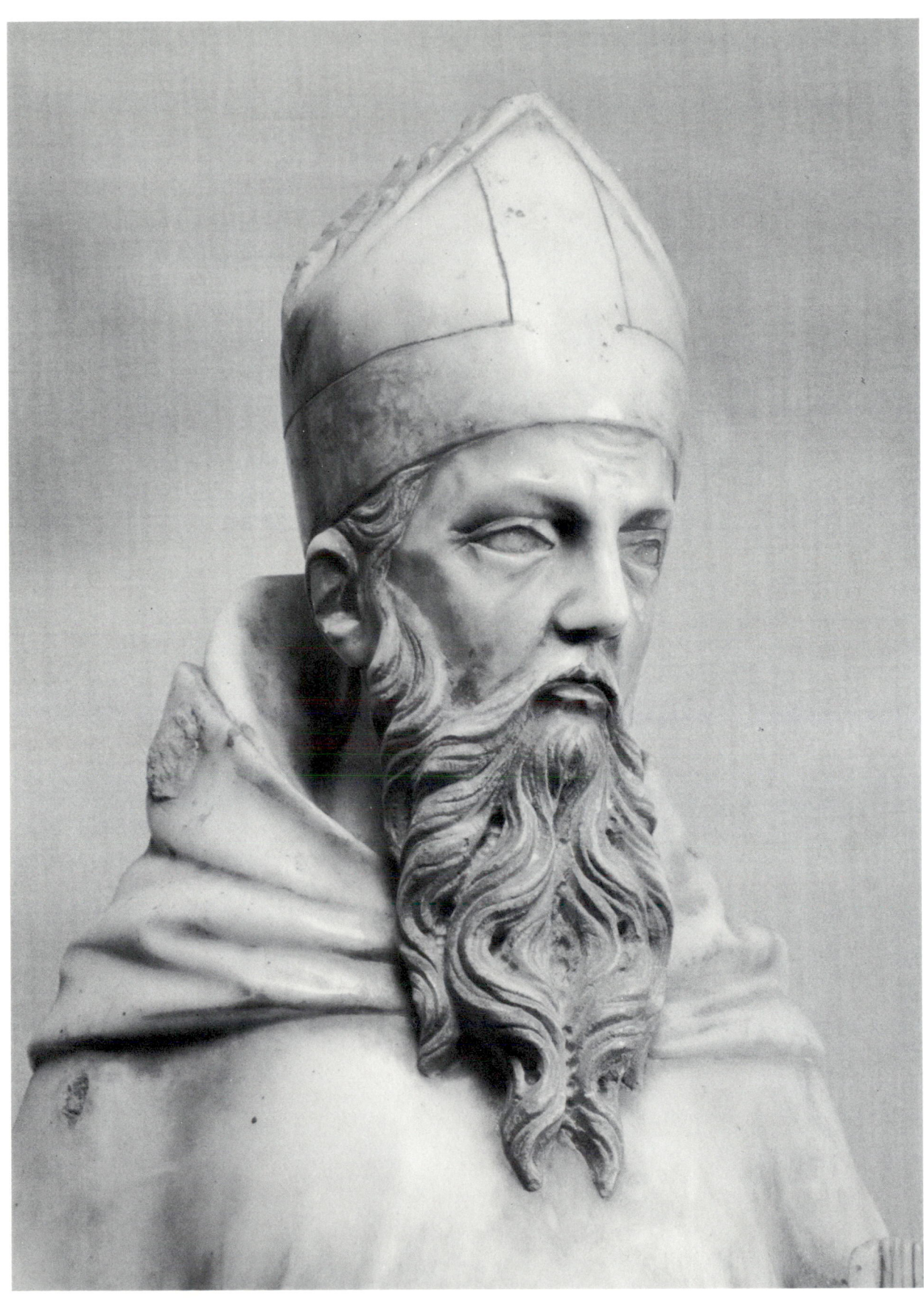

131. Nino Pisano: *Bishop Saint*, detail. Oristano, San Francesco

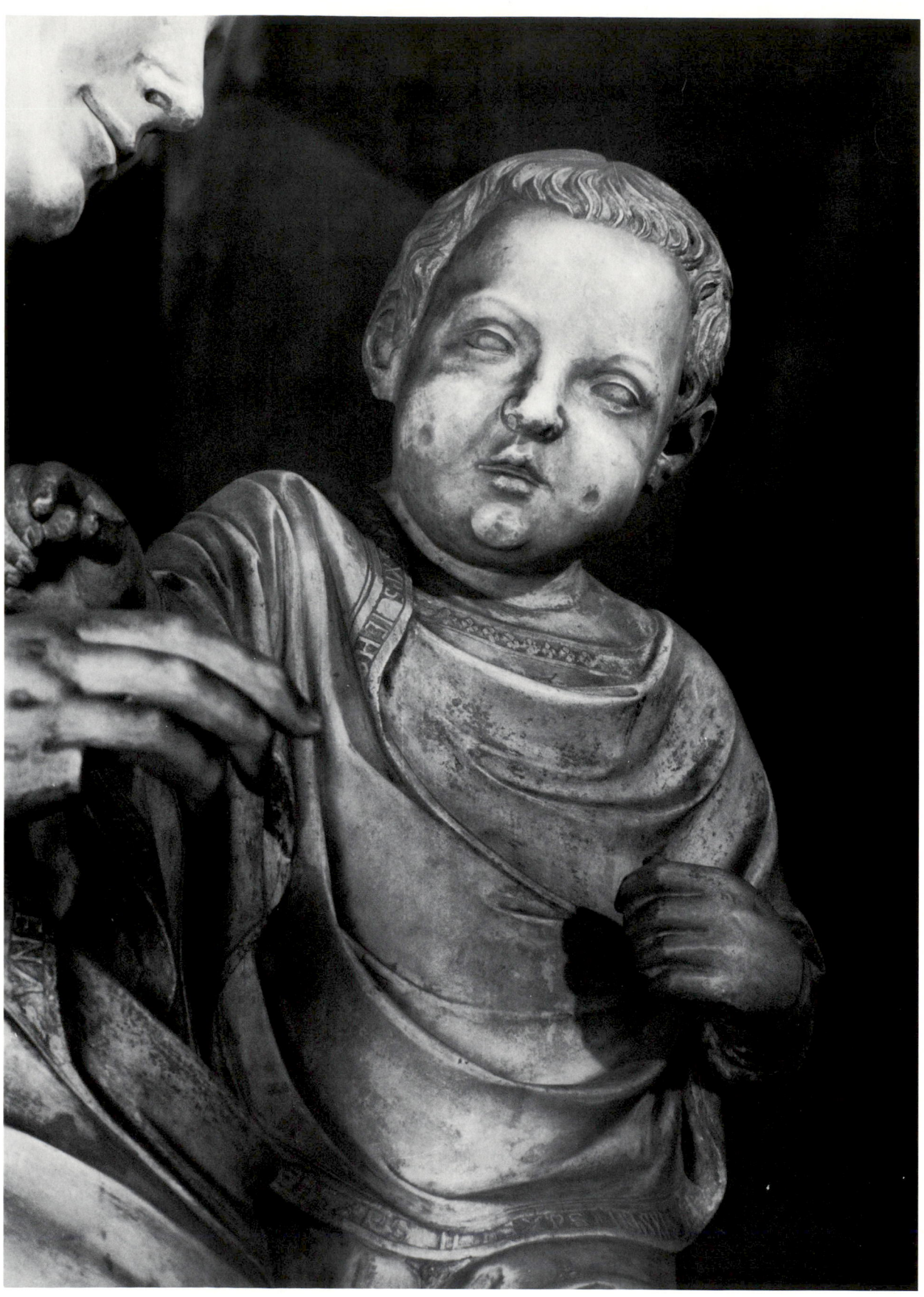

132. Andrea Pisano: *Madonna and Child*, detail. Pisa, Sta. Maria della Spina

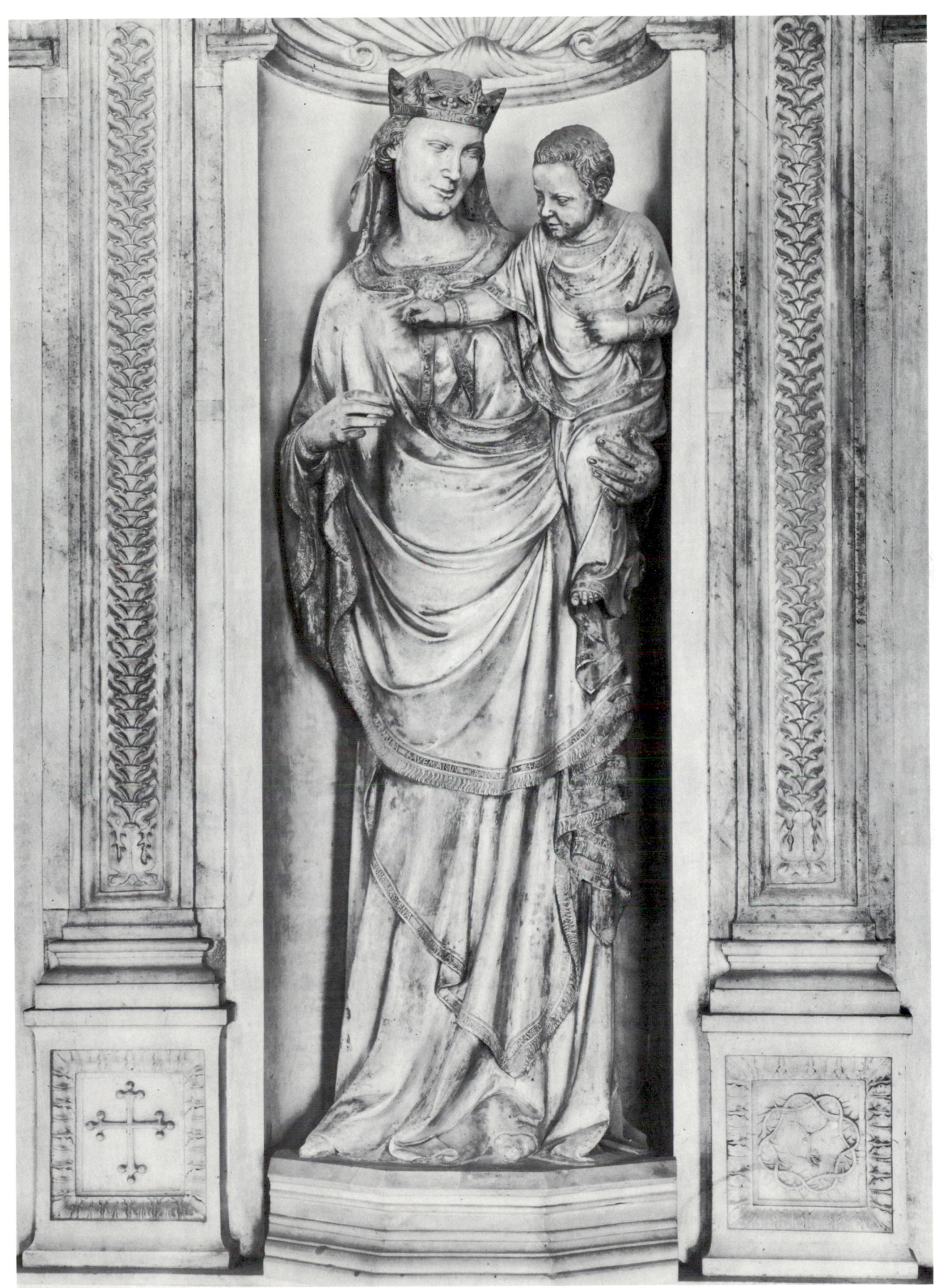

133. Andrea Pisano: *Madonna and Child* (ht 170 cm). Pisa, Sta. Maria della Spina

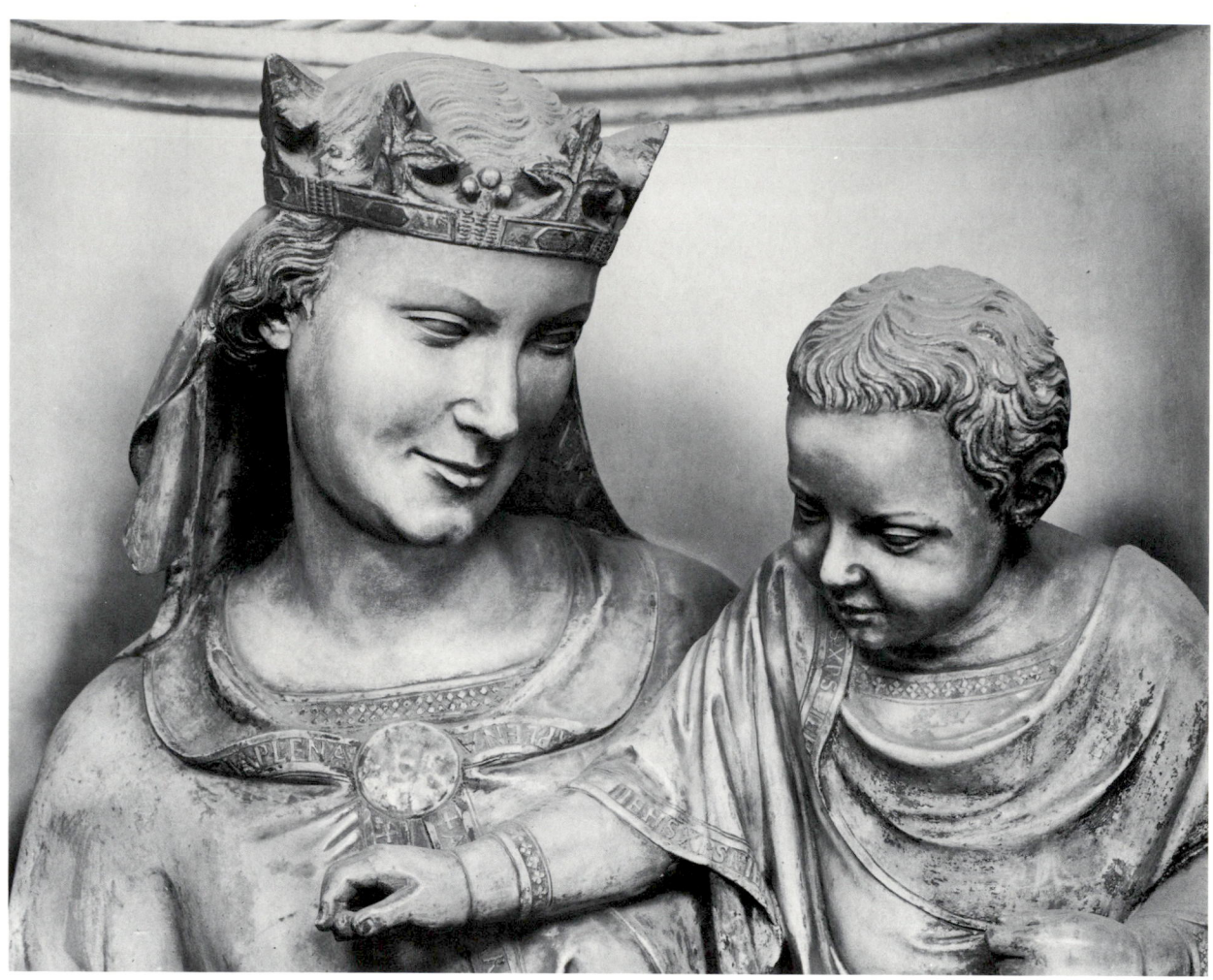

134. Andrea Pisano: *Madonna and Child,* detail. Pisa, Sta. Maria della Spina

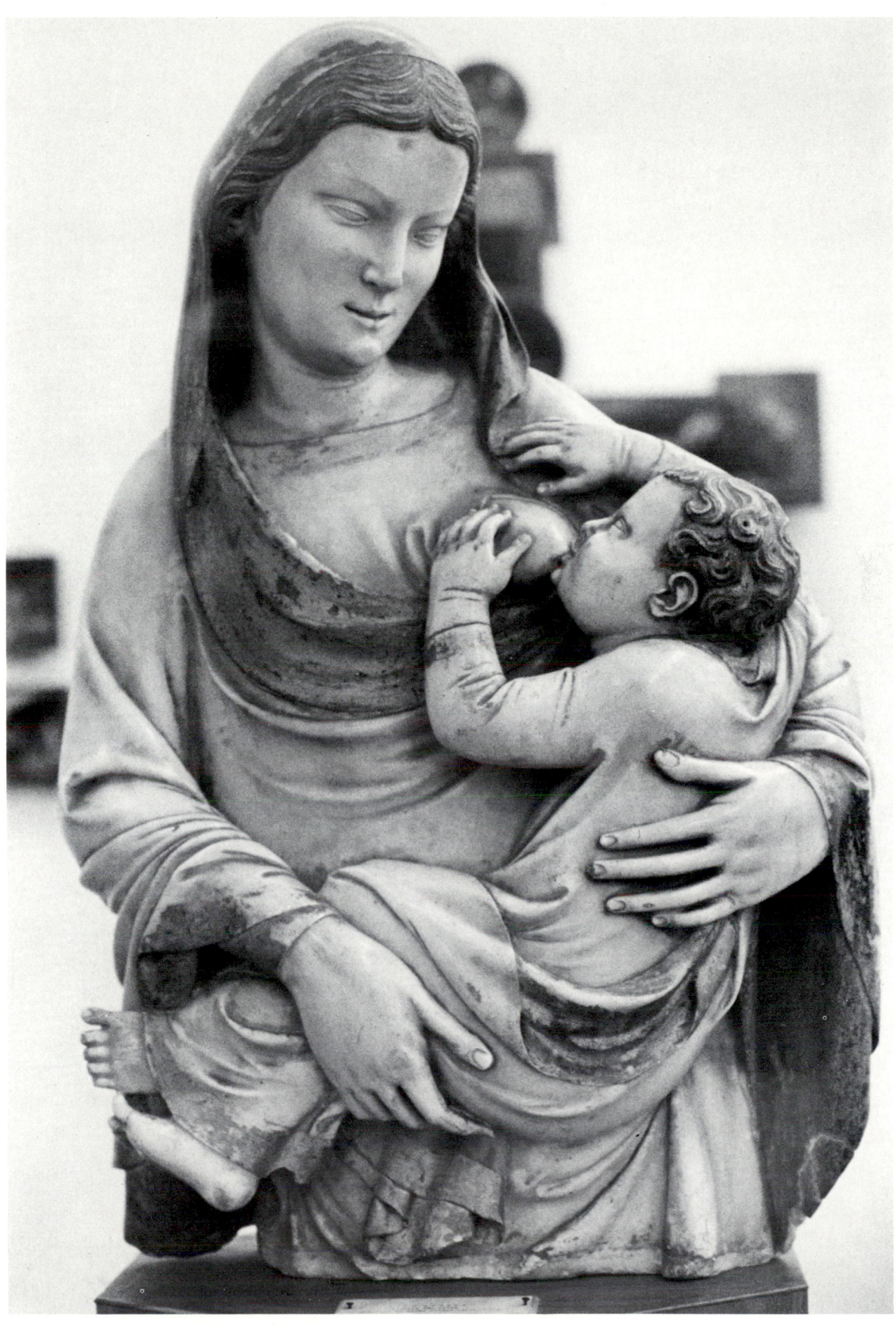

135. Andrea Pisano: *Madonna del Latte* (ht 91 cm). Pisa, Museo di San Matteo

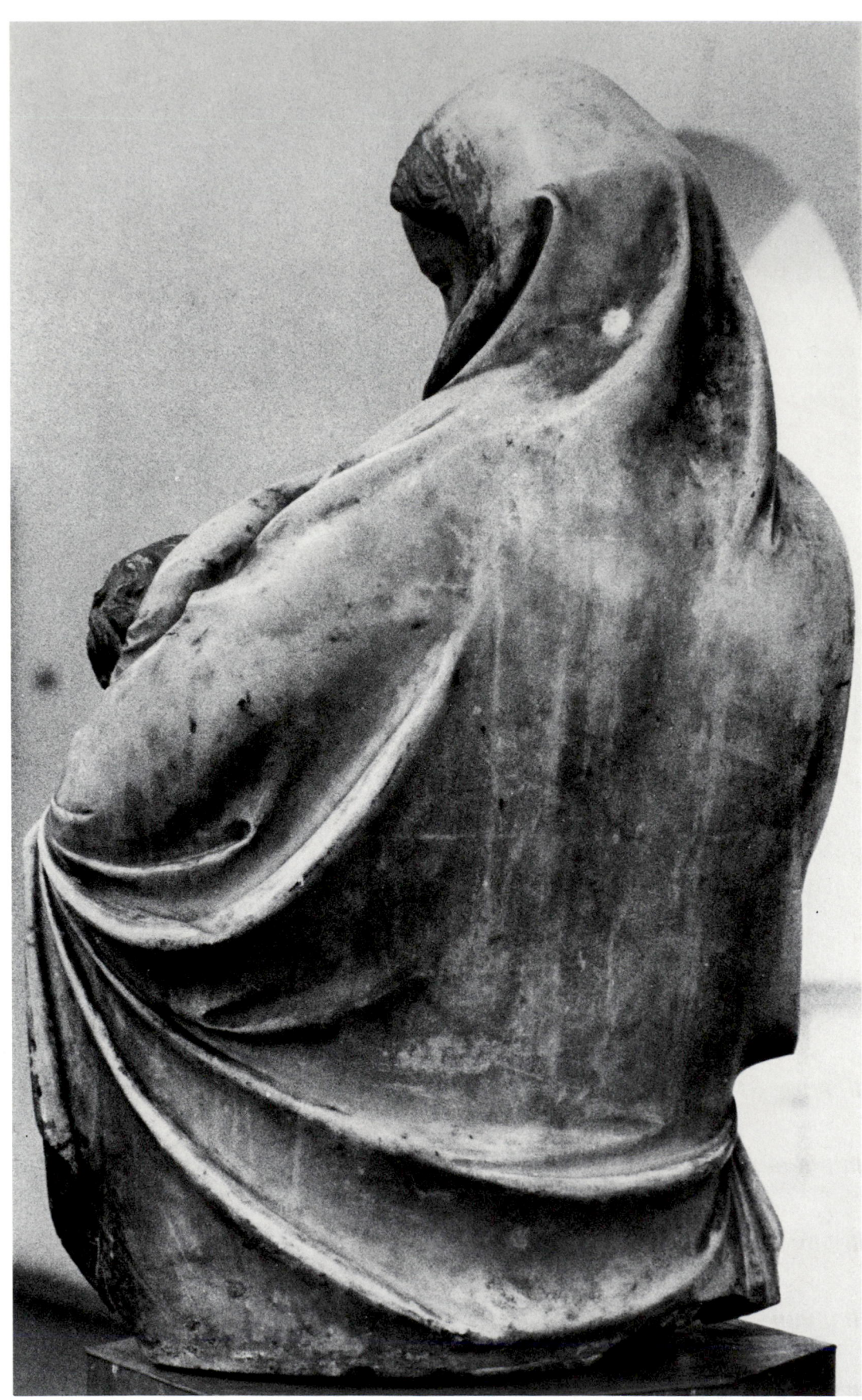

136. Andrea Pisano: *Madonna del Latte*. Pisa, Museo di San Matteo

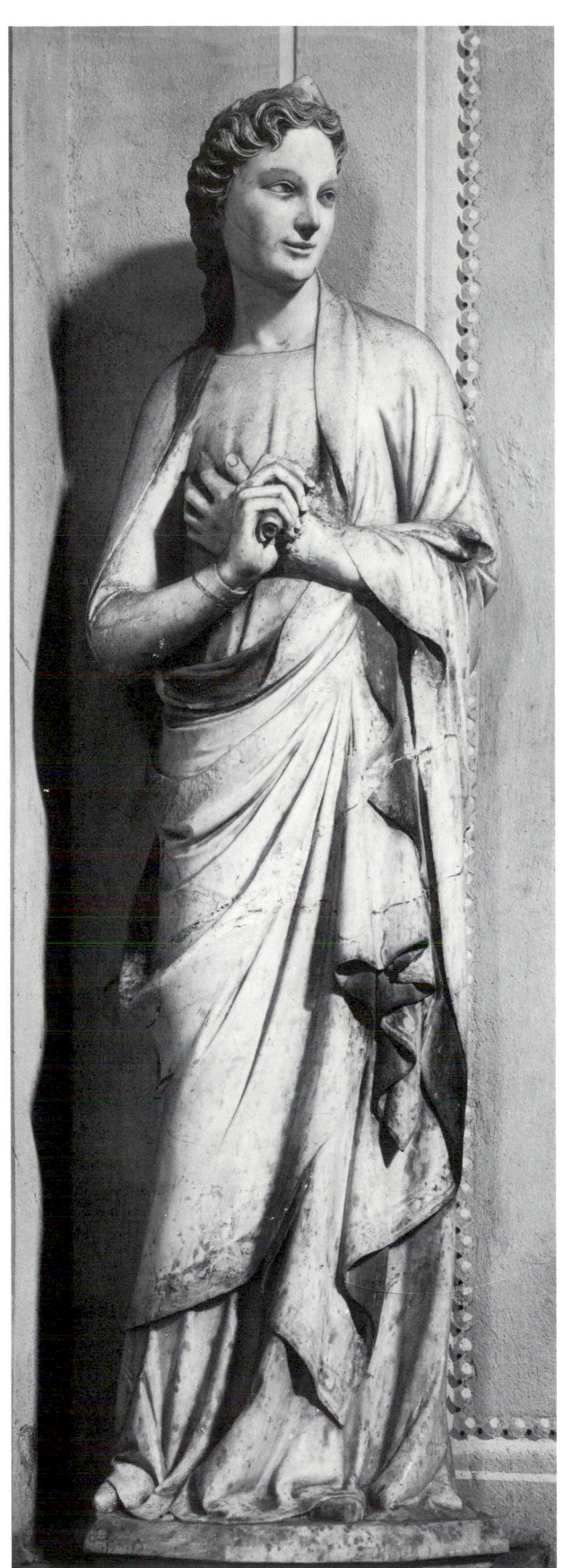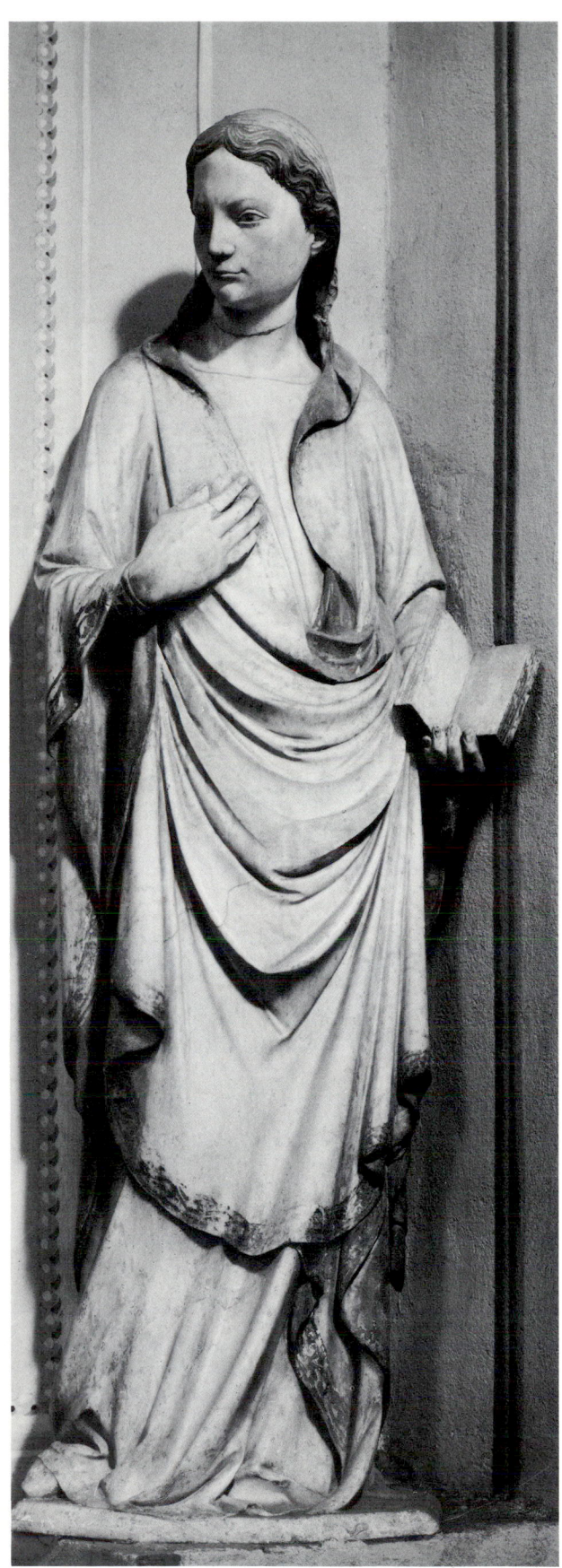

137. Master of the Sta. Caterina Annunciation: *Angel of the Annunciation* (ht 168 cm). Pisa, Sta. Caterina

138. Master of the Sta. Caterina Annunciation: *Virgin of the Annunciation*. Pisa, Sta. Caterina (ht 170 cm)

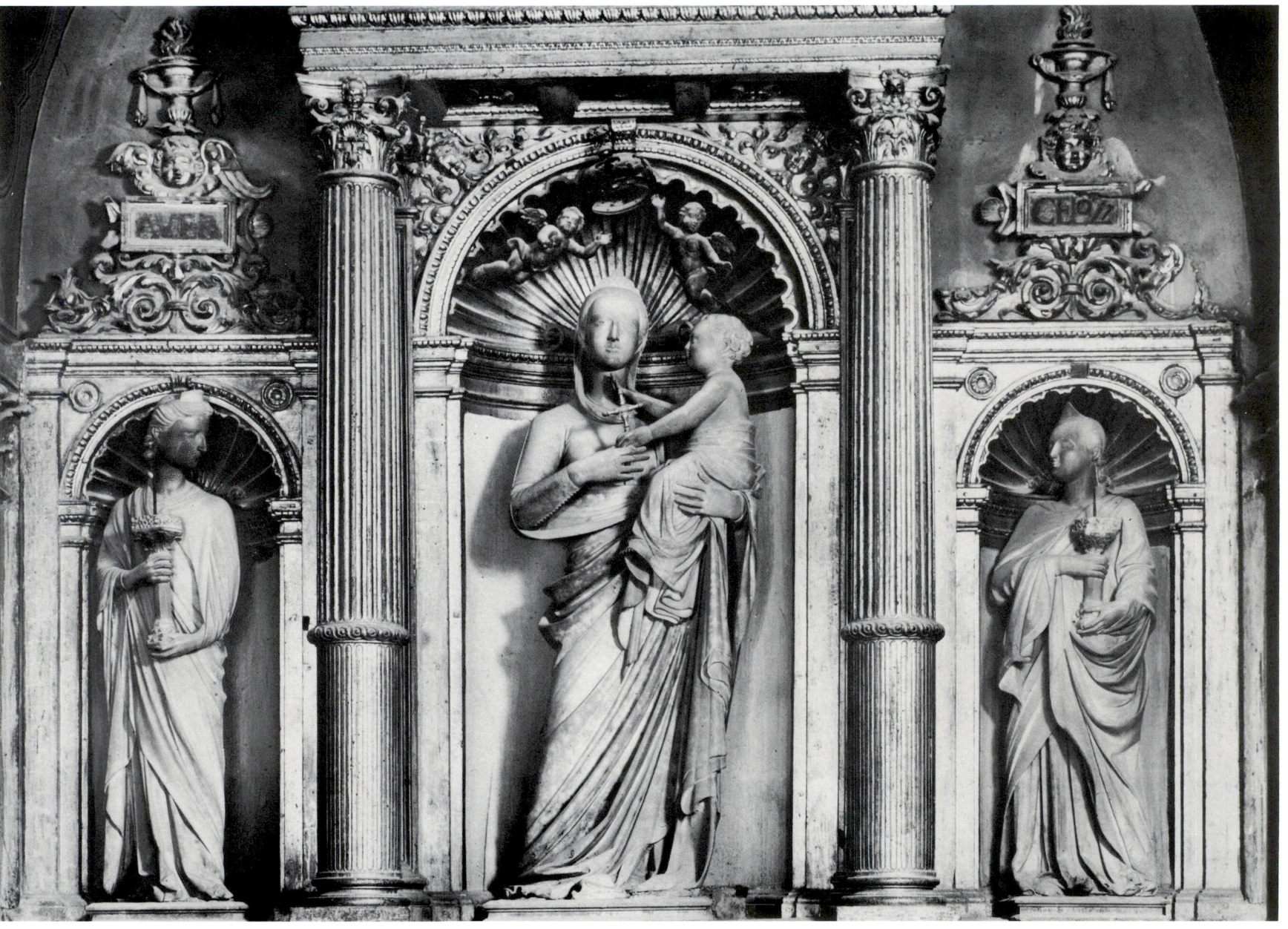

139. Alberto Arnoldi: *Madonna and Child and Saints*. Florence, Bigallo

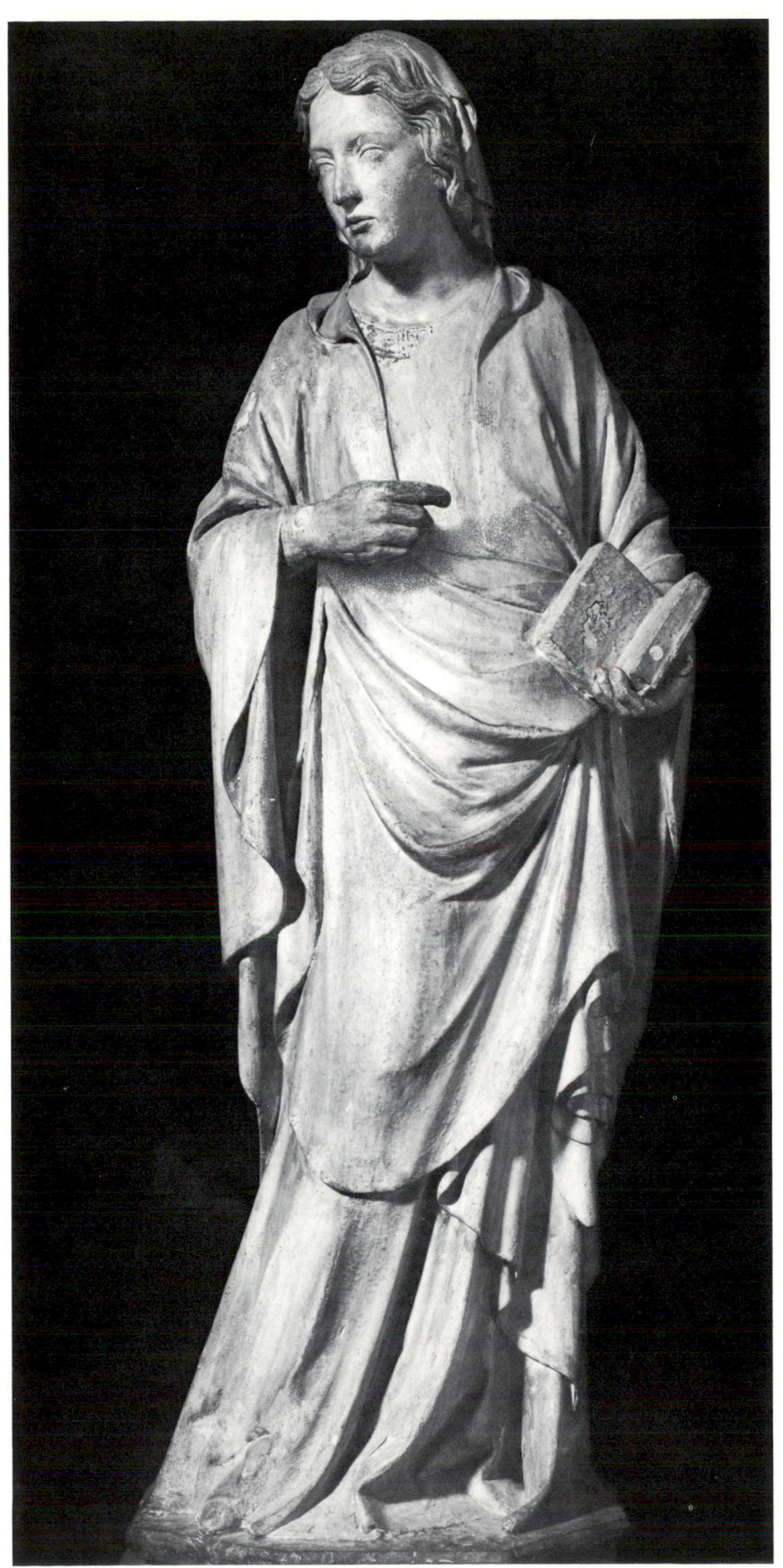

140. Follower of Nino Pisano: *Virgin Annunciate* (ht 168 cm). Pisa, Museo di San Matteo

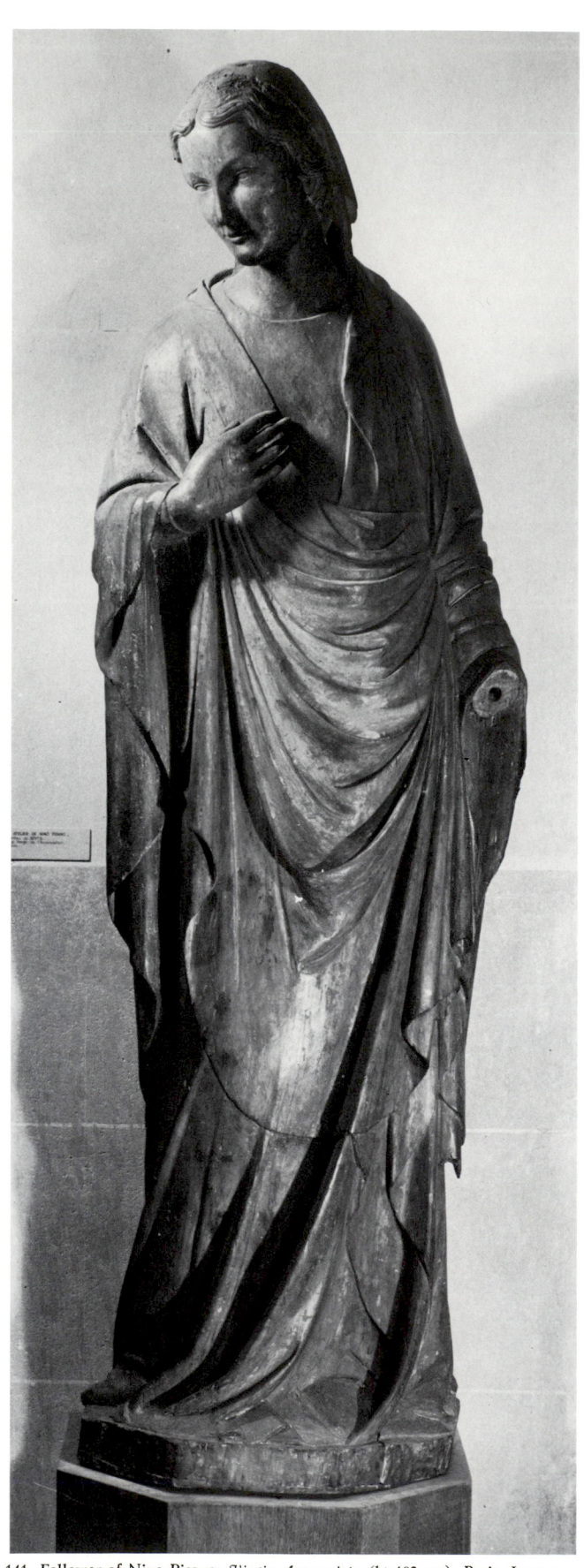

141. Follower of Nino Pisano: *Virgin Annunciate* (ht 182 cm). Paris, Louvre

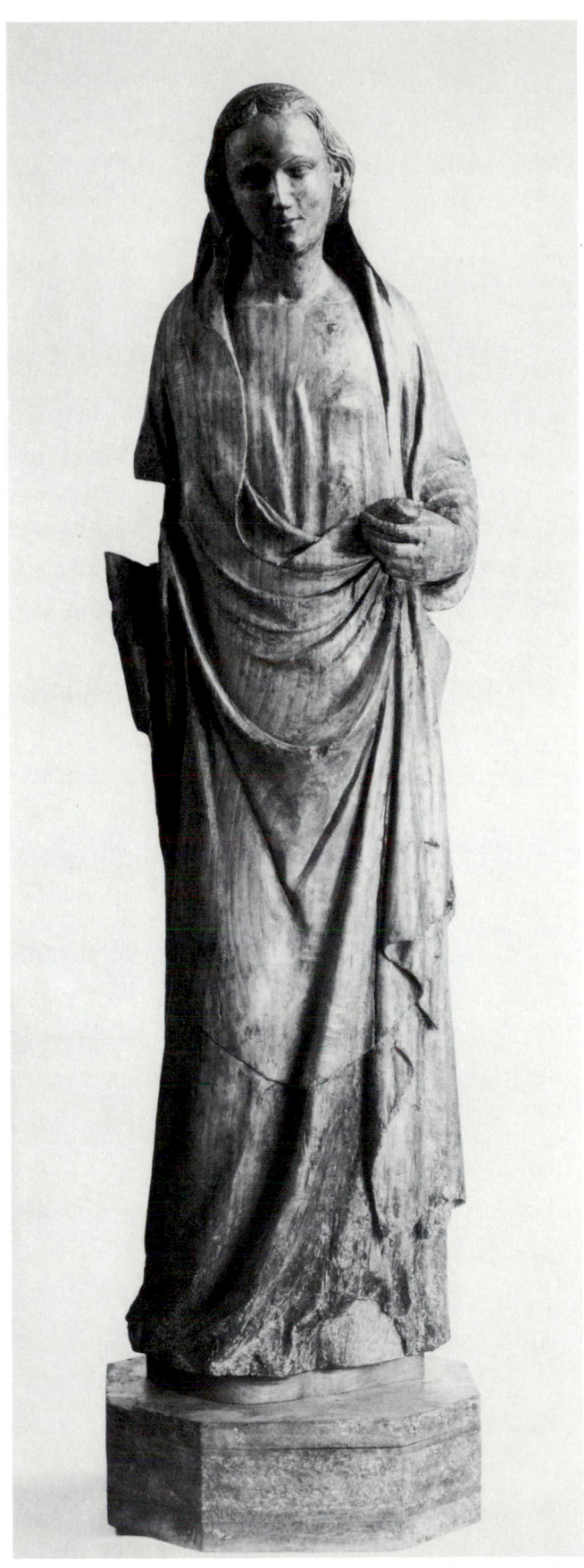

142. Nino Pisano workshop: *Virgin Annunciate* (ht 146 cm). Pontedera, Sto. Crocifisso

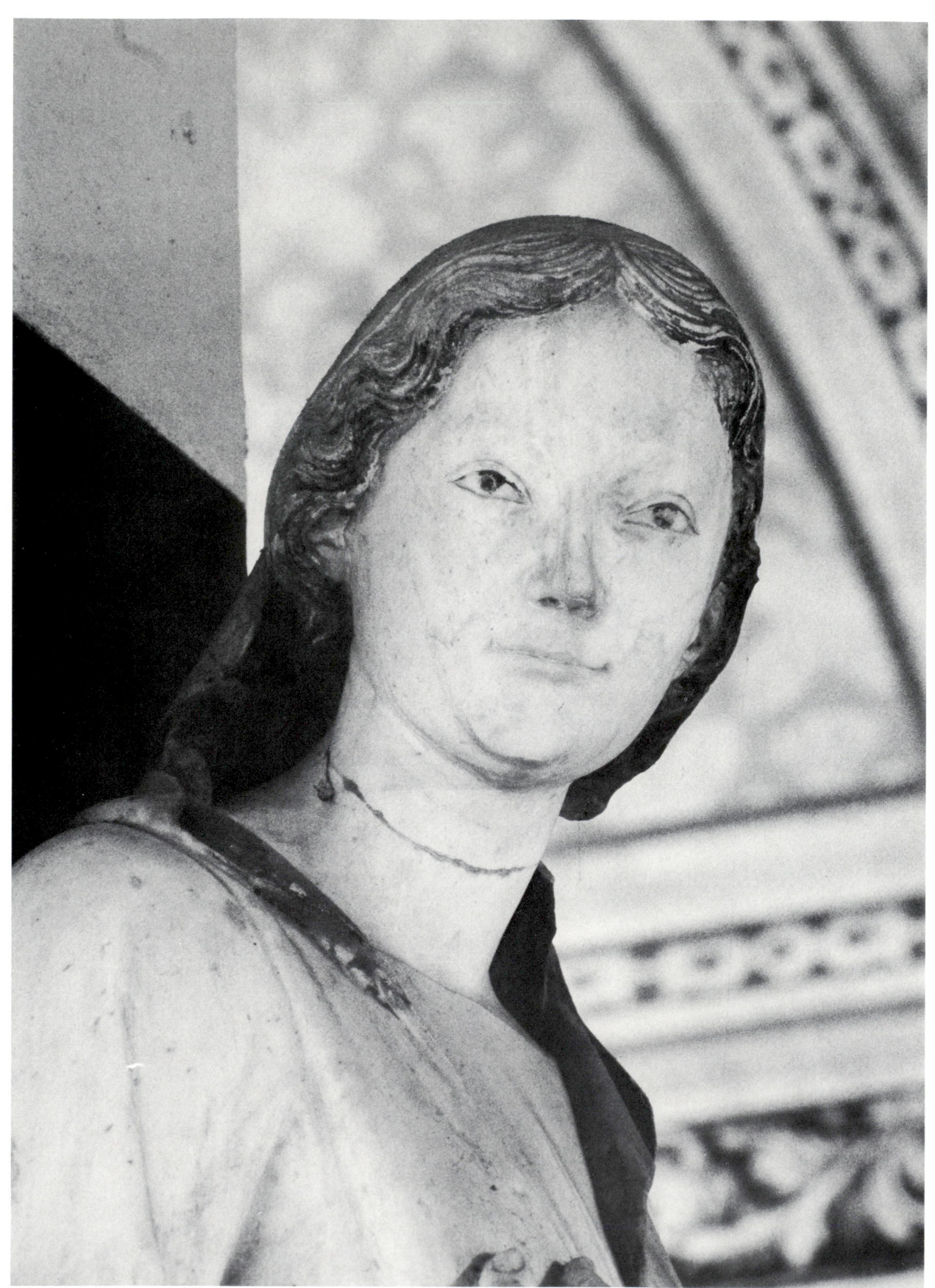

143. Master of the Sta. Caterina Annunciation: *Virgin of the Annunciation*, detail. Pisa, Sta. Caterina

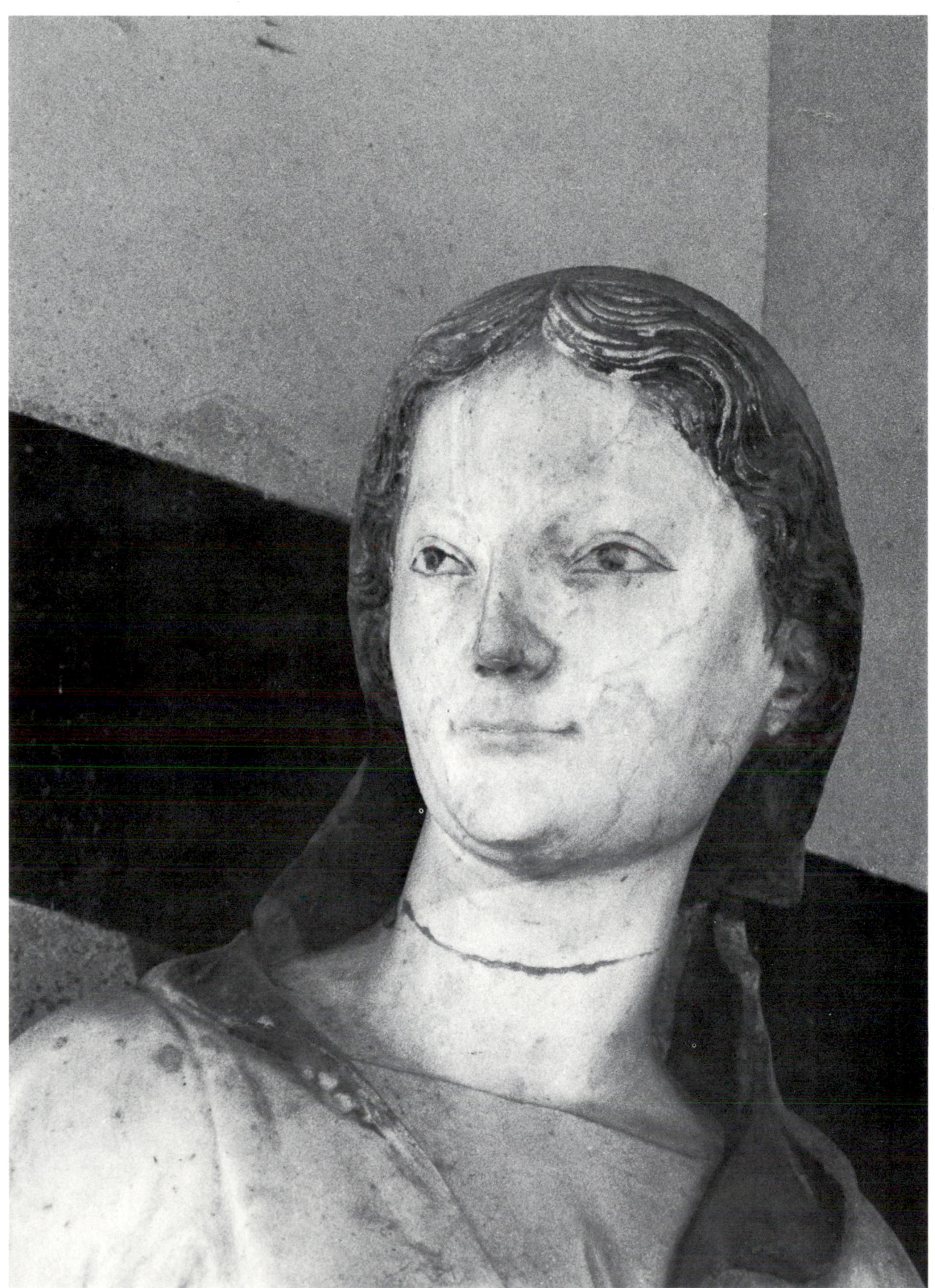

144. Master of the Sta. Caterina Annunciation: *Virgin of the Annunciation*, detail. Pisa, Sta. Caterina

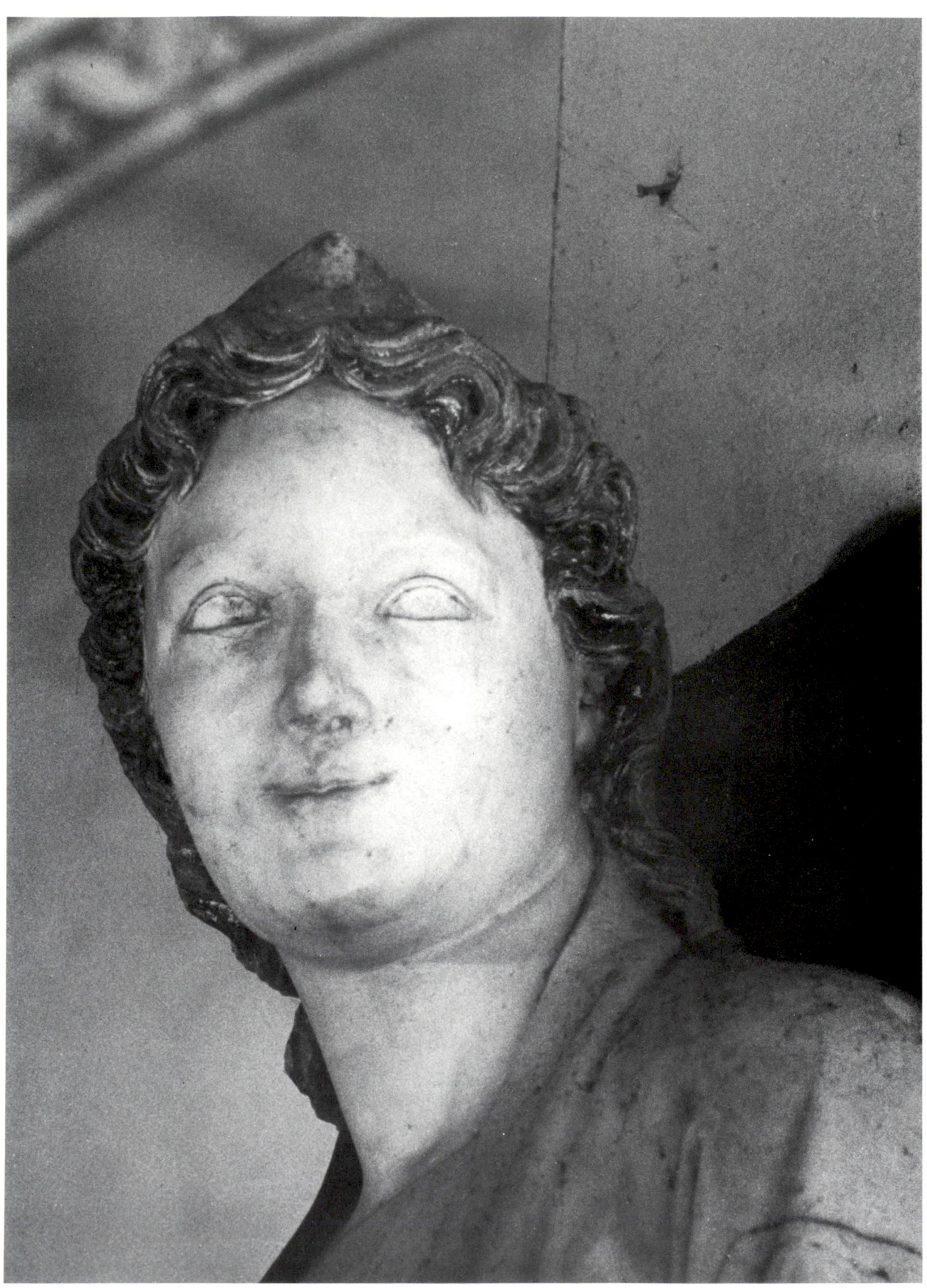

145. Master of the Sta. Caterina Annunciation: *Angel of the Annunciation*, detail. Pisa, Sta. Caterina

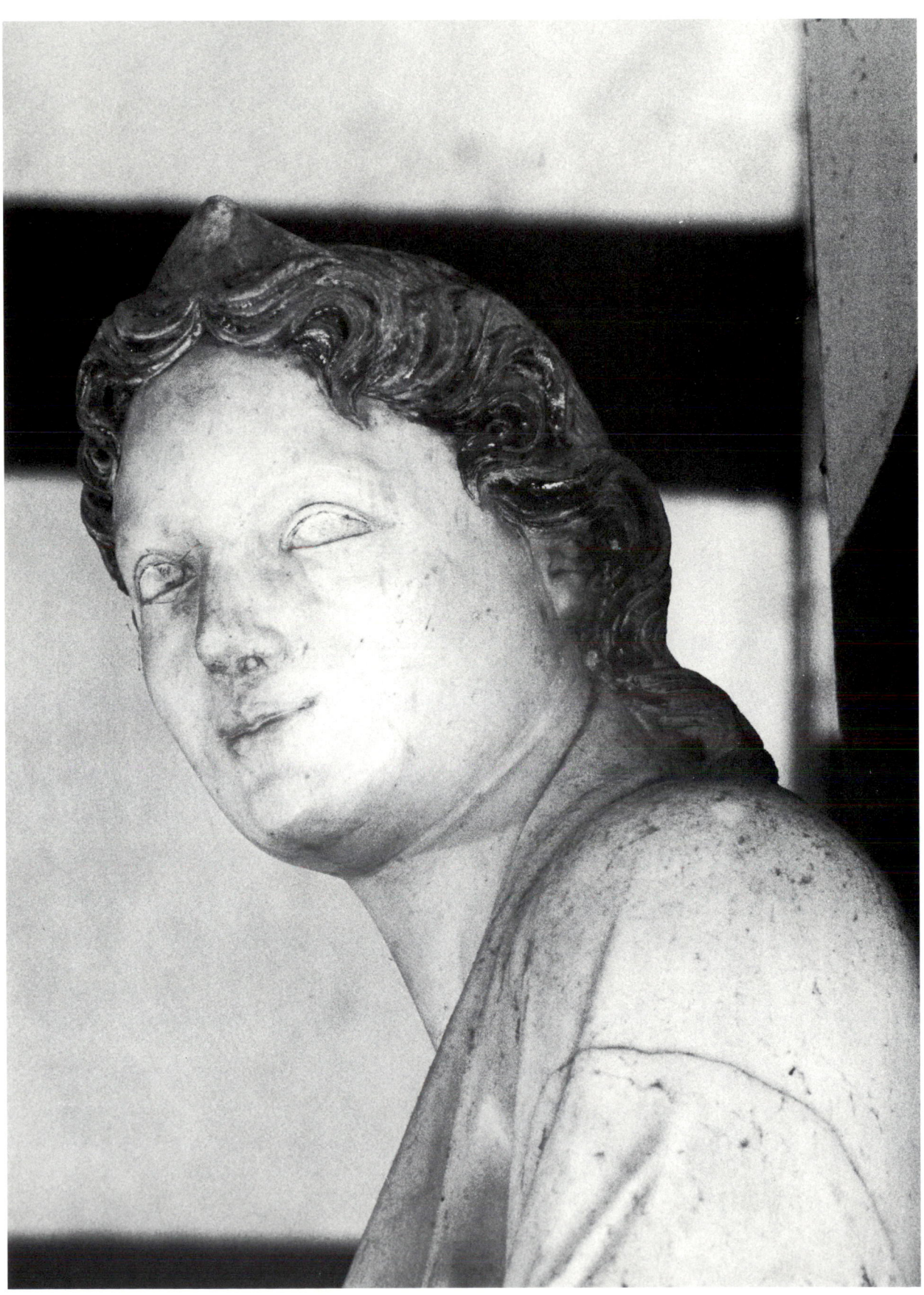

146. Master of the Sta. Caterina Annunciation: *Angel of the Annunciation*. Pisa, Sta. Caterina

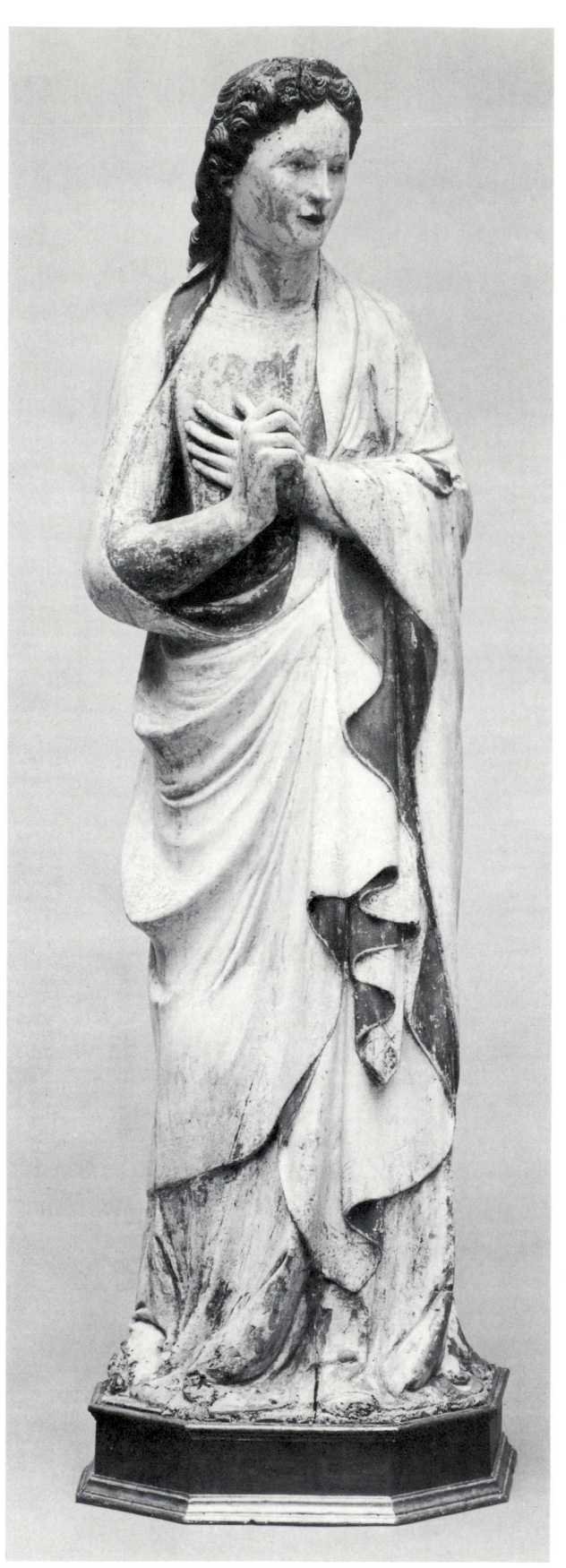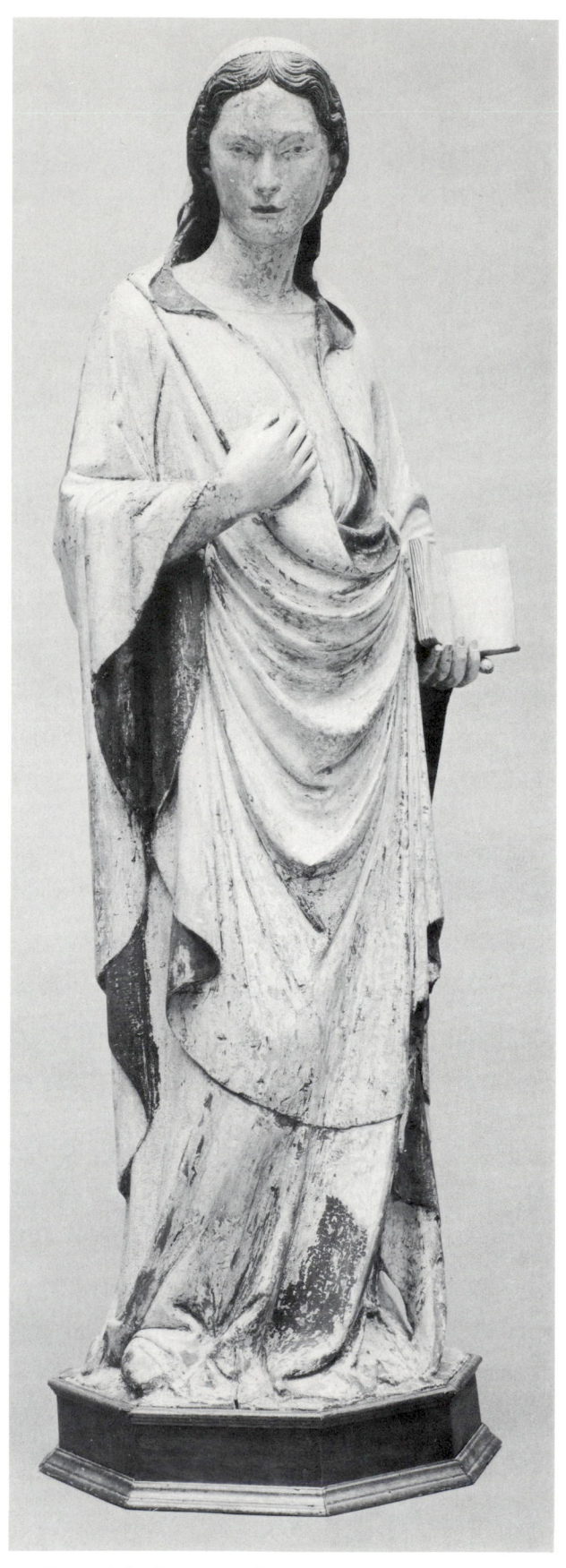

147. *Angel of the Annunciation* (ht without plinth 159.4 cm). Washington, D.C., National Gallery

148. *Virgin of the Annunciation* (ht without plinth 162.3 cm). Washington, D.C., National Gallery

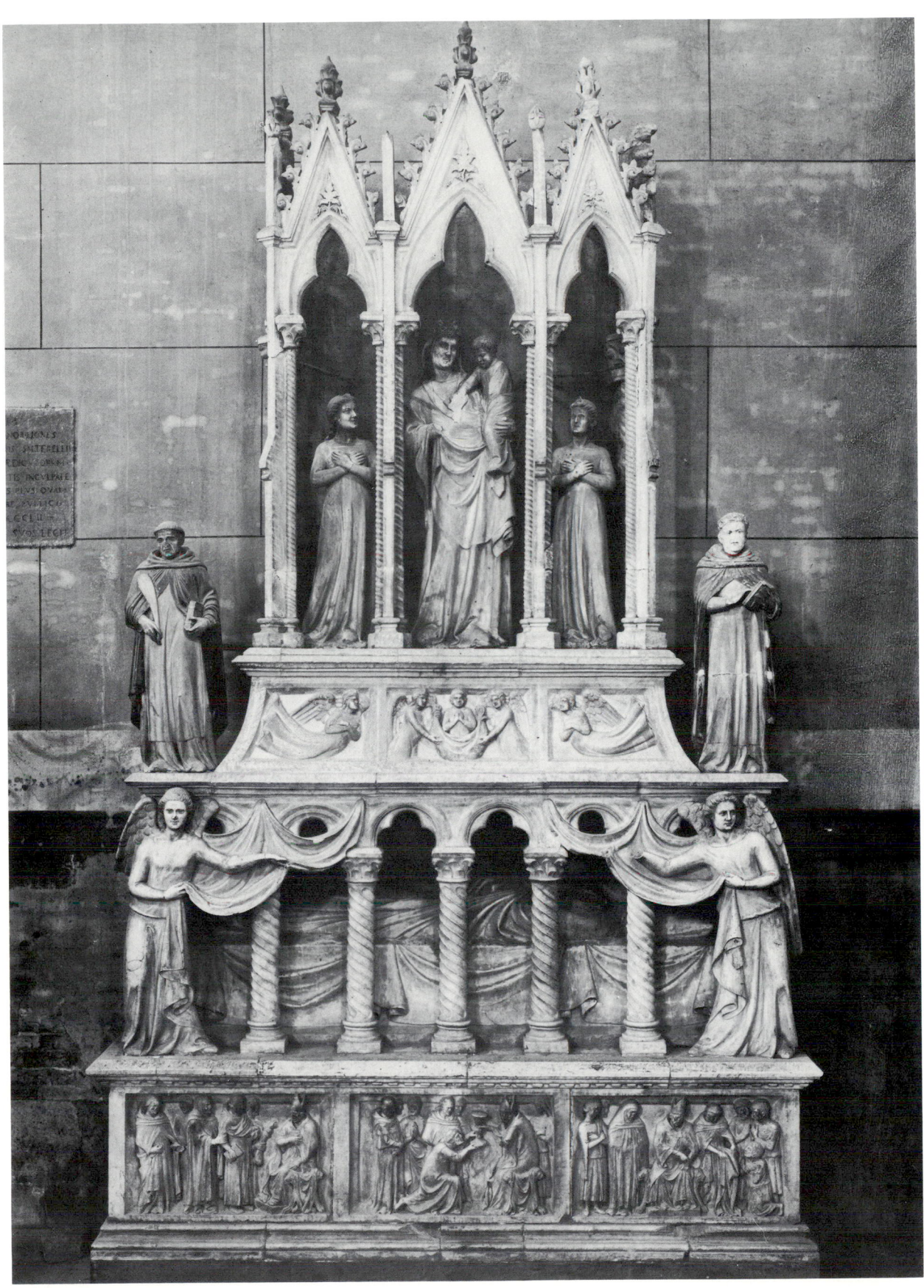

149. Andrea Pisano workshop: Saltarelli Monument. Pisa, Sta. Caterina

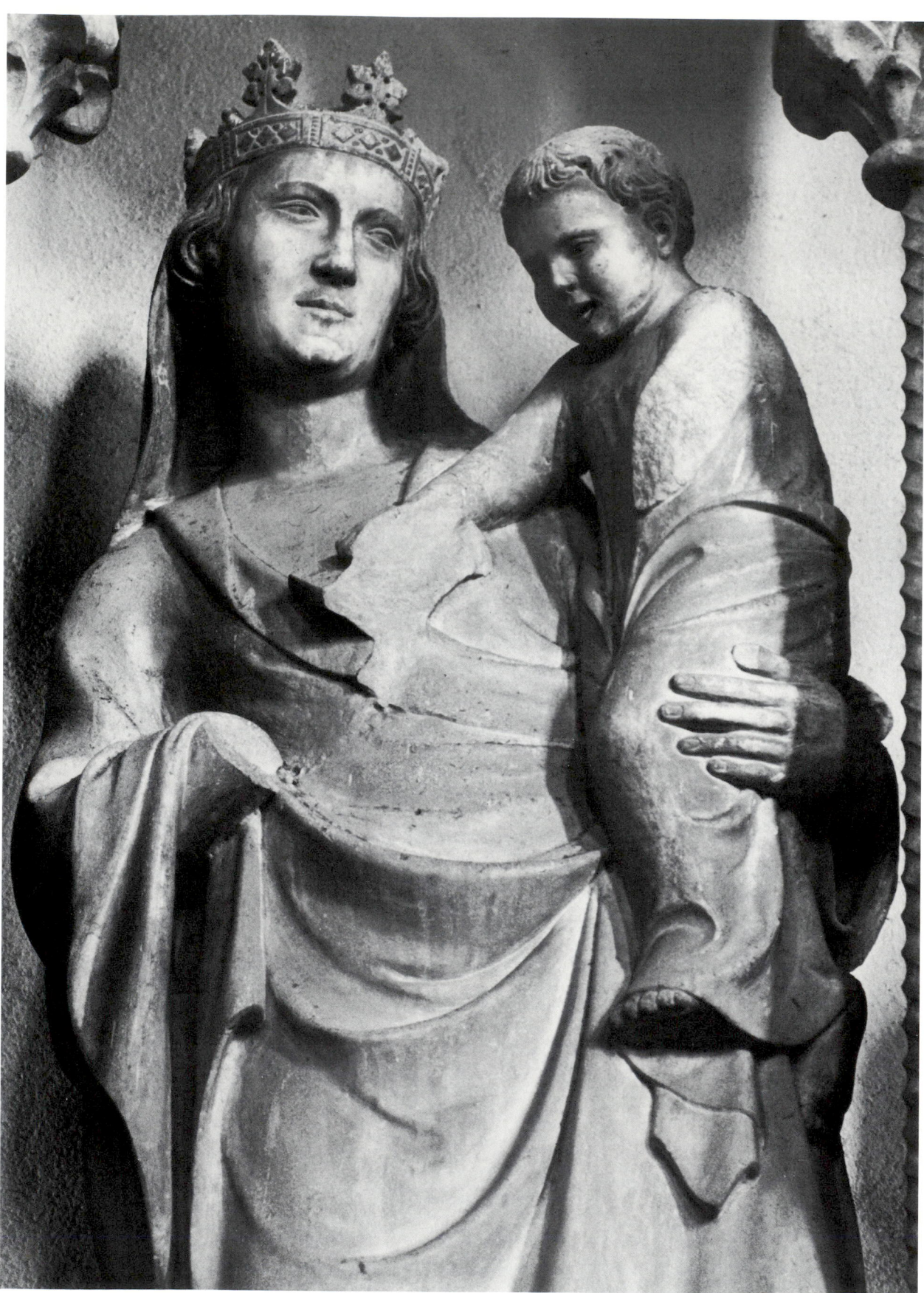

150. Andrea Pisano: *Madonna and Child*, detail Saltarelli Monument. Pisa, Sta. Caterina

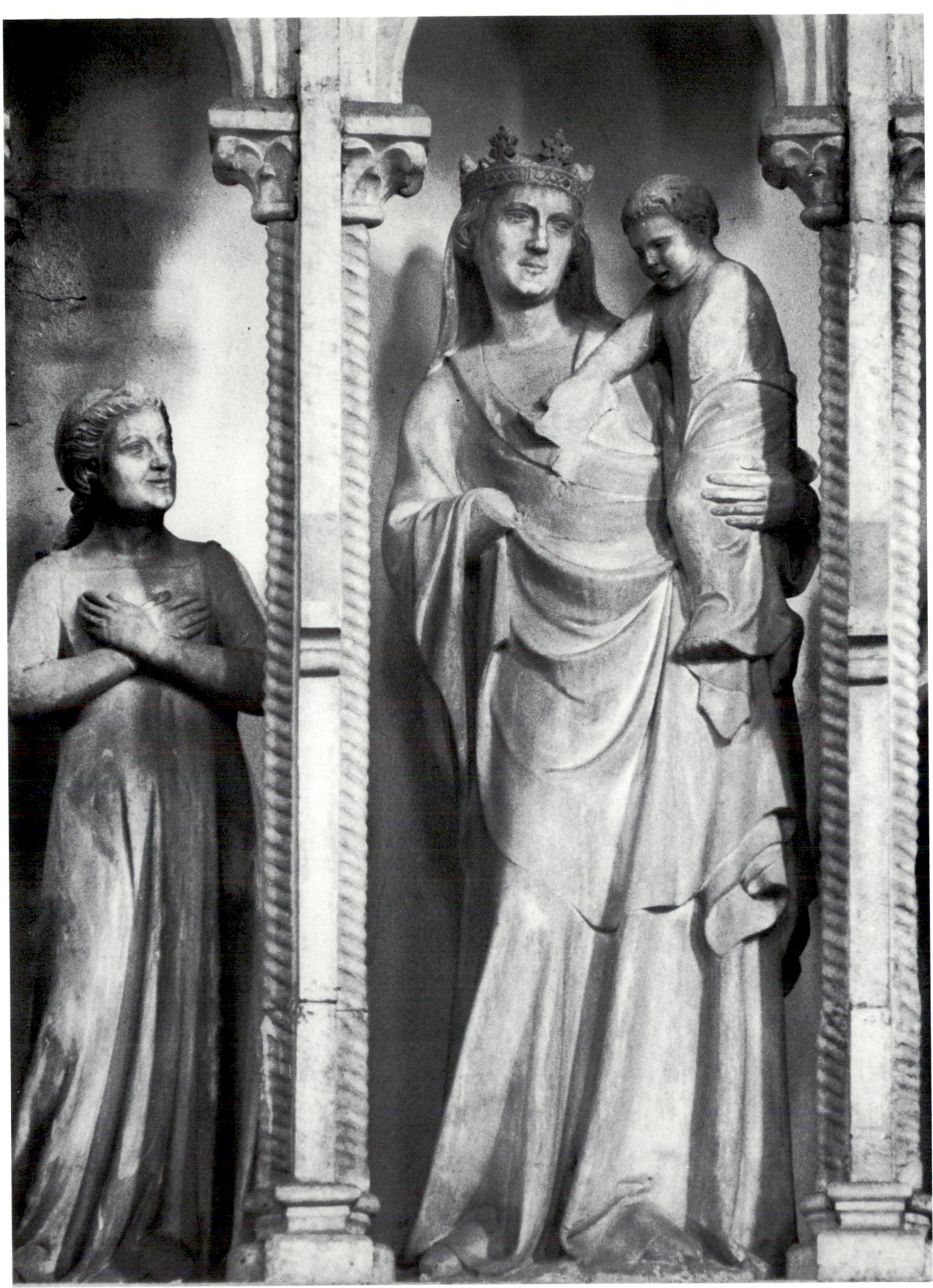

151. Andrea Pisano and workshop: Saltarelli Monument, detail. Pisa, Sta. Caterina

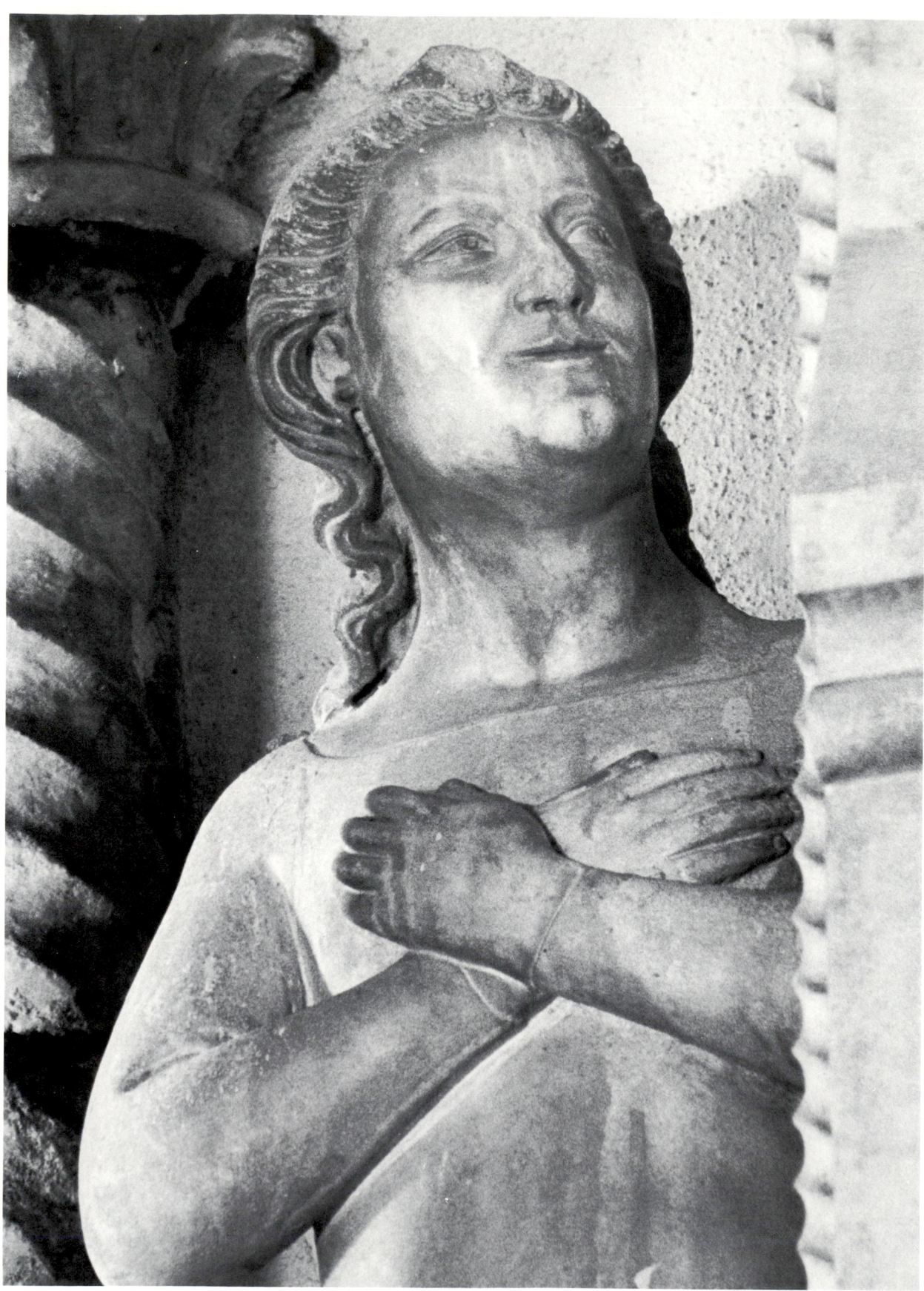

152. Andrea Pisano workshop: *Angel*. Saltarelli Monument. Pisa, Sta. Caterina

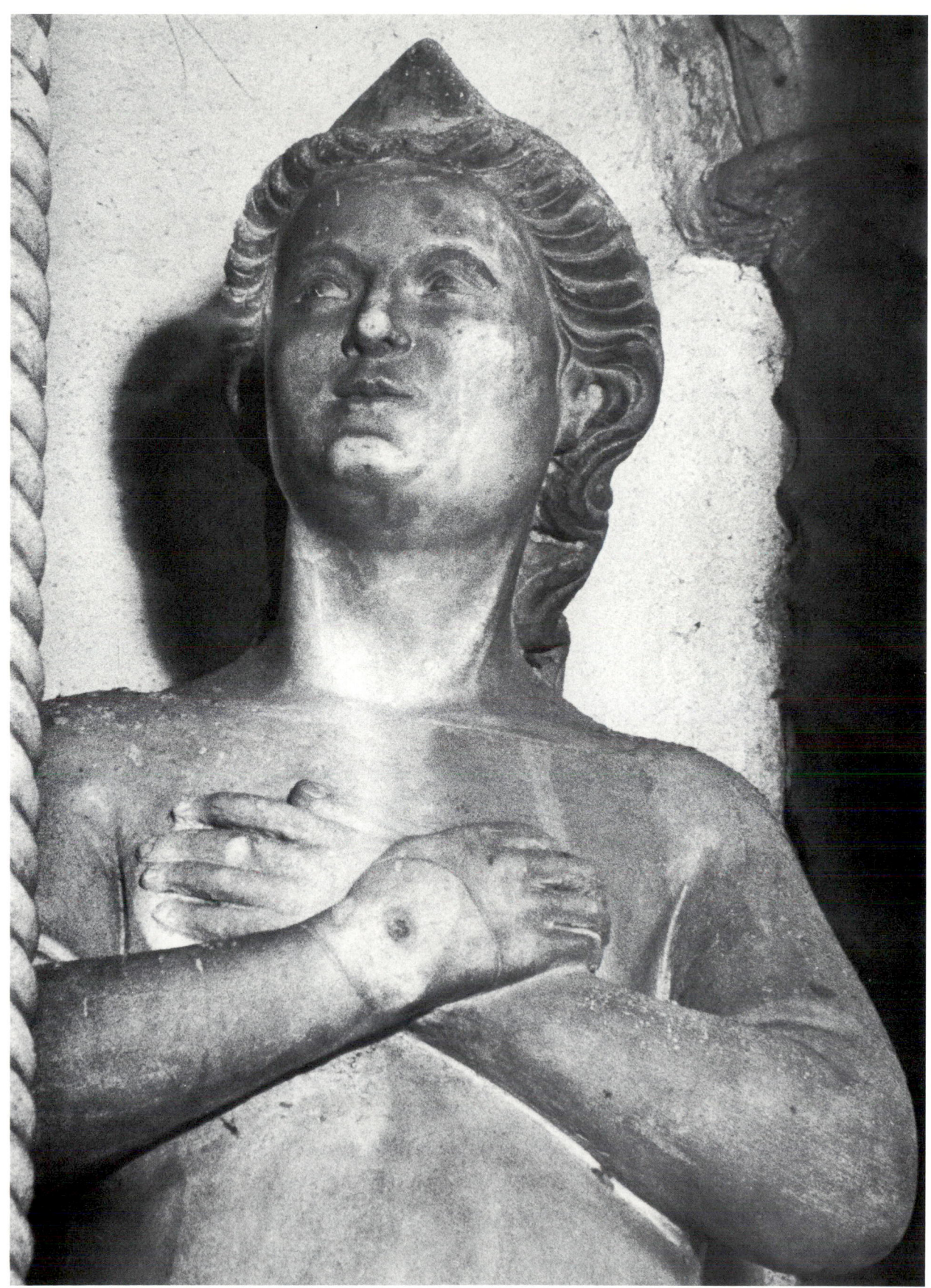

153. Nino Pisano: *Angel*. Saltarelli Monument. Pisa, Sta. Caterina

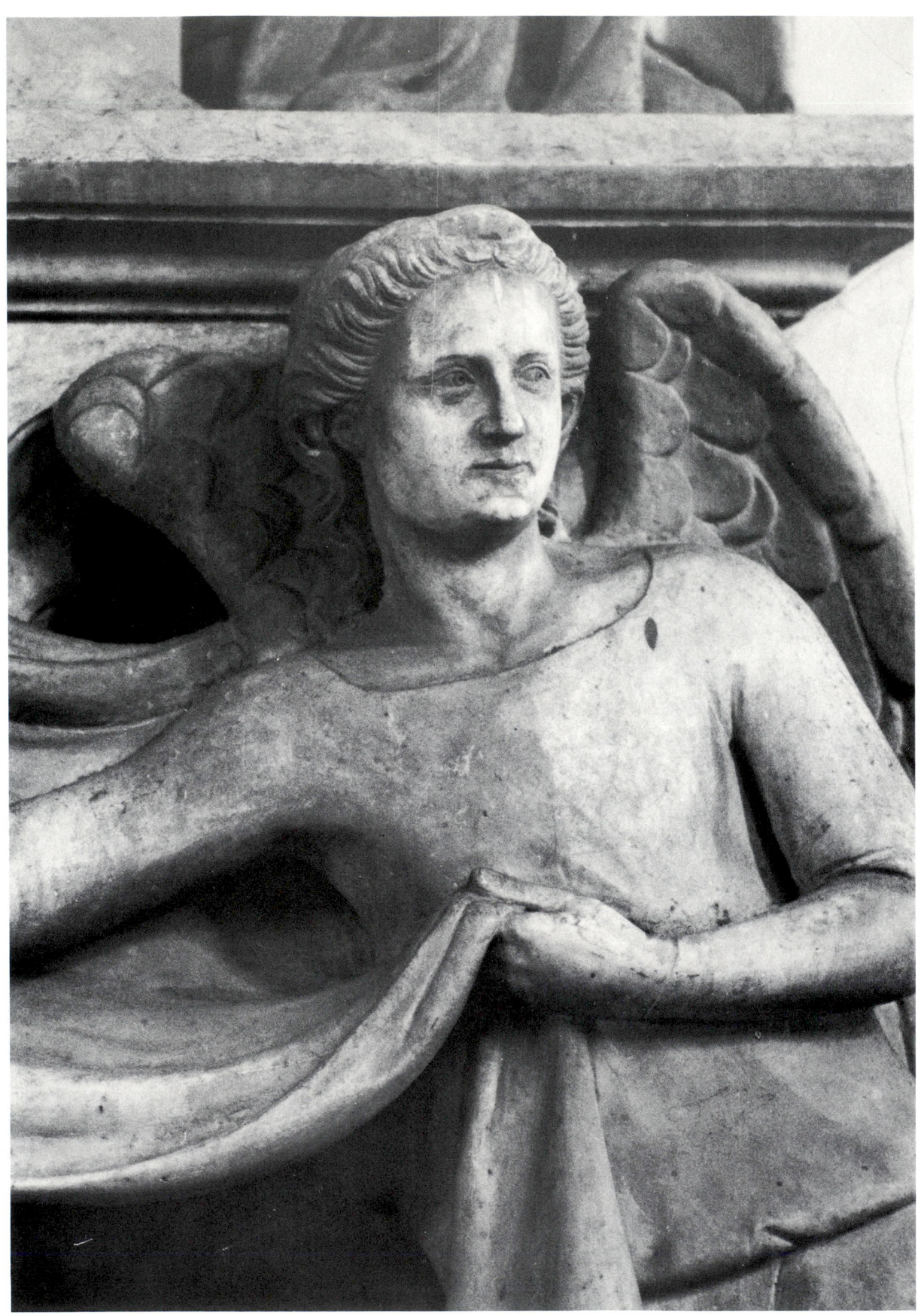

154. Andrea Pisano workshop: *Angel*. Saltarelli Monument. Pisa, Sta. Caterina

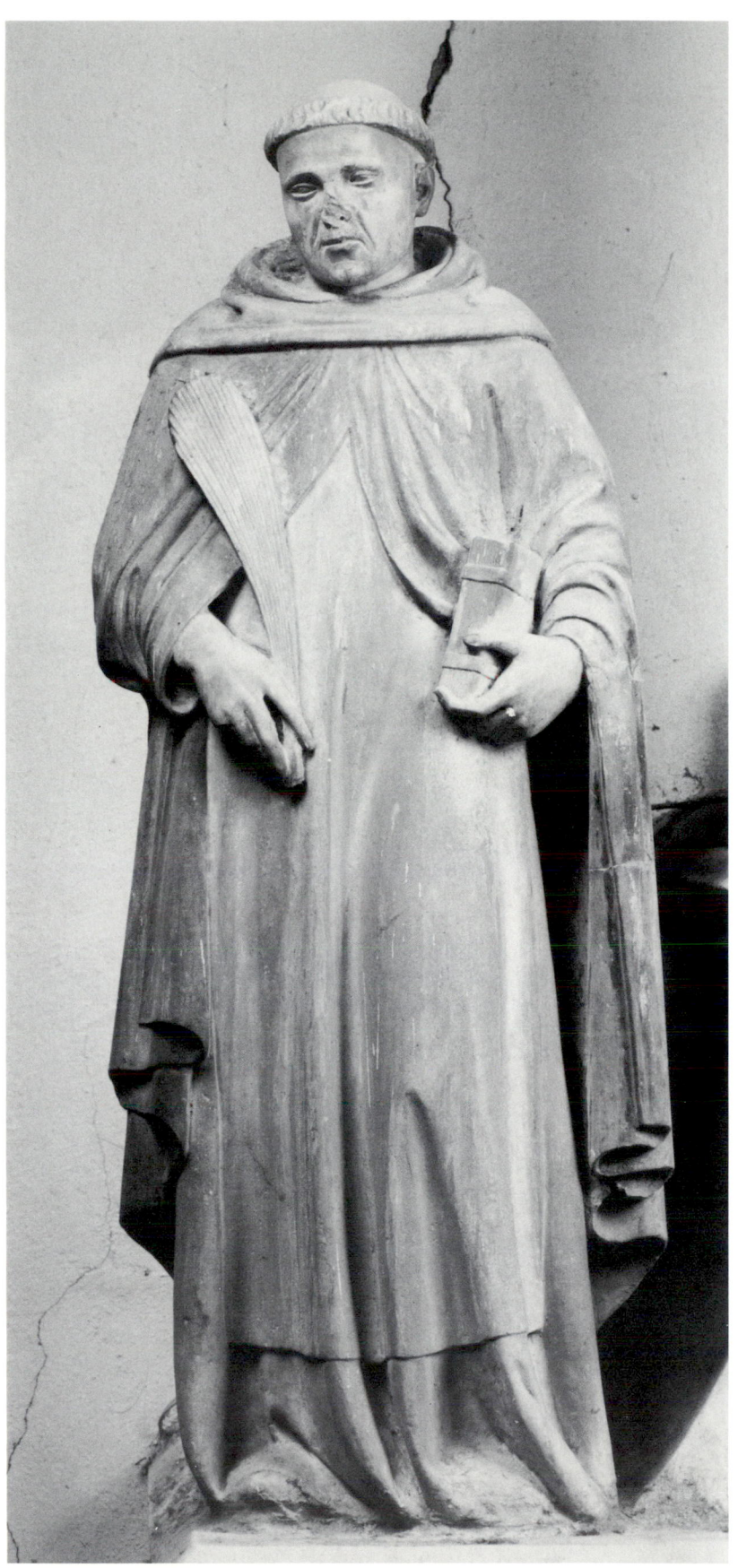

155. Andrea Pisano workshop (Assistant of Nino): *Saint*. Saltarelli Monument. Pisa, Sta. Caterina

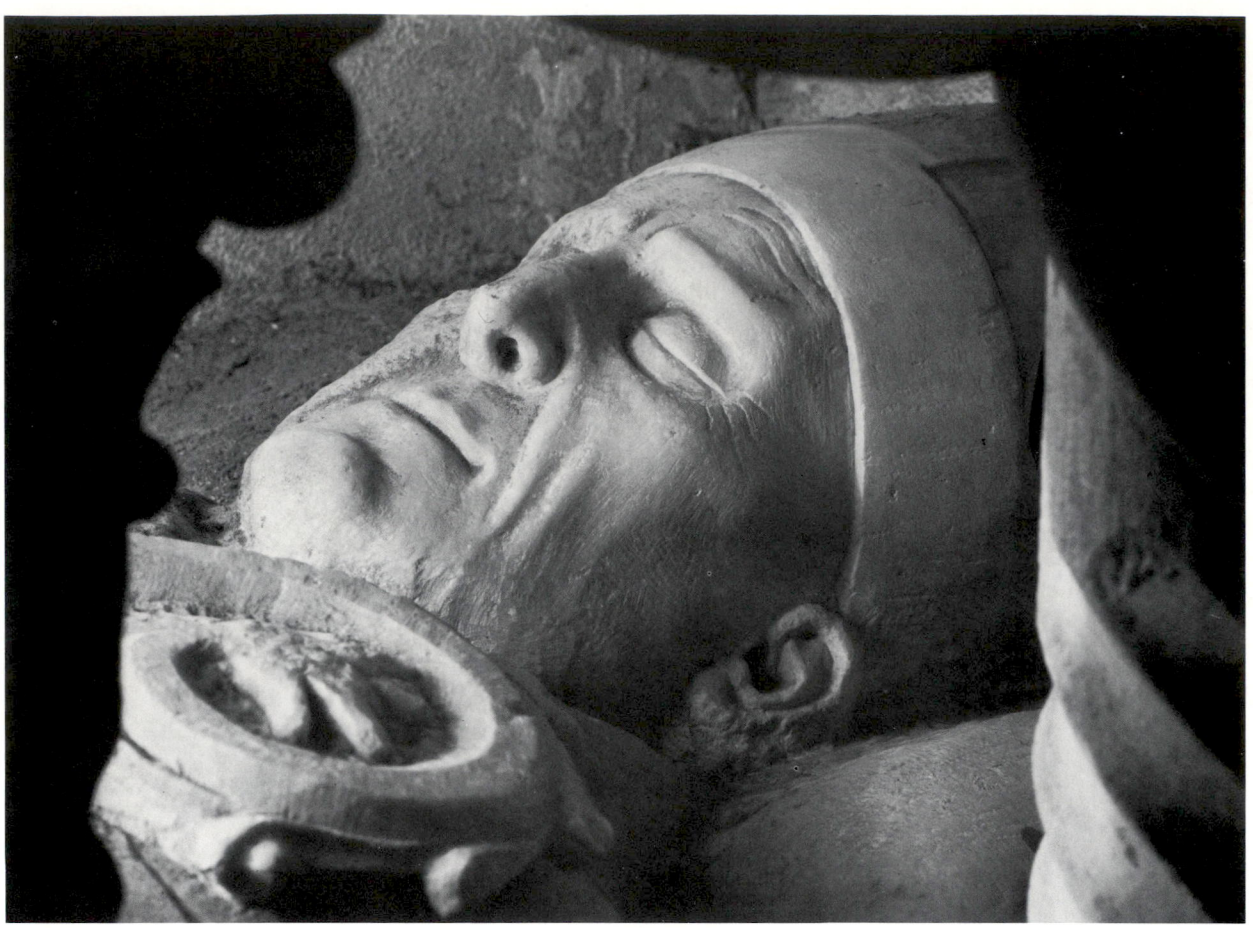

156. Nino Pisano: Simone Saltarelli, detail. Saltarelli Monument. Pisa, Sta. Caterina

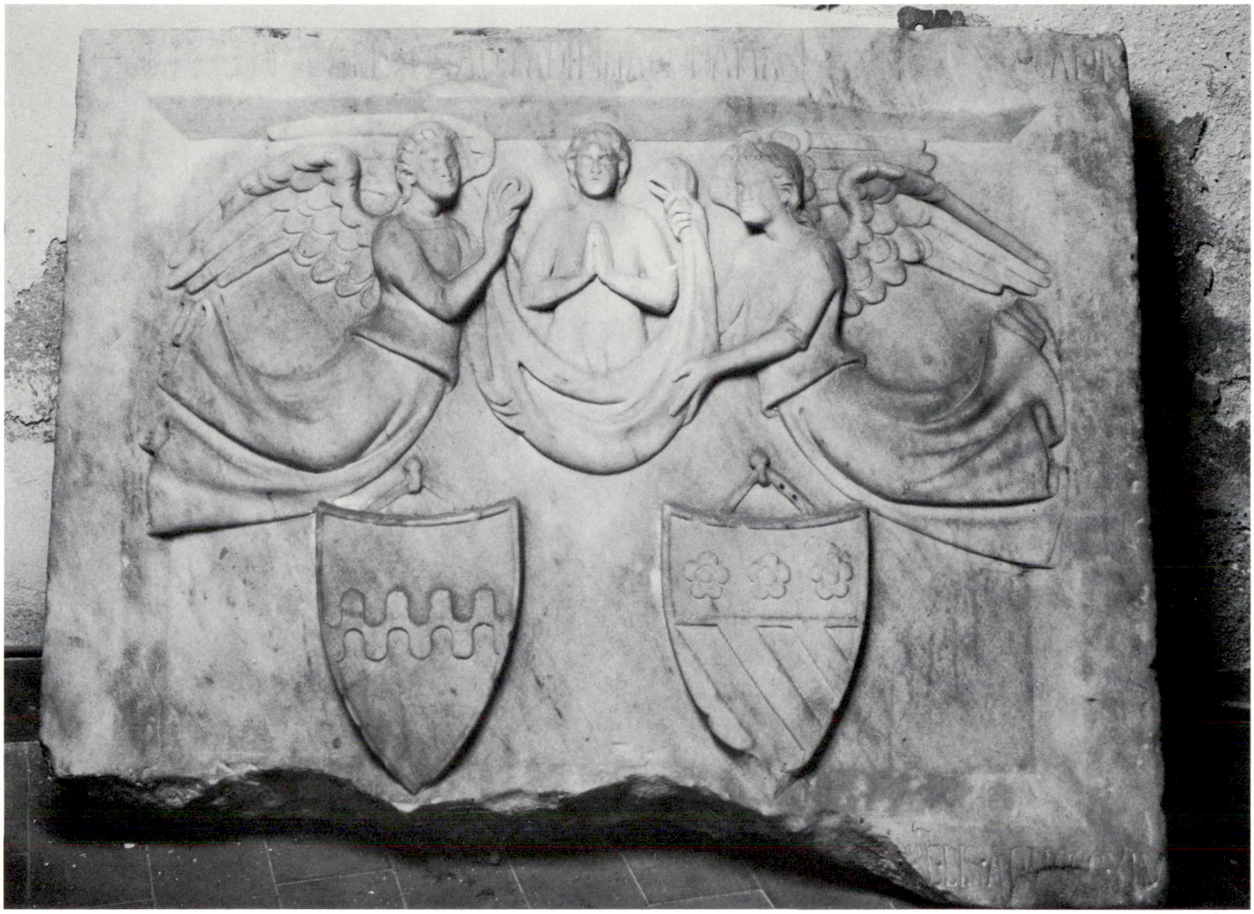

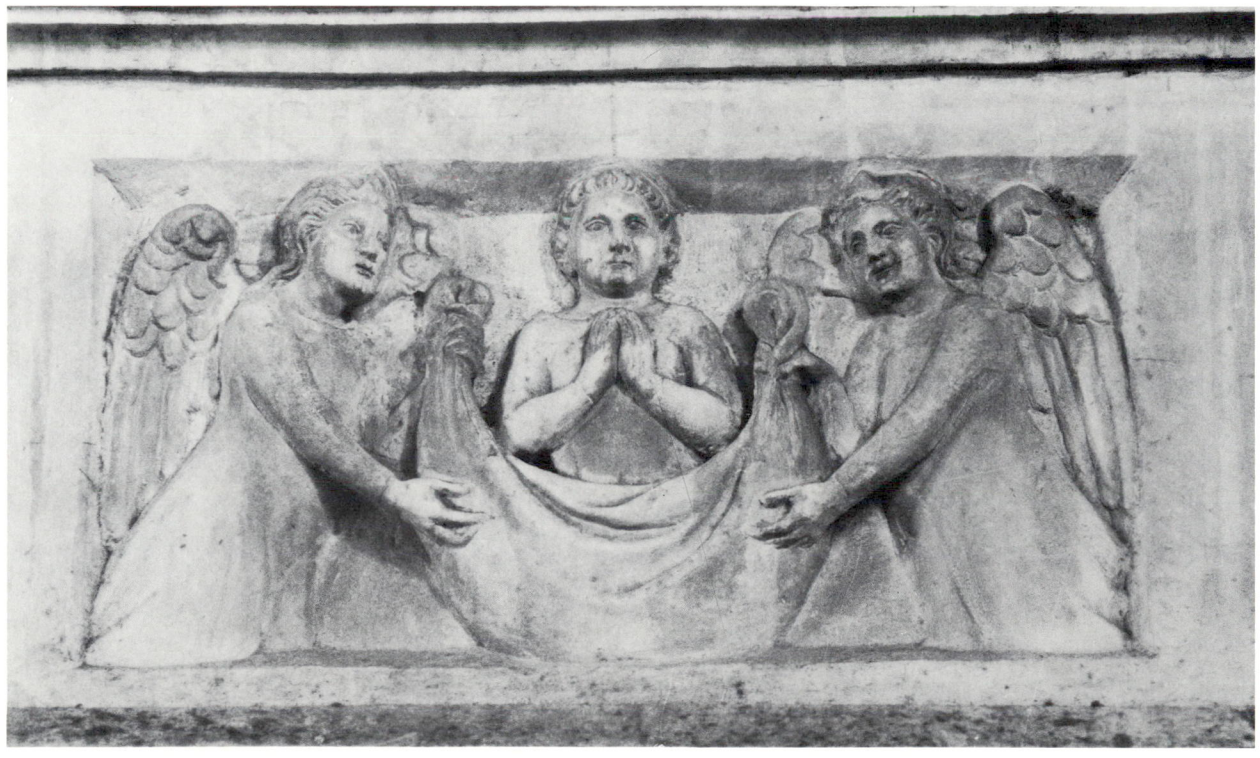

157. Andrea Pisano workshop: Tomb Slab (ht 75 cm, width 95 cm). Cagliari, Museo Nazionale

158. Andrea Pisano workshop: Saltarelli Monument, detail. Pisa, Sta. Caterina

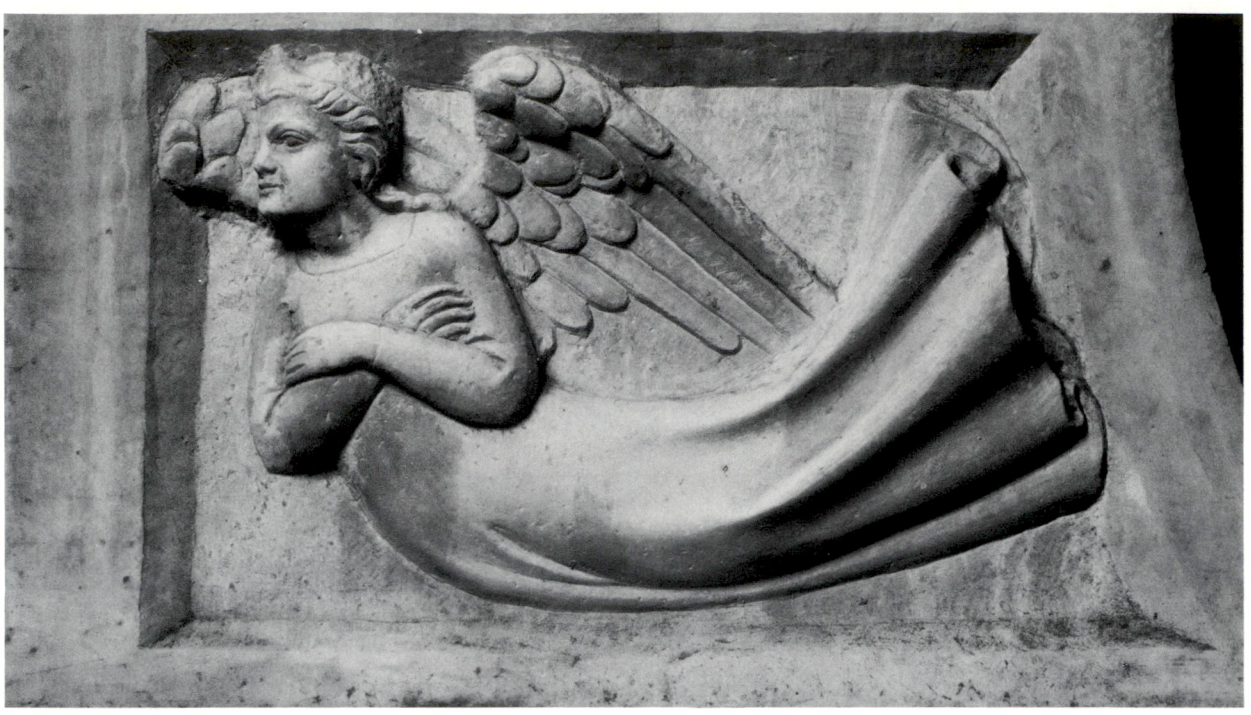

159. **Andrea Pisano** workshop: Saltarelli Monument, detail. Pisa, Sta. Caterina

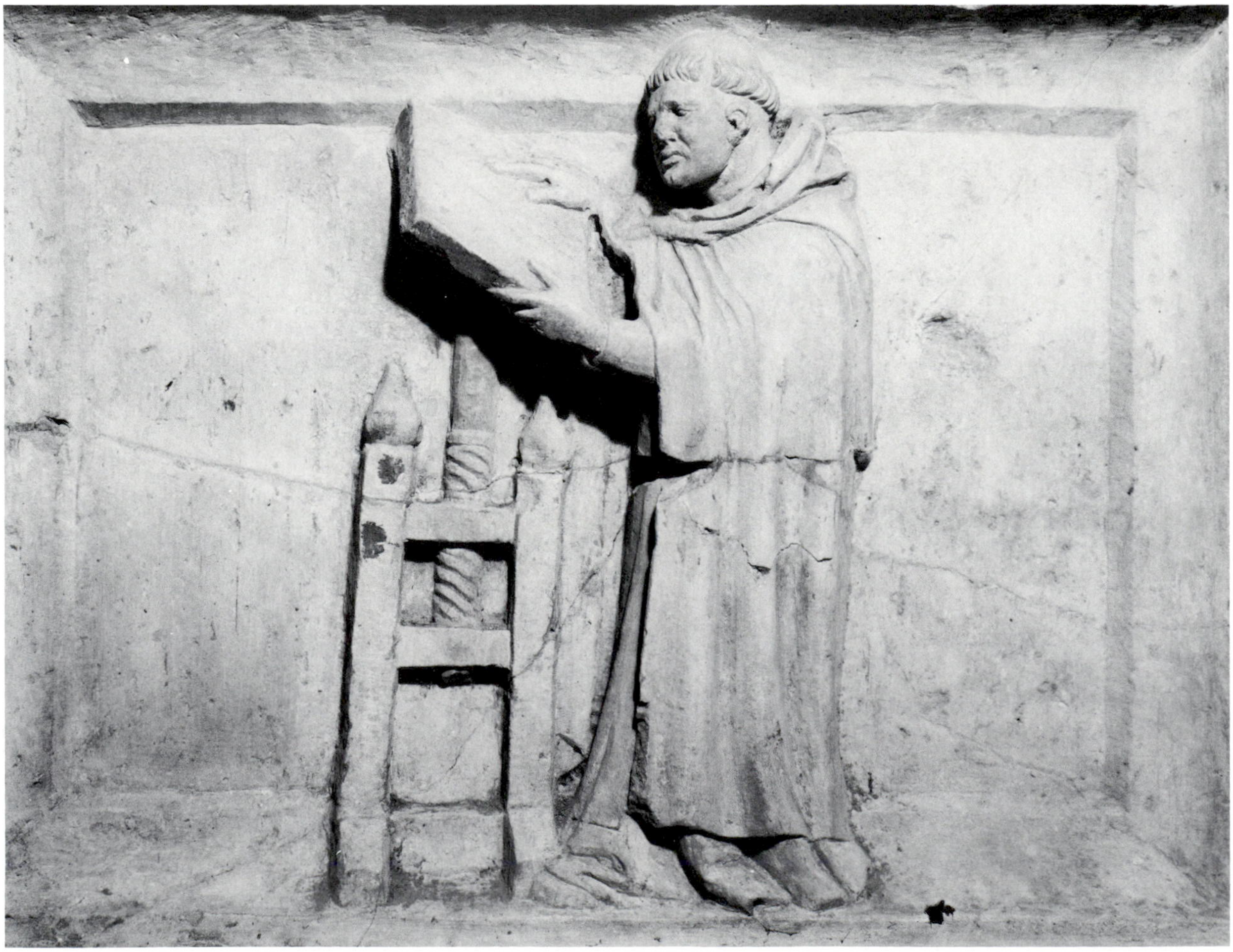

160. **Andrea Pisano** workshop: Saltarelli Monument, detail. Pisa, Sta. Caterina

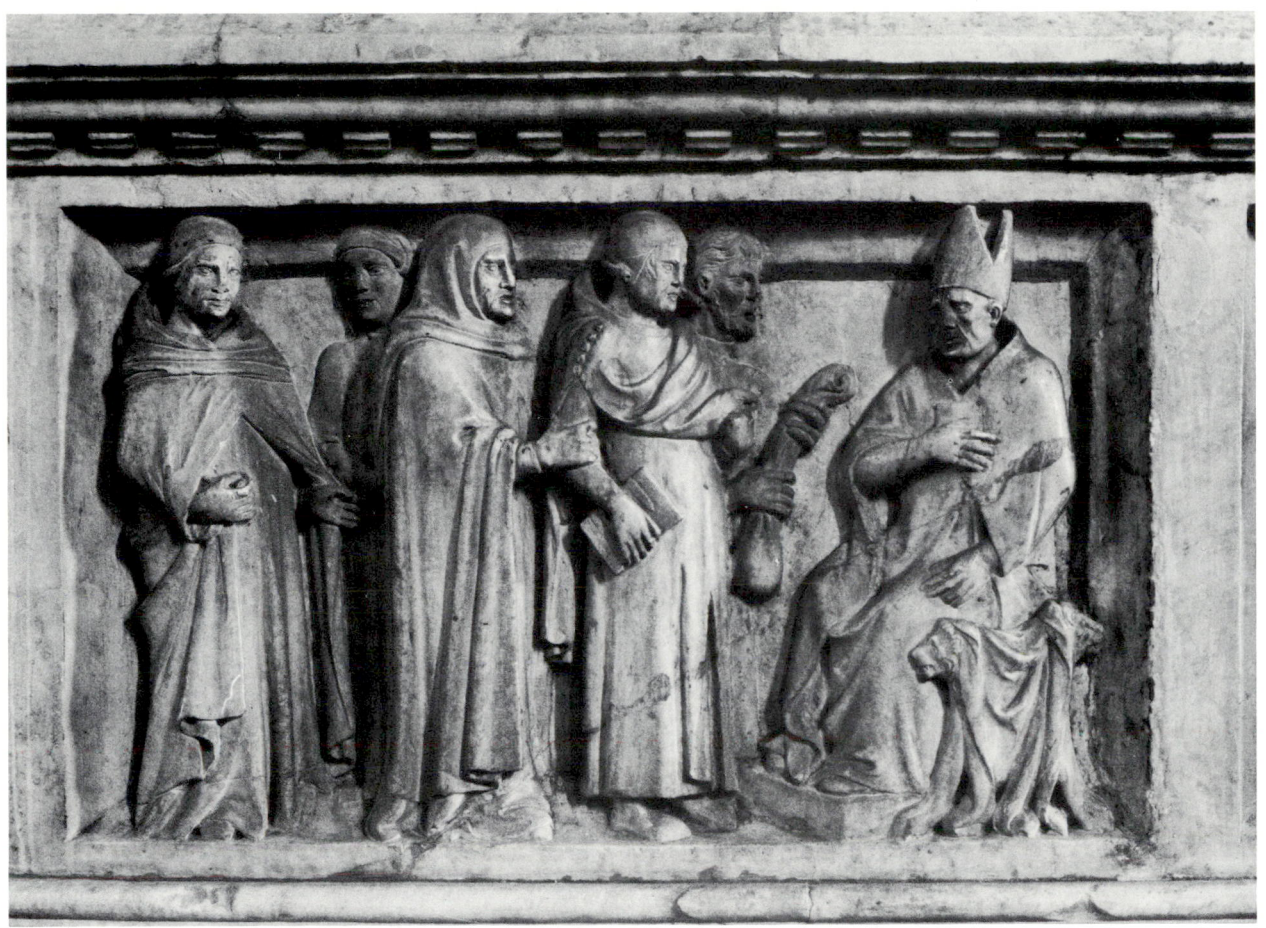

161. Andrea Pisano workshop: Saltarelli Monument, detail. Pisa, Sta. Caterina

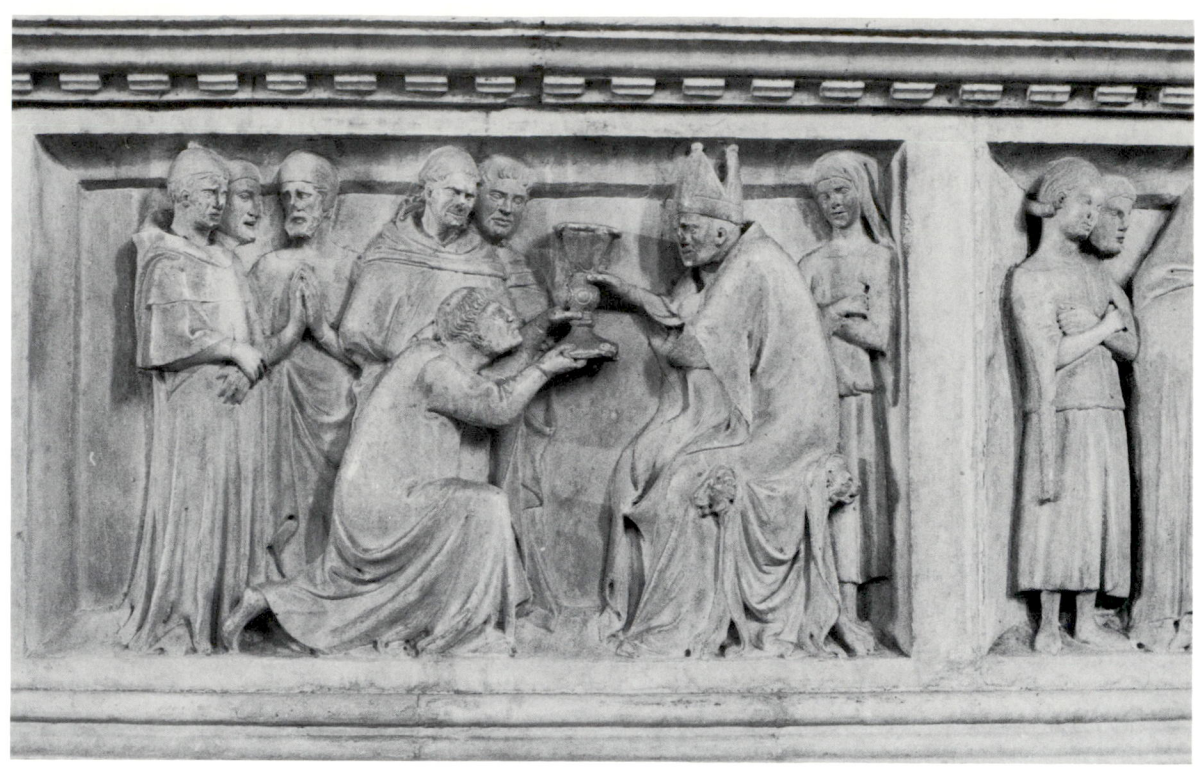

162. Andrea Pisano workshop: Saltarelli Monument, detail. Pisa, Sta. Caterina

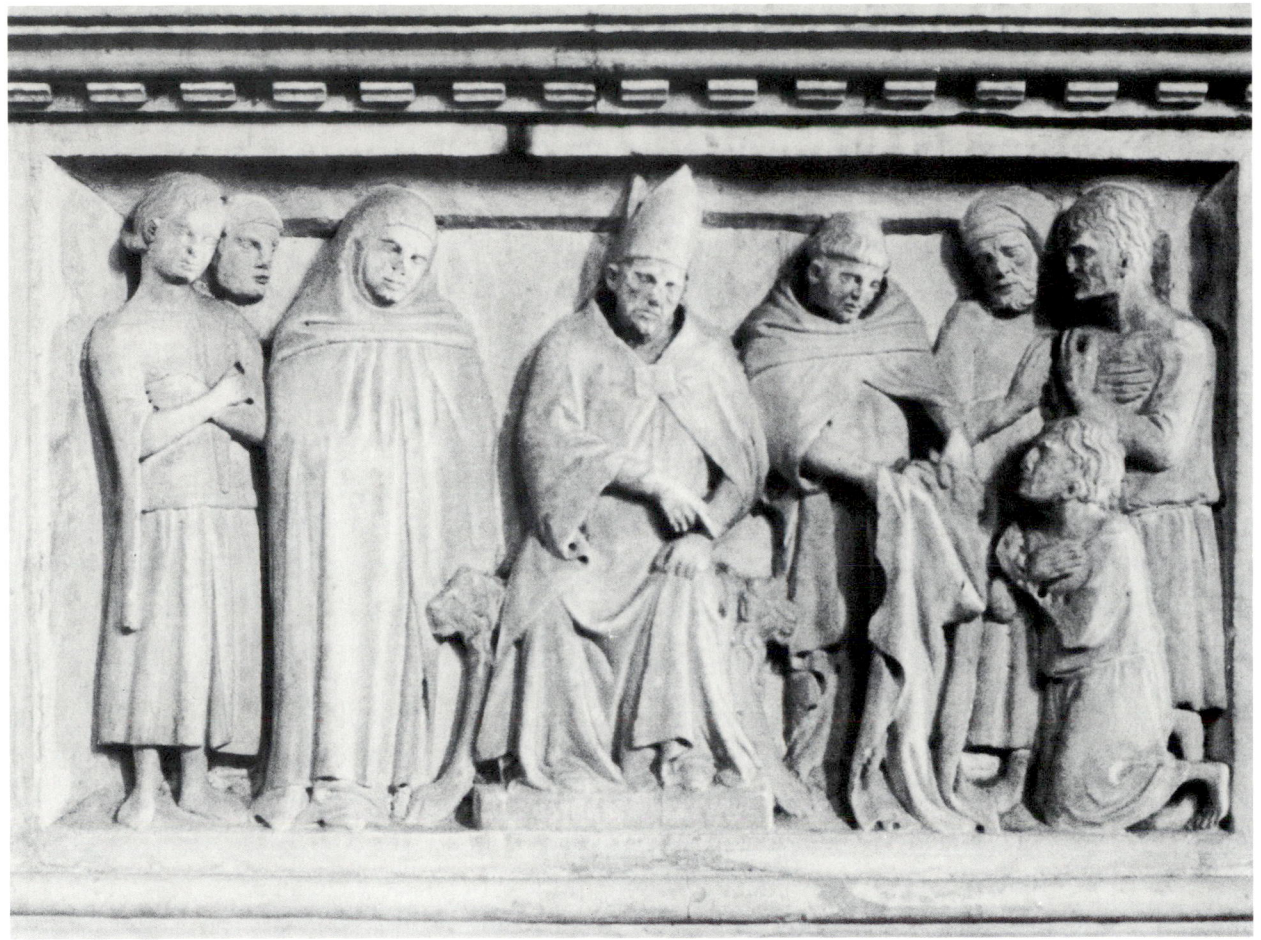

163. Andrea Pisano workshop: Saltarelli Monument, detail. Pisa, Sta. Caterina

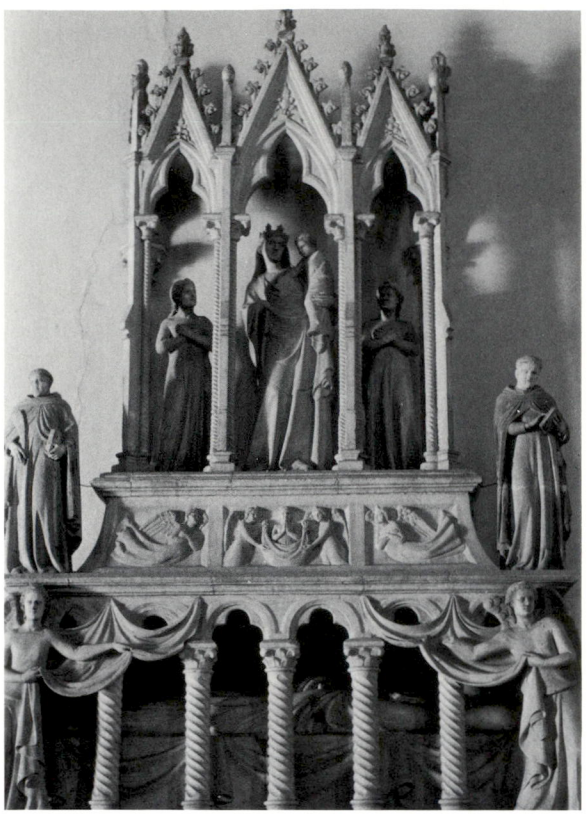

164. Andrea Pisano workshop: Saltarelli Monument, detail. Pisa, Sta. Caterina

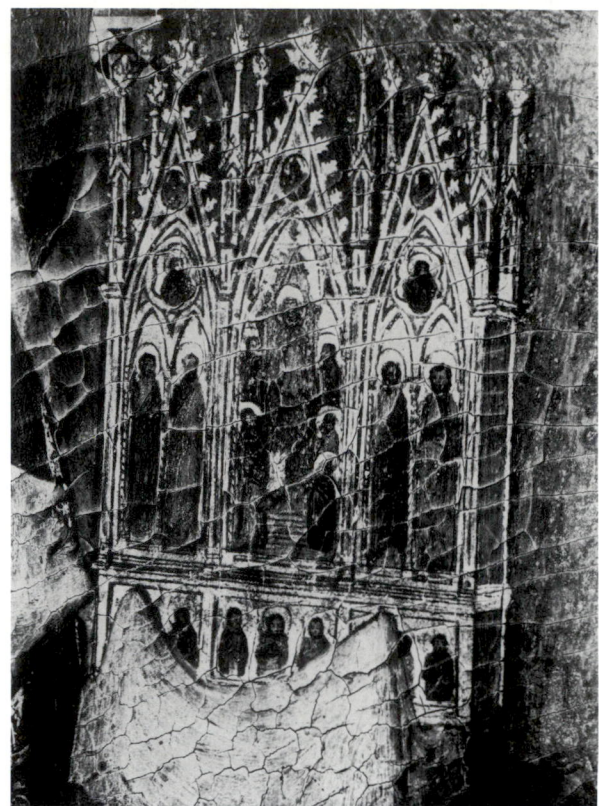

165. Giotto workshop: Stefaneschi Altarpiece, detail. Vatican Museum

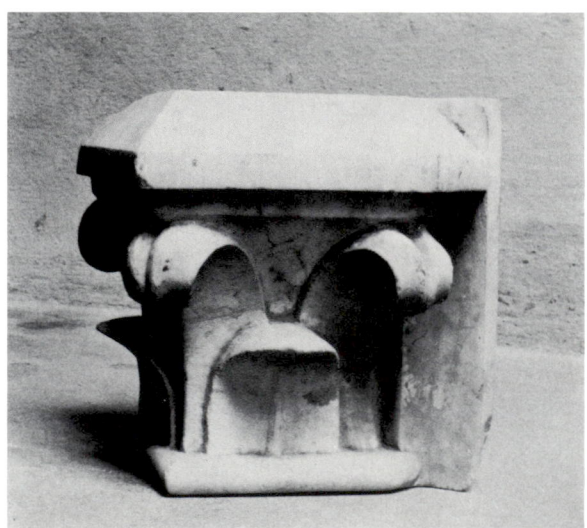

166. Andrea Pisano: Capital from Campanile. Florence, Museo dell'Opera del Duomo

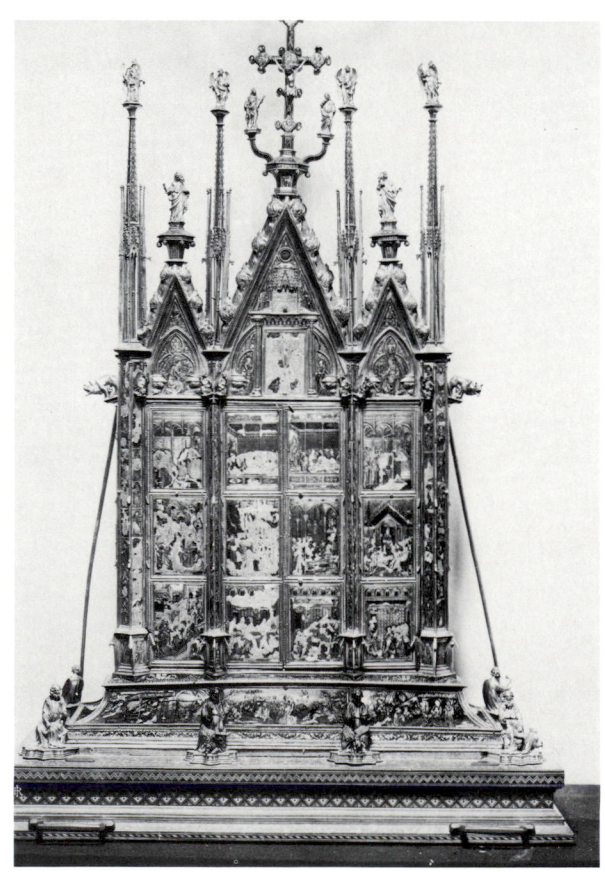

167. Ugolino di Vieri: Reliquary of the Holy Corporal. Orvieto Cathedral

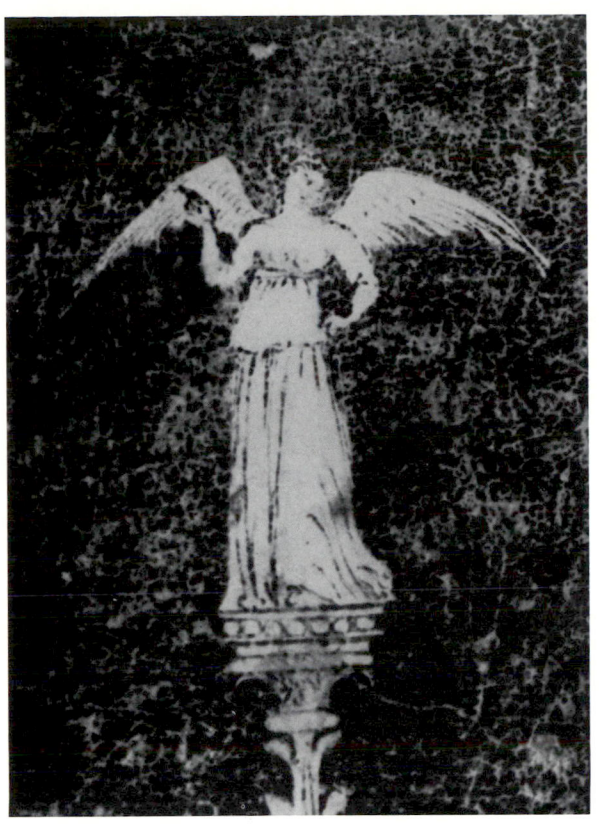

168. Campanile drawing, detail. Siena, Museo dell'Opera del Duomo

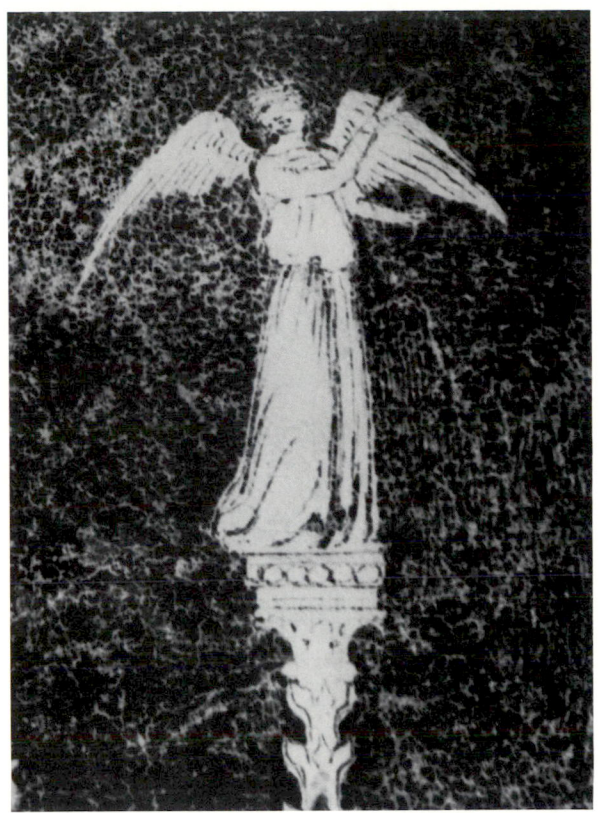

169. Campanile drawing, detail. Siena, Museo dell'Opera del Duomo

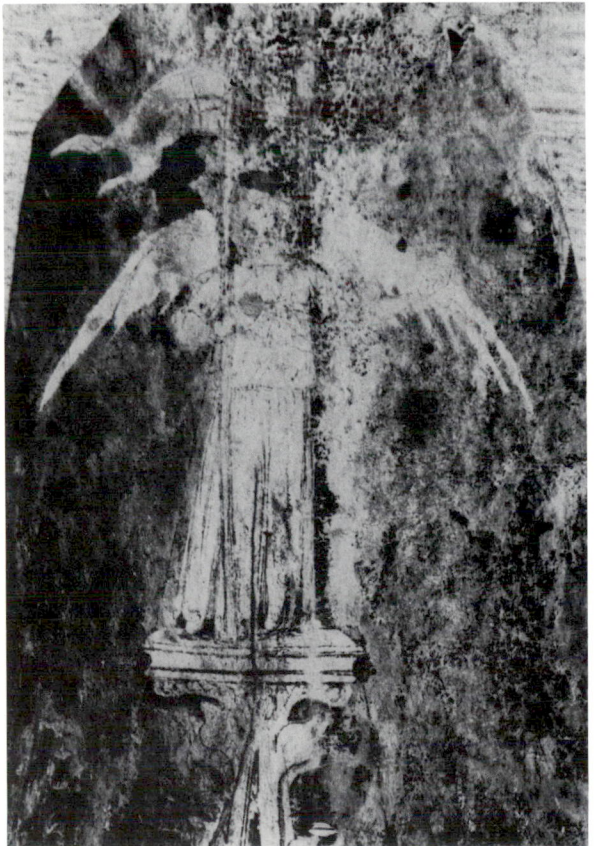

170. Campanile drawing, detail. Siena, Museo dell'Opera del Duomo

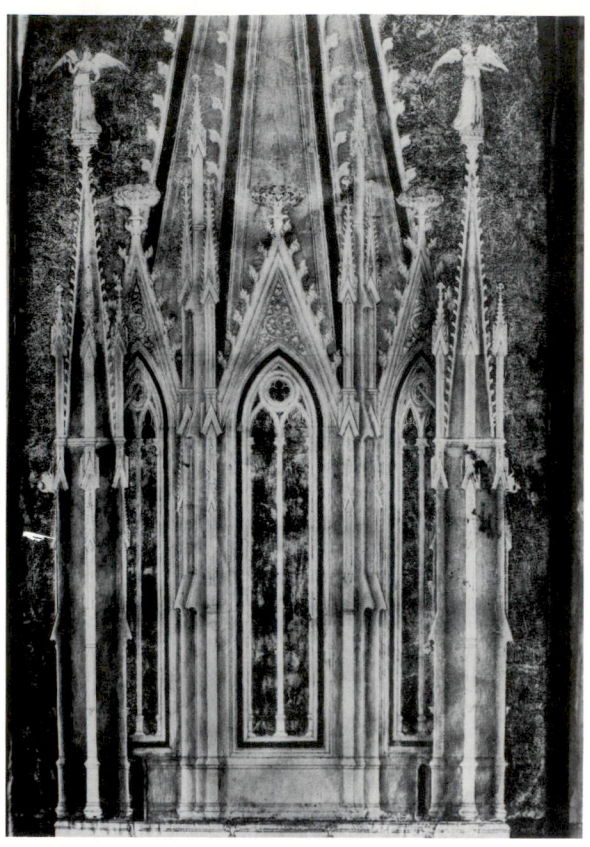

171. Campanile drawing, detail. Siena, Museo dell'Opera del Duomo

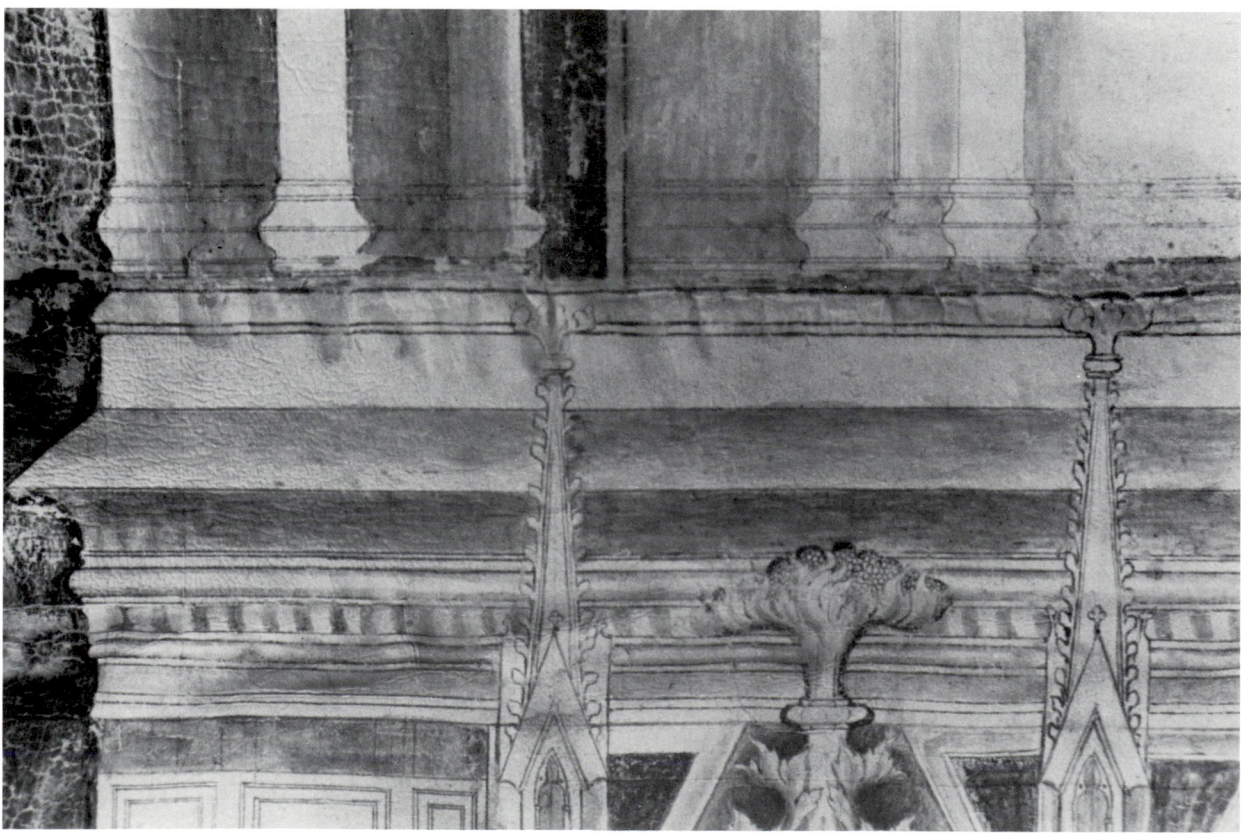

172. Campanile drawing, detail. Siena, Museo dell'Opera del Duomo

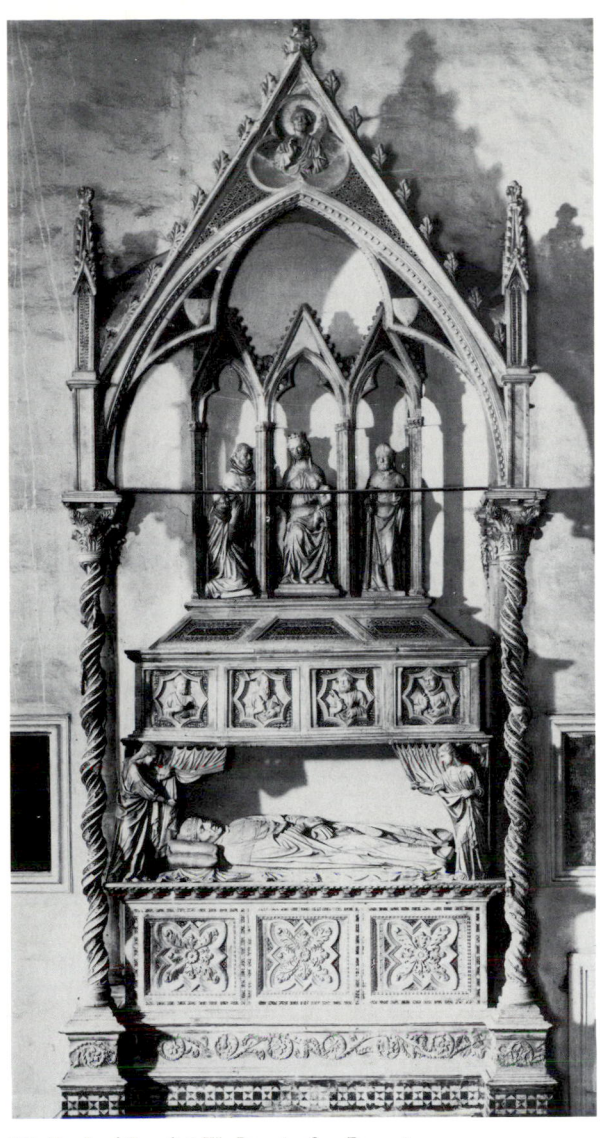

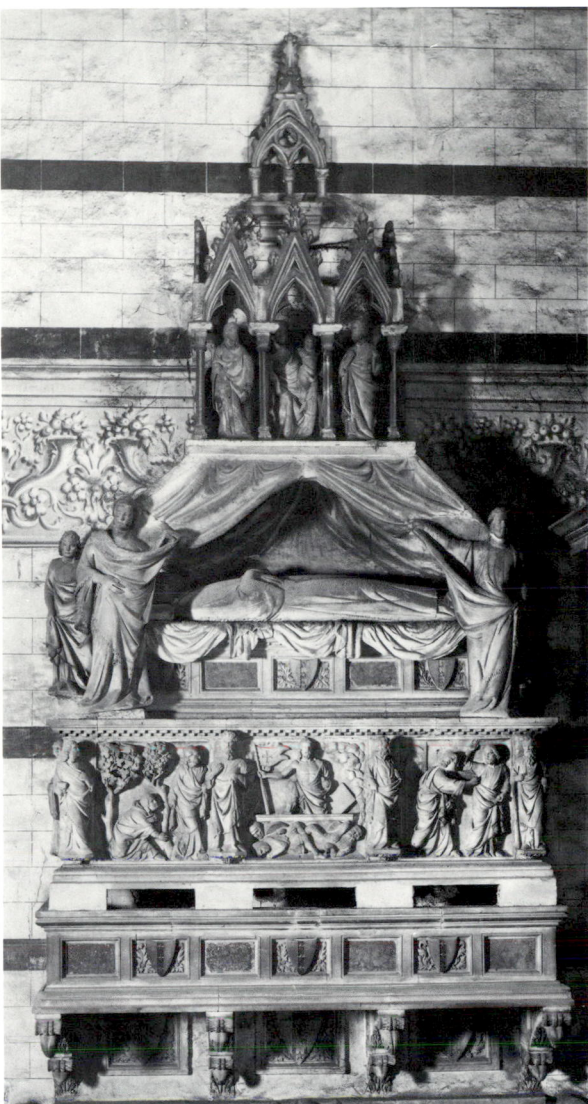

173. Tomb of Benedict XI. Perugia, San Domenico

174. Tino di Camaino: Petroni Monument. Siena Cathedral

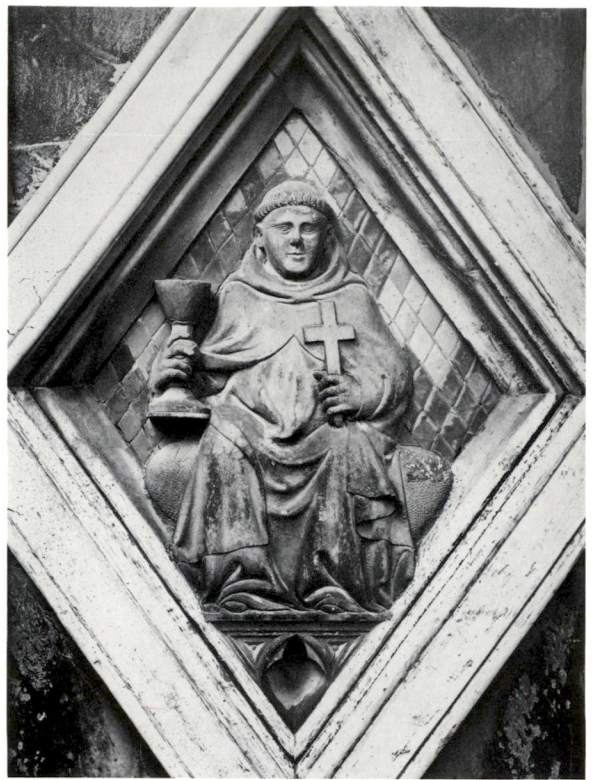

175. Campanile relief. Florence, Museo dell'Opera del Duomo

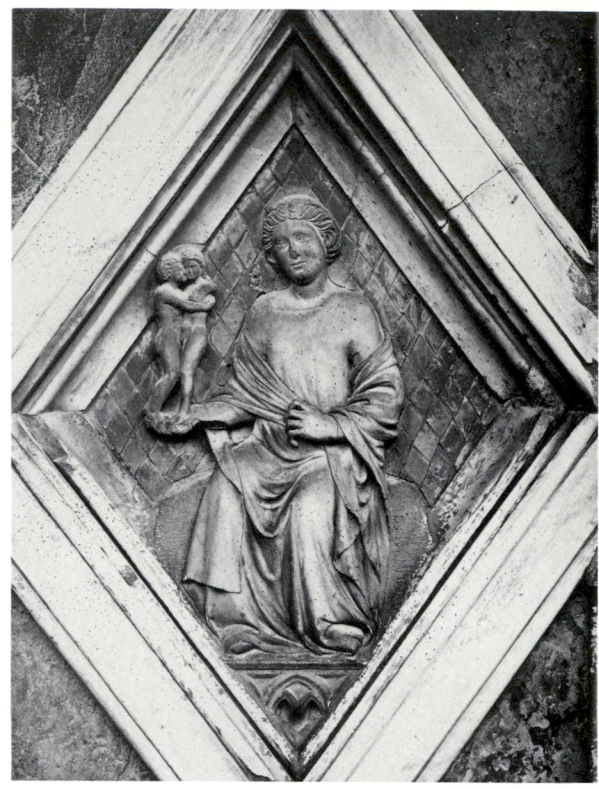

176. Campanile relief. Florence, Museo dell'Opera del Duomo

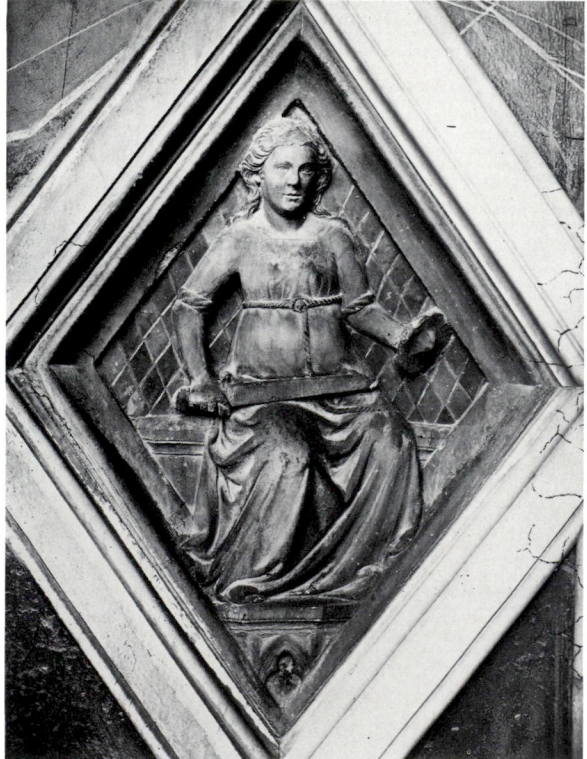

177. Campanile relief. Florence, Museo dell'Opera del Duomo

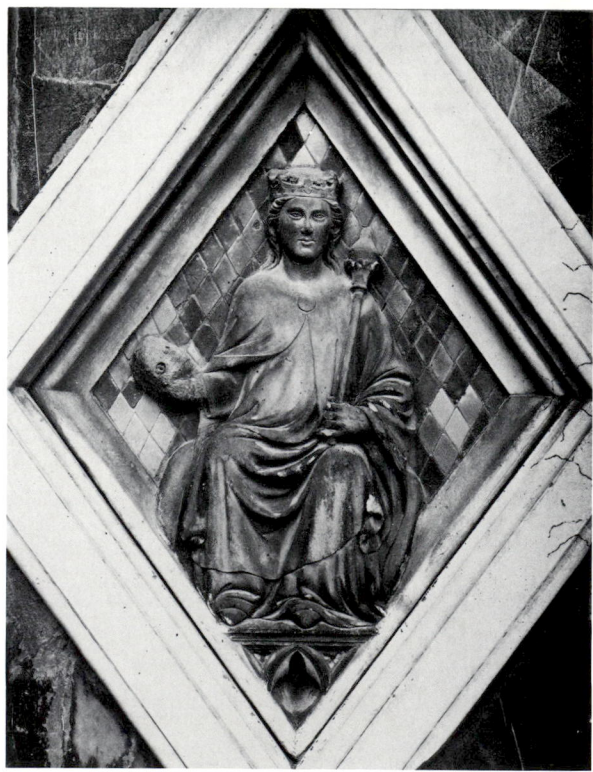

178. Campanile relief. Florence, Museo dell'Opera del Duomo

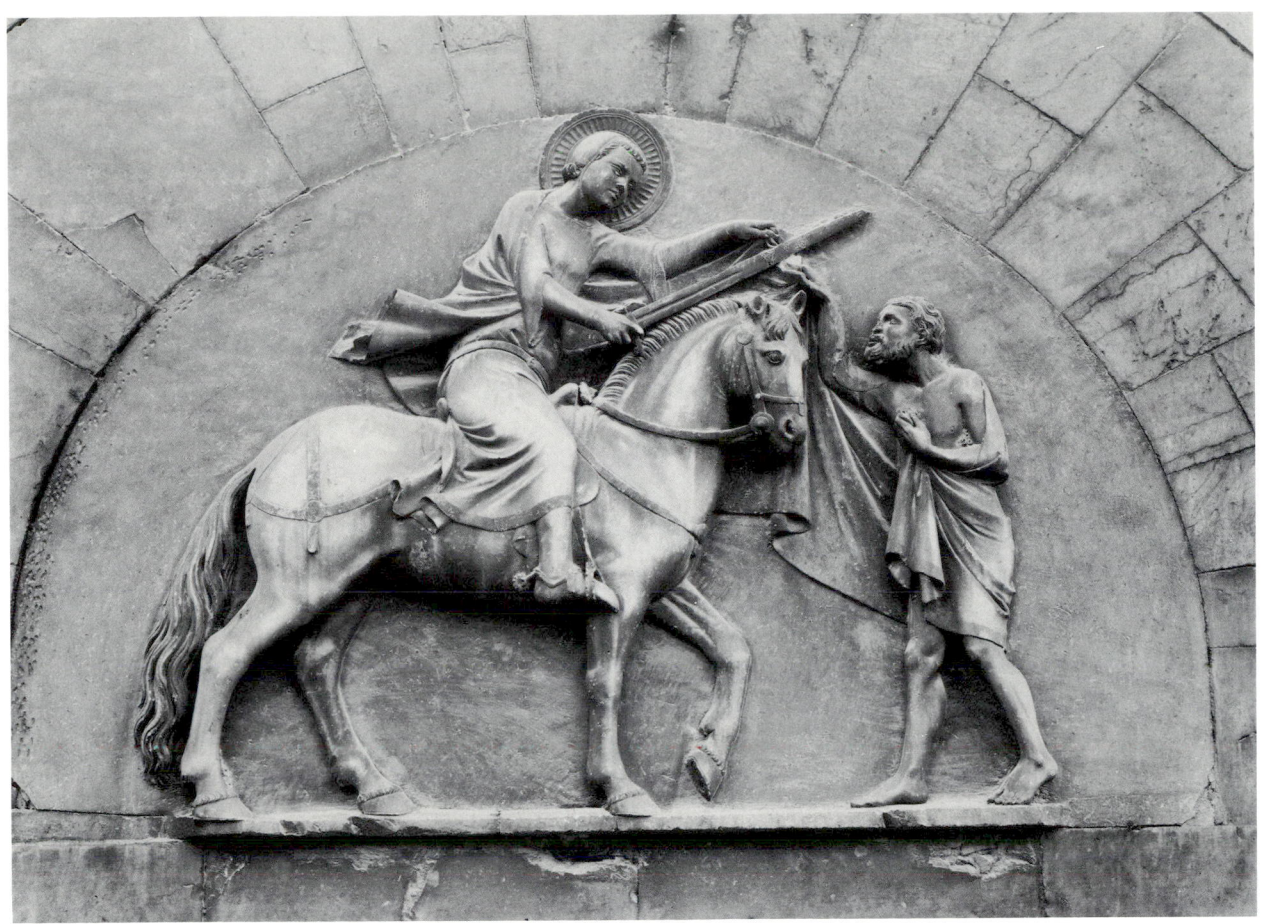

179. Andrea Pisano workshop: *St. Martin and the Beggar*, relief. Pisa, San Martino

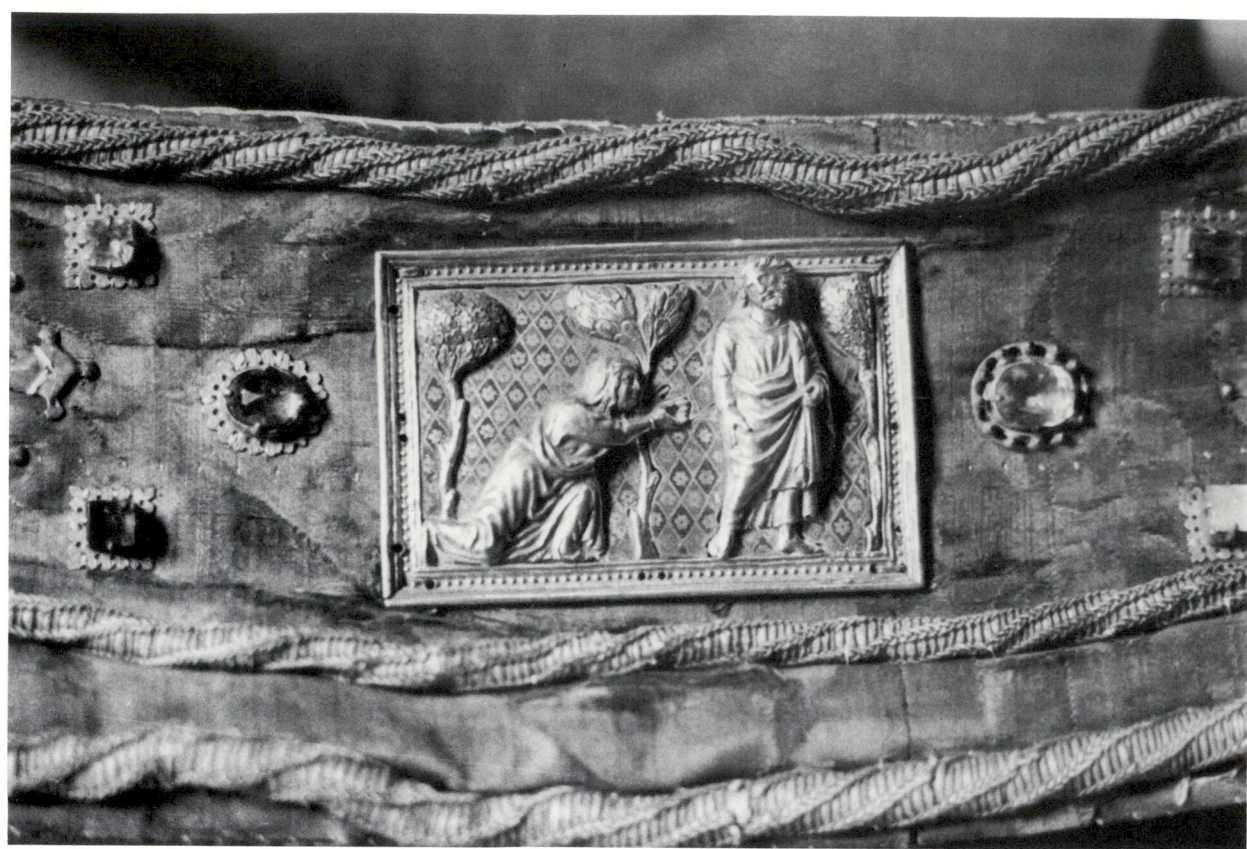

180. Sacra Cintola, detail. Pisa, Museo di San Matteo

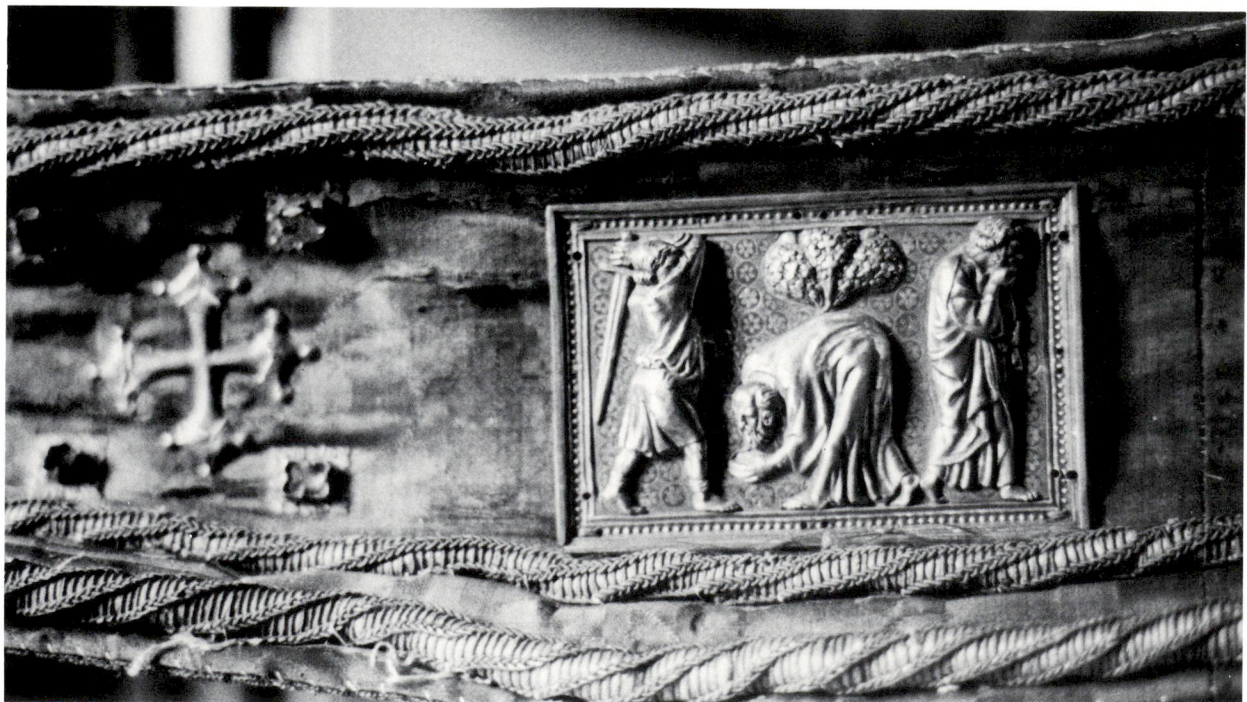

181. Sacra Cintola, detail. Pisa, Museo di San Matteo

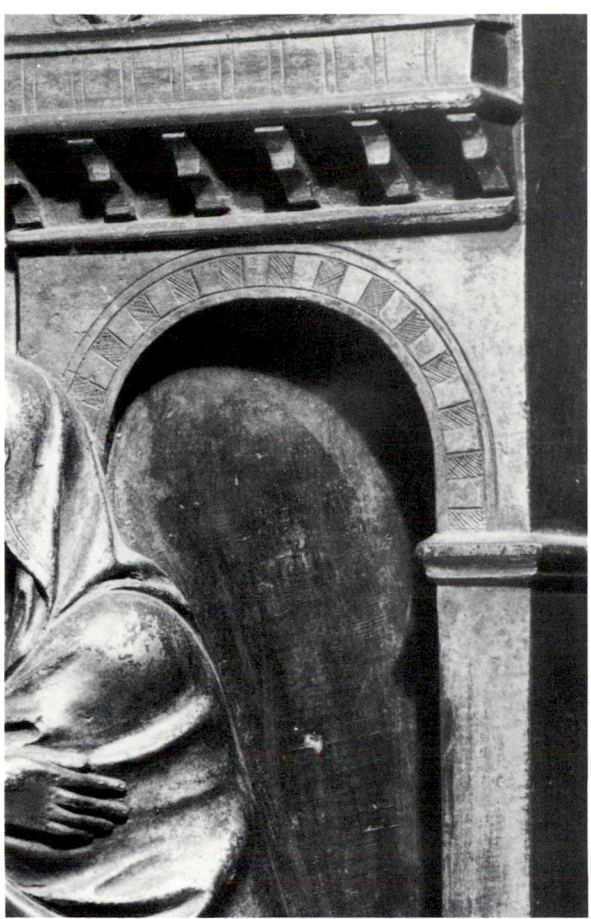

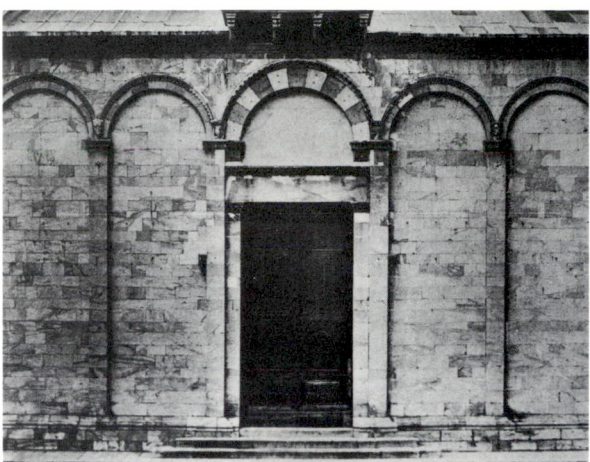

183. Pisa, Camposanto, entrance

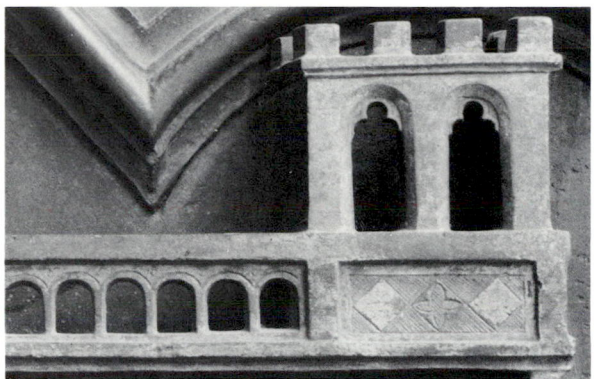

182. Andrea Pisano: *Visitation*, detail. Florence, Baptistry doors

184. Andrea Pisano: *Presentation of Baptist's Head to Herodias*, detail. Florence, Baptistry doors

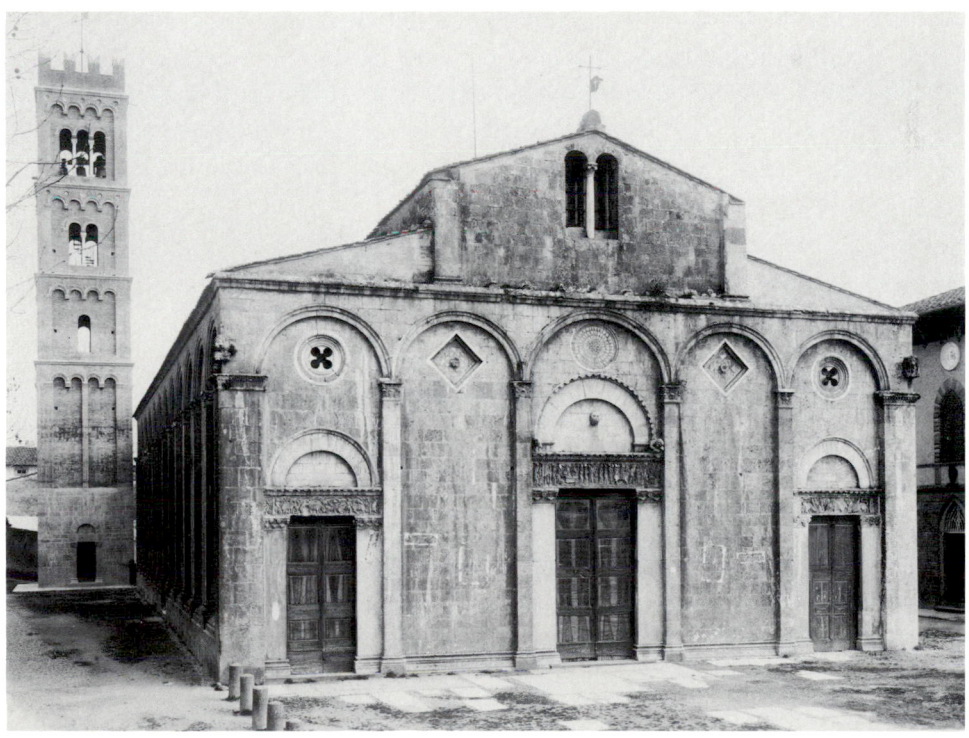

185. S. Casciano Presso Pisa, Pisa

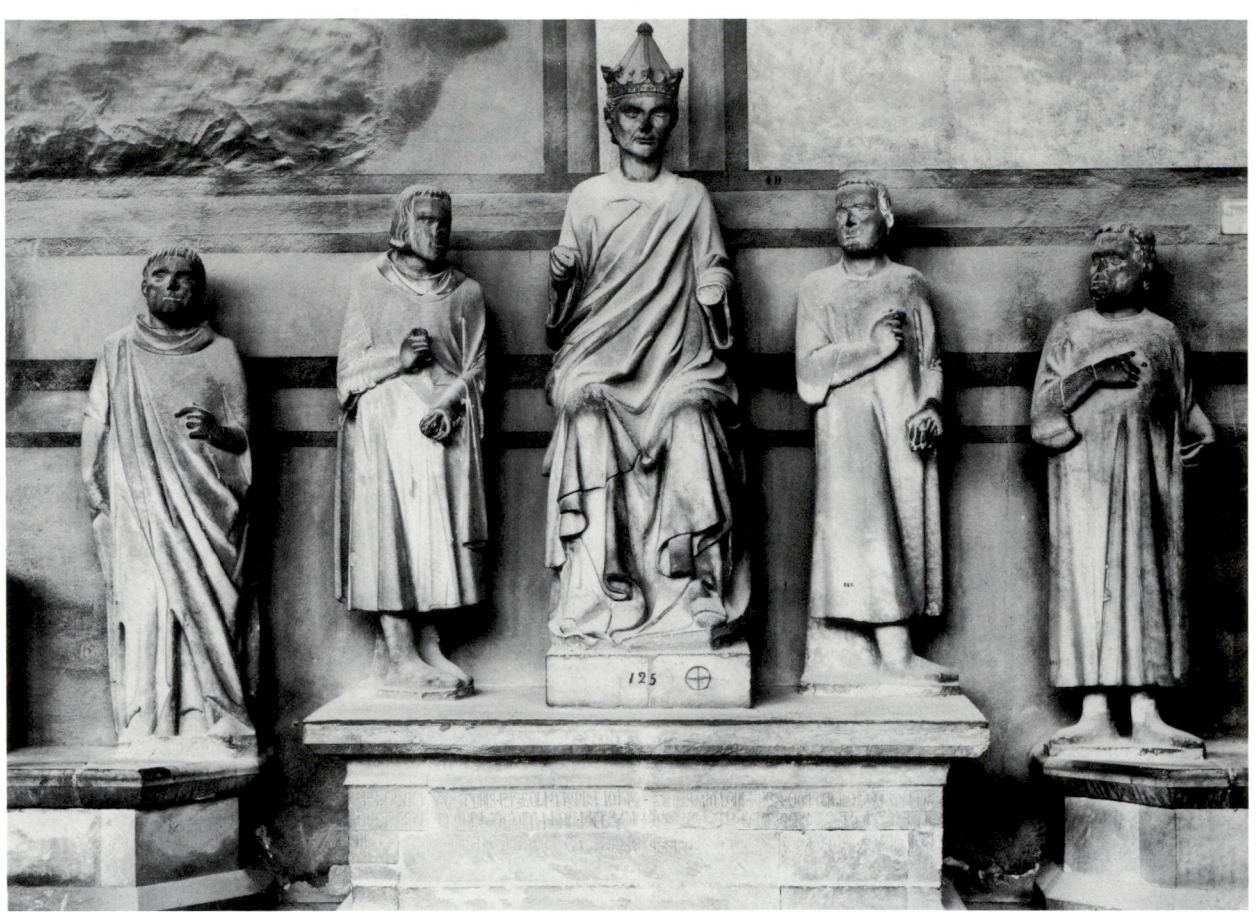

186. Tino di Camaino: Monument of Henry VII, detail. Pisa, Camposanto

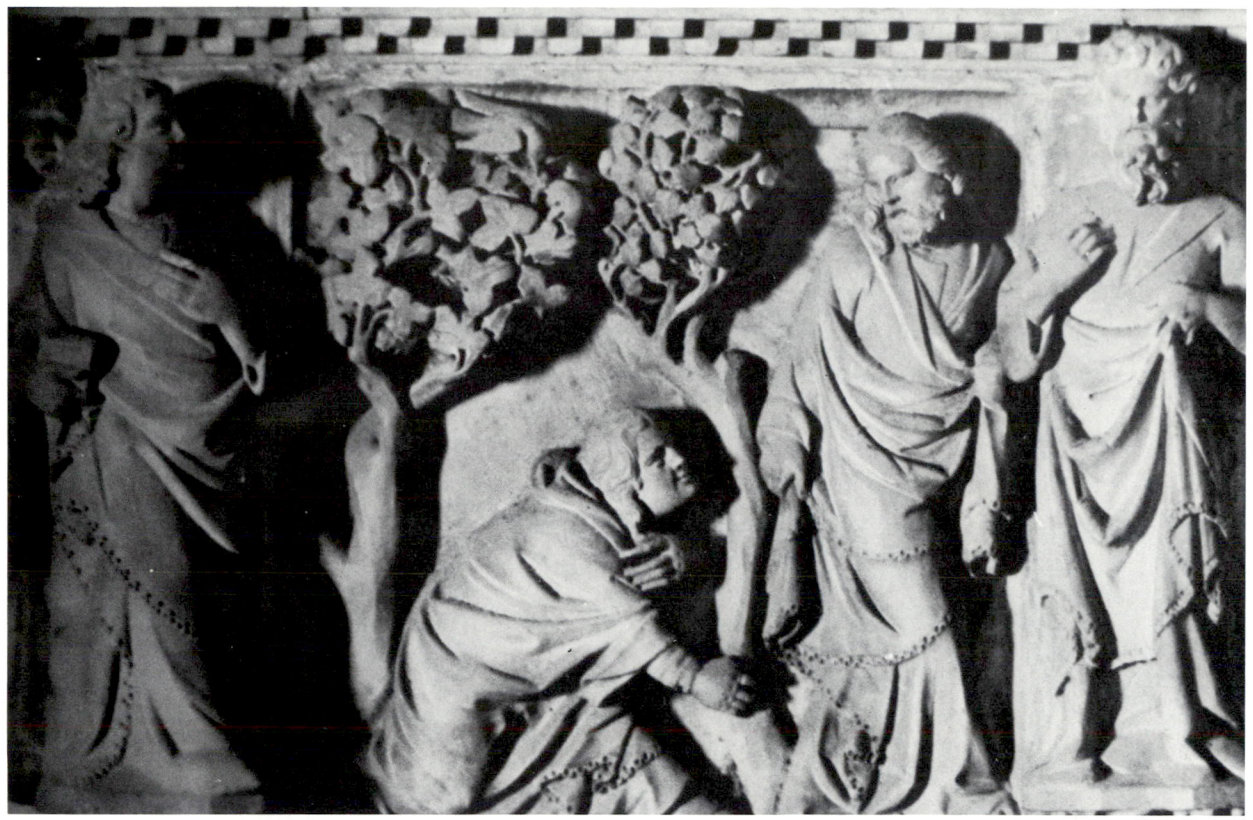

187. Tino di Camaino: *Noli Me Tangere*. Petroni Monument. Siena Cathedral

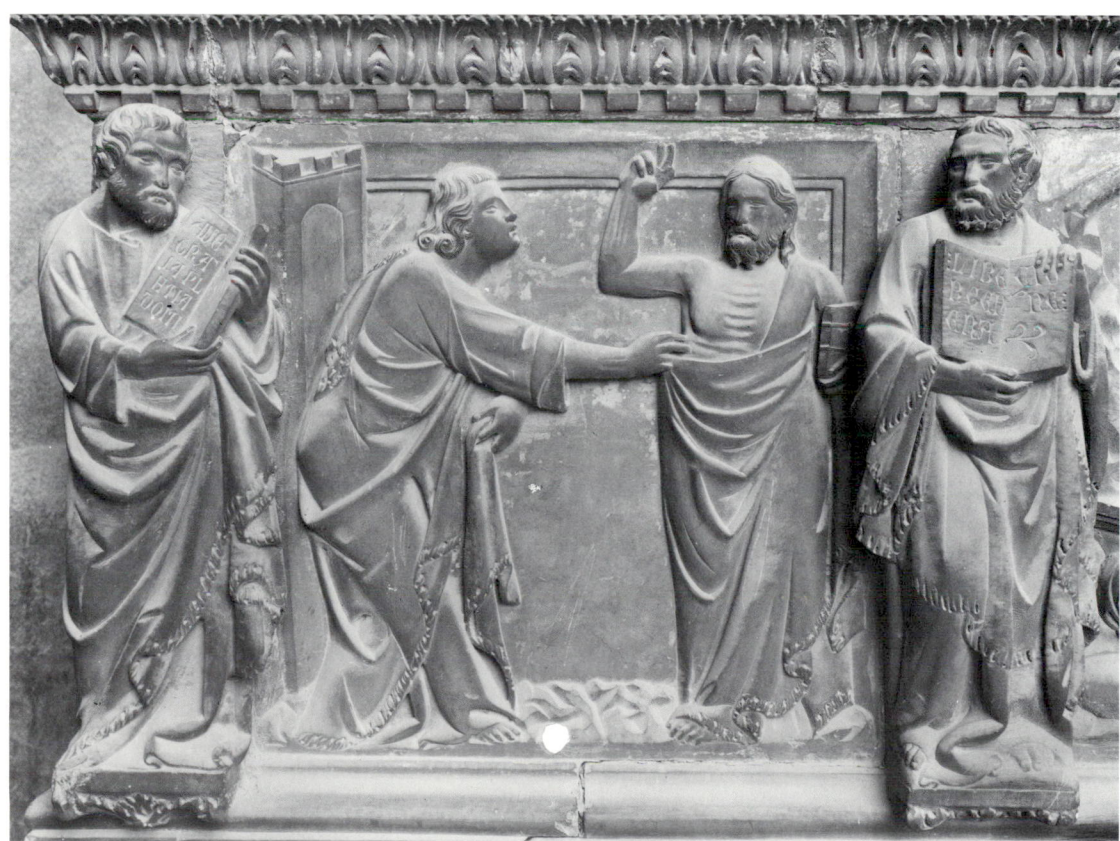

188. Tino di Camaino: *Doubting Thomas*. Delle Torre Monument. Florence, Sta. Croce

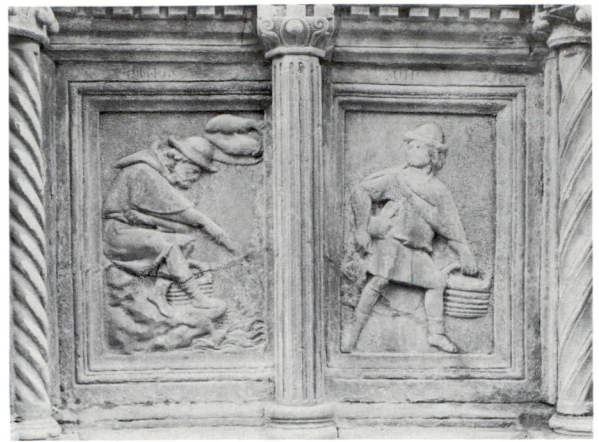

189. Nicola Pisano: Fontana Maggiore, detail. Perugia

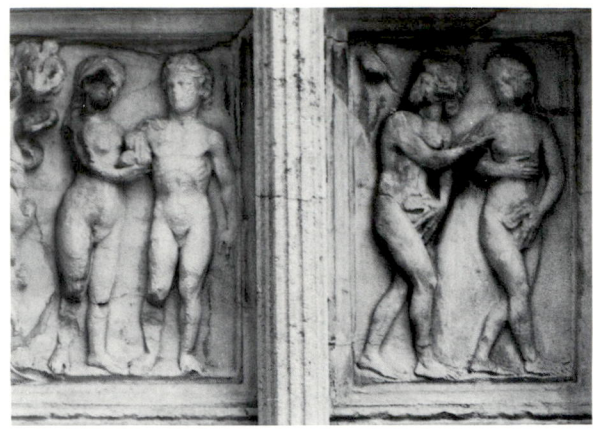

190. Nicola Pisano: Fontana Maggiore, detail. Perugia

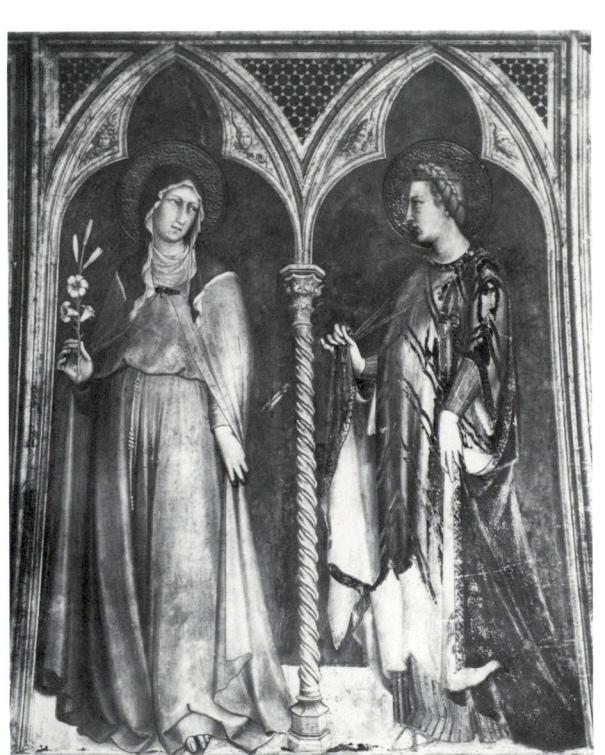

191. Simone Martini: *St. Claire and St. Elizabeth*. Assisi, San Francesco

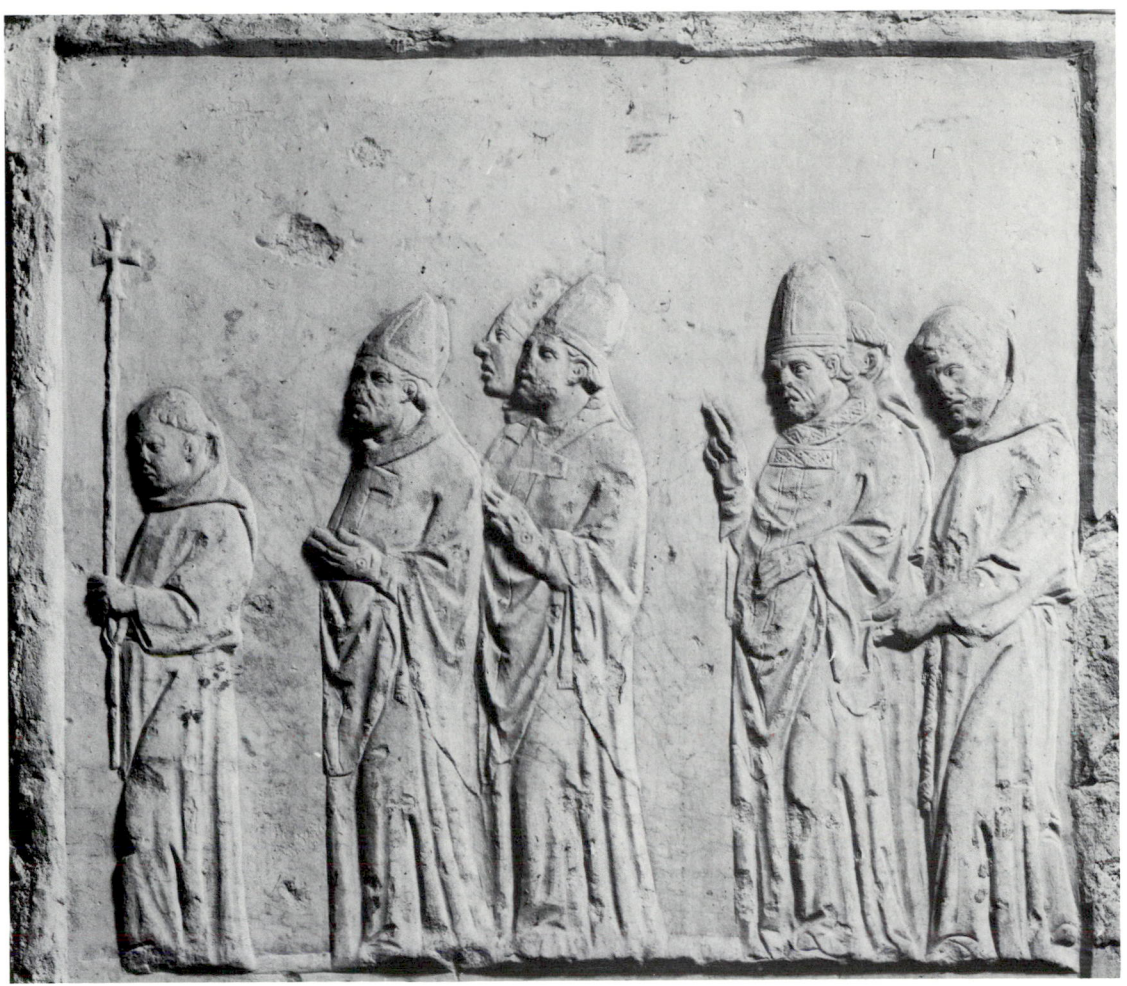

192. Consecration relief. Siena, San Francesco

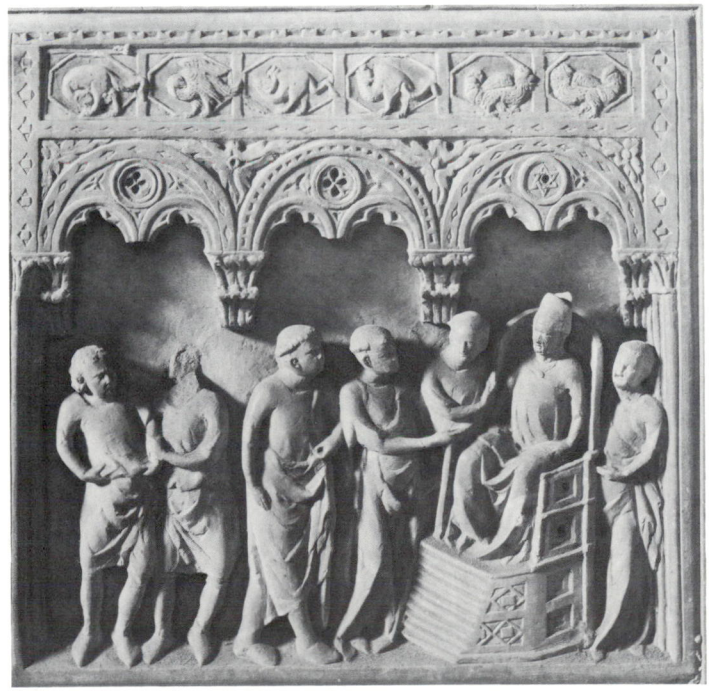

193. Goro di Gregorio: Arca di San Cerbone, detail. Massa Marittima Cathedral

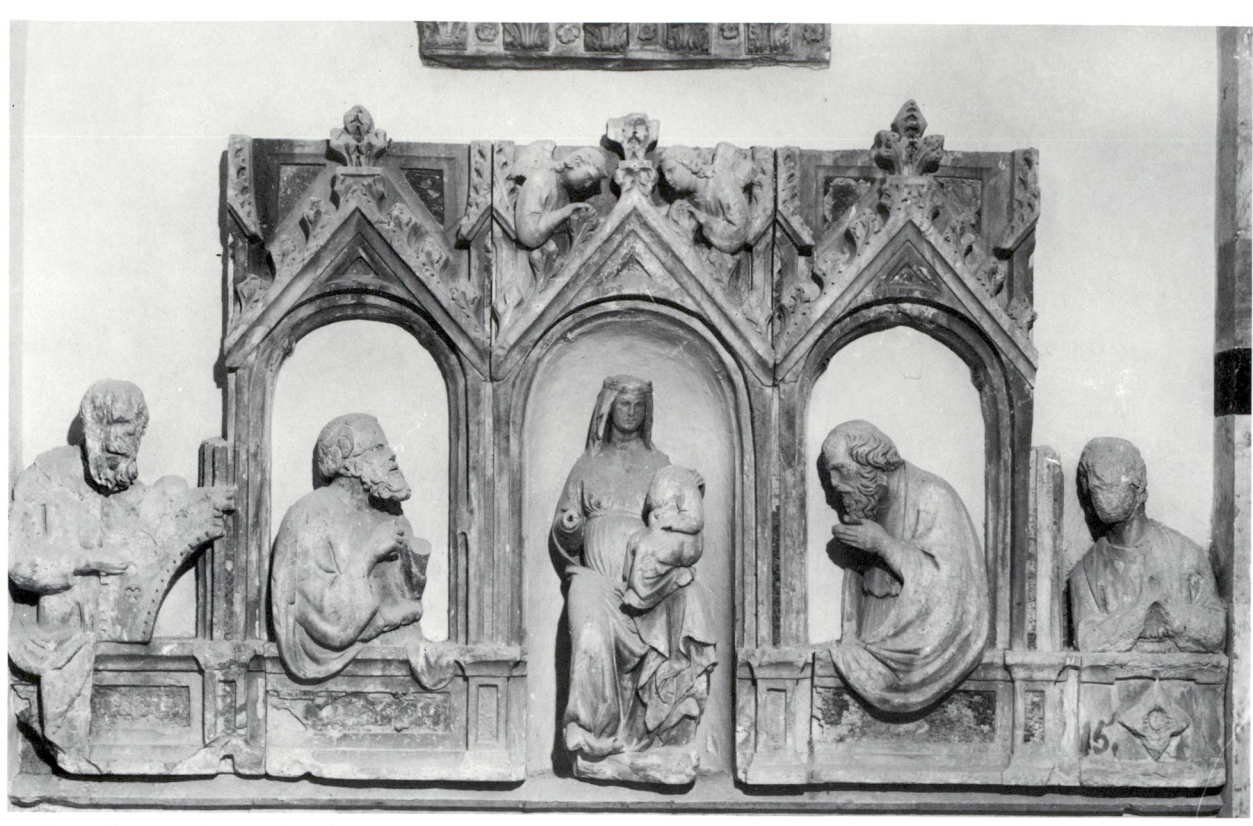

194. Figures from around rose window of Cathedral. Siena, Museo dell'Opera del Duomo

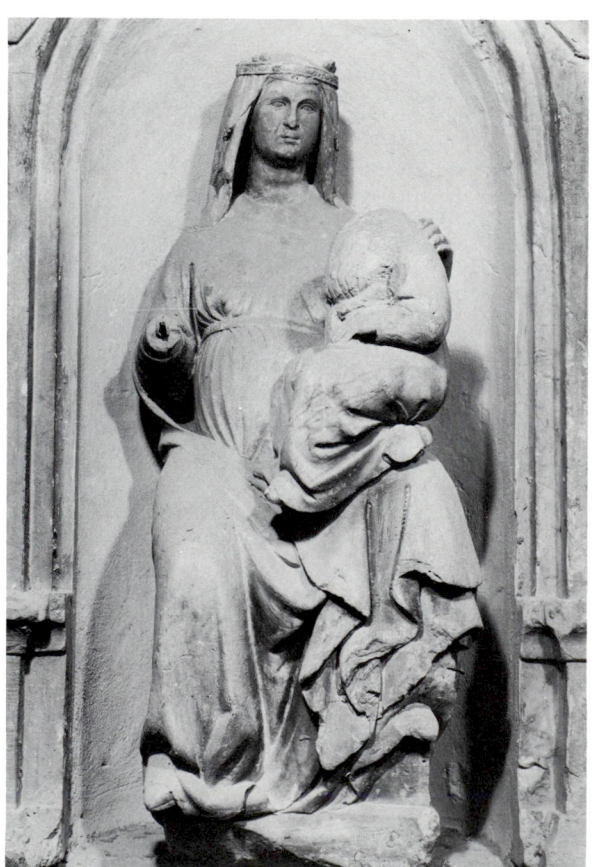

195. *Madonna* from around rose window of Cathedral. Siena, Museo dell'Opera del Duomo

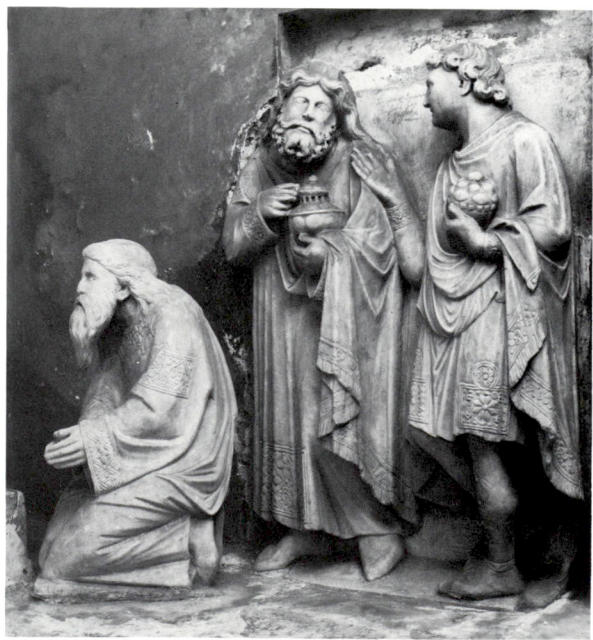

196. Arnolfo di Cambio: *Praesepe*, detail. Rome, Sta. Maria Maggiore

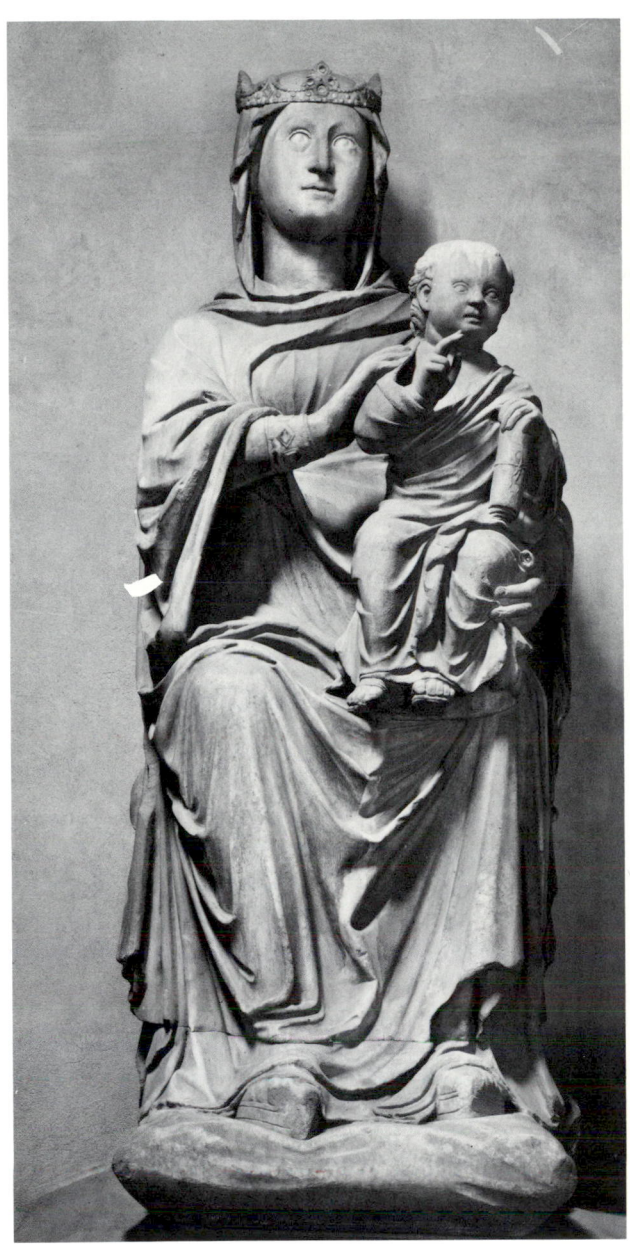

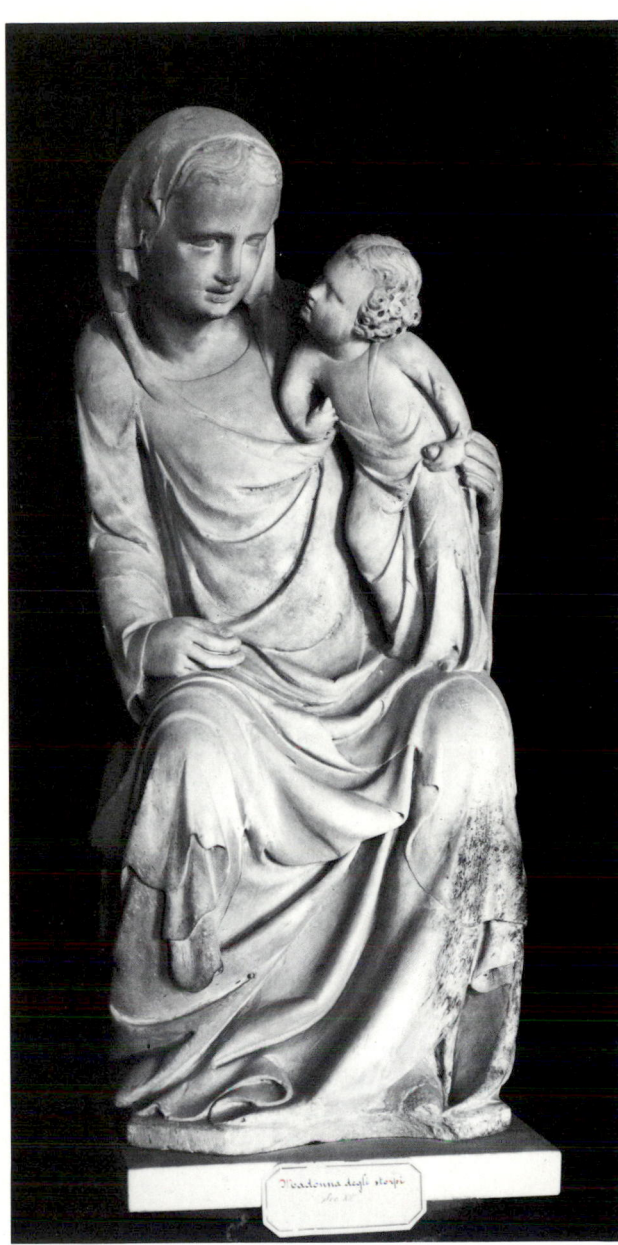

197. Arnolfo di Cambio: *Madonna and Child*. Florence, Museo dell'Opera del Duomo

198. Goro di Gregorio: *Madonna degli Storpi*. Messina, Museo Nazionale

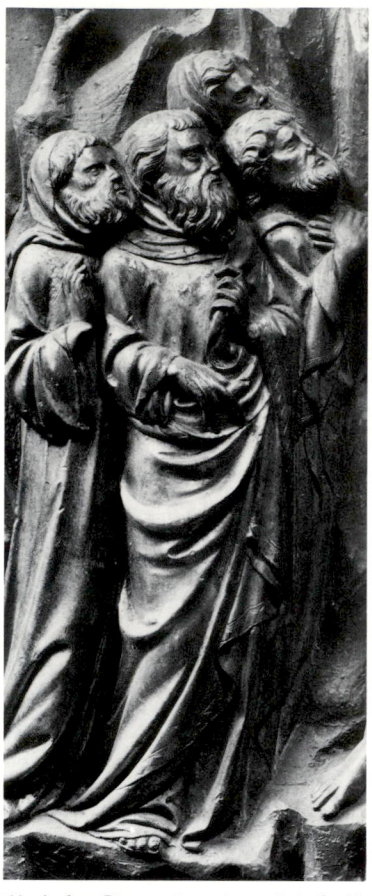

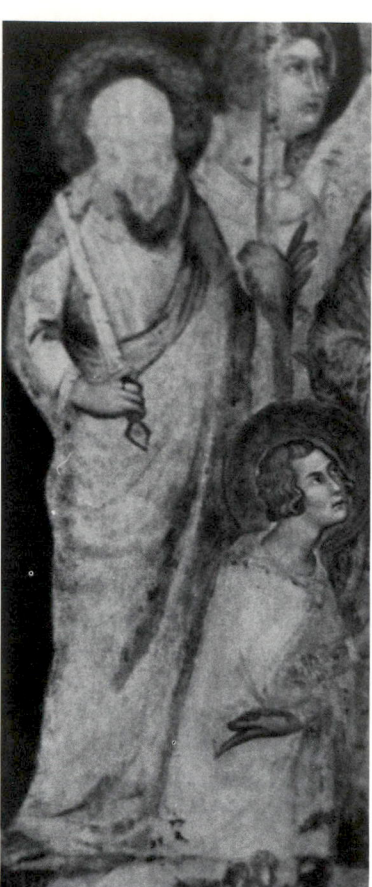

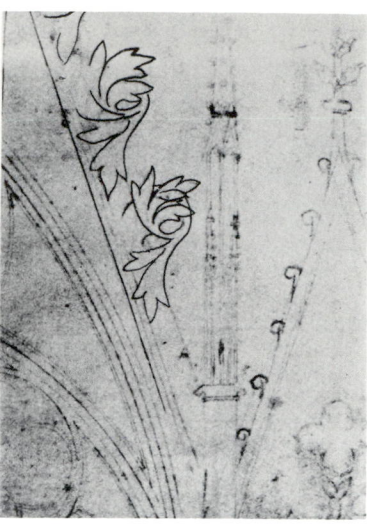

201. Design B, Strasbourg Cathedral. Strasbourg, Musée de l'Oeuvre Notre Dame

199. Andrea Pisano: *Ecce Agnus Dei*, detail. Florence Baptistry doors

200. Simone Martini: *Maestà*, detail. Siena, Palazzo Pubblico

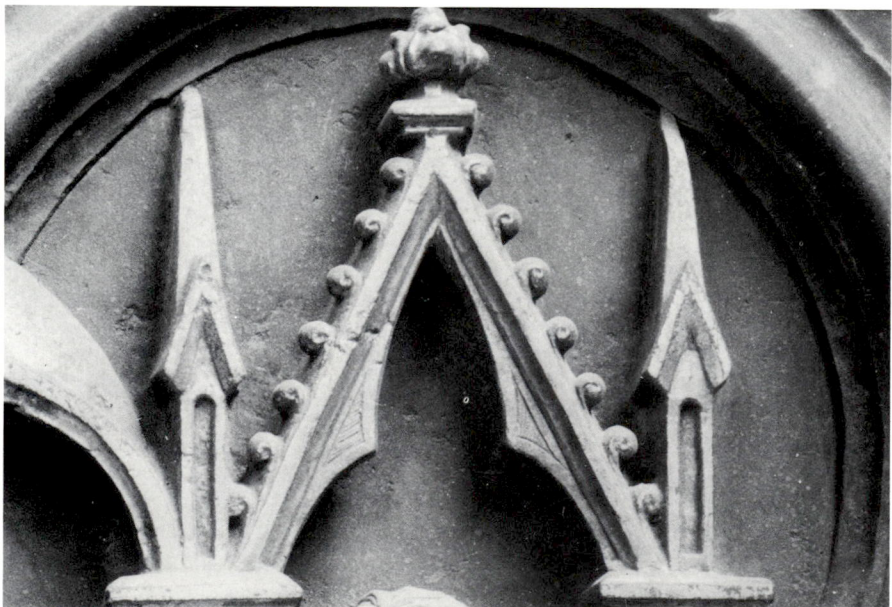

202. Andrea Pisano: *The Entombment*, detail. Florence, Baptistry doors

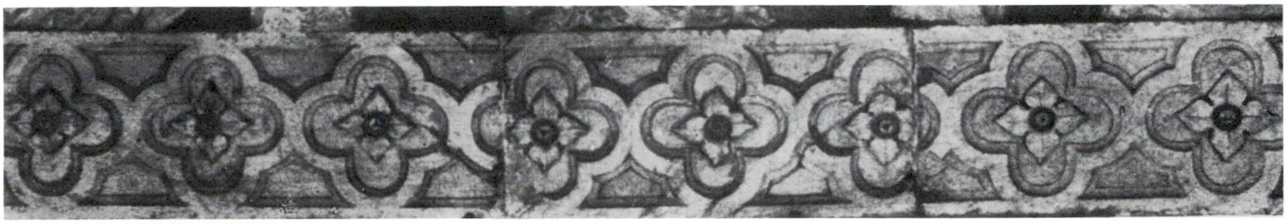

203. Tabernacle detail. Arezzo, Archbishop's Palace

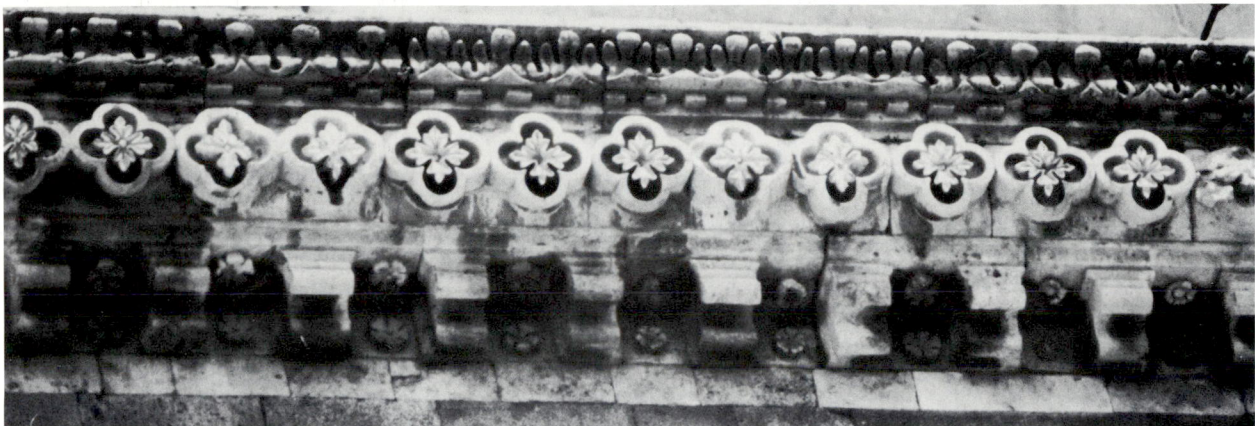

204. Orvieto Cathedral. Exterior side aisle cornice

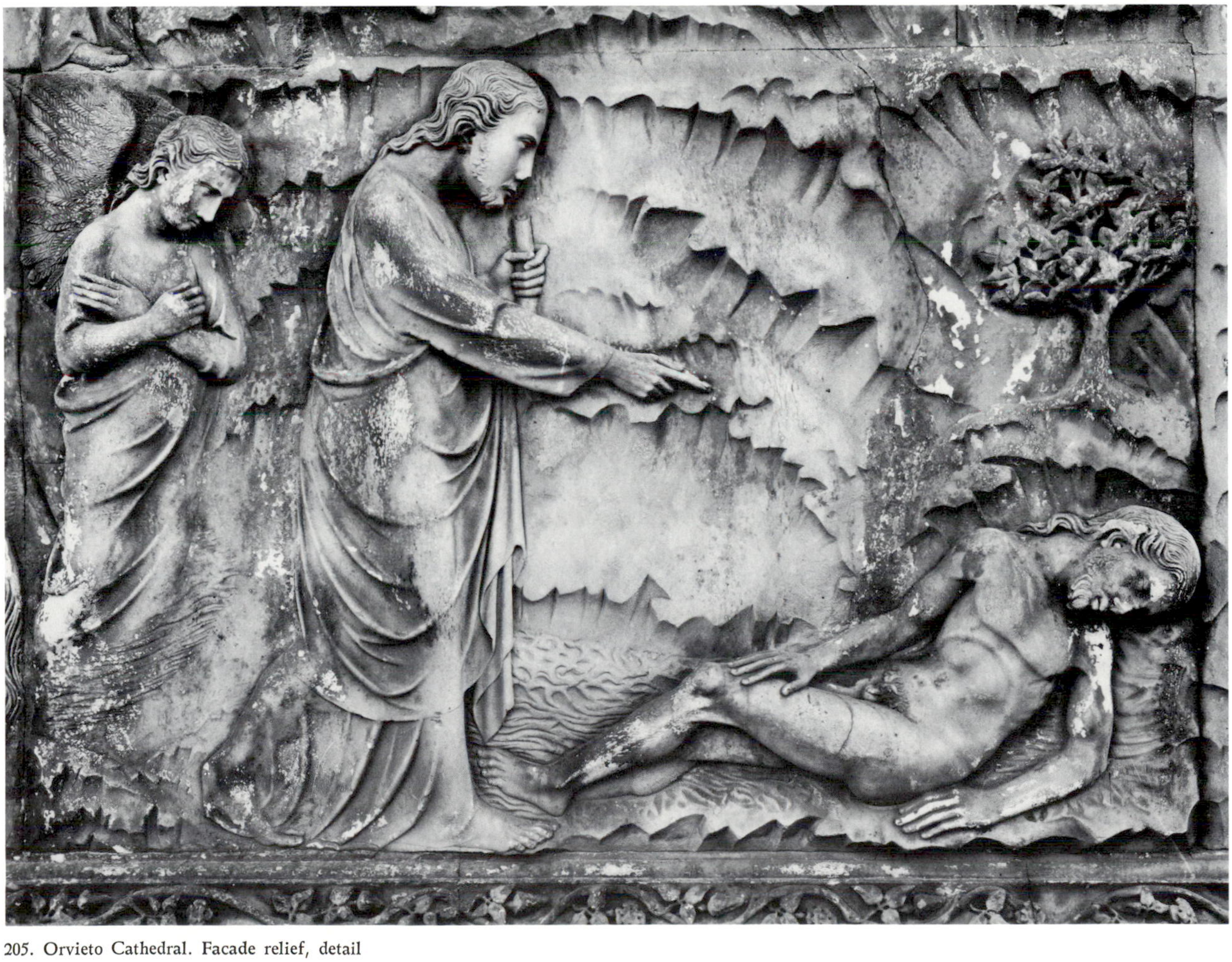

205. Orvieto Cathedral. Facade relief, detail

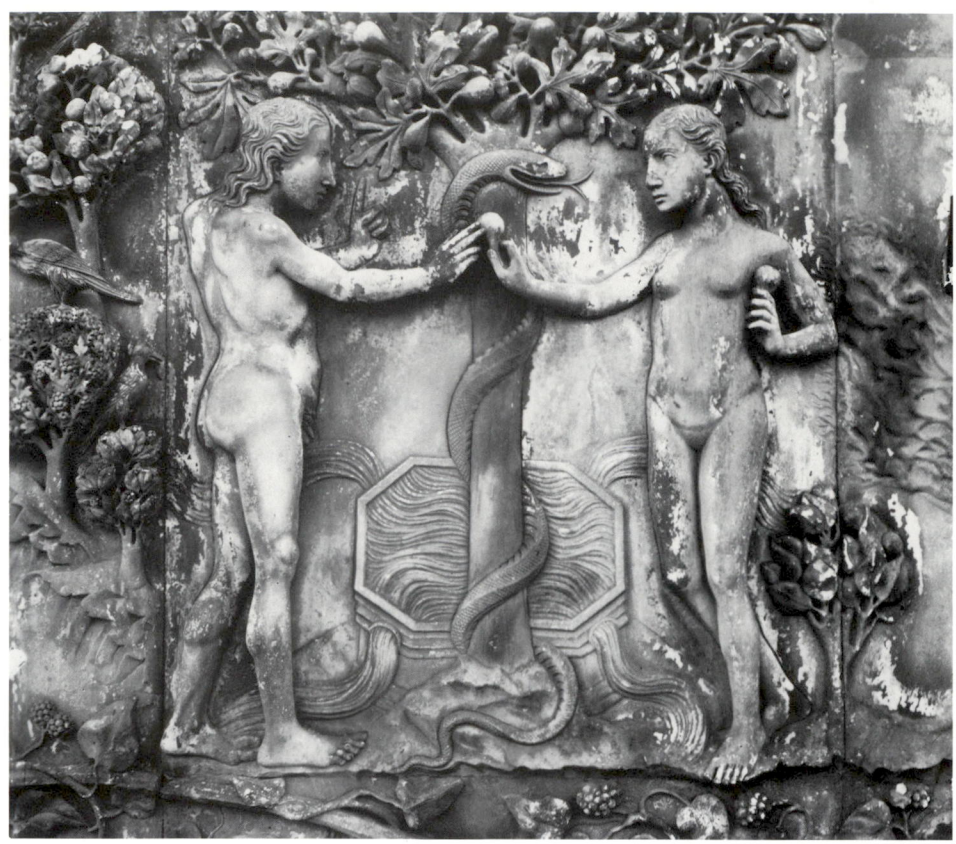

206. Orvieto Cathedral. Facade relief, detail

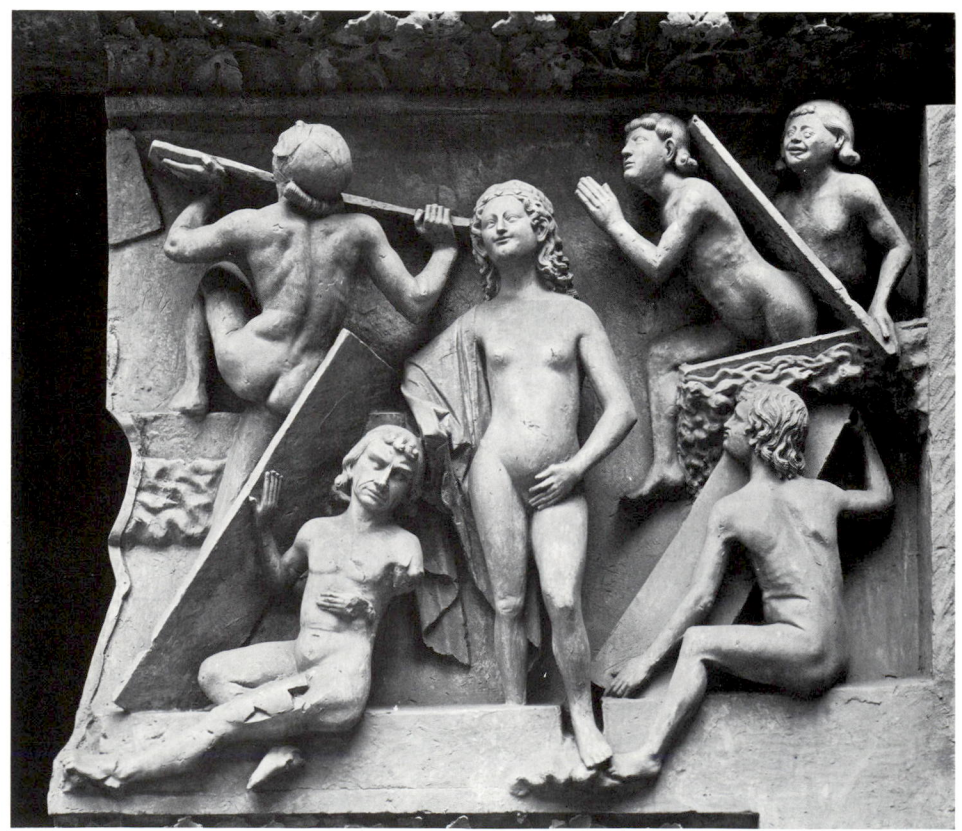

207. *Last Judgment*, detail. Bourges Cathedral

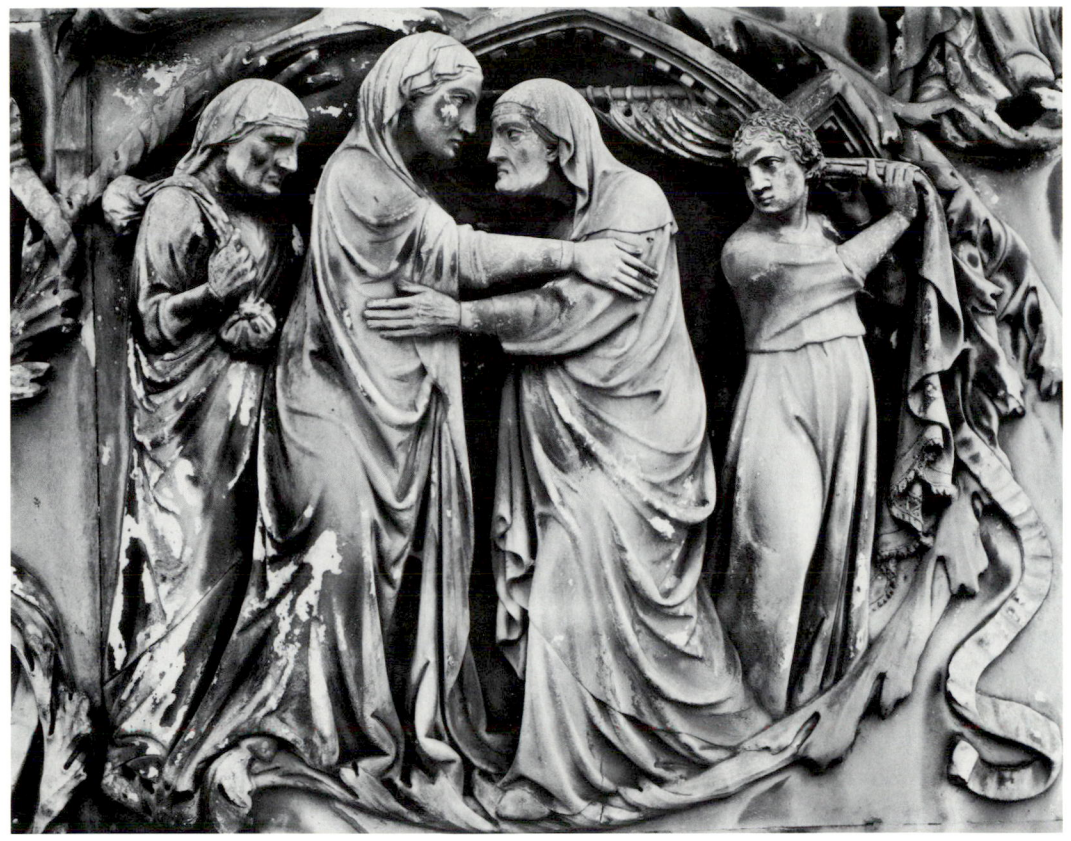

208. Orvieto Cathedral. Facade relief, detail

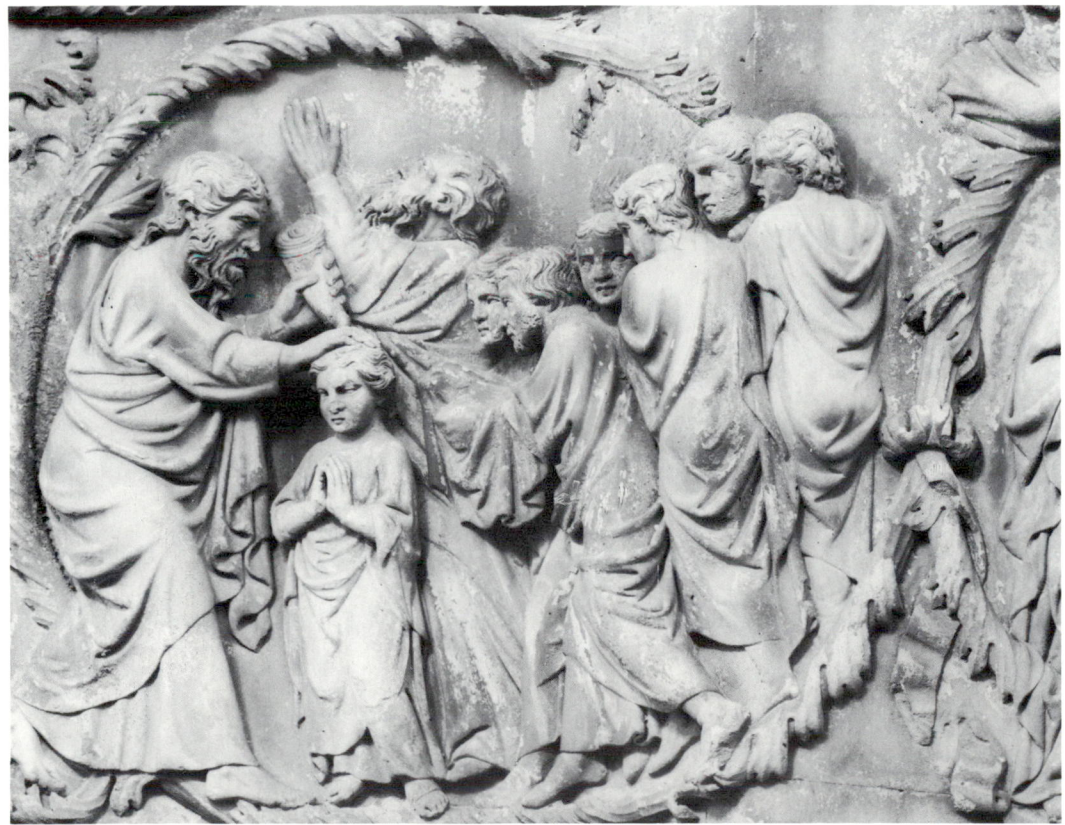

209. Orvieto Cathedral. Facade relief, detail

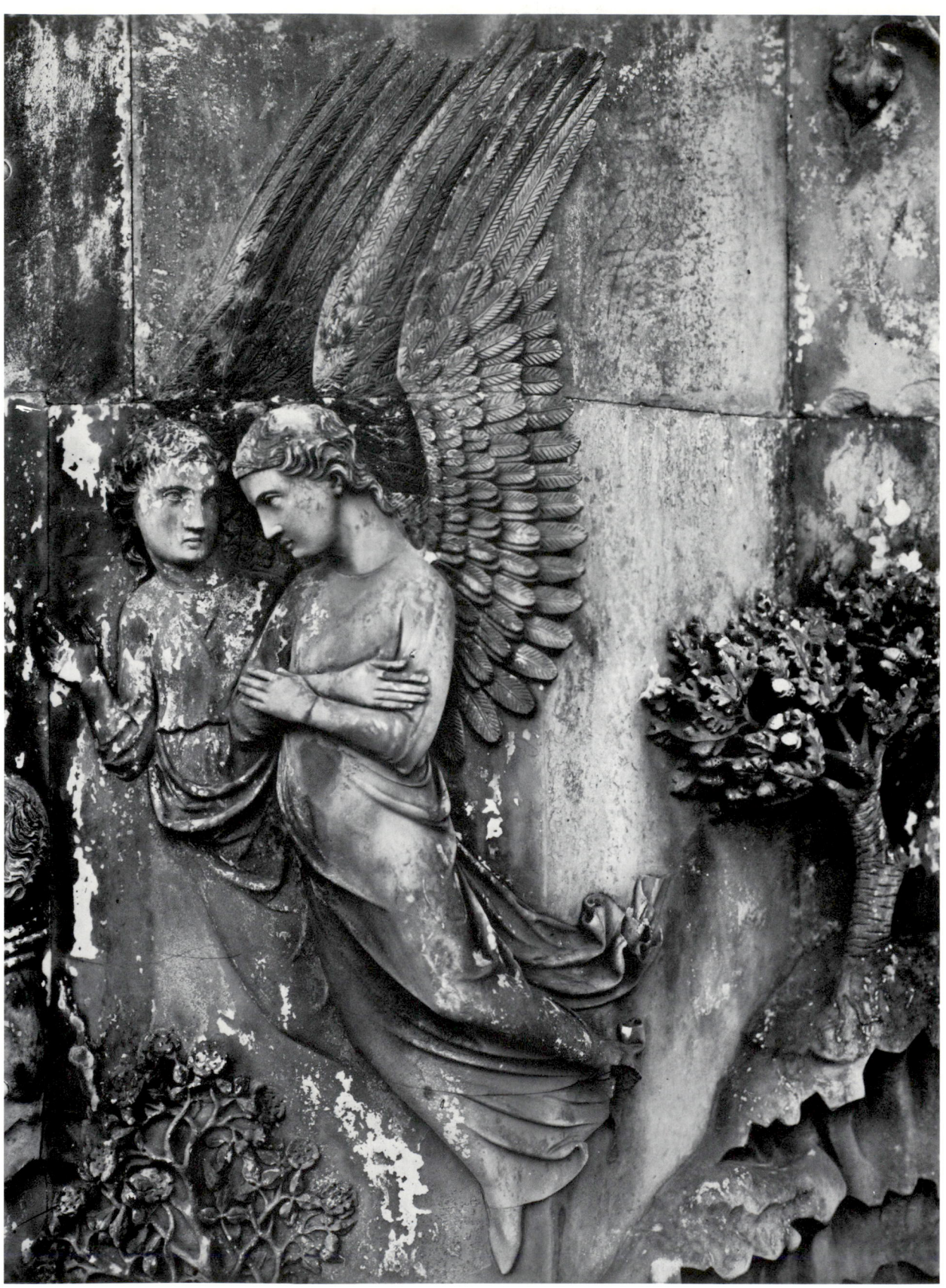

210. Orvieto Cathedral. Facade relief, detail

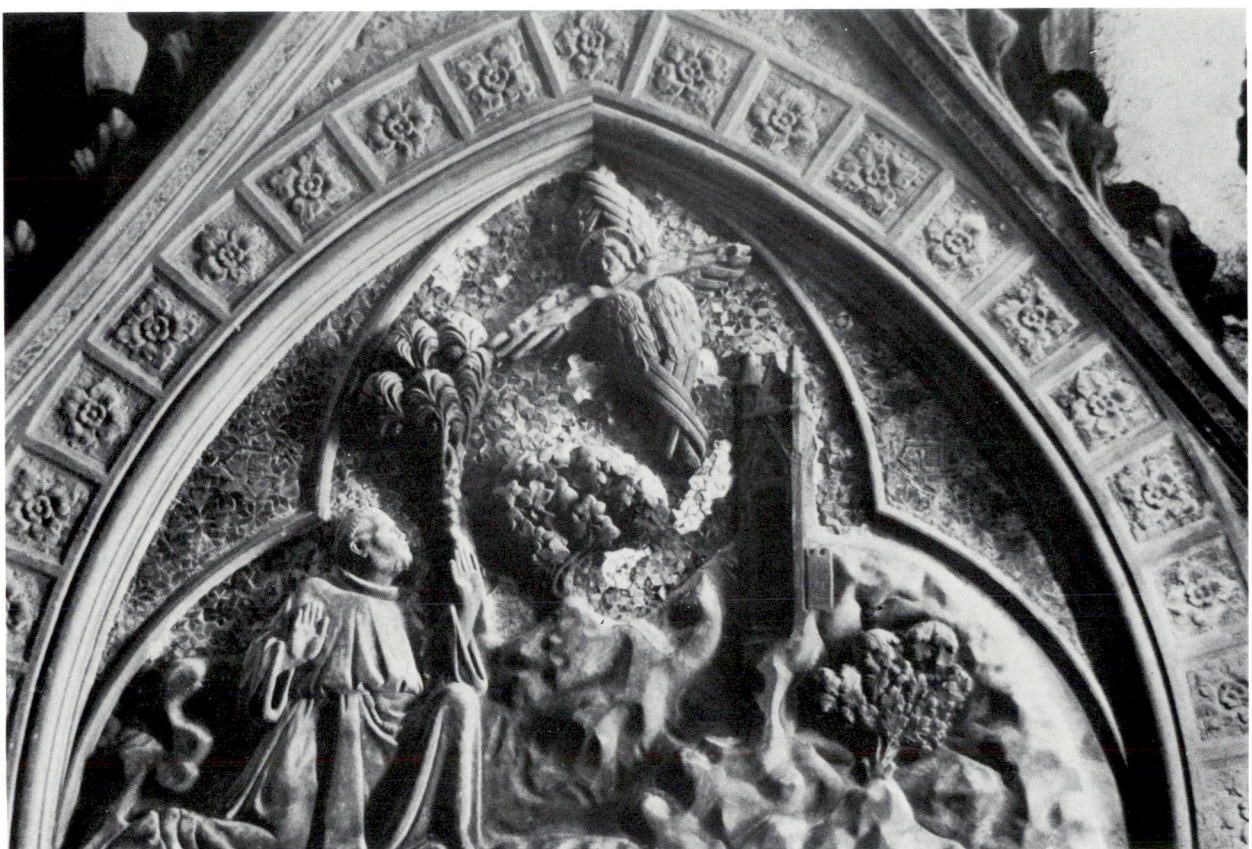

211. Tino di Camaino: Tomb of Catherine of Austria, detail. Naples, San Lorenzo

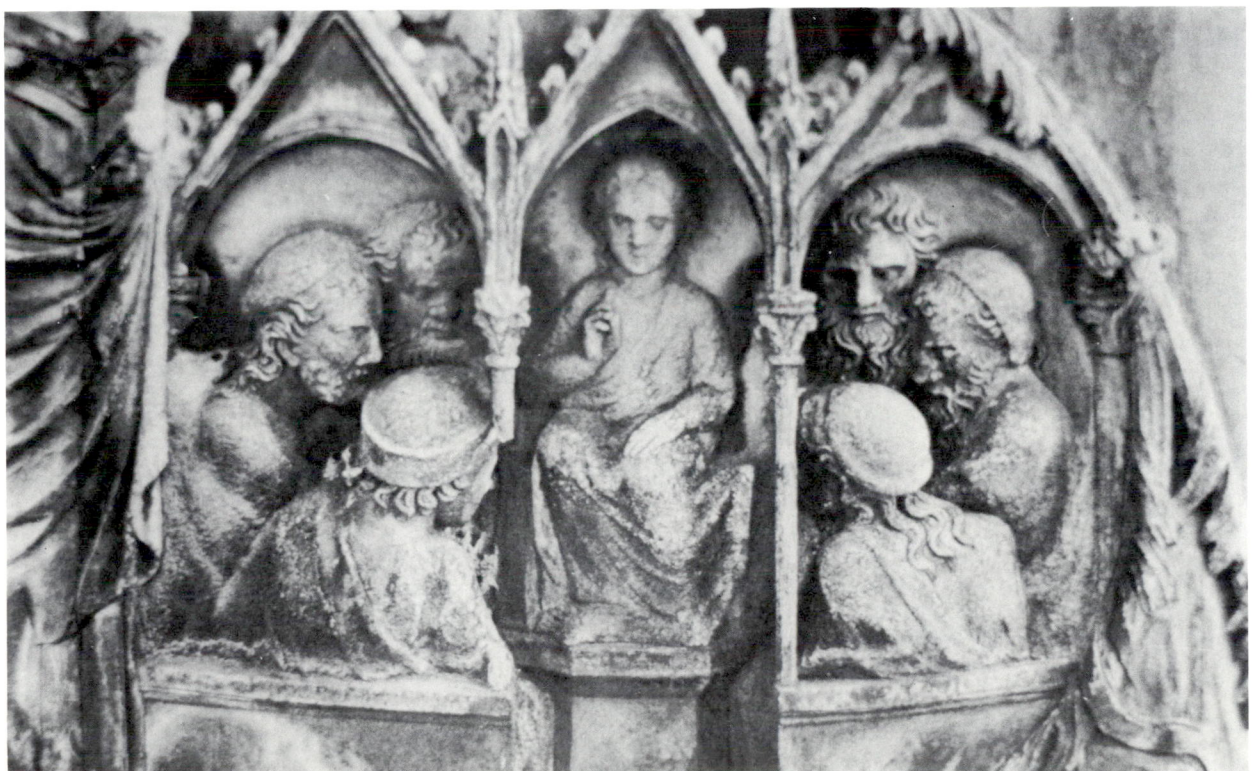

212. Orvieto Cathedral. Facade relief, detail

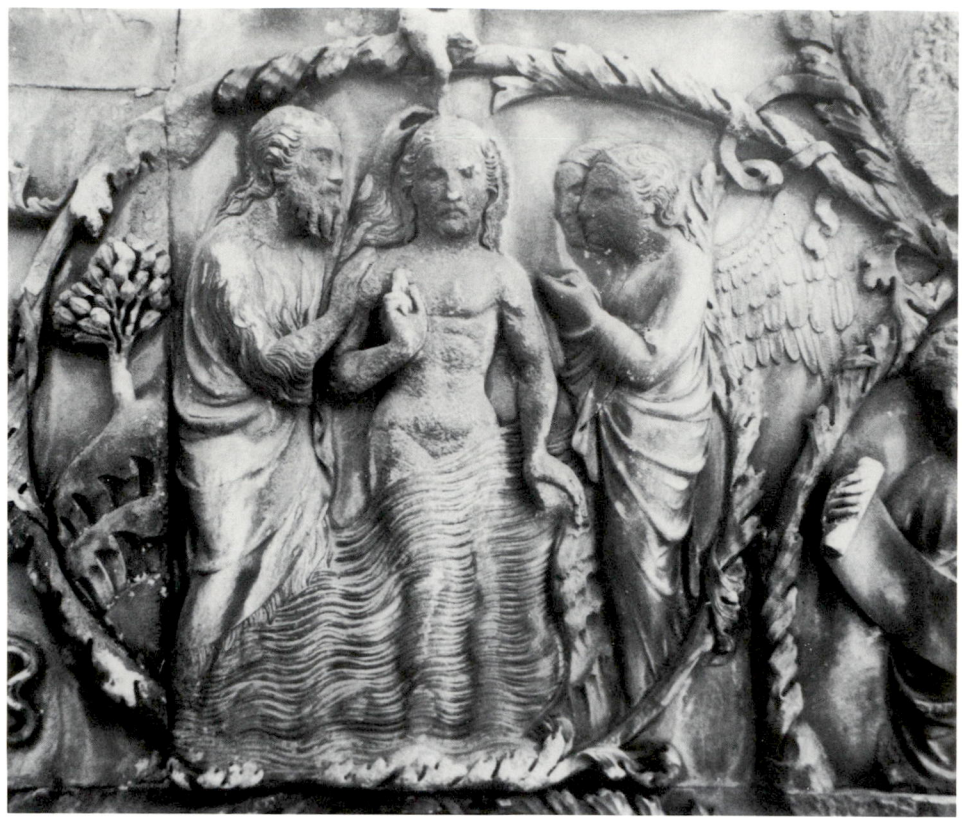

213. Orvieto Cathedral. Facade relief, detail

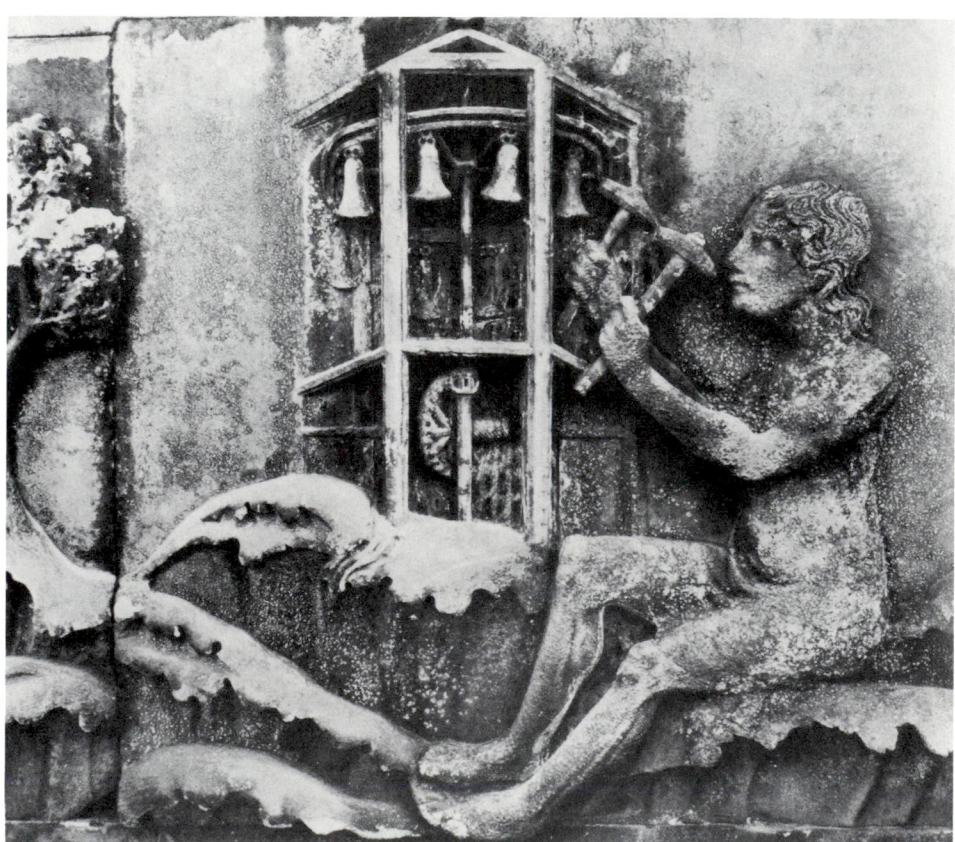

214. Orvieto Cathedral. Facade relief, detail

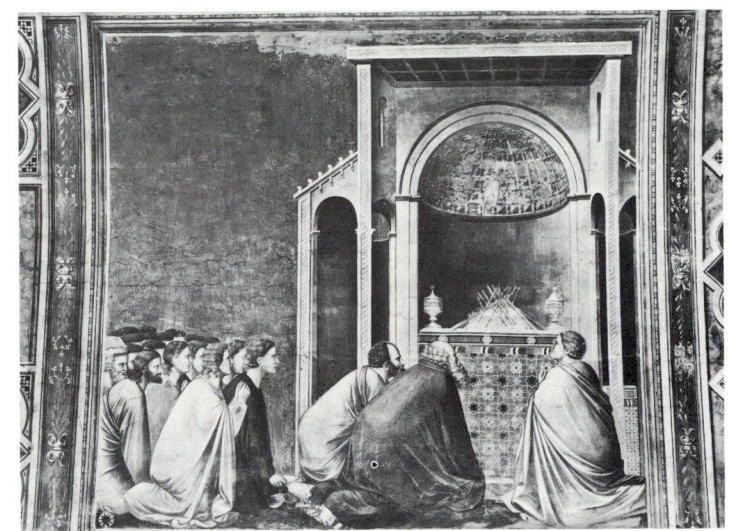

215. Giotto: *Watching of the Rods*. Padua, Arena Chapel

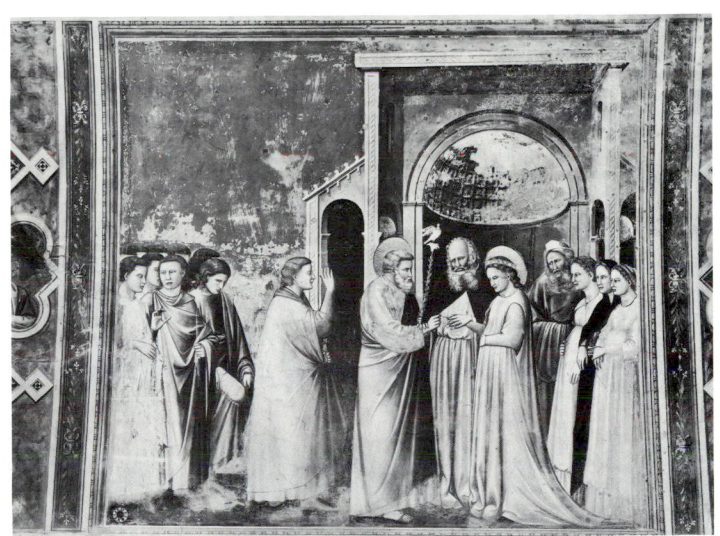

216. Giotto: *Marriage of the Virgin*. Padua, Arena Chapel

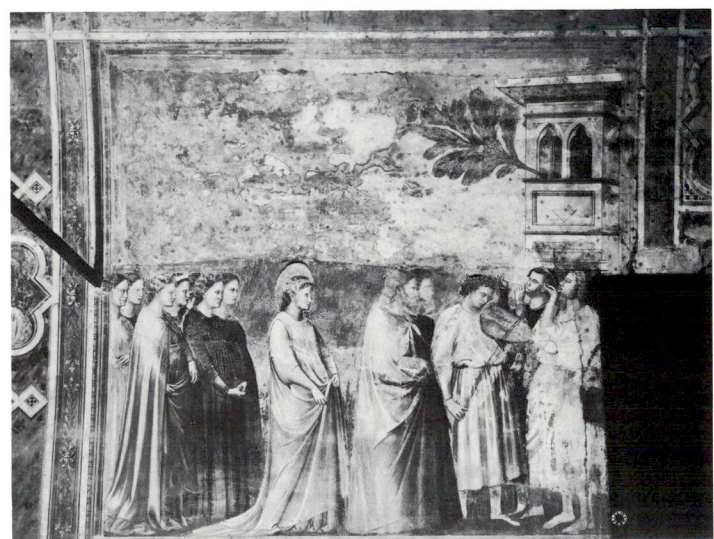

217. Giotto: *Wedding Procession*. Padua, Arena Chapel

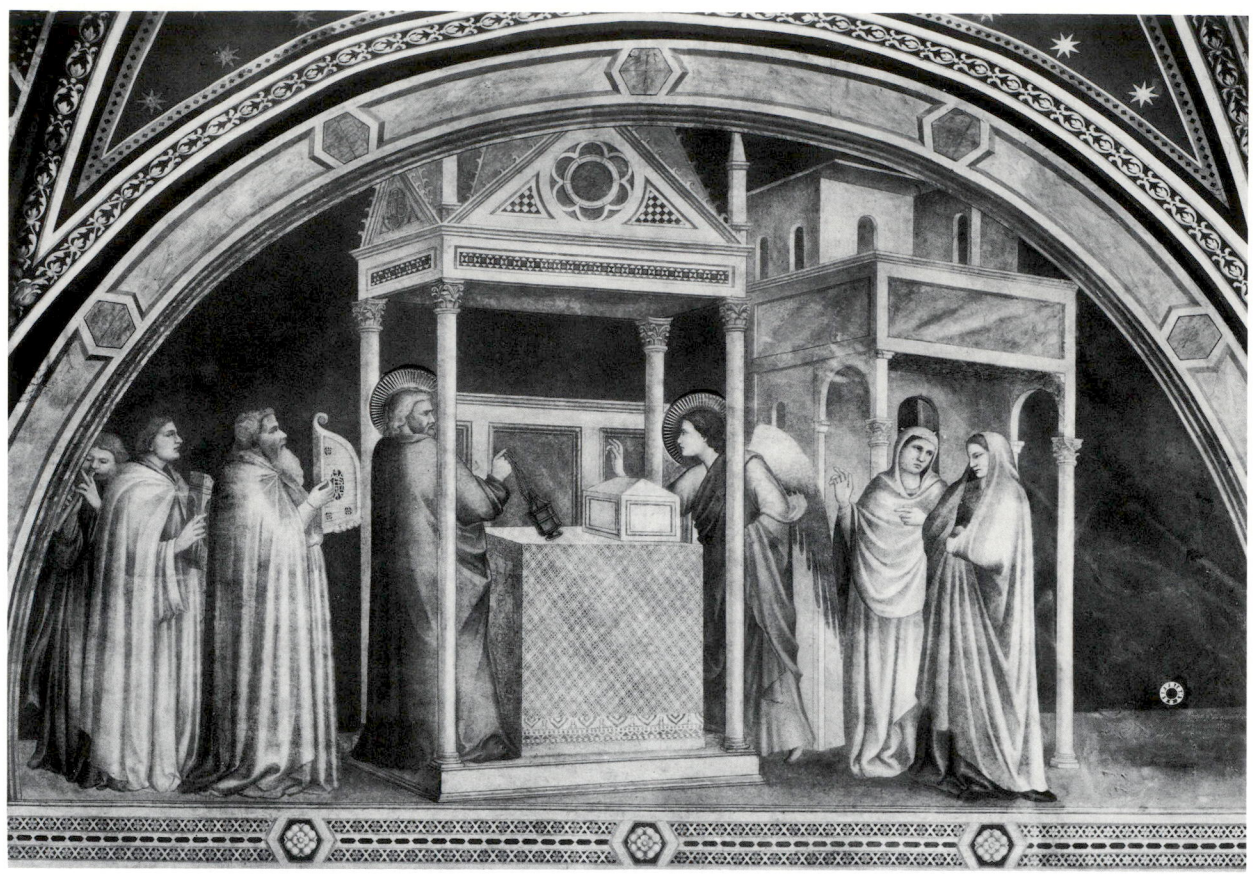

218. Giotto: *Annunciation to Zacharias*. Florence, Sta. Croce

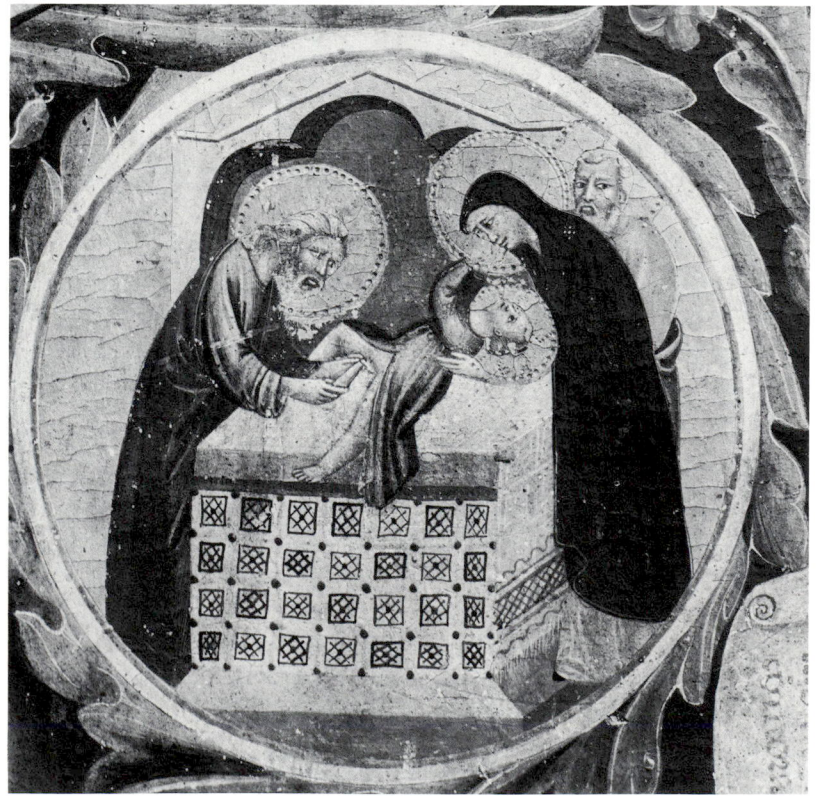

219. Pacino di Bonaguida: *Tree of Life*, detail. Florence, Accademia

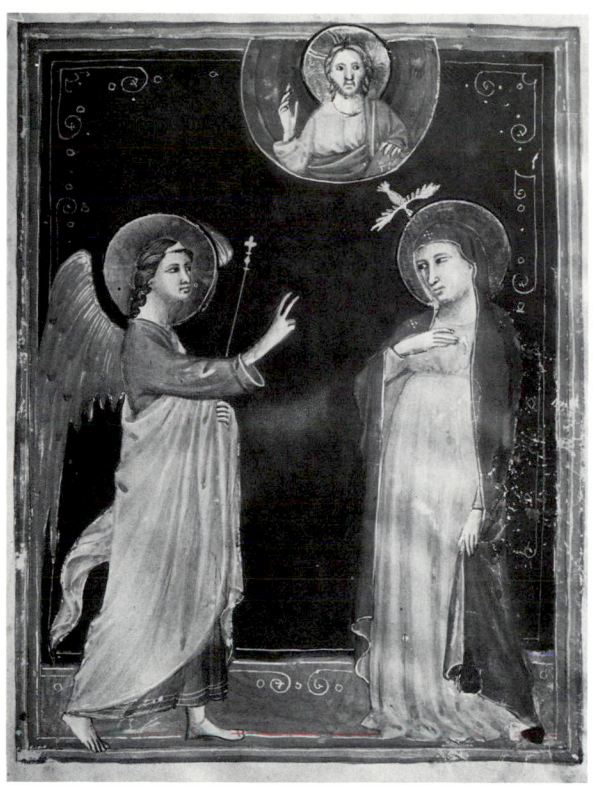

220. Pacino di Bonaguida: *The Annunciation*. New York, Morgan Library

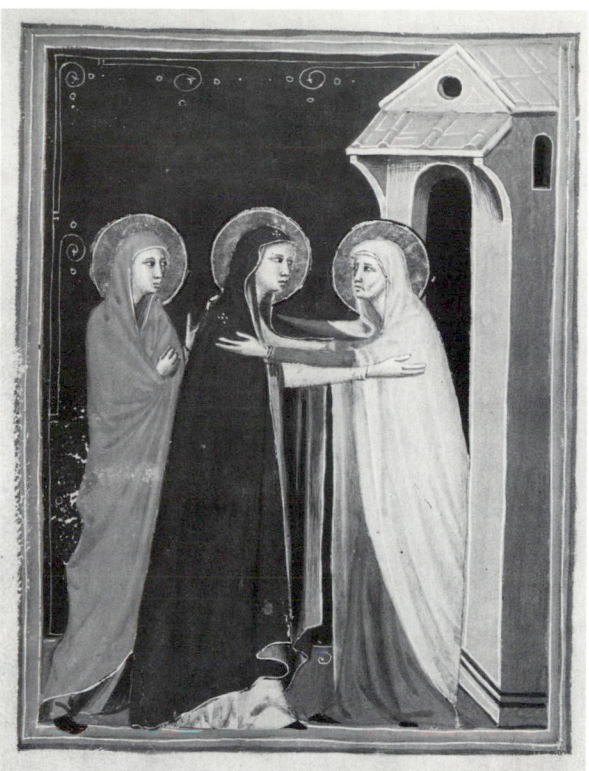

221. Pacino di Bonaguida: *The Visitation*. New York, Morgan Library

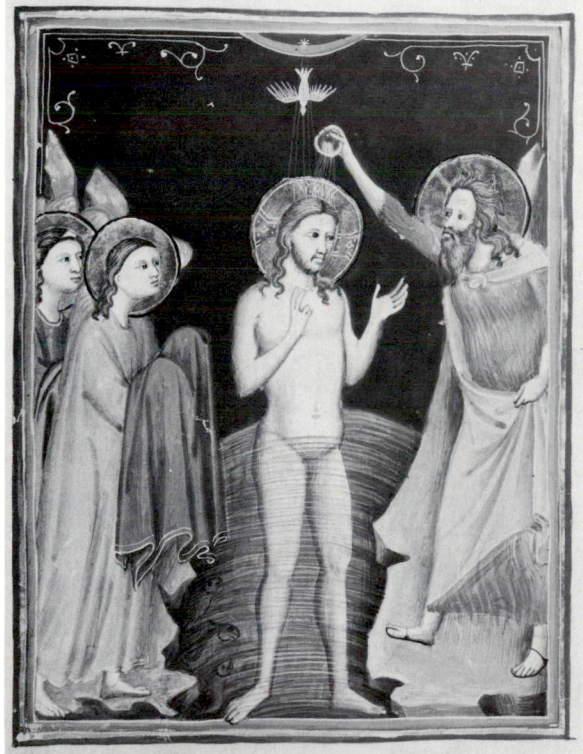

222. Pacino di Bonaguida: *Baptism of Christ*. New York, Morgan Library

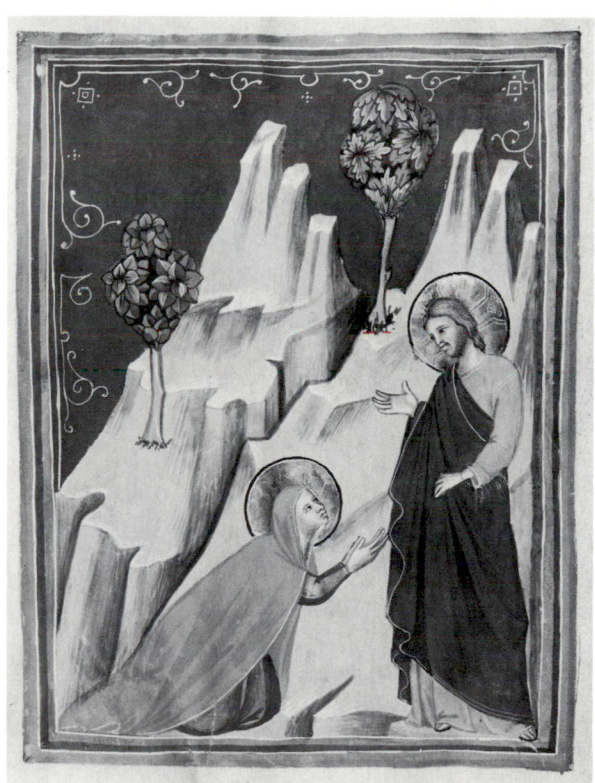

223. Pacino di Bonaguida: *Noli Me Tangere*. New York, Morgan Library

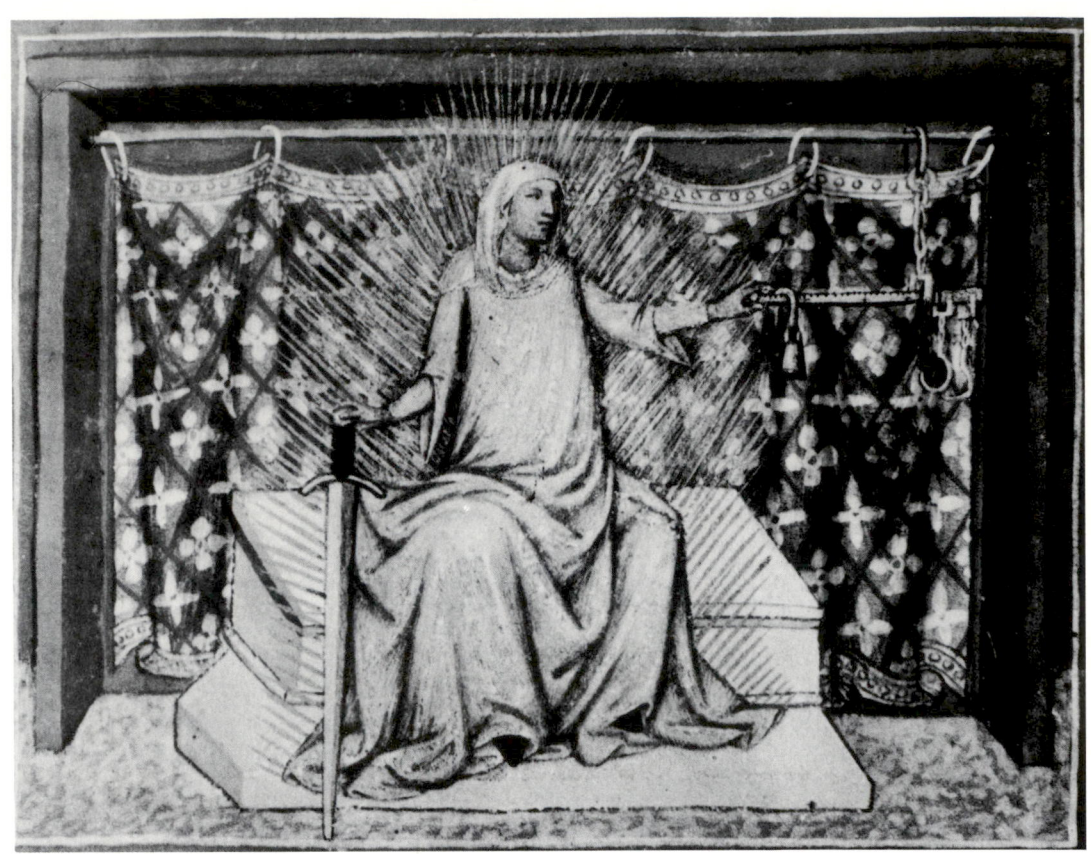

224. Francesco da Barberino: *Virtue* from Documenti d'Amore. Rome, Vatican Library

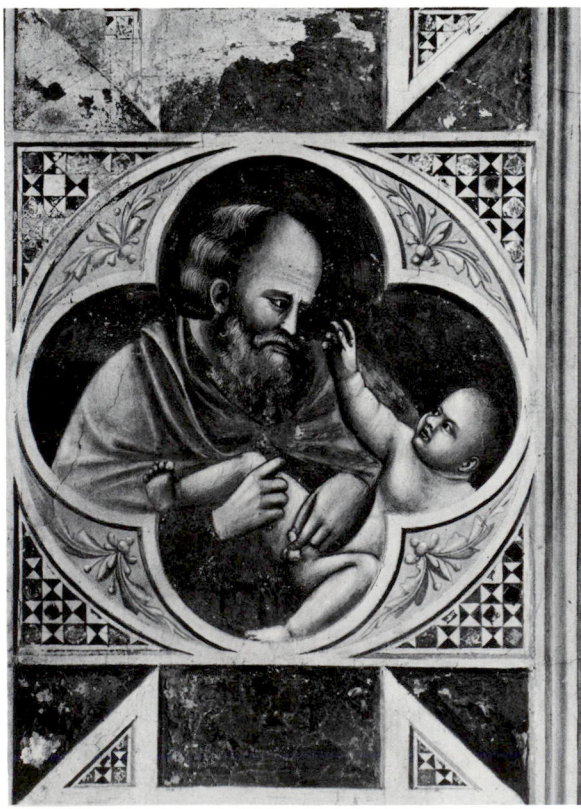

225. Giotto: *The Circumcision*. Padua, Arena Chapel

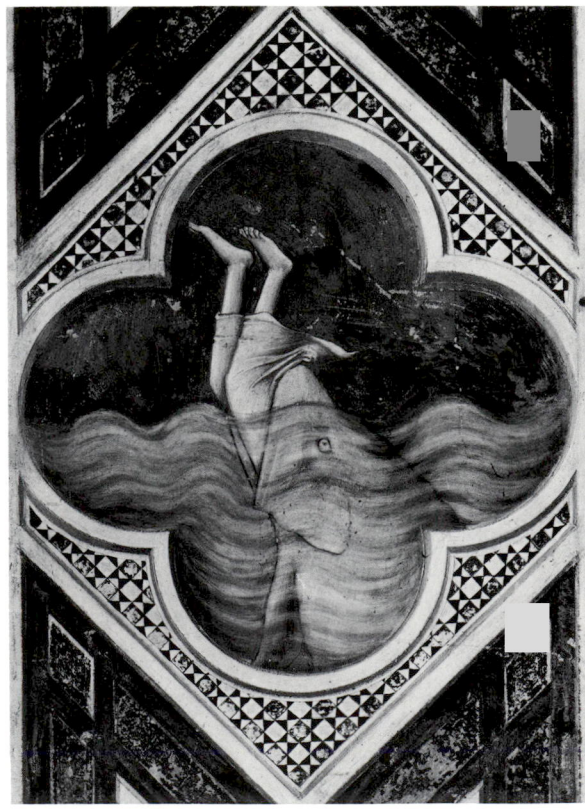

226. Giotto: *Jonah*. Padua, Arena Chapel

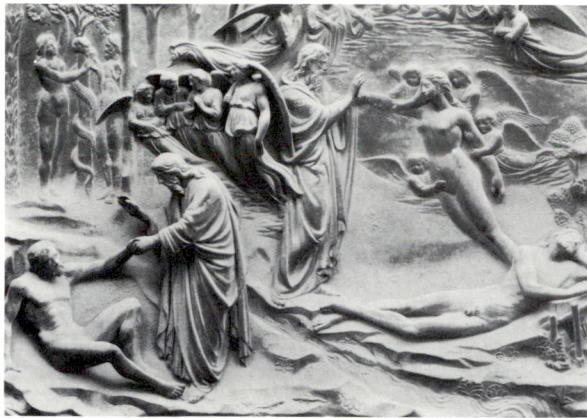

227. Ghiberti: *Genesis*. Gates of Paradise. Florence, Baptistry

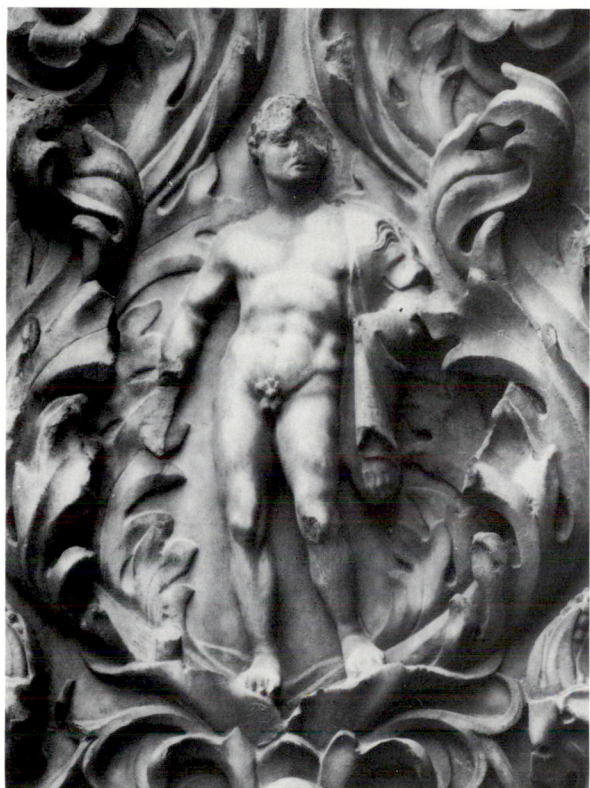

228. Florence Duomo, Porta della Mandorla, detail

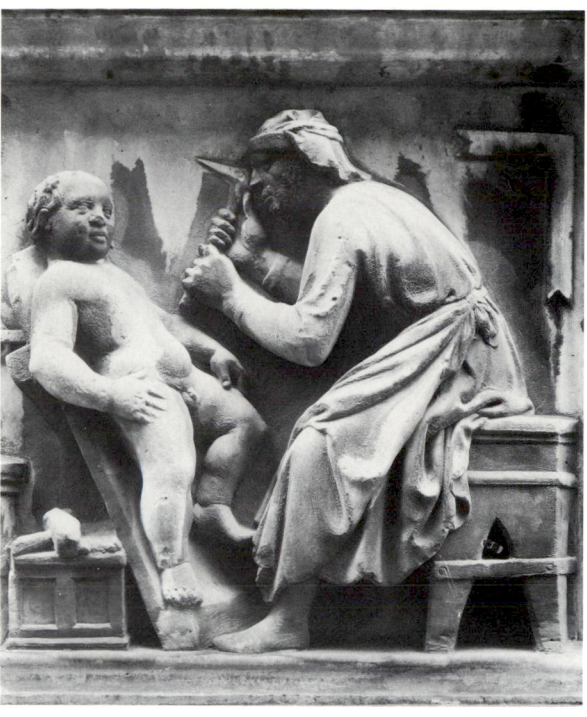

229. Nanni di Banco: *Sculpture*, detail. Florence, Or San Michele

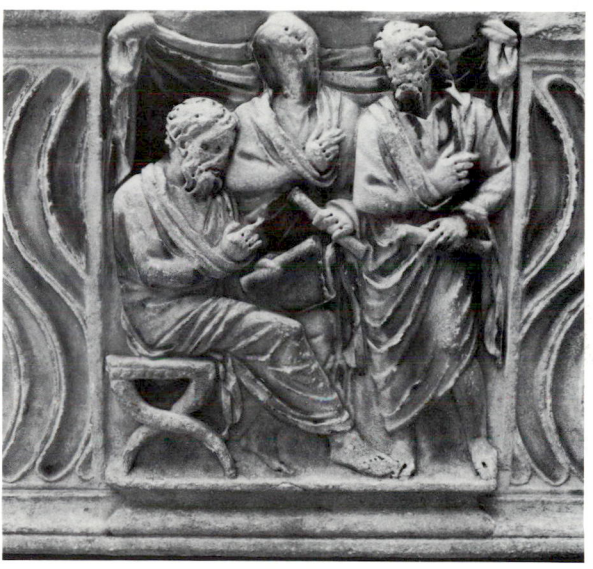

230. Roman sarcophagus, detail. Florence, Corner Borgo S. Jacopo and Via Guicciardini

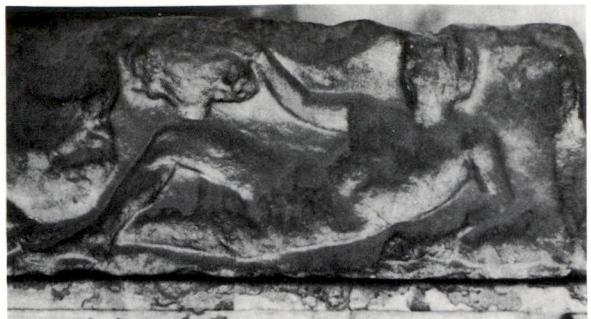

231. Roman sarcophagus, detail. Pisa, Camposanto

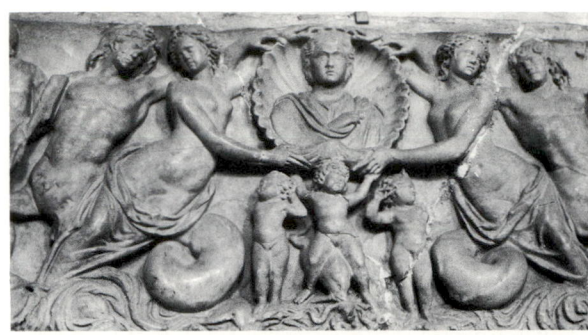

232. Roman sarcophagus front. Siena, Museo dell'Opera del Duomo

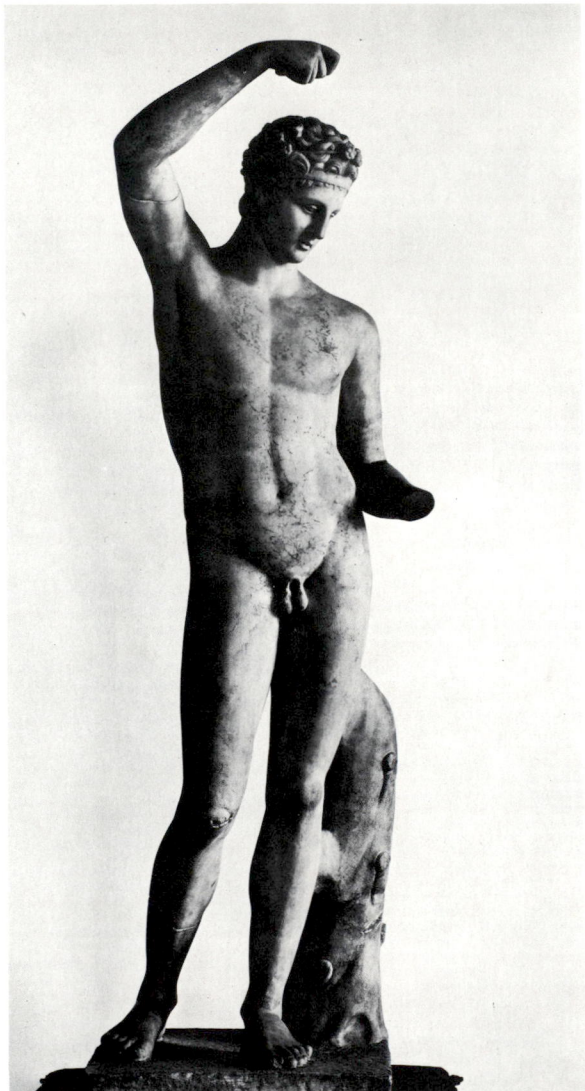

233. Roman statue. Dresden, Skulpturensammlung

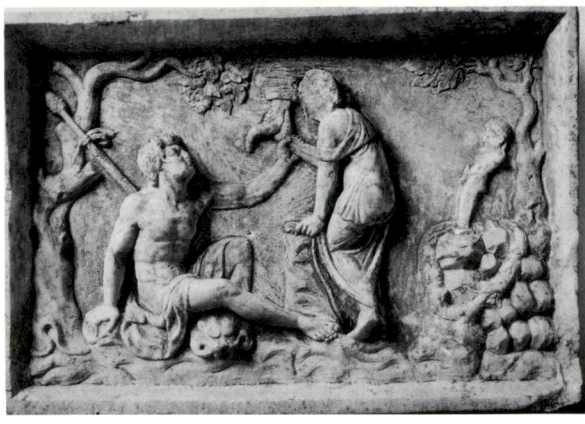

234. Roman relief. Berlin (East), Staatliche Museen zu Berlin

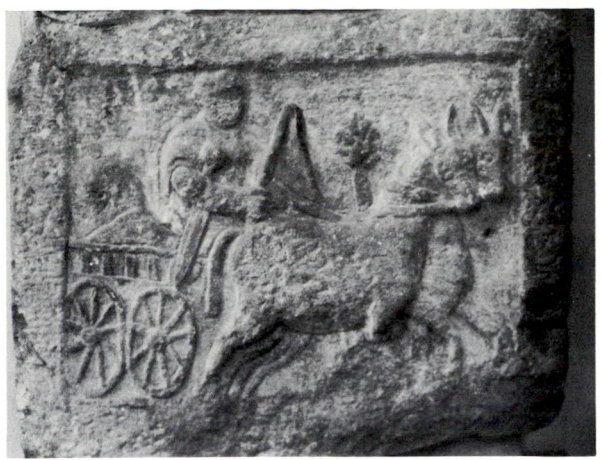

235. Roman relief. Strasbourg. Musée de l'Oeuvre Notre Dame

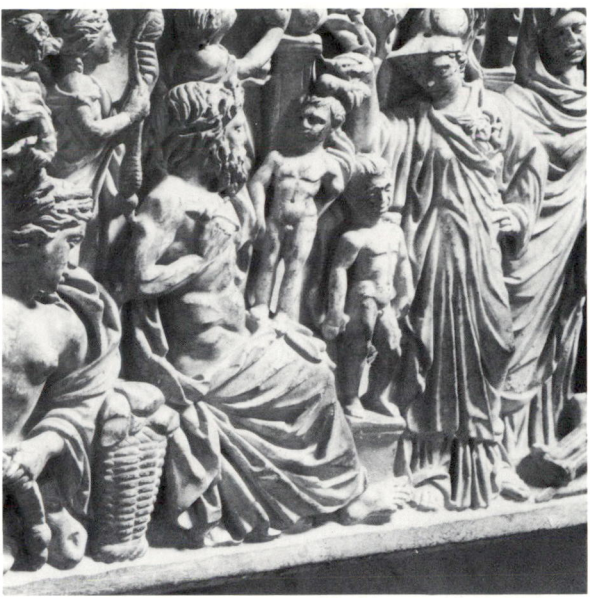

236. Roman sarcophagus. Rome, Museo Capitolino

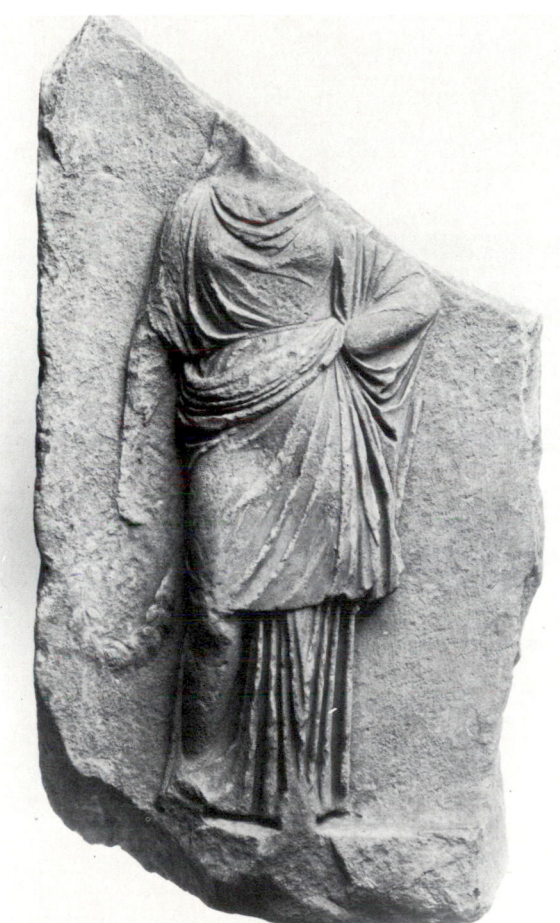

237. Attic relief. Cambridge, Fitzwilliam Museum

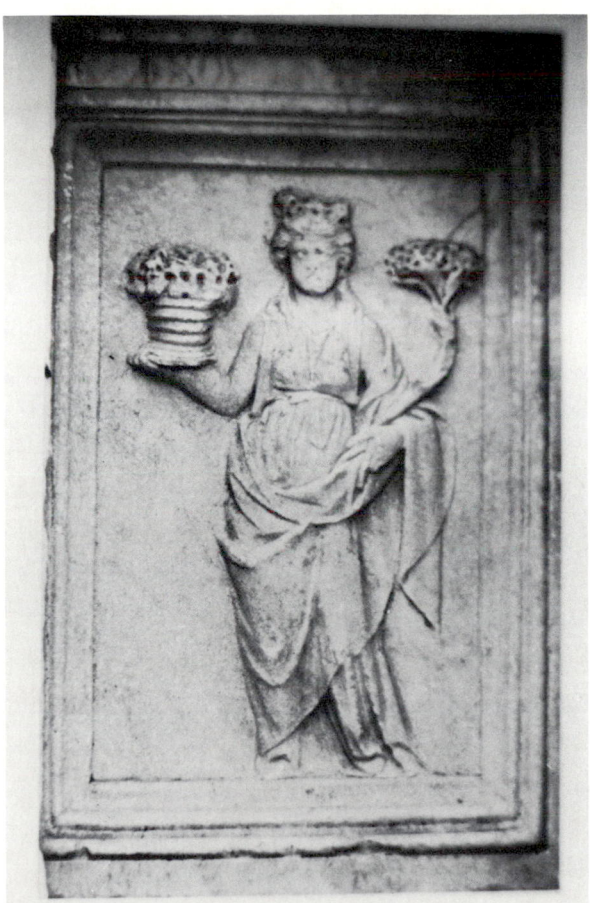

238. Nicola Pisano: *Uxor*. Perugia, Fontana Maggiore

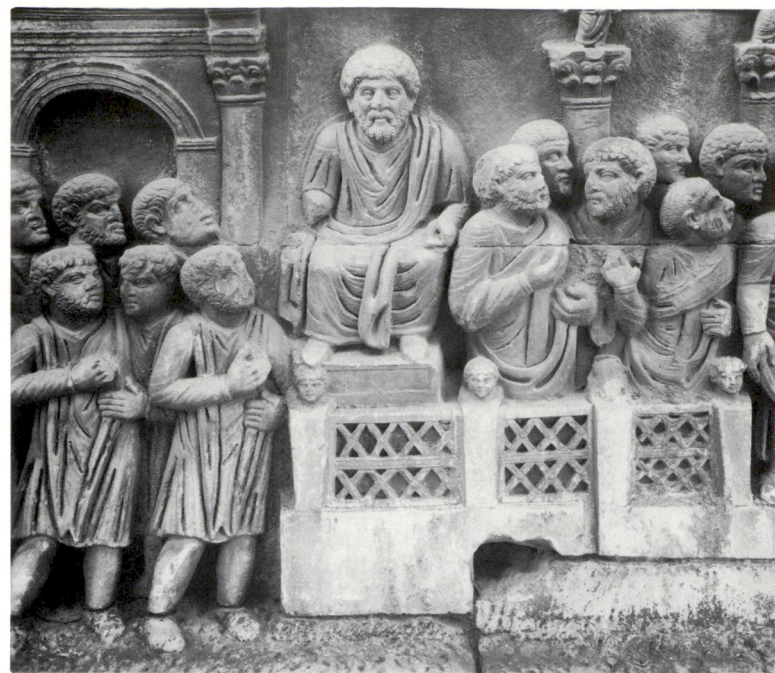

241. Roman relief, Tomb of a skipper. Location unknown

239. Arch of Constantine, detail. Rome

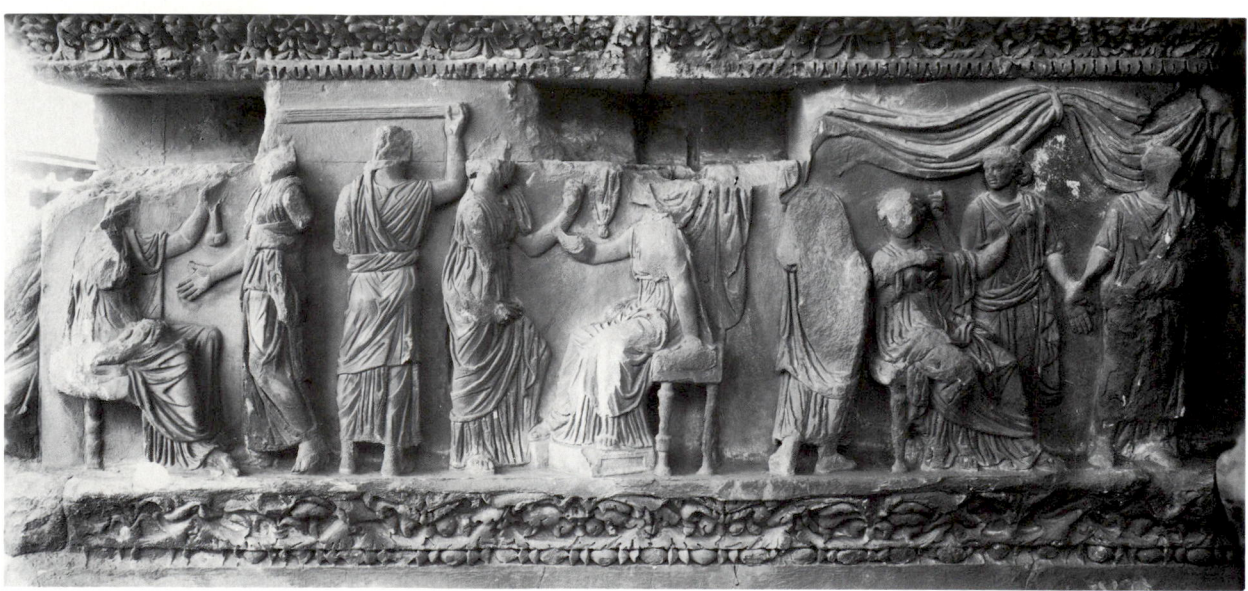

240. Minerva frieze. Rome, Forum of Nerva

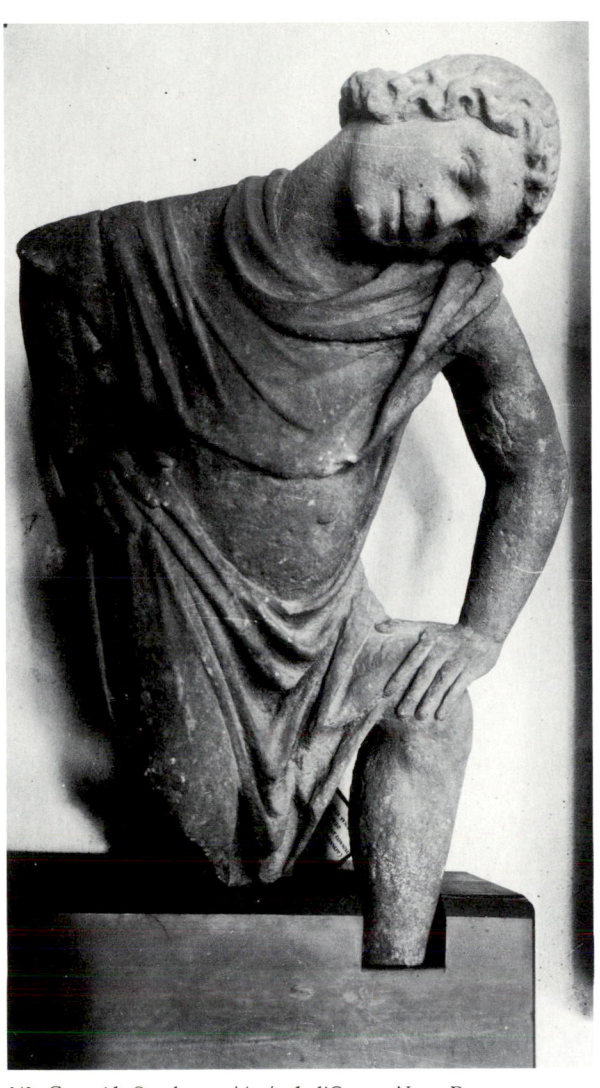

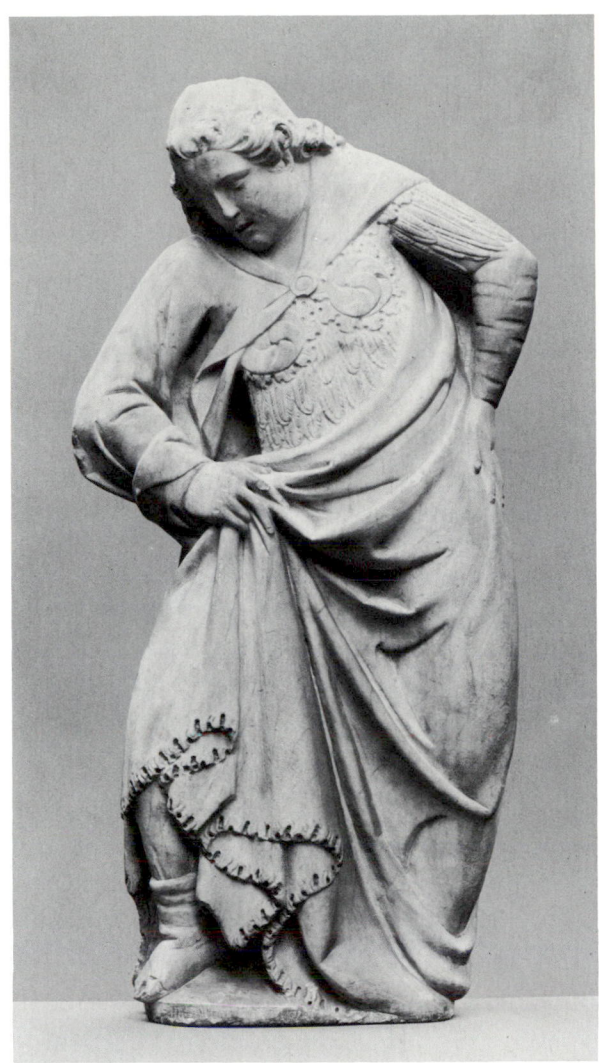

242. Caryatid. Strasbourg, Musée de l'Oeuvre Notre Dame

243. Tino di Camaino: Caryatid. Frankfurt am Main, Liebieghaus.

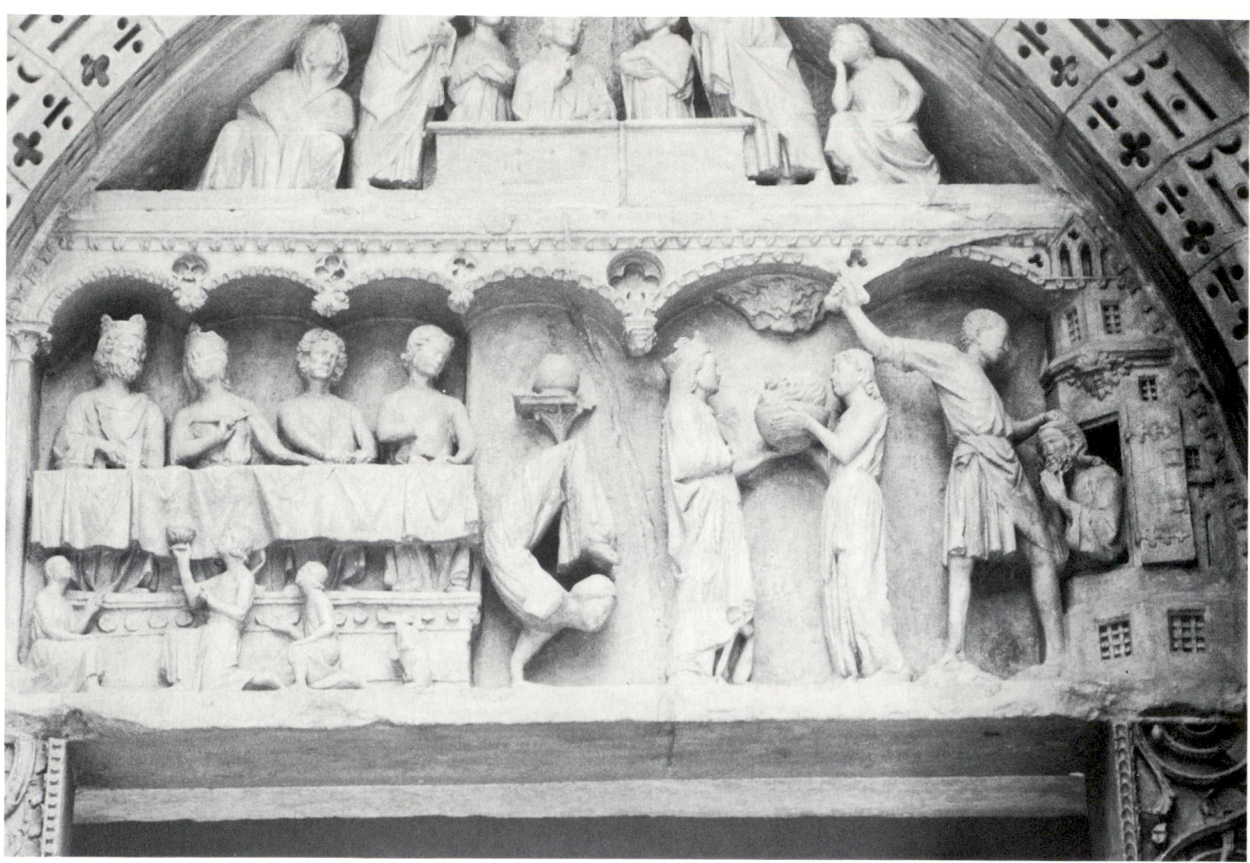

244. *Dance of Salome*. Rouen Cathedral

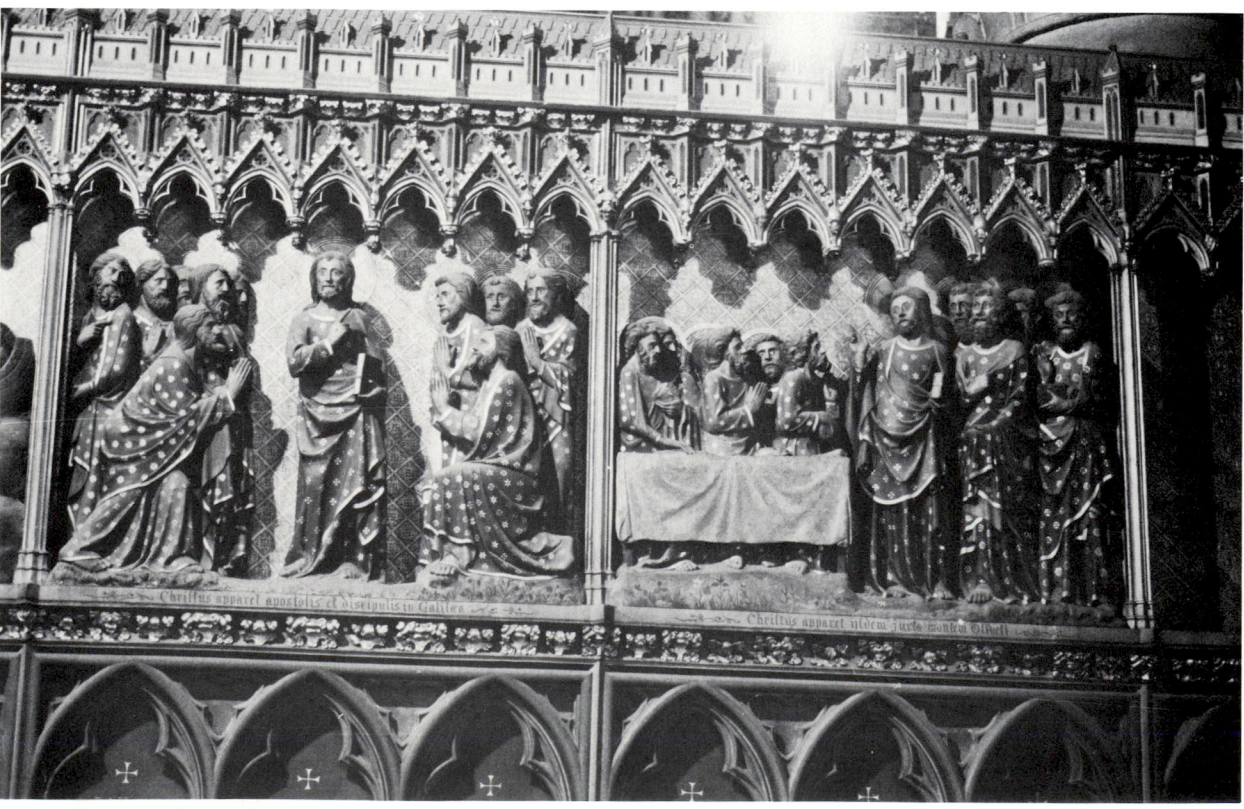

245. Choir screen, detail. Paris, Notre Dame

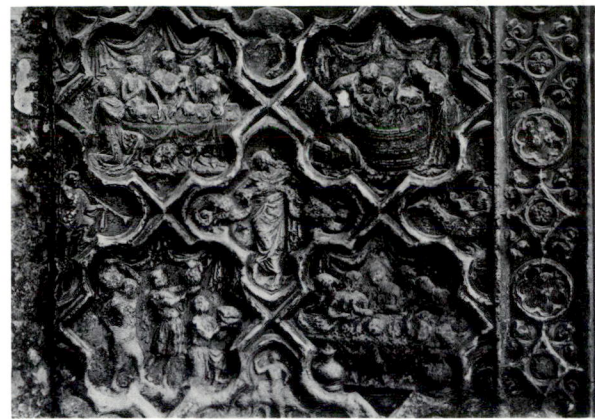

246. Medallion. Auxerre Cathedral, facade

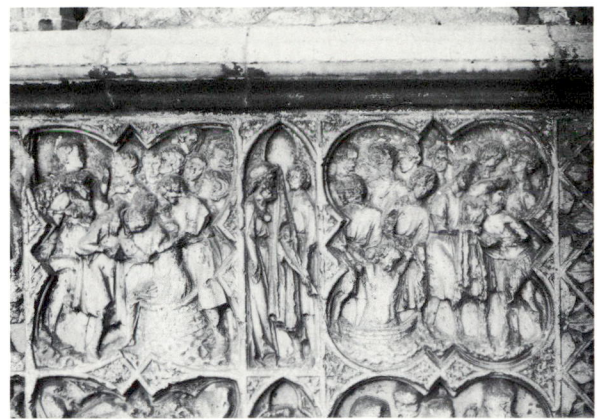

247. *The Story of the Prodigal Son.* Auxerre Cathedral, facade

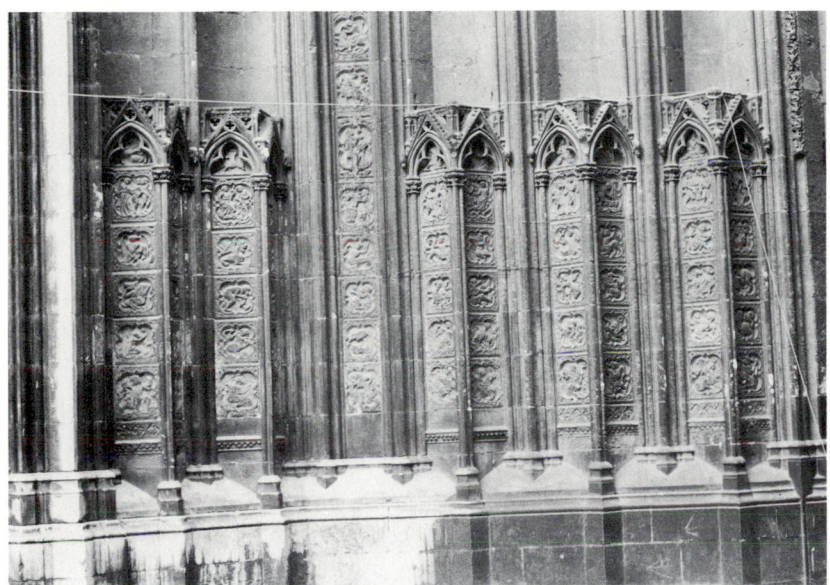

248. Rouen Cathedral, Portail des Libraires

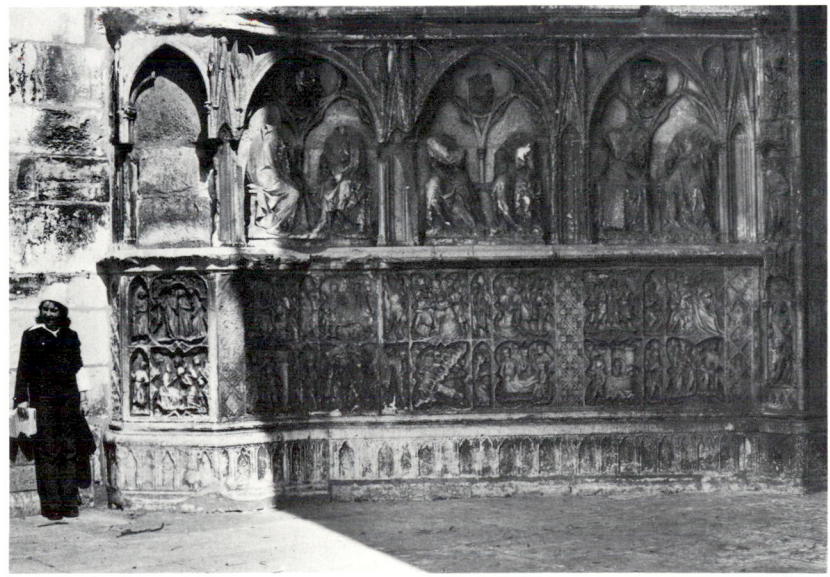

249. Auxerre Cathedral. Facade, detail

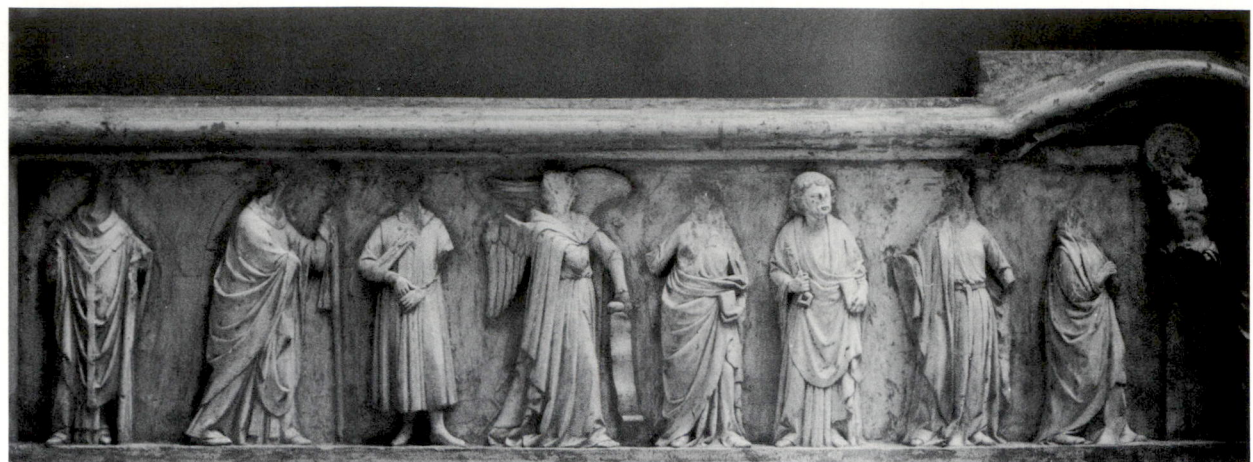

250. Altar retable from St. Germer-de-Flye (plaster cast). Paris, Musée des Monuments Français

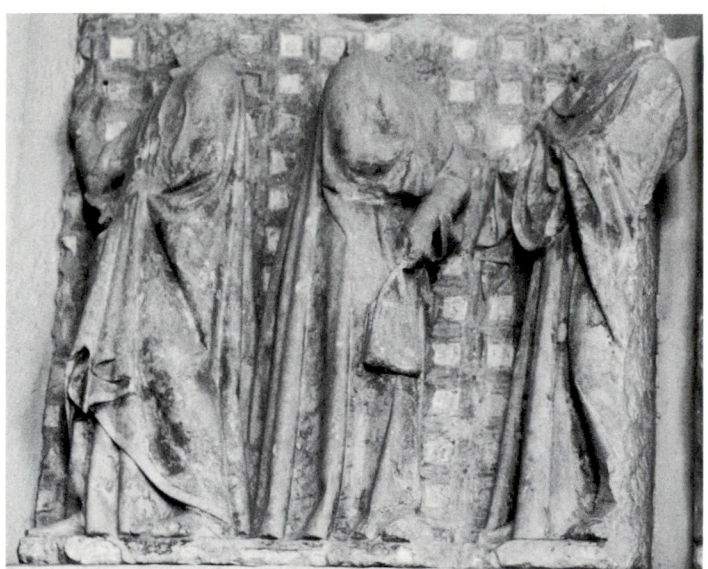

251. Fragment of the Jubé of Bourges Cathedral. Paris, Louvre

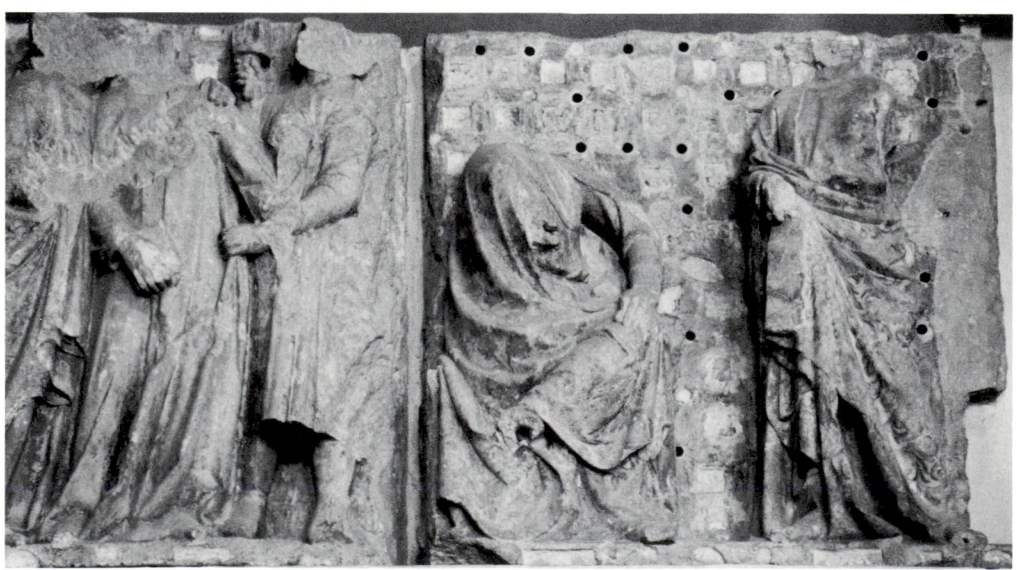

252. Fragment of the Jubé of Bourges Cathedral. Paris, Louvre

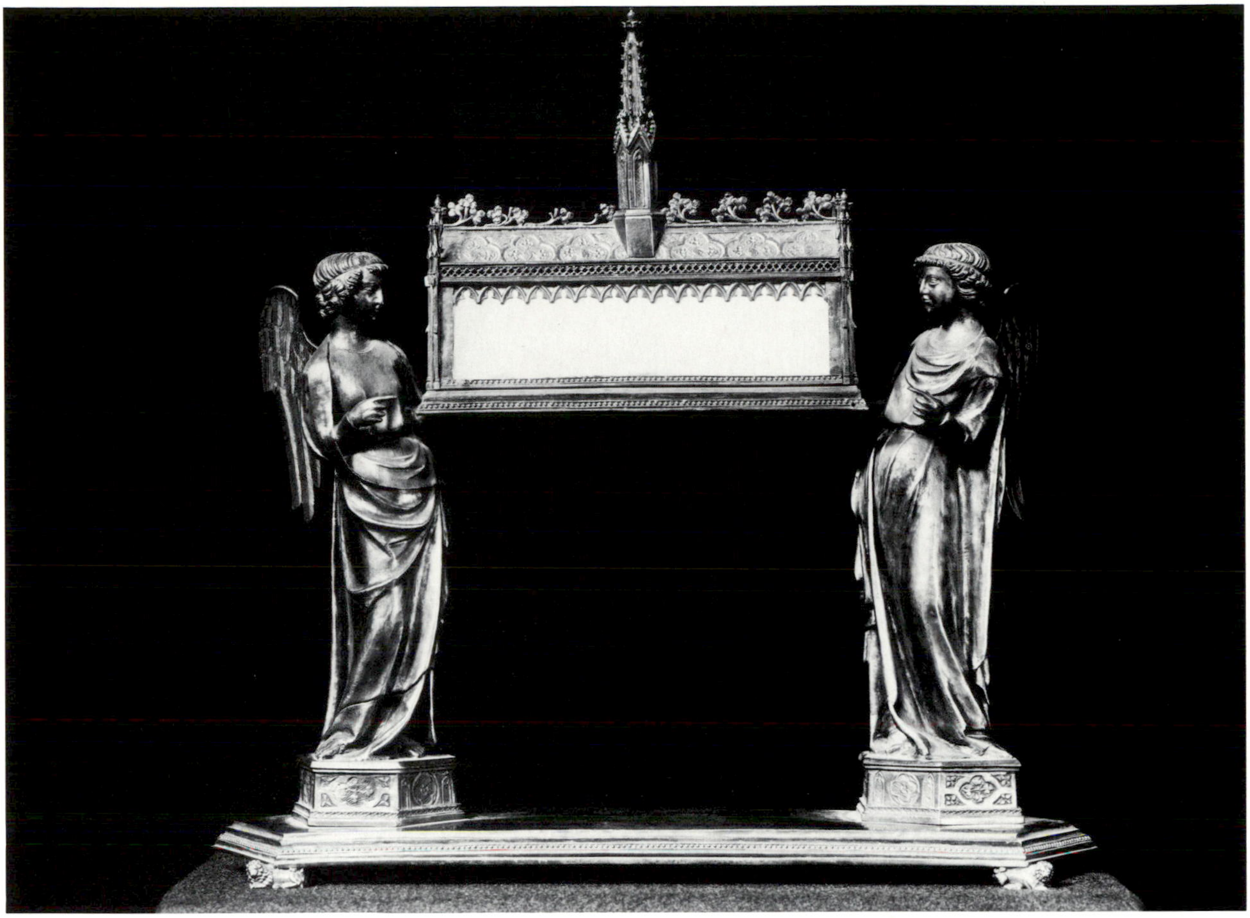

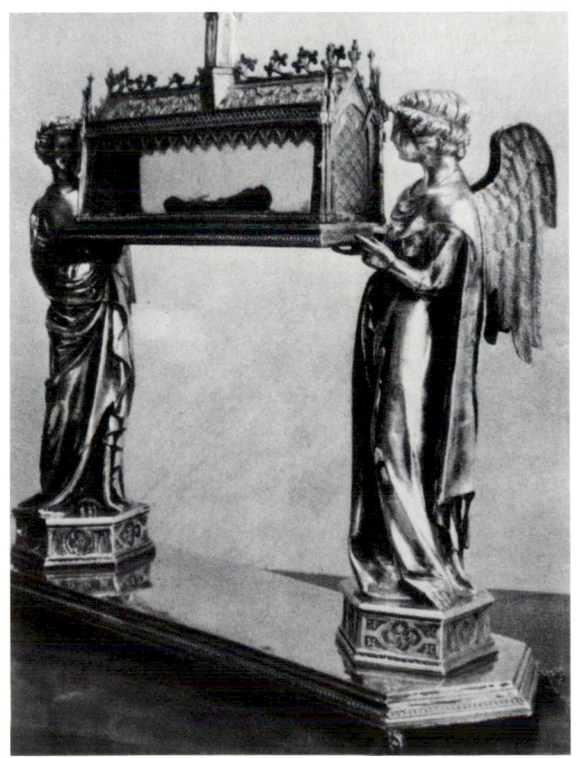

253. Reliquary. Bologna, San Domenico

254. Reliquary. Bologna, San Domenico

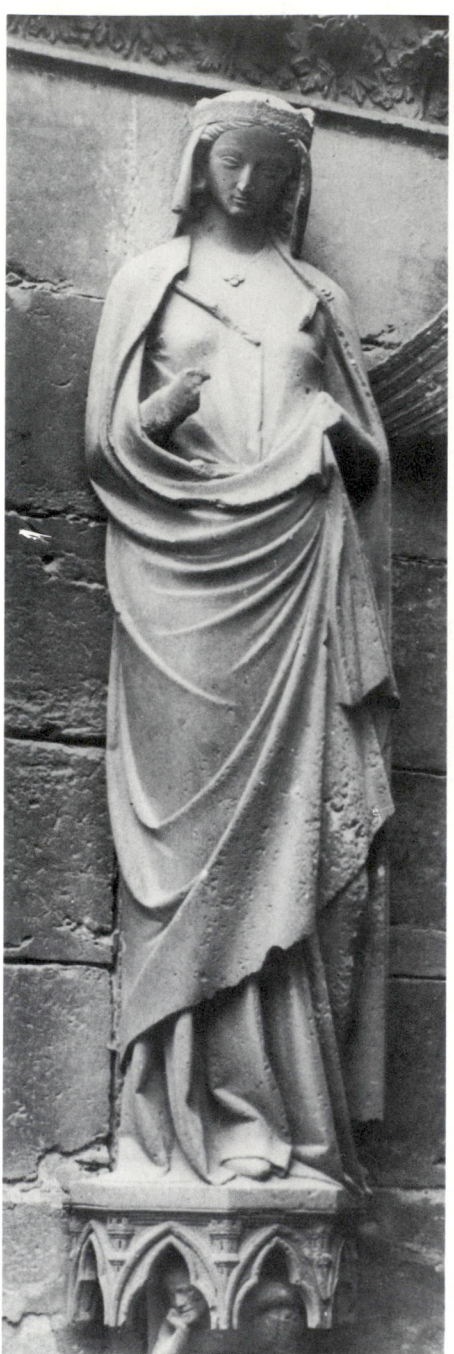

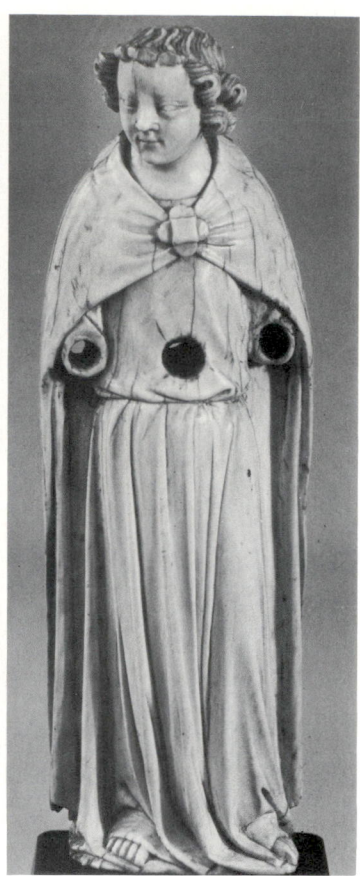

257. Ivory Angel. New York, Metropolitan Museum of Art

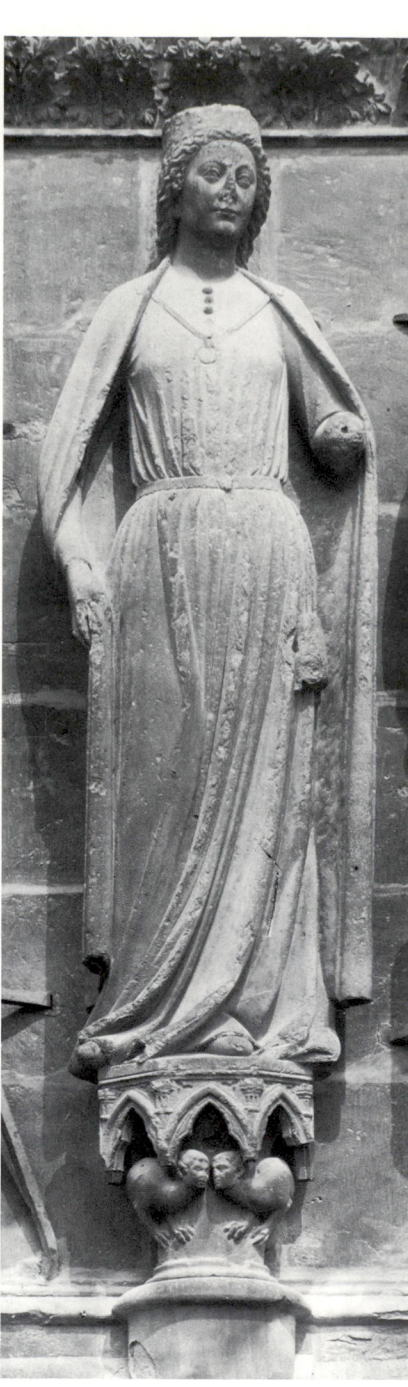

255. Reims Cathedral, west facade, detail

256. *Queen of Sheba*. Reims Cathedral

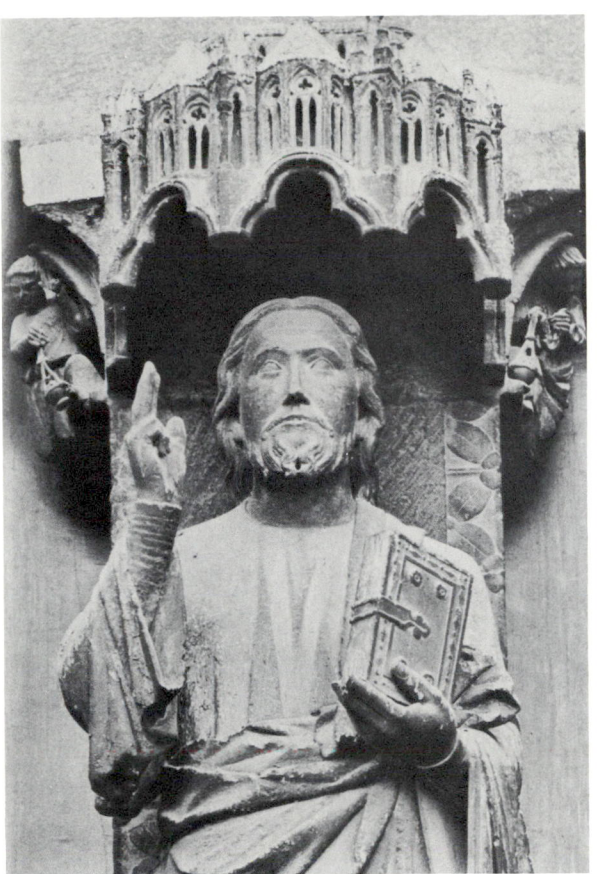

258. *Beau Dieu*. Amiens Cathedral

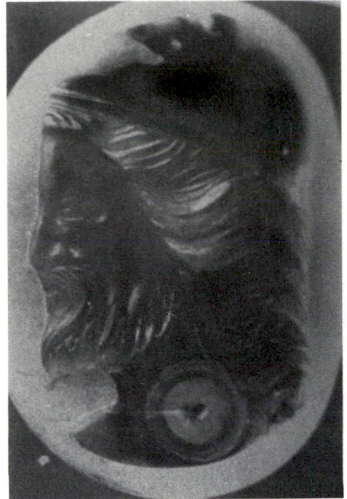

259. French cameo. Royal Coin Cabinet, The Hague (Museum)

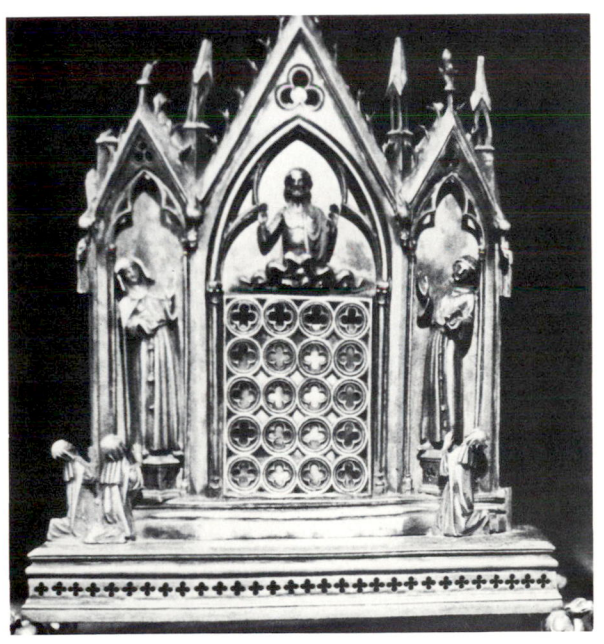

260. French reliquary. Assisi, San Francesco

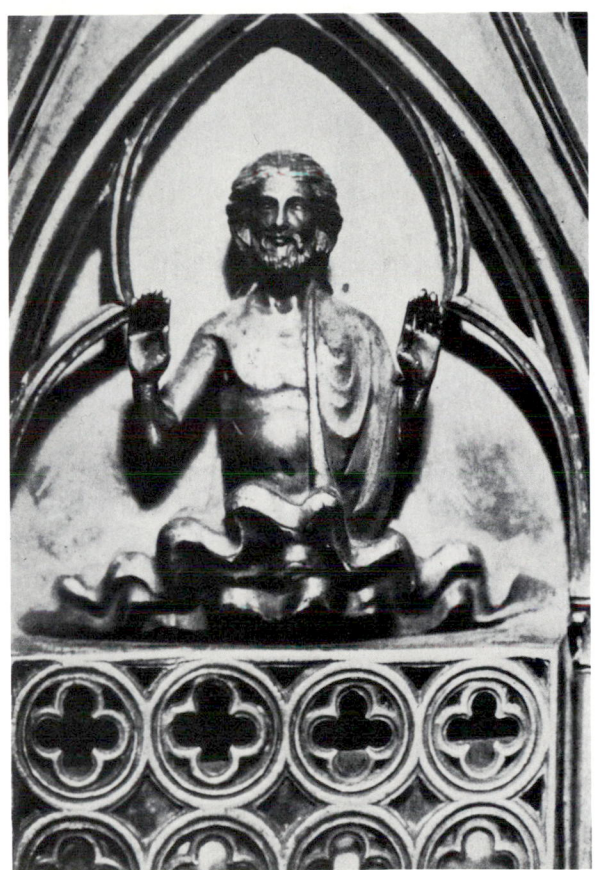

261. French reliquary. Assisi, San Francesco

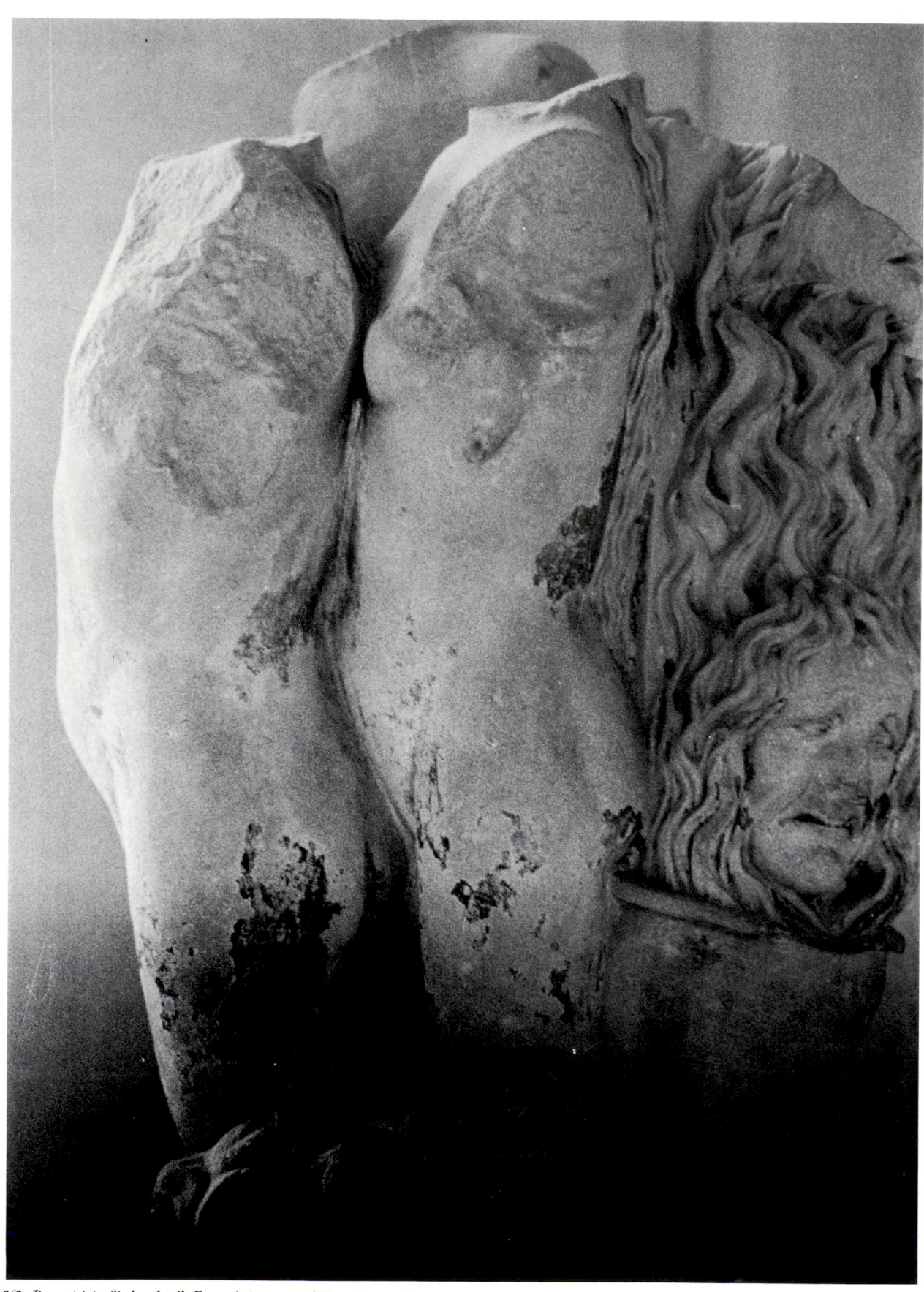

262. *Descent into Limbo*, detail. From choir screen of Notre Dame, Paris. Paris, Louvre

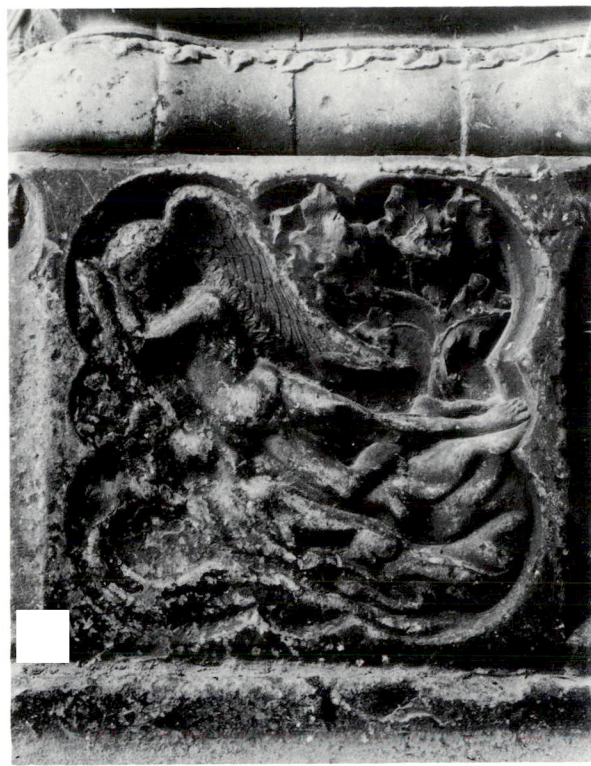

263. *Eros*. Auxerre Cathedral

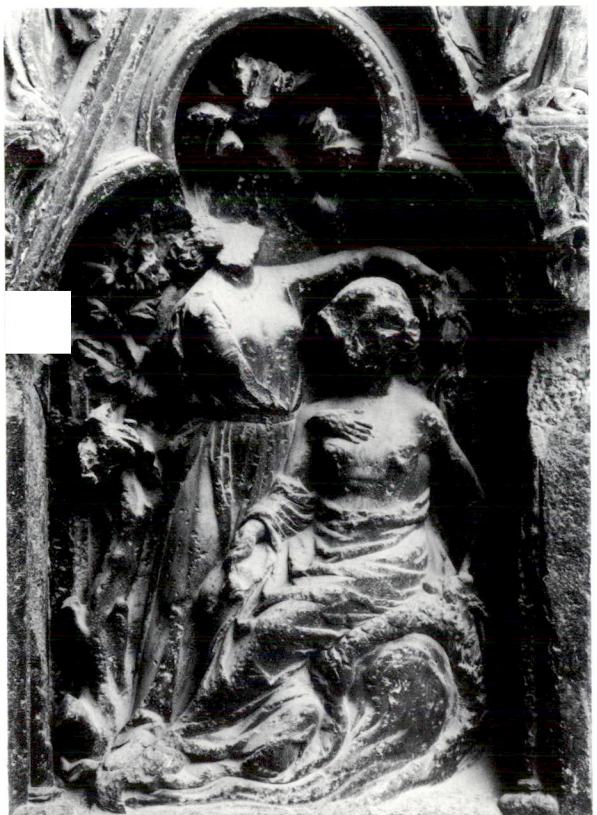

264. *Bathsheba*. Auxerre Cathedral

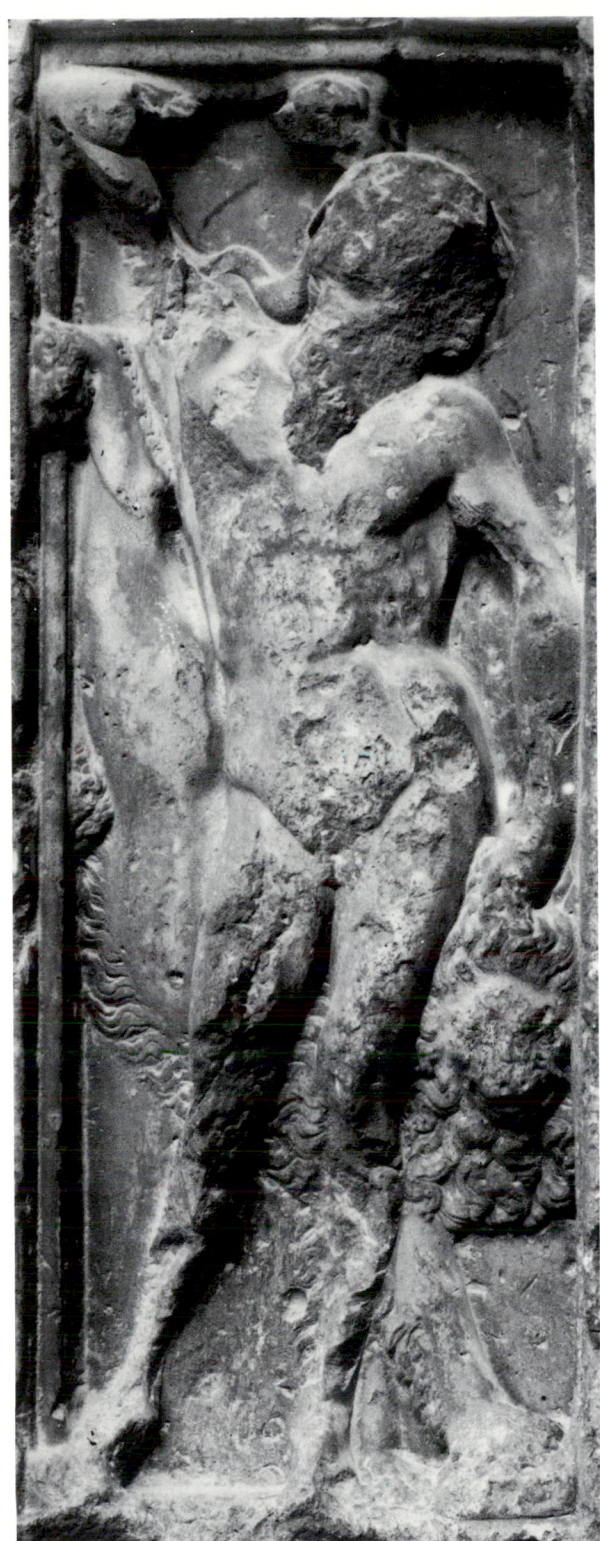

265. *Hercules*. Auxerre Cathedral

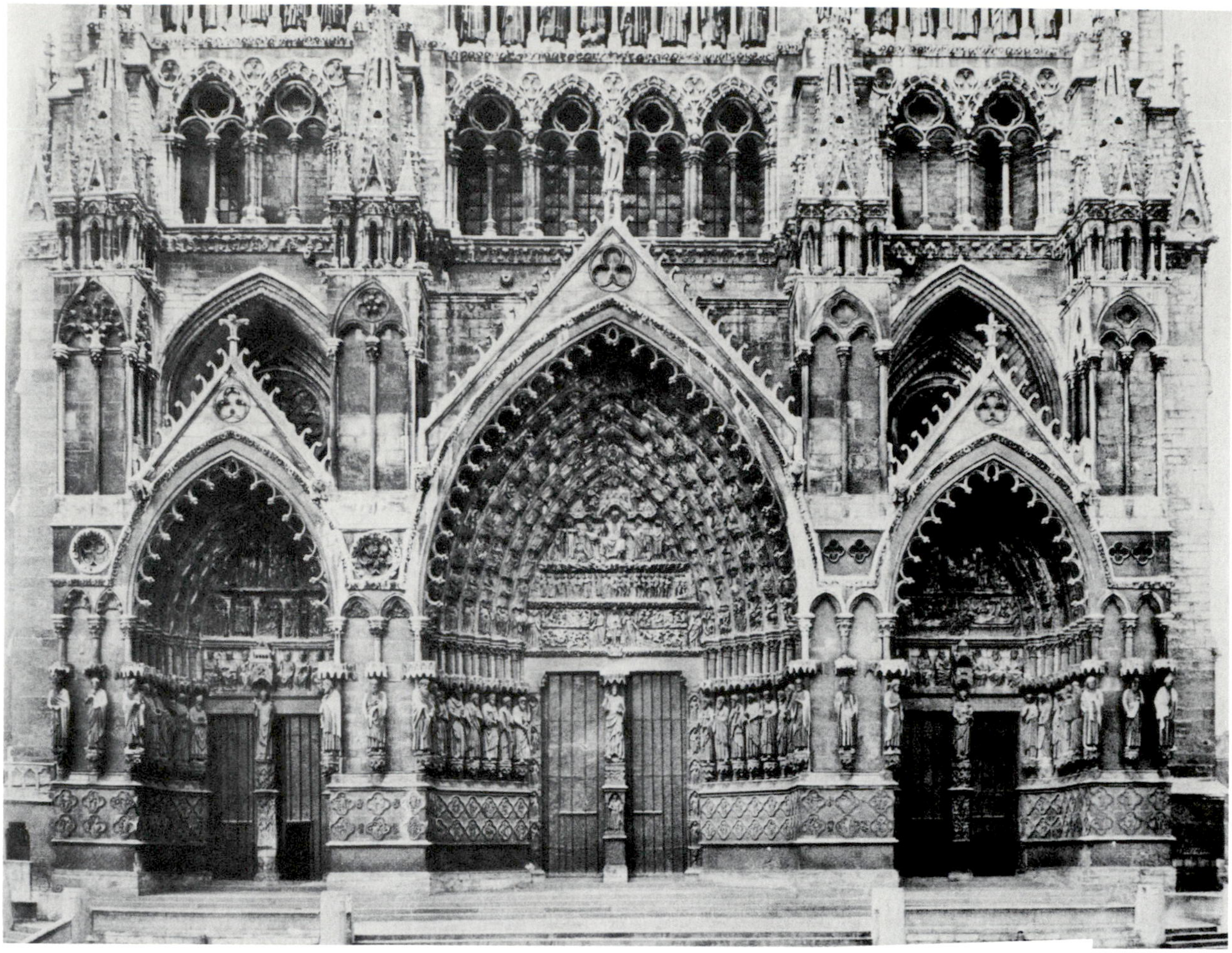

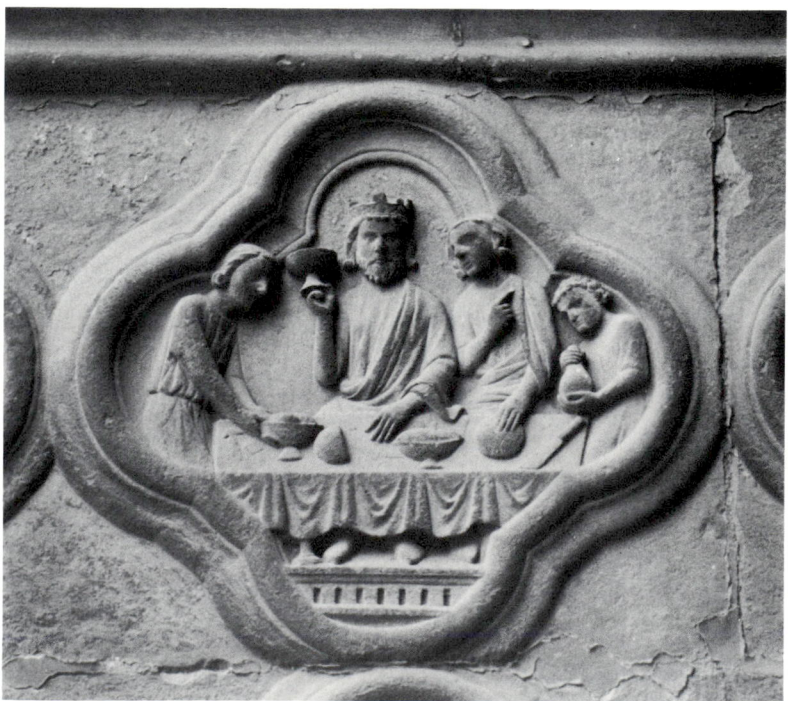

266. Amiens Cathedral, facade

267. Amiens Cathedral, facade, detail

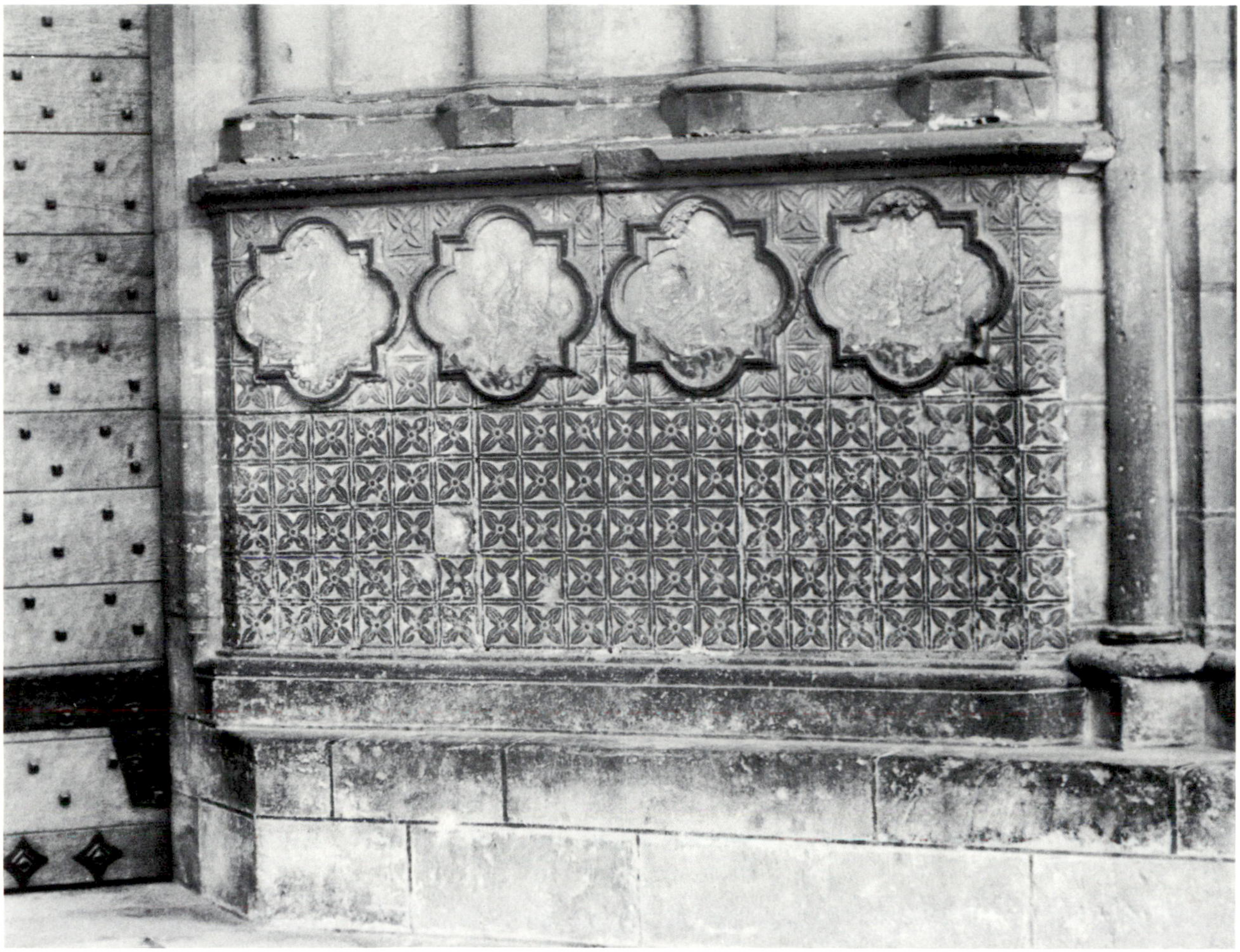

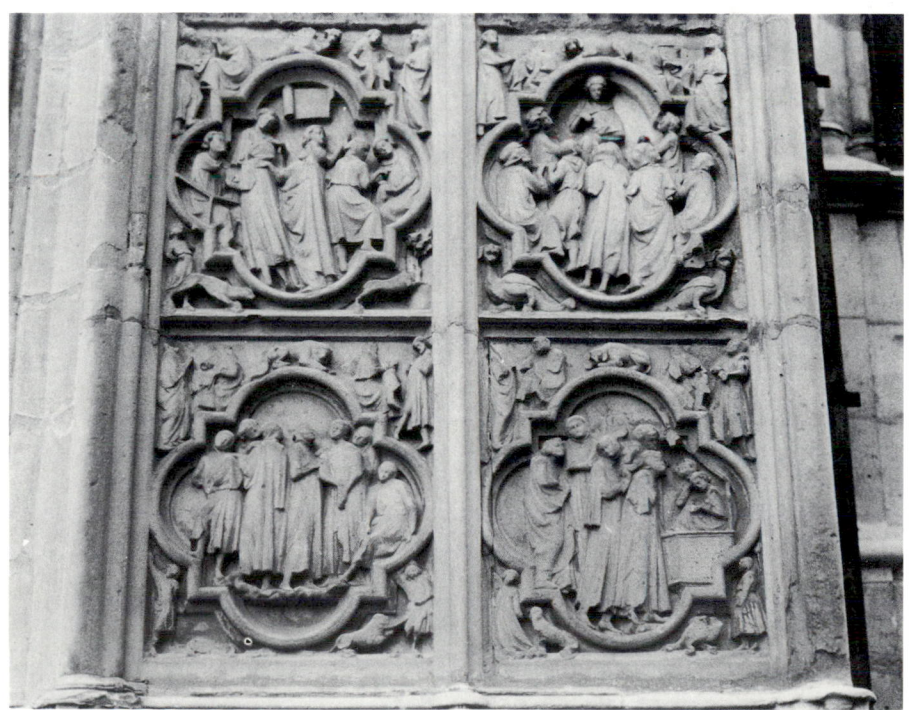

268. Noyon Cathedral, facade, detail

269. Paris, Notre Dame. South transept detail

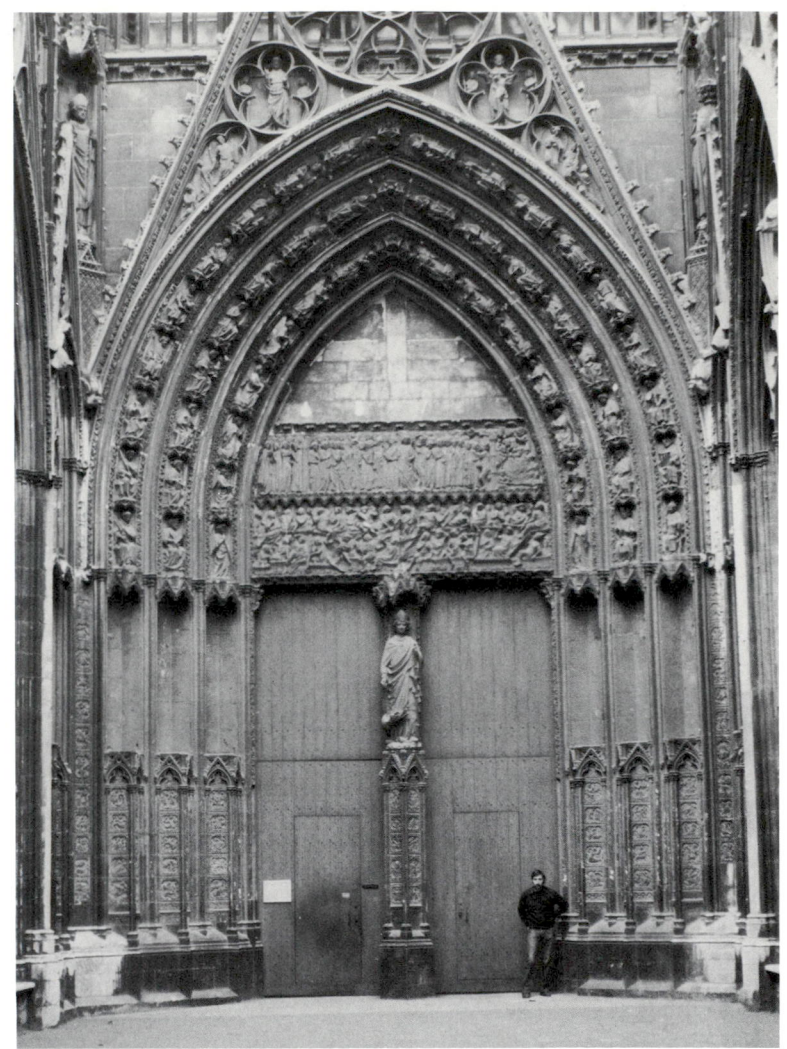

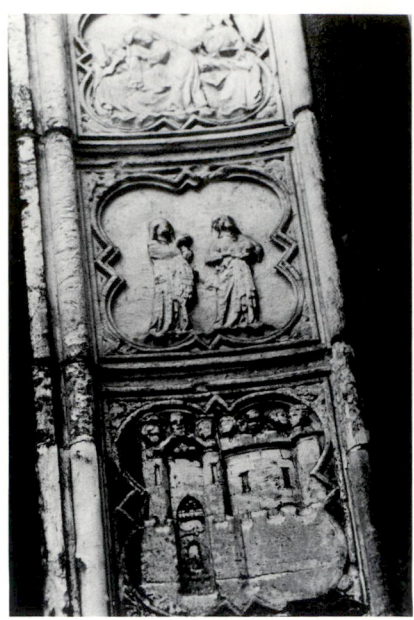

271. Rouen Cathedral. Portail de la Calende

270. Rouen Cathedral. Portail de la Calende

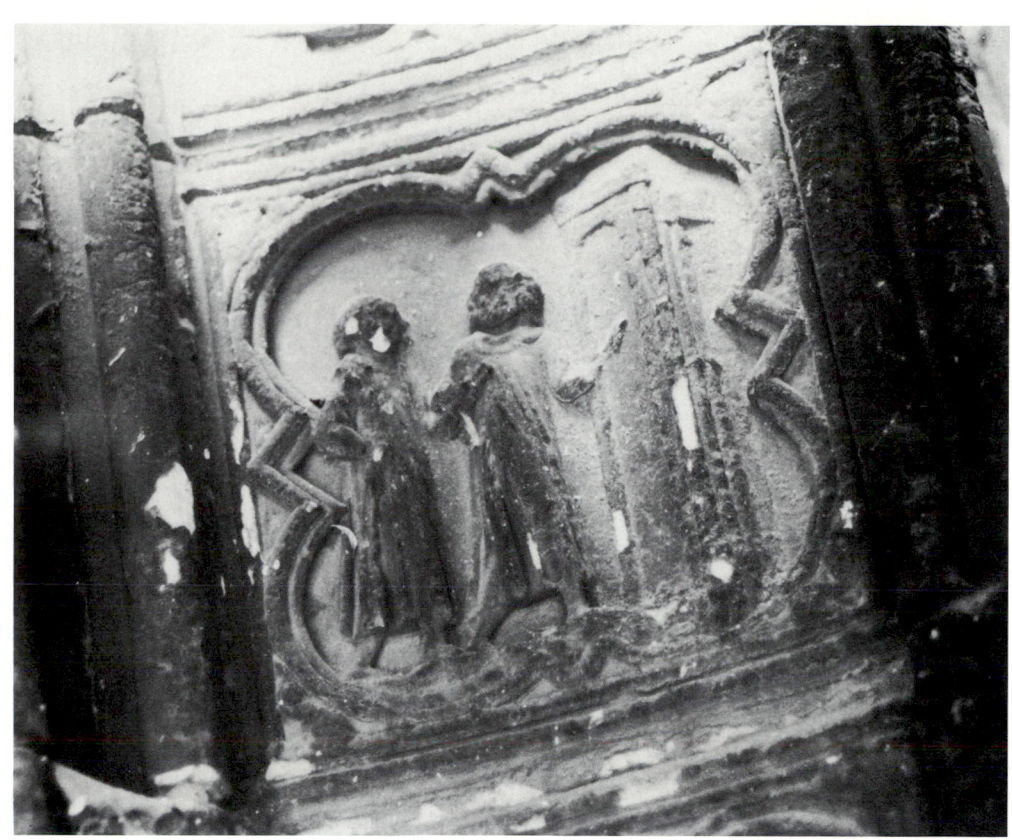

272. Rouen Cathedral. Portail de la Calende

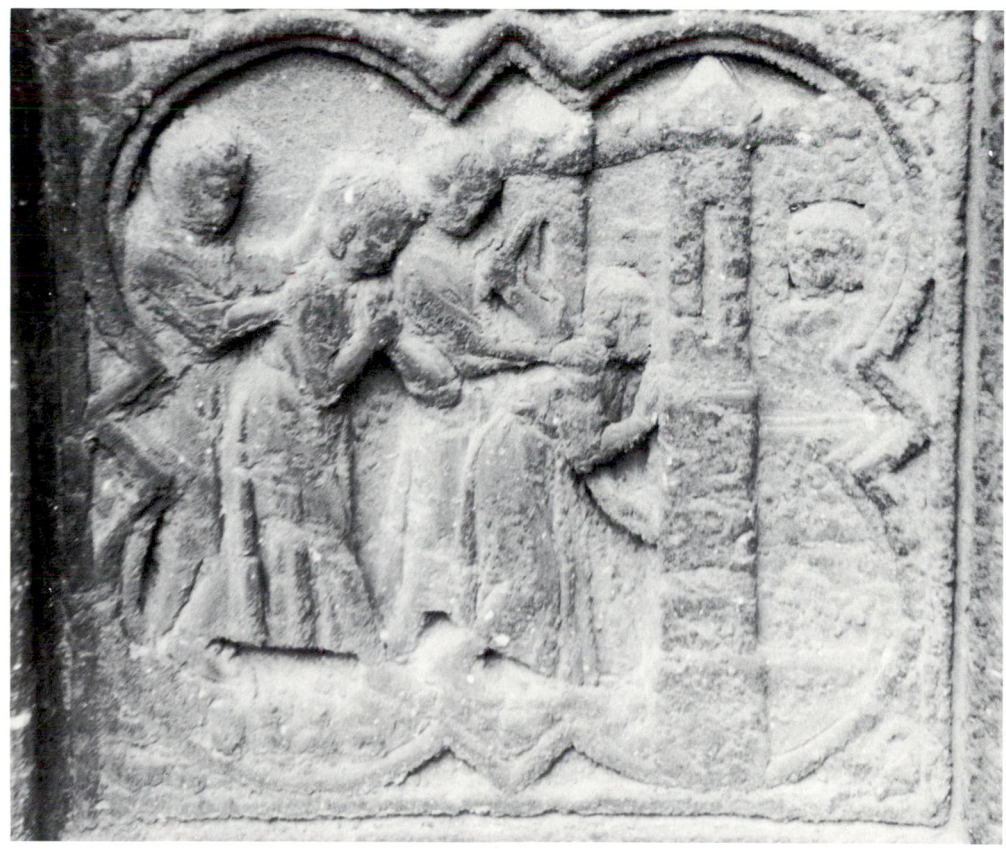

273. Rouen Cathedral. Portail de la Calende

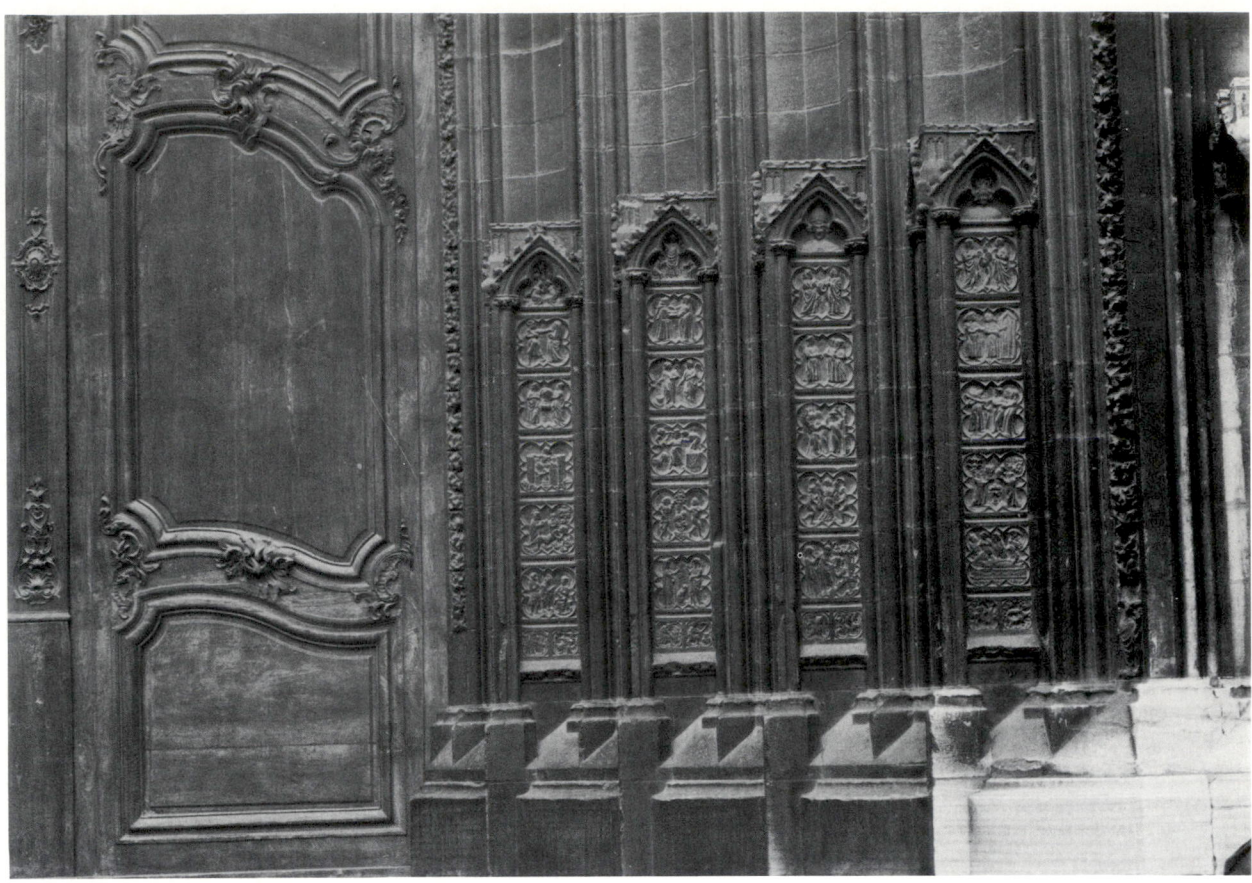

274. Lyon Cathedral. Facade, detail

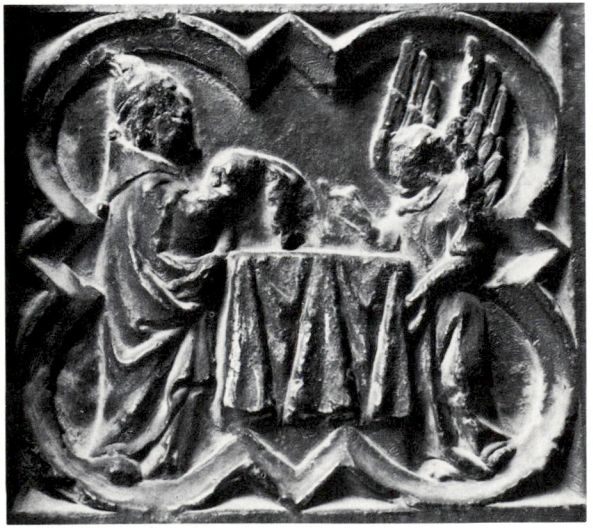

275. *Annunciation to Zacharias.* Lyon Cathedral

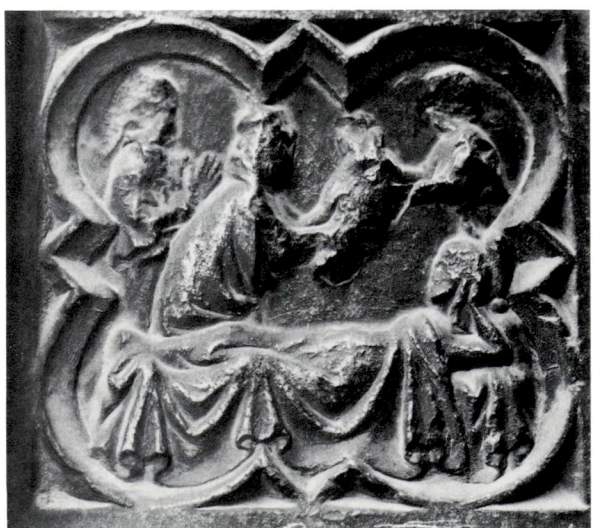

276. *Birth of Baptist.* Lyon Cathedral

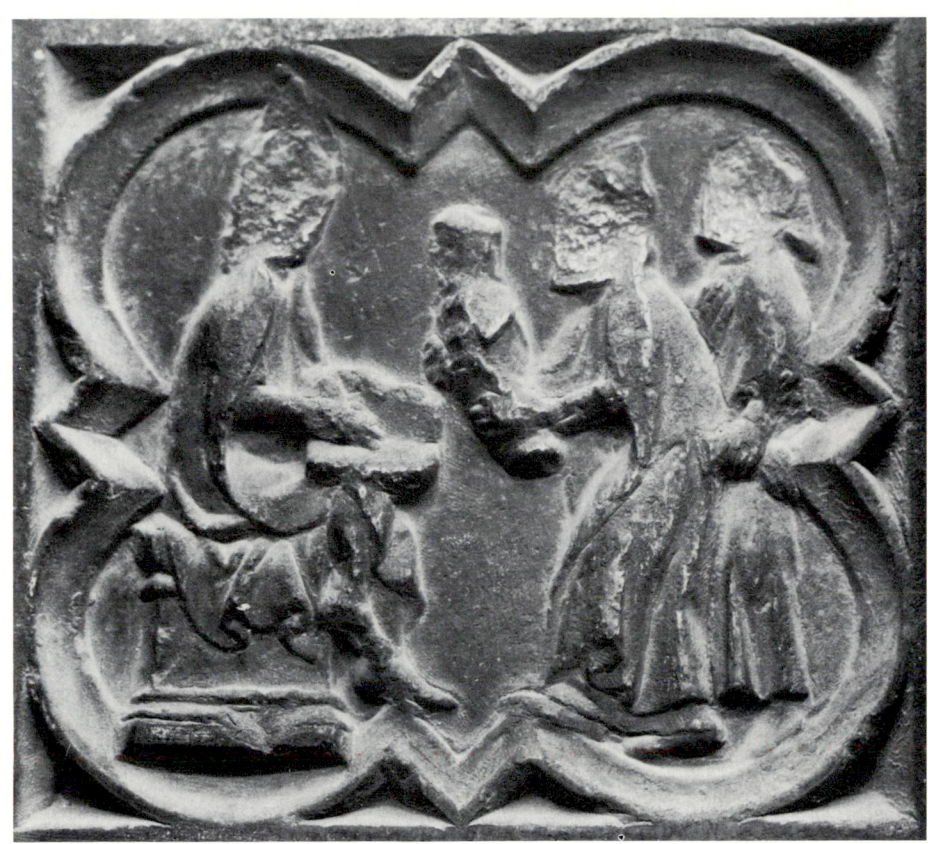

277. *Naming of Baptist.* Lyon Cathedral

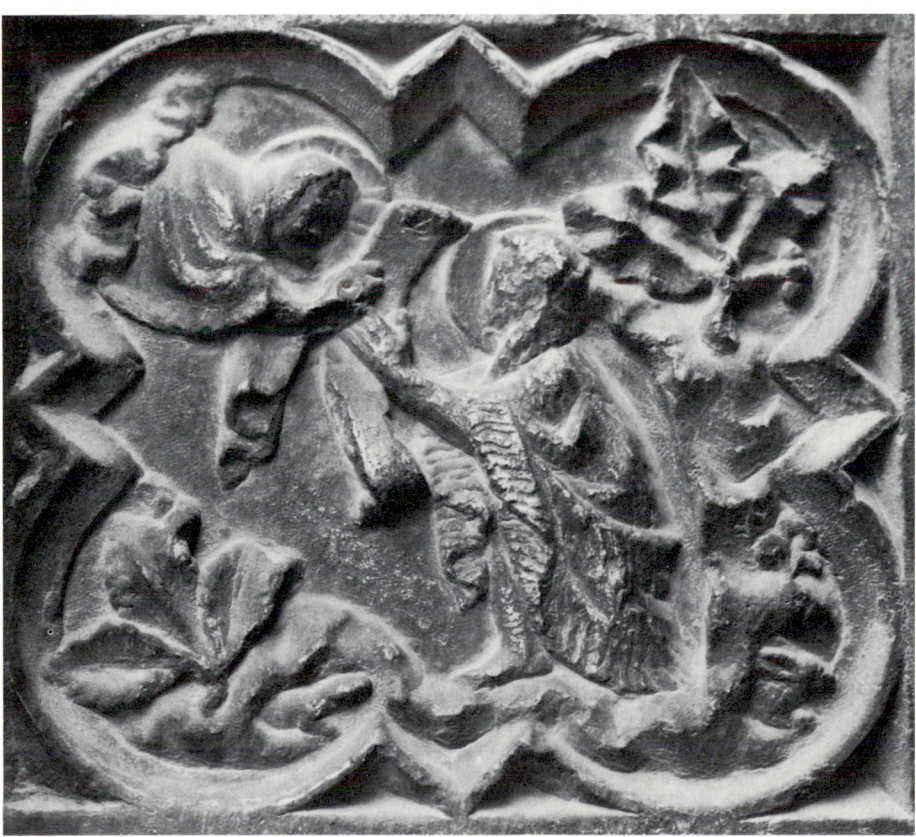

278. *John Receives His Mission.* Lyon Cathedral

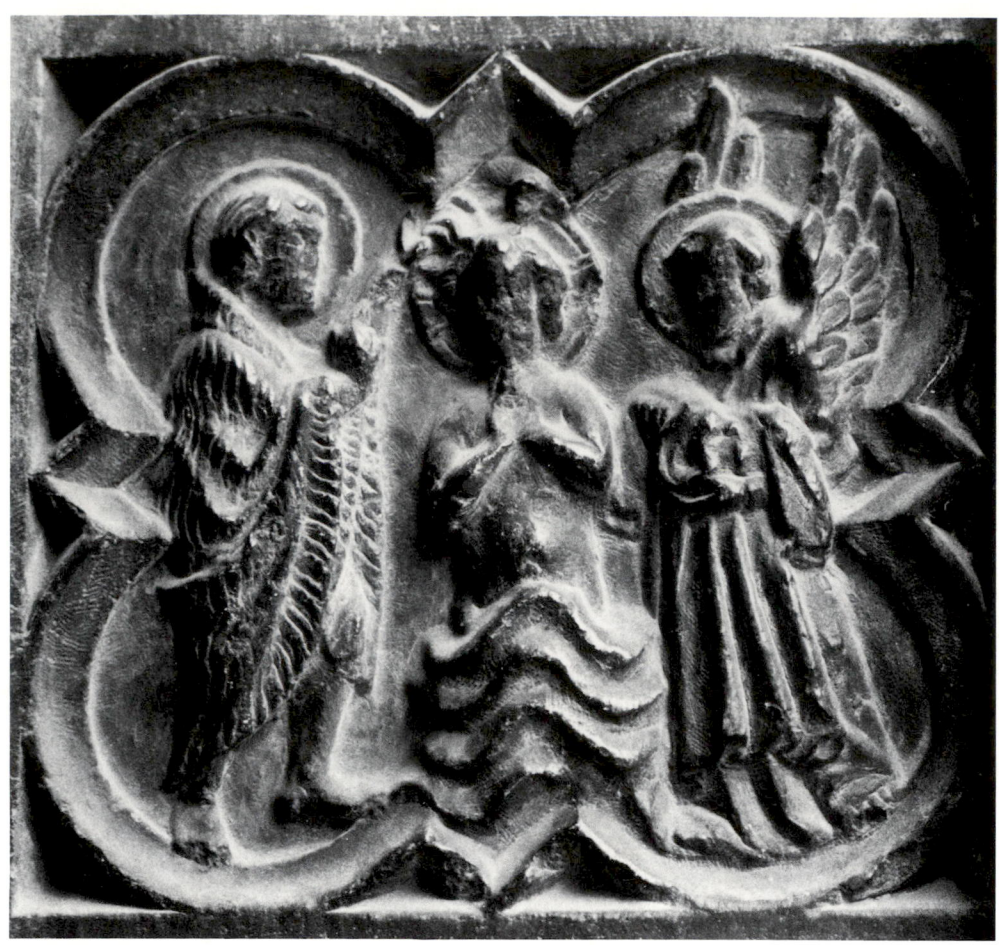

279. *Baptism of Christ*. Lyon Cathedral

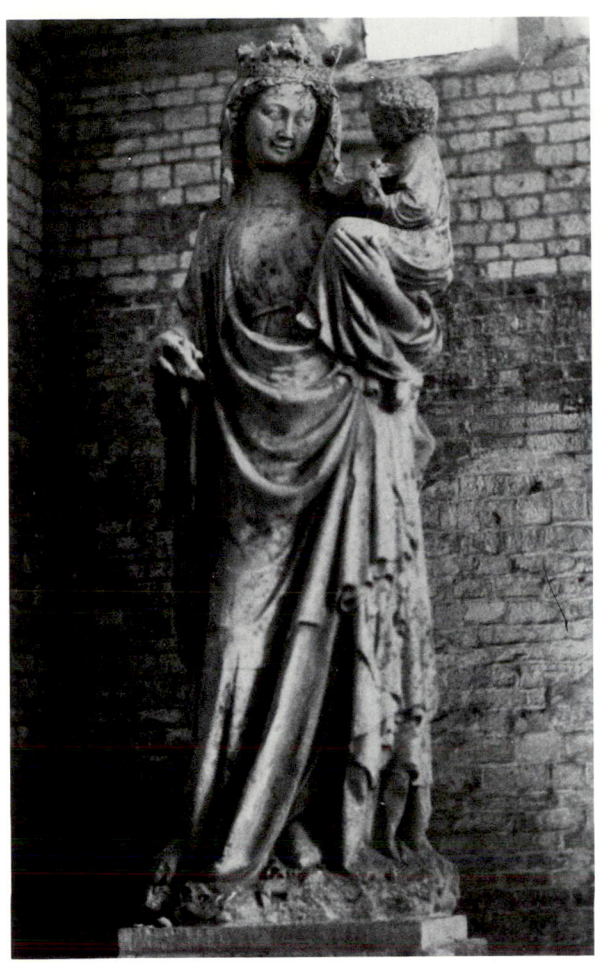

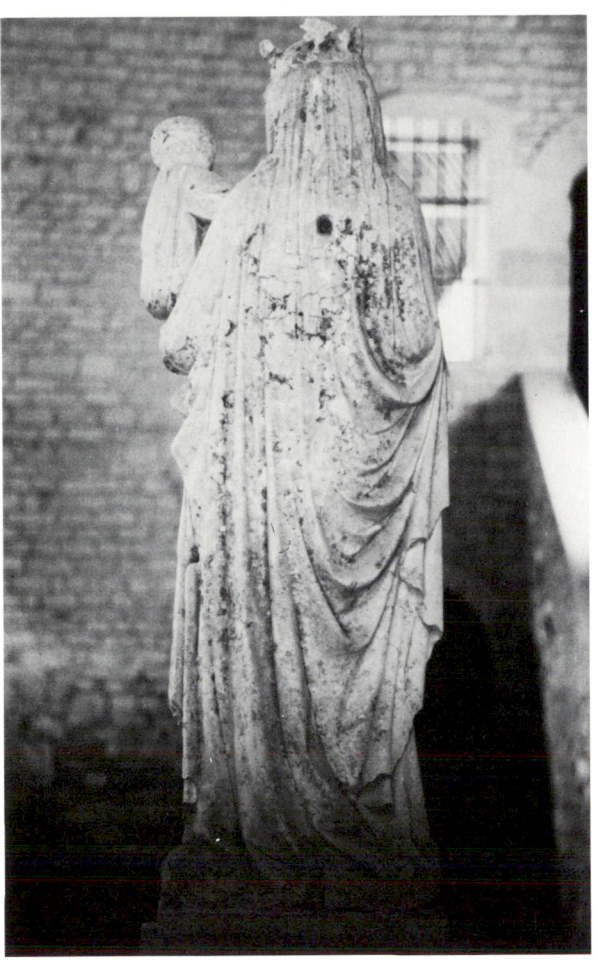

280. *Madonna and Child*. Fontenay Abbey

281. *Madonna and Child*. Fontenay Abbey

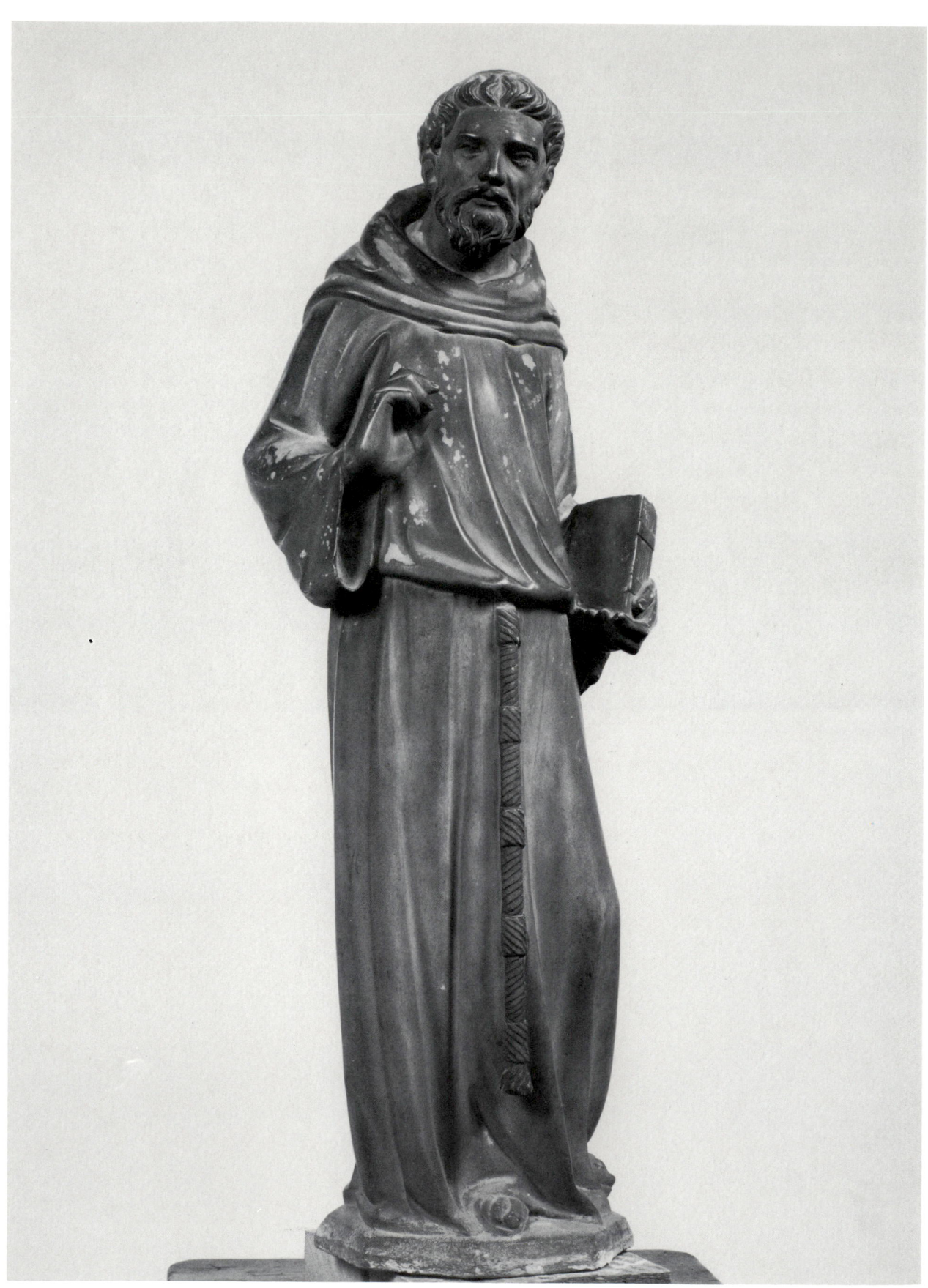

282. Nino Pisano: *San Francesco* (ht = 78 cm). Pisa, Opera del Duomo

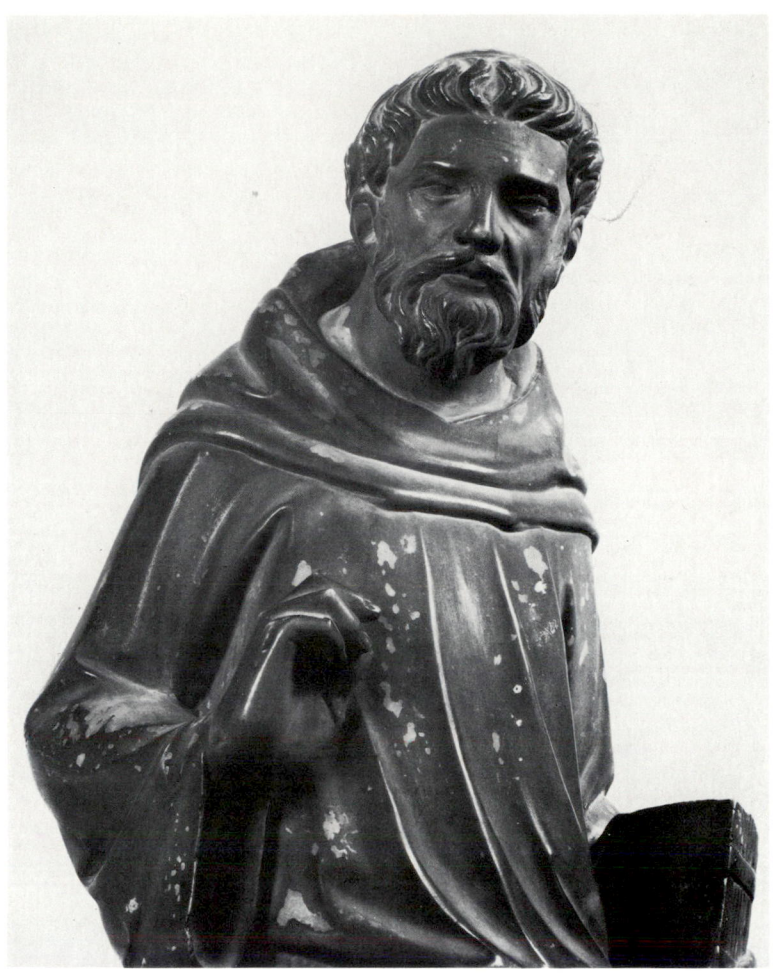

283. Nino Pisano: *San Francesco*. Pisa, Opera del Duomo

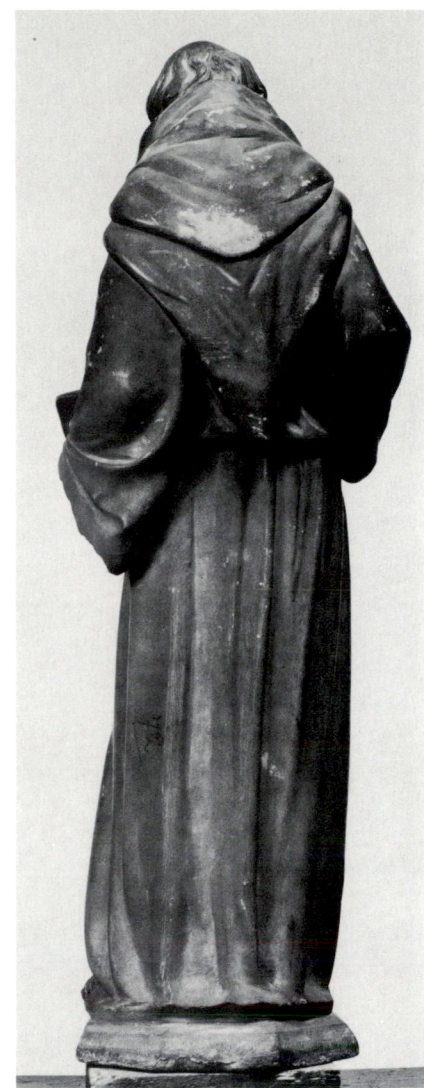

284. Nino Pisano: *San Francesco*. Pisa, Opera del Duomo

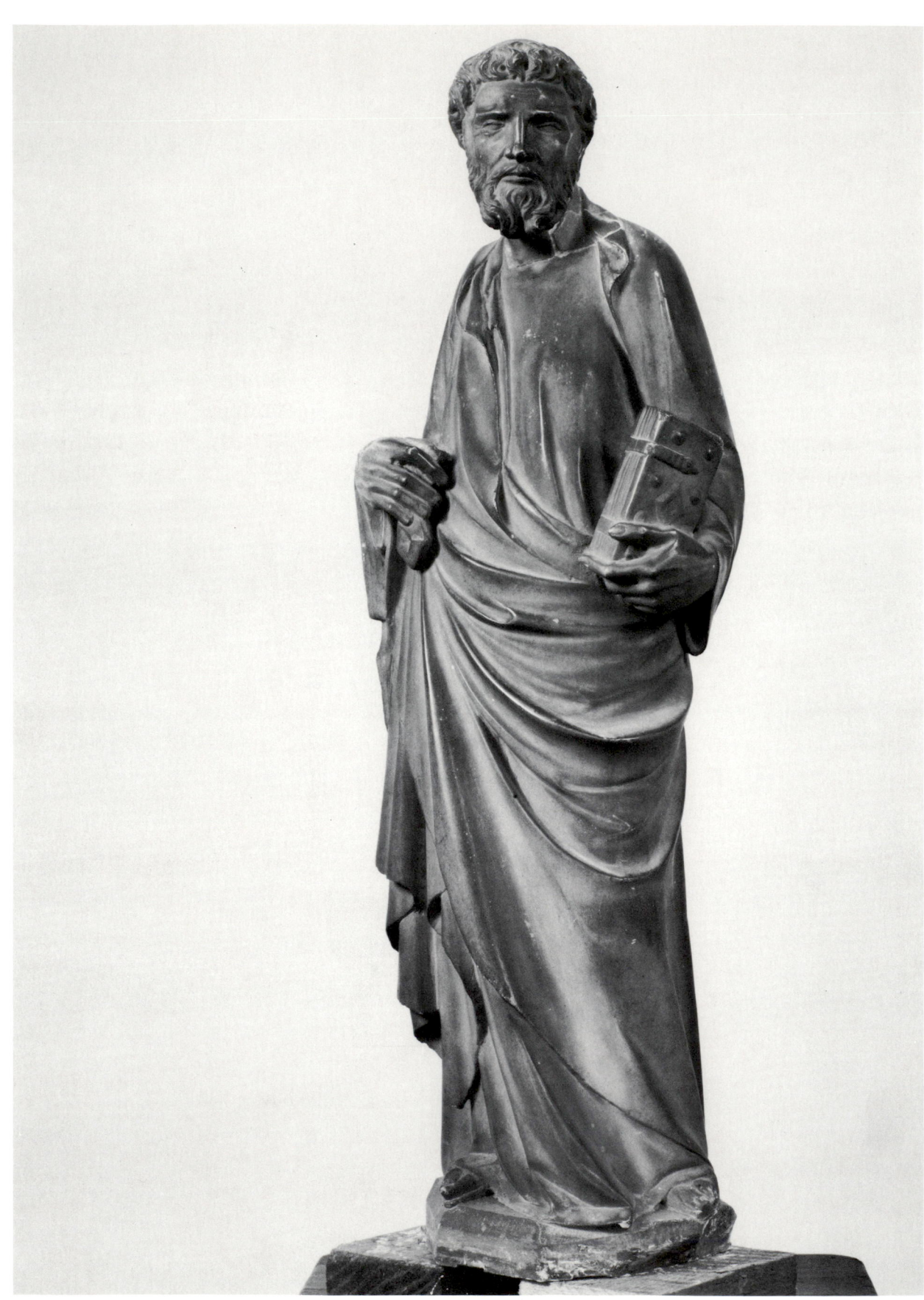

285. Nino Pisano workshop (Tommaso?): *San Pietro* (ht 80 cm). Pisa, Opera del Duomo

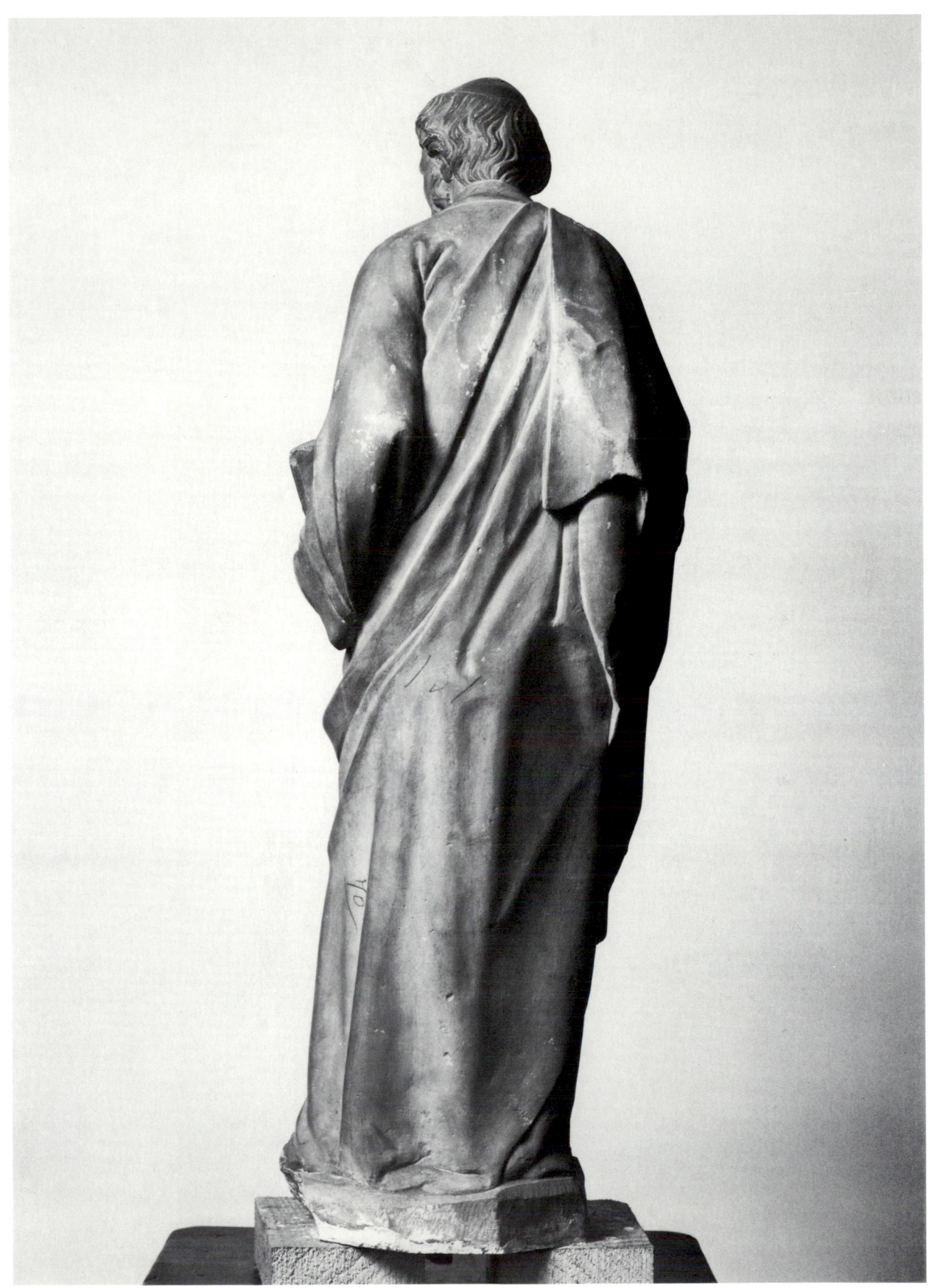

286. Nino Pisano workshop (Tommaso?): *San Pietro*. Pisa, Opera del Duomo

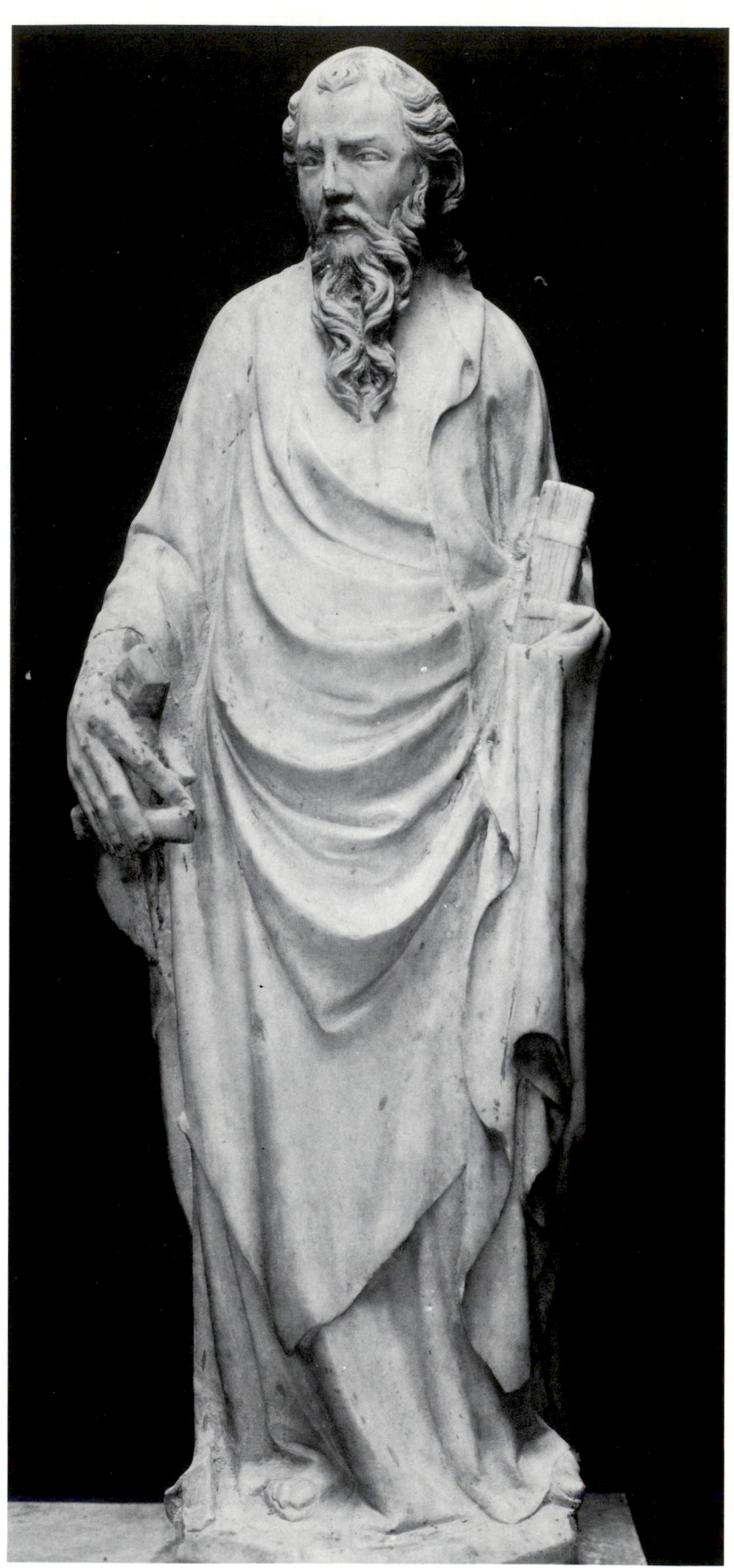

287. Tommaso Pisano: *San Paolo* (ht 80 cm). Pisa, Museo di San Matteo

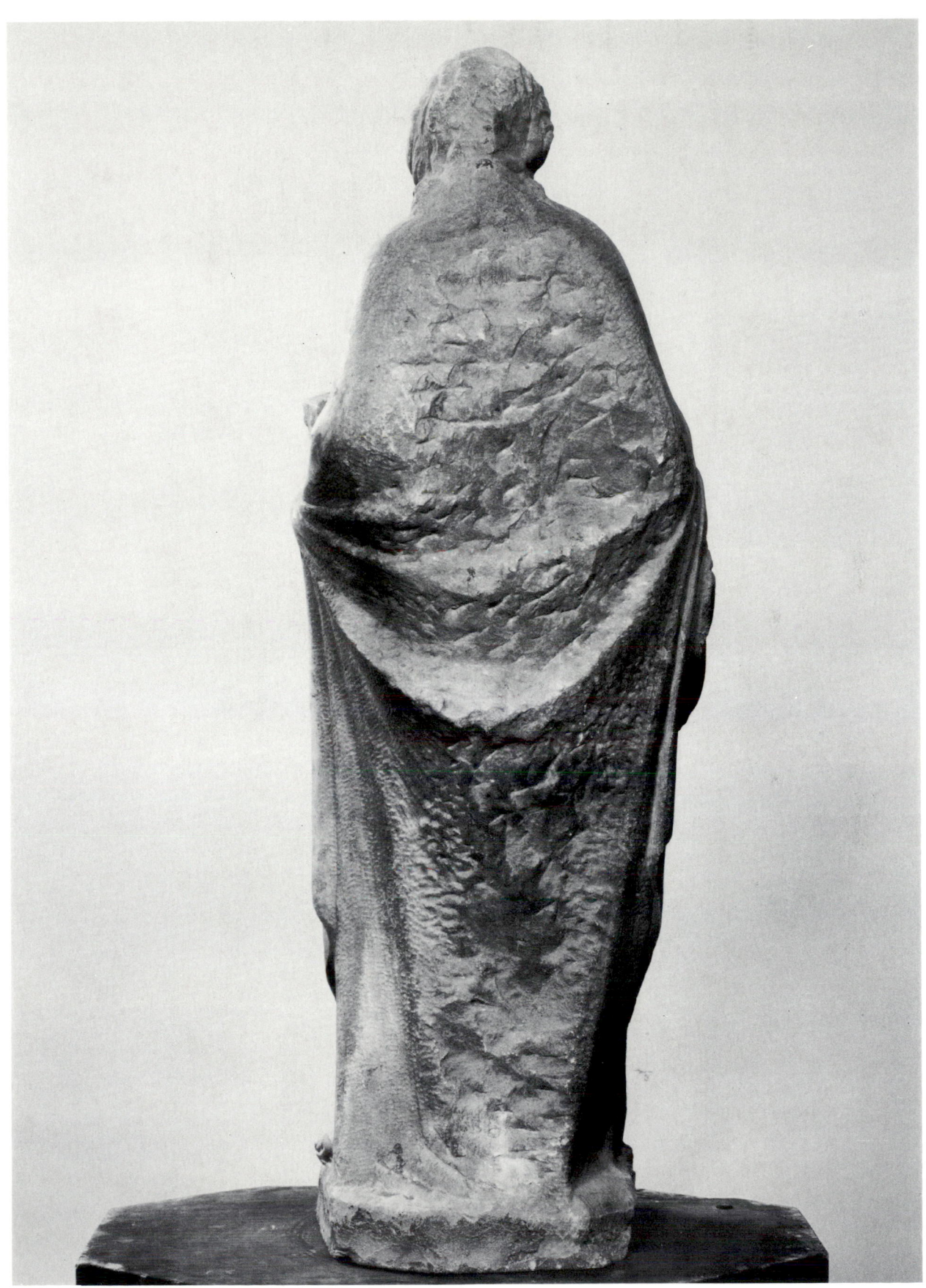

288. Tommaso Pisano: *San Paolo*. Pisa, Museo di San Matteo

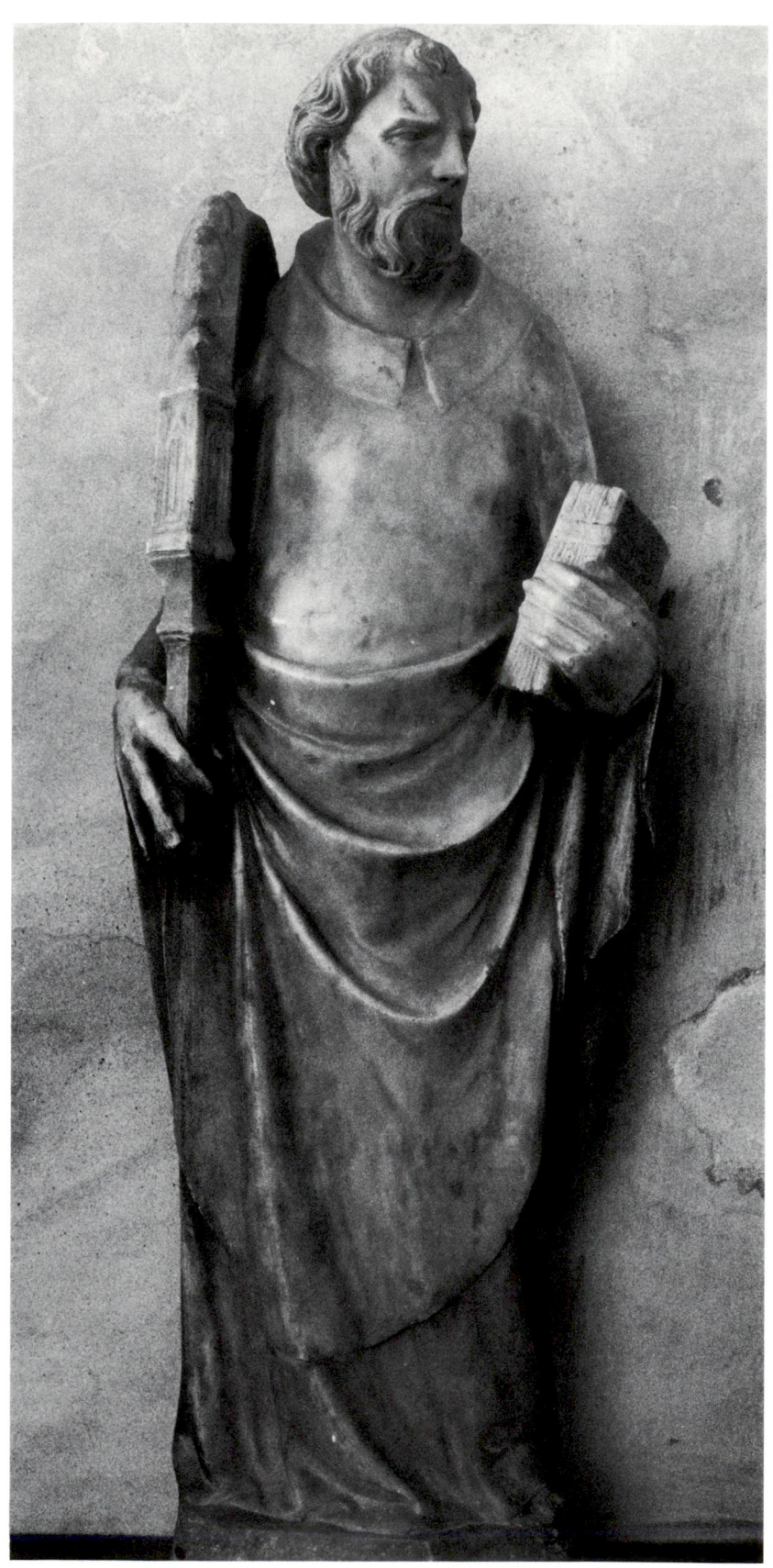

289. Tommaso Pisano: *Saint* (ht 80 cm). Pisa, Museo di San Matteo

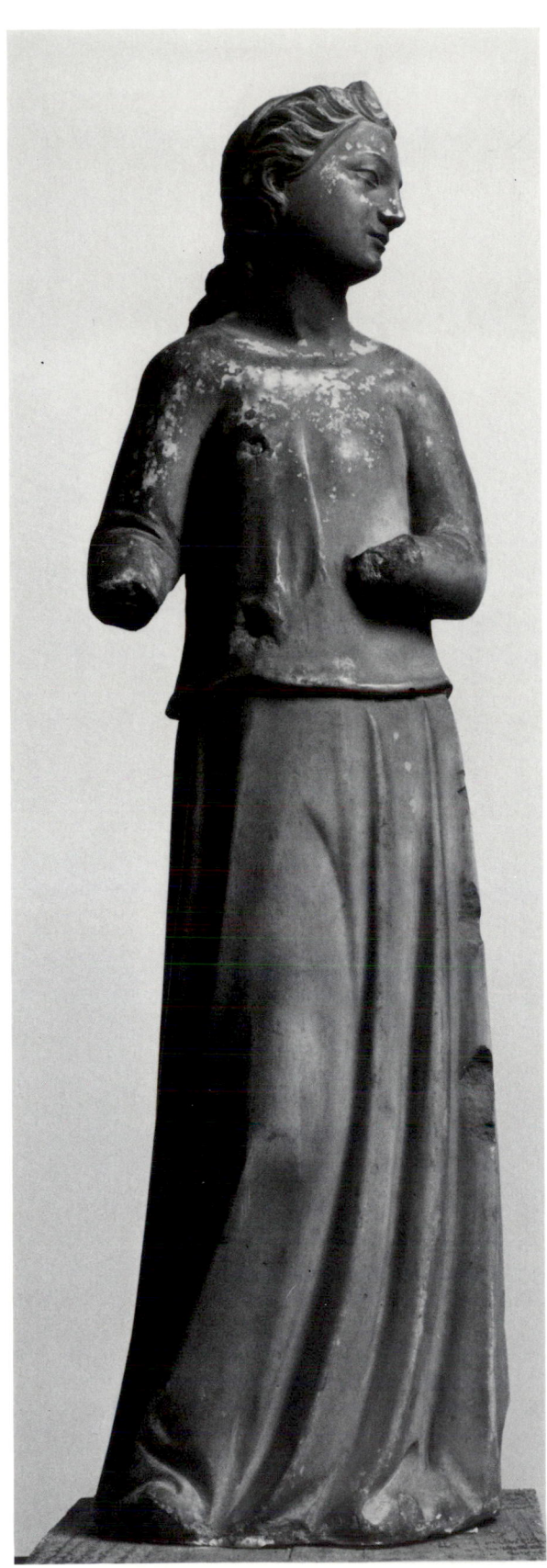 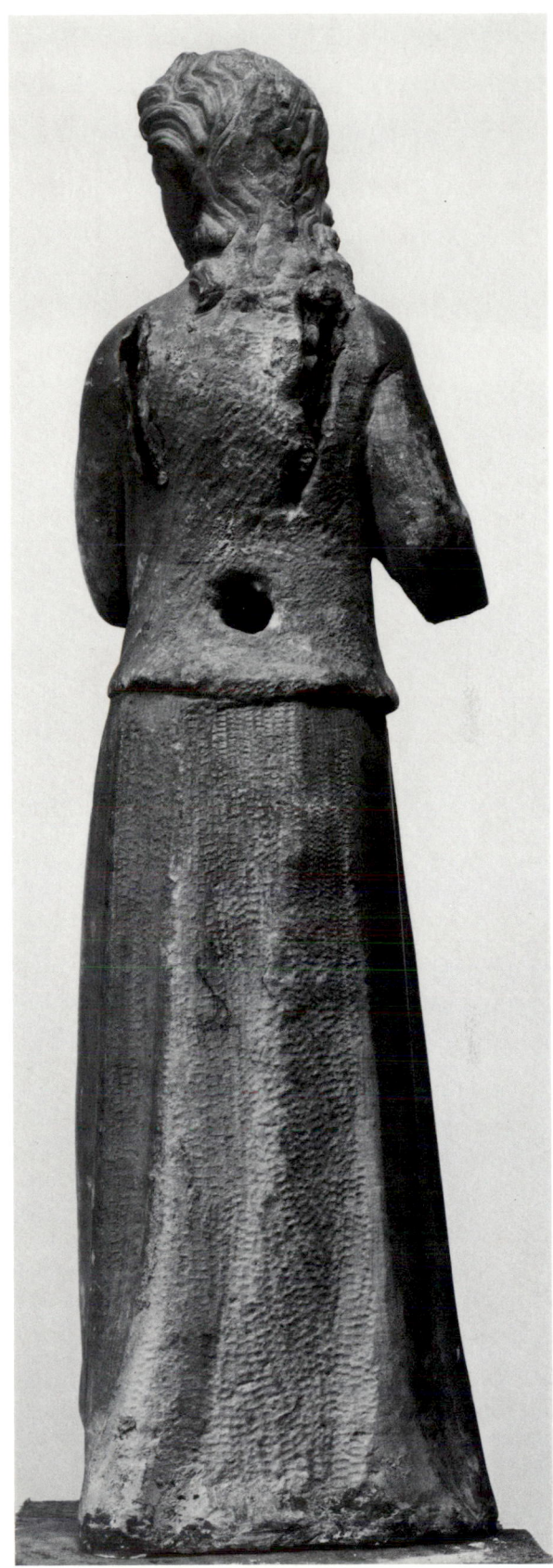

290. Nino Pisano workshop: *Angel* (ht 61 cm). Pisa, Opera del Duomo   291. Nino Pisano workshop: *Angel*. Pisa, Opera del Duomo

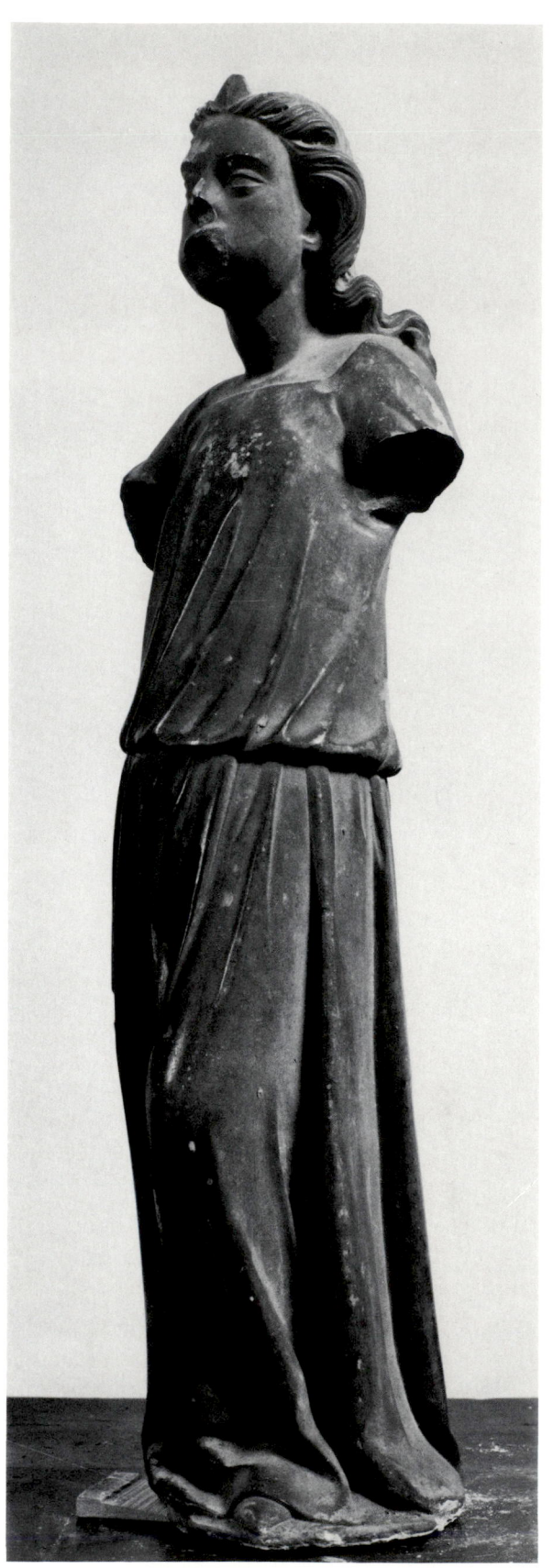 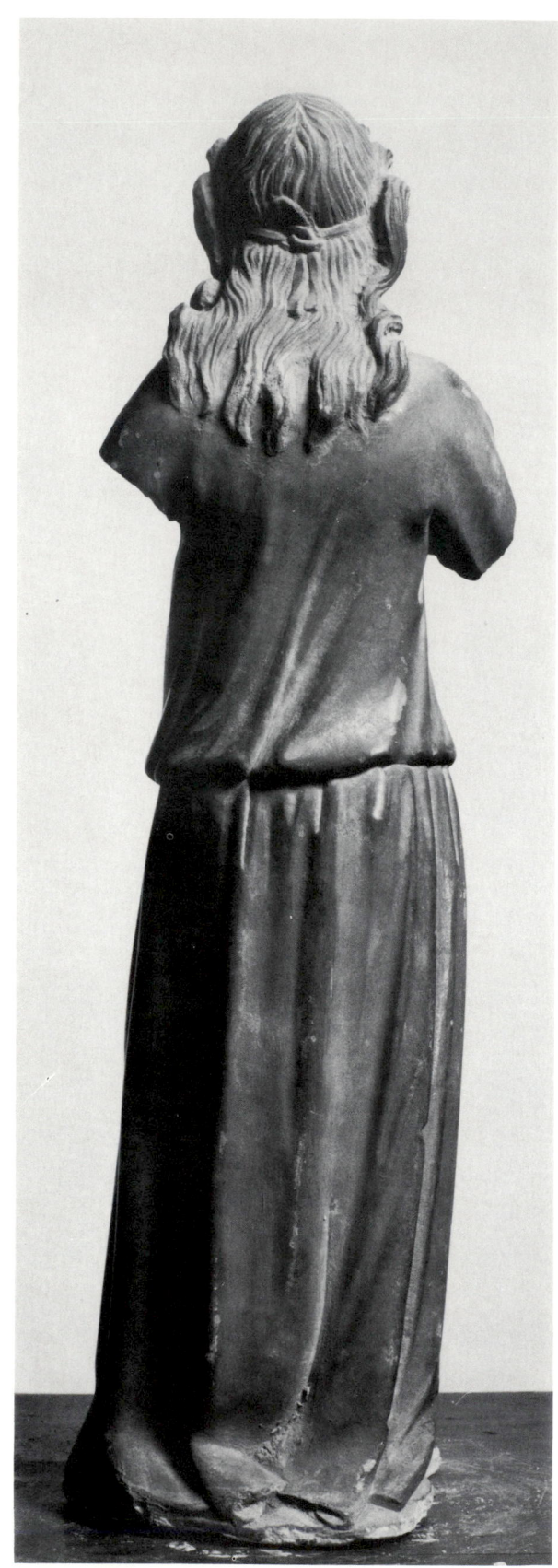

292. Nino Pisano workshop: *Angel* (ht 50 cm). Pisa, Opera del Duomo

293. Nino Pisano workshop: *Angel*. Pisa, Opera del Duomo

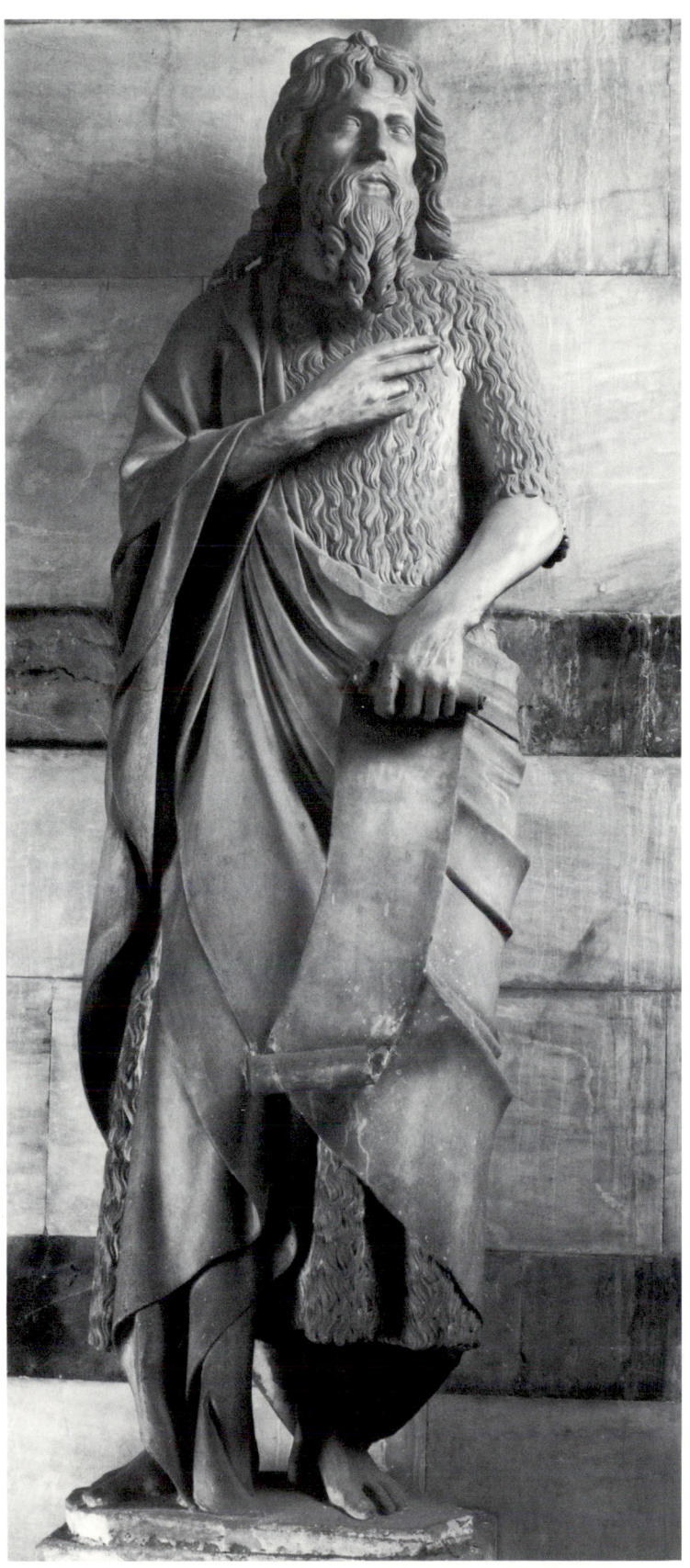

294. Tommaso Pisano: *John the Baptist* (ht 162 cm). Pisa, Sta. Maria della Spina

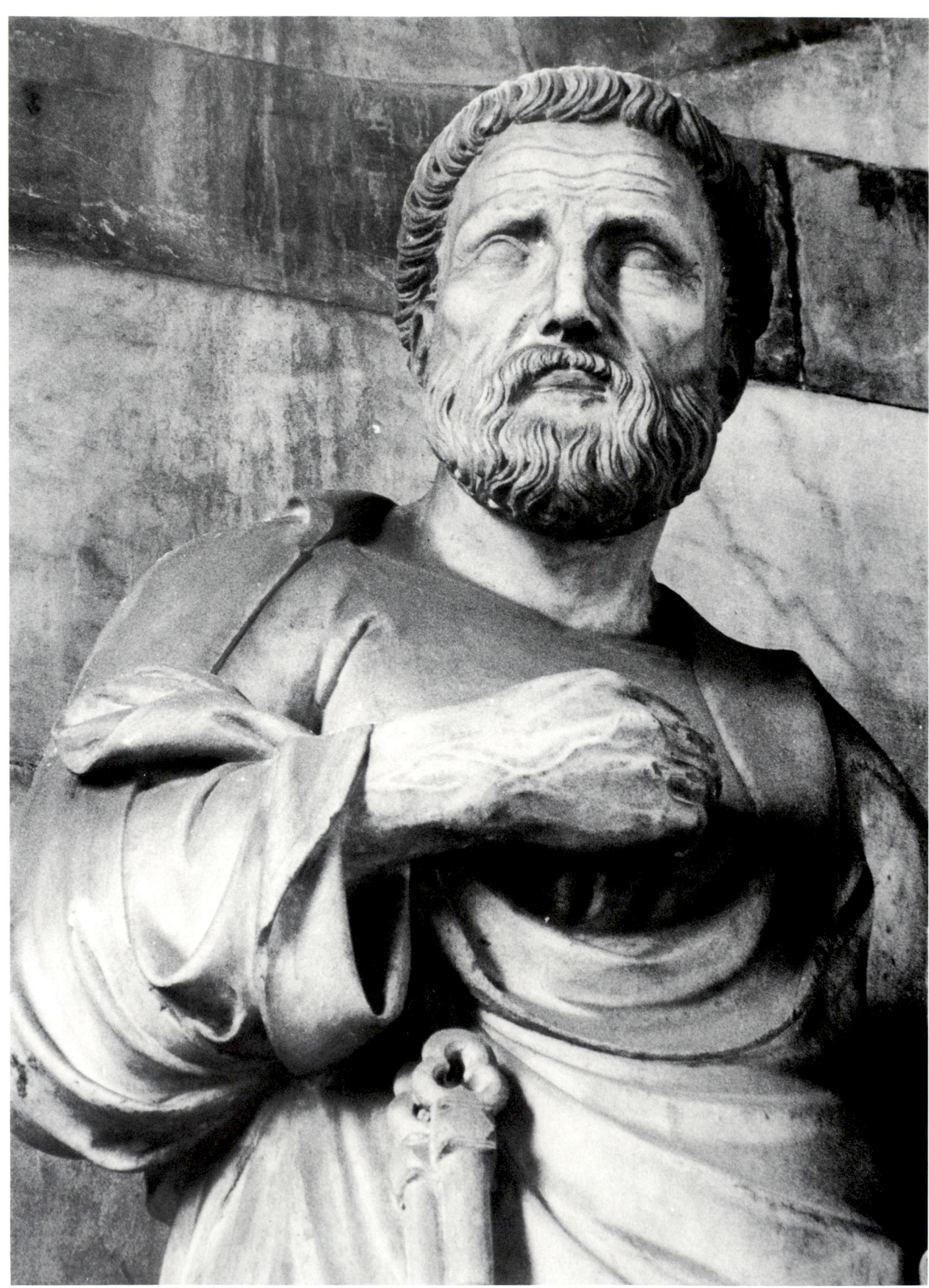

295. Nino Pisano: *St. Peter*, detail. Pisa, Sta. Maria della Spina

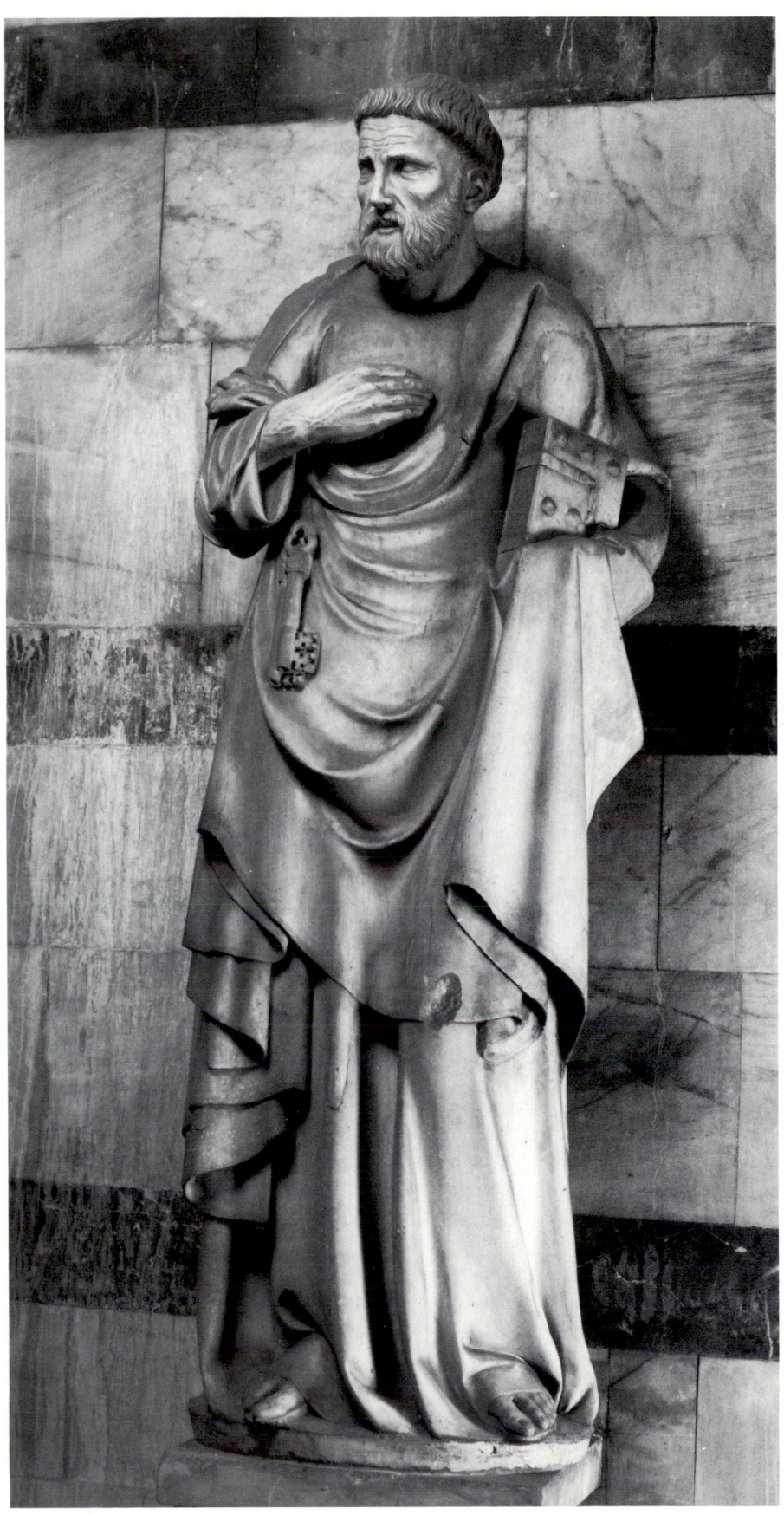

296. Nino Pisano: *St. Peter* (ht 168 cm). Pisa, Sta. Maria della Spina

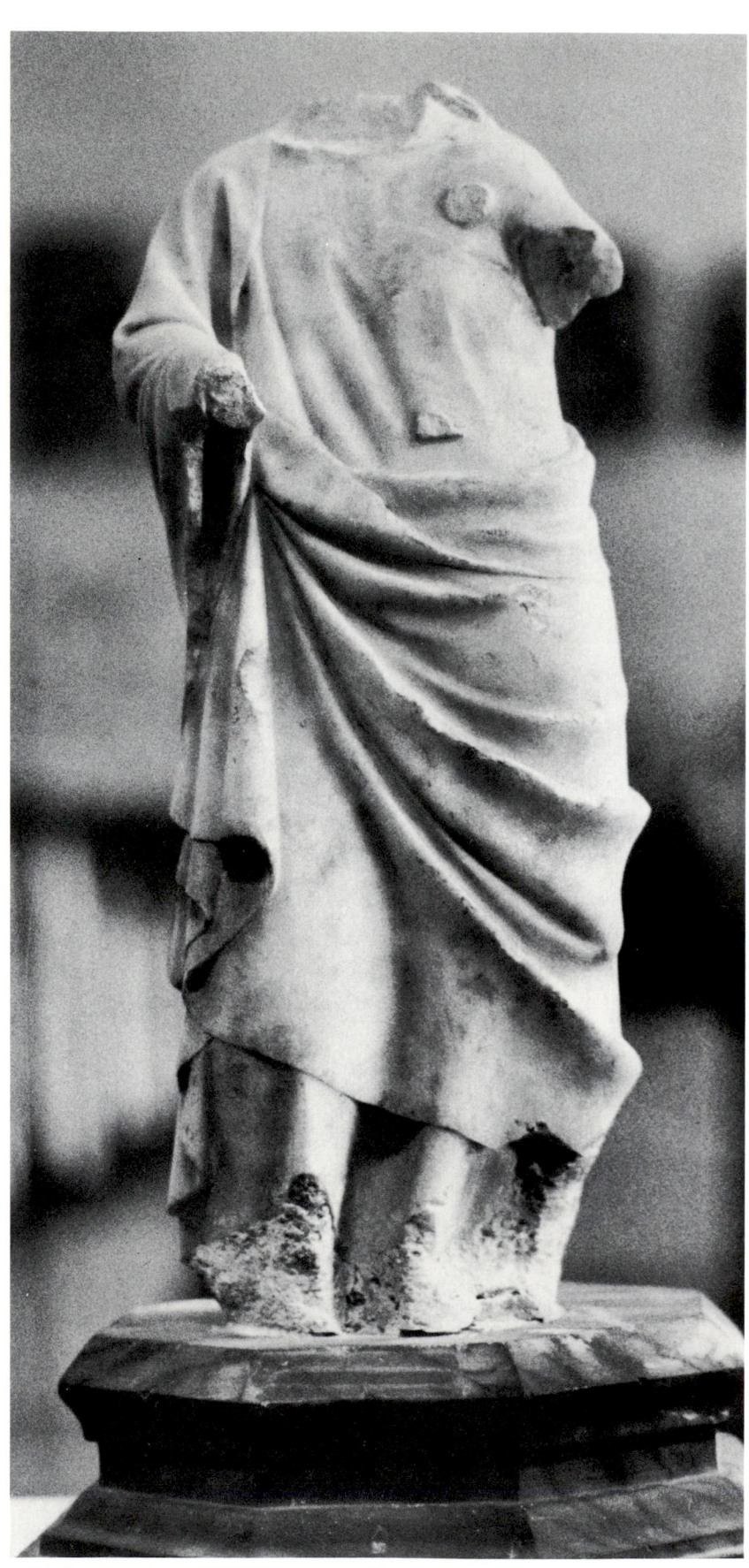

297. Andrea Pisano: *Angel* (ht 47 cm). Orvieto, Museo dell'Opera del Duomo

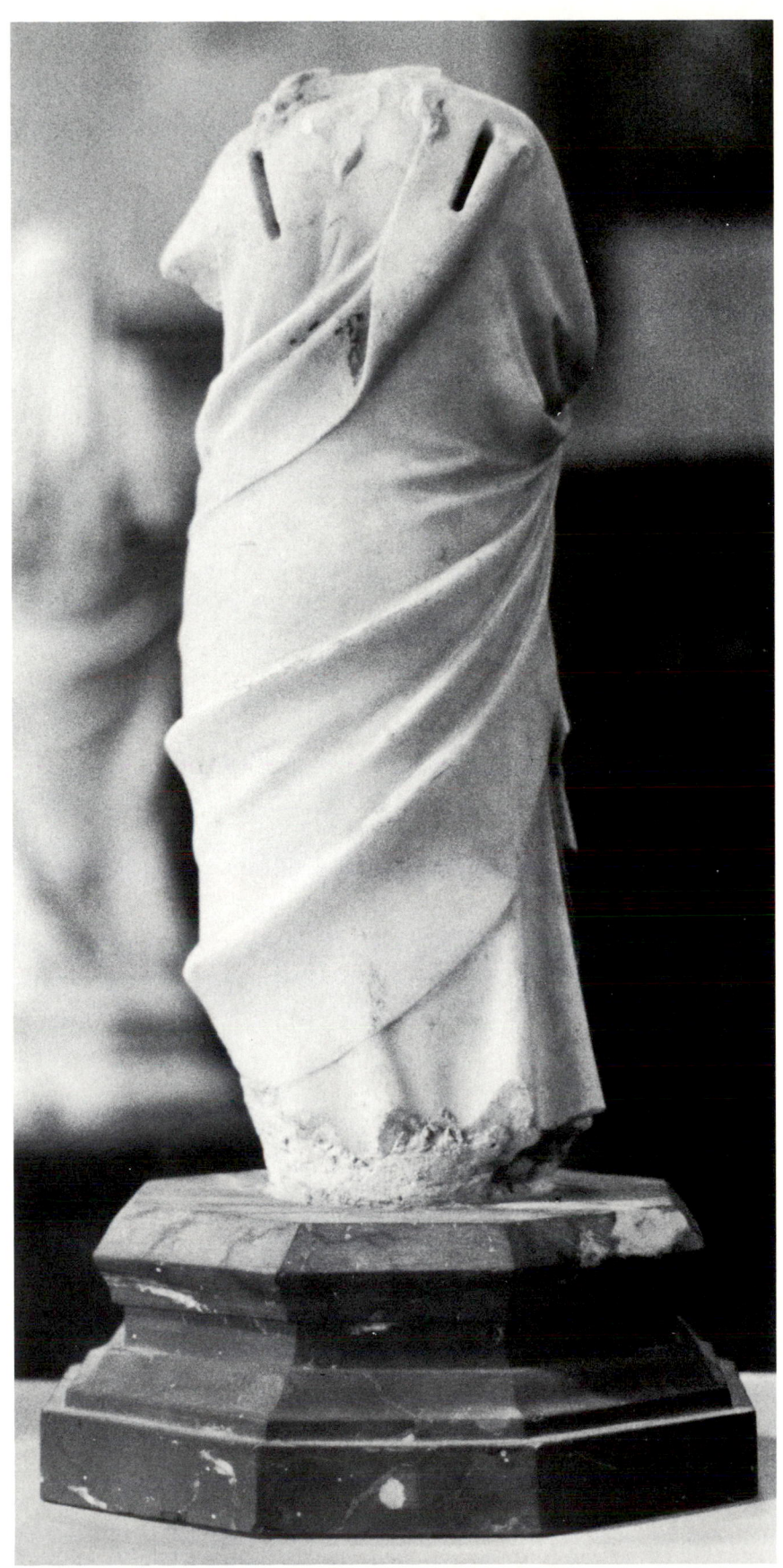

298. Andrea Pisano: *Angel*. Orvieto, Museo dell'Opera del Duomo

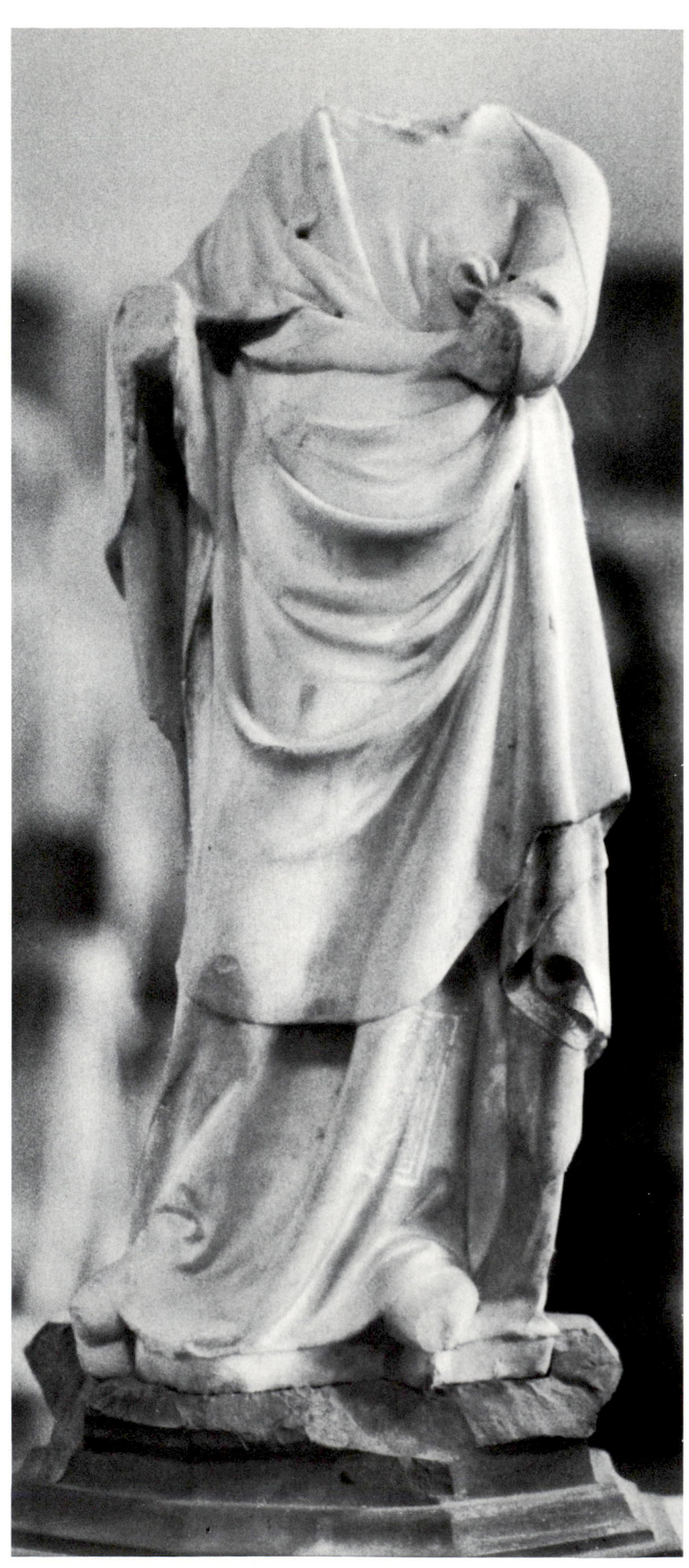

299. Nino Pisano: *Angel* (ht 53 cm). Orvieto, Museo dell'Opera del Duomo

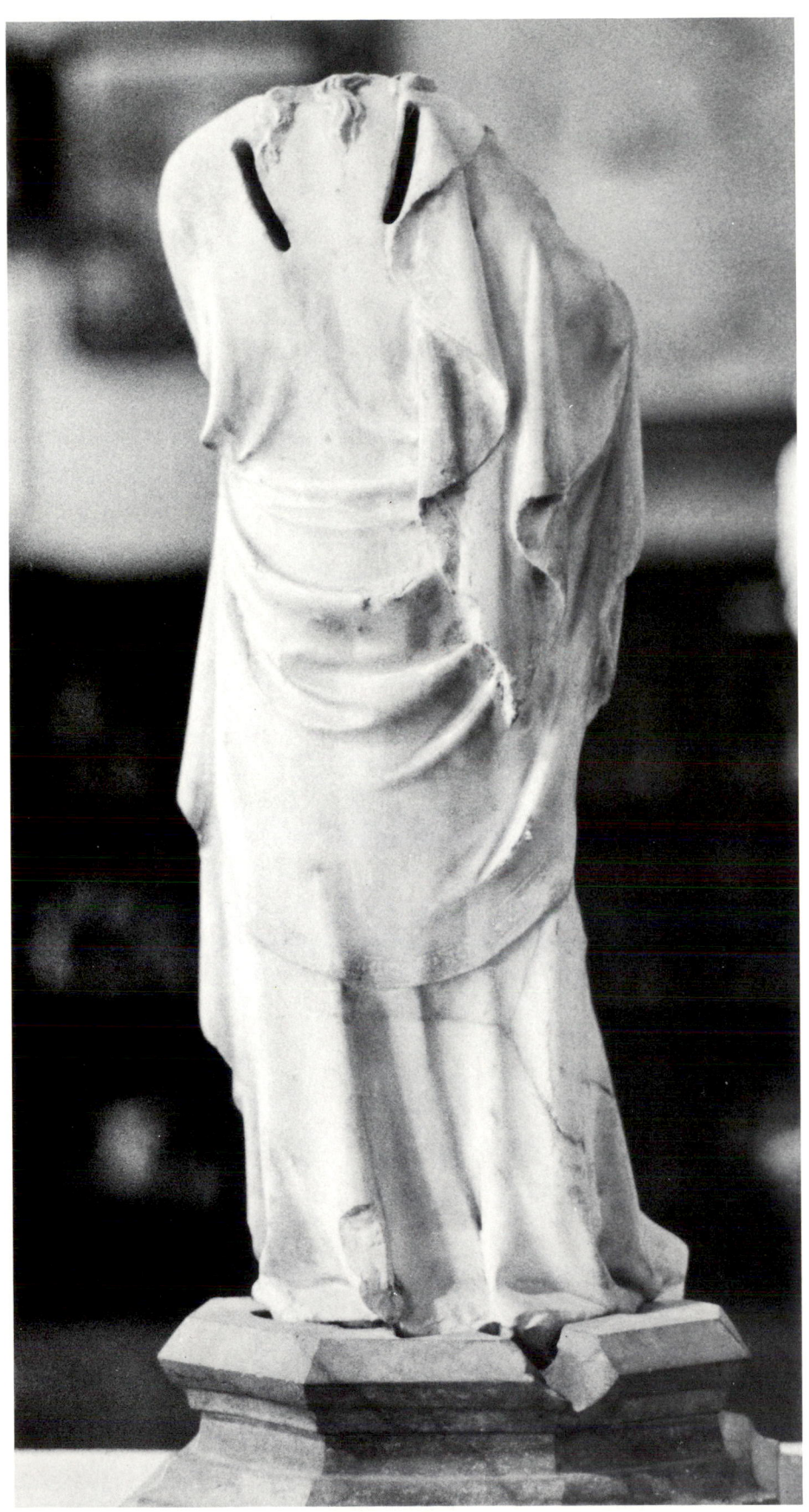

300. Nino Pisano: *Angel*. Orvieto, Museo dell'Opera del Duomo

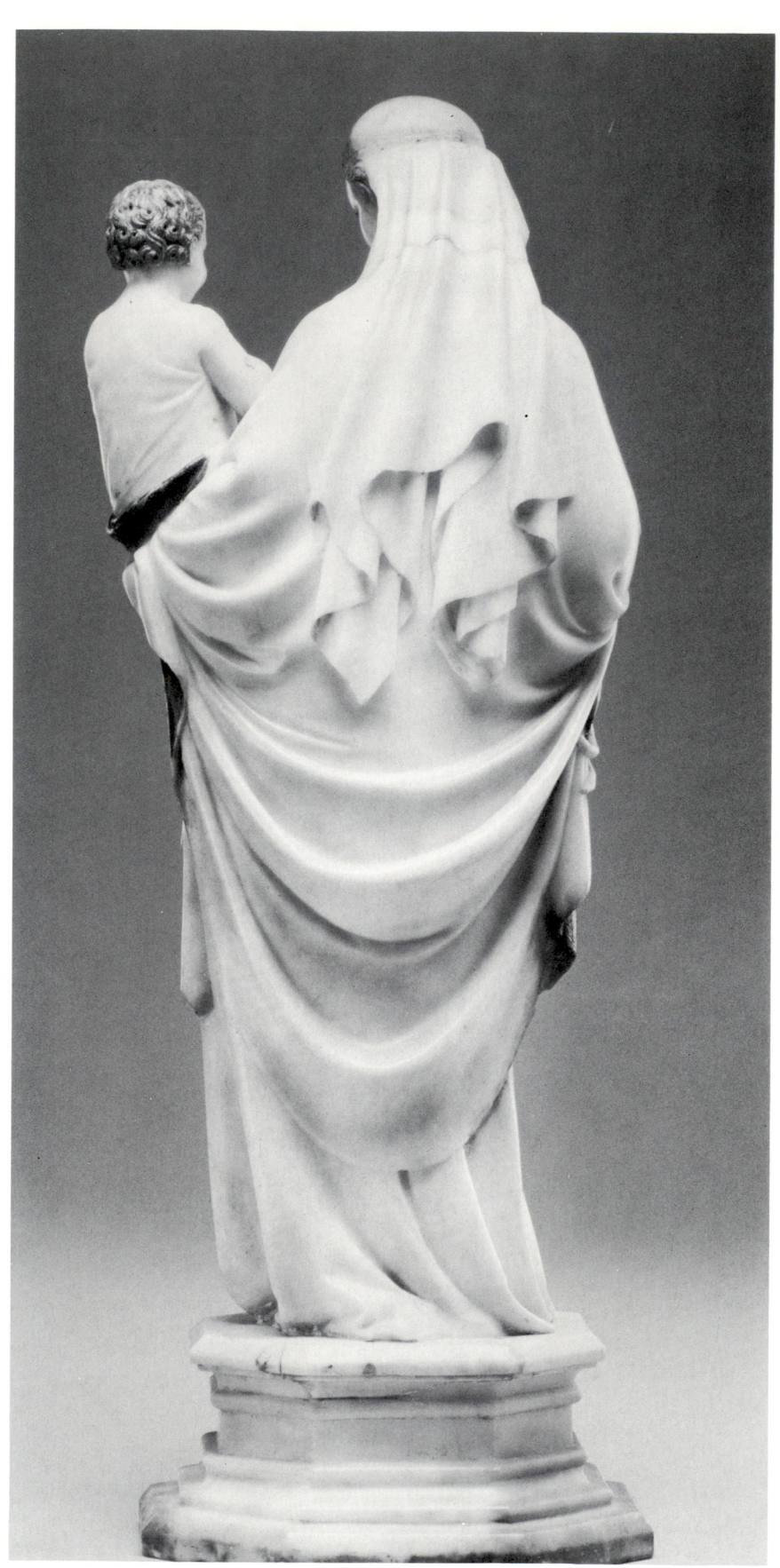

301. Nino Pisano: *Madonna and Child*. Detroit Institute of Arts

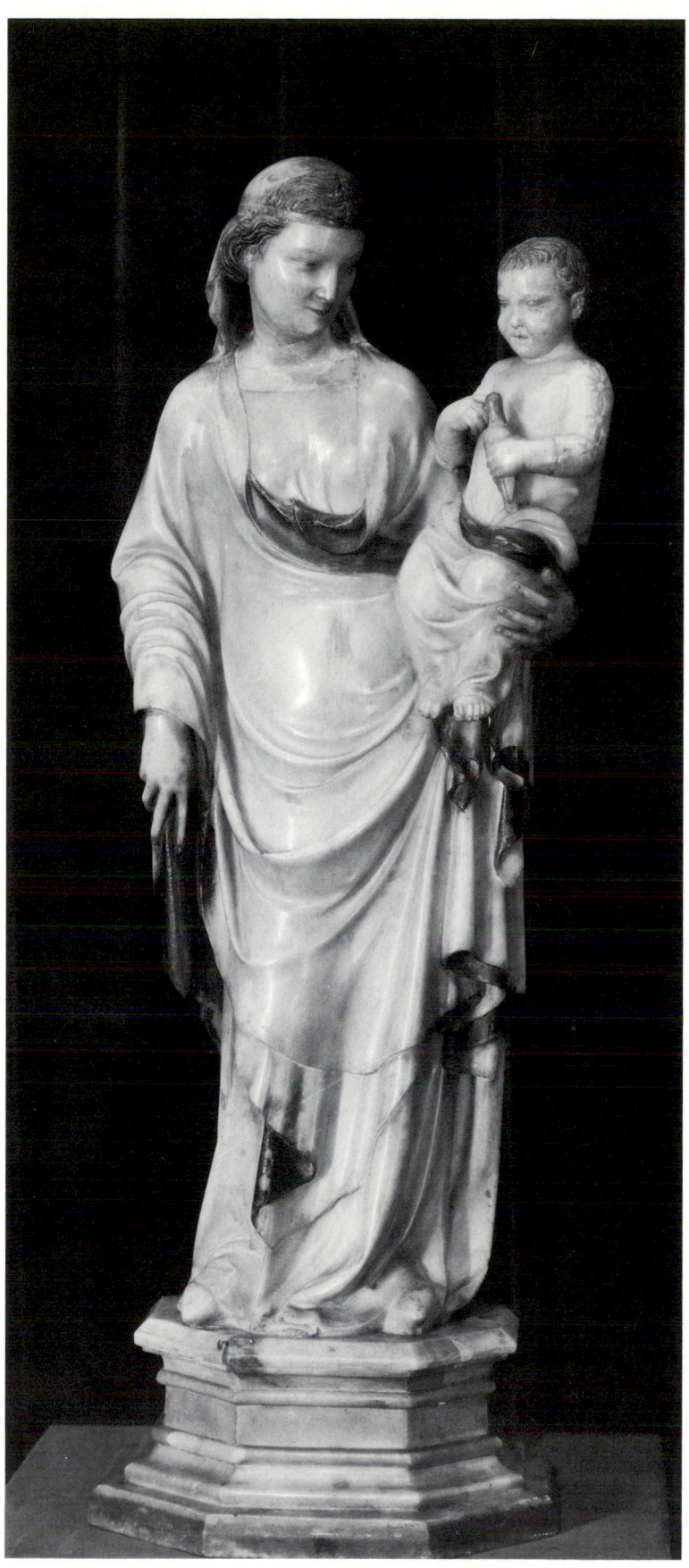

302. Nino Pisano: *Madonna and Child* (ht 76.2 cm). Detroit Institute of Arts

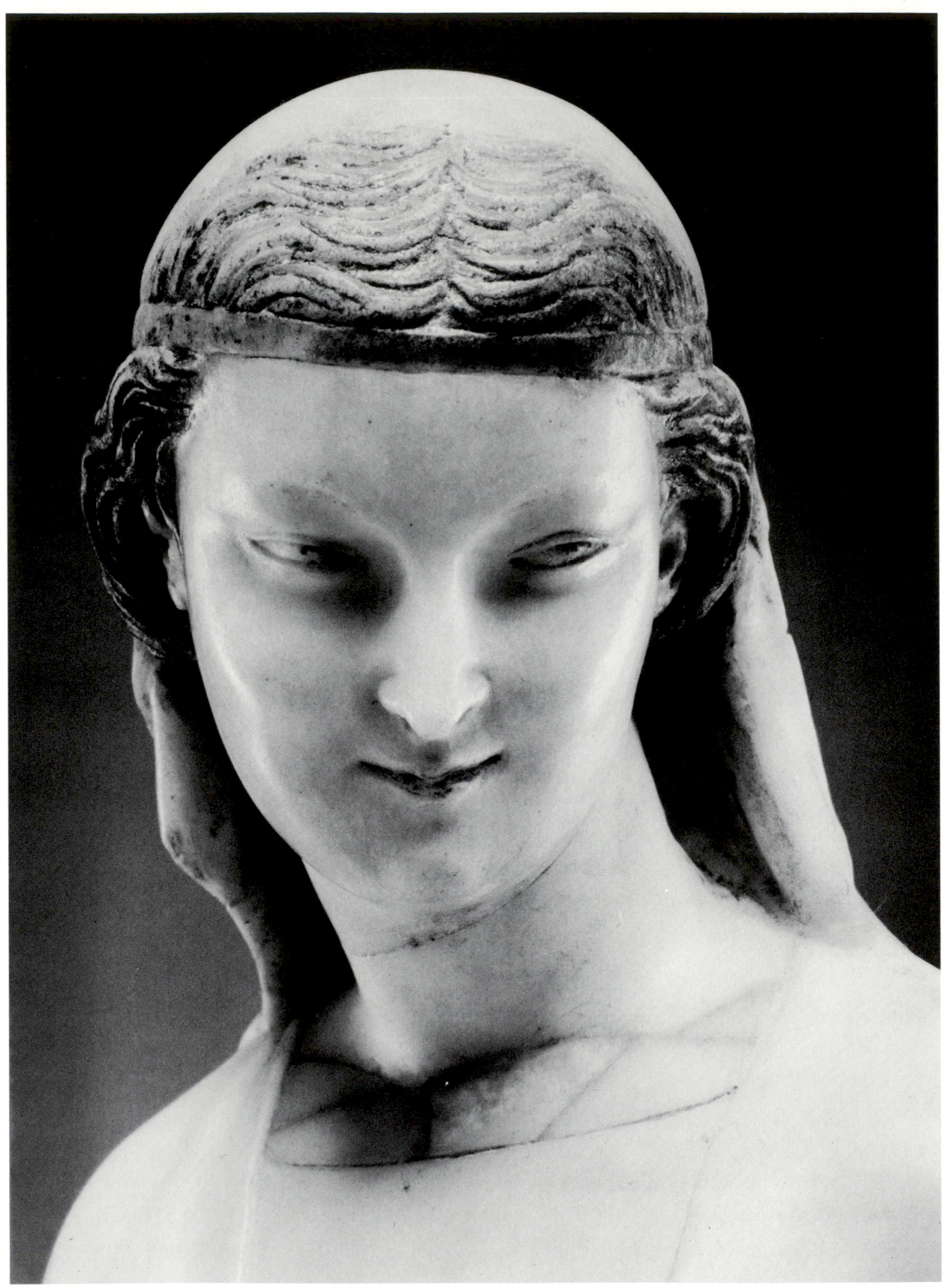

303. Nino Pisano: *Madonna and Child*, detail. Detroit Institute of Arts.

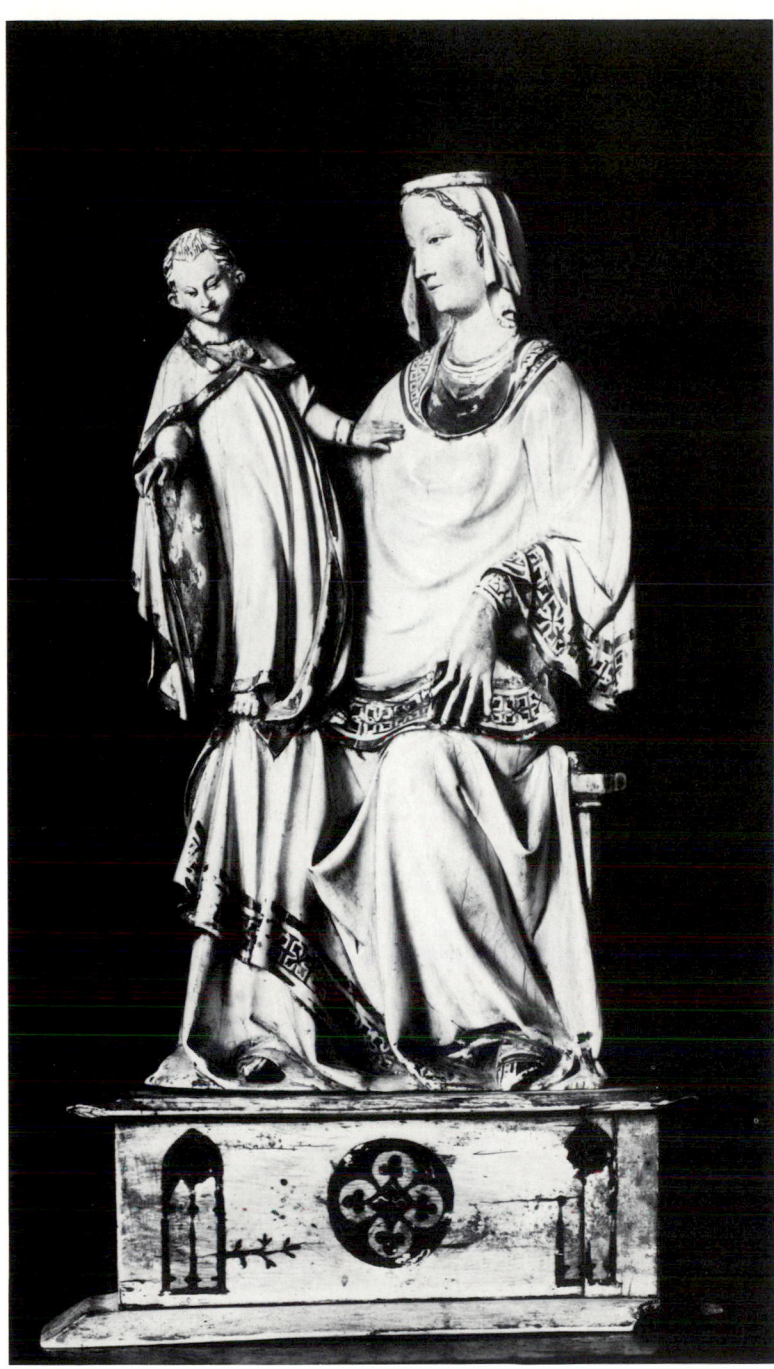

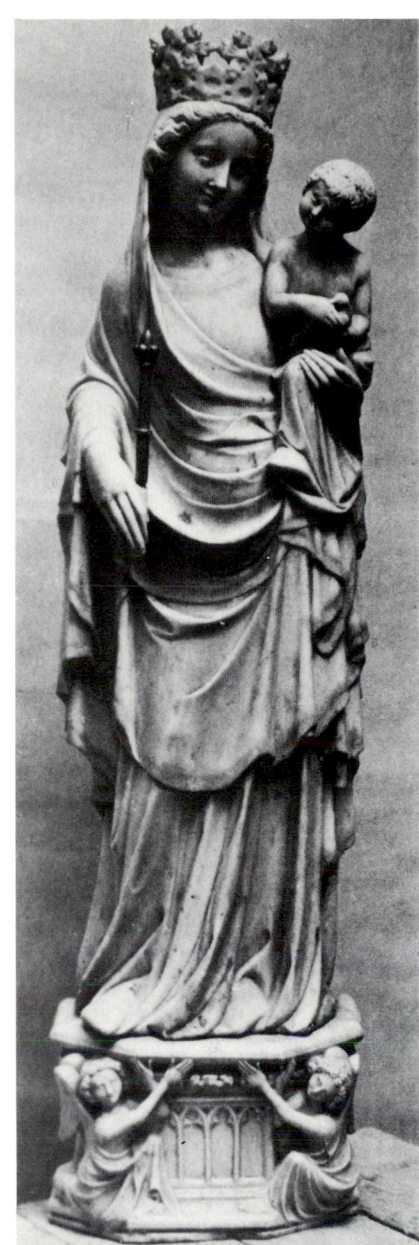

305. *Virgin and Child.* Bouée (Loire-Atlantique), parish church

304. *Virgin and Child*, ivory. Assisi, San Francesco

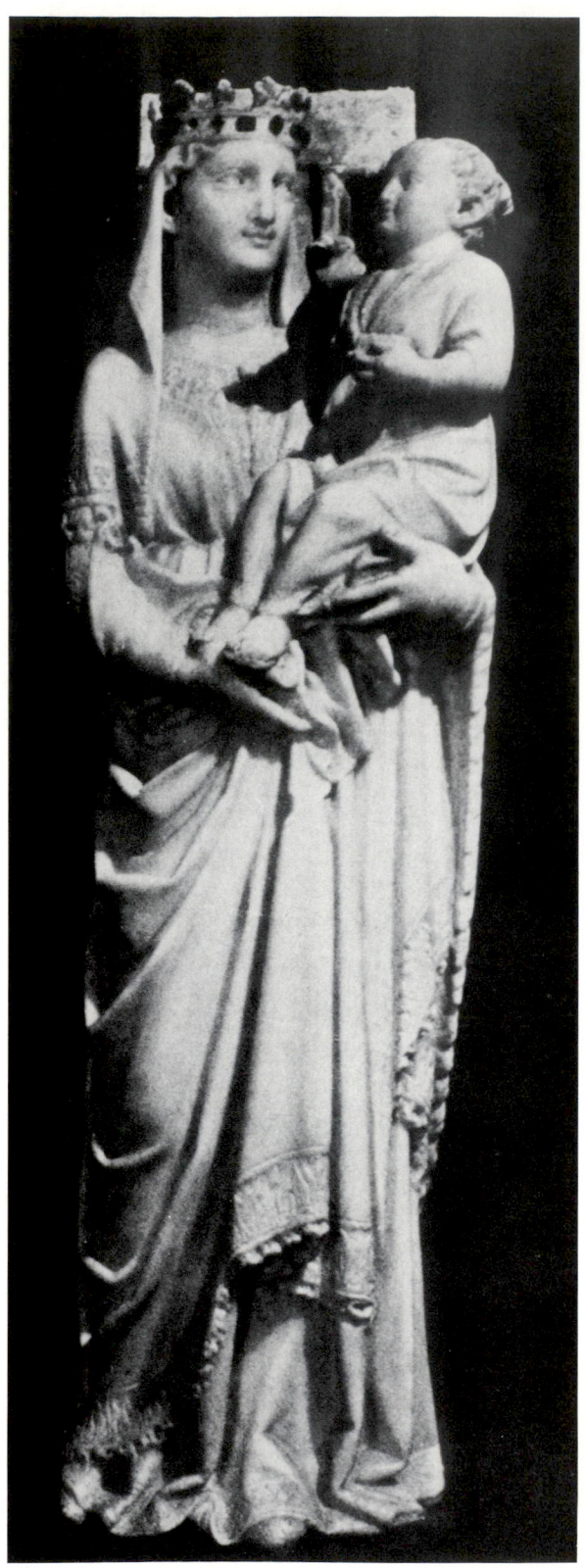

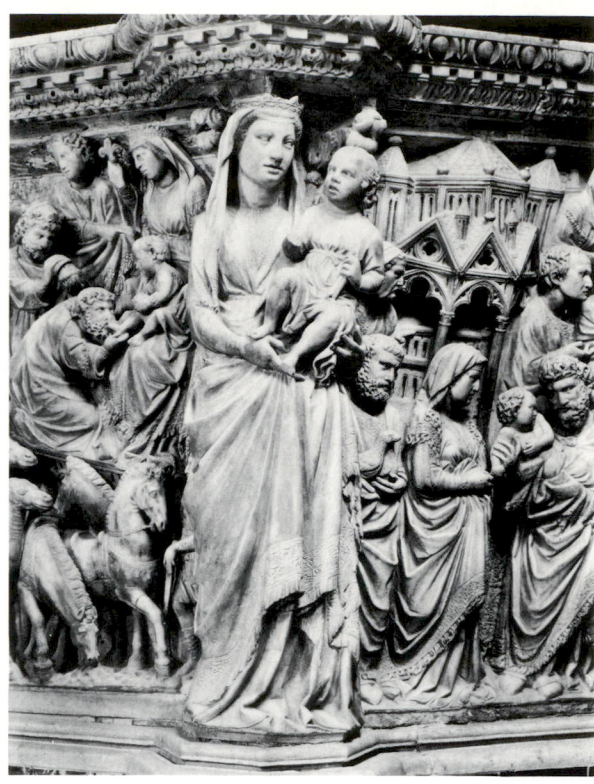

307. Nicola Pisano: Pulpit, detail. Siena Cathedral

306. Nicola Pisano: *Arca di San Domenico*, detail. Bologna, San Domenico

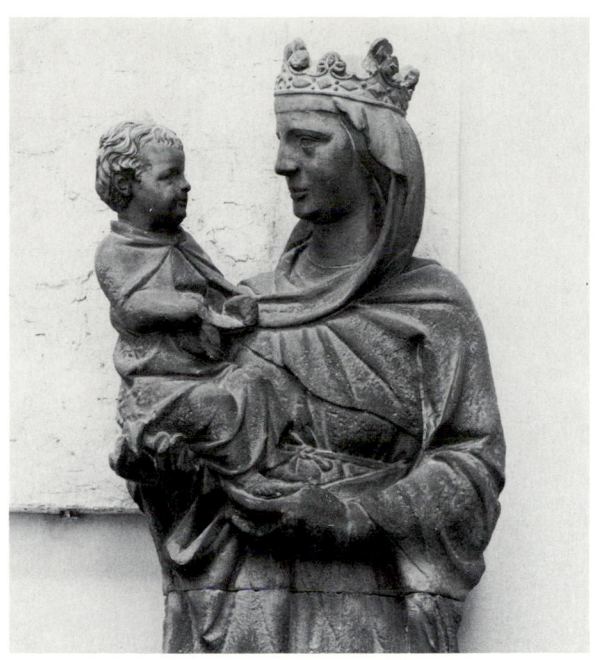

308. Giovanni Pisano: *Madonna and Child*. Pisa, Camposanto

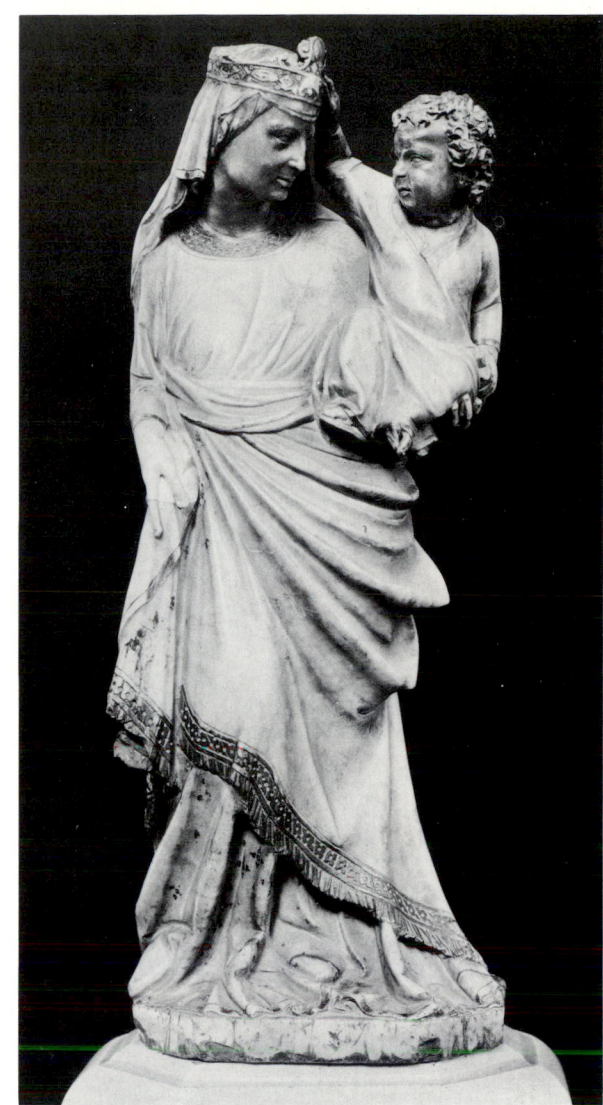

309. Giovanni Pisano: *Madonna and Child*. Prato Cathedral

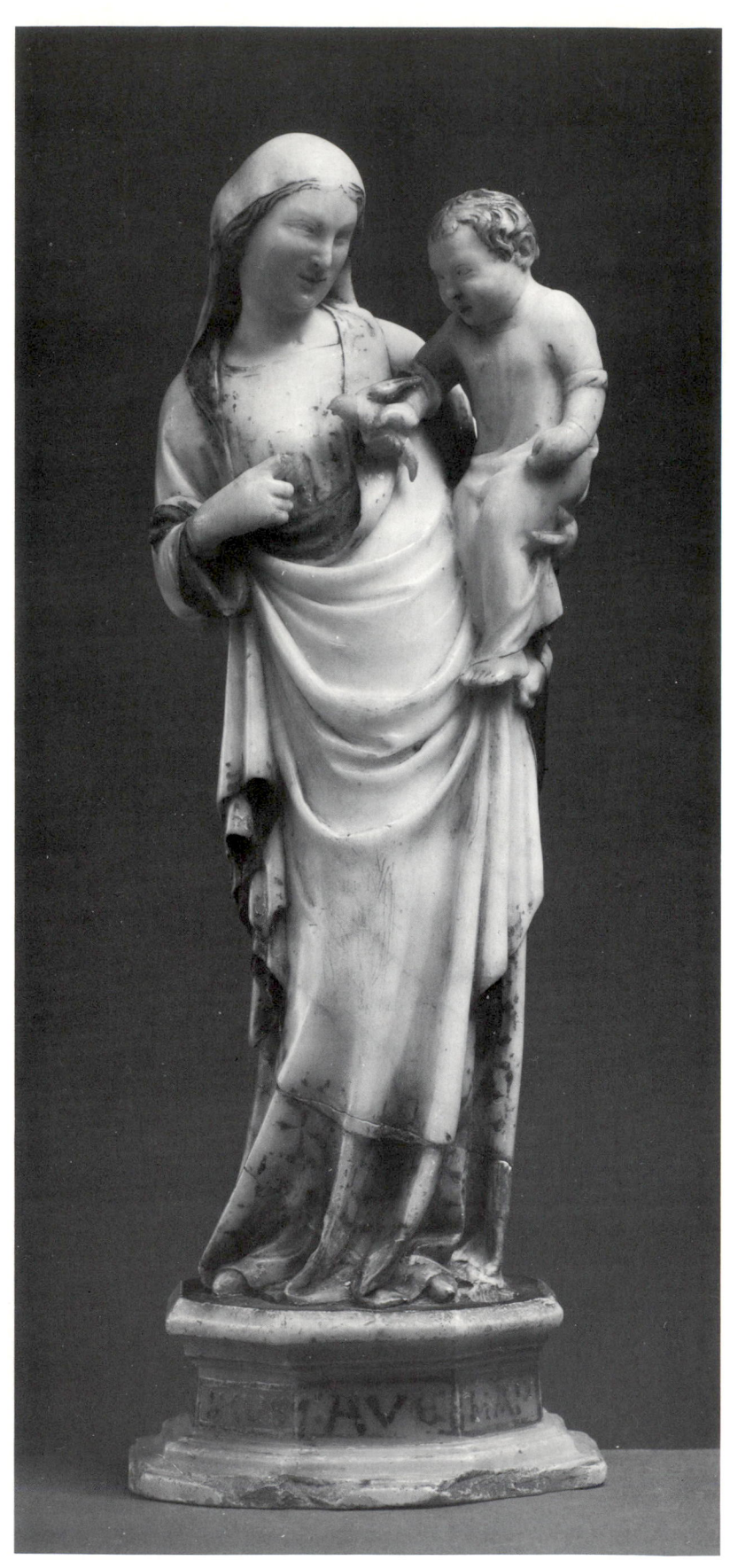

310. Follower of Nino Pisano: *Madonna and Child* (ht 35 cm). Berlin, Staatliche Museen (Dahlem)

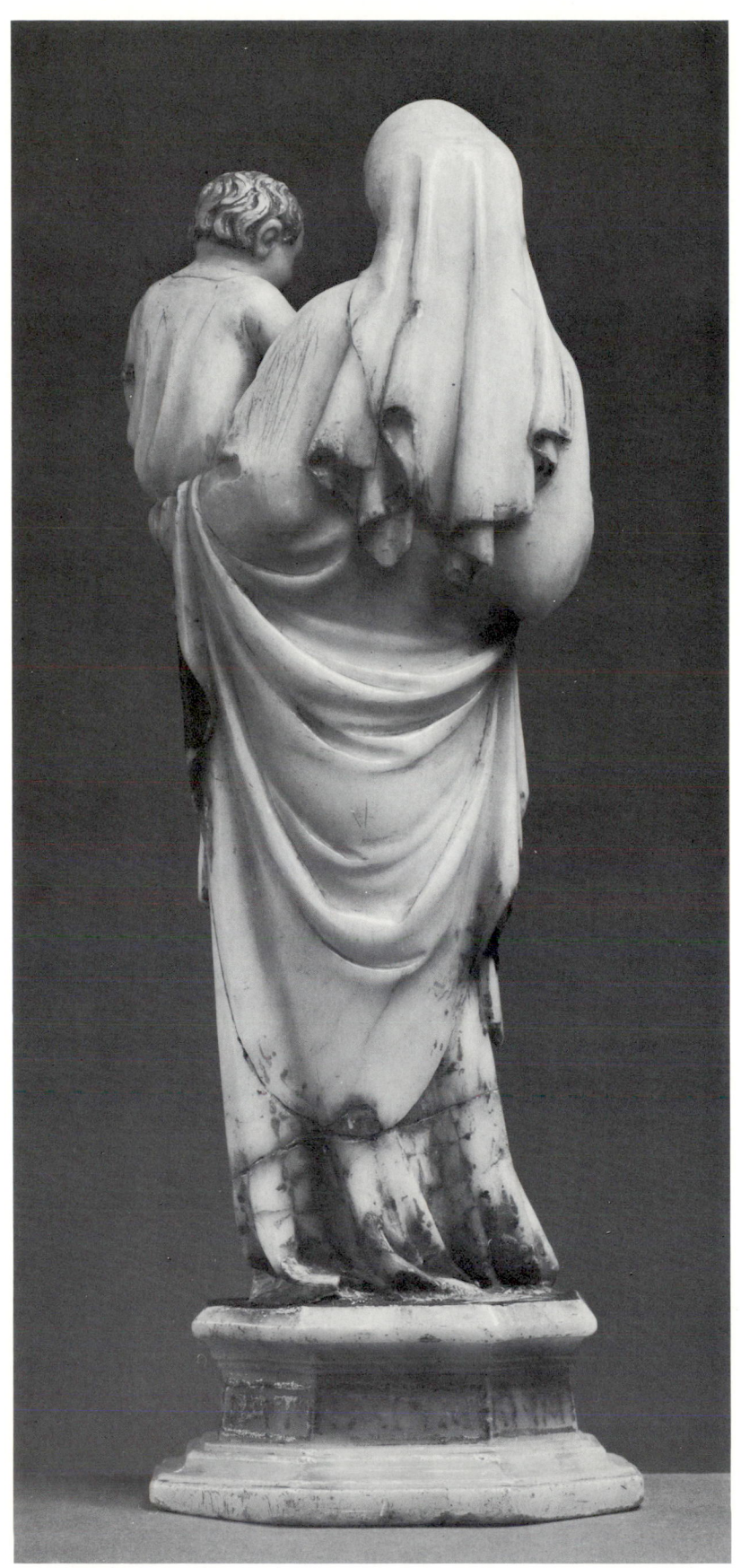

311. Follower of Nino Pisano: *Madonna and Child*. Berlin, Staatliche Museen (Dahlem)

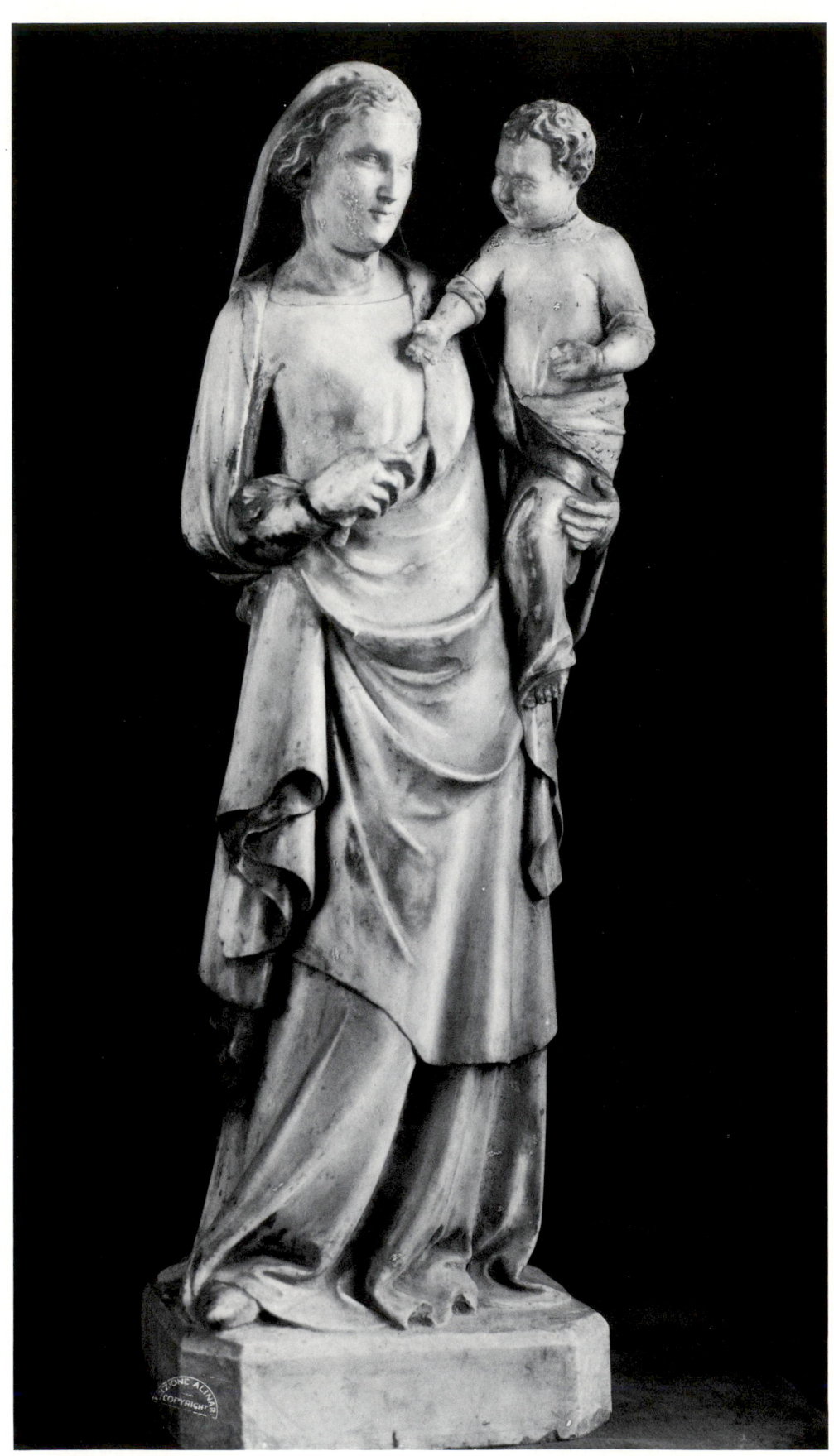

312. Follower of Nino Pisano: *Madonna and Child* (from Sta. Maria a Mantignano) (ht 60 cm). Florence, Archivescovile

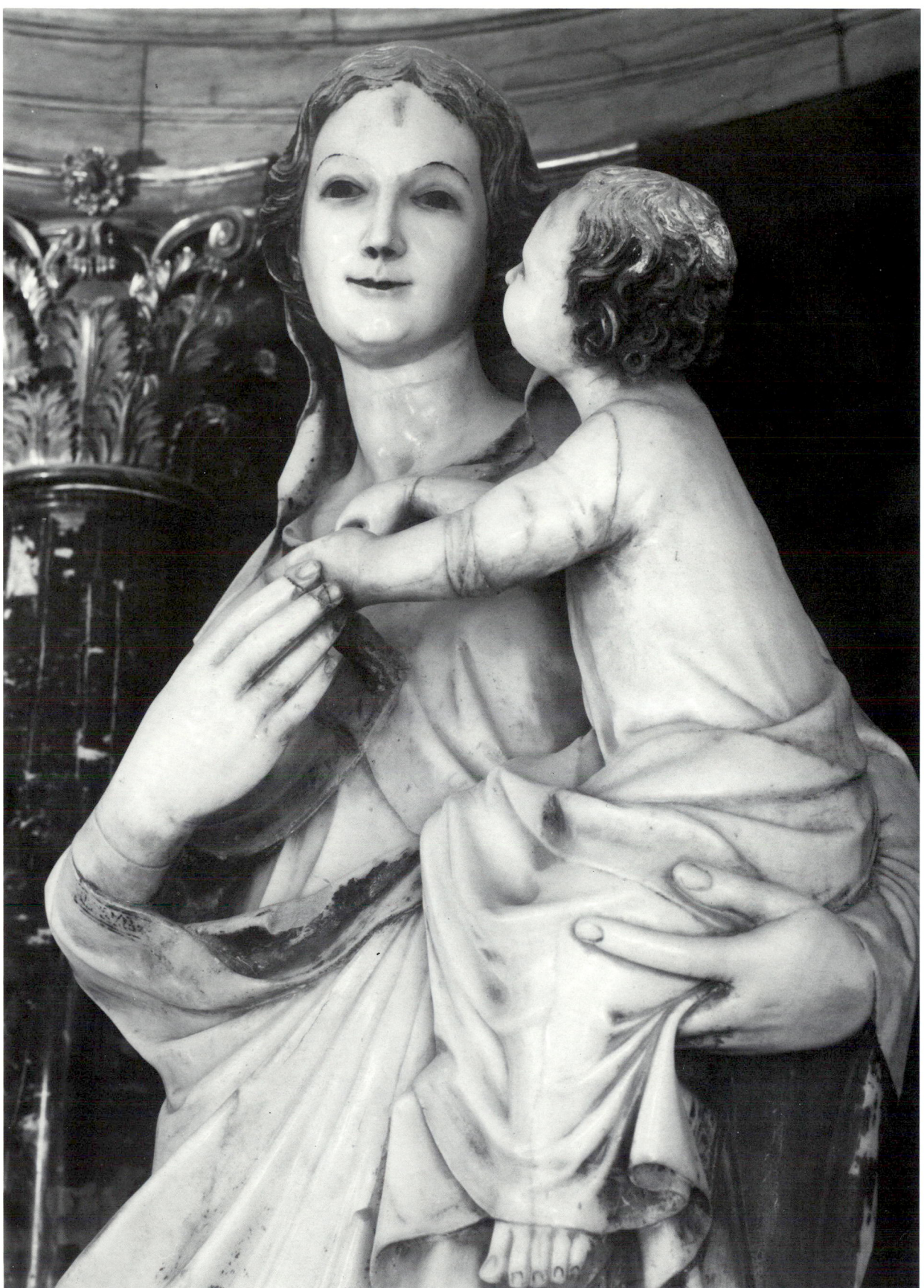

313. Master of the Sta. Caterina Annunciation (?): *Madonna and Child*. Trapani, Santissima Annunziata

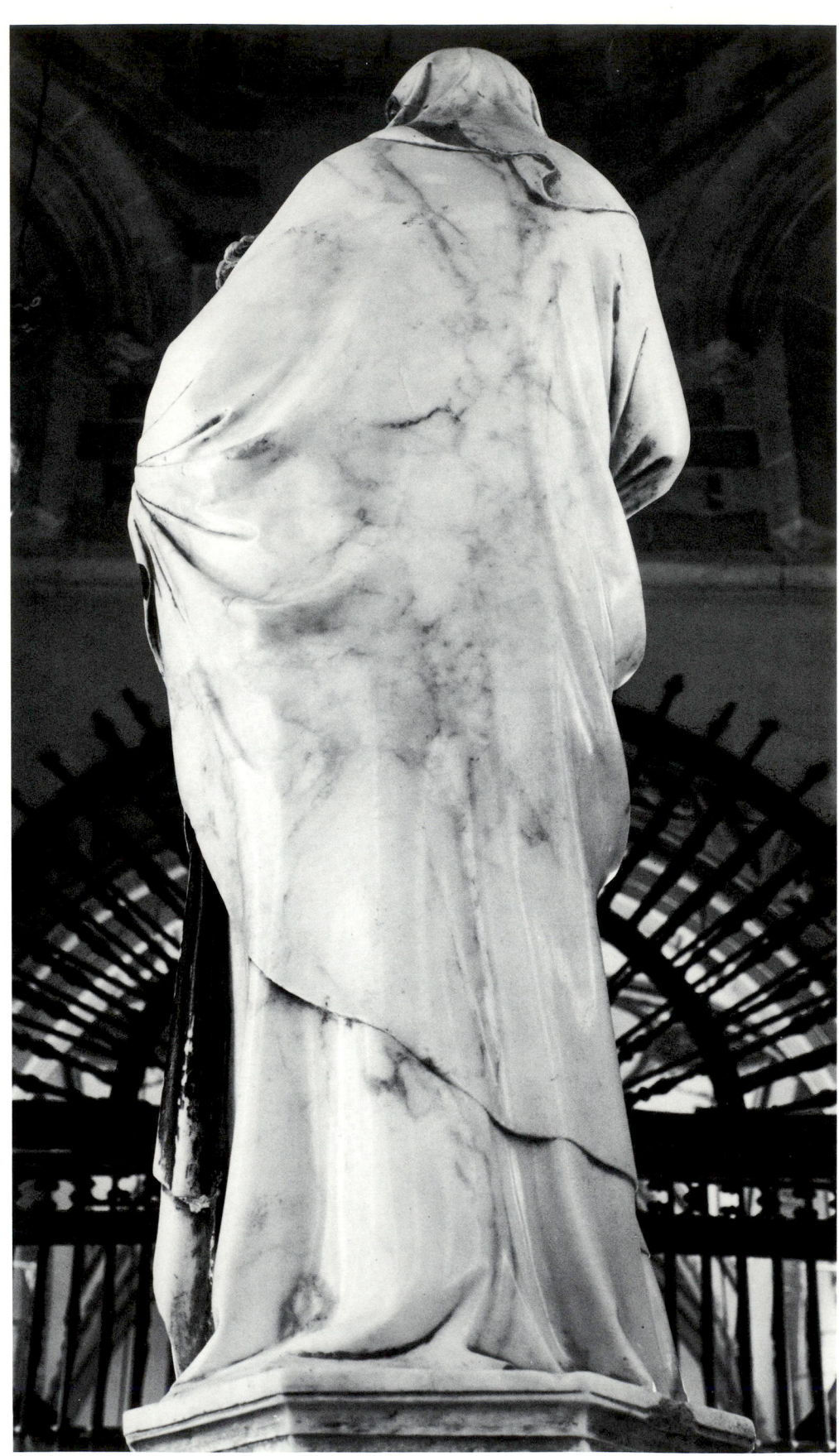

314. Master of the Sta. Caterina Annunciation (?): *Madonna and Child*. Trapani, Santissima Annunziata

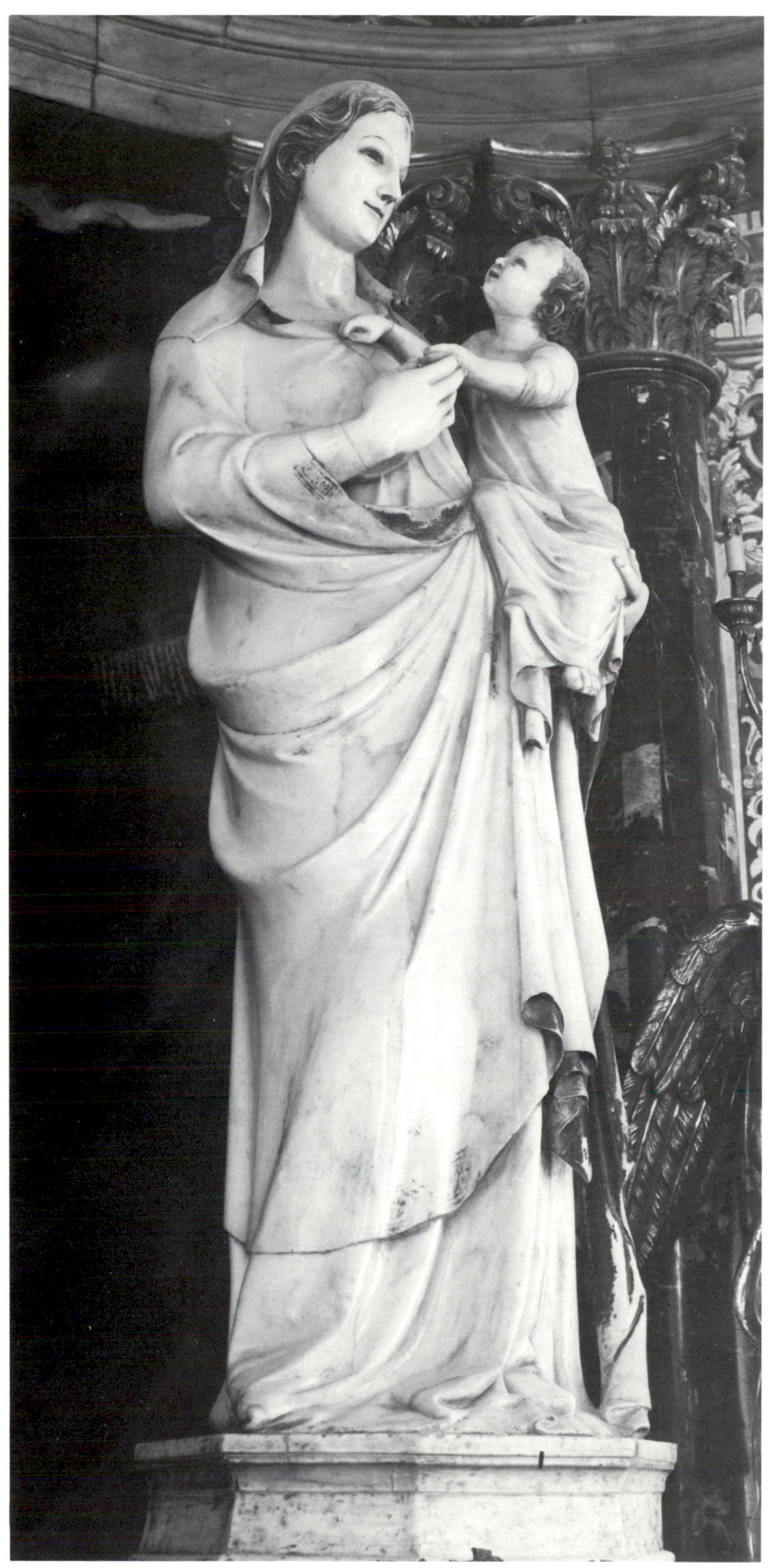

315. Master of the Sta. Caterina Annunciation (?): *Madonna and Child*. Trapani, Santissima Annunziata

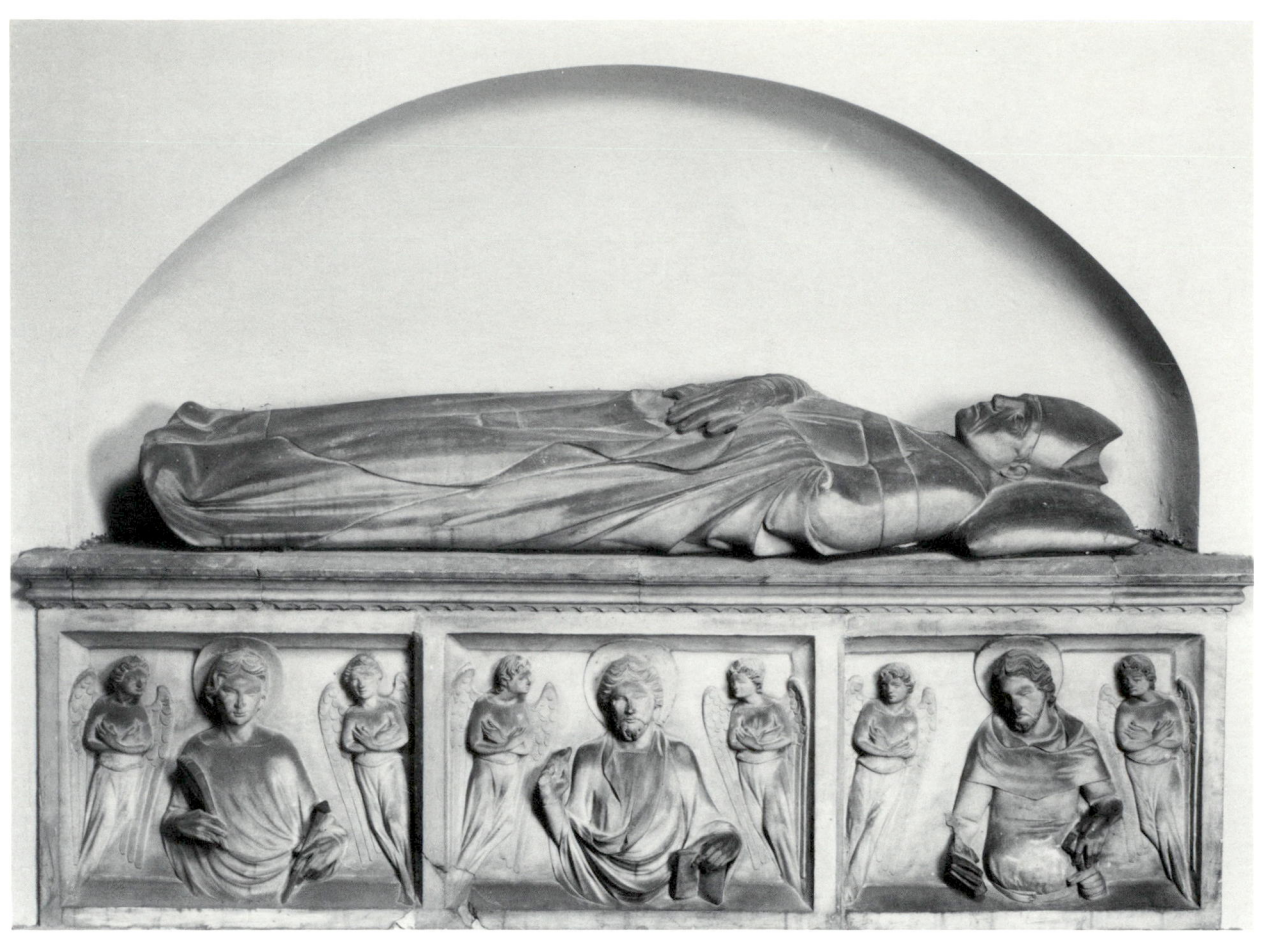

316. Nino Pisano and workshop: "Scherlatti" Monument (reliefs from Moricotti tomb) (sarcophagus: ht 51 cm, width 197 cm). Pisa, Camposanto

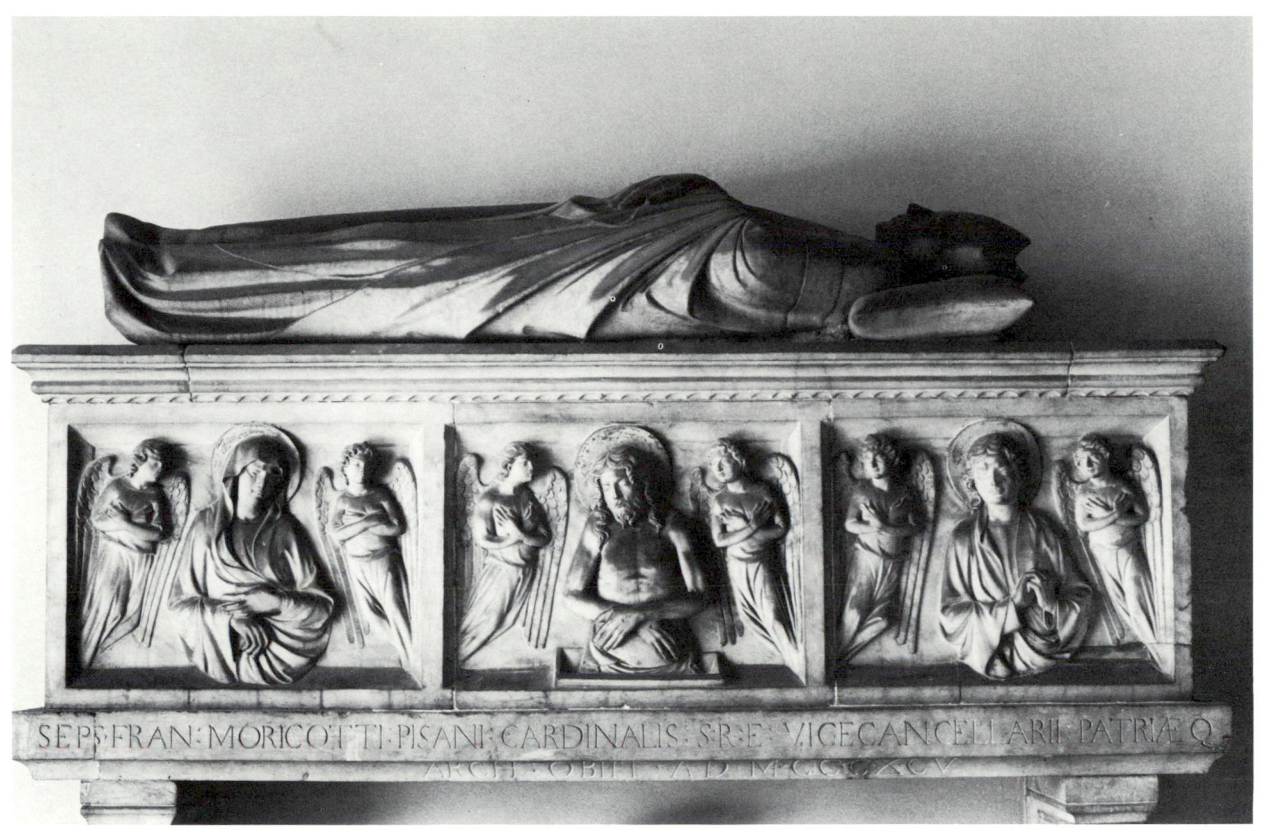

317. Nino Pisano and workshop: "Moricotti" Monument (reliefs from Scherlatti tomb) (sarcophagus: ht 51 cm, width 199 cm). Pisa, Camposanto

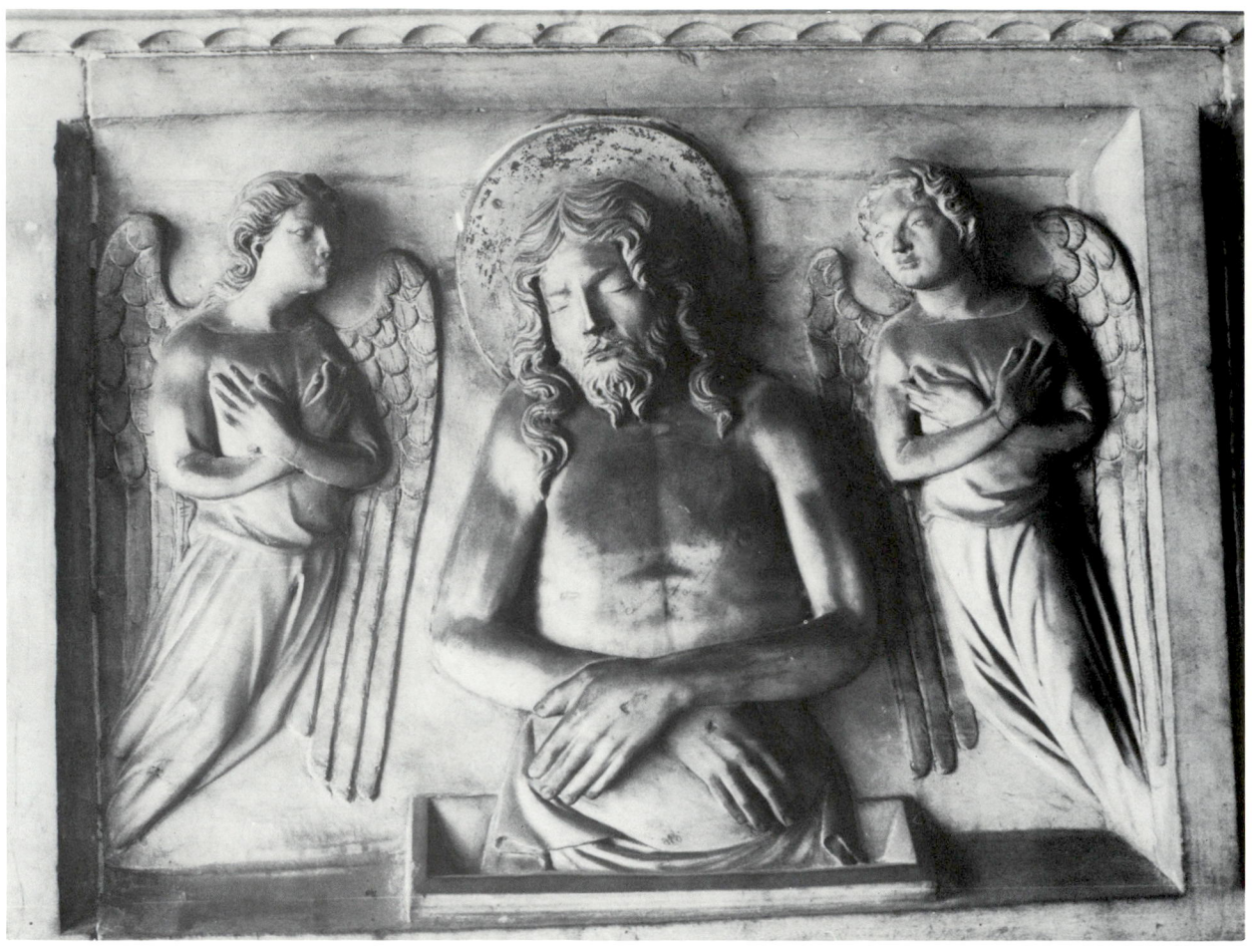

318. Nino Pisano: "Moricotti" Monument, detail. Pisa, Camposanto

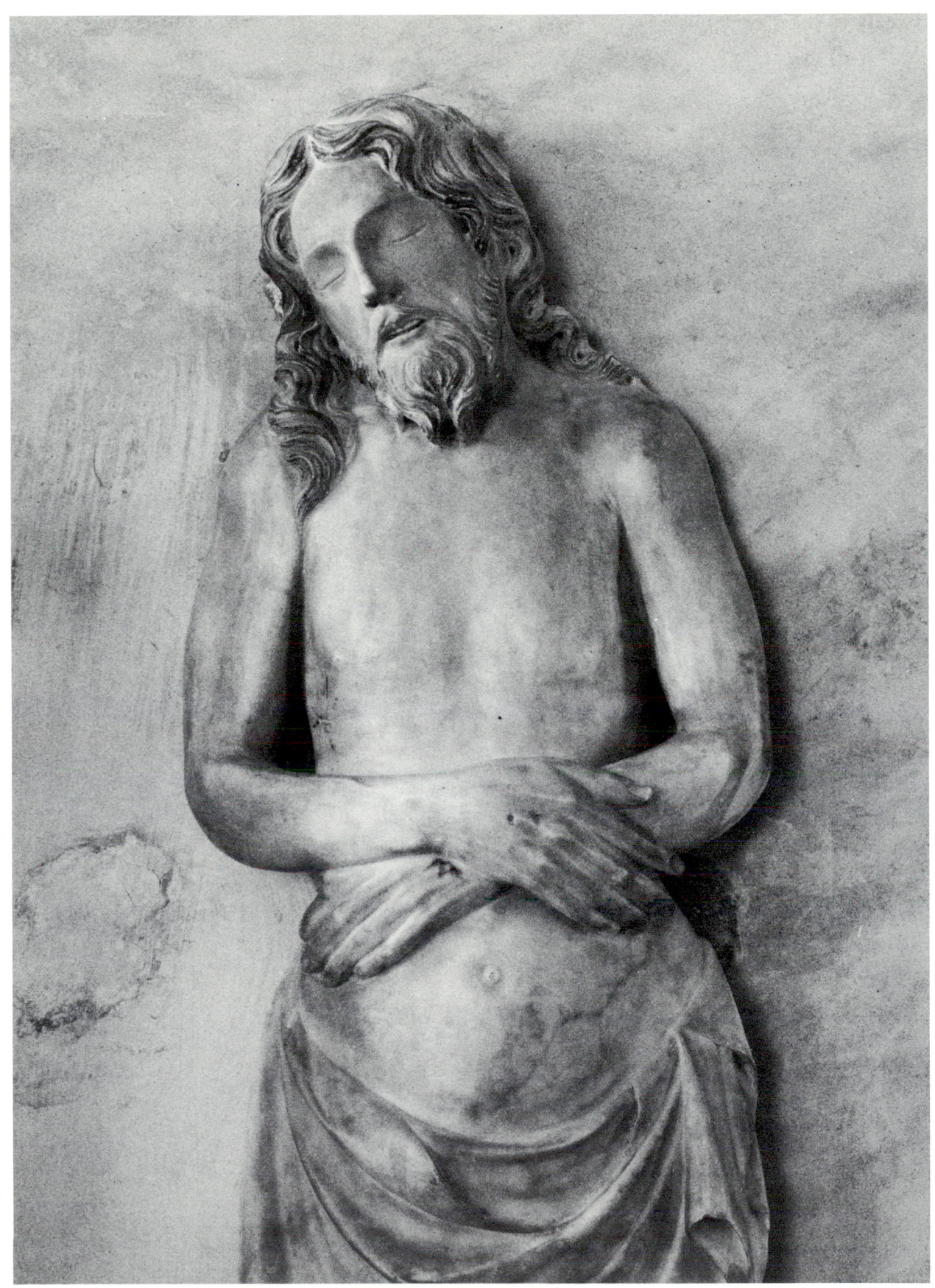

319. Nino Pisano: *Man of Sorrows* (ht 80 cm, width 35 cm). Pisa, Museo di San Matteo

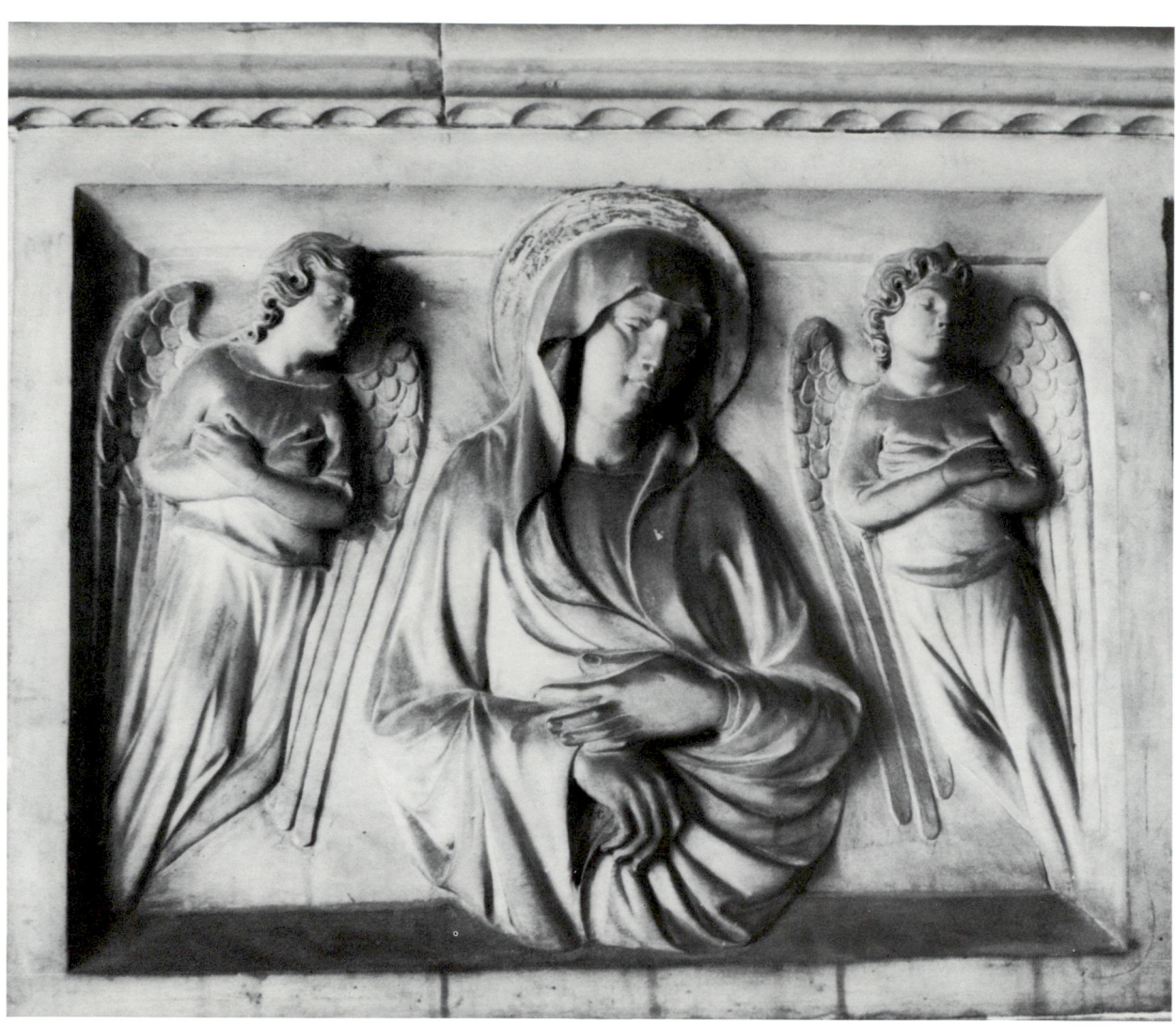

320. Nino Pisano: "Moricotti" Monument, detail. Pisa, Camposanto

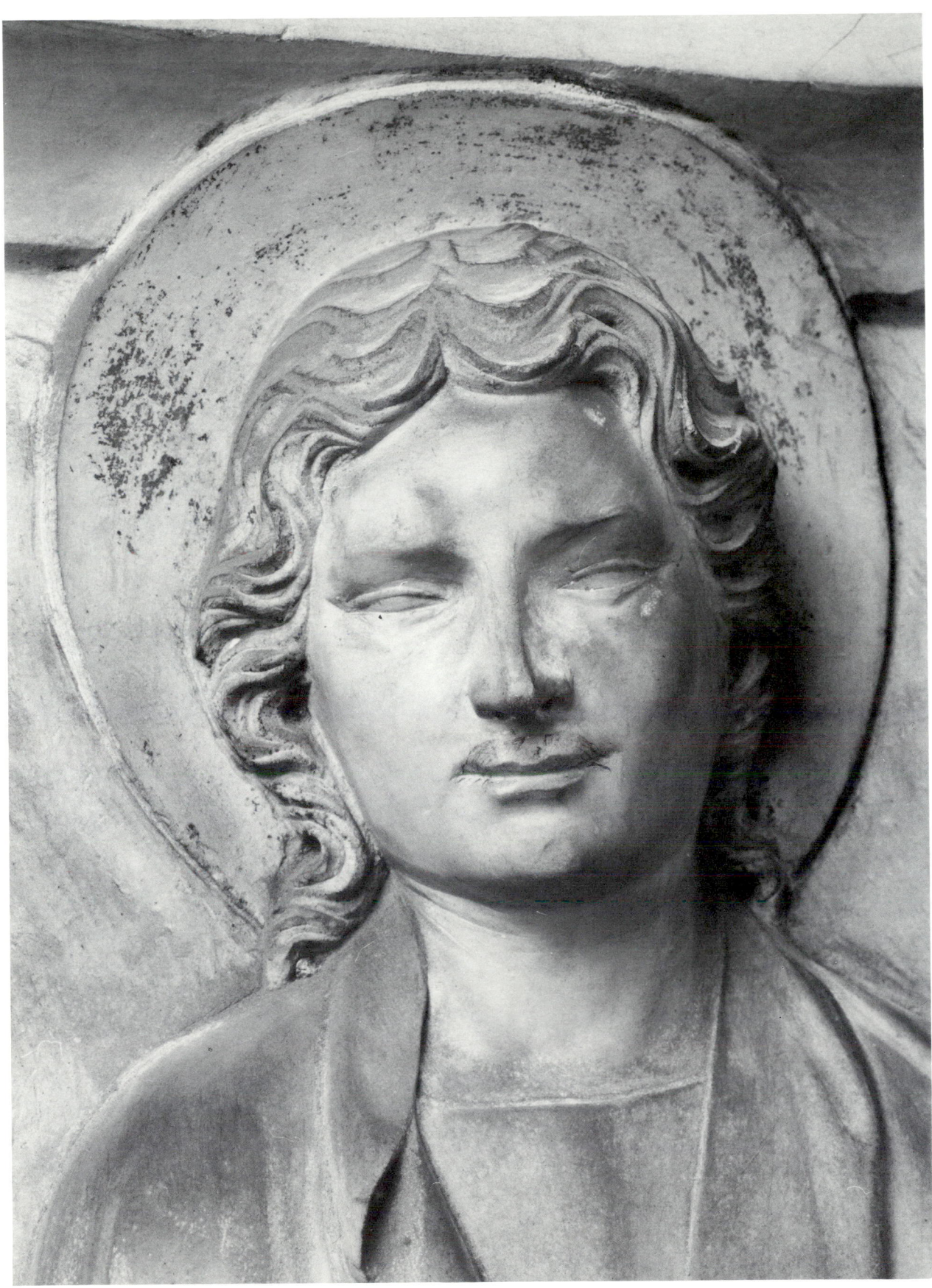

321. Nino Pisano: "Moricotti" Monument, detail. Pisa, Camposanto

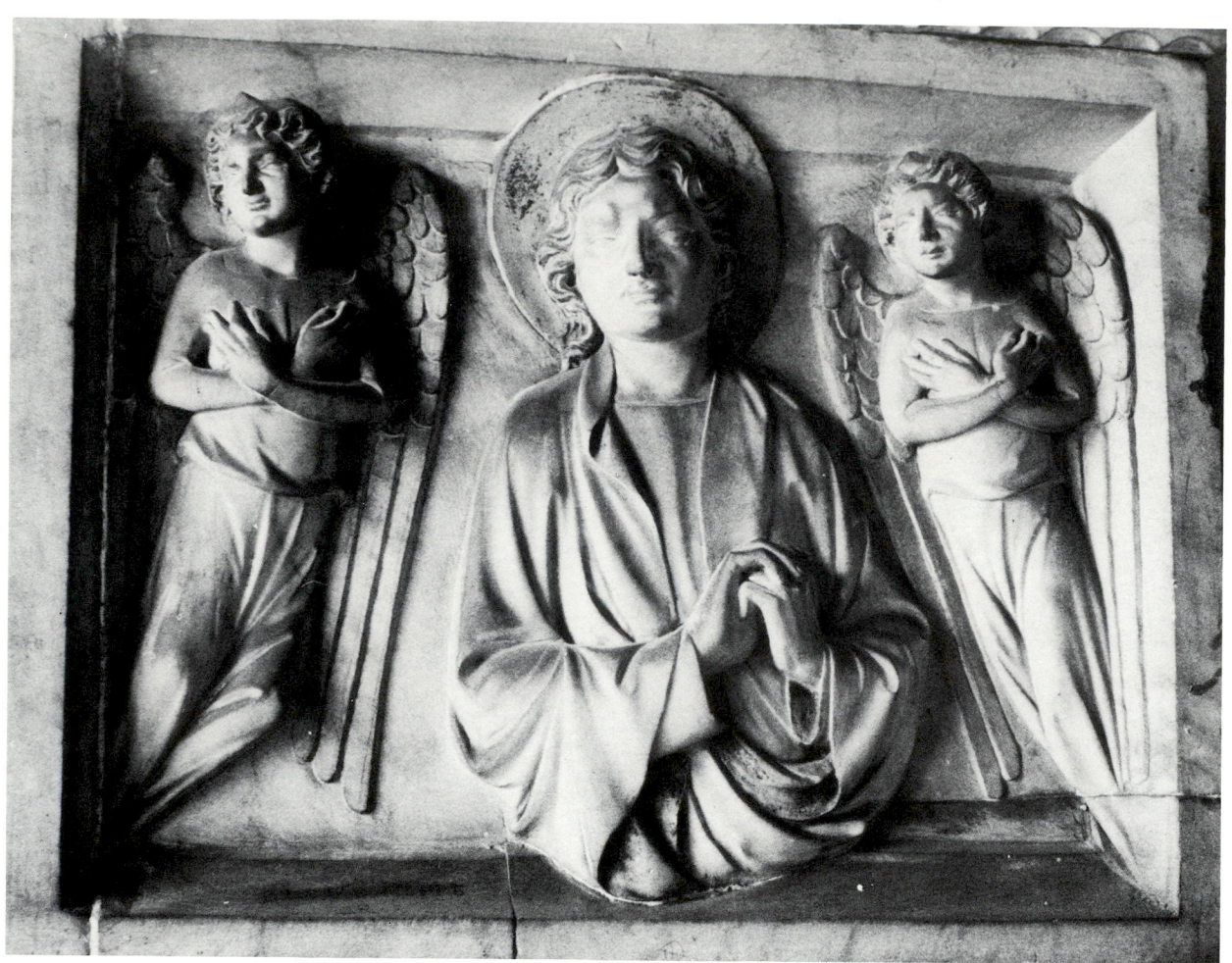

322. Nino Pisano: "Moricotti" Monument, detail. Pisa, Camposanto

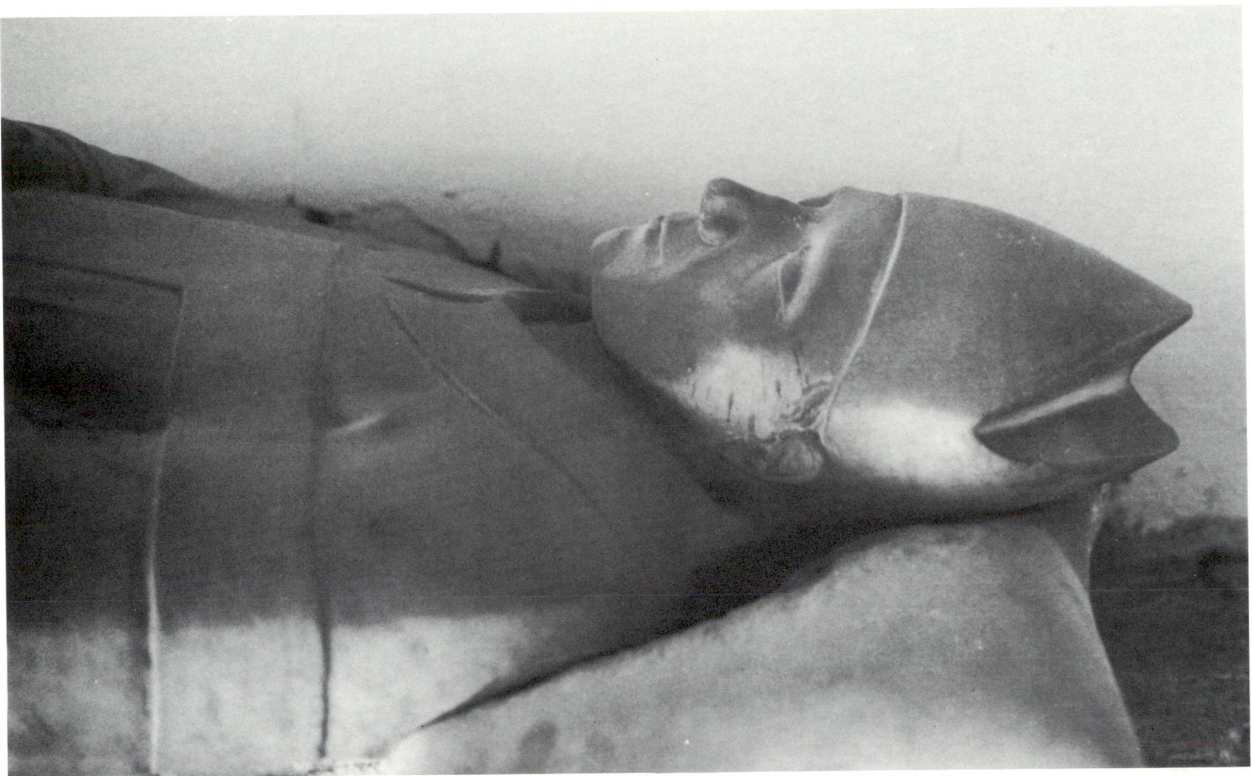

323. Nino Pisano workshop: Effigy of Moricotti, detail. Pisa, Camposanto

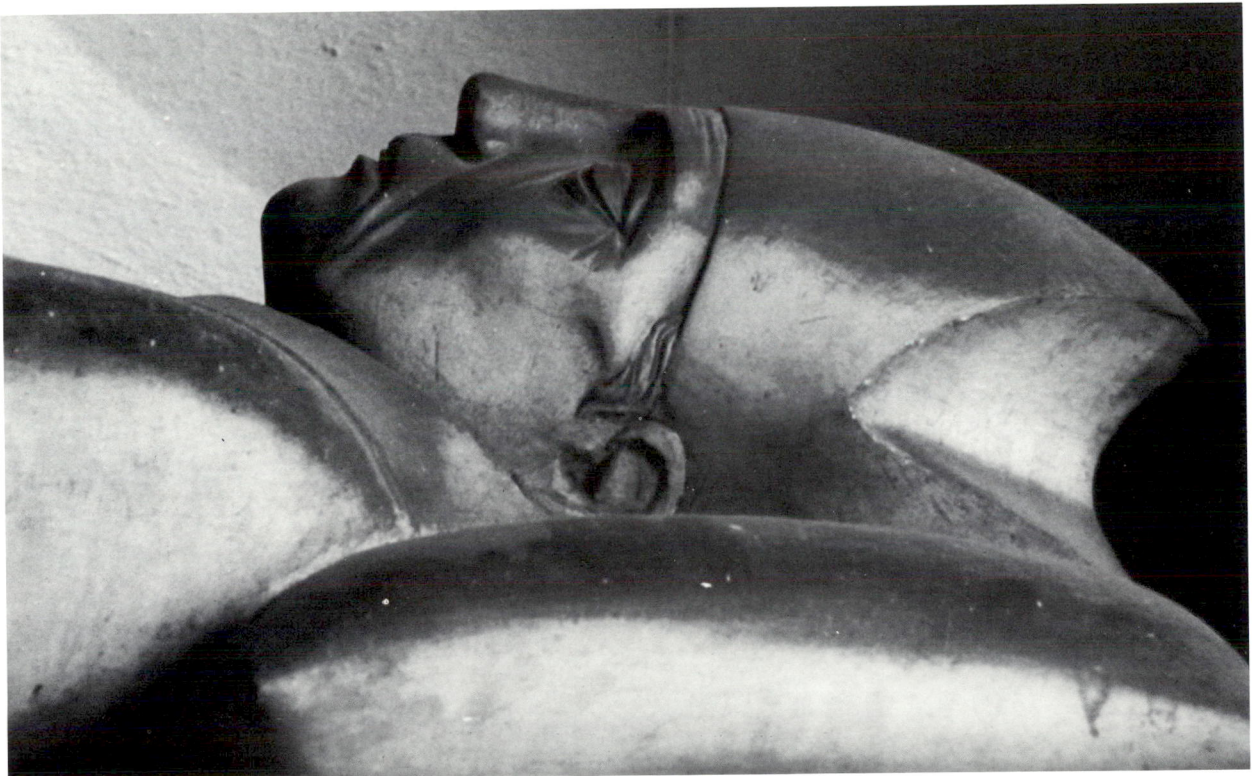

324. Nino Pisano: Effigy of Scherlatti, detail. Pisa, Camposanto

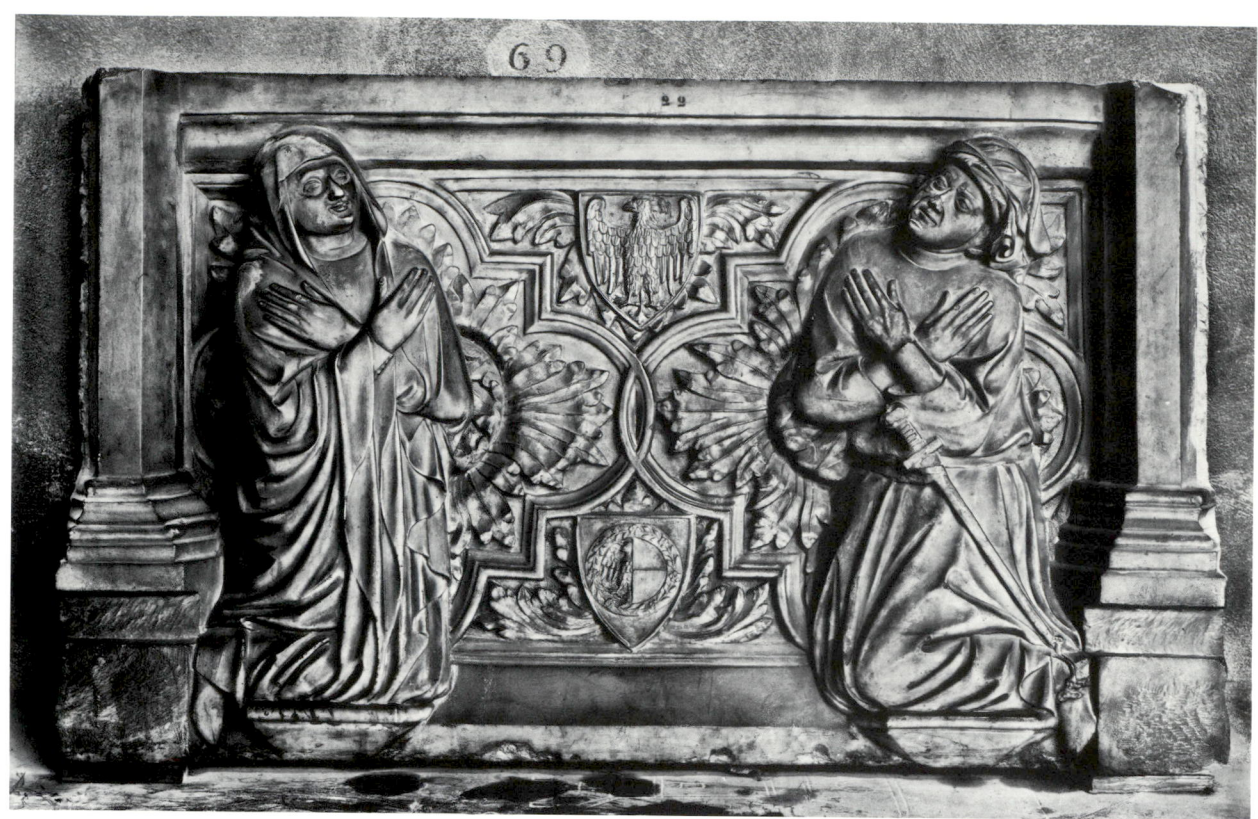

325. Upezzinghi Marriage Relief. Pisa, Camposanto

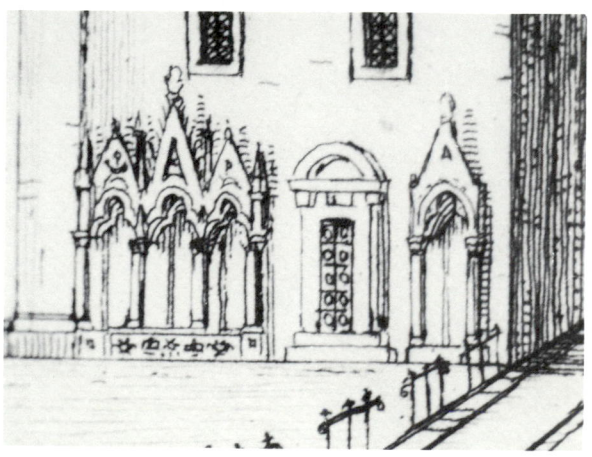

326. Polloni: Piazza San Francesco, detail. From *Vedute di Pisa*, 1835.

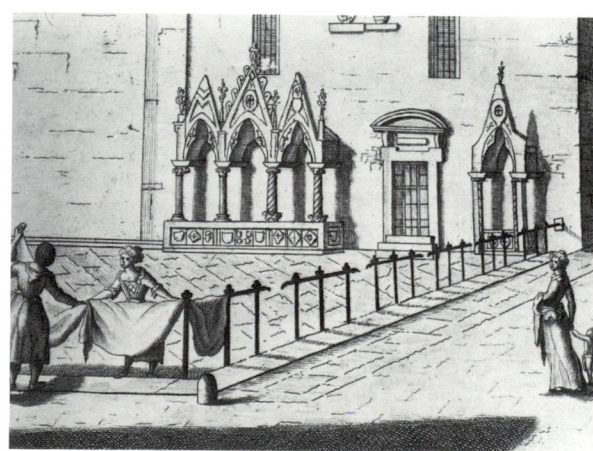

327. Ferdinando Fambrino: Piazza San Francesco, detail, engraving, 1783. Pisa, Soprintendenza

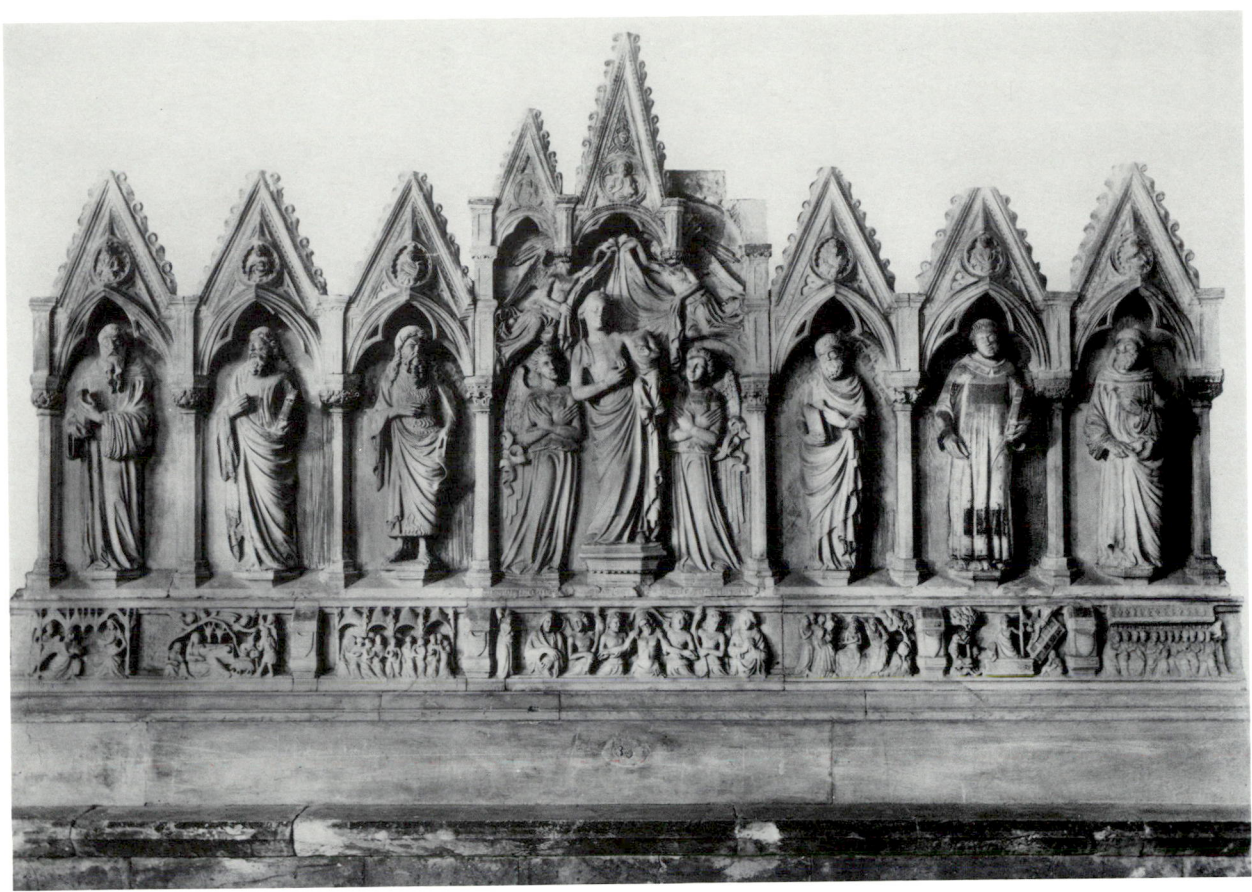

328. Tommaso Pisano: High Altar (width at base 385 cm). Pisa, San Francesco

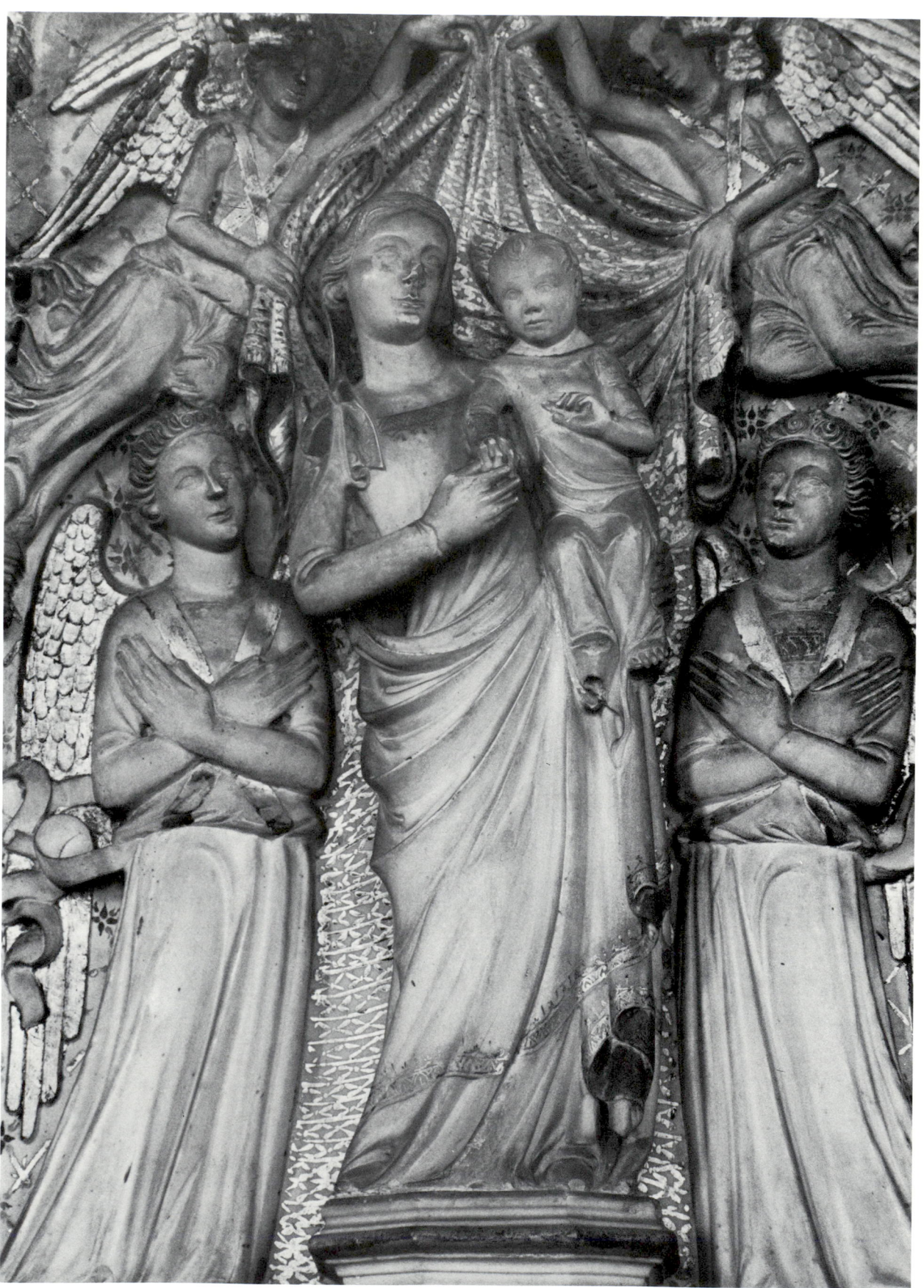

329. Tommaso Pisano: High Altar, detail. Pisa, San Francesco

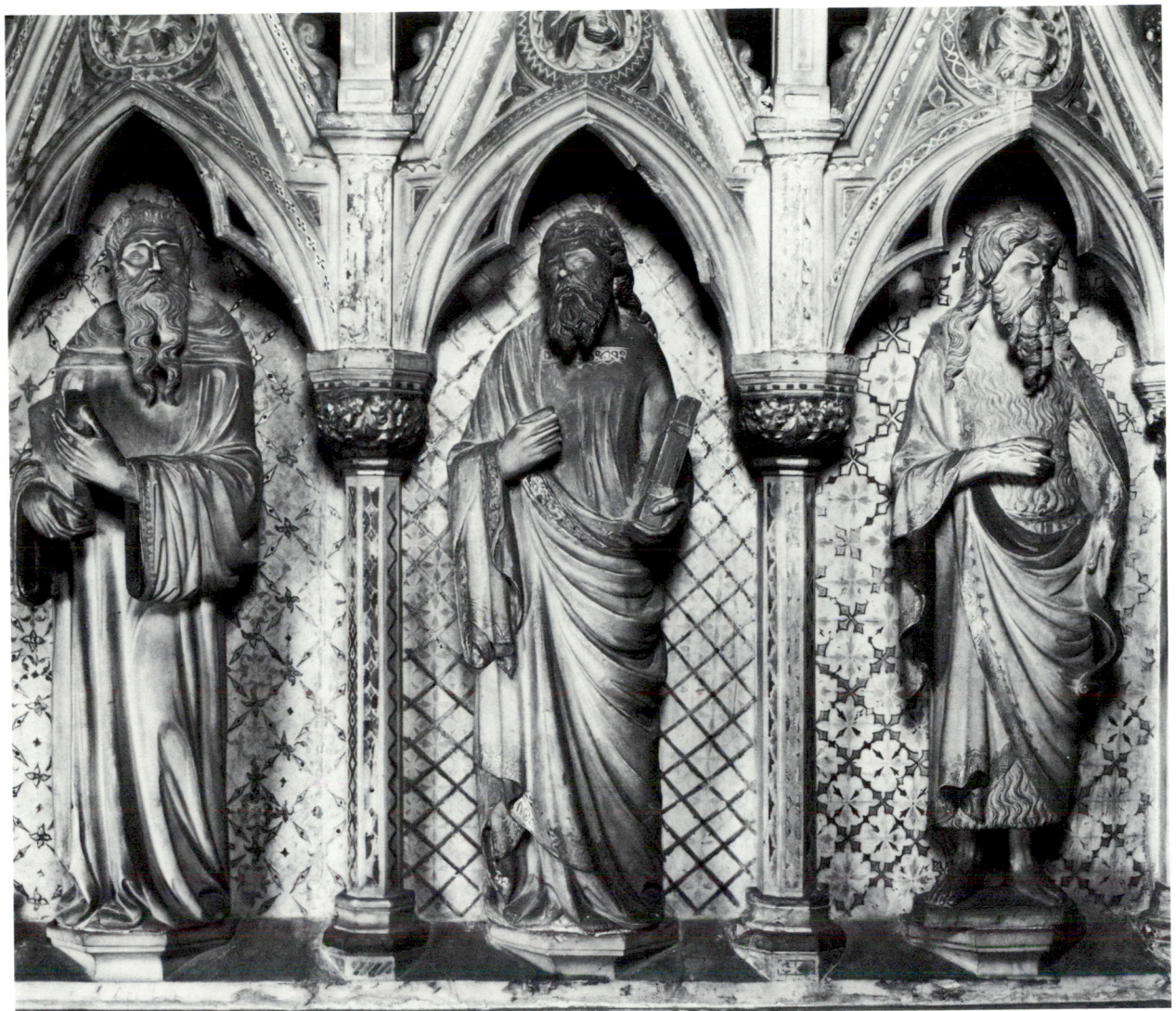

330. Tommaso Pisano: High Altar, detail. Pisa, San Francesco

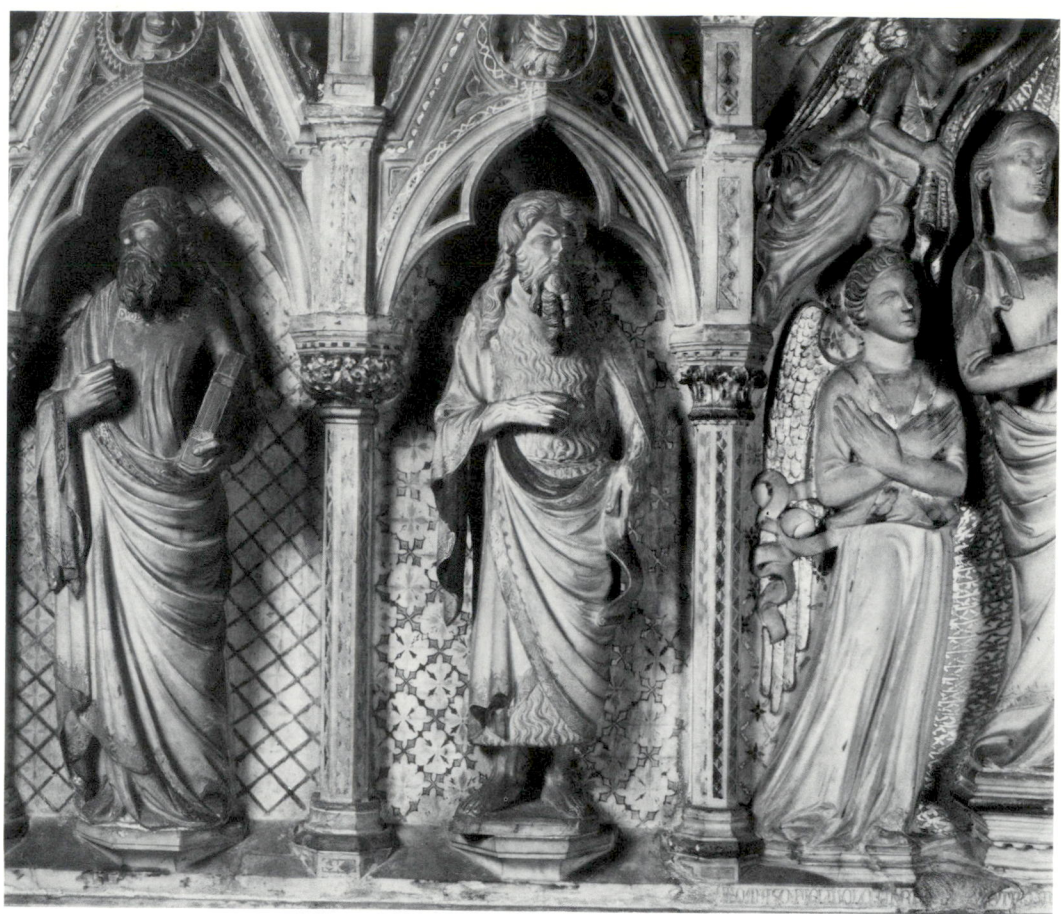

331. Tommaso Pisano: High Altar, detail. Pisa, San Francesco

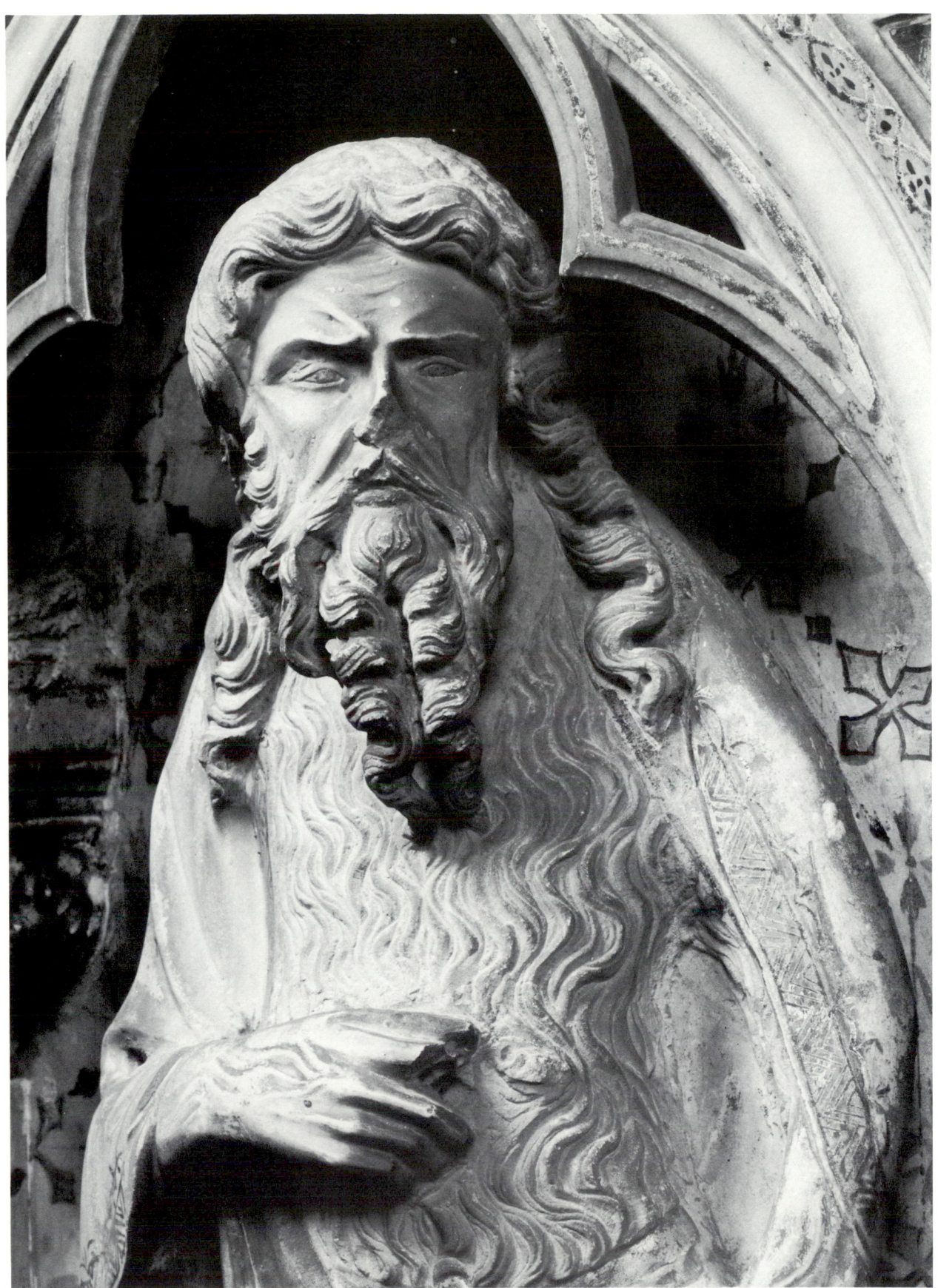

332. Tommaso Pisano: High Altar, detail. Pisa, San Francesco

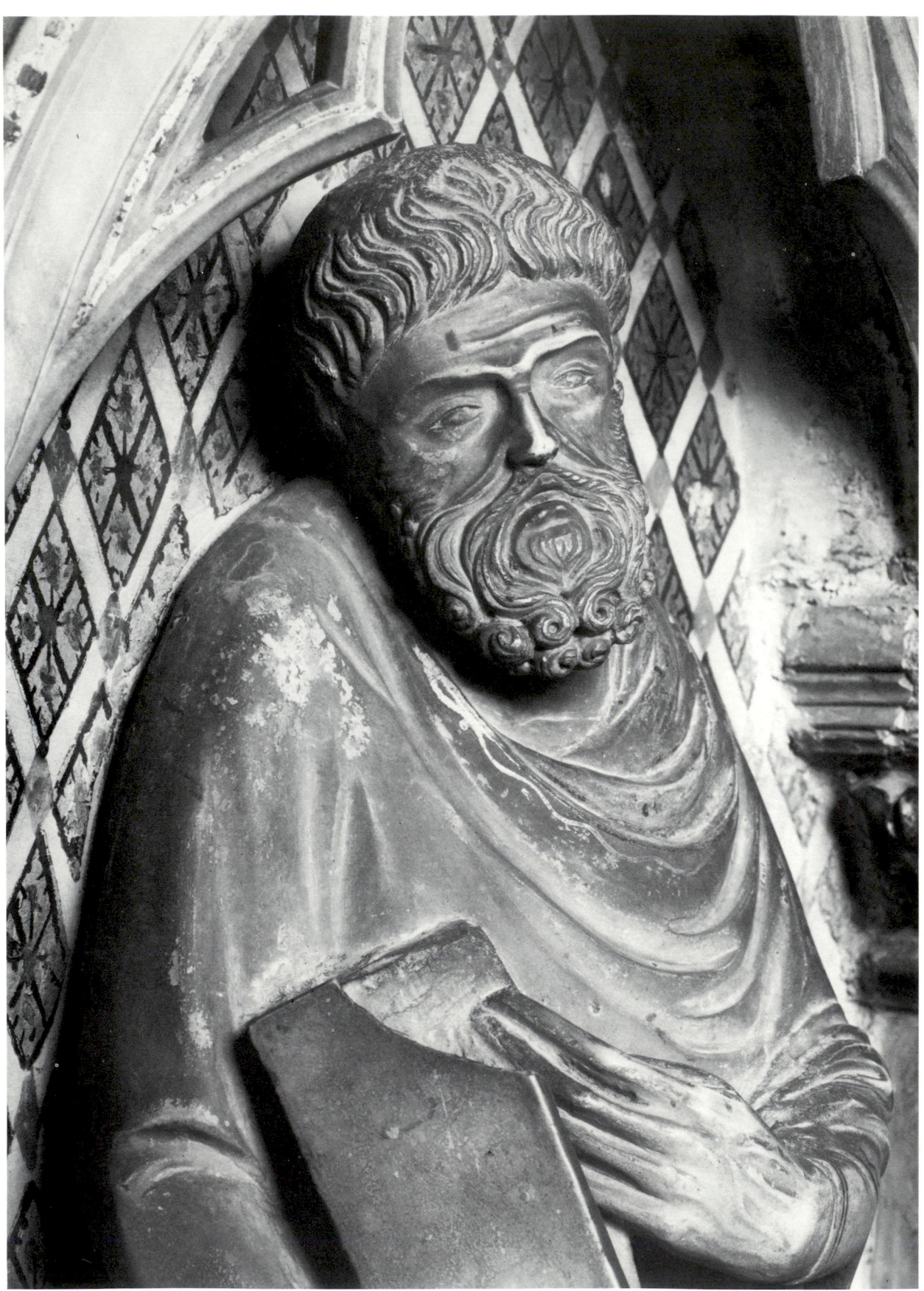

333. Tommaso Pisano: High Altar, detail. Pisa, San Francesco

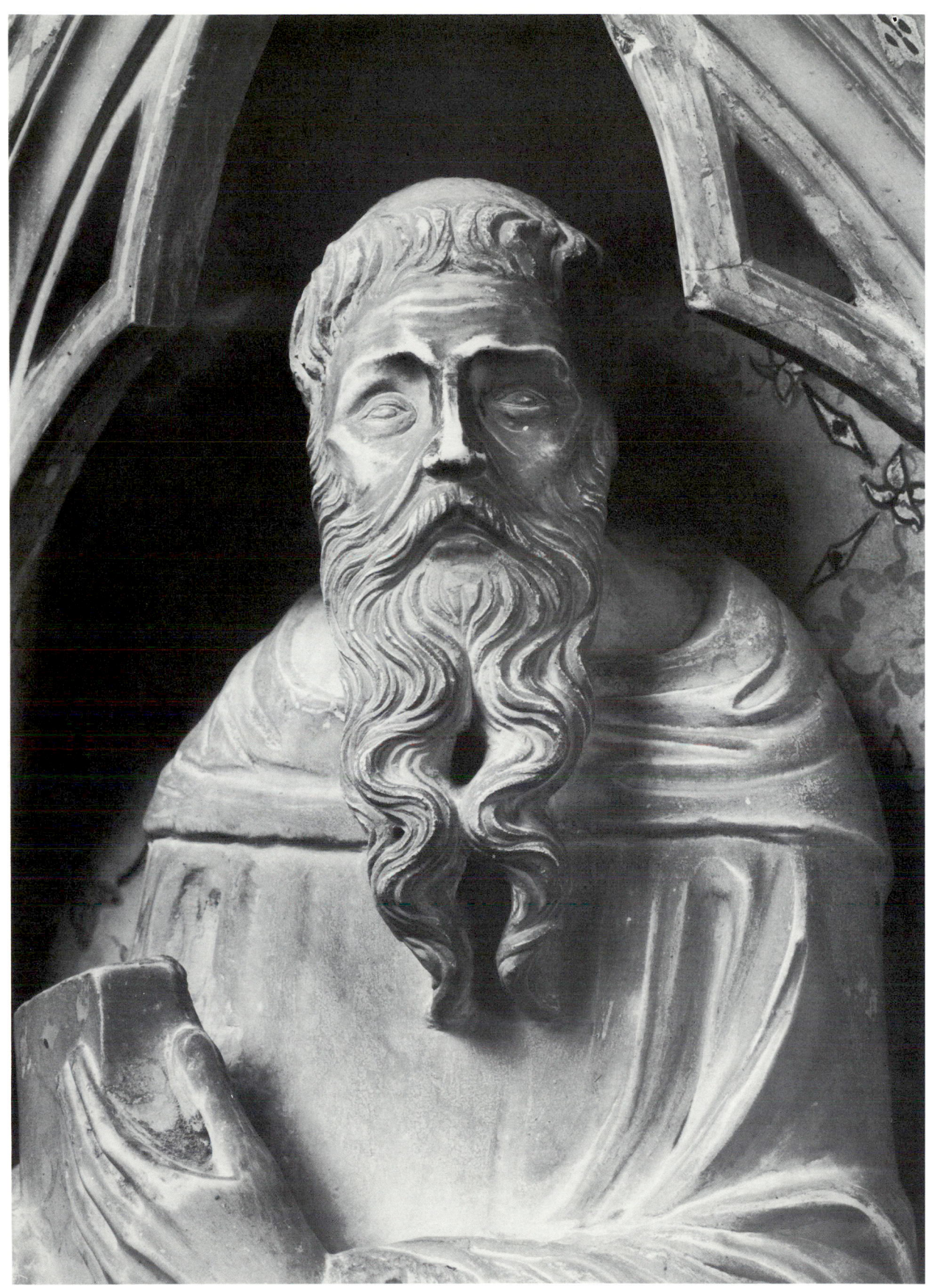

334. Tommaso Pisano: High Altar, detail. Pisa, San Francesco

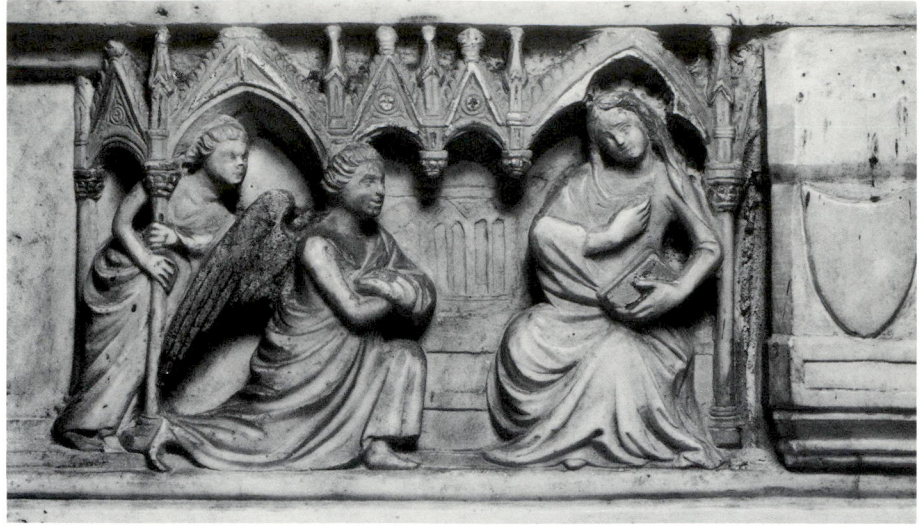

335. Tommaso Pisano: High Altar, detail. Pisa, San Francesco

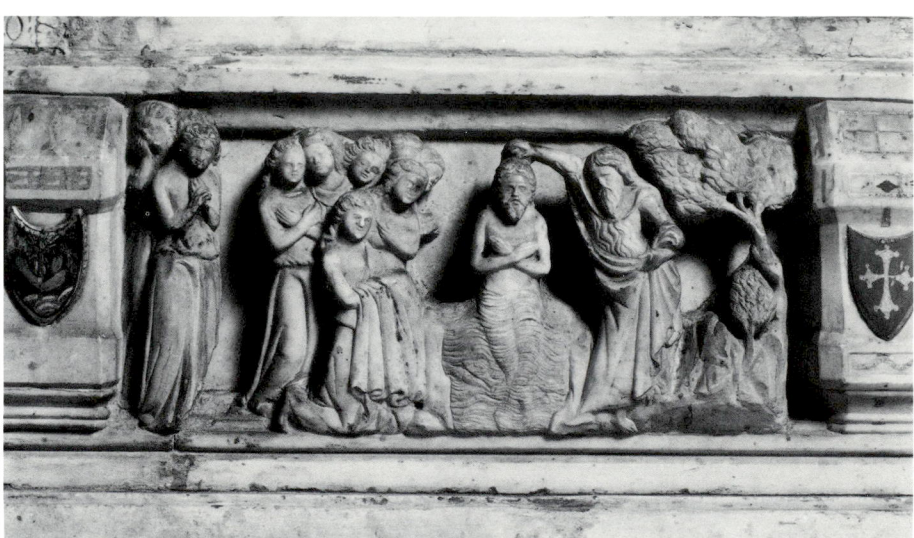

336. Tommaso Pisano: High Altar, detail. Pisa, San Francesco

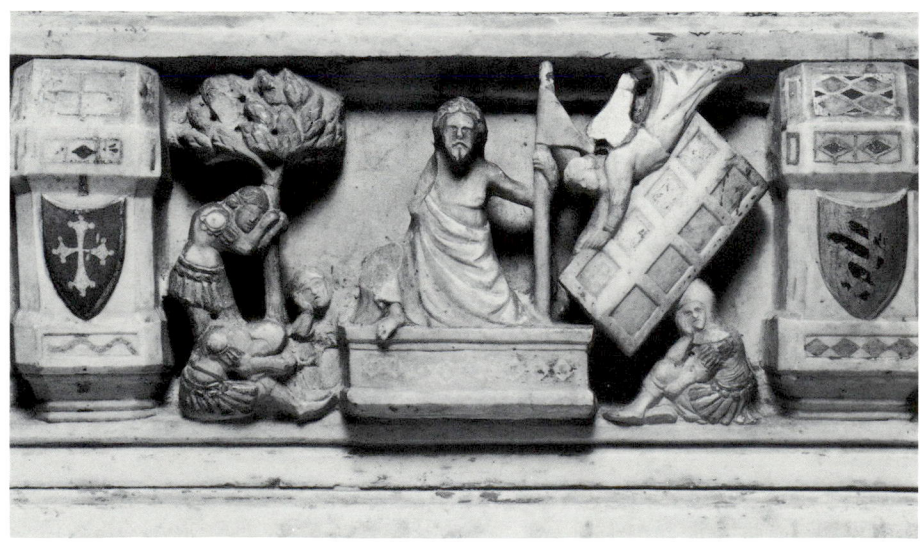

337. Tommaso Pisano: High Altar, detail. Pisa, San Francesco

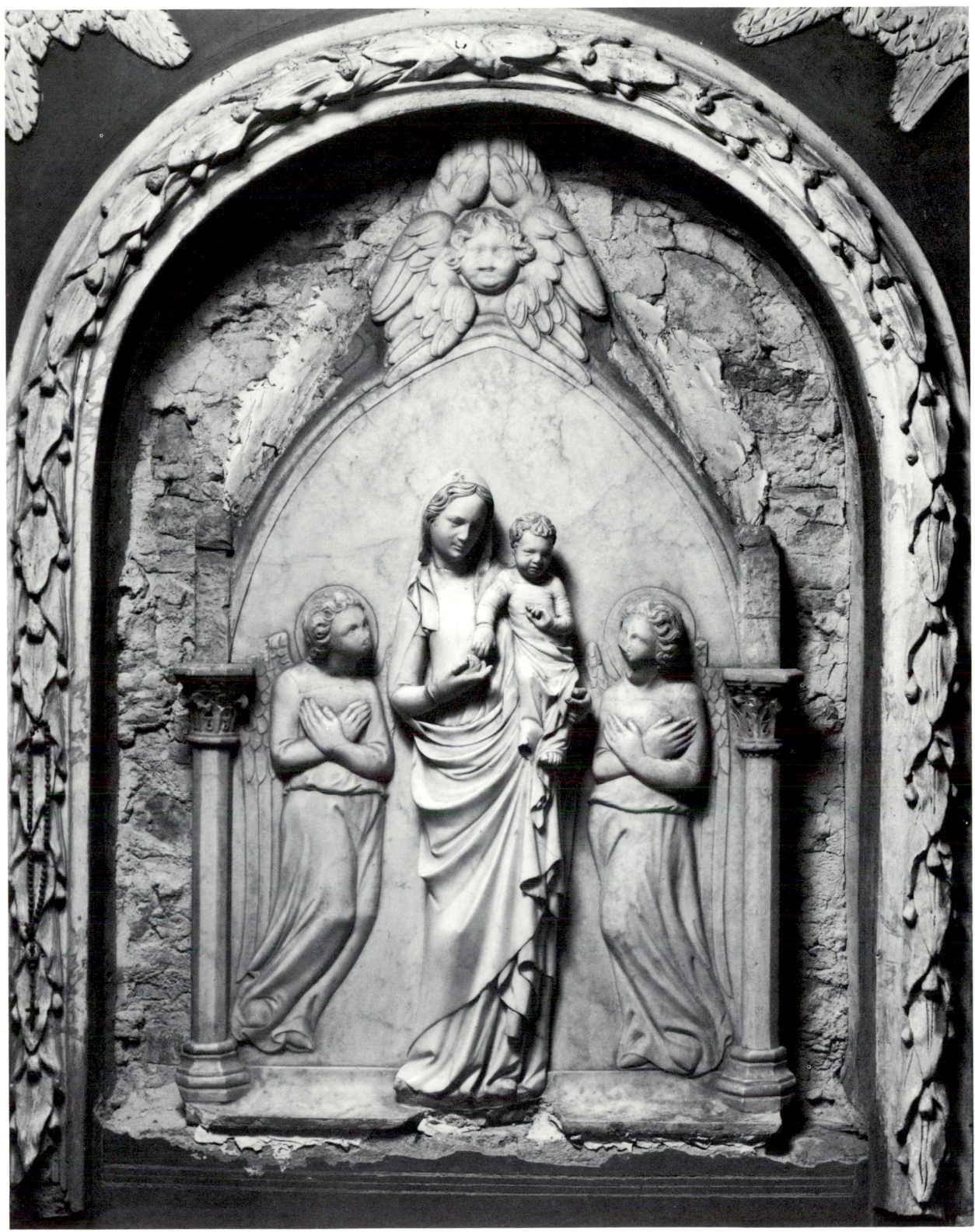

338. Follower of Nino Pisano: *Madonna and Child and Angels*. Arliano (Lucca), Pieve di San Giovanni Battista

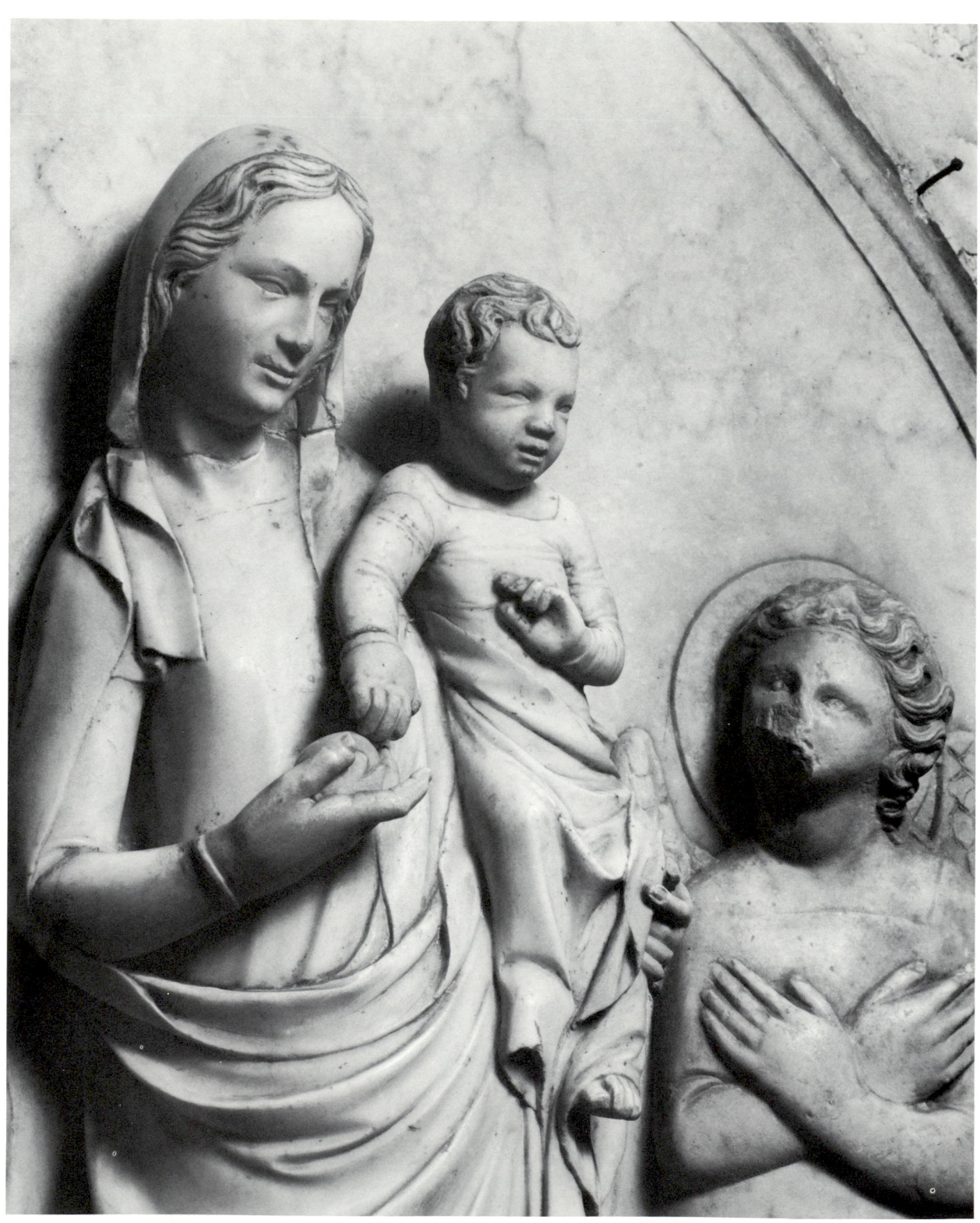

339. Follower of Nino Pisano: *Madonna and Child and Angels*, detail. Arliano (Lucca), Pieve di San Giovanni Battista

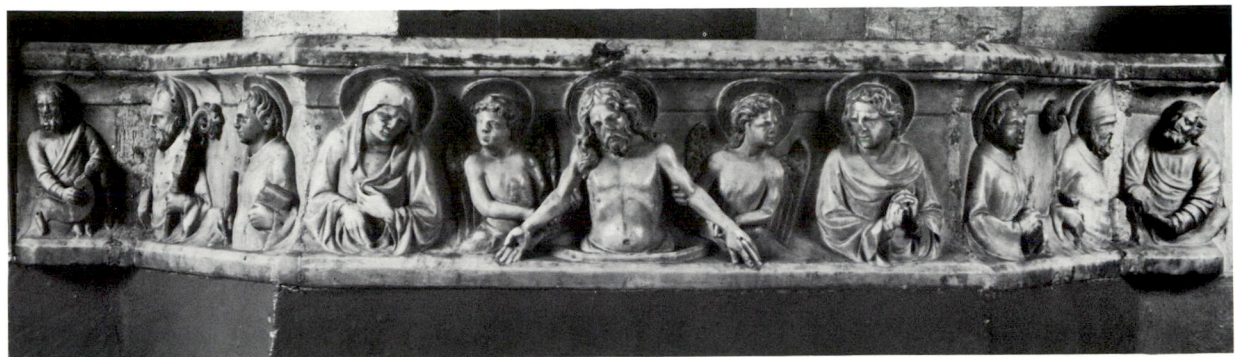

340. Late Trecento Tuscan workshop of Follower of Nino Pisano: *Man of Sorrows with Saints and Angels* (ht 27.5 cm). Lucca, San Martino

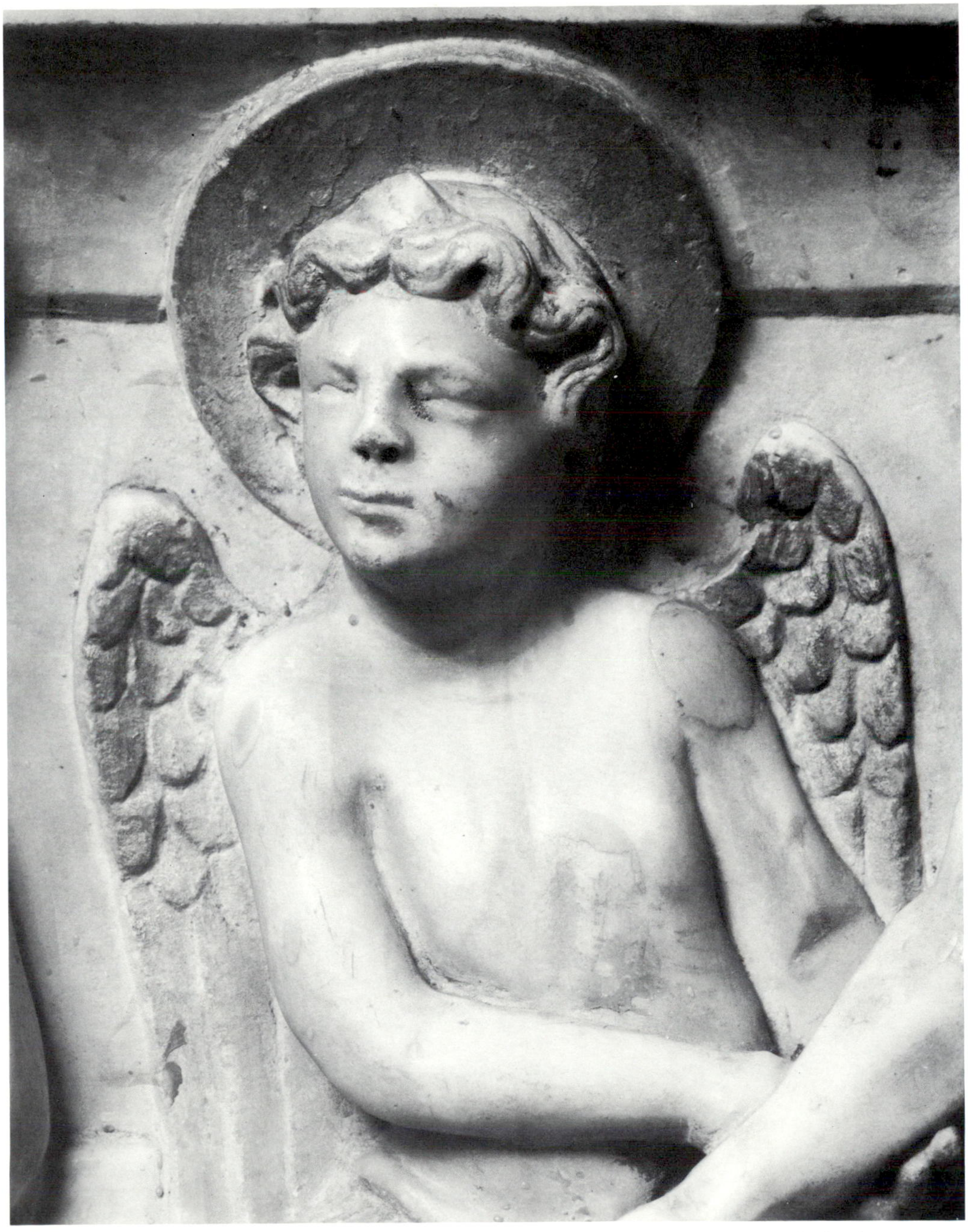

341. Late Trecento Tuscan workshop of Follower of Nino Pisano: *Man of Sorrows with Saints and Angels*, detail. Lucca, San Martino

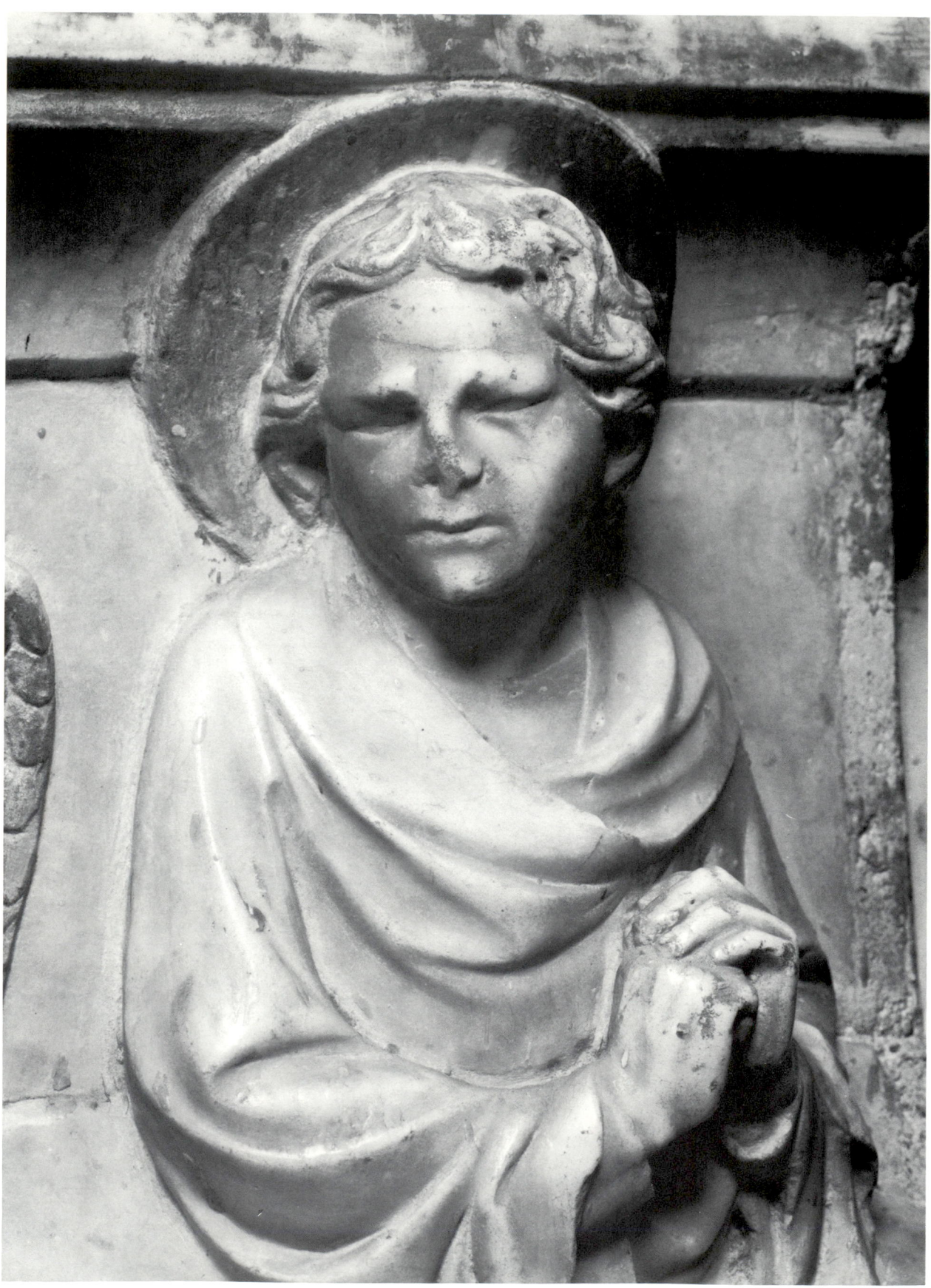

342. Late Trecento Tuscan workshop of Follower of Nino Pisano: *Man of Sorrows with Saints and Angels*, detail. Lucca, San Martino

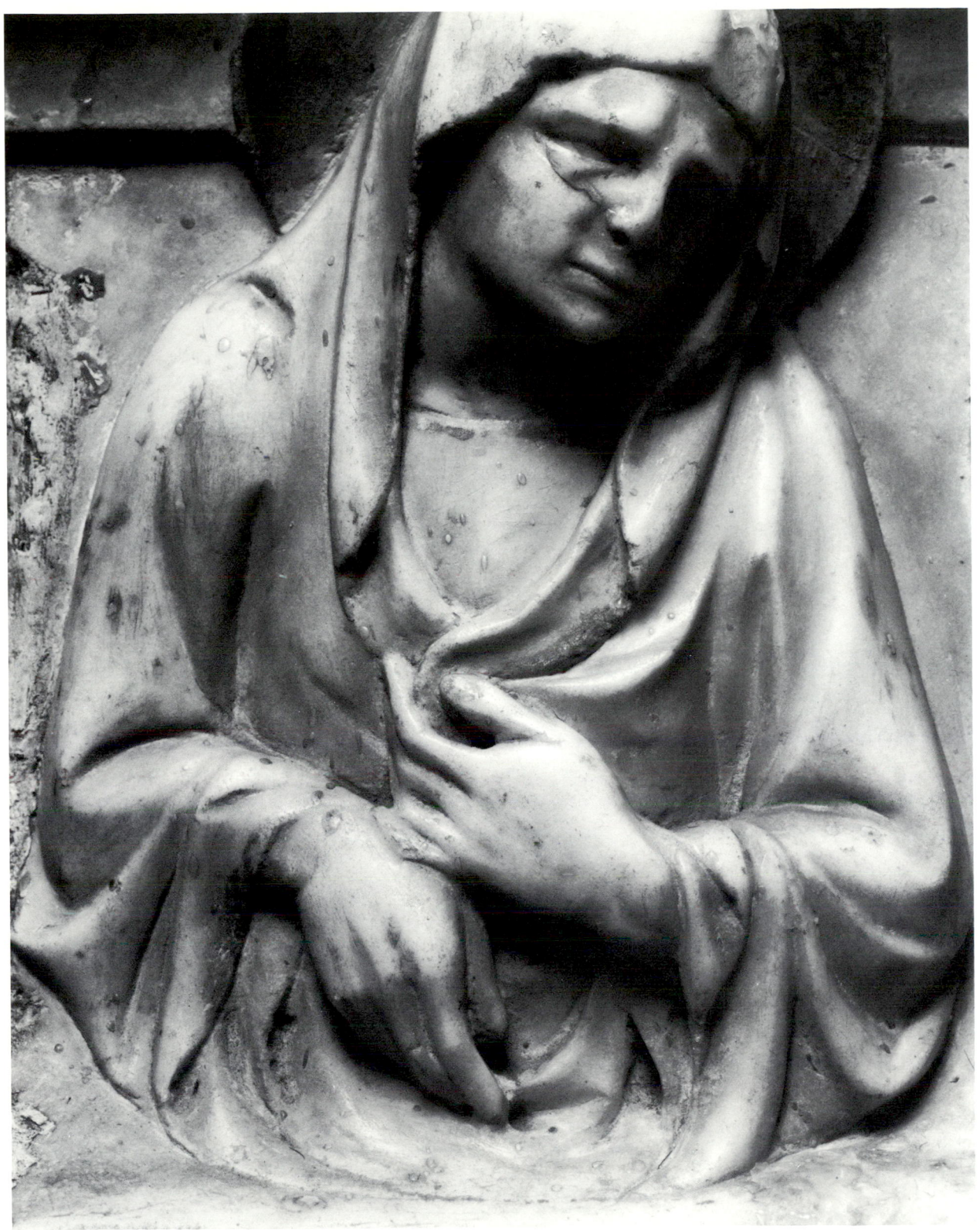

343. Late Trecento Tuscan workshop of Follower of Nino Pisano: *Man of Sorrows with Saints and Angels*, detail. Lucca, San Martino

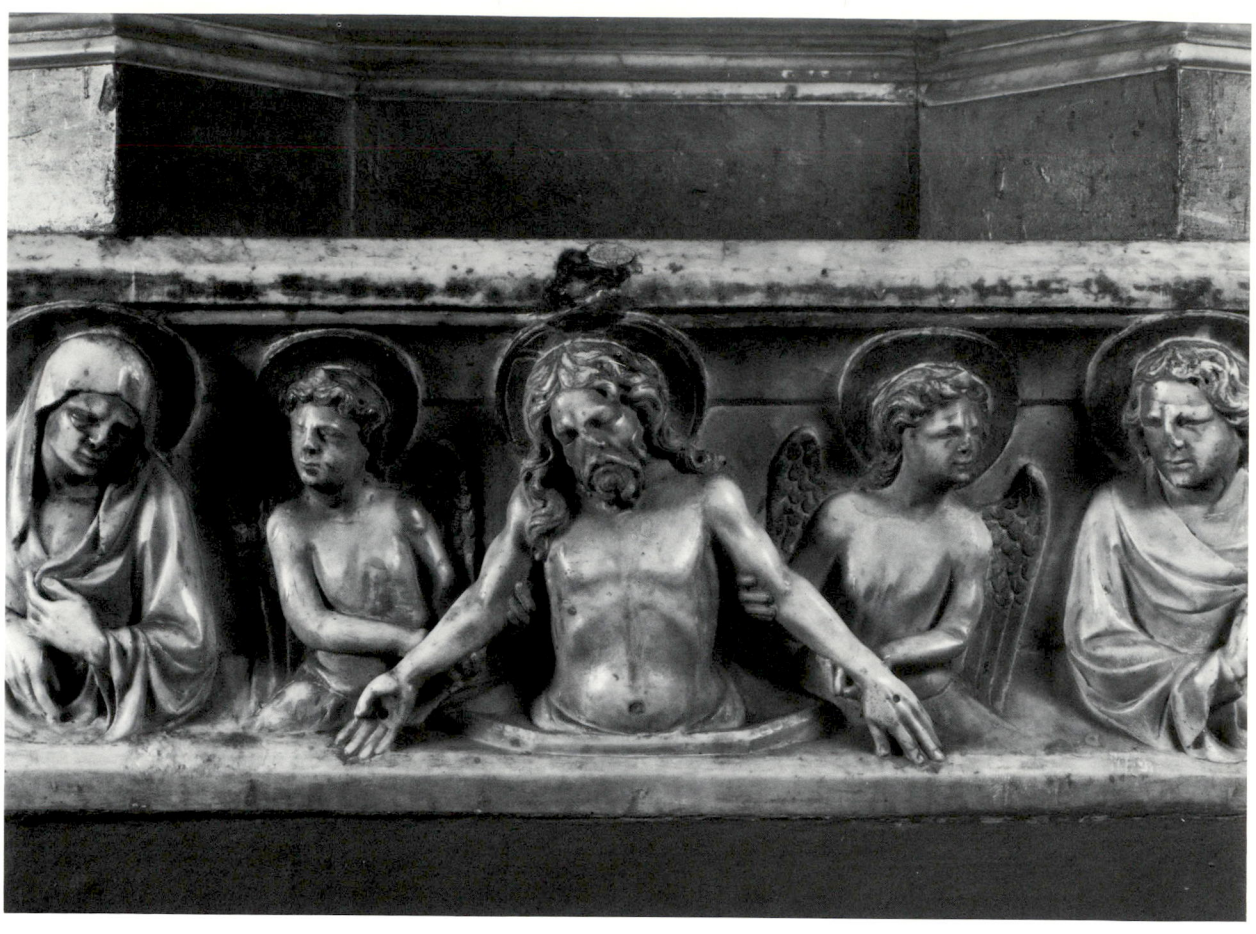

344. Late Trecento Tuscan workshop of Follower of Nino Pisano: *Man of Sorrows with Saints and Angels*, detail. Lucca, San Martino

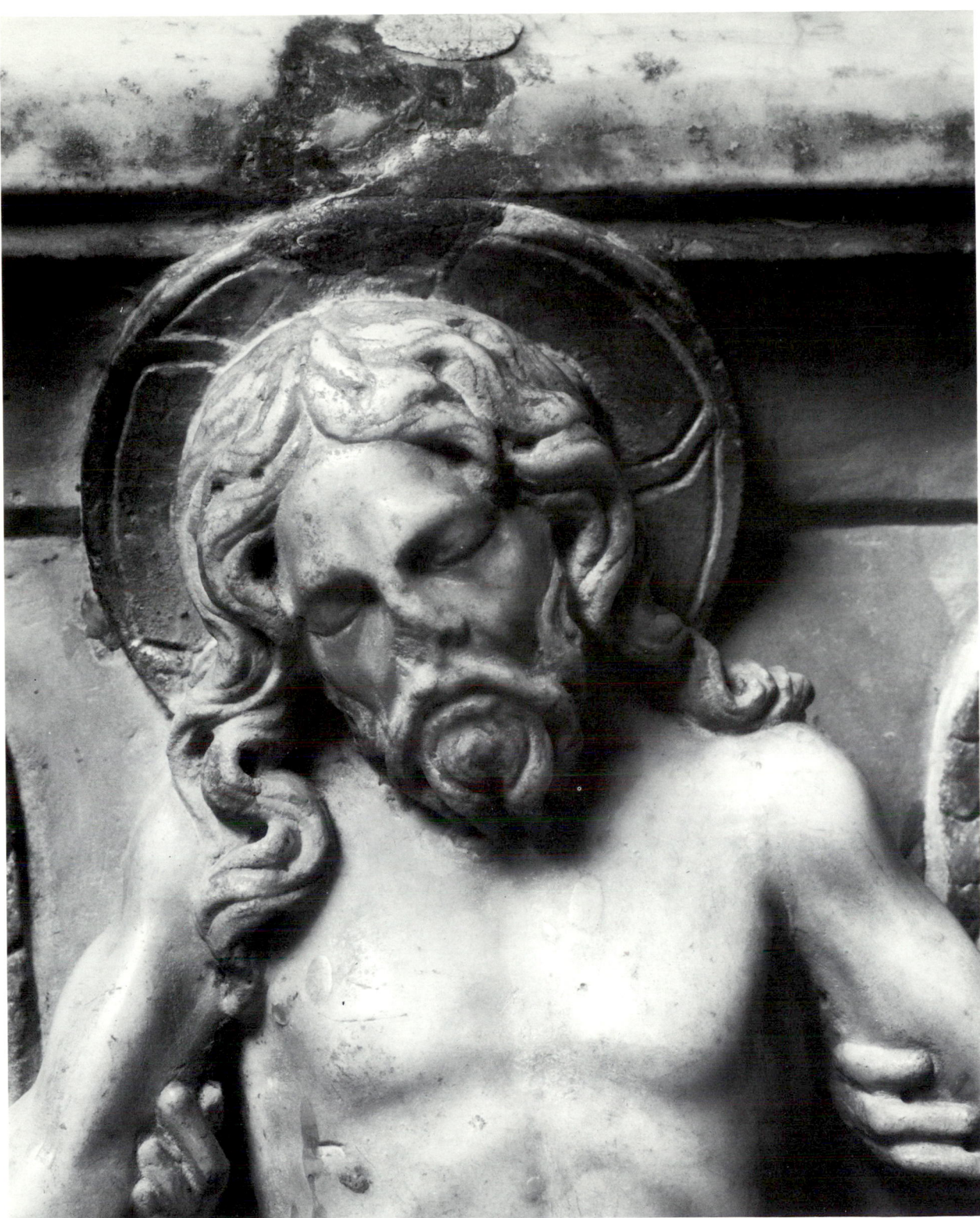

345. Late Trecento Tuscan workshop of Follower of Nino Pisano: *Man of Sorrows with Saints and Angels*, detail. Lucca, San Martino

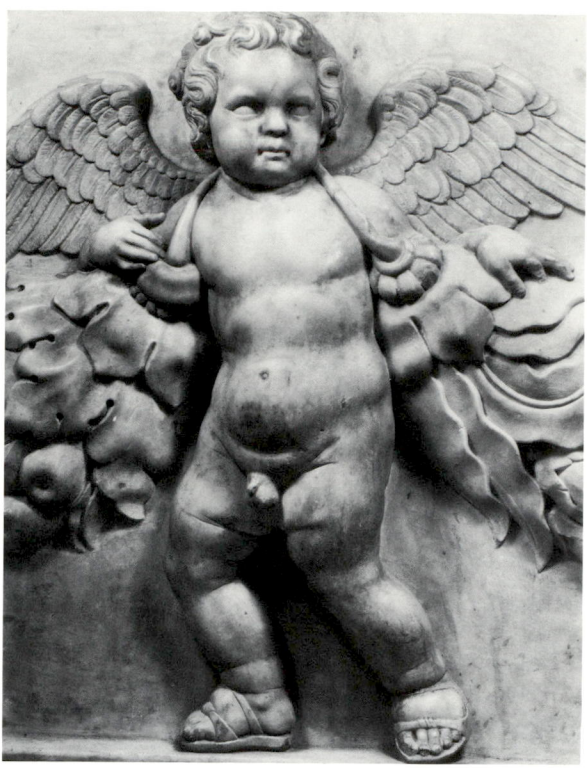

346. Jacopo della Quercia: Tomb of Ilaria del Carretto, detail. Lucca, San Martino

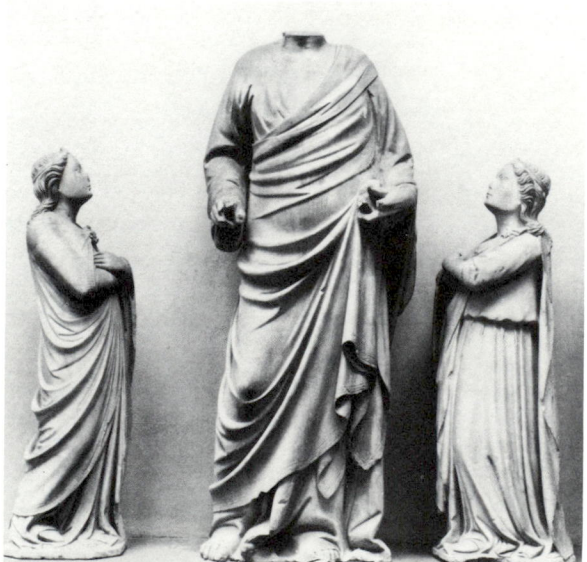

348. Piero di Giovanni Tedesco: *Adoring Angels*; Nanni di Banco(?): *Saint*. Florence, Museo dell'Opera del Duomo

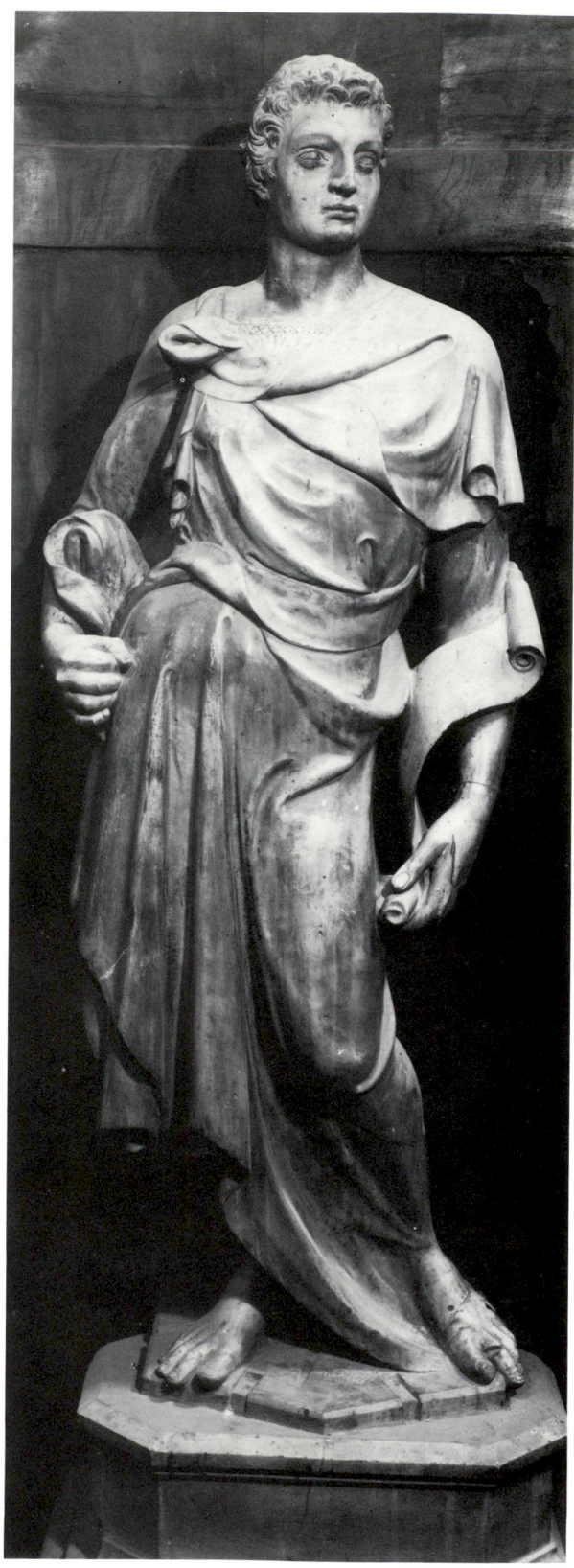

347. Nanni di Banco: Prophet from Porta della Mandorla. Florence Cathedral

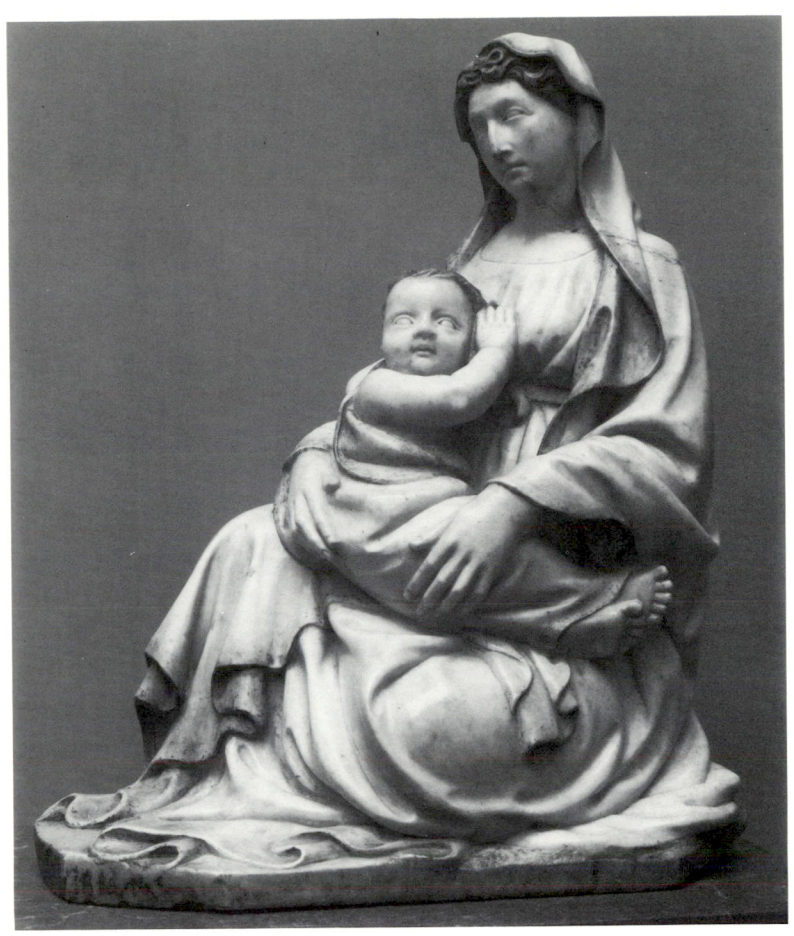

349. Jacopo della Quercia (?): *Madonna of Humility* (ht 58.4 cm, width 48.8 cm, depth 28.3 cm). Washington, D.C., National Gallery

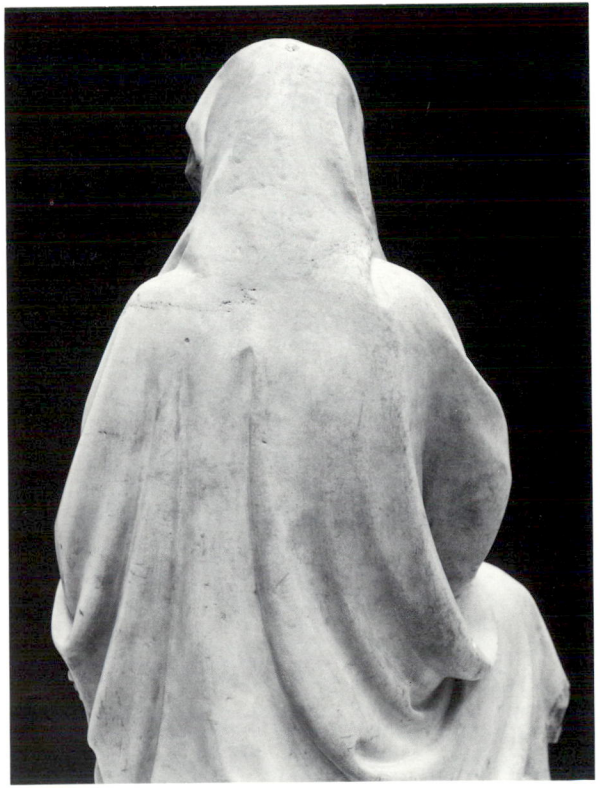

350. Jacopo della Quercia (?): *Madonna of Humility.* Washington, D.C., National Gallery